In the same series

YEATS ANNUALS Nos. 1, 2 Edited by Richard J. Finneran

YEATS ANNUALS Nos. 3–8, 10–11, 13 Edited by Warwick Gould

YEATS AND WOMEN
YEATS ANNUAL No. 9: A Special Number
Edited by Deirdre Toomey

THAT ACCUSING EYE
YEATS AND HIS IRISH READERS
YEATS ANNUAL No. 12: A Special Number
Edited by Warwick Gould and Edna Longley

YEATS AND THE NINETIES
YEATS ANNUAL No. 14: A Special Number
Edited by Warwick Gould

YEATS'S COLLABORATIONS
YEATS ANNUAL No. 15: A Special Number
Edited by Wayne K. Chapman and Warwick Gould

POEMS AND CONTEXTS
YEATS ANNUAL No. 16: A Special Number
Edited by Warwick Gould

INFLUENCE AND CONFLUENCE
YEATS ANNUAL No. 17: A Special Number
Edited by Warwick Gould

THE LIVING STREAM
YEATS ANNUAL No. 18: A Special Issue
Essays in Memory of A. Norman Jeffares
Edited by Warwick Gould

YEATS ANNUAL No. 19

W. B. Yeats in the New College, Oxford, rooms of G. K. Chettur, who, from 1918–21 was a Commoner of the College (1918–21). The photograph was taken by Chettur some time after Yeats had addressed the Oxford Majlis on 23 November 1919.

YEATS'S MASK

YEATS ANNUAL No. 19
A Special Issue

Edited by
Margaret Mills Harper and Warwick Gould

in association with the Institute of English Studies
School of Advanced Study, University of London

http://www.openbookpublishers.com

© 2013 Margaret Harper Mills and Warwick Gould, unless otherwise stated.

Copyright of individual chapters are maintained by the chapter author(s).

This entire volume is published under a Creative Commons Attribution-Non Commercial-NoDerivatives 4.0 International Public License (CC BY-NC-ND 4.0), which enables you to share, copy, distribute and transmit the work in its entirety for personal and non-commercial use, providing editor and author attribution is clearly stated.

However all the text and many of the individual chapters are licenced under the more permissive Creative Commons Attribution 4.0 International Public License (CC BY 4.0), which additionally allows you to share, copy, distribute, transmit, adapt, and re-use the material so licenced, even for commercial purposes. Any material copied or adapted in this way must be attributed to the editors and the respective authors (but not in any way that suggests that they endorse you or your use of the work).

Some images have all rights reserved by the copyright holder. This means that you are able to copy and redistribute the image as an integrated part of the entire chapter or volume, but you are not permitted to reuse the image in an alternative setting or work without obtaining permission from the copyright holder. For the full copyright statement relating to each image, please refer to the list of illustration (p. xiii).

Every effort has been made to identify and contact copyright holders; any omissions or errors will be corrected if notification is made to the publisher.

All attributions in relation to any part of this work should include the following information:

Mills Harper, Margaret and Gould, Warwick (eds.), *Yeats's Mask: Yeats Annual No. 19*, Cambridge, UK: Open Book Publishers, 2013. http://dx.doi.org/10.11647/OBP.0038

Further details about the various Creative Commons licenses are available at:

http://www.creativecommons.org/licenses/

ISBN Paperback: 978-1-78374-017-8
ISBN Hardback: 978-1-78374-018-5
ISBN Digital (PDF): 978-1-78374-019-2
ISBN Digital ebook (epub version): 978-1-78374-020-8
ISBN Digital ebook (mobi version): 978-1-78374-021-5
DOI: 10.11647/OBP.0038

Cover image taken from the cover design of *Wheels and Butterflies* (London: Macmillan, 1934). Artist unknown.

All paper used by Open Book Publishers is SFI (Sustainable Forestry Initiative), and PEFC (Programme for the Endorsement of Forest Certification Schemes) Certified.

Printed in the United Kingdom and United States by Lightning Source for Open Book Publishers

The bravest from the Gods but ask:
A house, a sword, a ship, a mask.[1]

---

[1] From *Wheels and Butterflies,* 157: see below, 369–78.

Contents

List of Illustrations	xiii
Abbreviations	xvii
Editorial Board	xxv
Notes on the Contributors	xxvii
Editors' Introduction	xxxiii
Acknowledgements and Editorial Information	xxxix

YEATS'S MASK

The Mask before *The Mask*
    WARWICK GOULD   3

The King's Threshold, *Calvary*, *The Death of Cuchulain*:
Yeats's Passion Plays
    ALEXANDRA POULAIN   49

To 'make others see my dream as I had seen it':
Yeats's Aesthetics in *Cathleen ni Houlihan*
    AISLING CARLIN   65

'Oxford Poets': Yeats, T. S. Eliot and William Force Stead
    DAVID BRADSHAW   77

Playing with Voices and with Doubles in Two of Yeats's Plays:
The Words upon the Window-pane and *A Full Moon in March*
    PIERRE LONGUENESSE   103

The Mask of Derision in Yeats's Prologue to *A Vision* (1937)
    ELIZABETH MÜLLER   121

A Vision and Yeats's Late Masks
    MARGARET MILLS HARPER   147

The *Mask* of *A Vision*
  NEIL MANN   167

'I beg your pardon?': W. B. Yeats, Audibility and
Sound Transmission
  EMILIE MORIN   191

Mask and Robe: Yeats's *Oxford Book of Modern Verse* (1936)
and *New Poems* (1938)
  MICHAEL CADE-STEWART   221

The Poem on the Mountain: A Chinese Reading
of Yeats's 'Lapis Lazuli'
  JERUSHA McCORMACK   261

The Manuscript of 'Leo Africanus', edited by
STEVE L. ADAMS and GEORGE MILLS HARPER
Reprinted from *Yeats Annual* 1   289

SHORTER NOTES

'My Dear Miss Brachvogel...' A Ms Version of a Yeats Quatrain
  PHILIP R. BISHOP   339

The Land Of Heart's Desire: Some Hitherto Unrecorded
Printings – 'Work in Progress'
  COLIN SMYTHE   351

Wheels and Butterflies: Title, Structure, Cover Design
  WARWICK GOULD   369

REVIEWS

W. B. Yeats and Lady Gregory, *Where there is Nothing
and The Unicorn from the Stars: Manuscript Materials*,
ed. Wim Van Mierlo
  RICHARD ALLEN CAVE   381

The King's Threshold: Manuscript Materials, edited by Declan Kiely
  RICHARD ALLEN CAVE   389

W. B. Yeats, *At The Hawk's Well and The Cat and the Moon: Manuscript Materials*, ed. Andrew Parkin
RICHARD ALLEN CAVE   401

Karen E. Brown, *The Yeats Circle, Verbal and Visual Relations in Ireland, 1880–1939*
TOM WALKER   417

W. B. Yeats and George Yeats, The Letters ed. Ann Saddlemyer; *W. B. Yeats's 'A Vision': Explications and Contexts*, ed. Neil Mann, Matthew Gibson and Claire Nally
LAUREN ARRINGTON   421

Sean Pryor, *W. B. Yeats, Ezra Pound and the Poetry of Paradise*
STODDARD MARTIN   427

Writings on Literature and Art: G. W. Russell – A.E., edited and with an Introduction by Peter Kuch
NICHOLAS ALLEN   433

Joseph M. Hassett, *W. B. Yeats and the Muses*
MICHAEL CADE-STEWART   437

Michael McAteer, *Yeats and European Drama*
TARA STUBBS   441

R. F. Foster, *Words Alone: Yeats and his Inheritances*
GERALDINE HIGGINS   445

PUBLICATIONS RECEIVED   451

List of Illustrations

Cover Image: Taken from the cover design of *Wheels and Butterflies* (London: Macmillan, 1934), artist unknown. See pp. 369–78. Image in the public domain.

Frontispiece: W. B. Yeats in the New College, Oxford, rooms of G. K. Chettur, late 1919 or early 1920. Photograph by G. K. Chettur, and reproduced from his *The Last Enchantment: Recollections of Oxford* (Mangalore: The B. M. Bookshop, 1934, facing p. 40). Image in the public domain.

Plates

1.	Plaster cast of mask of W. B. Yeats by Kathleen Scott (née Bruce, later Lady Kennet), 1907. 17 1/2 in. (445 mm) high. Photograph courtesy and © The National Portrait Gallery, London. All rights reserved.	20
2.	The 'Palatium Arcanorum', frontispiece of Christian Knorr von Rosenroth's *Kabbala Denudata seu Doctrina Hebræorum transcendentalis et metaphysica atque theological etc.*, 1677. Photograph courtesy and © The British Library. All rights reserved.	42
3 a-b.	Yeats at the Microphone, very probably March 1937. Photographs of unknown authorship, courtesy Colin Smythe. Images in the public domain.	215
4.	Yeats's Lapis Lazuli mountain (given to him by Harry Clifton, and the inspiration of the poem 'Lapis Lazuli'), front view. Photograph courtesy and © of the National Library of Ireland. All rights reserved.	260
5.	*Mi Fu Honouring a Rock.* Photograph courtesy and © of the Shanghai Museum. All rights reserved.	270
6.	Detail from *"Ting Qin Tu": Listening to the Qin*, attributed to the Emperor Song Huizong (11th Century). Image in the public domain. See http://commons.wikimedia.org/wiki/File:Songhuizong8.jpg	274

7.	Writing on a rock-face in Huangshan, Anhui Province. Photograph © H. K. Tang, CC BY-NC-ND license. See: http://www.flickr.com/photos/ehktang/4066986112/	275
8.	Back side of Yeats's Lapis Lazuli mountain, with poem circled. Photograph courtesy and © of the National Library of Ireland. All rights reserved.	277
9.	First page of Lily Yeats's letter to her American friend, Clara Brachvogel. Image in the public domain.	341
10.	Photostat copy by Colin Smythe of inscribed front free endpaper of Lady Gregory's lost bookplate copy of Yeats's *Poems, 1899–1905*. Image in the public domain.	344
11.	W. B. Yeats's poem as inscribed in the Mosher Press edition of *The Land of Heart's Desire* (1908). Image in the public domain.	344
12.	Yeats's inscription in *The King's Threshold – A Play in Verse* (New York: Printed for Private Circulation [John Quinn], 1904). Courtesy Yeats Estate and Beinecke Rare Book and Manuscript Library, Yale University. Image in the public domain.	345
13.	Top page of John Quinn's set of the Cuala proofs of *Twenty-One Poems written by Lionel Johnson*: Selected by William Butler Yeats (1904), inscribed by Yeats and his two sisters. Lily Yeats's comment is 'Not to be pirated, Oct 27th. 1904.' Photograph courtesy and © private collector, all rights reserved.	349
14 a-f.	Images of various states and editions of In the Land of Heart's Desire [sic] published by the Thomas Y. Crowell Company of New York, c.1905 and later. Portrait by John Butler Yeats, remaining artwork of unknown authorship. Images in the public domain.	350-53
15 a-b.	Images of *The Land of Heart's Desire* [?1904]. Images in the public domain.	355
16 a-b.	Images of *The Land of Heart's Desire* published by the Walter H. Baker Company of Boston, 1919. Artwork of unknown authorship. Images in the public domain.	356

17 a-e.	Images of various states and editions of *The Land of Heart's Desire* published by Dodd, Mead, New York, c.1909. Artwork of unknown authorship. Images in the public domain.	360-61
18 a-f.	Images of various states and editions of *The Land of Heart's Desire* published by the Little Leather Library, New York, 1919 and later. Artwork of unknown authorship. Images in the public domain.	361-63
19 a-d.	Images of various states and editions of *The Land of Heart's Desire* [sic] published by the Shrewesbury Publishing Company, Chicago, after 1925. Images in the public domain.	365
20 a-d.	Images of various states and editions of *In the Land of Heart's Desire* [sic] published by the Haldeman-Julius Company as their Pockett and Little Blue Books Series, Girard, Kansas and Portland, Oregon, 1923 and after. Images in the public domain.	367-68
21-23.	The bronzes cast before 1929 from Hildo Van Krop's masks for *The Woman of the Sidhe*, Emer, and Cuchulain in *Vrouwe Emer's Groote Strijd*, the 1922 Dutch production of *The Only Jealousy of Emer*, and now in the Stadsschouwburg, Amsterdam. Photograph of unknown authorship, predating 1934. Image in the public domain.	370
24.	Title-page design of *Wheels and Butterflies* (London: Macmillan, 1934). Artwork of unknown authorship. Image in the public domain.	372
25.	Thomas Sturge Moore's original design for the spine and top board of *The Cutting of an Agate* (London: Macmillan, 1919). Image courtesy and © Senate House Library, University of London. All rights reserved.	375

Abbreviations

Au	*Autobiographies* (London: Macmillan, 1955).
AVA	*A Vision: An Explanation of Life Founded upon the Writings of Giraldus and upon certain Doctrines attributed to Kusta Ben Luka* (London: privately printed for subscribers only by T. Werner Laurie, Ltd., 1925). See also *CVA*.
AVB	*A Vision* (London: Macmillan, 1962).
Berg	Books and Manuscripts, The Berg Collection, New York Public Library (Astor, Lenox and Tilden Foundations).
*BIV*1, 2	*A Book of Irish Verse* (London: Methuen, 1895; 1900).
BL Add. MS	Additional Manuscript, The British Library, London (followed by number).
BL Macmillan	Later papers from the Macmillan Archive, British Library, London.
Bodley	Bodleian Library, Oxford.
Bradford	*Yeats at Work*, by Curtis B. Bradford (Carbondale and Edwardsville: Southern Illinois University Press, 1965).
Brotherton	Manuscript, The Brotherton Collection, Brotherton Library, University of Leeds.
CH	*W. B. Yeats: The Critical Heritage*, ed A. Norman Jeffares (London: Henley; Boston: Routledge & Kegan Paul, 1977).

CL1, 2, 3, 4	*The Collected Letters of W. B. Yeats: Volume I, 1865–1895*, ed. John Kelly and Eric Domville; *Volume II, 1896–1900*, ed. Warwick Gould, John Kelly, Deirdre Toomey; *Volume III, 1901–1904*, and *Volume IV, 1905–1907*, ed. John Kelly and Ronald Schuchard (Oxford: Clarendon Press, 1986, 1997, 1994, 2005).
CL InteLex	*The Collected Letters of W. B. Yeats*, gen. ed. John Kelly, Oxford University Press (InteLex Electronic Edition) 2002. Letters cited by Accession number.
CM	*W. B. Yeats: A Census of the Manuscripts*, by Conrad A. Balliet, with the assistance of Christine Mawhinney (New York and London: Garland Publishing, Inc., 1990).
CVA	*A Critical Edition of Yeats's* A Vision *(1925)*, ed. George Mills Harper and Walter Kelly Hood (London: Macmillan, 1978).
CW1	*The Poems*, second edition (New York: Scribner, 1997), ed. Richard J. Finneran and replacing *The Poems: Revised* (New York: Macmillan, 1989; London: Macmillan, 1989), *PR*, which replaced *The Poems: A New Edition* (New York: Macmillan, 1983; London: Macmillan London Ltd., 1984), *PNE*, as the first volume of *The Collected Works of W. B. Yeats* (formerly *The Collected Edition of the Works of W. B. Yeats*).
CW2	*The Plays*, ed. David R. Clark and Rosalind E. Clark (New York: Scribner, 2001), volume II of *The Collected Works of W. B. Yeats* (formerly *The Collected Edition of the Works of W. B. Yeats*).
CW3	*Autobiographies*, ed. William H. O'Donnell and Douglas N. Archibald, assisted by J. Fraser Cocks III and Gretchen Schwenker (New York: Scribner, 1999), volume III of *The Collected Works of W. B. Yeats* (formerly *The Collected Edition of the Works of W. B. Yeats*).
CW4	*Early Essays*, ed. Richard J. Finneran and George Bornstein (New York: Scribner, 2007), volume III of *The Collected Works of W. B. Yeats* (formerly *The Collected Edition of the Works of W. B. Yeats*).

CW5	*Later Essays*, ed. William H. O'Donnell, with assistance from Elizabeth Bergmann Loizeaux (New York: Charles Scribner's Sons, 1994), volume V of *The Collected Works of W. B. Yeats* (formerly *The Collected Edition of the Works of W. B. Yeats*).
CW6	*Prefaces and Introductions: Uncollected Prefaces and Introductions by Yeats to Works by other Authors and to Anthologies edited by Yeats*, ed. William H. O'Donnell (London: Macmillan, 1988), volume VI of *The Collected Works of W. B. Yeats* (formerly *The Collected Edition of the Works of W. B. Yeats*).
CW7	*Letters to the New Island* ed. George Bornstein and Hugh Witemeyer (London: Macmillan, 1989), volume VII of *The Collected Works of W. B. Yeats* (formerly *The Collected Edition of the Works of W. B. Yeats*).
CW8	*The Irish Dramatic Movement*, ed. Mary FitzGerald and Richard J. Finneran (New York: Scribner, 2003), volume VIII of *The Collected Works of W. B. Yeats* (formerly *The Collected Edition of the Works of W. B. Yeats*).
CW9	*Early Articles and Reviews: Uncollected Articles and Reviews written between 1886 and 1900*, ed. John P. Frayne and Madeleine Marchaterre (New York: Scribner, 2004), volume IX of *The Collected Works of W. B. Yeats* (formerly *The Collected Edition of the Works of W. B. Yeats*).
CW10	*Later Articles and Reviews: Uncollected Articles, Reviews, and Radio Broadcasts written after 1900*, ed. Colton Johnson (New York: Scribner, 2000), volume X of *The Collected Works of W. B. Yeats* (formerly *The Collected Edition of the Works of W. B. Yeats*).
CW12	*John Sherman and Dhoya*, ed. Richard J. Finneran (New York: Macmillan, 1991), volume XII of *The Collected Works of W. B. Yeats* (formerly *The Collected Edition of the Works of W. B. Yeats*).
CW13	*A Vision: The Original 1925 Version*, ed. Catherine E. Paul and Margaret Mills Harper (New York: Scribner 2008), volume XIII of *The Collected Works of W. B. Yeats* (formerly *The Collected Edition of the Works of W. B. Yeats*).

CWVP1–8	*The Collected Works in Verse and Prose of William Butler Yeats*, 8 vols. (Stratford-on-Avon: The Shakespeare Head Press, 1908).
DC	*Druid Craft: The Writing of The Shadowy Waters, Manuscripts of W. B. Yeats*, transcribed, edited & with a commentary by Michael J. Sidnell, George P. Mayhew, David R. Clark (Amherst: The University of Massachusetts Press, 1971).
Diaries	*Lady Gregory's Diaries 1892–1902*, ed. James Pethica (Gerrards Cross: Colin Smythe, 1996).
E&I	*Essays and Introductions* (London and New York: Macmillan, 1961).
Emory	Books and Manuscripts in the Robert W. Woodruff Library, Emory University.
Ex	*Explorations*, selected by Mrs W. B. Yeats (London: Macmillan, 1962; New York: Macmillan, 1963).
FFTIP	*Fairy and Folk Tales of the Irish Peasantry*, edited and selected by W. B. Yeats (London: Walter Scott, Ltd., 1888).
G-YL	*The Gonne-Yeats Letters 1893–1938: Always Your Friend*, ed. Anna MacBride White and A. Norman Jeffares (London: Hutchinson, 1992).
Harvard	Manuscript, Houghton Library, Harvard University.
HRHRC	Books and Manuscripts, Harry Ransom Humanities Research Center, University of Texas at Austin.
I&R	*W. B. Yeats: Interviews and Recollections*, ed. E. H. Mikhail, 2 vols. (London: Macmillan, 1977).
IFT	*Irish Fairy Tales* edited with an introduction by W. B. Yeats (London: T. Fisher Unwin, 1892).
J	*W. B. Yeats: A Classified Bibliography of Criticism*, second edition, revised and enlarged by K. P. S. Jochum (Urbana and Chicago: University of Illinois Press, 1990). Item nos. or page no. preceded by 'p.'.
JBYL	*Letters to his Son W. B. Yeats and Others 1869–1922 by J. B. Yeats*, edited with a Memoir by Joseph Hone and a Preface by Oliver Elton (London: Faber and Faber, 1944).

Kansas	Manuscripts in the Kenneth Spencer Research Library, University of Kansas, Lawrence.
L	*The Letters of W. B. Yeats*, ed. Allan Wade (London: Rupert Hart-Davis, 1954; New York: Macmillan, 1955).
LBP	*Letters from Bedford Park: A Selection from the Correspondence (1890–1901) of John Butler Yeats*, edited with an introduction and notes by William M. Murphy (Dublin: The Cuala Press, 1972).
LDW	*Letters on Poetry from W. B. Yeats to Dorothy Wellesley*, with an introduction by Kathleen Raine (London and New York: Oxford University Press, 1964).
Life 1	*W. B. Yeats: A Life, I: The Apprentice Mage*, by R. F. Foster (Oxford and New York: Oxford University Press, 1997).
Life 2	*W. B. Yeats: A Life, II: The Arch-Poet*, by R. F. Foster (Oxford and New York: Oxford University Press, 2003).
Lilly	Manuscript in the Lilly Library, Indiana University, Bloomington.
LJQ	*The Letters of John Quinn to W. B. Yeats*, ed. Alan B. Himber, with the assistance of George Mills Harper (Ann Arbor: UMI Research Press, 1983).
LMR	*"Ah, Sweet Dancer": W. B. Yeats and Margot Ruddock, A Correspondence*, ed. Roger McHugh (London and New York: Macmillan, 1970).
LNI	*Letters to the New Island* by W. B. Yeats, edited and with an introduction by Horace Reynolds (Cambridge, MA: Harvard University Press, 1934).
LRB	*The Correspondence of Robert Bridges and W. B. Yeats*, ed. Richard J. Finneran (London: Macmillan, 1977; Toronto: Macmillan of Canada, 1978).
LTWBY1, 2	*Letters to W. B. Yeats*, ed. Richard J. Finneran, George Mills Harper and William M. Murphy, with the assistance of Alan B. Himber, 2 vols. (London: Macmillan; New York: Columbia University Press, 1977).
MBY	Manuscript in the Collection of Michael Butler Yeats.

McGarry	*Places Names in the Writings of W. B. Yeats* by James P. McGarry, edited with additional material by Edward Malins and a Preface by Kathleen Raine (Gerrards Cross: Colin Smythe Ltd., 1976).
Mem	*Memoirs: Autobiography – First Draft: Journal*, transcribed and edited by Denis Donoghue (London: Macmillan, 1972; New York: Macmillan, 1973).
Myth	*Mythologies* (London and New York: Macmillan, 1959).
Myth 2005	*Mythologies*, ed. Warwick Gould and Deirdre Toomey (Houndmills, Basingstoke: Palgrave Macmillan, 2005).
MYV1, 2	*The Making of Yeats's 'A Vision': A Study of the Automatic Script*, by George Mills Harper, 2 vols. (London: Macmillan; Carbondale and Edwardsville, Ill.: Southern Illinois University Press, 1987).
NLI	Manuscripts in the National Library of Ireland, Dublin.
NLS	Manuscripts in the National Library of Scotland, Edinburgh.
NYPL	Manuscripts in the New York Public Library.
Norwood	Manuscripts, Norwood Historical Society, Day House, Norwood, Mass.
OBMV	*The Oxford Book of Modern Verse 1895–1935*, selected by W. B. Yeats (Oxford: Clarendon Press, 1936).
Princeton	Manuscript in the Scribner Archive, Firestone Library, Princeton University.
Quinn Cat.	Complete Catalogue of the Library of John Quinn sold by auction in five parts [with printed prices] (New York: The Anderson Galleries, 1924), 2 v.
SB	*The Speckled Bird by William Butler Yeats: an Autobiographical Novel With Variant Versions: New Edition, incorporating recently discovered manuscripts*, edited and annotated by William H. O'Donnell (Basingstoke: Palgrave Macmillan, 2003).
SQ	*A Servant of the Queen: Reminiscences*, by Maud Gonne MacBride, ed. A. Norman Jeffares and Anna MacBride White (Gerrards Cross: Colin Smythe, 1994).

SS	*The Senate Speeches of W. B. Yeats*, ed. Donald R. Pearce (Bloomington: Indiana University Press, 1960; London: Faber and Faber, 1961).
TB	*Theatre Business: The Correspondence of the First Abbey Theatre Directors: William Butler Yeats, Lady Gregory and J. M. Synge*, ed. Ann Saddlemyer (Gerrards Cross: Colin Smythe; University Park: Pennsylvania State University Press, 1982).
TSMC	*W. B. Yeats and T. Sturge Moore: Their Correspondence, 1901–1937*, ed. Ursula Bridge (London: Routledge and Kegan Paul; New York: Oxford University Press, 1953).
UP1	*Uncollected Prose by W. B. Yeats, Vol I*, ed. John P. Frayne (London: Macmillan; New York: Columbia University Press, 1970).
UP2	*Uncollected Prose by W. B. Yeats, Vol II*, ed. John P. Frayne and Colton Johnson (London: Macmillan, 1975; New York: Columbia University Press, 1976).
VBWI	*Visions and Beliefs in the West of Ireland*, collected and arranged by Lady Gregory: with two Essays and Notes by W. B. Yeats with a foreword by Elizabeth Coxhead (Gerrards Cross: Colin Smythe Ltd.; New York: Oxford University Press, 1970).
VP	*The Variorum Edition of the Poems of W. B. Yeats*, ed. Peter Allt and Russell K. Alspach (New York: Macmillan, 1957). Cited from the corrected third printing of 1966.
VPl	*The Variorum Edition of the Plays of W. B. Yeats*, ed. Russell K. Alspach, assisted by Catherine C. Alspach (London and New York: Macmillan, 1966). Cited from the corrected second printing of 1966.
VSR	*The Secret Rose, Stories by W. B. Yeats: A Variorum Edition*, ed. Warwick Gould, Phillip L. Marcus and Michael J. Sidnell, second edition, revised and enlarged (London: Macmillan, 1992).
Wade	Allan Wade, *A Bibliography of the Writings of W. B. Yeats*, third edition, revised by Russell K. Alspach (London: Rupert Hart-Davis, 1968). Cited by item no. and/or page no. preceded by 'p.'.

WWB1, 2, 3	*The Works of William Blake Poetic, Symbolic, and Critical,* edited with lithographs of the illustrated *"Prophetic Books"*, *and a memoir and interpretation* by Edwin John Ellis and W. B. Yeats, 3 vols. (London: Bernard Quaritch, 1893).
YA1, 2, etc.	*Yeats Annual* (London: Macmillan, 1982–) cited by no.
YAACTS	*Yeats: An Annual of Critical and Textual Studies*, ed. Richard J. Finneran (publishers vary, 1983–1999) cited by no.
YGYL	*W. B. Yeats and George Yeats: The Letters*, ed. Ann Saddlemyer (Oxford: Oxford University Press, 2011).
YL	*A Descriptive Catalog of W. B. Yeats's Library*, by Edward O'Shea (New York and London: Garland Publishing, 1985).
YO	*Yeats and the Occult*, ed. George Mills Harper (Toronto: Macmillan of Canada; Niagara Falls, NY: Maclean-Hunter Press, 1975).
YP	*Yeats's Poems*, edited & annotated by A. Norman Jeffares, with an appendix by Warwick Gould (London: Macmillan, 1989). Cited from the second, revised edition of 1991.
YT	*Yeats and the Theatre*, ed. Robert O'Driscoll and Lorna Reynolds (Toronto: Macmillan of Canada; Niagara Falls, New York: Maclean-Hunter Press, 1975).
YVP1, 2, 3, 4	*Yeats's Vision* Papers (London: Macmillan, 1992; Palgrave 2001), gen. ed. George Mills Harper, assisted by Mary Jane Harper, *Vol. 1: The Automatic Script: 5 November 1917–18 June 1918*, ed. Steve L. Adams, Barbara J. Frieling and Sandra L. Sprayberry; *Vol. 2: The Automatic Script: 25 June 1918–29 March 1920*, ed. Steve L. Adams, Barbara J. Frieling and Sandra L. Sprayberry; *Vol. 3: Sleep and Dream Notebooks, Vision Notebooks 1 and 2, Card File*, ed. Robert Anthony Martinich and Margaret Mills Harper; Vol. 4: *"The Discoveries of Michael Robartes" Version B ["The Great Wheel" and "The Twenty-Eight Embodiments"]*, ed. George Mills Harper and MargaretMills Harper assisted by Richard W. Stoops, Jr.

Editorial Board

Seamus Deane
Denis Donoghue
Jacqueline Genet
Margaret Mills Harper
John Harwood
K. P. S. Jochum
John Kelly
Edna Longley
Phillip L. Marcus

William H. O'Donnell
Yukio Oura
Marjorie Perloff
James L. Pethica
Ronald Schuchard
Michael J. Sidnell
Colin Smythe
C. K. Stead
Katharine Worth

Series Editor: Warwick Gould
Research Editor: Deirdre Toomey

Notes on the Contributors

Lauren Arrington is Lecturer in Literature at the Institute of Irish Studies, University of Liverpool. Her book, *W. B. Yeats, the Abbey Theatre, Censorship, and the Irish State*, was published by Oxford University Press in 2010. She is currently writing *Revolutionary Lives: Constance and Casimir Markievicz*, a biography which will be published by Princeton University Press.

Philip R. Bishop, independent scholar, writer-essayist, bibliographer, book collector and ABAA/ILAB bookseller, is the compiler of *Thomas Bird Mosher: Pirate Prince of Publishers* (New Castle DE: Oak Knoll Press; London: The British Library, 1998) and contributes to numerous publications and exhibitions. He has assembled one of the world's largest book and MS collections on Mosher and the Mosher Press, and maintains the website: www.ThomasBirdMosher.net. His collecting, memoirs and the *Collected Letters of Thomas Bird Mosher* are his longer term projects.

David Bradshaw is Professor of English Literature at Oxford University and a fellow of Worcester College. As well as numerous articles and essays on all aspects of modernism, he has edited, among other volumes, *The Hidden Huxley* (1994), *A Concise Companion to Modernism* (2003), *The Cambridge Companion to E. M. Forster* (2007), *A Companion to Modernist Literature and Culture* (with Kevin J. H. Dettmar, 2006), Waugh's *Decline and Fall*, Ford's *The Good Soldier*, Woolf's *Carlyle's House and Other Sketches*, Huxley's *Brave New World* and Oxford World's Classics editions of Lawrence's *The White Peacock* and *Women in Love*, and Woolf's *Mrs Dalloway, Selected Essays, To the Lighthouse* and *The Mark on the Wall and Other Short Fiction*. He is Co-Executive Editor (with Professor Martin Stannard) of the 42 volume Oxford University Press edition of *The Complete Works of Evelyn Waugh*.

Michael Cade-Stewart is currently pursuing a British Academy post-doctoral fellowship at King's College London, where he is researching a history of poetic rhythm from Wordsworth to Auden using innovative digital tools. His PhD (2013) was undertaken at the Institute of English Studies (also University of London) and examined the effects of Yeats's reading for the *Oxford Book of Modern Verse* (1936) upon his subsequent poems. He has also published on the form of Yeats's 'News for the Delphic Oracle' in the *South Carolina Review* (43:1).

Aisling Carlin (née Mullan) is an independent scholar specialising in modern Irish Theatre. Her thesis, 'Religious Transformations in the Drama of W. B. Yeats and J. M. Synge' was completed at Queen's University in 2009. Her current research focuses on concepts of ritual, tragedy and utopia. She has presented papers at the 'Yeats and Mask' conference at Lille, IASIL conferences and the Synge Summer School.

Warwick Gould is Professor of English Literature in the University of London (at Royal Holloway) and Senior Research Fellow of the Institute of English Studies (in the School of Advanced Study), of which he was Founder-Director 1999–2013. He is co-author of *Joachim of Fiore and the Myth of the Eternal Evangel in the Nineteenth and Twentieth Centuries* (1988, rev. 2001), and co-editor of *The Secret Rose, Stories by W. B. Yeats: A Variorum Edition* (1981, rev. 1992), *The Collected Letters of W. B. Yeats, Volume II, 1896–1900* (1997), and *Mythologies* (2005). He has edited *Yeats Annual* for thirty years.

Margaret Mills Harper is Glucksman Professor of Contemporary Writing in English at the University of Limerick, Ireland. She is the author of *Wisdom of Two: the Spiritual and Literary Collaboration of George and W. B. Yeats* (Oxford: Oxford University Press, 2006) and *The Aristocracy of Art: James Joyce and Thomas Wolfe* (Baton Rouge: LSU Press, 1990). She has co-edited two of the four volumes of *Yeats's "Vision" Papers* (Basingstoke: Macmillan, 1992 and 2001). With Catherine Paul, she has edited *A Vision* (1925) and is now preparing *A Vision* (1937) for *The Collected Works of W. B. Yeats* (New York: Scribner, 2008 and 2014).

Geraldine Higgins is Associate Professor of English and Director of Irish Studies at Emory University. Her most recent book, *Heroic Revivals from Carlyle to Yeats* examines the flexibility of heroic identity in a range of Revival writers. She has also published a book on Brian

Friel for the 'Writers and their Work' series and several articles on Yeats and popular culture. She is currently curating a major exhibition on 'Seamus Heaney: The Music of What Happens' which will open at Emory in February 2014.

Pierre Longuenesse is a graduate of the Ecole Normale Superieure in Paris and holds a PhD from Paris 4 Sorbonne. He is currently Associate Professor in Drama studies at Artois University in France. His publications include *Yeats dramaturge, la voix et ses masques* (2012) along with articles in French journals such as *Etudes Théâtrales, Registres, Théâtre/Public* and *Etudes Irlandaises*. He is also an actor, and Director of Compagnie du Samovar, a professional theatre company based in Paris.

Neil Mann has taught in Britain, Finland and Spain. He has written primarily on *A Vision* and related matters, maintaining the website, www.yeatsvision.com and a blog on aspects of *A Vision*, yeatsvision.blogspot.co.uk. He has also co-edited the collection of essays *W. B. Yeats's 'A Vision': Explications and Contexts* (Clemson University, 2012). He was involved with the exhibition on W. B. Yeats at the National Library of Ireland, and currently works at the Berg Collection, New York Public Library.

Stoddard Martin is a writer, lecturer and publisher. His academic books include *Wagner to the Waste Land, California Writers, Art, Messianism and Crime, Orthodox Heresy* and *The Great Expatriate Writers*, published by Macmillan. He edited anthologies of Byron, Nietzsche and D. H. Lawrence in the Duckworth 'Sayings of' series, which he helped to devise. He has reviewed widely on literature and culture, and his essays have appeared in anthologies including *George Moore: Dublin, Paris, Hollywood*. He has taught at Harvard, Oxford, Łódź and Warsaw universities and is an Associate Fellow of the Institute of English Studies, University of London.

Jerusha McCormack's work focused on Oscar Wilde and his disciple, John Gray: first through an academic biography, then through a fictionalized account in *The Man Who Was Dorian Gray* (2000), during her long career at UCD. Two volumes of edited essays reflect current interests: *Wilde the Irishman* (1998) and *China and the Irish* (2009; Mandarin edition, 2010), for which her own essay explores the relationship of Oscar Wilde and a fourth-century Chinese sage called Zhuangzi (Chuang Tsŭ). Over the past eight years she has served as Visiting Professor at Beijing Foreign Studies University where she helped found the first multidisciplinary Irish Studies Centre in China.

Emilie Morin is Lecturer in the Department of English and Related Literature at the University of York. Her research interests lie in Irish and European modernism, and her publications include *Samuel Beckett and the Problem of Irishness* (Palgrave, 2009).

Elizabeth Müller is an Associate Professor at the University of Nantes. She has published numerous articles on Yeats including 'Yeats and the Figure of the Bard', 'Reshaping Chaos: Platonic Elements in Yeats's *A Vision* and Later Poetry' and 'The Cult of Dionysus in the Work of W. B. Yeats'; '"The Embattled Stance": Resistance in Yeats's Late Poetry', and '"Of Golden King and Silver Lady": Yeats and the pre-Socratic Philosophers'. With Meg Harper and Alexandra Poulain, she has also co-organized conferences on Yeats at the University of Lille III, at Emory University, and at the Catholic University of Paris where she also lectures. Her book on Yeats and Dante is forthcoming.

Alexandra Poulain is Professor of Irish Literature and Drama at the Université Charles de Gaulle – Lille 3. Her recent books include *Homo Famelicus: le théâtre de Tom Murphy* (Presses Universitaires de Caen, 2008), *Hunger on the Stage* (Scholars Press, 2008), co-edited with Elisabeth Angel-Perez, *Endgame ou le théâtre mis en pièces* (Presses Universitaires de France, 2009), also with Elisabeth Angel-Perez, and *Passions du corps dans les dramaturgies contemporaines* (Septentrion, 2010). Her current project is on versions of the Passion narrative in modern Irish drama.

Colin Smythe is presently working on a new bibliography of W. B. Yeats, correcting, enlarging, and updating that by Allan Wade (3rd edition, 1968). He is General Editor of his publishing company's Irish Literary Studies Series (53 titles) and (with the late T. R. Henn) of the *Coole Edition of Lady Gregory's Works* (16 volumes so far published), and with Henry Summerfield, of *the Collected Works of G. W. Russell (AE)*. He is also Sir Terry Pratchett's literary agent and first publisher. He received an Hon. LLD from Dublin University for services to Irish Literature in 1998.

Tara Stubbs is a University Lecturer in Literature and Creative Writing at the Department for Continuing Education, Oxford University (OUDCE). Her monograph, *American Literature and Irish Culture, 1910–1955: the Politics of Enchantment*, was published this year by Manchester University Press. It uses a transatlantic framework to consider the ways in which American modernist fiction and poetry was rejuvenated and shaped by cultural and political movements in Ireland during the period. She has worked as a Research Assistant on the *Collected Letters of W. B. Yeats*, and has published articles and book chapters on Yeats and the Ghost Club, Thomas McGreevy, and Bernard Shaw.

Tom Walker is the Ussher Lecturer in Irish Writing at Trinity College Dublin. He has published essays in *The Cambridge Quarterly, The Review of English Studies* and *The Oxford Handbook of Modern Irish Poetry* (Oxford University Press, 2012), and is completing a monograph on the poetry of Louis MacNeice.

Editors' Introduction

THE MASK, a symbolic object used for disguise, as protection, and in performance in many cultures and for most of human history, has been associated with practices as various as ancient religious ritual and contemporary psychoanalysis. That the Mask had an enduring fascination for Yeats, and that a number of principles that are useful in reading his work can be understood by means of the concepts associated with it, is hardly a surprising notion. Indeed, the opposite is true. Yeats's Mask is one of the ideas that spans his oeuvre, from poems like 'The Mask', to prose texts such as *Per Amica Silentia Lunae*, to plays that use physical masks, to recurring characters like Cuchulain and influences like that of Wilde, to take several obvious examples. As early as two years after the poet's death, Louis MacNeice could mention in passing 'Yeats's favourite doctrine of the Mask', knowing his fellow admirers of the poet would agree with its importance, and a decade had not passed before Richard Ellmann entitled his influential literary biography *Yeats: The Man and the Masks*.[1] Both MacNeice and Ellmann began their respective studies with notions of poetry and poets that were commonplaces of the time, that, in Ellmann's words, 'a poet has what Thomas Nashe called a "double soul". The relation of the man and the poet is close but it is not simple.'[2]

---

[1] Louis MacNeice, *The Poetry of Yeats* (New York: Oxford University Press, 1941), 107; Richard Ellmann, *Yeats: The Man and the Masks* (New York: Macmillan, 1948).

[2] Ellmann, 4–5. Ellmann's book appeared in the same year as A. Norman Jeffares's *W. B. Yeats: Man and Poet* (London: Routledge and Kegan Paul, 1949) which explores doubleness in a less theorized way. The two books were the first significant biographically based studies after Joseph Hone's and made rival claims on the critical attention of the public.

MacNeice begins his preface with the same assumption, that there is a doubleness of 'man' and 'poet', and that this binary is crucial:

> There is not, to my knowledge – nor do I think there can be – any satisfactory definition of the relationship of poetry to life. I am convinced however, that there is such a relationship and that it is of primary importance; I am also convinced that a poem is a thing in itself, a self-contained organism, a 'creation' – I might almost say, saving the presence of philosophers, an absolute.[3]

Despite Ellmann's reference to Nashe,[4] and MacNeice's to 'philosophers' (or 'Dr Johnson', in the sentence that follows the quotation above), MacNeice and Ellmann, writing when and where they did, were likely to consider the mortal self and the aesthetic creation of an artistic self or mask as two distinct items, an easy extension of the assumption that reality falls into that handy structure of Art and Life. To a large degree, Yeats shared this assumption.

Such assumptions are now part of a historical context available for analytical exposure. Moreover, contemporary Yeats studies can now take advantage of decades of superb textual and archival scholarship. Yeats's work as a dramatist, rhetorician, and theoretical occultist is now recognized, and correspondingly interdisciplinary scholarship has been pursued. It is, therefore, timely to revisit the Mask. Its obviousness as a relevant term in Yeats studies has ironically contributed to its being overshadowed in the critical landscape: as a commonplace, it can be used in service of other arguments more often than focused on directly. Yet it is not difficult to imagine a number of benefits of reanimating the Mask in light of recent scholarship. After all, the Mask brings into focus a number of concepts fascinatingly relevant to the study of Yeats. For instance, a mask as an object connected with the human body as well as a common synecdoche for notions of self and agency, among others, make it vital to investigations of his form and technique, including poetic and dramatic voice. Insofar as masks are ritual objects in a number of the early religious and philosophical

---

[3] MacNeice, vii.

[4] Nashe's passage reads: 'As sweet Angelicall queristers they are continually conuersant in the heauen of Arts, heauen it selfe is but the highest height of knowledge, he that knowes himself & all things else, knowes the meanes to be happie : happie, thrice happie are they whom God hath doubled his spirite vppon, and giuen a double soule vnto to be Poets.' (*The Unfortunate Traveller or, The Life of Jack Wilton* (London: 1594), quoted from the edition by H. B. Brett-Smith (Oxford: Basil Blackwell, 1927, Percy Reprints), 42.

systems of which Yeats was a student, our increased awareness of the details of his spiritual and intellectual development should lead (as it does in several essays in this collection) to understanding the Mask as a continuum rather than one element in a more or less stable binary. In that masks have been common in theatrical practices for millennia, as well as finding dense use in theatrical practice in the late nineteenth and early twentieth centuries (for example, in the theories of Edward Gordon Craig), much can be learned by focusing on the Mask about Yeats's dramaturgy no less than his intellectual excitement in his studies in classic Athenian drama and Japanese Nó tradition. As Emily Morin argues, Yeats found himself an actor on a different kind of stage in his often overlooked work with the BBC. Many of the essays in this collection use manuscript and newly discovered material to find connections that may surprise readers (as they did the editors) with their apt examinations, in areas that in retrospect seem obvious. Of course, we should look into the ubiquitous narratives of Christ's Passion, the Chinese verses engraved on the sculpture described in the poem 'Lapis Lazuli', personal questions Yeats asked himself about how to control his temper, or the massive reading he undertook to prepare to edit *The Oxford Book of Modern Verse*, to take a few examples from the essays that follow. In general, all the contributors are less interested in finding a completed 'Mask' than noting precise internal variations and probably also the inherent inconsistencies of the idea, the alien quality of finding, in Yeats's words, that when the hero of classical epic found his mask 'hanging upon some oak of Dodona', 'another's breath came and went within his breath upon the carven lips, and that his eyes were upon the instant fixed upon a visionary world' and that, 'all religious men have believed that there is a hand not ours in the events of life' (*Per Amica Silentia Lunae, CW5* 11; *Myth* 335–36).

Given the doubling or multiplicity of Yeats's masks, and the performativity at the heart of the concept of the Mask, it is appropriate that this volume started its life as twin conferences. In the spring of 2009, Alexandra Poulain and Margaret Mills Harper hosted scholars at their respective universities, the Université Charles de Gaulle – Lille III and Georgia State University, to investigate ideas of mask and voice in Yeats's work. The calls for papers described the aims of the conferences thus:

Yeats's impressive array of personae or masks combines with the conscious manipulation of voice, ranging from the remote and dignified to the trivial and lowly. Variations on voice and mask are decisive modalities of Yeats's effort to recreate an oral tradition and thus contribute to the elaboration of Ireland's cultural identity. On the other hand, they also relate to his histrionic propensity for 'remaking himself' simultaneously with his own creation. Whether collective or individual, 'identity' is thus envisaged as plural and dynamic, as performance rather than essence.

Thus, this paradoxical ontology of 'voice and mask' in turn calls attention to the element of theatricality at the heart of Yeatsian aesthetics, in dramatic and non-dramatic forms alike. It also invites analyses of the ways in which literature overlaps with, and sometimes seeks to absorb, other art forms, in particular music and the visual arts; central to Yeats's oeuvre, for instance, is the tension and constant alternation between stasis and kinetic energy.[5]

Part of the aim of the twin conferences was to explore differences that would arise from the different settings, of the various papers as well as musical and theatrical performances and displays of archival materials, which were a feature of both events. The two universities at which the conferences took place are outside expected centres of research on Yeats and therefore, the organizers reckoned, possible sites for new ideas, but they are also both locations that might attract significant participants from a range of disciplinary and methodological specialisms. The Université de Lille is a major centre for Irish Studies in Europe and easily accessible from Paris as well as Ireland and the United Kingdom; the research opportunities at Georgia State University include, for the purposes of Yeats study, the links between Irish Studies there and Emory University, also located in Atlanta. The conveners of the conferences felt also that the linked events would be likely to further transatlantic collaboration, a goal that has been met in numerous ways, including the present issue of the Yeats Annual.

---

[5] 'La voix et le masque dans l'oeuvre de W. B. Yeats: le théâtre des identités', 6–7 février 2009, Université Charles-de-Gaulle, Lille III. In addition to Professors Poulain and Harper, the scientific committee of the French conference included Prof. Carle Bonnafous-Murat (Université de la Sorbonne Nouvelle, Paris III) and Dr. Elizabeth Muller (Université de Nantes); keynote speakers were Nicholas Grene (Trinity College Dublin) and Jacqueline Genet (Université de Caen). Yeats's Anniversary Conference: 'Voice and Mask: Performing Identities', 15–16 May 2009, Georgia State University, Atlanta, Georgia. In addition to Professors Harper and Poulain, the organizing committee included Prof. Geraldine Higgins (Emory University) and Dr. Elizabeth Muller; keynote speakers were James Pethica (Williams College) and James Flannery (Emory University).

Many thanks are due, first and foremost to Alexandra Poulain, for her inspiration and work on the project; also to Geraldine Higgins and Elizabeth Müller for their work in transforming the events into this publication.

The 'Voice and Mask' project has expanded. The collection now includes some essays developed from presentations given at the two conferences and others that were not part of the original events. This issue of the *Yeats Annual* fills out the contours of what we hope are informational as well as provocative new readings and directions for further thought on this subject. The essays are ordered in roughly chronological sequence, beginning with Warwick Gould's analysis of the development of the concept of the Mask before its fully developed form in about 1918, to Michael Cade-Stewart's study of the connections Yeats made from his wide reading in contemporary English-language poetry in his role of editor of *The Oxford Book of Modern Verse* and his multiple masks as presented in *New Poems*.

In addition to the essays published here for the first time, we are happy to reprint 'The Manuscript of "Leo Africanus"', a dialogue in letters written by Yeats in 1915 between himself and the sixteenth-century travel writer Johannes Leo Africanus (al-Hasan ibn Muhammad al-Wazzan al-Fasi). The dialogue, a significant experiment featuring Yeats's assumption of the Mask of a spirit who arrived in séance, and later as a Frustrator in the sessions of automatic writing with George Yeats, forms a significant part of the 'phantasmagoria' of Yeats's spiritual experimentation. The edited text with accompanying essay by Steve L. Adams and George Mills Harper, first published in *Yeats Annual* No. 1 edited by Richard J. Finneran, has long been difficult of access; now that *Yeats Annual* is published digitally, it is possible to redress this situation.[6] As a final chapter of the essays in this *Annual*, the 'Leo Africanus' letters offer a concrete sense of what the concept meant to Yeats: aesthetics here blend seamlessly into serious, even agonizing, personal commitment to the Mask, an exploration that is challenging as only that 'of all imaginable things | The most unlike' (*VP* 371) can be.

Margaret Mills Harper and Warwick Gould
October 2013

---

[6] We thank Steve L. Adams, Margaret Mills Harper, Ann Christian Harper, Richard Edmond Finneran and Catherine Finneran for their permission and encouragement to republish this essay.

Acknowledgements and Editorial Information

Our chief debt of gratitude is to the Yeats Estate over many years for granting permission (through A. P. Watt Ltd., now part of United Agents Partnership, Ltd.) to use published and unpublished materials by W. B. Yeats. Our contributors are further indebted to Caítriona Yeats and to the Yeats family for making unpublished materials available for study and for many other kindnesses, as is the Editor.

A number of helpful librarians include Dr Declan Kiely of the Pierpont Morgan Library, New York, Professor Thomas F. Staley, Dr Cathy Henderson and Dr Richard Oram at the Harry Ransom Humanities Research Center, Austin, Catherine Fahy at the National Library of Ireland, all of whom have provided us with materials and research assistance. At the British Library, the Curator of the Macmillan Archive, Dr Elizabeth James, renders invaluable assistance to the Editor, while the research librarians at the Robert W. Woodruff Library at Emory University are equally generous and prompt in recovering specialist materials. Dr Karen Attar in Special Collections at the Senate House Library, University of London has been unfailingly helpful, especially in respect of the Thomas Sturge Moore Collection. Riette Sturge Moore (who died in 1995) allowed us to use in the livery of the *Yeats Annuals* the rose symbol adapted from Thomas Sturge Moore's designs for the H. P. R. Finberg translation of *Axël* (1925). Linda Shaughnessy of A. P. Watt (now United Agents Partnership), Professors Roy Foster, FBA and John Kelly on behalf of Oxford University Press, are generous with permissions. Individuals, institutions and estates which gave permission for the reproductions of images in the Plate section are thanked within the legends. Every effort has been made to trace copyright holders, and while some images are by unknown photographers, the editor would be grateful to acknowledge any omissions in the next issue.

At Open Book Publishers, William St. Clair FBA, Rupert Gatti and Alessandra Tosi provided patient assistance and invaluable advice to facilitate our transfer to Open Access publishing. Members of the Advisory Board continue to read a large number of submissions and we are grateful to them, and also to Mr R. A. Gilbert and other specialist readers who offered valuable assistance.

The present number of Yeats Annual was set in Caslon SSi by Zoe Holman of the Institute of English Studies. Readers will recall that Caslon Old Face was the typeface which Yeats himself preferred for Cuala Press books.

Deirdre Toomey as Research Editor of this journal continues to take up the challenges which routinely defeat contributors, finding innumerable ways to make good articles better by means of her restless curiosity and indefatigable reading. All associated with the volume (as well as its readers) continue to be grateful for her persistence with intractabilities.

Contributions for *Yeats Annuals No. 20* are largely in place, and those for *No. 21* should reach me, preferably by email, by 1 June 2014 at:

The Institute of English Studies,
University of London
Senate House, 239
Malet Street
London WC1E 7HU
United Kingdom
E-mail warwick.gould@sas.ac.uk.

Yeats Annual is offered to its publishers in camera-ready form. A style sheet, instructions for the submission of articles to the Editorial Board and consequent editorial procedures will be found at our website, http://www.ies.sas.ac.uk/publications/yeats-annual, where it is also possible to find full information about, and to purchase, in-print numbers from the Yeats Annual backlist. The website is being further developed to complement the online and print availability of the current issues through the publisher's website (http://www.openbookpublishers.com).

Professor John Kelly of St. John's College, Oxford is General Editor of *The Collected Letters of W. B. Yeats*. Later years of the letters are now available in the InteLex electronic edition, which presently includes only the first three fully annotated volumes as well as the

'B' text of all subsequent letters which have come to light. Priority in the publication of newly discovered letters remains, however, with the print-based volumes, the fifth of which is now in proof at the Clarendon Press. Colin Smythe (PO Box 6, Gerrards Cross, Bucks, SL9 8XA, UK, cpsmythe@aol.com) is completing his revision of the Wade-Alspach *Bibliography* for the Clarendon Press, while an authorised edition of *Yeats's Occult Diaries, 1898–1901* is being prepared by Deirdre Toomey and myself. We continue to revise A. Norman Jeffares' *New Commentary on the Poems of W. B. Yeats*. All the above would be very grateful to hear of new letters, and to receive new information from readers.

We are grateful to receive offprints and review copies and other bibliographical information (acknowledged at the end of each volume).

Warwick Gould

YEATS'S MASK

The Mask before *The Mask*

Warwick Gould

PREAMBLE

VISIT A MAJOR EXHIBITION at a well-known gallery and you will find paper masks of historical characters enduringly popular in the gift shop. Watch a political rally or demonstration and masks worn by protestors fix, define and arraign the villains and reproject their grotesqueries back through global media. The essence of the mask is its 'immobility',[1] its stillness, its capture of character through characteristic, in some 'eternal moment'.[2]

Such simplicity is, however, far from what is variously implied by the term 'Mask' in the work of Yeats. Having developed the concept towards that of the Anti-Self until around the publication of *Per Amica Silentia Lunae* in 1917, he then italicized it as a technical term, the *Mask* of *A Vision*. Yeats claimed that his Instructors came to give him 'metaphors for poetry' (*AVB* 8), but *A Vision* elaborates many

---

[1] 'Who can forget the face of Chaliapine as the Mogul King in *Prince Igor*, when a mask covering its upper portion made him seem like a phoenix at the end of its thousand wise years, awaiting in condescension the burning nest, and what did it not gain from that immobility in dignity and in power?' (*E&I* 226–27, first collected in *Certain Noble Plays of Japan: From the Manuscripts of Ernest Fenollosa, chosen and finished by Ezra Pound, with an introduction by William Butler Yeats* [Churchtown, Dundrum: Cuala, 1916], vii–viii).

[2] A catch-phrase in Yeats, ultimately from St Thomas Aquinas via Villiers de l'Isle Adam, which is discussed below.

existing metaphors. The italics of *Mask* signify a distinction: and it is not one without difference.³ As he creates and whirls his terms together in an 'arbitrary, harsh and difficult' symbolic system, they change meanings (*AVB* 23). As Neil Mann says

'The *Mask* that appears in *A Vision*, however, seems to have dwindled into a cipher circling the clock-face of the lunar phases along with the other *Faculties*, its function delimited by the System's geometry. It retains enough of its former traits to give a sense of *A Vision*'s continuity with Yeats's previous thought but is at root a different concept.'⁴

Yeats's theories of the Mask have been readily and fruitfully applied to the themes and techniques of his poems, as well as in his theatre, in teaching his work. 'The Mask' (and here I mean that doctrine which reaches its apogee in 1918) has seemed to provide an entry-point accessible and fruitful – especially for undergraduates – to the more recondite speculations of *A Vision* via the mid-career foothills of *Per Amica Silentia Lunae* and certain poems. However, as our sense of Yeats's life and thought has been thickened by the publication of his letters and the patient day-by-day filling in of the chronology of his activities, it becomes obvious that much previous criticism is compromised if it attempts to use the undifferentiated terminology of Mask/*Mask* as a skeleton key to unlock his work. A further difficulty is that 'Things thought too long can be no longer thought' (*VP* 564). The dominant influence of Richard Ellmann's

---

³ A similar distinction is insisted upon by Yeats in the italicization of the Daimon in sixty-nine places in *A Vision* (both versions). The issue is complicated, however, by sometimes uncapitalized and uniformly unitalicized usages of 'Daimon' from 1896 onwards, in thirteen places in essays, prefaces, his unpublished Autobiography (1916–7), *Autobiographies* (dating from 1922 and 1928), and in *Pages from a Diary written in 1930*. 'Daemon' is preferred in the twenty-two earlier usages of the word in *Per Amica Silentia Lunae* and 'Swedenborg, Mediums, and the Desolate Places'. Yeats's motto, of course, in the Order of the Golden Dawn, was 'Demon est Deus Inversus', ultimately taken from Madame Blavatsky's *The Secret Doctrine* I, 99, and *passim*, esp. section XI, 'Demon est Deus Inversus' which opens with the remark 'This symbolical sentence, in its many-sided forms, is certainly dangerous and iconoclastic in the face of all the dualistic later religions, or rather theologies, and especially so in the light of Christianity (1888 ed., p. 443). Madame Blavatsky uses 'Daimon' and 'Daemon' indifferently. See also *CL2* 52, n. 8 which comments that 'Demon est Deus Inversus' is an 'early and occult expression of [Yeats's] enduring belief that polarity and opposition are constitutive of a final unity', a remark which points to the relation between a self and its Mask throughout his life.

⁴ See below, 168.

1948 study *Yeats: The Man and the Masks* long after it was superseded (as he himself knew[5]) is a salutary reminder that until that sudden exhaustion of a ruling idea, overdue change can be hard to effect.

Anachronism is a problem compounded for a generation which has been encouraged to seek answers to the problems of literary texts via the application of post-structuralist literary theory. The allure of applying readings of *A Vision* back into texts before (say) those poems collected in *The Wild Swans at Coole* (1917) is dangerously anachronistic. Formulations of Mask doctrine before *Per Amica* are little studied but have their own integrity. The currency of the term obscures the origin of the thought and erases its unique character when it was at its most influential both as ethic and aesthetic.

My aim, then, is to trace the Mask to its root-tip and review the idea prior to its major exfoliation in *Per Amica Silentia Lunae*. Of the 647 'masks' in the electronically searchable canon,[6] 247 fall in *AVA* and 248 in *AVB*. The remaining 152 usages fall very unevenly: 34 in *Collected Plays*, 32 in *Memoirs*, 29 in *Autobiographies*, 26 in *Later Essays*, nine in *Essays and Introductions*, six in *Uncollected Prose 2*, five in *Explorations*, five in *Poems*, three in *The Secret Rose*, two in *Uncollected Prose 1*, and one, very singular usage in Yeats's preface to *Letters to the New Island*. The figures confirm an increasing reliance on the *Mask* as a technical term in the System, but many prior to 1918 may be ignored as objective descriptions of theatrical devices. I start with a brief anthology of Yeats's remarks c.1908–9 as a vantage point from which to look before and after. The sudden flowering of statements about the Mask in his diary shows that that which had been long-meditated suddenly crystallized as an ethical and aesthetic doctrine

---

[5] Ellmann conceded in a conversation in Oxford in late 1983 that the thesis of the book was flawed, especially that concerning the relation between Yeats and Michael Robartes and Owen Aherne in Ch. VI, 'Robartes and Aherne: Two Sides of a Penny'. Recognising that the then recently reissued book (Penguin, 1979) continued to dominate approaches to the study of Yeats, he found it impossible to update – as he had done with his life of James Joyce – preoccupied as he was with completing his life of Oscar Wilde, and with so much new work going forward on the authorized life of Yeats, then being taken over from the late Leland Lyons by Roy Foster, and the editing of Yeats's letters (in which I was involved).

[6] The 1998 Chadwyck-Healey *W. B. Yeats Collection* is a highly unreliable guide, with a poor search engine which sometimes miscounts multiple usages on a single page. Checking is therefore ultimately an item by item process. The figures given above do not distinguish between overlap, e.g., between *Memoirs* and 'Estrangement' in *Autobiographies*. See Warwick Gould, 'Yeats Digitally Remastered', *YA14* 334–49. For usages in his letters, see below, 19, n. 32.

during his rereading of his then recently published *Collected Works in Verse and Prose*. This is unsurprising.[7] In the following remarks one discerns the confluence of several earlier lines of thought.

THE MASK: A SELECT ANTHOLOGY

Identifying his 'worst fault' as a tendency to be detained by 'petulant combativeness', Yeats seems to have embarked on some disciplined 'anger-management'.

It is always inexcusable to lose one's self-possession. It always comes from impatience, from a kind of spiritual fright at someone who is here and now more powerful, even if only from stupidity. I am never angry with those in my power. I fear strangers; I fear the representatives of the collective opinion, and so rage stupidly and rudely, exaggerating what I feel and think ... Last night there was a debate on a political question at the Arts Club. I was for a moment inclined to use arguments merely to answer something said by one speaker or the other. *In pursuit of the mask I resolved to say only fanciful and personal things, and so to escape out of mere combat.* I did so, and I noticed that all the arguments which had occurred to me earlier were said by someone or other. Logic is a machine; one can leave it to itself; unhelped it will force those present to exhaust the subject. The fool is as likely as the sage to speak the appropriate answer to any assertion. If an argument is forgotten, somebody will go home miserable. You throw your money on the table, and you receive so much change. Style, personality (deliberately adopted and therefore a mask), is the only escape from all the heat of the bargaining, from all but the sight of the money changers (*Mem* 137–39, emphasis added; cf., 'Estrangement' 2, *Au* 461; *CW3* 341).

'Mask' seemingly springs into this 14 January 1909 entry on his old problem of Irish political rhetoric, but I will return to its submerged current of thought a little later.

'To oppose the new ill-breeding of Ireland, which may in a few years destroy all that has given Ireland a distinguished name ... I can only set up a secondary or interior personality created by me out of the tradition of myself, and this personality (alas, to me only possible in my writings) must be always

---

[7] In 1926 he told Pamela Travers 'oracularly' that '"When I get an idea for a poem ... I take down one of my own books and read it and then I go on from there". Moses explaining his tablets couldn't have moved me more'. See P. L. Travers, 'Only Connect', *The Openhearted Audience*, ed. Virginia Havilland (Washington: Library of Congress, 1980), 9–11, also quoted in *YA18* xxvi–vii.

gracious and simple. It must have that slight separation from immediate interests which makes charm possible, while remaining near enough for fire. Is not charm what it is, perhaps, because it is an escape from mechanism? So much of the world as is dominated by the contest of interests is a mechanism. The newspaper is the roar of the machine. Argument, the moment acknowledged victory is sought, becomes a clash of interests. One should not, above all not in books, which sigh for immortality, argue at all if one is not ready to leave to another apparent victory. In daily life one becomes rude the moment one grudges to the clown his perpetual triumph.[8]

Having latched onto the Mask as a necessity in social and public life, Yeats began to apply it as a personal ideal after a crisis in his private life, his unhappy sexual consummation with Maud Gonne. On 23 January 1909 he wrote

It seems to me that love, if it is fine, is essentially a discipline, but it needs so much wisdom that the love of Solomon and Sheba must have lasted for all the silence of the Scriptures. In wise love each divines the high secret self of the other and, refusing to believe in the mere daily self, creates a mirror where the lover or the beloved sees an image to copy in daily life. Love also creates the mask.[9]

In the lecture 'Friends of my Youth' (9 March 1910) at the Adelphi Club, Yeats pondered the Rhymers' Club's escape from Rhetoric via what he called 'personality' and 'personal utterance' (*YT* 29–30). Adapting a nostrum from Goethe "'No man ever learned to know himself by contemplation. We learn to know ourselves by action only'" (*YT* 31), he developed the equation between personality and the Mask.

---

[8] *Mem* 142, cf., 'Estrangement', *Au* 463; *CW3* 342–43. The passages given here were in fact first published in 1911 in a short series of notes 'about argument, for the argumentative drama presses upon you in England' entitled 'The Folly of Argument', in *The Manchester Playgoer* (June 1911). With so much of his thinking being about authorship and style (in which conjoined subjects lay the current application of his thinking about the Mask to drama), Yeats prefaced this small gathering with the thought that, at 'some crisis in our Theatre's affairs, because I found that I could do no premeditated writing, I began a diary of casual meditations. Having no set form I could begin and end them when I liked, and as they were but for my own reading, it was not necessary to write them over again. The Diary is now a considerable book and I find I turn to it continually to find out my own settled opinions.' See *UP2* 394–96.

[9] *Mem* 144–45, cf., *Au* 464; *CW3* 343. 'The Mask', the first significant love poem to use the theme, was drafted after 8 August, 1910 (*Mem* 258–59) and published in *The Green Helmet and Other Poems* (Dublin: Cuala) on the last day of September, 1910. See *VP* 263.

Man knows himself by action only, by contemplation, never; and this mysterious thing, personality, the mask, is created half consciously, half unconsciously, out of the passions, the circumstances of life' (*YT* 77).

The potential of a 'secondary or interior personality' was, however, 'alas, to me only possible to me in my writings' for writing remained for the moment more latent, but his perpetual reverie about authors and authorship was filled with it.

[between 23 and 28 Jan] There is a relation between discipline and the theatrical sense. If we cannot imagine ourselves as different from what we are and try to assume that second self, we cannot impose a discipline upon ourselves, though we may accept one from others. Active virtue as distinguished from the passive acceptance of a current code is therefore theatrical, consciously dramatic, the wearing of a mask. It is the condition of arduous full life. One constantly notices in very active natures a tendency to pose, or a preoccupation with the effect they are producing if the pose has become a second self. One notices this in Plutarch's heroes, and every now and then in some modern who has tried to live by classical ideas, in Oscar Wilde, for instance, and less obviously in men like Walt Whitman. Wordsworth is so often flat and heavy partly because his moral sense has no theatrical element, it is an obedience, a discipline which he has not created. This increases his popularity with the better sort of journalists, the *Spectator* writers, for instance, with all who are part of the machine and yet care for poetry (*Mem* 151).

[On or after 26 Jan., [1909] All my life I have been haunted with the idea that the poet should know all classes of men as one of themselves, that he should combine the greatest possible personal realization with the greatest possible knowledge of the speech and circumstance of the world. Fifteen or twenty years ago I remember longing, with this purpose, to disguise myself as a peasant and wander through the West, and then shipping as a sailor. But when one shrinks from even talking business with a stranger, and is unnatural till one knows a man for months, because one underrates or over-rates all unknown people, one cannot adventure far. The artist grows more and more distinct, more and more a being in his own right as it were, but more and more loses grasp of the always more complex world. Some day setting out to find knowledge, like some pilgrim to the Holy Land, he will become the most romantic of all characters. He will play with all masks.[10]... Comedy is joyous because all assumption of a part, of a personal mask, whether the individualized face of comedy or the grotesque face of farce, is a display of energy, and all energy is joyous. A poet creates tragedy from his

---

[10] *Mem* 151–52. In 'Presences' (November 1915), Yeats contrives to 'play with all masks' (*VP* 358).

own soul, that soul which is alike in all men, and at moments it has no joy, as we understand that word, for the soul is an exile and without will. It attains to ecstasy, which is from the contemplation of things which are vaster than the individual and imperfectly seen, perhaps, by all those that still live. The masks of tragedy contain neither character nor personal energy. They are allied to decoration and to the abstract figures of Egyptian temples. Before the mind can look out of their eyes the active will perishes, hence their sorrowful calm. Joy is of the will which does things, which overcomes obstacles, which is victorious. The soul only knows changes of state. These changes of state, or this gradually enlarging consciousness, is the self-realization of modern culture. I think the motives of tragedy are connected more with these changes of state than with action. I feel this but cannot see my way clearly. But I am hunting truth too far into its thicket. It is my business to keep close to the impression of the senses, and to daily thought. Yet is not always the tragic ecstasy some realization or fulfilment of the soul in itself, some slow or sudden expansion of it like an overflowing well? Is not that what we mean by beauty? (*Mem* 152–53)

Jan. 28 [1909]. The tragic mask expresses a passion or mood, a state of the soul; that only. (The mask of musician or of the dying slave.) The mask of comedy an individual. (Any modern picture.) The mask of farce an energy; in this the joyous life by its own excess has become superficial, it has driven out thought. (Any grotesque head.) Then these are connected in some way with the dominant moods of the three classes which have given the cradles, as it were, to tragedy, comedy, and farce: aristocracy, the middle class, and the people – exaltation, moral force, labour (*Mem* 153).

I think that all happiness depends on the energy to assume the mask of some other self; that all joyous or creative life is a rebirth as something not oneself, something which has no memory and is created in a moment and perpetually renewed. We put on a grotesque or solemn pained face to hide us from the terrors of judgement, invent an imaginative Saturnalia where one forgets reality, a game like that of a child, where one loses the infinite pain of self-realisation. Perhaps all the sins and energies of the world are but its flights from an infinite blinding beam (*Mem* 191).

In life courtesy and self-possession, and in the arts style, are the sensible impressions of the free mind, for both arise out of a deliberate shaping of all things, and from never being swept away, whatever the emotion, into confusion or dullness.[11]

---

[11] *E&I*, 253. Dated 'August 1907' in 'Poetry and Patriotism' in *Poetry and Ireland: Essays by W. B. Yeats and Lionel Johnson* (Churchtown, Dundrum: Cuala, 1908), 9, and in *CWVP8* (also Dec. 1908), 102.

'Mask' being typically clustered with such concepts as 'discipline' 'self-possession', 'oratory', 'courtesy', 'style', and 'theatrical sense', it now becomes possible to see the imperative for such a thing, implicit in this famous remark of eighteen months before. Such statements reflect a *fin de siècle* (indeed Paterian) fascination with the coincidence of aesthetics and ethics.

THE FIN DE SIÈCLE MASK

While the full context of writing about the Mask in the 1890s lies beyond my scope,[12] it is worth recalling that by 1914 it was a matter of such commonplace as to merit casual recollection. In that year Yeats recalled of Olive Schreiner that 'Twenty-five years ago ... she lived in the East End of London because only there could she see the faces of people without a mask. To this Oscar Wilde replied that he lived in the West End because nothing interested him but the mask'.[13] As ever, Wilde's conversation was but a dress rehearsal for his writing, and such sentiments appeared in 'The Decay of Lying'. Wilde read the proofs to Yeats on Christmas Day, 1888 (*Au* 134–5; *CW3* 147) and therefore could have heard Wilde read 'what is interesting about people in good society ... the mask that each of them wears, not the reality that lies behind the mask'.[14] There

---

[12] Max Beerbohm's *The Happy Hypocrite* (London: John Lane, The Bodley Head, 1897) would be an excellent point of departure for such a study. See A. Norman Jeffares, 'Yeats's Mask', *English Studies XXX*, 6 (Dec., 1949), 289–98, collected in Jeffares's *The Circus Animals* (London: Macmillan, 1970), 3–14, at 6. The whole subject may be pursued through the indices to *J*.

[13] *UP2* 412. The context was the Poetry banquet in his honour in Chicago in 1914. Having opened with the allusion to Wilde's memory of Schreiner, Yeats said: 'After a week of lecturing I am too tired to assume a mask, so I will address my remarks especially to a fellow craftsman [Vachel Lindsay], whose 'General William Booth Enters into Heaven' had 'a strange beauty', and you know Bacon said, "There is no excellent beauty without strangeness"'. 'Strangeness' in Court Masque as a form was sought by Ben Jonson, and Bacon's phrase to the effect that 'excellent beauty' required 'high grave dignity and strangeness' had filtered to Yeats via Pater and Poe and via Baudelaire's 'Le beau est toujours bizarre'. See *CL2* 448, n. 6; *CW9* 179 & 548; *Ex* 181.

[14] See *The Complete Works of Oscar Wilde*, IV, *Criticism: Historical Criticism, Intentions, The Soul of Man*, ed. Josephine M. Guy (Oxford: Oxford University Press, 2007), 80. Yeats owned *Intentions* in the Leipzig: Heinemann and Balestier, 1891 edition: see *YL* 2268.

are of course, numerous bold paradoxes about the Mask throughout the essays, which culminate with the last sentence of 'The Truth of Masks':

A Truth in art is that whose contrary is also true ... it is only in art-criticism that we can realize Hegel's system of contraries. The truths of metaphysics are the truths of masks.[15]

There are, again as Wilde saw, Paterian answers to the problems posed by considering the aesthetic as a guide to the serious life. In the essay on 'Style', Pater, in fleshing out the idea that '"The style is the man"', comes close to the idea of Mask in showing how expression is 'the finer accommodation of speech to that vision within'.[16] Style, then, is formative of behaviour, as Wilde saw, and not just in such well-known texts as *The Picture of Dorian Gray*. In 'The Decay of Lying' Vivian is bold enough to disclose 'the secret that Truth is entirely and absolutely a matter of style; while Life – poor, probable, uninteresting human life ... will follow meekly after him ...'.[17] The argument continues through various *obiter dicta* in the other *Intentions* essays and culminates in 'The Truth of Masks', but the best early statement is that of 'The Artist as Critic':

Use Love's Litany and the words will create the yearning from which the world fancies that they spring. Have you a grief that corrodes your heart? Steep yourself in the language of grief, learn its utterance from Prince Hamlet and Queen Constance, and you will find that mere expression is a mode of consolation, and that Form, which is the birth of Passion, is also the death of pain.[18]

---

[15] *Ibid.,* 228.
[16] Walter Pater's essay on 'Style' may be found in *Appreciations* (London: Macmillan, 1889, reprinted 1901), 5–38 at pp. 35, 16.
[17] *The Collected Works of Oscar Wilde,* IV, 88–89.
[18] *Ibid.,* IV, 196. The idea is developed in later mss of 'The Portrait of Mr W. H.': 'It is never with impunity that one's lips say Love's Litany. Words have their mystical power over the soul, and form can create the feeling from which it should have sprung. Sincerity itself, the ardent, momentary sincerity of the artist, is often the unconscious result of style, and in the case of those rare temperaments that are exquisitely susceptible to the influences of language, the use of certain phrases and modes of expression can stir the very pulse of passion ... and can transform into a strange sensuous energy what in its origin had been mere aesthetic impulse.' The essay had been published as a story in *Blackwood's Edinburgh Magazine*, July, 1889, but this passage was not published until 1921. See *The Artist as Critic: Critical*

If Wilde could boast that he had stood 'in symbolic relation' to his time because he had 'summed up all systems in a phrase and all philosophies in an epigram',[19] it was left to Yeats to turn the mask, an epigram, back into a system. But it seems more important to acknowledge that the Mask begins in a continual reverie about authorship. Yeats's various remarks about literary style – its making, and its necessity – can be reconciled sometimes only with difficulty, but 'the Mask' is the practical tool and symbol whereby it is done. He remarks, for example, in 'Ego Dominus Tuus', 'A style is learned by sedentary toil | And by the imitation of great masters',[20] having said elsewhere, and with approval in recalling a conversation with Synge, 'Style comes from the shock of new material'.[21] Yeats's texts have within their field of allusion many of the 'great masters'; he has learned from imitating.[22] But behind *literary* style there is the more general field of human behaviour to be governed by style according to the *fin-de-siècle* sense that an ethic and an aesthetic might and indeed should be one and the same.

THE MASK IN BEDFORD PARK

When in 1934 Horace Reynolds sent 'a bundle of photographic copies' of articles Yeats had published in American newspapers, Yeats 'noticed' that in later life he had 'worked out with the excitement of discovery things known in my youth as though one forgot and

Writings of Oscar Wilde, ed. Richard Ellmann (London: W. H. Allen, 1970), 152–220 at 199.

[19] See *The Complete Works of Oscar Wilde*, II, *De Profundis, 'Epistola: In Carcere et Vinculis'*, ed. Ian Small (Oxford: Oxford University Press, 2005), 95, 163.

[20] *VP 370*. In the drafts, the idea is more complex. The 'masters' are 'masters of our speech' and their imitation is pursued 'By writing and rewriting'. See 'The Wild Swans at Coole' *Manuscript Materials by W. B. Yeats*, ed. Stephen Parrish (Ithaca and London: Cornell University Press, 1994), 284–85.

[21] *Mem* 105; repeated in 'The Bounty of Sweden' (*Au* 531). The phrase may recall Pater: 'the chief stimulus of good style is to possess a full, rich, complex matter to grapple with' (Pater, *Appreciations*, op. cit., 16).

[22] 'A mask: that is what I needed', says that 'novice' narrator, Umberto Eco. Narrating *'about* the Middle Ages' compelled him to narrate *'in* the Middle Ages', compelling the reading and rereading of medieval chroniclers 'to acquire their rhythm and their innocence', and therefore bringing with it the inevitability of intertextual echoes of earlier writers. 'Books always speak of other books' is of course one of the major themes of his novel. See Umberto Eco, *Reflections on* The Name of the Rose (London: Secker and Warburg, 1985), 19–20.

rediscovered oneself'. Many of these had been learned in the Bedford Park Clubhouse theatre, through the production of plays which, with the inherent alienation of a 'pastoral theme', had helped Yeats to 'avoid[] every oratorical phrase or cadence' in reworking *The Countess Cathleen*.

My isolation from ordinary men and women was increased by an asceticism destructive of mind and body, combined with an adoration of physical beauty that made it meaningless. Sometimes the barrier between myself and other people filled me with terror; an unfinished poem, and the first and never-finished version of *The Shadowy Waters* had this terror for their theme. I had in an extreme degree the shyness – I know no better word – that keeps a man from speaking his own thought. Burning with adoration and hatred I wrote verse that expressed emotions common to every sentimental boy and girl, and that may be the reason why the poems upon which my popularity has depended until a few years ago were written before I was twenty-seven. Gradually I overcame my shyness a little, though I am still struggling with it and cannot free myself from the belief that it comes from lack of courage, that the problem is not artistic but moral. I remember saying as a boy to some fellow student in the Dublin art schools, "The difference between a good draftsman and a bad is one of courage". I wrote prose badly ... [my] prose, unlike verse, had not those simple forms that like a masquer's mask protect us with their anonymity (*LNI*, 1934, vii–xiii).

Yeats rebelled against the authorial anonymity which writing for W. E. Henley's S*cots Observer* and '*National Observer*' entailed, 'in the puritanism of [his] twenties'. Taking a nationalistic stance, he sought nevertheless to exclude rhetoric and opinion as a 'first discipline in creative prose' (*Mem* 38). While he contrasted Lionel Johnson's self-possession with his own 'provincial ... clumsiness', he quickly saw through Johnson's poised self-creation by means of his faked, perfect dramaticules of imaginary conversations with his famous 'puppets' (*CW5* 90). Self-mastery came only slowly, but as Irish oratory and rhetoric yielded to his own self-possession, it became clear that its style in itself was but 'high breeding in words and argument' (*E&I* 253). For Yeats, the essence of Byron, Shelley, and Keats was not 'character for its own sake', but 'the mask for some mood or passion, as in Byron's "Manfred" and in his "Don Juan"' with their 'great types, great symbols of passion and of mood ...'[23] It had not been thus in Ireland, until 'The Dublin Hermetic Society' had started writing 'many curious and some beautiful lyrics' in c.1882 when 'seven youths

[23] 'Nationality and Literature' (1893), *UP1* 270–71.

began to study European magic and Oriental mysticism'. Their main conviction, Yeats tells us, was

> that the poets were uttering, under the mask of phantasy, the old revelations, and that we should truly look for genii of the evening breeze and hope for the final consummation of the world when two halcyons might sit upon a bough and eat once-poisonous herbs and take no harm ... These periodical meetings started a movement ...[24]

THE ETERNAL MOMENT: THE OCCULT MASK OF 1896

'Old revelations' under the 'mask of phantasy' reach their *fin de siècle* apogee in *Rosa Alchemica*, first published in *The Savoy* in April 1896, and gathered as the first of a triptych of occult stories as the culmination of *The Secret Rose* in 1897. Back into the *penseroso* life of a Dublin scholar and would-be alchemist comes the magus, Michael Robartes, who tries to seduce him into the Order of the Alchemical Rose with incantations to which selective quotation cannot do justice, and vision-inducing incense.

> He had ... become in my waking dream a shuttle weaving an immense purple web whose folds had begun to fill the room ... 'They have come to us; they have come to us', the voice began again; 'all that have ever been in your reverie, all that you have met with in books. There is Lear ... and he laughs because you thought yourself an existence who are but a shadow, and him a shadow who is an eternal god; and there is Beatrice, ... and there is the mother of the God of humility ... but she holds in her hand the rose whose every petal is a god; and there ... is Aphrodite ... I made a violent effort which seemed almost to tear me in two, and said with forced determination, 'You would sweep me away into an indefinite world which fills me with terror; and yet a man is a great man just in so far as he can make his mind reflect everything with indifferent precision like a mirror.' I seemed to be perfectly master of myself, and went on ... 'I command you to leave me at once, for your ideas and phantasies are but the illusions that creep like maggots into civilisations when they begin to decline, and into minds when they begin to decay.' I ... struggled hopelessly ... and I knew that I ... was conquered at last ... and as I was swirled along ... a multitude of pale hands were reaching towards me, and strange gentle faces bending above me, and half-wailing and half-caressing voices uttering words that were forgotten the moment they were spoken. I ... felt my memories, my hopes, my thoughts, my will, everything I held to be myself, melting away; then I seemed to rise through

---

[24] 'A New Poet', 1894, *UP1* 336.

numberless companies of beings who were, I understood, in some way more certain than thought, each wrapped in his eternal moment, in the perfect lifting of an arm, in a little circlet of rhythmical words, in dreaming with dim eyes and half-closed eyelids. And then I passed beyond these forms, which were so beautiful they had almost ceased to be, and, having endured strange moods ... I passed into that Death which is Beauty herself, and into that Loneliness which all the multitudes desire without ceasing. All things that had ever lived seemed to come and dwell in my heart, and I in theirs; and I had never again known mortality or tears, had I not suddenly fallen from the certainty of vision into the uncertainty of dream ... I awoke to find myself leaning upon the table and supporting my head with my hands. I saw ... Michael Robartes watching me ... 'I will go wherever you will', I said, 'and do whatever you bid me, for I have been with eternal things' (*VSR* 132–36. *Myth 2005* 181–83).

This 'eternal moment' is based on an Aquinian doctrine found in Villiers de L'Isle Adam's *Axël*, which Yeats had read before reviewing its première in Paris in 1894, with Maud Gonne translating for him: 'Car l'éternité, dit excellemment saint Thomas, n'est que la pleine possession de soi-même en un seul et même instant'.[25] It is fundamental to his subsequent re-applications of the phrase that here, in his first usage of it, it is associated with god-like heroes – Roland, Hamlet, Lear, Beatrice, Faust – who 'are always making and unmaking humanity, which is indeed but the trembling of their lips' from their mythic afterlives in the minds of readers.[26] Yeats's web of self-allusion provides his early sources for the idea of eternal self-possession.[27] In the *Summa Theologica* (Part I, *Quaestio* 10),

---

[25] *Axël* (Paris: Maison Quentin, 1890), 35; *YL* 2200. See *Myth 2005* 183, 372, n. 9; 384, n. 37; *CW9* 234–37. The latest editors of *AVA*, while drawing on my Review of *A Critical Edition of Yeats's A Vision (1925)*, ed. George Mills Harper and Walter Kelly Hood (London: Macmillan, 1978) in *Notes and Queries*, October 1981, N.S. Vol. 28, n. 5, 458–60 for clarification of the Aquinian source, cite only the 1925 H. P. R. Finberg translation for which, of course, Yeats wrote the introduction: see *CW13* 253, n. 148; *YL* 2201, whilst omitting any reference to Yeats's earliest use of the phrase.

[26] See *VSR* 133–34; *Myth 2005* 181–82; and, more generally on Yeats and Theatrum Mundi, Warwick Gould, '"A Crowded Theatre": Yeats and Balzac' in *Yeats the European*, ed. A. Norman Jeffares (Gerrards Cross: Colin Smythe Ltd., 1989), 69–90.

[27] See Warwick Gould, *Notes and Queries*, October 1981, 458–60. The idea remains with Yeats: see, e.g., in *On the Boiler* where he remarks of the final triumph of the Will: 'It has, as it were, thrust up its arms towards those angels who have, as Villiers de l'Isle Adam quotes from St Thomas Aquinas, returned into themselves in an eternal moment' (*CW5* 247).

Aquinas tests the Boethian doctrine that eternity is 'interminabilis vitae tota simul et perfecta possessio',[28] returning to the matter in the *Summa Contra Gentiles* (I, 15), in discussing God's eternity, but it is in the *quaestio* referred to above that he draws from Boethius's definition a distinction between aeviternity and eternity which, though never formulated as such by Yeats, comes close to the essence of his thinking. Yeats, as so often, has grasped and almost wilfully misinterpreted a central theological tenet in coming to philosophy via occultism, to formulate a key statement towards his eventual if somewhat mysterious idea of 'Beatific Vision' (*CVA* xii, *CW13* xv, *VP* 824), and in *AVA* the 'eternal moment' occurs when the soul 'com[es] into possession of itself forever in a single moment' (*CVA* 73; *CW13* 61).

Mythologies (2005) allowed for easy comparison of a complex of Yeats's associated ideas of the love of God for the uniqueness of the individual soul in its 'eternal moment', a state of eternal self-possession. 'The Voice' in *The Celtic Twilight* offers an entry point to what to Yeats seemed 'the root of Christian mysticism': 'no human soul is like any other human soul, and therefore the love of God for any human soul is infinite, for no other soul can satisfy the same need in God' (*Myth 2005* 46). Experiences behind the *pensée* recorded in Yeats's as yet unpublished *Visions* notebook between 14 July and 20 September 1898 indicate that his experiences were probably 'not true trance' (unlike the experience imagined for *Rosa Alchemica*) its being 'unusual' for Yeats to experience 'passive mysticism', his 'nature' having been 'shaped by thaumaturgy' (*Myth 2005* 46; 261, n. 2; 262 nn. 5 & 6). Under the mysterious glamour of Robartes, *Rosa Alchemica*'s narrator travels to the Connemara coast by train

> ... it seemed to me I was so changed that I was no more, as man is, a moment shuddering at eternity, but eternity weeping and laughing over a moment; and when ... Michael Robartes had fallen asleep, as he soon did, his sleeping face, in which there was no sign of all that had so shaken me and that now kept me wakeful, was to my excited mind more like a mask than a face. The fancy possessed me that the man behind it had dissolved away like salt in water, and that it laughed and sighed, appealed and denounced at the bidding of beings greater or less than man (*VSR* 144; *Myth 2005* 183 & n. 44).

When the initiation ceremony – in essence an orgiastic, drug-fuelled dance with immortal presences – begins, the narrator as initiate is

---

[28] *De Consolatione Philosophiae*, V, 6.

ushered in to the central chamber by Robartes, but not before an initial (and accurate) pre-vision of rejection.

I put my hand to the handle, but the moment I did so the fumes of the incense, helped perhaps by his mysterious glamour, made me fall again into a dream, in which I seemed to be a mask, lying on the counter of a little Eastern shop. Many persons, with eyes so bright and still that I knew them for more than human, came in and tried me on their faces, but at last flung me into a corner laughing; but all this passed in a moment (*VSR* 136–37; *Myth 2005* 188).

In the orgy, he drops out of a dance in the central hall, under a ceiling upon which is an 'immense rose wrought in mosaic', and stands, 'watching the

> coming and going of those flame-like figures; until gradually I sank into a half-dream, from which I was awakened by seeing the petals of the great rose, which had no longer the look of mosaic, falling slowly through the incense-heavy air, and, as they fell, shaping into the likeness of living beings of an extraordinary beauty. Still faint and cloud-like, they began to dance, and as they danced took a more and more definite shape, so that I was able to distinguish beautiful Grecian faces and august Egyptian faces, and now and again to name a divinity by the staff in his hand or by a bird fluttering over his head; and soon every mortal foot danced by the white foot of an immortal; and in the troubled eyes that looked into untroubled shadowy eyes, I saw the brightness of uttermost desire as though they had found at length, after unreckonable wandering, the lost love of their youth. Sometimes, but only for a moment, I saw a faint solitary figure with a veiled face, and carrying a faint torch, flit among the dancers, but like a dream within a dream, like a shadow of a shadow, and I knew by an understanding born from a deeper fountain than thought, that it was Eros himself ... a voice cried to me from the crimson figures, 'Into the dance! there is none that can be spared out of the dance; into the dance! into the dance! that the gods may make them bodies out of the substance of our hearts'; and before I could answer, a mysterious wave of passion, that seemed like the soul of the dance moving within our souls, took hold of me, and I was swept, neither consenting nor refusing, into the midst. I was dancing with an immortal august woman, who had black lilies in her hair, and her dreamy gesture seemed laden with a wisdom more profound than the darkness that is between star and star, and with a love like the love that breathed upon the waters; and as we danced on and on, the incense drifted over us and round us, covering us away as in the heart of the world, and ages seemed to pass, and tempests to awake and perish in the folds of our robes and in her heavy hair. Suddenly I remembered that her eyelids had never quivered, and that her lilies had not dropped a black petal, nor shaken from their places, and understood with

a great horror that I danced with one who was more or less than human, and who was drinking up my soul as an ox drinks up a wayside pool; and I fell, and darkness passed over me. I awoke suddenly as though something had awakened me, and saw that I was lying on a roughly painted floor, and that on the ceiling, which was at no great distance, was a roughly painted rose, and about me on the walls half-finished paintings. The pillars and the censers had gone; and near me a score of sleepers lay wrapped in disordered robes, their upturned faces looking to my imagination like hollow masks ... (*VSR* 145–48; *Myth 2005* 188–90)

This is an entirely new perspective on the hollowness and immobility of the mask. Its essential vacancy is seen as a human vessel to be filled and possessed by the whim of immortal presences, themselves fixed types of god or hero whose 'trembling lips make and unmake humanity. Yeats calls these presences 'the Moods', a difficult enough concept and a separate topic for discussion of such books as *The Secret Rose* and *The Wind Among the Reeds*.[29] Robartes is a magus, his temptation a thaumaturgical act (if not merely a drug-induced hallucinatory delusion: such is the element of the fantastic in the whole triptych). If the immortal presences can summon humans, so suitably inducted humans can summon immortal powers, a procedure we see attempted time after time with such women as Maud Gonne, Dorothea Hunter, and Nora Hopper in the rituals of the Celtic Mystical Order, a couple of years later.

What emerges from this whole two-way congress between the human questers and immortals – gods, spirits, archetypes – is that the Mask has now an occult purpose and function, but not yet a sense of the Anti-Self. And yet two of the heroes of these stories, the narrator and Owen Aherne, are divided men who, rejecting occult temptation, are held on the margins. They are not voteens but lead 'threshold' lives, praying best 'in poor chapels', held back from being 'swept away' as it were into the 'indefinite world'.[30] And the 'splitting' of Yeats into Aherne, Robartes and the triptych's Narrator presages the monopolylogue with 'principles of the mind' in *The Wind Among the Reeds*, Yeats's first attempt to 'play with all masks'.[31]

---

[29] A subject explored at some length in my Yeats International Summer School Lecture, 'Yeats's Fatal Book', 2007.

[30] *VSR 172; Myth 2005* 205. 'William Blake and his Illustrations to the *Divine Comedy*' affirms that beauty is 'the one mask through which can be seen the unveiled eyes of eternity' , *E&I* 139; *CW4* 103.

[31] In a seminar at the Institute of English Studies, 2012, Oliver Soden contrasted monopolylogue in the public readings by Charles Matthews and Charles Dickens

A harbinger of the occult mask might be found in Yeats's powerful early criticism of a draft of Olivia Shakespear's story, Beauty's Hour, in 1894. Yeats discerned that the hero, Gerald, wanted 'a slight touch more of definition'

> Might he not be one of those vigerous fair haired, boating, or cricket playing young men, who are very positive, & what is called manly, in external activities & energies & wholly passive & plastic in emotional & intellectual things? I met just such a man last winter. I had suspected before that those robust masks hid often and often a great emotional passivity and plasticity but this man startled me. He was of the type of those who face the cannons mouth without a tremour, but kill themselves rather than face life without some girl with pink cheeks, whose character they have never understood, whose soul they have never perceived, & whom they would have forgotten in a couple of months.[32]

The thought, though not exactly developed, was evidently reapplied when Yeats wrote a now lost letter to Maud Gonne, c.20 March 1899 which, to judge from her reply, must have asked her whether she had adopted a mask (*CL2* 377). The question can be inferred from her reply of 22 March 1899, 'No I do not think I wear a mask, & I do not think I am lonely though I am a little *outside* of life – & do not *want* to get back *into* life again' (*G-YL* 104–05). There was every reason to ask such a question at this time, so soon after Yeats had learned of her double life, her two children, and her relationship with Lucien Millevoye, and after she had turned down his proposal of marriage. The 'spiritual marriage', which she proposed, seemed an attractive second best as they worked together on the plans for a Celtic Mystical Order, work which allowed him to reflect on the

---

from the latter's own work, with Eliot's 'interpersonality' of 'different voices' in *The Waste Land*. For Ellmann's later view on the absence of the narrator from his *Yeats: the Man and the Masks* see above, n. 4.

[32] *CL1* 396–97, 6 August 1894. Olivia Shakespear took his advice and the story was published in the August and September 1896 issues of *The Savoy*. Yeats had also suggested a number of magical and mystical books for 'Dr Trefusis' in the story to read, including books by Jacob Boehme and St John of the Cross. There are 99 usages of 'mask' and 91 of 'masks' in the rather less easily searchable *CL InteLex* edition (the search tools do not discriminate between Yeats's usages and those of his editors, and manual checking is essential). In extracting a few I concentrate on usages before c.18 August 1918, when letters to Iseult Gonne suddenly show that the system of *A Vision* is being developed (*CL InteLex* 3472).

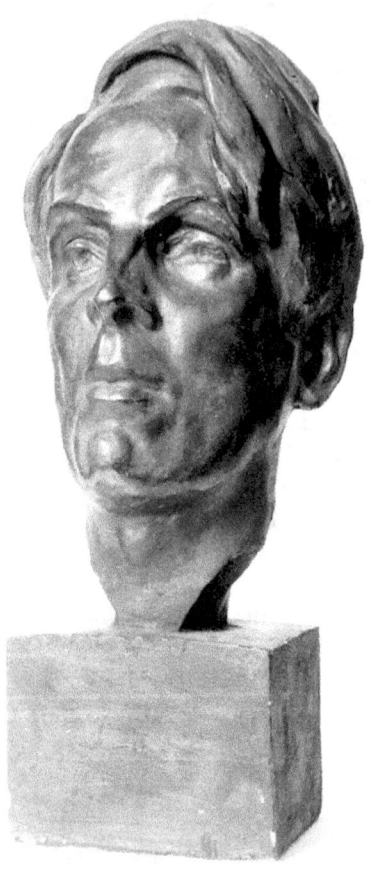

Plate 1. Plaster cast of mask of W. B. Yeats by Kathleen Scott (née Bruce, later Lady Kennet), 1907. 17 1/2 in. (445 mm) high. Photograph courtesy and © The National Portrait Gallery, London. All rights reserved.

profound differences between them.³³ If the lost letter belongs to a private dialogue in which the concept of the mask was being accorded an occult significance, then it is possible that such later summaries as the following passage from *The Trembling of the Veil* (1922) may have roots in this grim period.

As life goes on we discover that certain thoughts sustain us in defeat, or give us victory, whether over ourselves or others, and it is these thoughts, tested by passion, that we call convictions. Among subjective men (in all those, that is, who must spin a web out of their own bowels) the victory is an intellectual daily re-creation of all that exterior fate snatches away, and so that fate's antithesis; while what I have called 'the Mask' is an emotional antithesis to all that comes out of their internal nature. We begin to live when we have conceived life as tragedy.³⁴

If such is the case, then the sudden development of the metaphor into theories of behaviour and of creativity in the 1908–1909 journal is an outgrowth of the idea. Summing up the theatrical potential of the Mask in *Certain Noble Plays of Japan* (1916), Yeats traced a potential audience reaction to that stillness of theatrical masks in which 'the fine invention of a sculptor ... a work of art ... the nobler for lacking curiosity, alert attention, all that we sum up under the famous word of the realists, 'vitality' is lacking. It is a reaction that takes us straight back to the mask as used in *Rosa Alchemica*:

It is even possible that being is only possessed completely by the dead, and that it is some knowledge of this that makes us gaze with so much emotion upon the face of the Sphinx or of Buddha.³⁵

If an origin for the Mask is to be found in occult thought, then a remark by 'J. J. N.' in 1899 that he followed Yeats's 'occult maxim,

---

³³ 'My own seership was, I thought, inadequate; it was to be Maud Gonne's work and mine. Perhaps that was why we had been thrown together. Were there not strange harmonies amid discord? My outer nature was passive ... but I knew my spiritual nature was passionate, even violent. In her all this was reversed, for it was her spirit only that was gentle and passive and full of charming fantasy, as though it touched the world only with the point of its finger ... I, who could not influence her actions, could dominate her inner being. I could therefore use her clairvoyance to produce forms that would arise from both minds ... a spiritual birth from the soul of a man and a woman ... I believed we were about to attain a revelation' (*Mem* 124–25).

³⁴ *Au*, 189, first collected in *Four Years* (Churchtown, Dundrum: Cuala, 1921), 83.

³⁵ The passage immediately precedes the words quoted above, n. 1.

"Lead your reactions, be not led by them'" is intriguing.[36] Nevertheless I cannot think of any specific GD sources for masks (as distinct from hoodwinks[37]) in ritual writings or teachings or in ceremonies, and if the mask does have a ceremonial occult source, it perhaps goes back to the Dublin Hermetic Society.

REREADING HIMSELF IN 1908–09

Around the period of the 1908–09 Diary masks of other sorts bore in on Yeats's attention. A cast purporting to be Dante's death mask – a souvenir, perhaps, brought back from Ravenna by Symons – hung on his wall in Woburn Buildings by June 1904.[38] He had seen the Mask of Hathor at MacGregor Mathers's house in Auteuil.[39] In 1908 Edward Gordon Craig launched his periodical, *The Mask*, which served intermittently as a vehicle for his theatrical theories and designs until 1929, theories and designs which impinged on Yeats (who collected copies of it and wrote for it) in a number of ways. Kathleen Bruce's bronze life mask of Yeats, done with inclusion in *The Collected Works in Verse and Prose* in mind though not reproduced in that shrine of Yeats's permanent self-images, is found in Plate 1 of the present volume, and its making was a major preoccupation of the spring of 1908 (*CL InteLex* 851, 853 etc, 10 April 1908 and later). From c.1907 Yeats had worked on a tragedy, later emerging as *The Player Queen*, frustrated by the thought of 'every player finding or not finding ... the Antithetical Self' (*VPl* 761). By 17 August 1908, he

---

[36] See 'Some Irish Men and Women, No 37 Mr. W. B. Yeats' by 'J. J. N.', *New Ireland*, 21 January 1899. 'J. J. N.' is possibly James Joseph Nolan who was inducted into the Golden Dawn much later as 'Justa Sequor', on 31 May 1909 and who described himself as 'Editor, 10 New Fetter Lane'. See R. A. Gilbert, *The Golden Dawn Companion* (Wellingborough: Aquarian Press, 1986), 173.

[37] If an anachronistic reference can be excused, the 'Introduction to the Neophyte Ceremony: God Forms and Stations in the 0 = 0', one learns that in the uninitiated neophyte is '[t]hrice bound and hoodwinked' and led by the Hierophant who represents his 'Higher and Divine Genius, which in his blindness he cannot realize himself.' See Israel Regardie, *The Golden Dawn: A Complete Course in Practical Ceremonial Magic etc.* (St. Paul, MN: Llewellyn Publications, 1986), 114.

[38] See *YA5*, frontispiece, a reproduction of 'W. B. Yeats in his study in Woburn Buildings' from *The Tatler*, 157, 29 June 1904.

[39] In her *Flowering Dusk* (Toronto: Longmans, 1945) Ella Young describes Mathers's house: 'The mantelpiece displays the richest collection of Egyptian treasures I have ever seen outside of a museum. A mask of Hathor fascinates me ...' (105–06).

dispatched a draft of 'The Mask', intended then as a lyric for that play, to its inspirer, Mabel Dickinson: the inspiration by then was 'a couple of years' old (*VP* 263; *CL IntelLex* 1141). Like Shelley's magus, Zoroaster, who '[m]et his own image walking in the garden',[40] Yeats confronted himself in his own *Collected Works in Verse and Prose* in late 1908, and this provided the precise context in which and moment at which 'The Mask' came back in its new form to crystallize and to dominate his thinking. Amid a good deal of satisfaction with the fairly serviceable self-image he found there, the old itch to revise quickly asserted itself.

Dec. 13 [1908]. Have been looking through Collected Works, volume VII. I now see what is wrong with 'Tables of the Law'. The hero[41] must not seem for a moment a shadow of the hero of 'Rosa Alchemica'. He is not the mask but the face. He realizes himself. He cannot obtain vision in the ordinary sense. He is himself the centre. Perhaps he dreams he is speaking. He is not spoken to. He puts himself in place of Christ. He is not the revolt of multitude. What did the woman in Paris reveal to the Magi? Surely some reconciliation between face and mask? Does the narrator refuse this manuscript, and so never learn its contents? Is it simply the doctrine of the Mask? The choosing of some one mask? Hardly, for that would but be the imitation of Christ in a new form. Is it becoming mask after mask? Perhaps the name only should be given, 'Mask and Face'. Yet the nature of the man seems to prepare for a continual change, a phantasmagoria. One day one god and the next another. The imitation of Christ as distinguished from the self-realization of the 'Tables of the Law'. What of it? Christ is but another self, but he is the supernatural self.

SELF-REALIZATION THROUGH STYLE

Between 23 and 28 January 1909, in the very period at which the word 'Mask'; seems to pop so unexpectedly into his brooding over various aspects of his own behaviour and writing, Yeats had begun to

---

[40] Percy Bysshe Shelley, *Prometheus Unbound*, I, 192–93, in *The Poetical Works of Percy Bysshe Shelley*, ed. William Bell Scott (London: George Routledge, 1880), 207. Yeats's copy was presented to him and inscribed '... from his affectionate friend, | Katharine Tynan. | January 24th 1888' (*YL* 1908).

[41] *Mem* 138; *VSR* 267. I read this obscure note as suggesting that the 'hero' is not the narrator, that it is Aherne who must not seem the 'shadow' of Robartes, and who does sacrifice himself but not 'among those for whom Christ died' (*Myth 2005* 199; *VSR* 163).

project plans for yet more tinkering with *The Adoration of the Magi*.⁴²
'Wisdom is a butterfly', as he later wrote, 'the crooked road of intuition'
is opposed to abstraction or a code of rules, and is opposed to dogma
(*VP* 338, 827). But equally, 'sincerity' as an artistic ambition has its
perils. Yeats's practical experience in the theatre had shown him this,
during a formative phase of his own play-writing and awakening
sense of the possibilities of both masque as a form and masks as a
device for theatrical estrangement. A letter to Mrs Patrick Campbell
in 1901 must suffice here as example. While Yeats saw little merit in
Björn Björnson's *Beyond Human Power* in November 1901, he wrote
to Mrs Patrick Campbell:

> Your acting seemed to me to have the perfect precision and delicacy and
> simplicity of every art at its best. It made me feel the unity of the arts in a
> new way. I said to myself, that is exactly what I am trying to do in writing,
> to express myself without waste, without emphasis. To be impassioned and
> yet to have a perfect self-possession, to have a precision so absolute that
> the slightest inflection of voice, the slightest rhythm of sound or emotion
> plucks the heart-strings ... I happened to have in my pocket 'The Revelation
> of Divine Love', by the Lady Julian, an old mystical book my hand strayed
> to it all unconsciously. There was no essential difference between that work
> and your acting; both were full of fine distinction, of delicate logic, of that
> life where passion and thought are one (*CL3* 122, c.19 Nov, 1901).

Shortly after Yeats had reread himself in his own *Collected Works in
Verse and Prose,* Synge's death was followed by the grim episode of
Yeats's unsuccessful attempt to get a death mask of Synge. Synge's
brother, a member of the Plymouth Brethren, forbade such a move:

> I went ... at the request of various people to get leave for a death mask to be
> taken with a view to a bust but the coffin was closed & the brother would

---

⁴² 'When I rewrite "The Adoration of the Magi" I see clearly that the message given to the old men must be a series of seemingly arbitrary commands: a year of silence, certain rules of diet, and so on. Without the arbitrary there cannot be religion – is the idea, because there cannot be the last sacrifice, that of the spirit. The recorder should refuse the care of the MS on hearing that it contains not wisdom but the supernaturally sanctioned arbitrary, the commanded pose which would make all definite. Mere wisdom would die, he knows, like any other living breath. The tree has to die before it can be made into a cross' (*Mem* 147; *VSR* 163). For its later publication in *Estrangement: Being some fifty thoughts from a Diary kept by William Butler Yeats in the year Nineteen Hundred and Nine* (Dublin: Cuala, 1926) the passage is revised: thus instead of the recorder's refusing 'the care of the MS' the passage reads 'The old men should refuse to record the message on hearing' (6).

not open it – a queer looking man in black clothes that did not fit, very pious I believe, & I think by his manner hating us all.[43]

Yeats never mentions the episode in the Diary, but its presence pervades its writing.[44]

For the last three months finding myself unable to do any kind of serious writing which required continuity of mood I have kept a diary philosophical and meditative. It is now quite a big book and has resulted in my being able to systemize my exasperations. It also contains the impressions made upon one, day by day, of the news of Synge's illness and death. I don't think anything I could have done would have made Synge's family consent to the taking of the Death Mask. They are indeed a strange obstinate people, Plymouth Brothers, who probably hate everything he did ...[45]

By 1910 he was able to declare in 'The Tragic Theatre',

in mainly tragic art one distinguishes devices to exclude or lessen character, to diminish the power of that daily mood, to cheat or blind its too clear perception. If the real world is not altogether rejected it is but touched here and there, and into the places we have left empty we summon rhythm, balance, pattern, images that remind us of vast passions, the vagueness of past times, all the chimeras that haunt the edge of trance; and *if we are painters, we shall express personal emotion through ideal form, a symbolism handled by the generations, a mask from whose eyes the disembodied looks, a style that remembers many masters, that it may escape contemporary suggestion;* or we shall leave out some element of reality as in Byzantine painting, where there is no mass, nothing in relief, and so it is that in the supreme moment of tragic art there comes upon one that strange sensation as though the hair of one's head stood up (*UP2* 388, emphasis added).

The mask thus becomes a device for estrangement, for alienation from selfhood, thereby to facilitate self-contemplation. A sampling of various *pensées* shows Yeats meditating on this theme. Augustus

---

[43] *CL InteLex* 1122, to Lady Gregory [26 March 1909].

[44] Only *Estrangement: Being some fifty thoughts from a Diary kept by William Butler Yeats in the year Nineteen Hundred and Nine* (1926) and *The Death of Synge, and other passages from an old Diary* (1928) appeared from the Cuala Press. The whole 'Journal' is in *Memoirs* (1972).

[45] 'The right place for such a bust is the Municipal Gallery, so it is necessary, as well as desirable ... that [Hugh Lane] choose the artist ... [I]n the absence of the death mask it may be better to content ourselves with a medallion ... of which the subscribers could get small replicas, but I propose to leave the whole thing to Hugh Lane, who is our expert (*CL InteLex* 1148, to John Quinn, 5–7 May 1909).

John's etching (now frontispiece to *AVB*) 'in a Birmingham gallery' made Yeats 'shudder[]' at himself, depicted as

> an unshaven, drunken bar-tender, and then I began to feel John had found something that he liked in me, something closer than character, and by that very transformation made it visible. He had found Anglo-Irish solitude, a solitude I have made for myself, an outlawed solitude (*Ex* 308).

Excluding portraiture, some recondite areas of self-discovery[46] were available only through the arduous cultivation of style and the daring of the Mask, as in the 1910 essay, 'J. M. Synge and the Ireland of his Time':

> how hard ... is that purification from insincerity, vanity, malignity, arrogance, which is the discovery of style. But life became sweet again when I had learnt all I had not learnt in shaping words, in defending Synge against his enemies, and knew that rich energies, fine, turbulent or gracious thoughts, whether in life or letters, are but love-children (*E&I* 318–19).

By 1911 and with the help of Craig, Yeats was planning to put the Fool of *The Hour-Glass* and the Blind Man from *On Baile's Strand* into masks, a plan frustrated when there was no one to make a mask of leather.[47] Craig insisted on seeing the finished masks. Yeats was 'so anxious to get Masks' because he 'despair[ed] of getting good performances of my work under the conditions of the stage at present'. He sought to pay Craig for the design work by writing for *The Mask*, and to secure Craig's designs 'for the "Hour Glass" Fool' and one 'for

---

[46] See, e.g., any context where Yeats reflects upon 'the state of mind which is, of all states of mind not impossible, the most difficult ... because only the greatest obstacle that can be contemplated without despair rouses the will to full intensity' (*Au* 194–95; see also 272–73). Achieving such a Mask can involve betrayal of the seemingly solid self in the discovery of other selves, the price also paid by the double agent, who betrays as 'a tribute to our unlived lives'. See John le Carré, *A Perfect Spy* (London: Hodder and Stoughton, 1986), 121–22.

[47] 'I am very much excited by the thought of putting the fool into a mask & rather amused at the idea of an Angel in a golden domino. [*The Hour-Glass*] I should have to write some words into the play. They fear to meet the eyes of men being too pure for mortal gaze or the like. Craig evidently wants to keep what is supernatural from being too inhuman. If the masks work right I would put the fool & the blind man in 'Baile's Strand' into masks. It would give a wildness, & extravagance that would be fine. I would also like the Abbey to be the first modern theatre to use the mask' (*CL InteLex* 1450, 21 October 1910). See *Plays for an Irish Theatre* (Stratford-upon-Avon & London: A. H. Bullen, 1913), xiv. A design of the Fool in his mask by Edward Gordon Craig appeared facing p. 65.

the Blind Man in Bailes Strand'.⁴⁸ He did not actually get masks in a play until the 2 April, 1916 charity performance of *At the Hawk's Well* in London. By 5 March, he was excited about Dulac's first mask, 'a greek head and helmet with the look of something older, perhaps Egyptian. Cuchulain will be a wonderful figure, magnificent in face and in dress, and it is quite easy to speak in a mask. I put it on and recited in it. He had begun an old man's mask for the other speaking character' (*CL InteLex* 2879). On 2 April he wrote to John Quinn

> I am tired out with the excitement of rehersing my new play in which Masks are being used for the first time in serious drama in the modern world. Ainley who is hero wears a mask like an Archaic Greek statue ... If ... Balfour & Sargent and Ricketts, & Sturge More & John & the Prime Minister and a few pretty ladies will come & see it ... I shall be happier than Sophocles I shall be as lucky as a Japanese dramatic poet at the Court of the Shogan.⁴⁹

FINGER OR CLAY?⁵⁰

George Mills Harper's edited collection *Yeats and the Occult* (1975) offered presentations of Yeats's accounts of the automatic writing of Elizabeth (Bessie) Radcliffe in 1912–13, and the results of forensic investigations with Everard Feilding of the Society for Psychical

---

⁴⁸ *CL InteLex* 1463, 19 November 1910. Yeats was also trying to persuade Bullen to include them in *Plays for an Irish Theatre*, and would even pay for their reproduction himself, but the plan for their use in the Dublin production did not come off (*CL* InteLex 1469, 5 December 1910. See also 1466, 1469, 1472, 1480, 1486–87, 1572; *VPl* 644–45).

⁴⁹ Yeats enclosed a cutting from *The Observer* headed 'Masks on the Stage. New W. B. Yeats Play for a Charity' which included the following 'Lady Cunard has organised a performance at Lady Islington's, for the Social Institutes' Union for Women and Girls, of which the Countess of Ancaster is the President. It provides dinners for many thousand factory girls and munition workers ... Mr. Henry Ainley will act the hero, and Ito, the Japanese dancer, will take the part of the hawk's spirit. Masks will be used for the first time in serious drama in the modern world. The masks and costumes have been designed and executed by Mr. Edmund Dulac. Mr. Henry Ainley will wear a mask resembling an archaic Greek sculptured face ... The performance is under the patronage of Queen Alexandra, who will be present' (*CL InteLex* 2923).

⁵⁰ '... I am in the place where the Daemon is, but I do not think he is with me until I begin to make a new personality, selecting among those images, seeking always to satisfy a hunger grown out of conceit with daily diet; and yet as I write the words "I select", I am full of uncertainty not knowing when I am the finger, when the clay.' (*CW5* 31–32).

Research into the allegedly bleeding oleographs in a church in Mirebeau in 1914.[51] After surveying an immense amount of evidence, the 'Preliminary Examination of the Script of E[lizabeth R[adcliffe]' (finished on 8 October, 1913) reveals above all wariness with 'spirits' who came through in séances, each claiming to be the shade of a person whose life was recorded in standard reference works. While the essay comes down in favour of 'the spiritistic hypothesis' to account for 'supernatural phenomena', that was a position of which Yeats grew less certain, as he added revisions covering the possibilities of secondary and tertiary personalities, adding notes as late as 7 June 1914 (*YO* 134, 136–37, 146, 155, 171).

The essay on the bleeding oleographs is largely unrelated, but the reverence of the Abbé Vachère at Mass in Mirebeau Yeats finds moving rather than suspect, and he begins to see the alleged miracle – later tests at the Lister Institute ruled out human blood – as having a place

> in spiritual drama ... I had felt the reverence one always feels in contemplation of the reverence of others, but now I tested my own beliefs by the intensity of those about me. I too had my conception of the Divine Man, and a few days before had schemed out a poem, praying that somewhere upon some seashore or upon some mountain I should meet face to face with that divine image of myself. I tried to understand what it would be if the heart of that image lived completely in my heart, and the poetry full of instinct full of tenderness for all life it would enable me to write, and then I wondered what it would be if the head awoke within my head, and here my understanding was less clear and my attention strayed to the Latin words of the Mass, returning presently to the hands, and trying vainly to discover their spiritual meaning. Thoughts out of the Kabbala and out of Swedenborg who has arranged the heavens as a vast man, the angels and the souls making the members of his body. I know that I prayed in my fashion ... (*YO* 187).

The poem which shortly shaped itself from this Mass in the Abbé's private chapel on 12 May 1914, was 'The Fisherman', drafted on 4 June, 1914 (*VP* 347–48). Like Shelley's Zoroaster again, the idea of the 'face to face' meeting with a 'divine image of myself' approaches

---

[51] See Arnold Goldman, 'Yeats, Spiritualism, and Psychical Research'; George Mills Harper and John S. Kelly, 'Preliminary Examination of the Script of E[lizabeth] R[adcliffe]'; George Mills Harper, '"A Subject of Investigation": Miracle at Mirebeau' (*YO* 108–29; 130–71; 172–89).

one concept inherent in the Mask, yet crucially lacks the idea of an opposite or anti-self.

From 1897 through the next decade, one thing dominated Yeats's joint work with Lady Gregory outside the Irish Literary Theatre, and that was the collecting of Kiltartan folklore. They had jointly planned a 'big book of folklore' of which much had been jointly drafted in the six folklore essays he alone had signed, but in the end Lady Gregory had continued alone to write it as *Visions and Beliefs in the West of Ireland* (1920), with various separately signed contributions by Yeats. His accompanying essay 'Swedenborg, Mediums, and the Desolate Places' was finished on 14 October 1914 and classifies the 'many analogies' [i.e., with Irish belief]

in modern spiritism ... [I] began a more careful comparison, going a good deal to séances for the first time and reading all writers of any reputation I could find in English or French. I found much that was moving, when I had climbed to the top story of some house in Soho or Holloway, and, having paid my shilling, awaited, among servant girls, the wisdom of some fat old medium. That is an absorbing drama, though if my readers begin to seek it they will spoil it, for its gravity and simplicity depends on all, or all but all, believing that their dead are near. I did not go there for evidence of the kind the Society for Psychical Research would value, any more than I would seek it in Galway or in Aran. I was comparing one form of belief with another ... and ... was discovering a philosophy. Certain things had happened to me when alone in my own room which had convinced me that there are spiritual intelligences which can warn us and advise us ... And yet I do not think I have been easily convinced ... I pieced together stray thoughts written out after questioning the familiar of a trance medium or automatic writer ... or arranged the fragments into some pattern, till I believed myself the discoverer of a vast generalization. I lived in excitement, amused to make Holloway interpret Aran, and constantly comparing my discoveries with what I have learned of mediaeval tradition among fellow students, with the reveries of a Neoplatonist, of a seventeenth-century Platonist, of Paracelsus or a Japanese poet. Then one day I opened *The Spiritual Diary* of Swedenborg, which I had not taken down for twenty years, and found all there, even certain thoughts I had not set on paper because they had seemed fantastic from the lack of some traditional foundation. It was strange I should have forgotten so completely a writer I had read with some care before the fascination of Blake and Boehme had led me away ... Nor should we think of spirit as divided from spirit, as men are from each other, for they share each other's thoughts and life, and those whom he has called celestial angels, while themselves mediums to those above, commune with men and lower spirits, through orders of mediatorial spirits, not by a conveyance of messages, but as though a hand were thrust within a hundred gloves,[52] one glove outside another, and so there is a continual influx from God to man. It flows to us through the evil angels as through the good, for the dark fire is the perversion of God's life and the evil angels have their office in the equilibrium that is our freedom, in the building of that fabulous bridge made out of the edge of a sword (*Ex* 30–32, 38; *CW5* 47–48, 52).

Elsewhere, Yeats accounts for folklore collecting with Lady Gregory in a style detached and yet moving: the anecdotes recounted to them were, said Yeats's view, 'my obsession', 'but a part' of a traditional experience which he had 'discussed only too much elsewhere' (*Au* 401).

Every night she wrote out what we had heard in the dialect of the cottages. She wrote, if my memory does not deceive me, two hundred thousand words, discovering that vivid English she was the first to use upon the stage. My object was to find actual experience of the supernatural, for I did not believe, nor do I now, that it is possible to discover in the text-books of the schools, in the manuals sold by religious booksellers, even in the subtle reverie of saints, the most violent force in history ... [N]either she nor those peasants were pagans. Christianity begins to recognize the validity of experiences that preceded its birth and were, in some sense, shared by its founders. When later she asked me to annotate and introduce her book, *Visions and Beliefs*, I began a study of 'Spiritualism' not only in its scientific form but as it is found among the London poor, and discovered that there was little difference except that the experience of the cottagers was the richer. Requiring no proof that we survive the grave, they could turn to what was dramatic or exciting and, though more ignorant than the townsmen, lacked vulgarity (*Au* 400–01).

The two streams of information, from Kiltartan and from Soho or Holloway could be further compared with evidence won with his fellow (and very middle-class) questers in the Society for Psychical Research, where what passed at the time as rigorous, quasi-scientific, sceptical experimentation and classification of a variety of experiences was carried on with a number of spirit mediums, or in the London Spiritualist Alliance, the séances of which he also attended. These were especially relevant, being sessions seemingly with believers in life after death and offering the best modern parallels to traditional belief and therefore of constructive significance.

---

[52] [Yeats's note] 'The Japanese Noh play *Awoi no Uye* has for its theme the exorcism of a ghost which is itself obsessed by an evil spirit. This evil spirit, drawn forth by the exorcism, is represented by a dancer wearing a "terrible mask with golden eyes".

LEO AFRICANUS

On 9 May, 1912 at a séance of Mrs Etta Wreidt's at W. T. Stead's Cambridge House, Wimbledon, 'a Spanish moor' appeared. His 'life is in Chambers' Biographical Dictionary', protested Yeats in the Radcliffe script, and therefore his appearance 'supported the theory of some unconscious action of the mind', the spirit control speaking overtly of the dictionary 'to give me evidence of his existence' (*YO* 146, 151, 170). This was Leo Africanus, and despite Yeats's noting on a report of the séance, 'First appearance of Leo', he may actually have been coming back into Yeats's life. '[S]hortly' after Yeats had consulted Dr George Sigerson's daughter, Bessy, on 11 December 1898, he had a séance in London with Charles Williams at which it seemed he had heard the medium to name 'Leonora Arguite'. 'Fifteen or twenty years later' it seemed to Yeats that the name could have been 'Leo Africanus' who, indeed, claimed that he was

> Leo my guide & seemed astonished that I had never heard of you. "I am Leo the writer" you repeated, & I would find you in the books or hear of you at Rome. You spoke too of your travels & said that you had been with me from childhood ... [53]

The laborious summaries of séances in the PIAL notebook[54] record with ever greater precision the sessions with such mediums as Etta Wreidt and Felicia Scatcherd between 1909 and 1915 at which Leo Africanus came through in various guises. Yeats and Leo courted each other very warily, and the exchange of letters between them, written by Yeats in December 1915, edited in 1980 and reprinted in this volume offers in retrospect a reasonable summary of their previous encounters in séances. It is possible to be slightly more precise about certain details than were Harper and Adams given the subsequent discovery of so many more of Yeats's letters (i.e., to the then living), but the bones of the story are well laid out in their edited transcript. Yeats's letter to his then occasional mistress, Alick Schepeler, on 26 Dec. 1915 from Stone Cottage, tells us that he is 'writing a letter to Leo Africanus, my "daimon" & reading Landor'.[55] Leo Africanus (al-Hasan ibn Muhammad al-Wazzan) in fact had been

---

[53] *YA1* 23–24, and 313. The Bessy Sigerson notes are in his as yet unpublished 'Visions' notebook of the late nineties.

[54] NLI 36,276 (2).

[55] *CL InteLex* 2838.

a Cordovan Moor who, from 1492 travelled in northern Africa and Asia Minor. Falling into the hands of Venetian corsairs, he was sent to Leo X at Rome, where he lived twenty years, and accepted Christianity, but returned to Africa and his old faith, and died at Tunis in 1552. He wrote (1526) an account of his African travels in Italian (first printed 1559 [as the *Della descrittione dell'Africa*]), long the source of information as to the Soudan.

Or so said the entry in *Chambers's Biographical Dictionary*, where Yeats found him snugly between Leo III the Isaurian, Byzantine Emperor (717–741), and, two one-line entries away, Leonardo da Vinci.[56] Yeats remained suspicious of mediums, audiences (including himself), and others who could summon controls and *soi-disant* ghosts from common reference sources.[57] Rather than bother with Robert Brown's 1896 Hakluyt Society re-edition of John Pory's translation of 1600 to which this entry directed him, Yeats procured a copy of the 1600 translation itself.[58]

At the end of the exchange of letters, Yeats writes that:

I am not convinced that in this letter there is one sentence that has come from beyond. [*sic*] my own imagination but I will not use a stronger phrase. The morning I began it I found my mind almost a blank though I had prepared many thoughts. I could remember nothing except that I intended to begin with an analysis of the axiom that one could not seek an unknown cause, till one has exhausted the known causes. I wrote till I came to line — page — & finding that that page was but a plea for solitude I remembered that an image that gave itself your name said speaking through a certain seer

---

[56] *Chambers's Biographical Dictionary: The Great of all Times and Nations*, ed. David Patrick and Francis Hindes Groome (London and Edinburgh: W. & R. Chambers, 1897, 1911), 584; *YL* 365. Chambers's also has an entry on Yeats himself from 1897 onwards 'favourably known as a poet': see 990.

[57] Yeats was 'not at all impressed & thought Mrs Wreidt who is perhaps a ventriloquist of some kind looks up guides for her visitors in Chambers when [she] knows nothing of their [dead] friends & relatives' (*YA1* 23 and below 313).

[58] *A geographical historie of Africa, written in Arabicke and Italian by Iohn Leo a More, borne in Granada, and brought up in Barbarie. ; Wherein he hath at large described, not onely the qualities, situations, and true distances of the regions, cities, townes, mountaines, riuers, and other places throughout all the north and principall partes of Africa; but also the descents and families of their kings ... gathered partly out of his owne diligent obseruations, and partly out of the ancient records and chronicles of the Arabians and Mores. Before which, out of the best ancient and moderne writers, is prefixed a generall description of Africa, and also a particular treatise of all the maine lands and isles vndescribed by Iohn Leo. And after the same is annexed a relation of the great princes, and the manifold religions in that part of the world*; translated and collected by Iohn Pory, lately of Goneuill and Caius College in Cambridge (Londini: Impensis Georg. Bishop, 1600).

that your mission was to create solitude. At one other moment I felt that curious check or touch[59] in the mind that sometimes warns me, that a line of argument is untrue. Yet I think there is no thought that has not occurred to me in some form or other for many years passed; if you have influenced me it has been less to arrange my thoughts. I am be[ing] careful to keep my [style] broken, & even abrupt believing that I could but keep sensitive to influence by avoiding those trains of argument & deduction which run on railway tracks. I have been conscious of no sudden illumination. Nothing has surprised me, & I have not had any of those dreams which in the past have persuaded me of some spiritual presence. Yet I am confident now as always that spiritual beings if they cannot write & speak can always listen. I can still put by difficulties (*YA1* 38–39 & n. 89).

Thus does Yeats sit in judgement upon Leo. Roy Foster (whose excellent summary of the imaginary conversation misdates its drafting forward by a year) finds that 'Leo Africanus' 'ends as irresolutely as it begins'.[60] I find it subtly judicious. The revels now are ended, and the 'light in the tower window' (*VP* 377) is put out as a writer dismisses a character he has animated if not invented. The stroke of genius is the dialogic form, and at the same time in Stone Cottage, Yeats had Pound reading Landor to him. These letters are a stern imaginary conversation, in which Yeats writes his own position and serves to record what he projects as those of the traveller in an epistolary development of Socratic (or Wildean) dialogue. The arch 'The Poet and the Actress' conversation follows in 1916, as the practical and theatrical uses of the Mask are debated with an actress who only lightly masks Mrs Patrick Campbell, a dialogue which draws upon the completed but then unpublished poem, 'Ego Dominus Tuus' (*YA11* 123–43).

Séance, then, was a new dramatic *mise-en-scène* in which the poet could 'play with all masks'. Weird and wonderful characters turn up as controls, the historical span is limitless; they might be deceitful, might be secondary personalities, nothing is definite, everything has

---

[59] Cf., 'We are always in contact with the phantom of Coleridge ... [w]ith souls who have almost as it seems in the words of St. Thomas "entered into the eternal possession of themselves as in one single moment". The sense of contact, may perhaps come with any clearness & detail but two or three times, but afterwards there is always I think an occasional soft touch as it were, the sudden sensation of some one present, or at moments of difficulty a faint voice' (from 'Spiritus Mundi', an unpublished draft of *Per Amica Silentia Lunae* currently being edited for publication in a later volume of *Yeats Annual*. See also *CW5* 19).

[60] *Life 2*, 71 *& ff.*, at 74.

possibility. But it is to Leo, self-confessedly 'a brooding & braggart shade',[61] 'sent to give you confidence & solitude' (*YA1* 29 and below, 322), that belongs the master stroke of posing (or being postulated) as Yeats's opposite. In a sense he completes the difficulty lingering from the occult stories, for neither Robartes, Aherne, nor any other Mask can make that claim. As such, he points the way forward to the renewed fictions of the Robartes set, the Menippean *satura* in both versions of *A Vision*. An Archdeacon Hare to Walter Landor, he provoked the fullest response: 'I shall dine late; but the room will be well lighted, the guests few and select'.[62] Studying oppositional writers, such as Landor, and Morris, steered *Per Amica Silentia Lunae* to Yeats's deepest thoughts about authorship.[63]

TEXTS FOR EXPOSITION

Séance, like folklore collection, was an obsessive avocation for Yeats. A born writer, his poems came as the intermittent by-product of a consciousness which needed to experiment with (and issue in) many other forms. This can be seen in the period after 1908 as 'play[ing] with all masks', but on a formal level, poems begat prose and prose, poems – a relatively unstudied subject which could take its point of departure from Yeats's clue 'To some extent I wrote these poems as texts for exposition', a passage which occurs in a 1922 retrospective concession that certain poems were obscure without access to the record of thought from which they had arisen, and/or to which they gave rise.[64]

Thus, when Michael Robartes and other named characters appeared in the titles and notes of *The Wind Among the Reeds* they emerged less as 'actual personages', from *The Secret Rose* and

---

[61] '[Even] in this I am not wholly stable, for at times I am aware of a constraint upon my thoughts or my passion deepens because of one who is remote & silent & whom while I lived in Rome I was forbidden to call Mahomet' (*Ibid.*).

[62] A remark which of course gave rise to the closing lines of 'To a Young Beauty' (*VP* 335): see 'Archdeacon Hare and Walter Landor' in *Imaginary Conversations*, edited with biographical and explanatory notes by Charles G. Crump (London: J. M. Dent & Co., 1891, 1909), IV, 427 (*YL* 1081).

[63] See, e.g., *CW5* 6–7; 15–16.

[64] *A Vision* had been intended to make 'possible' a simpler poetry: 'I need no longer write poems like "The Phases of the Moon" nor "Ego Dominus Tuus", nor spend barren years ... striving with abstractions that substituted themselves for the play I had planned' (*CW13* lv; *CVA* xii).

elsewhere in his writings to date, than as 'principles of the mind' (*VP* 803). The train of connexion is hugely important in the gradual evolution of the Mask, because it marks a conscious move from the employment of fictional characters to heteronyms which, while they might be antitypes of each other (as are Aherne and Robartes), are not necessarily anti-selves of the author, except as postulated (and changing) 'principles of the mind'. And while letters of 1917 allegedly from Robartes to Aherne are quoted in the notes to 'An Image from a Past Life' and 'The Second Coming' in *Michael Robartes and the Dancer* (1920), we are not actually told the circumstances of his resurrection until the note keyed to 'The Phases of the Moon', 'The Double Vision of Michael Robartes', and 'Michael Robartes and the Dancer' in *Later Poems* (1922):

> Years ago I wrote three stories in which occurs [*sic*] the names of Michael Robartes and Owen Aherne. I now consider that I used the actual names of two friends, and that one of these friends, Michael Robartes, has but lately returned from Mesopotamia where he has partly found and partly thought out much philosophy. I consider that John Aherne is either the original of Owen Aherne or some near relation of the man that was, and that both he and Robartes, to whose namesake I had attributed a turbulent life and death, have quarrelled with me. They take their place in a phantasmagoria in which I endeavour to explain my philosophy of life and death, and till that philosophy has found some detailed exposition in prose certain passages in the poems named above may seem obscure. To some extent I wrote them as a text for exposition.—1922 (*VP* 821).[65]

Prior to the notes to *Michael Robartes and the Dancer*, there is little published evidence of the huge body of interdependent work except

---

[65] The passage was slightly altered after *A Vision* (1925) had appeared: see *VP* 820–21. On 13 February 1922, Yeats wrote to Allan Wade of Robartes; 'I have brought him back to life. My new story is that he is very indignant because I used his real name in describing a number of fictitious adventures, and that because I called my fictitious hero by his name, many people have supposed him to be dead. He lived for years in Mesopotamia, but when the war came there returned to England for a short time. In England he got into communication with a certain John Aherne, and through him got into correspondence with me, and finally conveyed to me, without quite forgiving me, the task of editing and publishing the philosophy which he has discovered among certain Arabian tribes. That philosophy now fills a very large tin box upon which my eyes at this moment are fixed, I am giving it to the world in fragments, poems, notes, and a Cuala volume [*Michael Robartes and the Dancer*, 1920]' (*CL Intelex* 4068; *L* 676–77). More Robartes fictions appear in notes to such books as *Four Plays for Dancers* (London: Macmillan, 1921) *The Cat and the Moon and Certain Poems* (Dublin: Cuala, 1924): see *VPl* 566–67; 777–79, 789–91.

for the obvious relation between the proem to *Per Amica Silentia Lunae* and its extended reverie. One must recall that at the time, 'Swedenborg, Mediums, and the Desolate Places' had not been published. The 'Preliminary Examination of the Script of E[lizabeth R[adcliffe]', 'The Poet and the Actress', 'Leo Africanus' and much else necessarily less finished or even in jottings or fragments lay unpublished in his lifetime, some even to this day.

So it is important to recognise that 'Leo Africanus' and 'Ego Dominus Tuus' were written at the same time, Yeats even spending the Christmas of 1915 (as we have seen), drafting 'Leo Africanus' in Stone Cottage and reading Landor (or having Ezra Pound do so for him).[66] Dialogic form is the crucial ingredient of all these activities, in spirit investigations, in prose, in new poems, and in the relation between all of these activities, as the dating of 'Ego Dominus Tuus' reveals. First published in *Poetry* (Chicago) in October 1917 and *The New Statesman* November 17, 1917 (on which date it also appeared in the Cuala Press edition of *The Wild Swans at Coole*), it became the proem to *Per Amica Silentia Lunae* (published on both sides of the Atlantic on 18 January 1918) and was gathered into *The Wild Swans at Coole* (London: Macmillan, 11 March, 1919). However, a penultimate MS, entitled 'The Self & the AntiSelf' is dated 'Dec 5. 1915'.[67] In the two *Per Amica* publications, the poem is emphatically dated *'December* 1915'. With *'Ille'* addressed by *Hic*[68] as he traces magical shapes on the sands beside the Streamstown river, his lamp burning beside a book left by Michael Robartes, the date effectively declares ownership and habitation of Thoor Ballylee for 'Ille' from that date. The completed poem thus would seem to predate the purchase of Thoor Ballylee by over 15 months, but 'The Self & the AntiSelf' anticipates even the opening of negotiations for the purchase by ten months.

---

[66] See John Kelly, *A Yeats Chronology* (Basingstoke: Palgrave Macmillan, 2003), 183; *CL InteLex* 2831, 19 December 1915; 2838, 26 December 1915; 2844, 26 January 1916. On the last of these occasions, Yeats tells Lady Gregory of Landor's 'great occasional beauty but much repetition of a few dominant thoughts'. It also seems that Landor had obligingly turned up in a séance of Bessie Radcliffe's on 15 July 1913 (*YO* 149).

[67] 'The Wild Swans at Coole', *Manuscript Materials*, 298–99, 301, 305.

[68] The 'this man'/ 'that man' formulation, in this case a self-division, echoes William Morris's use of 'Haec' ('this woman') and 'Ille' ('that man') as the speaker names in a song lyric found in 'Ogier the Dane' from his *The Earthly Paradise* (London: F. S. Ellis, 1868), 665–66, cf., *Life* 2, 30.

On 2 October, 1916, Yeats wrote to William F. Bailey from Coole:

For years I have coveted Ballylee Castle, on this property, or what was this property and which has now been bought by the C[ongested] D[istricts] B[oard]. It has got a tolerably good roof on it, good rough old Elizabethan chimney pieces, and I could restore it to some of its original stern beauty and have a place to keep my pictures and my books. At present it is worth nothing to anybody, and will soon become ruinous, and that will make the neighbourhood the poorer of romance. Now I want to know if I could get it from the Congested Districts Board. The tenant who had possession of it says he hears they are going to lock it up. He says also that a couple of acres have been kept with it, which would be useful to keep a few trees which are there now from being cut down. I might not be able to live there for some little time, but I should be sorry if I found it had been possible to get it and that it has slipped away. You would do me a great service if you would find out informally if such a purchase was possible. I need not say I could not give much for it, especially as I should have to lay-out money in doing it up ...[69]

Yeats had found an 'asylum for his affections' long before he actually possessed it. His first visit must have been between 20 June and c.15 November 1898, during which period he stayed at Coole and Tulira. He and Russell had spent time seeing visions in the nearby Lydacaun Castle, a similar Norman tower house, though uninhabitable. Ballylee, on the other hand, was occupied by Patrick Spellman, Master of the Loughrea Workhouse. Yeats returned there again in the summer of 1899 (*Myth 2005* 225–26), wholly absorbed in the lore and local memory of Mary Hynes as immortalized in the poetry of Antoine Raftery and collected by Douglas Hyde. He wrote "'Dust hath Closed Helen's Eye'" for *The Dome* (October, 1898), collecting it in the 1902 edition of *The Celtic Twilight*. In 1924 he added a note: 'Ballylee Castle, or Thoor Ballylee, as I have named it to escape from the too magnificent word "castle" is now my property, and I spend my summers or some part of them there' (*Myth 2005* 14–19). In the poem's opening 'Hic' addresses 'Ille', unmistakeably the inhabitant of Thoor Ballylee:

> Hic. On the grey sand beside the shallow stream
> Under your old wind-beaten tower, where still
> A lamp burns on beside the open book

---

[69] *CL InteLex* 3043. Further letters followed between Yeats and Sir Henry Doran, and others of the Land Commission, Dublin, on 10 November 1916 (3068); 27 March 1917 (3202, accepting price of £35.0.0).

> That Michael Robartes left, you walk in the moon,
> And, though you have passed the best of life, still trace,
> Enthralled by the unconquerable delusion,
> Magical shapes. (*VP* 367)

There is no explanatory note on Robartes, nor on his book. Yeats had killed him off in 1896: the Connemara temple is stormed by angry fisherfolk, and the narrator flees, leaving Robartes lying with the 'hollow masks' of the dancers, still in a drugged swoon on the dancing-floor (*VSR* 148–49; *Myth 2005* 190–91). Nor does the narrator rescue the vellum book which gives the history and rituals of the Order (while, as we have seen, in *The Wind Among the Reeds* he is merely a 'principle of the mind' rather than an 'actual personage').

In fact, the majority of the fictions of what Michael Sidnell, following Yeats's comment about 'The Gift of Harun Al-Rashid' has grouped as the Robartes 'set' (*VP* 830; *YO* 226) were unpublished until Volume 4 of *Yeats's* Vision *Papers* appeared in 2001.[70] Those that were published as notes to poems indeed held ground for *A Vision* (1925). In that work, Menippean *satura*, or such learned play goes a step further, with yet further steps to come in *A Packet for Ezra Pound* and *A Vision* (1937). 'Ego Dominus Tuus' is proleptic, its 'open book' a text for 'exposition' in 'An Alphabet' and '*Spiritus Mundi*', later published as *Per Amica Silentia Lunae*, a down payment on possession of the tower, an anticipation of habitation, all the more remarkable for seemingly preceding his courtship of Georgie Hyde-Lees.[71]

The formal potential was huge, as 'principles of the mind' were mastered in the self-division dramatized in the dialogue of 'Hic'

---

[70] Notes to poems ultimately depend on 'The Robartes-Ahearne [sic] Dialogues', including 'The Discoveries of Michael Robartes', drafted in 1918 as Yeats struggled to find an overall form for what became *A Vision* (1925): see *YVP4*.

[71] Yeats and Georgie Hyde-Lees 'probably' met on 22 November 1915 and 'may have discussed marriage' (Kelly, *A Yeats Chronology*, 182). On 30 September 1917 George's mother wrote that she had been 'very much afraid that Mr Yeats meant to propose to my daughter in Nov [19]15' and that she did not then 'consider him free to do so' (see John Harwood, *Olivia Shakespear and W. B. Yeats* [London: Macmillan, 1988], 157). Ann Saddlemyer thinks that 17, 21, or 22 November was 'profoundly significant ... in occult terms, an initiatory moment': see her *Becoming George: The Life of Mrs W. B. Yeats* (Oxford: Oxford University Press, 2002), 80, 687. At the time, Yeats's mistress was Alick Schepeler (*CL Intelex* 2808, 2816, 12 & 17 November 1915). The date in 'Anima Mundi' (9 May 1917), can suggest that the 'stair' is the winding stair of the tower: in fact the 'gilded Moorish wedding-chest' with its 'barbarous words' was at the time in 17, Woburn Buildings (*CW5* 32; *Myth* 366).

and 'Ille'. There had of course been the dialogic *The Wanderings of Oisin* (based on 'The Dialogue of Oisin and Patrick' and the equally dialogic 'Lay of Oisin on the Land of Youths as he related it to Saint Patrick'[72]), earlier 'conversation poems' such as 'Adam's Curse', the colloquy-within-narrative of 'The Grey Rock', or 'The Two Kings' (*VP* 204–06; 270–86), but it is in *The Wild Swans at Coole* that dialogic form comes back in a new way as a special projection via masks of 'the dialogue of the mind with itself' as Matthew Arnold had called it.[73] Much as Yeats had misgivings about the self-doubts of modernity (and indeed its 'modern hope' of self-discovery and the 'gentle, sensitive mind', *VP* 367–68), his interest in the free play of 'principles of the mind' was now to be fleshed out with numerous traditional identities – 'Shepherd and Goatherd', 'The Saint and the Hunchback' – types classified in yet another conversation not written for another two and a half years, 'The Phases of the Moon' (written in July 1918), a dialogue between heteronyms he had invented, forgotten and resurrected, Aherne and Robartes. As they pass by the tower, declining to stop and preferring to imagine Yeats 'crack[ing] his wits | Day after day', Yeats, now in possession of 'mysterious wisdom' won through his marriage and its toil of automatic writing, has the last 'laugh[]' on these characters of his own creation, an entirely new vein of work having opened up (*VP* 377).

Both the almost fully drafted 'The Self & the AntiSelf' (dated 'Dec 5. 1915') and the almost fair copy on which that title has been changed to 'Ego Dominus Tuus' (dated 'Dec. 1915') site the disciplined, objectifying, internal debate 'On the grey sands beside

---

[72] See *Transactions of the Ossianic Society for the Year 1856*, IV (Dublin: Ossianic Society, 1859) 3–63; 234–79.

[73] See Arnold's 'Preface to the First Edition of *Poems*' (1853) in *The Poems of Matthew Arnold*, ed. Kenneth Allott (London: Longman, 1969, 1979) second edition, ed. Miriam Allott, 654. *Empedocles on Etna* he found revealed 'much that we are accustomed to consider as exclusively modern ... the calm the cheerfulness, the disinterested objectivity have disappeared; the dialogue of the mind with itself has commenced.' Such 'doubts ... discouragement' were more characteristic of Hamlet and Faust, and excluded the poem on the ground that 'no poetical enjoyment can be derived [when] 'suffering finds no vent in action; in which a continuous state of mental distress is prolonged, unrelieved by incident, hope or resistance; in which there is everything to be endured, nothing to be done. In such situations there is inevitably something morbid, in the description of them something monotonous. When they occur in actual life, they are painful, not tragic; the representation of them in poetry is painful also' (655–56). For Yeats's endorsement and consequent omission of Wilfred Owen from *OBMV*, see *E&I* 336, 354, *CW5* 199, *CW13* 243, 255.

the shallow sea | Under your old wind-beaten Tower ...'. Yeats clearly wanted a single syllable at the end of the line, and either had not yet come to 'stream' or wished for some reason to occlude the location of the dialogue. Ballylee is c.15 km from the shallow Kinvarra Bay. And while there is indeed sand beside the Streamstown River at Ballylee, it does not have quite the scope for geomancy that one would find on a tidal sea-shore.

A tower, a light in the window, a mysterious book left by a magus, a seashore, geomantic drawings on the sand: the geography is of course phantasmagorical, but well before Yeats actually went to Ballyllee and the Streamstown river, such associations were beginning to form in his mind, and would continue to be rich inspiration to him right through to *The Tower* and *The Winding Stair* (see 'A Dialogue of Self and Soul', *VP* 470). A cluster of associations crystallises in 'The Phases of the Moon' (1918), where Yeats has Robartes speculate that he had 'chosen' Thoor Ballylee because of 'Il Penseroso' and 'Prince Athanase', and Samuel Palmer's 'The Lonely Tower' etching which illustrates the former by alluding to the latter.

> *Robartes.* ...
> We are on the bridge; that shadow is the tower,
> And the light proves that he is reading still.
> He has found, after the manner of his kind,
> Mere images; chosen this place to live in
> Because, it may be, of the candle-light
> From the far tower where Milton's Platonist
> Sat late, or Shelley's visionary prince:
> The lonely light that Samuel Palmer engraved,
> An image of mysterious wisdom won by toil;
> And now he seeks in book or manuscript
> What he shall never find. (*VP* 372–73)

What Robartes has in mind is the following passage:

> Or let my lamp at midnight hour,
> Be seen in some high lonely tow'r,
> Where I may oft outwatch the Bear,
> With thrice-greatest Hermes, or unsphere
> The spirit of Plato, to unfold
> What worlds, or what vast regions hold
> The immortal mind, that hath forsook
> Her mansion in this fleshly nook:
> And of those Demons that are found
> In fire, air, flood, or under ground,

>   Whose power hath a true consent
>   With planet, or with element.[74]

and

> His soul had wedded Wisdom, and her dower
> Is love and justice, clothed in which he sate
> Apart from men, as in a lonely tower,
> Pitying the tumult of their dark estate – [75]

In the 'Prince Athanase' fragment, the tower simile becomes actual. Prince Athanase is schooled by the elderly Zonoras, and his tower's lamp may be seen from far out in the Balearic Sea 'gleam[ing] from the turret, | 'Piercing the stormy darkness like a star | Which pours beyond the sea one steadfast beam' (*Ibid*, ll. 187–91). For Yeats, meditating on Shelley's 'Ruling Symbols' in 1900, 'half-ruined towers upon ... hilltops were '"towers of thought"' (in Shelley's own words: '"towers of thought's crowned powers"'[76]) because Yeats thought it

> hard ... to forget a symbolical meaning, I believe Shelley had more than a romantic scene in his mind when he made Prince Athanase follow his mysterious studies in a lighted tower above the sea.[77]

Yeats twice refers to the geomantic stanza describing Cythna's reveries in *The Revolt of Islam*:

> At a comparatively early time Shelley made his imprisoned Cythna become wise in all human wisdom through the contemplation of her own mind, and write out this wisdom upon the sands in 'signs' that were 'clear elemental shapes, whose smallest change' made 'a subtler language within language', and were 'the key of truths which once were dimly taught in old Crotona'.[78]

---

[74] John Milton, 'Il Penseroso', ll. 85–96, as found in *The Shorter Poems of John Milton*, with twelve illustrations by Samuel Palmer, Painter and Etcher (London: Seeley & Company, 1889), 27, plate and description, 29–30: see also *NC* 173–75.

[75] Percy Bysshe Shelley, 'Prince Athanase: A Fragment', ll. 31–34, in *The Poetical Works of Percy Bysshe Shelley*, ed. William Bell Scott (*YL* 1908). The facing page, 511, has been dog-eared.

[76] 'From those skiey towers | Where thought's crowned powers | Sit watching your dance, ye happy Hours': see Percy Bysshe Shelley, *Prometheus Unbound* IV, 103, Bell Scott edition, 250 and below, 43

[77] The 'sea', like Shelley's 'rivers, caves and caves with fountains' being 'a very ancient symbol': see *E&I* 86–87, 290–99; *CW5*, 66, *ll* 88 & ff., 9–10.

[78] *E&I* 78, see also 86; *CW5* 60, see also 65. See the celebrated stanzas xxxi–ii, Canto VII, *The Revolt of Islam*, ll. 3091–3108.

Plate 2. The 'Palatium Arcanorum', frontispiece of Christian Knorr von Rosenroth's *Kabbala Denudata seu Doctrina Hebræorum transcendentalis et metaphysica atque theological etc.*, 1677. Photograph courtesy and © The British Library. All rights reserved.

Such declarations of a heritage as personal and as symbol-laden as the history of his own poetic knowledge are found right through until 'Blood and the Moon' (written in August 1927).

I

Blessed be this place,
More blessed still this tower;
A bloody, arrogant power
Rose out of the race
Uttering, mastering it,
Rose like these walls from these
Storm-beaten cottages –
In mockery I have set
A powerful emblem up,
And sing it rhyme upon rhyme
In mockery of a time
Half dead at the top.

II

Alexandria's was a beacon tower, and Babylon's
An image of the moving heavens, a log-book of the sun's
  journey and the moon's;
And Shelley had his towers, thought's crowned powers
  he called them once.

I declare this tower is *my* symbol; I declare
This winding, gyring, spiring treadmill of a stair is *my*
  ancestral stair;
That Goldsmith and the Dean, Berkeley and Burke have
  travelled there. (*VP* 480–81, emphases added)

This cluster of 'symbolical meaning' went back at least to 1888 when Katharine Tynan presented Yeats with his Shelley. The 'mysterious wisdom' had been given 'a local habitation' by means of study of MacGregor Mathers' translation of Knorr Von Rosenroth's *Kabbala Denudata*, which must have led Yeats back to the 1677 edition in the British Museum, the frontispiece of which shows a neophyte approaching the 'Palatium Arcanum', by the shore of a turbulent sea.[79] This frontispiece may itself have provided a visual source for

---

[79] For Yeats's copies of S. L. MacGregor Mather's translation of the *Kabbala Denudata*, see also, *YL* 1292, 1292a.

the Temple of the Alchemical Rose on the shores of Connemara, where the 'grey, leaping waves', as of 'some indefinite and passionate life, which has begun to war upon our orderly and careful days' were 'covering [the temple] with showers of white foam'.[80] The point serves to show that while the history of Yeats's sources for symbolical obsessions is a very old approach to his work, nothing really gets left behind. In Boehme's word (and in modern magical doctrine) the imagination (and so for Yeats 'imaginative possessions', or the gathered symbol-hoard), 'creates and substantiates as it goes'.[81]

Walking towards Urbino in 1907, Yeats glimpsed a 'mediaeval tower' that induced a vision of

> an old man, erect and a little gaunt, standing in the door of the tower, while about him broke a windy light. He was the poet who had at last, because he had done so much for the word's sake, come to share in the dignity of the saint. He had hidden nothing of himself, but he had taken care of 'that dignity ... the perfection of form ... this lofty and severe quality ... this virtue.'[82] And though he had but sought it for the word's sake, or for a woman's praise, it had come at last into his body and his mind. Certainly as he stood there he knew how from behind that laborious mood, that pose, that genius, no flower of himself but all himself, looked out as from behind a mask that other Who alone of all men, the countrypeople say, is not a hair's-breadth more nor less than six feet high. He has in his ears well-instructed voices, and seeming-solid sights are before his eyes, and not, as we say of many a one, speaking in metaphor, but as this were Delphi or Eleusis, and the substance and the voice come to him among his memories which are of women's faces; for was it Columbanus or another that wrote, 'There is one among the birds that is perfect, and one perfect among the fish'?[83]

This poet of Yeats's vision stands on the threshold of his tower. The liminality of the poet of *Per Amica Silentia Lunae* distinguishes him from the Saint, the Hero, and the Money-Changers of the 'Chambers of Commerce and of Commons' (*Myth* 332–33; *CW5* 9). Then there

---

[80] *VSR* 138, *Myth 2005* 184 & Pl 6; *YO* frontispiece and Pl. 2 of this volume.

[81] See *Myth 2005* 394, n. 62; *UP2* 151; *YL* 209, cf., *CW5* 72.

[82] Verlaine had lectured in Oxford in 1893 while Yeats was in Dublin: his translated words came to Yeats, probably via Arthur Symons, and perhaps in redacted form (*CW4*'s note are evasive). The remembered words were, for Yeats in 1906, a profound ethical and aesthetic turning point: see 'The Tree of Life' (*E&I* 270–72; *CW4* 197–99).

[83] *E&I* 291; *CW4* 211–12, emphasis added.

is Geomancy, or sand divination, on his mind at various points in his life and beautifully turned into an *Arabian Nights* travesty in 'The Dance of the Four Royal Persons', a commentary upon the poem 'Desert Geometry, or, The Gift of Harun al Raschid', otherwise known as 'The Gift of Harun al Rashid.[84] An experience with Lucy Middleton and George Pollexfen at Rosses Point which led to 'Regina, Regina Pigmeorum, Veni' first published in the 1893 *The Celtic Twilight*, includes the troubling phrase (over which he fretted again in 1914), 'the sands of vision' (*Myth 2005* 37 and 251, n. 11). 'The Boy who would become Vizier' in *The Arabian Nights* stands behind the geomantic experience envisaged at the opening of 'Anima Mundi'.[85]

'No mind can engender till divided in two', Yeats reminds us in analyzing the minds of Keats, Shelley and Synge (*Au* 345; *CW3* 263), but the progeny is not merely the resultant work but also the mastery of the self. It is Yeats who banishes Robartes and Aherne after their exposition of 'The Phases of the Moon', and the order is issued from the commanding heights of his writer's desk in the tower. In the voice of 'Ille', it is Yeats who trumps 'Hic' at the end of 'Ego Dominus Tuus' because 'I seek an image, not a book'. The argument is over, self-discovery is ongoing.

> I call to the mysterious one who yet
> Shall walk the wet sands by the edge of the stream
> And look most like me, being indeed my double,
> And prove of all imaginable things
> The most unlike, being my anti-self,
> And, standing by these characters, disclose
> All that I seek ...[86]

In exactly the same way, Leo Africanus, having been summoned for disputation, had been dismissed. It has not been the purpose of this

---

[84] *CW13* 10–12; *CVA* 9–11. See Warwick Gould, 'A Lesson for the Circumspect: W. B. Yeats's Two Versions of *A Vision* and the *Arabian Nights*' in The Arabian Nights *in English Literature: Studies in the Reception of* The Thousand and One Nights *into British Culture*, ed. Peter L. Caracciolo (Basingstoke: Macmillan, 1988), 244–80, at pp. 250–60.
[85] See *Myth* 343; *CW5* 17, and Gould, '"A Lesson for the Circumspect"', 245–46.
[86] *VP* 370–71. Roy Foster thinks the 'anti-self' is a reference to Leo Africanus (*Life2* 31–32), but it seems to me that although the poem and the dialogue were written at the same time, Yeats's search for an anti-self was a perennial stylistic necessity.

article to take the Mask through its exfoliation in the system of *A Vision*. Beyond that system, however, lies Yeats's great theme. Simply summarized, the Mask endures as the 'First Principle' of Yeats's 'A General Introduction for my Work':

A poet writes always of his personal life, in his finest work out of its tragedies, whatever it be, remorse, lost love or mere loneliness; he never speaks directly as to someone at the breakfast table, there is always a phantasmagoria. Dante and Milton had mythologies, Shakespeare the characters of English history, of traditional romance; even when the poet seems most himself, when Raleigh and gives potentates the lie, or Shelley 'a nerve o'er which do creep the else unfelt oppressions of mankind', or Byron when 'the heart wears out the breast as the sword wears out the sheath', he is never the bundle of accident and incoherence that sits down to breakfast; he has been re-born as an idea, something intended, complete. A novelist might describe his accidence, his incoherence, he must not, he is more type than man, more passion than type. He is Lear, Romeo, Oedipus, Tiresias; he has stepped out of a play and even the woman he loves is Rosalind, Cleopatra, never The Dark Lady. He is part of his own phantasmagoria and we adore him because nature has grown intelligible, and by so doing a part of our creative power.[87]

If the phantasmagoria is a crowd of masks,

Memory is a series of judgments and such judgments imply a reference to something that is not memory; that something is the *Daimon*, which contains within it, co-existing in its *eternal moment*, all the events of our life, all that we have known of other lives, or that it can discover within itself of other *Daimons* (*AVB* 192; see also 193, 214, emphasis added).

In essence, it is memory of this order, in its 'eternal moment', memory of all he had read or written and rewritten and of what he

---

[87] *E&I* 509, cf., 'The arts are all the bridal chambers of joy. No tragedy is legitimate unless it leads some great character to his final joy. Polonius may go out wretchedly, but I can hear the dance music in 'Absent thee from felicity awhile', or in Hamlet's speech over the dead Ophelia, and what of Cleopatra's last farewells, Lear's rage under the lightning, Oedipus sinking down at the story's end into an earth 'riven' by love? Some Frenchman has said that farce is the struggle against a ridiculous object, comedy against a movable object, tragedy against an immovable; and because the will, or energy, is greatest in tragedy, tragedy is the more noble; but I add that 'will or energy is eternal delight', and when its limit is reached it may become a pure, aimless joy, though the man, the shade, still mourns his lost object. It has, as it were, thrust up its arms towards those angels who have, as Villiers de l'Isle Adam quotes from St Thomas Aquinas, returned into themselves in an eternal moment' (*CW5* 247). The ideas in this further passage (from *On the Boiler*) hark back to those explored on 28 January 1909, in the Diary.

done and not done, 'perpetually coming up to Judgement', that sent Yeats continually backward so as to take forward the realisations of the Mask.[88] There should be nothing unexpected here, for *Theatrum Mundi* had always been at the heart of Yeats's multivalent world view. 'Man can embody truth but he cannot know it', he wrote, trying to 'put all into a phrase', '"expression" is a part of "study"'. At his last – and writing – Yeats magnificently 'embod[ied]', and substantiated, his own best Masks 'in the completion of [his] life'.[89]

[88] Amid the numerous examples of self-allusion which demonstrate Yeats's dependence on the written in new writing, one passage in 'Leo Africanus' stands out: 'And so I passed from dream crisis to crisis [,] the same dreams returning again & again, but some power that seemed from beyond my mind seemed working with them & changing their form & colour. At Rome I had seen Michael Angelo at work upon the scaffolding in the Sistine Chapel, & once I had been in his studio & watched him drawing from the model. The events in life & the earlier dreams were like that model but gradually were so changed, that [they] resembled more what I saw in Adam or Sybil when the scaffolding was taken away. But now in my state of waking I did not seem to wholly wake, for side by side with the streets of Fez, or desert I seemed to see another world that was growing in weight & vividness, the double of yours, but vaster & more significant. Shades came to me from [that] world & returned to it again. Some of them I recognized. Those who were dead a long time I recognized for the most part with difficulty some because they were handsomer & some because they were terrible to look at like some strange work of art' (see *YA1* 31; and below 325). The relation between this passage as donnée and 'Long-Legged Fly' ll. 21–30 (*VP* 617–18) seems marked.

[89] *CL InteLex* 7362, to Lady Elizabeth Pelham, 4 January 1939.

The King's Threshold, *Calvary*, *The Death of Cuchulain*: Yeats's Passion Plays

Alexandra Poulain

FOR THOSE PLAYWRIGHTS and theatre practitioners who challenged the primacy of realism on the stage at the turn of the twentieth century, the dramatic treatment of ghosts often became the test of a new conception of theatre which set itself the task of making the invisible visible. Maeterlinck strove to display 'immense invisible and fateful powers'[1] in his plays, and experimented with marionettes to create a theatre in which 'it seems that the dead are talking to us [...] in august voices'.[2] Edward Gordon Craig saw Shakespeare's ghosts as 'the visualised symbols of the supernatural world which enfolds the natural',[3] and to him their appearance among the living on the stage was 'a clear command from Shakespeare that the men of the theatre shall rouse their imagination and let their reasonable logic slumber'.[4] Yeats concurred with this conception of a theatre freed from the tyranny of dramatic illusion. His plays are peopled by shadows who

---

[1] 'd'énormes puissances, invisibles et fatales'. Maurice Maeterlinck, Preface to his *Théâtre* (1901), in *Oeuvres 1, Le Réveil de l'âme, Poésies et essais*, ed. Paul Gorceix (Bruxelles: Editions Complexe, 1999), 496. My translation.

[2] 'Ce sont des morts qui semblent nous parler [...] d'augustes voix'. Maurice Maeterlinck, 'Menus Propos – le théâtre', *La Jeune Belgique* (1890), *op. cit.*, 463, my translation.

[3] Edward Gordon Craig, 'On the ghosts in the tragedies of Shakespeare', in *On the Art of the Theatre* (London: William Heinemann, 1911), 264.

[4] *Ibid.*, 266.

mingle with the living, and much of his aesthetic innovation originates from his experiments with the dramatic treatment of ghosts and their disruption of the natural order. The plays under discussion do not just resort to ghosts, but seek to dramatise death itself – not as an allegorical figure (as in the medieval mysteries), but as an event which takes place within the central character's dislocated body and mind. It is of course by no means uncommon, or even remotely original, to have a character die on the stage; but in these three plays death is the *drama* itself (in the etymological sense of 'action'). Pushing back the limits of theatre, Yeats invents a dramaturgy which seeks to probe the absolutely unknowable experience of death, expanding the infinitesimal moment of the crossing from life to death into the substance of a whole drama. These three plays, featuring a Poet, a Saint and a Hero, differ greatly in subject and tone. In the present essay they are considered as formal variations on the common pattern of the 'Passion play'. Of the three, only *Calvary* really qualifies as a Passion play in the literal sense of a dramatic representation of the Passion of Christ; yet the other two can be seen as profane revisitings of the Christian paradigm. Yeats was not the only one to turn to medieval theatre for an alternative dramaturgy, sequential rather than organicist, free of the dictate of the Aristotelian 'beautiful animal'[5]: Ibsen's *Peer Gynt* (1876), Strindberg's *The Road to Damascus* (1898), the German *stationendrama* of the 1920's, Claudel's *The Satin Shoe* (1929) and *The Book of Christopher Columbus* (1933), to name but a few, are all modelled on the Passion play[6] which is still a favourite form in contemporary drama.[7] However, Yeats's plays stand out in that they are concerned solely with the protagonist's dying moments,

---

[5] In his *Poetics*, Aristotle compares the plot of a tragedy to a 'living organism' whose 'beauty depends on magnitude and order' : like a 'beautiful animal', it should form an ideally proportioned whole. The image of the 'beautiful animal' is at the core of Aristotle's organicist conception of tragedy. Aristotle, *Poetics*, vii, 140b34–1451a15.

[6] Passion Plays evolved from liturgical drama and medieval Easter plays and focus on the life and sufferings of Christ. Thus they are to be distinguished from Mystery plays (dramatic representations of Biblical episodes) and miracle plays (re-enactments of miracles performed by Saints). Yeats displayed a life-long interest in the dramaturgical potential of the Passion Play, as testified by his own plays *Calvary* (1920) and *Resurrection* (1927), and his support of Lady Gregory's *The Story Brought by Brigit* (1924). In this paper, however, I use the term 'Passion Play' is a broader sense, to point to a dramaturgy which revolves on the staging of a death, in a religious or secular context.

[7] See J-P. Sarrazac, *Jeux de rêves et autres détours* (Paris : Circé, 2004), 36 & ff.

his motionless journey through the various stages of death, not towards death as in the traditional model of the Passion play. They are structured in successive, discrete tableaux or 'stations', but these stations occur after the catastrophe which has already befallen the protagonist and started the dying process. In what follows, the dramaturgy of *The King's Threshold* (1903), *Calvary* (1920) and *The Death of Cuchulain* (1939) as three 'Passion plays' is approached together as a prolonged experiment with the limits of theatrical possibilities.

SACRIFICE

Passion, of course, primarily implies physical suffering. All three plays are structured around a central image, the martyred body of the sacrificial victim who has 'chosen death' (*VPl* 258) and endures it ritualistically. While this connects them both to the Christian Passion play and to Greek tragedy,[8] I am concerned more specifically with the ways in which they recycle images of starvation and incorporation borrowed from the Christian ritual of the Eucharist. In the beginning of *The King's Threshold* Seanchan asks his Oldest Pupil to repeat the answer he made at Candlemas when asked how a man should guard poetic images:

> *Oldest Pupil.* I answered – and the word was half your own –
> That he should guard them, as the men of Dea
> Guard their four treasures, as the Grail King guards
> His holy cup, or the pale, righteous horse
> The jewel that is underneath his horn,
> Pouring out life for it, as one pours out
> Sweet heady wine ... But now I understand;
> You would refute me out of my own mouth [...] (*VPl* 265)

The familiar metaphor of blood-as-wine, whose resonance is magnified by the contiguous evocation of the Holy Grail, tropes the Poet as a Christ-like figure who offers up his flesh and blood in sacrifice. As the starving Seanchan's flesh melts away, leaving only 'a bag of bones', his voice is being incorporated by his pupils ('the word was half your own'). The passage is even suggestive of a form

---

[8] One important dramaturgic model for the three plays is Aeschylus' *Prometheus Bound*.

of cannibalistic ritual, a profane Eucharist which allows Seanchan to refute his Pupil 'out of his own mouth.' When Seanchan dies, his defiant last words ('King! King! Dead faces laugh', *VPl* 310) are allowed to resonate in the cues of the Oldest and Youngest Pupils, in a slightly spooky number of post-mortem ventriloquism (literally: speaking out of their stomachs). Reflecting on the metamorphosis of the poet's voice after his death, Auden was to give a memorable account of this process when he wrote that 'The words of a dead man | Are modified in the guts of the living' (the 'dead man' in his case was, of course, Yeats himself[9]).

The King's Threshold thus appropriates elements of the Christian Passion, but there is no parodic intent to these borrowings. The play features the characteristic Yeatsian tension between the sublime and the burlesque, but the burlesque elements are contained within the tragic structure and do not contaminate the greatness of Seanchan's sacrifice. In the first version, which ended happily with the victory of the Poet and the King's repentance, a prologue was spoken by a dishevelled Old Man in his dressing-gown and slippers, clearly a first avatar of the Old Man in *The Death Of Cuchulain*. His main function was to justify the happy ending, which went against the grain of source material and history, and indeed against Yeats's better instinct.[10] The play was heavily revised, and when Yeats eventually changed the ending to a tragic one, he removed the prologue and added burlesque characters (such as the cripples and the Mayor) within the body of the drama. While the prologue provided an ironic frame to the whole play, however, the cripples and the Mayor only embody the sort of down-to-earth mediocrity against which Seanchan is poised, and serve as foils to the sublimity of his sacrifice. Sacrifice, on the contrary, is treated ironically in both *Calvary* and *The Death of Cuchulain*, where burlesque elements consistently undermine the solemnity of tragedy. *Calvary* takes up one image

---

[9] W.H. Auden, 'In Memory of W. B. Yeats', in *Another Time* [1940] (London: Faber and Faber, 2007).

[10] Cf. Yeats's note to the play in the Cuala Press *Seven Poems and a Fragment* (1922): 'I had originally intended to end the play tragically and would have done so but for a friend who used to say "O do write comedy & have a few happy moments in the Theatre". My unhappy moments were because a tragic effect is very fragile and a wrong intonation, or even a wrong light or costume will spoil it all. However the play remained always of the nature of tragedy and so subject to vicissitude' (*VPl* 316).

from *The King's Threshold* but uses it as a minor-key parody of the central dramatic tableau of Christ's sacrifice. In the beginning of *The King's Threshold*, the Oldest Pupil tries to convince Seanchan of the futility of his hunger-strike:

> And though I all but weep to think of it,
> The hunger of the crane, that starves himself
> At the full moon because he is afraid
> Of his own shadow and the glittering water,
> Seems to me little more fantastical
> Than this of yours. (*VPl* 263)

The image, used derisively in the earlier play, recurs in *Calvary* in the musicians' inaugural song. In Yeats's iconography the white heron is the purely subjective counterpart to Christ's objective personality, his inverted image on the other side of the mirror in which he contemplates himself in deathly narcissistic fixation, at the risk of becoming 'fishes' diet'.[11] (*VPl* 780–81). Before Christ appears on the stage to perform the foundational act of Christian culture, the song bizarrely disrupts and distorts its elements and dreams up a surreal parody of Eucharist in the unreal conditional, where the Christic fish ('ichtus') literally eat up the starving heron.[12]

Finally, the parodic intent is most conspicuous in *The Death of Cuchulain*, where suggestions of cannibalistic absorption again recur in a decidedly burlesque context. Cuchulain's executioner is the Blind Man who had spent the duration of *On Baile's Strand* cooking and devouring a chicken. Cuchulain's head is to be cut off with the Blind Man's carving-knife ('I keep it sharp because it cuts my food') and carried in the bag he uses 'to carry what I get at kitchen doors' (*VPl* 1060) – the prototypical doggy-bag. What actually happens to the head is left for us to imagine, and it is surely a blessing that it only reappears in the stylised, abstract form of the 'black parallelogram' after the blackout.

---

[11] On heron symbolism in Yeats see Warwick Gould, 'Lionel Johnson comes the first to mind' *YO* 272–77, esp. n. 45, and *Myth 2005* 126–28, 293, n. 1; 335, n. 16; 399, n. 1; 418, n. 51.

[12] See Jacqueline Genet, *Le Théâtre de William Butler Yeats* (Villeneuve d'Ascq: Presses du Septentrion, 1995), 336.

PERFORMANCE: 'The man that dies has the chief part in the story'[13]

A consequence of the sacrificial imagination which runs through the three plays and connects them to the dramaturgy of the medieval Passion is their self-conscious theatricality. Death is not just endured, but displayed publicly, and it is precisely this gesture of display which makes it efficient as sacrifice. The motif is treated seriously – even solemnly – in *The King's Threshold*, ironically in *Calvary* and *The Death of Cuchulain*. In *The King's Threshold*, Seanchan's hunger-strike is a political gesture: it needs to be witnessed by the greatest number, since its purpose is to bring shame on the King's name. The steps where he lies dying are a stage on which he showcases his emaciated body while the rest of the cast file past him. As in Kafka's story 'The Hunger Artist', which traces the unimpressive artistic career of a professional faster, the paradoxical show consists solely in Seanchan's entirely passive enduring of hunger, and the marks it imprints on his body, registered and amplified in his interlocutors' cues ('he's such a bag of bones!', *VPl* 286). Seanchan's drawn-out torture on the stage, as each new visitor tempts him with an offer of food which he rejects, is concomitant with the rumour of rising discontent gathering momentum offstage. The play, however, ends not with insurrection, but with the dialogue of the Youngest and Oldest Pupils, two directorial figures competing for the right to impose their own ending on Seanchan's performance after his death: 'triumphant music' and loud songs, or 'solemn music from the strings' (*VPl* 311). The play's ending seems to be improvised in view of the audience as the contestants debate over the choice of music and give contradictory instructions to the musicians, thus displaying the theatrical nature of Seanchan's performance of martyrdom which it befalls them to finish in style.

In *Calvary*, Christ may be 'dreaming his passion through', as the narrator-musician tells us, yet the dream is real enough for the physical effects of the torture (the carrying of the cross, and crucifixion) to affect the character's performance of his death. The narrator's voicing of this paradox has a didascalic import

> The cross that but exists because He dreams it
> Shortens His breath and wears away His strength. (*VPl* 781)

---

[13] *VPl* 309; cf., *AVA* 10.

Indeed, the shortness of Christ's cues is an index of his physical dislocation, offered as spectacle to a 'mocking crowd' which is not embodied on the stage, but evoked in the musician's narrative:

> Those that are behind
> Climb on the shoulders of the men in front
> To shout their mockery [...] (*VPl* 781)

We too, the refined, over-educated audience in the theatre, absorb (and respond to) the show of Christ's martyrdom like our grotesque counterparts on the stage: indeed the image is oddly reminiscent of the Abbey audience during the *Playboy* riots. Public humiliation is part of the torture Christ endures, yet it is the spectacular nature of his death (the fact that it is being watched by onstage and offstage audiences) which confers to it the dignity of Passion. That *Calvary* does not merely replay Christ's Passion, but also the hundreds of Passion plays which have come before, each ritualistically re-enacting Christ's performance, further sharpens our awareness of the quintessentially theatrical nature of Passion. It is, then, supremely ironic that in the final section of the play, the Roman soldiers should perform a dance for the benefit of Christ, stealing the show and recasting him as spectator:

> *Second Roman Soldier* Come now; let us dance
> The dance of the dice-throwers, for it may be
> He cannot live much longer and has not seen it.
> (*VPl* 786)

Running counter to the aesthetic protocol defined by Seanchan in The King's Threshold ('The man that dies has the chief part in the story'), the episode divests Christ of the aura of martyrdom and sends him back to invisibility. Christ's cry of despair ('My father, why hast Thou forsaken me?') is heavy with the frustration of the upstaged actor.

A similar kind of ironic displacement is at work in *The Death of Cuchulain*. Cuchulain's staging of his own death is nothing if not histrionic: displaying his gaping wounds, tied up Christ-like upon his pole, Cuchulain prepares to 'die upon [his] feet', giving the performance of his life (*VPl* 1057). All he needs is an audience. As Peter Ure has observed, Cuchulain is robbed of the tragic, poetically satisfactory death he anticipates when Aoife, just as she is about to kill him in revenge for the murder of her son, exits for no valid reason, and is replaced by the burlesque Blind Man (of *On Baile's Strand*) who proceeds to cut him up like a piece of meat: 'The story in which revenge would have meaningfully completed work, life, and death is carefully built up but does not resolve into its climax; the actual ending runs against it'.[14] However, the bitter irony of the ending lies not just in the incompletion of the tragic-heroic pattern, but in the fact that Cuchulain's executioner turns out to be a *blind* man, on whom Cuchulain's posturing is entirely lost. Instead of taking in the carefully composed tableau of the Passion of Cuchulain, a profane Calvary, the blind man takes the butcher's approach and horribly feels his way from Cuchulain's feet upwards, searching for the proper joint, dissecting his body in words before he does it in the flesh: 'Your shoulder is there, | This is your neck. Ah! Ah! Are you ready, Cuchulain!' (*VPl* 1061) *The King's Threshold* thus provides an initial paradigm which *Calvary* and *The Death of Cuchulain* revisit sarcastically, magnifying theatricality yet ultimately denying the martyr his fifteen minutes of glory. The ironic twist which robs the martyr of his performer's visibility is a particularly cruel aspect of Yeats's modernised version of the Passion, a kind of theatrical death which offers a sardonic counterpoint to the literal death which constitutes the core of the drama in the three plays.

DRAMA: 'Lie down upon the threshold'[15]

The prologues of *The King's Threshold* and *The Death of Cuchulain* create the fiction that what is happening on the stage is being improvised: both mention the material conditions of the productions (the scarcity of actors in the earlier play, the difficulties the Old Man encountered in his capacity as stage manager and casting director in the latter) and show us the creative process itself, the progressive assembling of Yeats's new dramaturgy against the conventions of realistic theatre. The end of the Old Man's tirade in *The Death of Cuchulain* ('I spit three times. [...] I spit! I spit! I spit!' *VPl* 1052) parodies the traditional three knocks which announce the beginning of the performance in bourgeois theatre and thus vociferously dismisses that sort of theatre. Rejecting the model of the well-made play and its promises of realism, dynamic dialogue, plot-twists

---

[14] Peter Ure, *Yeats the Playwright* (London: Routledge & Kegan Paul, 1963, 1969), 82.
[15] *VPl* 291.

and satisfactory resolution, Yeats replaces it with an alternative dramaturgy which he brings to its most radical expression in the three plays I am concerned with, in which it is the process of death itself which is being dramatised: catastrophe has already taken place, so that there is no 'action' to speak of, only a theatrical situation.

The eponymous 'threshold' of the earlier play (the steps before the royal palace) is clearly a metaphor for a metaphysical threshold, that which separates life from death. The time-span of the play is the time it takes Seanchan to cross the threshold, but that moment is artificially stretched out and Seanchan seems to be perpetually suspended in the action of dying. He envisages himself poised at the 'edge' of the living world, ready to take the jump:

> I lie rolled up under the ragged thorns
> That are upon the edge of those great waters
> Where all things vanish away, and I have heard
> Murmurs that are the ending of all sound.
> I am out of life [...] (*VPl* 287)

The paradoxical phrase 'I am out of life' points to his liminal situation, no longer alive, yet not quite dead since he is still there to say it. The play is made up of a succession of sequences in which the king's mediators (the pupils, the Mayor, Brian, the Chamberlain, the Monk, the Girls, the Soldier, the Princesses, and eventually Fedelm) successively fail to persuade him to discontinue his hunger-strike. The King thus delegates his presence and voice until the penultimate sequence when he comes to beg Seanchan in person, to no avail. He is an authorial figure in the text, who arranges the order of appearance of the cast and even provides them with their lines ('Persuade him to eat or drink.' 'Promise a house with gras and tillage land...' *VPl* 260, 262) Yet King Guaire, who has given in to his courtiers' demands and banished the poet from the State council, has forfeited all claims to authority. While the Poet's word, for whose dignity he is prepared to shed his own blood, has the terrible power of making and unmaking kings, the King's word, which he delegates to all and sunder, is shown to be vacuous and inefficient from the start. The play thus writes itself against his authority, inexorably unrolling Seanchan's own scenario, which the king announces in frustration in the opening sequence: 'he has chosen death: Refusing to eat or drink...' (*VPl* 258). The real author is of course Seanchan, whose death is a foregone conclusion. It is already well under way when the play begins, and we are constantly being reminded of it by the spectacle of Seanchan's starving body, and by the cues of Seanchan's visitors who perpetually, obsessively anticipate the inevitable denouement. The stage direction '*He dies*' at the end of the play merely brings the process to completion. The whole play is thus arrested 'upon the threshold' (*VPl* 291), a fraction of time expanded dramaturgically in terms of spatial location. When Seanchan does die, his body is immediately carried offstage, beyond the threshold.

In *Calvary* we witness the very last stages of the Passion of Christ, as he stumbles under the burden of the cross then stands stretched out upon it, awaiting death. As in *The King's Threshold*, 'the man that dies' has in fact already started dying when he enters. The first word we hear, sung by the First Musician, is 'Motionless', and it contains the whole dramaturgy of the play. Christ (just as his counterpart the heron) remains entirely static throughout, and all that happens on stage merely delays the inevitable outcome. Here, however, the actual crossing of the threshold is not represented on the stage, as if Christ never reached the moment of death; yet the First Musician, setting the scene at the beginning, tells us that 'Good Friday's come, | The day whereon Christ dreams his Passion through' (*VPl* 781). Christ is dreaming back his own death from beyond the threshold, so that the whole play seems caught in a paradoxical time loop, perpetually performing two contradictory movements, forward (toward the moment of death) and backward, from beyond death back to the final moments of life, the live man hurrying to his death, the dead man dreaming it back. What lies beyond can never be represented, because the experience of death consists in returning to the threshold of death: combining stasis with circularity, the structure of the play sacrilegiously suggests a sort of purgatorial vicious circle, anticipating such Beckett shorts as *Not I* and *Play*.

The Death of Cuchulain, too, is a variation on a well-known story, and should we be less familiar with 'the old epics' than the Old Man who speaks the prologue expects us to be, the title leaves little doubt as to the conclusion of the play. The hero's imminent death is also repeatedly announced by Eithne Inguba and Aoife, whose voices merge in choric incantation:

> *Eithne*: If, thinking what you think, you can forgive,
> It is because you are about to die (*VPl* 1055)
>
> *Eithne*: I might have peace [...]
> But that Cuchulain is about to die (*VPl* 1056)
>
> *Cuchulain*:   I cannot understand.
>
> *Aoife*: Because about to die! (*VPl* 1059)

However, there is more to the plot of *The Death of Cuchulain* than what the title promises – the death of Cuchulain. The time of the play is not arrested 'upon the threshold' of death as in the other two plays: instead the play is a triptych, in which Cuchulain appears successively alive, dying and dead. The play covers a number of events which undeniably qualify as 'action' (manipulation, revelation, a lovers' tiff, a battle lost and won, an ex-lovers' reunion, revenge, a sordid murder, a widow's lament) and even features such melodramatic devices as a forged message and a belatedly delivered letter – yet all these *peripeteia* are absorbed within the structure of the station-drama. There is no temporal continuum, but independent sequences separated by blackouts. Action proper occurs offstage, either before the start of the play (this even includes all the plots of the other plays of the Cuchulain cycle), or between sequences, and is retrospectively narrated in the sequences which bring Cuchulain face to face with successive interlocutors, all would-be executioners, until the moment of death proper – the decapitation which occurs between the penultimate and final sequences. Chronology is rough-handled – the Morrigu's narrative of the battle occurs after Cuchulain's death. This counter-realistic aesthetics of discontinuity and achronicity creates a sense of stasis: the play is constructed like a three-panelled retable, the central panel of which displays the now familiar picture of the dying man, tied to his post, suspended 'upon the threshold' of death. Death comes by virtue of a (literally) decisive gesture, decapitation, but it is crucial that Cuchulain is already mortally wounded when he returns from battle, so that the two sequences in the middle part (Cuchulain and Aoife, Cuchulain and the Blind Man) are located within the extended moment of the hero's death. The third part or panel, however, takes us beyond the threshold, into the realm of death itself.[16] The Morrigu greets us there with the resonant line 'The dead can hear me, and to the dead I speak' (*VPl* 1061). We too must be dead, then, and as ghosts we witness the final sequence of the inset play, Emer's dance of anger and mourning. To the challenge of representing death on the stage Yeats answers by dramatising the poignantly irreducible gap between life and death, between the living, fluid body of the dancer and the mineral *quidditas* of the black parallelogram, a metaphor of

---

[16] See Katharine Worth's remarks about the imagery of the door in the play. Katharine Worth, *The Irish Drama of Europe from Yeats to Beckett* (London: Athlone Press, 1978), 189–91.

Cuchulain's absence. The real tragedy of the play is Emer's failure to be reunited with Cuchulain. At first she is too far away to warn him in person of impending danger, and her efforts to supplement her voice with the letter, and her body with Eithne's, are to no avail. She comes too late; Cuchulain may be watching Emer's dance as a ghost among the other ghosts of the audience, but he cannot reach out to her anymore than we can.

The three plays thus experiment with ever more sophisticated formats of the Passion play to stage the crossing of the threshold between life and death, expanding the moment of death and absorbing all other elements of complication into the pattern of the station drama. Returning to the paradigm of the Passion play over the decades, Yeats gradually pushes the limits of the form as he endeavours not merely to stage this experience from an external viewpoint, but to capture it from within, as a subjective experience. Ultimately, what the plays attempt to dramatise is what befalls the subject when the subject ceases to be.

SUBJECTIVITY: 'He is delirious ...'[17]

The viewpoint in *The King's Threshold* remains external. The progressive collapse of Seanchan's mind is diagnosed clinically by the Mayor toward the end of the play: 'He is delirious now' (*VPl* 299). 'Delirium' (originally a term from agriculture, from the Latin *delirare*, 'to go off the furrow') signals the moment when the starving man's speech becomes dissociated from the here and now, the actual dramatic situation, and takes on poetic/prophetic resonances[18]. In the early moments of *The King's Threshold* Seanchan awakens from a dream of 'roast flesh', but soon recovers his clarity of mind. His first exchanges with his Oldest Pupil are written in the tradition of the Socratic dialogue: the master questions the pupil relentlessly until he brings him to change his mind, refuting him 'out of [his] own

---

[17] *VPl* 299.
[18] Likewise, in 'September 1913', Yeats evokes the 'delirium of the brave' to celebrate the past heroes who went off the furrow of ordinary lives lived only 'to pray and save', and whose voices, despite the poem's insistent claim that 'Romantic Ireland's dead gone', continue to sound through the poet's own voice, and to conjure an alternative vision of Ireland. W. B. Yeats, *Poems*, ed. Daniel Albright (London: Everyman, 1990), 159.

mouth.'[19] The incipit of the play thus displays Seanchan's superior reasoning abilities, the better to trace their disintegration as death progresses and reason gives way to vision. Seanchan's speech goes off the furrow of rationality, and his delirium culminates with the apocalyptic image of the leprous god in the sky. Poetry, the play suggests, has to do with the poet's commerce with death. The play's structure, however, is not affected by Seanchan's delirium, which is represented objectively, realistically. Seanchan's successive interlocutors exist independently of his delirium, and with them we witness Seanchan's departure from the bank of reality. The effect of approaching death is observable in his dislocated speech, but the subjective experience of death remains entirely out of reach of the audience.

Yeats's approach is entirely different in *Calvary*, which attempts to stage death from within, from the vantage point of 'the man that dies'. On the face of it, Christ is all but delirious: his speech remains remarkably composed to the end, his lines are rhythmically and syntactically balanced and conform to the original script of the Gospels ('O my father...') Those who clearly stray from the 'furrow' are Lazarus and Judas, the antithetical personalities who rebel against their fate, and refuse to be part of the divine scheme. Yet as the First Musician warns us, the play comes as a dream which Christ himself is dreaming. Christ's delirium is not contained in his speech, but in the palimpsestic structure of the play which rewrites the story of the Passion, deviating from the furrow of Scripture. There is no one to diagnose Christ's delirium in *Calvary*, because the whole play is his delirium, which is staged subjectively, from within – so that diagnosis must come in the first person: 'I am delirious', the play tells us, not 'he is delirious.' Yet the play goes further and questions the stability of this 'I' which it constructs. One difficulty comes from the 'white heron' which appears in the opening song, 'shiver[ing] in a dumbfounded dream.' It is a critical commonplace that the bird is Christ's anti-self or mask:[20] but if both are dreaming, who is dreaming whom? The play is a possible variation on the Taoist philosopher Zhuangzi's famous 'butterfly dream' (Zhuangzi dreams that he is a butterfly: or is it the butterfly who dreams that it is Zhuangzi?) Death is staged as

---

[19] Specifically, the passage is reminiscent of the *Crito*, which takes place after Socrates' condemnation, just before he drinks the poison. Crito begs Socrates to escape from prison, but Socrates, by the usual game of questions and answers, brings him to agree that it is fair he should commit suicide.

[20] See for instance Jacqueline Genet, *op. cit.*, 334 & ff.

the dissolution of identity, when self becomes mask. The neat symmetry which opposes Christ and the heron, one embodied dramatically, the other evoked lyrically, is further complicated by the status of the musicians in the play, in particular of the First Musician who acts as narrator and sets the scene of Christ's dream:

> *First Musician* The road to Calvary, and I beside it
> Upon an ancient stone. Good Friday's come,
> The day whereon Christ dreams His passion through. (*VPl* 781)

A figure of the playwright in the play, the Musician gives us an external, objective view of Christ, providing us with the structural key of the whole play (this is all a dream); yet at the same time, he tells us that he is part of the dream, a member of the crowd who watches on 'the road to Calvary'. Confusion increases when he intones a song in rhymed trimeters, expressing feelings which might be those of a bystander ('and I beside it') but are more plausibly Christ's: 'O but the mockers' cry | Makes my heart afraid...' (*VPl* 781). Voice is thus dissociated from body[21] in a striking dramatisation of the dissolution of self in death. From his ontological Moebius strip, inside and outside the dream, objective spectator-narrator and subjective voice of Christ's innermost feelings, the First Musician undermines our perception of Christ as unified self. The physical dislocation of crucifixion thus coincides with the dislocation of the I.

Yeats's project of staging death as the process of dissolution of the self is taken to completion in *The Death of Cuchulain*. When Cuchulain '*enters wounded*' after the battle, he expresses a sense of disorientation ('Where am I? Why am I here?') which suggests the beginning of delirium. The whole play is in fact structured like a dream, the extended delirium of the dying hero, but as Katharine Worth has remarked, whose dream it is remains an open question.[22] The final song seems to provide a definite answer when it states that 'an old man looking back on life | Imagines it [Cuchulain's body] in scorn'; yet the Old Man of the prologue, who allegedly recruited the street-singers and taught them their song, is clearly a fictional clown

---

[21] For an extensive study of such phenomena in Yeats's plays see Pierre Longuenesse's doctoral thesis, '"Singing Amid Uncertainty": Dramaturgie et pratique de la voix dans le théâtre de William Butler Yeats', Université de Paris-Sorbonne, 2008 and his Yeats dramaturge, *La voix et ses masques* (Rennes: Presses Universitaires de Rennes, 2012).

[22] *Op. cit.* p. 188.

who provides a burlesque image of both Yeats (who knew he was dying when he wrote the play) and Cuchulain. Cuchulain himself takes responsibility for the dream when he claims that 'I make the truth' (*VPl* 698), but this is only one instance of the proliferation of authorial figures in the play. The beginning of the play stages a contest between Maeve and Emer, who both try to impose their own scenario on Cuchulain: Maeve, like a manipulative playwright behind the scenes, has put Eithne 'in a trance' and taught her her lines, but Emer's letter 'tells a different story' (*VPl* 695). In the end, the Morrigu also emerges as a double of the playwright when she takes on the task of retrospective narration and then declares: 'I arranged the dance' (*VPl* 703). Strindberg had invented the dramaturgy of the dreamplay to create the paradox of a subjective theatre; in his dramatic exploration of the experience of death Yeats takes the form further and stages a dream without a dreamer – or with a plurality of authors/ dreamers. The play dreams the death of Cuchulain; it gives shape to the dying hero's delirium, yet what makes it so uniquely delirious is the splitting of the dreaming subjectivity. Death, the coming apart of the subject, is thus encoded in the structure of the play.

For Yeats, as for Craig, the task and privilege of theatre was to reveal the contiguity of the visible and invisible worlds, and to push back the borders of the unknowable. Reading those three plays together, I have tried to argue that they constitute three stages of a coherent aesthetic project which Yeats pursued from the beginning of his theatrical career to his dying day, that of inventing a dramaturgy with which he might stage the absolutely unknowable experience of death. Agamben, in *Remnants of Auschwitz*,[23] reminds us that etymologically the word 'martyr' means 'witness'. For the ethical subject to testify to his own suffering, he argues, he must lend his voice to another within himself, who has experienced such suffering that it has made him incapable of speaking (like the Muslim or *Muselmann* of the Nazi camps). To bear witness is always to bear witness to the impossibility of bearing witness, so that the witness (or martyr) must go through the experience of desubjectivation, of the dissolution of the speaking self, before he can testify. Experimenting with the form of the Passion play, Yeats invents a dramaturgy with which he can accommodate this paradox, and give voice to the martyrs who testify, impossibly, from beyond the threshold.

---

[23] Giorgio Agamben, *Remnants of Auschwitz: The Witness and the Archive*, trans. Daniel Heller-Roazen (New York: Zone Books, 1999).

To 'make others see my dream as I had seen it': Yeats's aesthetics in *Cathleen ni Houlihan*

Aisling Carlin

IT IS NOW WELL ESTABLISHED that Lady Gregory collaborated with Yeats in the writing of *Cathleen Ni Houlihan*. However, the extent and the implications of this collaboration remain incoherent. In 1962, Elizabeth Coxhead suggested Lady Gregory as primary author of the play, and in 1971 Daniel J. Murphy made the more absolute claim that Lady Gregory wrote the play 'in its entirety'.[1] Perhaps the most extensive and scholarly investigation of the play's authorship is James Pethica's 1988 article, published in the *Yeats Annual*.[2] Pethica's articulate examination of manuscripts and his comparative analysis of *Cathleen ni Houlihan* in the light of other writings by Lady Gregory (her folklore collections, the strongly nationalist essay 'Felons of the Land', and the play, *The Travelling Man*), placed a scholarly obligation on succeeding commentators to admit Lady Gregory's role as at least co-author, if not primary author, on this occasion. For Antoinette Quinn, the reappraisal of Lady Gregory's role is just one step in recognising 'the upstaging of real women by the nationalist

---

[1] Elizabeth Coxhead, *Lady Gregory: A Literary Portrait* (London: Macmillan, 1961), 68; Daniel J. Murphy, 'Lady Gregory, Co-Author and Sometimes Author of the Plays of W. B. Yeats', *Modern Irish Literature: Essays in Honour of William York Tyndall*, ed. Raymond J. Porter and James D. Brophy (New York: Iona College Press, 1972), 47.

[2] James Pethica, '"Our Kathleen": Yeats's Collaboration with Lady Gregory in the Writing of *Cathleen ní Houlihan*', *YA6* 3–31.

female icon' that followed these early productions.³ Nicholas Grene also supports this reassessment of authorship, referring to the play throughout *The Politics of Irish Drama* as *Kathleen ni Houlihan*, his spelling and textual citations derived from Lady Gregory's *Selected Writings*.⁴ In view of this critical re-assessment of authorship, Yeats's insistent appropriation of the play within his *Collected Works* strikes some as the wishful thinking and vanity of an otherwise unpopular playwright. This impression derives in some part from Lady Gregory's remarks, as noted by Elizabeth Coxhead:

> When her family...urged her to stake her claim, she always refused with a smile, saying that she could not take from [Yeats] any part of what had proved, after all, his one real popular success.⁵

The due acknowledgement of Lady Gregory's participation in the writing of *Cathleen ni Houlihan* cannot, and generally does not seek to, erase Yeats from the picture. However, any critical analysis based on Yeats as primary author requires resolution of the play's stylistic incongruity with his other early drama. Performing this task, Maria Tymoczko contextualizes the play in relation to popular melodrama and the *tableaux vivants*.⁶ Tymoczko highlights Yeats's early optimistic intention of using the theatre to affect a 'Unity of Being', claiming the popular theatre with its preordained iconographic meanings as the proper home of *Cathleen ni Houlihan*. For Tymoczko, *Cathleen ni Houlihan* can be safely attributed to Yeats because his vision at this stage was of a popular theatre. Deirdre Toomey helps clarify authorial roles by attributing the uncanny aspect of the play to Yeats and the *heimlich* aspect to Lady Gregory.⁷ More recently, Michael McAteer examined the occult ritualism of the play, paying particular attention to the play's interlocking conceptualisation of history, masculinity, and

---

³ Antoinette Quinn, 'Cathleen ni Houlihan Writes Back: Maud Gonne and Irish National Theater', *Gender and Sexuality in Modern Ireland*, ed. Anthony Bradley and Maryann Gialanella Valiulis (Amherst: University of Massachusetts Press, 1997), 47.
⁴ Nicholas Grene, *The Politics of Irish Drama: Plays in Context from Boucicault to Friel* (Cambridge: Cambridge University Press, 1999). Lady Gregory, *Selected Writings*, ed. Lucy McDiarmid and Maureen Waters (Harmondsworth: Penguin, 1995).
⁵ Coxhead, 68.
⁶ Maria Tymoczko, 'Amateur Political Theatricals, Tableaux Vivants, and *Cathleen ní Houlihan*', *YA10* 33–64.
⁷ Deirdre Toomey, 'Moran's Collar: Yeats and Irish Ireland', *YA12* 67.

marriage.⁸ McAteer discerns a symbolic pattern and radical politics in *Cathleen ni Houlihan* that developed from *The Land of Heart's Desire* in response to the criticism expressed by Frank Fay:

> The plays which Mr. Yeats wishes to see on the stage of his 'Theatre of Art' remind me of exquisitely beautiful corpses. *The Countess Cathleen* and *The Land of Heart's Desire* are undoubtedly charming, aye, and moving too; but they do not inspire; they do not send men away filled with the desire for deeds.⁹

Despite reassessment of *Cathleen ni Houlihan* as a piece of Yeatsian drama, in line with its first promotion and performance as a play by Yeats, this range of critical response shows that debate still pertains as to the populist versus esoteric aesthetics contained, and how exactly to configure these within Yeats's theory of art.

The aim here is to further prove Yeats's justification in taking *Cathleen ni Houlihan* as primarily his creation, notwithstanding Lady Gregory's collaboration. This justification comes to light in considering the allegorical and symbolical aspects of the play as serving a specific purpose within Yeats's broader theory of art. The realistic setting and statuesque acting style veil a finely crafted 'spirit drama' which bears all the hallmarks of Yeats. The duplicity of a linear surface meaning and an underlying cyclical and symbolic meaning was carefully plotted and constructed by Yeats in accordance with the principles of Greek tragedy. As Oedipus discovers in his solving of the riddle, *Cathleen ni Houlihan* offers the spectator a choice of meanings through which Yeats communicates the 'tragic crisis' (*Au* 332) which constitutes the play's theme. The tragic crisis is fundamentally an aesthetic crisis and a choice between allegoric or symbolic historical frames, between what is named and what is suggested. Read allegorically, *Cathleen ni Houlihan* traces a Gothic dimension to Irish history, not only in terms of colonial rule, but also in terms of a Celtic Christianity long suppressed by Roman rule. The deduction of political allegory from the play perpetuates a linear history which

---

⁸ Michael McAteer, '"Stranger in the House": Alienation and History in *The Land of Heart's Desire* and *Cathleen ni Houlihan*', *Irish Theatre in England*, Irish Theatrical Diaspora Series 2, ed. Richard Cave and Ben Levitas (Dublin: Carysfort Press, 2007), 35–51.

⁹ Frank J. Fay, *Towards a National Theatre: The Dramatic Criticism of Frank J. Fay*, ed. Robert Hogan (Dublin: The Dolmen Press, 1970), 52.

Yeats called 'the confident logic ... the way of a marching army' (*E&I* 318). *Cathleen ni Houlihan* is Yeats's attempt to transfigure this militaristic and deadening historical trajectory using a symbolic art. The Old Woman's transfiguration into a young girl is a symbolic representation of a historical transformation that is both iconoclastic and iconographic. It is only through recognition of the play's symbolic significance, dependent on the power of suggestion which is the antithesis of allegorical meaning, that this historical transformation can be fully understood. In essence, Yeats sought a renewal of the religious imagination that gave birth to the young and beautiful Cathleen ni Houlihan, but which had now sunken through the outworn and repetitive labours of old age into a hypnotic entrapment within a Gothic allegory. Read in this way, Yeats was not reaffirming the popular consumption of Irish iconography as exhibited by Inghinidhe na hEireann and the *tableaux vivants*, but rather he sought to transfigure the allegorical reduction of a once sacred national icon to what he deemed the level of idolatry, through symbolic suggestion.

Yeats's views on allegory and symbolism are developed in the 1898 essay on William Blake entitled, 'Symbolism in Painting', following on from the 1897 essay, 'William Blake and his Illustrations to the *Divine Comedy*'. In keeping with Blake, Yeats considered allegory as reading 'a meaning – which had never lacked its voice or its body – into something heard or seen, and loved less for the meaning than for its own sake' (*E&I* 147). On the other hand, symbolism 'gave dumb things voices, and bodiless things bodies' (*E&I* 147). The key difference here is that allegory simply *per*ceives an already given reality; in contrast, symbolism actually brings new life, it transfigures *per*ception into *con*ception, what is named history into what is born anew. Thus a truly symbolic art shatters past memories and engenders a new historical source. For Yeats then, to accomplish a symbolic art is to discover a new form of religious expression, a perfection through which history starts afresh:

A person or a landscape that is a part of a story or a portrait, evokes but so much emotion as the story or the portrait can permit without loosening the bonds that make it a story or a portrait; but if you liberate a person or a landscape from the bonds of motives and their actions, causes and their effects, and from all bonds but the bonds of your love, it will change under your very eyes, and become a symbol of an infinite emotion, a perfected emotion, a part of the Divine Essence; for we love nothing but the perfect, and our dreams make all things perfect, that we may love them. Religious and visionary people, monks and nuns, and medicine-men and opium-eaters, see symbols in their trances; for religious and visionary thought is thought about perfection and the way to perfection; and symbols are the only things free enough from all bonds to speak of perfection (*E&I* 148–49).

Carried to extremes, the choice of literary modes is nothing less than a spiritual choice, a theme which appears throughout Yeats's early works including *The Countess Cathleen*, *The King's Threshold* and the essay 'Magic'. In 'Symbolism in Painting' Yeats draws an association between allegory and 'the Daughters of Memory', in whose hands history becomes languid, frustrated, and embittered. For Yeats, an unfettered reliance on allegory signifies spiritual danger: allegory permits entrenchment of the historical memory, breeding the obsession that makes 'a stone of the heart' (*VP* 394). In keeping with Blake, Yeats believed symbolism liberates from and transcends a vengeful hatred using the imagination, which is itself love and beauty and the forgiveness of sin (*E&I* 111–15). Like tragedy, with its roots in the yearly cycle of nature, the symbolic imagination possesses the secret to spiritual renewal, that is, the ability to overturn loss, destruction and death and to bear new life.[10]

This distinction between allegory and symbolism is important in discerning the type of revolution envisaged by Ycats in *Cathleen ni Houlihan*. Essentially, *Cathleen ni Houlihan* exposes the spiritual peril involved in physical force nationalism, as evidenced in the sectarian atrocities which took place during 1798 rebellion. As early as 1894, Yeats guarded against the human cost of sudden revolution and was wary of the collective energy seeking historical justice. In correspondence with Alice Milligan Yeats wrote:

> I have often noticed that Irish men who have no personal dignity or nobility will yet have a true & devoted love for their country & I have made a story to describe this & put the song into it. My experience of

---

[10] This conceptualisation of tragedy derives from Aristotle's *Poetics* in which Aristotle assigns the origins of tragedy to 'the authors of the Dithyramb' '*Poetics*', *The Basic Works of Aristotle*, ed. Richard McKeon, introduction by C. D. C. Reeve (New York: The Modern Library, 2001), 1458. For further explanation of the Dithyramb, see Jane Ellen Harrison, *Ancient Art and Ritual* (1913; London: Thornton Butterworth, 1927), 101; and Gilbert Murray, 'Excursus on the Ritual Forms preserved in Greek Tragedy', *Themis*, 341–63 and *Five Stages of Greek Religion* (1912; London: Watts & Co., 1935), 60. Also relevant to the discussion of the evolution of ritual and religion, see Sir James G. Frazer's *The Golden Bough: A Study in Magic and Religion*, edited and introduced by Robert Fraser (Oxford: Oxford University Press, 1994).

Ireland, during the last three years, has changed my views greatly, & now I feel that the work of an Irish man of letters must be not so much to awaken or quicken or preserve the national idea among the mass of people but to convert the educated classes to it on the one hand to the best of his ability, & on the other – and this is the more important – to fight for moderation, dignity and the rights of the intellect among his fellow nationalists (*CL 1*: 399).

Yeats's qualified presentation of nationalism here is important to the interpretation of *Cathleen ni Houlihan* because the story referred to is his 1894 publication, 'Kathleen-Ny-Hoolihan', later reprinted in *The Secret Rose* as 'Hanrahan and Cathleen, the Daughter of Houlihan' (*VSR* 205–09; 102–05; *Myth 2005* 153–55). Significantly, Cathleen is not a physical presence in the story but rather a suggested one, finding similarity to the suggested offstage presence of the young Cathleen of the later play, "a young girl…[with] the walk of a queen" (*VPl* 231) and of whom Yeats would sing, "Your Mother Eire is always young" ('Into the Twilight', *VP* 148). In the story, Cathleen is brought to mind through the imagination of Hanrahan and a motley band of social outcasts. Margaret Rooney, with whom Hanrahan lodges, is described as having 'no good name at that time, and it was the priest routed her out of the place at last', while her companion, Mary Gillis, is described as having 'much the same story as herself'. Cathleen ni Houlihan is revealed here amongst a people whom time would sooner forget, whose lives fall outside the margins of history – that is, women of ill-repute, 'bocachs and beggars and blind men and fiddlers', and Hanrahan who, with his stories of the Fianna, belongs to an almost extinct bardic culture (*Myth 2005* 153).

The Cathleen envisaged by this party is not an Old Woman of the roads, nor is her chastity a likely condition of their love. This Cathleen is she who abides throughout the storm that breaks 'courage … like an old tree in a black wind', she who quells the '[a]ngers that are like noisy clouds', she who transcends the 'heavy flooded waters' which are 'our bodies and our blood' (*Ibid.* 154–55). In this imaginative vision, Cathleen performs the role of fertility goddess to a human world that suffers misery and mortality just as nature suffers. Rather than conducting a doom-laden call to arms and betraying an erotically charged Gothic fascination with death, Hanrahan's Cathleen stands inviolable before the futility of imminent disaster and spiritual obliteration.

Thus read in relation to *Cathleen ni Houlihan* it is possible to distinguish Yeats's alternative to allegory and what is named, through elucidation of the symbolism of the play and what the names suggest. The play's religious meaning – the proposal of a spiritual revolution and thus a new historical birth – is grasped through the suggestive power of all characters on stage. The names Peter, Bridget, Michael, Delia, and Patrick are no less important than Cathleen ni Houlihan. In the marriage of Peter and Bridget there is signification of the Irish Catholic alliance with Rome (St. Peter) and the Christianization of pagan Ireland: 'Brigid' was originally a pagan goddess who came to be appropriated into Christianity as an Irish saint. Michael bears a name association with Michael of the heavenly host, archangel of the Church Militant, often pictured as brandishing a flaming sword; Delia is a Greek name derived from the birth of the goddess Artemis on the island of Delos. Through the symbolism of their names, the prospective marriage of Michael and Delia implies the wedding of a Christian male with a pagan goddess. Finally, in Patrick there occurs not just a name association with St. Patrick, first apostle and patron saint of Ireland, but also a totemic association with Cuchulain, as demonstrated in the wish for a greyhound pup.

Through these names, Yeats evokes a history of religion extending much further back than 1798. Actually in operation in *Cathleen ni Houlihan* is a historical cycle lasting 2000 years, arriving at the possibility of a last analysis in the rebellion of 1798. Turning to Cathleen then, a key question must be asked of her religious identity and function. Since Rosalind Clark's illuminating study of the radical changes imposed on poetic representations of the female Sovereignty during the course of Ireland's colonial history, the interpretation of *Cathleen ni Houlihan* as an intrinsically nationalist allegory has faced new challenges.[11] Rather than celebrate Cathleen's youthful rejuvenation, the focus has been on the blood sacrifice demanded by the old woman. Drawing comparisons with vampirism and the Hag of Beare, Cathleen has at last come to be politically identified by Lionel Pilkington as 'a Unionist *deux ex machina*' who disrupts and nullifies the anticipated economic development of the cosy Irish homestead.[12] However, approached in this way, Pilkington again superimposes a political and allegorical framework upon the play, a logical development of Clark's argument that through Yeats,

[11] Rosalind Clark, *The Great Queens: Irish Goddesses from the Morrigan to Cathleen ni Houlihan*, Irish Literary Studies 34 (Gerrards Cross: Colin Smythe, 1991).
[12] Lionel Pilkington, *Theatre and the State in Twentieth Century Ireland: Cultivating the People* (London and New York: Routledge, 2001), 32.

Cathleen 'became interested in the sacrifice of her subjects, not their prosperity'.[13] Yet crucially, this malevolent Cathleen is fact an intentional device employed by Yeats to confront his audience with the realisation of just how desecrated the national memory had become, in fact no longer functioning as an image of unity – the perfection of love and forgiveness of sins. Yeats hereby sought to awaken a realization of personal complicity and collective sin in the perpetuation of national disharmony. As Winny of the Cross-Roads testifies, the appearance of the Old Woman is no cause for jubilation; she is an omen, 'the strange woman that goes through the country whatever time there's war or trouble coming' (*VPl* 216). Her chastity and her descent from sovereign to peasant are not attributes that bode well in Yeats's aristocratic and strongly anti-Puritan schema. As for Oedipus, so too does Cathleen's identity as national icon contain more than one truth. In *Cathleen ni Houlihan* Yeats ironically suggests that the cure to Irish Gothic history, with its appendage totemic tendencies and the human sacrifice of war/rebellion, is the alchemical restoration of Cathleen to all her transcendental grandeur, an emblem of the kingdom's fertility to be envisioned by power of the mind, rather than greeted as a physical presence with offerings of food and money.

Interpreted in line with Yeats's discussion of allegory, the Old Woman's incantatory lines gain an ominous fatalism, in fact the fatalism of damnation. Whilst assuming the appearance of heroism, the substance of the Old Woman's words is laden with irony. 'They will have no need of prayers, they will have no need of prayers' (*VPl* 228) she says, not because they have a place reserved for them in heaven but because they will be beyond all mercy having surrendered their spiritual agency. 'They that have red cheeks will have pale cheeks for my sake, and for all that, they will think they are well paid', she says, the word 'paid' clanging loudly in Yeats's repertoire with connotations of simony and materialism (*VPl* 229). And summoning those 'Daughters of Memory' who may be said to perpetuate Diarmuid and Dervogilla's curse in *The Dreaming of the Bones*, she sings, 'They shall be remembered for ever, | They shall be alive for ever, | They shall be speaking forever, | The people shall hear them for ever' (*VPl* 229). Everything uttered by the Old Woman contains an awful and terrible irony, a prophecy of both spiritual entrapment and physical alienation:

---

[13] Clark, 185.

'...many that have been free to walk the hills and bogs and the rushes will be sent to walk hard streets in far countries; many a good plan will be broken; many that have gathered money will not stay to spend it; many a child will be born and there will be no father at its christening to give it a name' (*VPl* 229).

With these words, Cathleen the Old Woman is exposed as a succubus of the nation's soul, feeding primarily on its masculine strength. Moreover, considering the fundamental significance of names to the play's power of suggestive meaning, this absence of a father at baptism seems to harbinger collapse into the absolute chaos of unmitigated hatred and violence. In short, this Cathleen ni Houlihan appearing in the form of an old woman is a mask worn by the angel of death, epitomising what Vincent Twomey describes as the 'angelism' of the nation, drawing people 'away from God by making the nation an end in itself, or...[by] claim[ing] divine status for one's own nation'.[14] Yeats was attempting to foreground for his audience the potential sacrilege of patriotism when the iconography is aged or hollowed out, thus defiled into idolatry.

The choice between allegory and symbol in *Cathleen ni Houlihan* is condensed in the Gillane family's response to the prospective marriage of Michael and Delia. Significantly, the parents focus on the material corollary of the marriage – the new clothes and the dowry. Compounding this materialism is the insinuation of simony, contained in Bridget's hope that they may turn the dowry to spiritual account by making Patrick a priest. In contrast, Patrick looks forward to his gift, a greyhound pup promised to him by Delia upon her entrance to the house as newly married bride. The young couple's fate pivots at the crossroad of these contrary desires. When Michael takes over from his parents in conversation with the Old Woman, he moves to the centre of a sacrificial site. This transition signals the confrontation of material desire with its moment of spiritual reckoning.

As argued by Michael McAteer, occult significance is attached to Bridget's offer of milk and here by extension, to Peter's offer of money. This offer of milk and money on the eve of the young couple's marriage instances a gross *mesalliance* and oversight on the parents' behalf. In keeping with McAteer's argument, milk and honey are accepted by the Fairy Child in *The Land of Heart's Desire*. The Old

---

[14] D. Vincent Twomey, *The End of Irish Catholicism?* (Dublin: Veritas, 2003), 28–29.

Woman's refusal of milk in *Cathleen ni Houlihan* establishes 'a complex engagement with the 'libidinal economy' of marriage in a particular historical and social situation'.[15] Notably, milk and honey are the food items traditionally associated with the nurture of youth; wine and bread on the other hand, are the food items associated with maturity, also the spiritual food of Christian sacrifice. Having crossed the offer of milk with the offer of money, the Gillane parents not only fail to correlate the food item appropriate to the Old Woman's age, but they corrupt the nature of that offer with the avaricious logic that also enshrined the marriage bargain. According to folk tradition, the offer of money was an insult to the fairy world, and it was also a taboo gift for such healers as Biddy Early (*UP2* 225). Given the supernatural aspect of Cathleen ni Houlihan, it can be seen that she would seek vengeance for the insult of the parents' offerings. In taking the body and blood of Michael, the son, the aged Cathleen therefore takes the physical equivalent of the spiritual error performed. Michael's enchantment with the Old Woman reflects the hypnotic element of ritual slaughter marking his transformation in the piece from passive voyeur to symbolic lamb. 'If anyone would give me help' proclaims the Old Woman, 'he must give me himself, he must give me all' (*VPl* 226). Therefore the religious identity and function of the aged Cathleen is that she ministers and performs a Black Mass before the witness of a packed theatre auditorium. Michael's exit with the Old Woman is the passing of a sacrificial victim into the pagan world of the Sidhe.

Michael's death is a consequence of his parents' materialistic and allegorical reduction of what was essentially a loving union between two young people. Having transacted spiritual wealth for material gain, Peter and Bridget must watch the supernatural forfeit – the loss of a much loved son. However, another reality comes into being simultaneously with this loss, and that is the miraculous vision beheld by Patrick upon returning to the house. Having been absent throughout the sacrificial scene, Patrick's return signals a religious transformation – significantly, it is through his eyes that Cathleen appears 'a young girl ... [with] the walk of a queen' (*VPl* 231). By appealing to the audience's visionary eye, Yeats compels an imaginative action which transcends the physical devastation played out onstage and it is through this vision that Yeats extends his hope for Irish nationalism. Through Patrick, perhaps the most overlooked

---

[15] McAteer, 46.

and most important player in the piece, Cathleen is envisaged as a young queen who commands a reverential love by virtue of her transcendent beauty. By drawing this relation through Patrick, Yeats implies an alternative association between 'home' and 'the stranger' than the 'libidinal economy' of marriage – here revealed is a symbolic image of dreamlike quality. It is only through recognition of allegory as a point of departure for envisaging symbolism that *Cathleen ni Houlihan* embodies a nationalistic agenda. Through the formation of an intangible visionary relation between Patrick and Cathleen, Yeats brings to birth the possibility of a new 2000 year historical cycle. Read in this light, the flaw of Peter and Bridget goes beyond their bourgeois materialism: it lies at the very heart of their marriage union and the founding principles of Christianity in Ireland as implied in their namesakes. *Cathleen ni Houlihan* is a condensation of Irish history, in all its idealism and failure, within a radical symbolic structure that seeks the liberation of that history from national allegories which hasten tragic crisis.

Cathleen ni Houlihan is a profoundly nationalist play, but not in the way it was first received or in subsequent allegorical interpretations. The nationalist solution offered here is one of religious transformation. The play is primarily and essentially religious in its conception and structure; its political dimension exists insofar as it asks a spiritual question of patriotism. Yeats duly emphasized the symbolic significance of the play:

...it may be said that it is a political play of a propagandist kind. This I deny. I took a piece of human life, thoughts that men had felt, hopes they had died for, and I put this into what I believe to be a sincere dramatic form. I have never written a play to advocate any kind of opinion and I think that such a play would be necessarily bad art, or at any rate a very humble kind of art. At the same time I feel that I have no right to exclude, for myself and for others, any of the passionate material of drama.[16]

Contrary to Marjorie Howes's claim that Yeats's purpose was to hypnotise his audience,[17] the possibility occurs that Yeats hoped to awaken Dublin audiences whom he believed to be fixated by the images and narratives of an outworn nationalism into an imaginative

---

[16] NLI 109 52 (i) (vi). Reprinted in Anthony Coleman, 'A Calendar for the Production and Reception of *Cathleen ni Houlihan*', *Modern Drama* 18.2 (1975), 137.

[17] Marjorie Howes, 'When the Mob becomes a People', *Yeats's Nations: Gender, Class and Irishness*, second edition (Cambridge: Cambridge University Press, 1998), 66–101.

vision of the moment of national rebirth. If anything, the popularity of the play and the compounding of an allegorical meaning at the expense of an intricate symbolic patterning must have been profoundly disappointing to Yeats. Indeed, Lady Gregory's conceit regarding her collaborative role, and her promotion of the play as a nationalist allegory, could have only diminished further Yeats's hopes for the play. Lady Gregory's grafting of the end of *Cathleen ni Houlihan* onto her translation of Douglas Hyde's *An Posadh*, highlights further an acute lack of insight and a failure to fathom the holistic integrity of symbolic art.[18] This failure to recognise Yeats's symbols, still prevalent in criticism to date, is a serious distortion of the play's meaning. For Stephanie Pocock, the often-cited 'The Man and the Echo' expresses Yeats's long held anxiety about the issue.[19] She writes:

> For the elderly Yeats, the incident evidences the breakdown in communication between artist and audience, validating his sense that, like the Man in his poem, his complex questions and spiritual struggles echo back to him reduced and twisted into statements of objective violence… The cry of wordless terror echoes the violence his words have caused…His words echo back to him, transformed into violent screams by a world in which he, and his words, are dangerously out of phase.[20]

To conclude, the complexity of structure and detail justifies Yeats's authorship of the play, and whilst Lady Gregory contributed her part, Yeats's role, as he so succinctly claimed, was he 'pared it to the bone' (*Au* 332).

---

[18] Douglas Hyde, *Selected Plays of Douglas Hyde 'An Craoibhin Aoibhinn'*, trans. Lady Gregory, selected and introduced by Gareth W. Dunleavy and Janet Egleson Dunleavy (Gerards Cross: Colin Smythe, 1991), 80–105. Hyde's Gaelic version is the verso page with Lady Gregory's translation on the recto. Lady Gregory's translation deviates from the original text, particularly in the closing section of the play in which she tries to emulate the transfiguration of Cathleen ni Houlihan in the person of the poet Raftery.

[19] Stephanie J. Pocock, 'Artistic Liminality: Yeats's *Cathleen ni Houlihan* and *Purgatory*', *New Hibernia Review* 12.3 (2008), 99–117.

[20] Pocock, 109.

© David Bradshaw, CC BY   http://dx.doi.org/10.11647/OBP.0038.04

'Oxford Poets':
Yeats, T. S. Eliot and William Force Stead

David Bradshaw

WITH THE ARRIVAL of William Force Stead in 1927, Worcester College, Oxford, secured its place among the footnotes of modern literary history.[1] College Chaplain from 1927 to 1930 and Chaplain and Fellow from 1930 to 1933, Stead was a friend of both Yeats and T. S. Eliot, and it was partly to thank Stead for baptising him as an Anglican in the summer of 1927 and arranging for his private confirmation by the Bishop of Oxford the following day that Eliot gave a rare, only partially documented and hitherto undated reading of *The Waste Land* at Worcester College.[2] This present article, centred on 'Oxford Poets', an unpublished talk that Stead gave at some point (probably in the early or mid-1960s) after he took up a Professorship of English at Trinity College, Washington, D.C., seeks not only to provide details of Eliot's Worcester reading, but, more significantly, to augment and in some small ways correct George Mills Harper's 1980 account of 'William Force Stead's Friendship with Yeats and Eliot'[3] by bringing to light Stead's own recollections of Yeats.

---

[1] An earlier version of this essay, 'The American Chaplain and the Modernist Poets: William Force Stead, W. B. Yeats and T. S. Eliot', appeared in the *Worcester College Record* (2011), 103-33.

[2] There are many letters from T. S. Eliot to Stead in the Beinecke Rare Book and Manuscript Library, Yale University, and these, alongside letters Eliot wrote to Stead that are now held in other repositories, will be published in due course as part of the multi-volume *Letters of T. S. Eliot* (London: Faber and Faber, 1988-).

[3] George Mills Harper, 'William Force Stead's Friendship with Yeats and Eliot', *Massachusetts Review*, 21:1 (Spring 1980), 9-38.

Harper begins his article by quoting from a 3 November 1951 letter Stead wrote to the Librarian of the University of Virginia enclosing four letters of recommendation that had been written in his favour by Yeats, Eliot, Edmund Blunden and D.C. Simpson, the latter, even in 1951, being rather less of a household name than the other three. We shall return to the testimonials from Yeats and Eliot in due course, but the first aspect of Harper's article that requires emendation is Stead's statement in his covering letter that he was 'a U. Va. poet of the ripe old vintage of 1908'. In an 'Autobiographical Note' now housed in the Enoch Pratt Free Library, Baltimore (which Stead may have written in 1945, if not before), he states that he was born in Washington on 29 August 1884 before offering this brief overview of his career as a schoolboy and undergraduate. 'In spite of all that could be done by the [Sidwell] Friends School, Washington, Tome Institute, and the University of Virginia', Stead writes, 'I remained impregnable to learning. At the University of Virginia I joined the Delta Phi fraternity, won a gold medal for poetry, was an Editor of *College Topics*, played a mandoline in the Glee Club, and poker with the Varsity Pikers.'[4] These diverse accomplishments help to explain, no doubt, why Stead failed to graduate from Virginia due to his inability to pass its maths requirement. This information and an account of Stead's post-Virginia life is set out in a detailed letter to Harper of 15 June 1975 from his son, Dom Julian Stead, quoted at the end of Harper's article (34-38), but since there are a number of discrepancies between Dom Julian's overview and my own research (which draws on a number of sources), I will now set down my own version of William Force Stead's career.[5]

On leaving the University of Virginia in 1907 (not 1908), Stead was accepted into the American Consular Service, his first post being US Vice-Consul in Nottingham. He was US Vice-Consul in Liverpool by the time he married, in 1911, Anne Francis

---

[4] William Force Stead, 'William Force Stead'. Autobiographical Note, stamped 'OCT-1945', William Force Stead Collection, MS 23, Series I, Box 1, Folder 3, Enoch Pratt Free Library, Baltimore. I would like to thank Dom Julian Stead for granting me permission to quote from the unpublished writings of his father.

[5] Dom Julian has supplemented his letter of 15 June 1975 by offering me guidance and information at every stage of my research and for all of his assistance and advice I am very grateful indeed. His letters and emails to me have now been deposited in the Worcester College archives.

Goldsborough, 'a Washington girl of the best style and society'.[6] Their first child, Philip Hugh Force Stead, was born in Chester in 1913, but not long afterwards Stead's life took a marked change of direction when he decided to train for the Anglican priesthood. He attended Ripon Clergy College in 1915 and Ridley Hall, Cambridge, in 1916, his first assignment as a clergyman being curate to the Vicar of Ross-on-Wye (1916-19).[7] It was here that he became friends with a Radley schoolboy, Henry Vere Fitzroy Somerset, a scion of the local gentry, who would go on to be elected to a Fellowship in History at Worcester College, Oxford, in 1921.

In 1919 Stead went up to Queen's College, Oxford, to read Theology. He took a Second in 1921, remained in Oxford for a year pursuing 'some special work in the philosophy of religion',[8] before being appointed Assistant Chaplain of St Mark's, Florence, in 1922. He remained in Florence until 1924, took his Oxford MA in 1925, and was Acting Curate of the Church of St. Mary and St. Nicholas, Littlemore, Oxford, when Somerset recommended him for the post of Chaplain of Worcester College. Stead's appointment was confirmed at the Governing Body meeting of 23 June 1927 (not '1926' as Harper has it on 19 and 29, footnote 30),[9] and he was reappointed as Chaplain on 17 June 1930, being elected to a Fellowship at the same meeting.[10] Stead thus became Worcester College's first American Fellow and its first salaried Chaplain,[11] having been on the point of resigning in May 1930 and moving back to the United States due to the increasing financial and emotional strain he was then under.[12]

Three years later Stead was forced to resign the Chaplaincy and his Fellowship in the run-up to his conversion to Roman Catholicism on

---

[6] Robert Sencourt, *T. S. Eliot: A Memoir*, ed. Donald Adamson (London: Garnstone Press, 1971), 105.

[7] *Crockford's Clerical Directory for 1918-19*, 50th Issue (London: Field and Queen, 1919), 1433. When the United States entered the War in 1917, however, Stead contributed to the American war effort by returning to the consulate in Liverpool for the remaining year of hostilities.

[8] 'William Force Stead', Enoch Pratt Free Library.

[9] Minutes, Governing Body, Worcester College Archives, WOR/GOV 3/2.

[10] Minutes, Governing Body, Worcester College Archives, WOR/GOV 3/2.

[11] E. Roberts to Stead, 21 July 1930; Stead to E. Roberts, 22 July 1930. William Force Stead Benefaction File, Worcester College.

[12] Stead to Richard Cobden-Sanderson, 18 May 1930, Special Collections, Morris Library, University of Delaware.

17 August 1933. 'I am sure that Worcester will lament, long lament the necessity you are under of leaving that excellent life, and all you were accustomed to do for the College. Why can't they fit you in? May not a Fellow be a Catholic?', his friend Edmund Blunden asked him on 13 August.[13] Stead, however, knew that for the time being he was *persona non grata* at Worcester, at least as far as the Provost was concerned. As Stead put it in a letter of the following year to Richard Cobden-Sanderson, when he was poised to visit Worcester for the first time since his resignation:

> You will not envy me my coming ordeal at Worcester College. The Provost is sore as hell with me; you know they created a new and special Fellowship for me in 1930, and then I not only resigned but joined the Church of Rome! Of all horrible things, especially in the cold fish like eyes of The Rev. F.J. Lys, Provost of Worcester and Vice Chancellor of Oxford. He is one of the old time drab and dreary Protestants who regard the Church of Rome as a purely Satanic Power. He would not have minded much if I had become a Buddhist or a Mohamedan ... But to become an R.C., is, in his eyes, to become a Devil Worshipper.
>
> When I went to say good bye to him last August he was out in his garden trimming his apple trees. He not only did not condescend to invite me for tea nor even to ask me into his house; he did not even come down from his ladder, but chatted coldly with me from a distance.[14]

In the same year that Stead resigned his Fellowship he brought out *Uriel: A Hymn in Praise of Divine Immanence*, his only volume of poetry to receive, in some quarters at least, anything like acclaim, though it was by no means his first book of verse. Sir Henry Newbolt told him that he had 'enjoyed [*Uriel*] more than any poem [he had] read for a long time',[15] while an article in the November 1933 number of *Blackfriars*, the monthly journal of the English Dominicans, hailed Stead as 'A New Catholic Genius' on the strength of it. It

---

[13] Edmund Blunden to William Force Stead, 13 August 1933, James Marshall and Marie-Louise Osborn Collection, Beinecke Rare Book and Manuscript Library, Yale University, MS 158, Box 1. There is a eulogy to Stead written after Blunden had been to dinner in Worcester on 22 February 1930 and a poem of 1 June 1930 by Blunden in celebration of Stead's imminent election to a Fellowship, as well as other poems and letters addressed to him by Blunden, in the James Marshall and Marie-Louise Osborn Collection. The Beinecke also holds collections of letters to Stead from Richard Cobden-Sanderson and Robert Sencourt (both in OSB MSS Box 3).

[14] Stead to Cobden-Sanderson, 17 April 1934, University of Delaware.

[15] Stead to Cobden-Sanderson, 28 March 1933, University of Delaware.

was written by his friend Gordon George (under his usual nom de plume of 'Robert Sencourt'), and although its pitch and title are ridiculously laudatory, it throws a valuable spotlight on Stead at this pivotal moment of his life and provides us with a flattering portrait of a man with whom both Yeats and Eliot were by then close friends:

[H]e is an excellent talker. A cliché, a truism, these...one hardly ever hears from his lips. He looks so straight at life that all he says is fresh and individual: his talk sparkles with the dew of truth, a truth which is fresh every morning. He is extraordinarily free from any sense of strain or of self-assertion: his conversation is quiet and modest and delightful in its sense both of the littleness of the self, and of the charm and importance of very little things...He is a keen watcher of the skies and is devoted to nature, especially the humanized nature which Virgil loved, and his garden has one of the best collections of lilies in Oxfordshire: he is something of a connoisseur, and with a very shrewd sense how to get the most for his money he has made his home in the most unspoilt and most picturesque village on the Thames, Clifton Hampden.[16] There, with the same shrewdness, he has collected Georgian furniture, and can seldom pass a shop with pictures that look anything like the period of Cox or William Turner. He takes little exercise except walking; though he likes to drive a large and silent car. But his specialities are inns and beer. If one wants to guide him on byways in the Cotswolds, it is no use thinking to do it by roads and villages: one must name the taverns; when he found that Prinknash Priory [Gloucestershire] was between *The William* and *The Air Balloon*, his heart warmed to it so that, from that moment, his heart was open to all that the ways of the Benedictines suggested to him. It was with them that he made up his mind to take the steps that would open to him the immediacy of Catholicism. For, though he never sought to alter the Protestant traditions of Worcester College Chapel, he had been for years in the habit of saying of Catholicism: 'It is the true Church.' The gift of faith, however, is something more than the power to discern that the faith of Rome is essential Christianity: it is the conviction that it would be intolerable to live without it. Such is the gift which came this summer to the poet: came at Prinknash...and so suddenly that most of his closest friends were taken by surprise. For not long before he had been inclined to say: 'It is an *iron* religion', and even to the last moment, he demanded every assurance that his conscience would not be coerced.[17]

---

[16] Stead lived at The Red House, Clifton Hampden, from 1928-39, 'the happiest period of my father's life' according to Dom Julian (Harper, 37).

[17] Robert Sencourt, 'A New Catholic Genius', *New Blackfriars*, 14.164 (November 1933), 924-35 at 925-26.

Stead was to be awarded an Oxford B.Litt. degree in 1936 for a thesis, supervised by Blunden, on the life and work of the Catholic poet and martyr Robert Southwell (1561-1595), and after resigning from Worcester in 1933 he had hopes of securing a position teaching English Literature at a university, possibly back in the USA (where he spent four or five months during the winter of 1933-34[18]) or at the University of Cairo, where George had connections. That his application to Cairo was successful[19] is not surprising given the collective distinction of the friends and ex-colleagues, such as Yeats and Eliot, who wrote him testimonials at this time. Even Provost Lys, having eventually climbed down from his ladder, drew attention in his reference of 16 November 1934 to Stead's 'considerable reputation' in the fields of poetry and literary criticism before adding that 'he is a man who can be trusted to carry out with all his power anything that he has undertaken, and is sure to be liked by those with whom he has to deal.'[20]

In the event, Stead did not take up a position at Cairo or any other university in the mid-1930s, but he did become a regular contributor to the literary press. The July 1938 number of the *Criterion*, for instance, carried an essay by Stead on Christopher Smart's cat Jeoffry. In words that are all too applicable to his own poetic *oeuvre*, Stead remarks of Smart that 'to read through his collected poems is to wander in a waste of tame, conventional verses, empty odes, flimsy ballads, and Prize Poems in Miltonic blank verse on the attributes of the Divine Being…He seemed unable to break through the crust of convention and to speak from the core of his being.'[21] Stead goes on to describe 'an unpublished and hitherto unknown manuscript' by Smart that he had 'recently examined.' In fact, Stead's discovery of Smart's *Jubilate Agno* (his edition of which was published in 1939 as *Rejoice in the Lamb: A Song from Bedlam*; it was set to music by Britten in 1943) was instrumental in putting this previously obscure eighteenth-century poet on the literary map, and in a piece he wrote

---

[18] Stead to Cobden-Sanderson, 30 December 1933; 10 January 1934; 17 April 1934, University of Delaware.
[19] Harper, 9.
[20] MS 23, Series III, Subseries 1, Enoch Pratt Free Library, Baltimore.
[21] William Force Stead, 'Christopher Smart's Cat', *Criterion*, 17.69 (July 1938), 679-85. Quote from 680.

about the *Jubilate* for the *TLS* Stead drew attention to its engaging oddity.[22]

As well as writing literary journalism and scholarly articles, Stead examined for the Oxford and Cambridge Schools Examination Board for a number of years after resigning his Fellowship, but on 12 August 1939, only a few weeks before the outbreak of the Second World War, he and his younger son Peter[23] (born on 20 November 1926) left Liverpool for the United States in order to visit his seriously ill father. The war, however, led to his American passport being cancelled[24] and Stead was unable to return to England until 1946.[25] He became a professor of literature at Trinity College, Washington in 1942 and ended up living in the United States for the rest of his life, although he revisited Europe almost annually, usually accompanied by Mrs Nancy Venable, a wealthy, cultured, domineering and possessive widow with whom he had fallen in love in 1939 and with whom he was to have a relationship more akin to that of a mother and child for the rest of his life. He died at her home in Baltimore on 8 March 1967. During the course of one of their Atlantic crossings Stead and Mrs Venable became friends with Tennessee Williams, who went on to portray him as the moribund poet Nonno in *The Night of the Iguana* (1961).[26]

*****

[22] William Force Stead, 'A Christopher Smart Manuscript: Anticipations of "A Song to David"', *TLS*, n. 1883 (5 March 1938), 152.

[23] Peter Force Stead adopted the religious name Julian when he became a Benedictine monk.

[24] Stead to Cobden-Sanderson, 10 December 1939, University of Delaware; Harper, 25, 37-38.

[25] When Stead and Peter took their holiday in America in 1939, Anne Francis Stead returned to Harborne Hall, Birmingham, which had become a Roman Catholic community of Sisters of the Retreat of the Sacred Heart in 1925, and which she had first entered in the late 1920s. When it was clear that her husband and son could not return, she remained at the convent and did not leave it until 1951, when she sailed for America in the hope of being reunited with Stead. Mrs Venable (for whom see further on in the main text), however, forbade Stead from meeting his wife and Anne had no choice but to live with her sisters in Easton, Maryland, where she died in 1959.

[26] Dom Julian comments in a letter to the author of 18 August 2011: 'if anybody today is curious to know what Stead was like in real life, they should see that film [1964].' See also Harper, 38.

While he was at Queen's and during the year he spent in Oxford before going to Florence, Stead got to know and was to remain friendly with a number of men who went on to become well-known writers. As well as Blunden, his circle included L. P. Hartley, Robert Graves, A.E. Coppard, Roy Campbell, Edgell Rickword, L.A.G. Strong, Richard Hughes, John Masefield and Robert Bridges. Stead later recalled his encounters with these men, and with other literary figures, in a talk entitled 'Oxford Poets':

The Sitwells were much in evidence, tho' they lived in London...Edith already looked like a Sienese Madonna in purple brocade and hung about with pearls; Osbert and Sacheverell looked like what they had recently been, young guardsmen, officers in a smart regiment...More diverse in effect were the 'Jolly Farmers.' None of us were farmers; we were a group meeting on Saturday evenings to read old plays, – Elizabethan and Jacobean – in an ancient public house called the Jolly Farmers. Comforted by a blazing fire on the hearth, a bowl of punch in front of the fire, and long clay pipes, we sat on the only furnishings in the room, hard wooden settles against the walls. We chose it as providing the right background, a shabby old ale-house unchanged since the days of our Elizabethan authors. But it had remained unaltered only because it was in one of the poorest and slummiest parts of Oxford.[27] And this gave rise to an astute suspicion; why were Oxford undergraduates lurking in such dark and thievish corners of the city?

One evening we looked up to see a black robed figure standing in the door; the black robes and black mortar board of the Senior Proctor. – We were 'progged'. The police had been watching; one or more had been secreted somewhere, listening to our readings. The language of Ben Jonson and Beaumont and Fletcher conveyed to the constabulary nothing more nor less than mutterings in an unknown tongue...We might be a band of Bolshevik conspirators.[28]

...The youngest of our group was the fabulous and flamboyant Roy Campbell. I didn't know what to make of him in those days...He was sort of half in and half out of the university; that is, he had been allowed to take up residence on condition that he passed his entrance examination at the end of the year.

Near the end of this period of probation I met him coming down the Cornmarket with a pile of books under his arm. 'Well' I said, 'I see you are

---

[27] The Jolly Farmers, Paradise Street, is still a pub and now far from shabby.

[28] In his autobiography, Vivian de Sola Pinto recalls a Proctorial raid on the Jolly Farmers when Yeats was present. He is said to have responded to the Proctors' request for his name with: '"William Butler Yeats, known as a poet throughout Europe and America"'. Vivian de Sola Pinto, *The City that Shone: An Autobiography (1885-1922)* (London: Hutchinson, 1969), 269.

getting to work.' – 'Work, hell', he replied, 'I am taking these over to pawn.' And that was as far as he got in Oxford.[29]

Stead goes on to evoke his memories of Graves, Blunden, Bridges and Masefield and his frequent visits to Lady Ottoline Morrell's Garsington Manor, but by far the most eminent of the 'Oxford Poets' he got to know at this time was Yeats. When Stead heard that Yeats was living in Oxford and 'liked people interested in poetry to drop in on Monday evenings' he could not contain his excitement: 'Why, since boyhood I had thought of him as the Magician Merlin harping in the Forest of Brocéliande' ('Oxford Poets'). He wrote to Yeats on 14 September 1920 enclosing a copy of his latest book of poems, the 'rather Pre-Raphaelite verses' of *Verd Antique*:

Dear Sir,
I have heard that you are kind and sympathetic toward the younger poets, and so I am venturing to send you my little volume. – As a matter of fact I am not so very young after all, having turned 30.
   What troubles me is ... do you think I am capable of writing poetry? This is only a small selection, but it is the best I have written. And I have always tried most honestly to be myself, and have most rigidly abstained from adopting any of the poses which have been fashionable during the last ten years.
   Yet very few papers have noticed my book, and the few who have, do not attach any significance to it. Especially was I hurt and crushed by this sentence in "The Nation", – "There is no ardour nor vision in it, no reality[,] no revelation of the beautiful[,] enigmatic face of life",[30] – this hurt me especially because the reviewer had some reason to be favourably disposed toward me, since my book was introduced to him by one of my best friends who is also a close friend of his.
   If there is no poetry in this book, then at 30 I can hardly hope ever to write poetry – And poetry is to me everything. – What do you think? – Please forgive me if you have no time for such letters (*LTWBY*2, 368).

It is noteworthy that Stead misrepresents his age in this letter: he was in fact thirty-six in September 1920, not thirty.

---

[29] William Force Stead, 'Oxford Poets', William Force Stead Collection, MS 23, Series II, Subseries 2, 'Other Writings, 1925-1965', Box 2, Folder 66, Enoch Pratt Free Library, Baltimore.
[30] Anon., 'A Bed of Verses', *Nation*, 27.22 (28 August 1920), 673-74.

Yeats, then living at 4 and 5 Broad Street, Oxford, and deeply involved in the occult investigations that would culminate in *A Vision*, replied to Stead on 26 September 1920 (*Life 1*, 113-117; 157-62):

Dear Mr. Stead,
I have been for days on the point of writing to you about your book of distinguished poems. But much work put off & still puts off the reading of it in any adequate way. I wonder if you would come & see me? I shall be in but not alone tomorrow evening. If you are free come in. In any case we will have a talk later on when I have read more (*CL InteLex* 3783).

Stead takes up the story in 'Oxford Poets':

Yeats lived at ... a delightful 17th century house now pulled down and replaced by vulgar commercial premises. An Irish maid led me to his study at the top of the house, up two flights of stairs with old oak bannisters carved in the twisted Jacobean fashion. I found the poet surrounded by his books and a small gathering, – his wife, an impressively silent lady, very striking with raven black hair, a beak-like nose, and brilliant eyes, – an equally striking looking Hindoo priest, with a round chocolate-colored face and a long flowing orange colored robe, – and, by way of contrast, Father Martindale, a Jesuit priest.[31]

Yeats at this time (1920) was about 55 and at the height of his powers. Under his wife's civilizing influence, and in honour of his guests, he was wearing a dinner jacket with black tie, his hair, still without a touch of grey, was carefully brushed and slicked down. His greeting had an old-fashioned air that combined formality and dignity with something that was modest and deferential.

...Yeats was vigorous, animated, confident, and controversial. I found him in the midst of a discourse on spiritualism and its evidences of survival. But every time he brought forward what seemed a convincing instance, Father Martindale found a naturalistic explanation. The learned Hindoo then offered some oriental marvels, but fared no better under the searchlight of the brilliant Jesuit.

Finally, Yeats could stand it no longer, he leapt from his chair, shook his finger in Father Martindale's face and exploded angrily, 'Father Martindale, you are an unbeliever!'

Yeats would subscribe to all the miracles of the Christian, Mohammedan and Mormon scriptures, the hidden powers of the monks of the Ganges and Euphrates, and the mountain-guarded secrets of Tibet, rather than listen to the most persuasive sceptic explaining one miracle away. A man born to believe, he said that when he first came to London he found the

---

[31] Cyril Charles Martindale (1879-1963) of Campion Hall, Oxford. I have not been able to identify the 'Hindoo priest'.

intelligentsia followers of Darwin, Huxley and Spencer, but he knew such doctrines could not be true; materialism, he said, is 'just too *dull* to be true.'

When we were leaving he lit a candle, and holding it above his head, lighted us down the stairs. At the door he asked me to wait a moment, and after the others had gone, he said he was interested in my little book, – I pricked up my ears, expecting some praise of my verses, – but he went on to explain that the spirits manifest themselves in various ways, most subtly and delicately by odours; as he took up my book, addressed in an unknown hand, he was visited by an odour of violets, – a friendly and favorable odour: would I care to come in the following Monday evening?

In fact, Yeats was so curious about Stead's 'odour of violets' that he wrote to him later that same evening (Monday 27 September) inviting him to dine with him and his wife 'on Friday next at seven o'clock. We shall be by ourselves & I do not think we shall lack things to talk of' (*CL InteLex* 3786) 'Two days later, in a notebook recording visionary experiences used in *A Vision* (1925)', Harper comments, 'Yeats recalled Stead's visit: "On Monday night a young man called Force Stead came, & a few minutes before he arrived I smelt violets, & communicator said this was to draw attention to him". As Yeats points out in the "Introduction to 'A Vision'", his Communicators or Controls were accustomed to announce their presence and pleasure by "whistlings" or "sweet smells" and their displeasure by bad smells or noises.'[32]

Had he known how privileged he was to give off such an aroma, Stead would no doubt have been beside himself with joy. As Yeats told Lennox Robinson on 16 March 1922, 'About the violets. One man here [in Ireland] was introduced to me by a smell of violets when I opened his letter asking if he might call. I found when he did that he had had the same dreams – certain precise symbols I and my wife have had for years. I have seen a great deal of him, much more than of any body else ...'.[33] The odour of violet was also Maud Gonne's favourite scent, and Yeats associated it with manifestations of sanctity. As he puts it in 'Oil and Blood':

> In tombs of gold and lapis lazuli
> Bodies of holy men and women exude
> Miraculous oil, odour of violet. (*VP* 483)

[32] Harper, 12-13.
[33] *CL InteLex* 4096. For other references to the odour of violets in the early 1920s, see the following letters to George Yeats regarding the madness of Francis Stuart: *CL InteLex* 3750 (30 July 1920); 3760 (4 August 1920) and 3763 (6 August 1920).

Elsewhere, Yeats asked Thomas Sturge Moore in 1928 how he accounted 'for the fact that when the Tomb of St Teresa was opened her body exuded miraculous oil & smelt of violets?' (*CL InteLex* 5072. 2 February [1928]), while in *A Vision* (1937) he recalled the signs his communicators had used in the early 1920s:

> Sweet smells were the most constant phenomena, now that of incense, now that of violets or roses or some other flower, and as perceptible to some half-dozen of our friends as to ourselves, though upon one occasion when my wife smelt hyacinth a friend smelt eau-de-cologne. A smell of roses filled the whole house when my son was born and was perceived there by the doctor and my wife and myself ... Such smells came most often to my wife and myself when we passed through a door or were in some small enclosed place, but sometimes would form themselves in my pocket or even in the palms of my hands ... When I spoke of a Chinese poem in which some old official described his coming retirement to a village inhabited by old men devoted to the classics, the air filled suddenly with the smell of violets, and that night some communicator explained that in such a place a man could escape those 'knots' of passion that prevent Unity of Being and must be expiated between lives or in another life (*AVB* 15-16)

Yet another reason why Yeats would have been intrigued by Stead's odour is because 'there was a connection between the smell of violets & the Tower symbol', as he was to put it one of his *Vision* notebooks on 2 May 1922.[34]

Stead became a regular at Yeats's Monday evening gatherings and he was also invited on other days of the week when he and the Yeatses would have supper together. 'At these times he was Willie and she was George', he remembered, '...an easy and intimate little party, but I was often puzzled in the hours that followed when we retired to his study':

> Yeats, who mistook me for a philosopher and a man of learning, went voyaging off into regions with which I was wholly unfamiliar.[35] He was then reading the Catholic theologian, Baron von Hugel, – and here I could offer a few comments; he was already interested in Byzantium, and I had a little knowledge of the Eastern Empire. But his range of interest – tho' he was not a man of learning – went far beyond my boundaries. For instance,

---

[34] *YVP3*, 104. See also 308.
[35] In a letter of 20 March 1921 (*CL InteLex* 3882), for example, Yeats asked Stead: 'What is the history of turpentine in ancient times? For what was it used? That if we knew it might explain tarebuith. What is calominth?'

he would open a volume on Art, *Apollo* by Reinach,[36] and ask me to compare the facial expressions in Greek and Roman sculpture, as representing the contrast between the subjective or instinctive life and the objective or rational life. This led to a discussion of the difference between the Greek and Roman civilizations, and to subjective and objective periods during the Christian era.

Here I was invited to follow his involved system of intersecting cones, as the objective age or civilization was moving up into the subjective, and the subjective age or civilization was moving down into the objective. These again were symbolised by the dark of the moon as the objective, and the light or full moon as the subjective, and the transition as the gradual rounding out of the dark into the light, and vice versa.

I was often quite lost, and even the poet himself, to whom this reading of character and history had come as a revelation, – partly thro' his wife, who had pronounced psychic powers, – even the poet would pause at times, drop his glasses, dangle them at the end of their ribbon, – look round and say:

'It is all very difficult.'

Other subjects were the Great Memory; the Pylons, or Gates of Knowledge, and the external existence of dreams: for instance, he was staying in a friend's house, Lady Gregory's, I believe, when he had a dream of Diana shooting an arrow at a star; he came down to breakfast and started to relate it to Arthur Symons, another guest in the house, only to find that Symons had had the same dream at the same time and had already embodied it in a poem.[37] What could this mean, but that the dream was not peculiar to one dreamer? Dreams have an external existence of their own and floating through the world, they may visit several dreamers at the same time.

I must have been useless as a source of information and ideas, but Yeats was lonely and felt rather neglected in Oxford; his was not the academic type of mind, and learned ladies bored him by asking, 'Mr. Yeats, what is your subject?' as though he were a don, with some narrow field of research. He soon adopted a blunt reply, – 'Astrology', and that floored them.

As a matter of fact, it was one of his many interests in occultism. I have heard him inveigh against the blind and irrational manner in which astrology has been ignored by the western mind without ever being disproved. Speaking of the subject one evening, he said it was by this science that Pico

---

[36] *Apollo, histoire générale des arts plastiques* by Salomon Reinach (1858-1932) was first published in 1904. It was translated into English and many other languages. The British edition, *Apollo: An Illustrated Manual of the History of Art throughout the Ages*, was revised and reprinted on a number of occasions.

[37] Yeats was actually staying at Tillyra Castle, the home of Edward Martyn, not at the home of Lady Gregory. For a comprehensive account of 'The Vision of the Archer', which occurred on the night of 14-15 August 1896, see *CL2* 658-63.

della Mirandola[38] had been able to foretell the year and day of his death. We were a group of 4 or 5, while Mrs. Yeats sat apart, quietly sewing by the fire, – very much 'out of it.' I remembered how Yeats looked over to her saying, 'But my wife knows more about this; she has been reading Pico's life. George, tell us something about Pico della Mirandola', – with a gentle courtesy drawing her into our circle.

Yeats welcomed almost any form of belief. He craved the supernatural. It was the only air he could live and breathe in. He was suffocated by materialism and irritated by scepticism. Once when I had brought an undergraduate with me, Yeats gave us a long discourse on re-incarnation. At the end my young friend ventured to observe that the theory of re-incarnation 'bristles with difficulties.' Yeats passed it off in sullen silence, but several times later on referred indignantly to 'that young man who said re-incarnation bristles with difficulties.'

The 'young man' was C.S. Lewis, and if Stead remained an awe-struck devotee, the Ulsterman was rather less impressed with Yeats and his extraordinary household. 'It was the weirdest show you ever saw', Lewis told his father in a letter of 19 March 1921. '... You sit on hard antique chairs by candlelight in an oriental looking room and listen in silence while the great man talks about magic and ghosts and mystics... It is a pity that the real romance of meeting a man who has written great poetry and who has known William Morris and [Rabindranath] Tagore and [Arthur] Symons should be so overlaid with the sham romance of flame coloured curtains and mumbo-jumbo.'[39]

Lewis developed his account of his 14 March 1921 visit to Yeats's house in a serial letter to his brother and during the course of it he also took the opportunity to disparage Stead, whom he called 'rather a punt...He is an undergraduate but also curate of a parish in Oxford. He writes poetry. The annoying thing is that it's exactly like mine, only like the bad parts of mine.' Before heading off to Broad Street, Lewis rendezvoused with Stead at his lodgings and he describes Stead's wife in this letter as 'a woman of implacable sullenness who refused even to say good evening to me...Stead was finishing a very nasty meal of cold fish and cocoa: but he soon put on his coat and after asking his lady why there were no stamps in the house and receiving no answer, swung out with me into the usual

---

[38] Giovanni Pico della Mirandola (1463-1494), esoteric philosopher and author of *Oration on the Dignity of Man* (1486), one of the foundational texts of Renaissance humanism.

[39] 'Family Letters 1905-1931', *The Collected Letters of C.S. Lewis*, ed. Walter Hooper, 3 vols. (San Francisco: Harper, 2004), I, 524-25.

Oxford theatrical night.'[40] Lewis goes on to describe the interior of Yeats's home in some detail:

> We were shown up a long stairway lined with rather wicked pictures by Blake – all devils and monsters – and finally into the presence chamber, lit by tall candles, with orange coloured curtains and full of things which I can't describe because I don't know their names. The poet was very big, about sixty years of age ... grey haired, clean shaven. When he first began to speak I would have thought him French, but the Irish sounds through after a time. Before the fire was a circle of hard antique chairs. Present were the poet's wife, a little man who never spoke all evening, and Father Martindale ... Everyone got up as we came in: after the formalities I was humbly preparing to sink into the outlying chair leaving the more honourable to Stead, but the poet sternly and silently motioned us into other ones ...
> Then the talk began. It was all of magic and cabbalism and the 'Hermetic knowledge'. The great man talked while the priest and Mrs Yeats fed him with judicious questions. The matter I admit was either medieval or modern, but the manner was so XVIII Century that I lost my morale.

Lewis told his brother that he found Stead's account of a recent dream especially risible and reports the scene as follows: 'YEATS (looking to his wife): "Have you anything to say about that, Georgie?" Apparently Stead's transcendental self, not important enough for the poet, has been committed to Mrs Yeats as a kind of ersatz or secondary magician...Try to mix Pumblechook,[41] the lunatic we met at the Mitre [Hotel, Oxford], Dr Johnson, the most eloquent drunk Irishman you know, and Yeat's [sic] own poetry, all up into one composite figure, and you will have the best impression I can give you.'[42]

Stead, on the other hand, as Harper takes pains to show, grew ever more enraptured with Yeats. They shared an interest in esoteric phenomena and corresponded about dreams, visions and the supernatural in a number of letters written between 1921 and 1924.[43] Indeed, they remained in intermittent touch throughout the decade

---

[40] Dom Julian, on the other hand, notes that Anne Stead was very friendly with Richard Cobden-Sanderson and his wife and with Vere Somerset.

[41] The nickname of G. Herbert Ewart (1857-1924) as well as a character in *Great Expectations*.

[42] *Collected Letters of C.S. Lewis*, ed. Hooper, I, 525-34; quotes from 529-32. Despite his contempt for what went on there, Lewis returned to Yeats's house with Stead on 21 March 1921: see 533-34.

[43] See Harper, 13-19.

and Harper concludes that they enjoyed 'an unbroken if not intimate relationship'.[44]

When Stead brought out *The House on the Wold and Other Poems* in late 1930 it coincided with perhaps the greatest crisis of his life. An earlier volume, *The Sweet Miracle* (1922), had been dedicated 'To Guy and Dorothy Trafford and with love to Cicely', while one of the poems in his 1924 collection, *Wayfaring*, called 'His Nymph Grazing', is about a girl with a voracious appetite. Its last four lines, hilarious and pathetic in equal measure, are:

> Though you've emptied half the larder,
> Nothing can subdue my ardour;
> Come and kiss me, pretty sinner,
> And love me, – like you love your dinner.[45]

Similarly, in his latest collection, *The House on the Wold*, there are further 'Nymph' poems dedicated 'To Cecilia, aged 8', 'To Cecilia, aged 9', 'To Cecilia, aged 11', 'To Cecilia, aged 15' and 'To Cecilia, aged 16'. As early as September 1926 Stead had told Somerset that he was 'in love' with his 'Nymph',[46] but by 1929-1930 he had become completely besotted with Cicely Trafford and things were rapidly getting out of hand.

Stead's wife seems to have suffered some kind of breakdown around this time and was then recuperating in Malvern while Stead himself was 'unutterably depressed about everything' as he put it in a letter to Cobden-Sanderson. Stead also mentions in this letter that his doctor had urged him to live 'a celibate life' but he preferred to live apart from his wife – 'I simply *can't* live with her as brother and sister'. His brother-in-law tried to persuade him to divorce Anne, but Stead knew that this would 'utterly crush her.' 'Also what is the use in divorcing her when the only other person I care for is the Nymph, and her mama, while kindness itself to me on all other subjects, is absolutely *ruthless* in her determination to tear that dear girl away from me and marry her to a county name and a county mansion?'[47]

---

[44] Harper, 19.

[45] William Force Stead, *Wayfaring: Songs and Elegies* (London: Richard Cobden-Sanderson, 1924), 34-36.

[46] Stead to Vere Somerset, 1 September 1926, Stead's Personal File, Worcester College.

[47] Stead to Richard Cobden-Sanderson, 7 February 1929, University of Delaware.

By the beginning of 1931 Stead's 'ardour' for Cicely Trafford was still as intense as ever, and when he sent a copy of *The House on the Wold* to Yeats on 8 January he also took the opportunity to describe the predicament in which he now found himself:

The Traffords have been my very great friends and patrons for many years, and their delightful William & Mary house, Hill Court, has been my 'English Home' as they always said, until recently – but gradually I fell so deeply and hopelessly in love with their daughter, my 'Nymph', that I confessed my devotions, like a fool – and that put an end to the best and brightest and sweetest episode in my dull and prosaic life…My wife you know lives apart from me, almost entirely in a convent.⁴⁸ So my heart went a wandering and lodged with the Nymph! She was only 8 and I was 30 when I first knew her; so that was alright. But alas for the tricks of time: she is now 22 and I am 44. So it is *not* alright. And having her taken away from me has hurt my feelings and soured my heart and left me empty and desolate. Why cannot I accept a desolation like this and make great poetry out of it, instead of growing soured and bitter? Pride is the trouble, I fear – and that is what made even the Angels fall!⁴⁹

All the evidence suggests that Stead's feelings for Cicely could not have been more fervent or sincere, but in the eyes of some of his friends he had made himself a laughing-stock through his doomed devotion to her. Eight months earlier, on 30 April 1930, for example, L.A.G. Strong had told Yeats:

Force Stead… is going through one of those troubled times popularly considered good for poets. His wife has left him, & entered a nunnery, where she claims to be happy. He has fallen in love, inaccessibly, with just such another, only higher up in the scale: a young girl whose blank gaze he fills mentally with spiritual condoms. She has an affection for him, but, when he protests devotion, she says he gives her the pip. This phrase makes him furious, & he broods for three months each time he provokes her to utter it. Her people regard him as a mixture of Wilde and Aleister Crowley, & won't have him near the place. Poor Stead: it is unkind to talk of him in this way, but one cannot help feeling a little impatient to see a man who knows as much as he knows acting in such a way. It isn't the being in love with her which is silly, but the way he goes about it, & the interpretations he puts on actions & remarks of hers which are plain from the other side of the street. That she could feel affection for him, without being in love, never entered his head… He won't divorce his

---

⁴⁸ Harborne Hall, Birmingham. See n. 25 above.
⁴⁹ *LTWBY2* 513.

wife, because if she is divorced the nuns won't keep her; & she knows how to play upon his kindness. I hope he will go off on his own, & find someone to look after him. He is much liked & respected by [Worcester] undergraduates. They come to him deeply worried by Bertrand Russell's book on marriage.[50] After combating its statements with the thirtieth undergraduate, he said to me "I've decided not to read it after all".[51]

In the event, it did not take long for Stead's relationship with the Trafford family to improve, but it would never recover its old intimacy, while his marriage seemed broken beyond repair.

'Are you back at Worcester. I had heard that you had given up your work as Chaplin?', Yeats enquired of Stead in a letter of 26 September 1934.[52] Stead replied promptly and in his last extant letter to Yeats, dated 29 September 1934, he wrote:

As for Worcester College, I remain a member of the Senior Common Room and dine there from time to time – perhaps you will dine with me there if you are in Oxford again – but I resigned my Fellowship in order to be received into the Catholic Church ... I felt that I wanted to be a Catholic, and I wanted it more and more, until I wanted it so badly that I was willing to resign my Oxford Fellowship...

Since becoming a Catholic I have had very wonderful experiences, such as when I took my hour's watch from 4 to 5 A.M. before the Blessed Sacrament in the Franciscan Church in Oxford [Greyfriars, Iffley Road]. There was continuous devotion day and night for 2 days and 2 nights – never a moment when there were not watchers engaged in prayer and meditation before an altar with the Sacrament exposed in the Monstrance surrounded by flowers and burning candles. I rose up soon after 3 – while it was still dark – motored into Oxford and took my hour's watch not as a duty but as a joy with a keen sense of spiritual influences and powers around me.[53]

It was not long after this (around November 1934) that Yeats must have written the short testimonial for Stead that is now held in the Stead Collection at the Enoch Pratt Library and a copy of which Stead sent to the University of Virginia Library in 1951. In his reference, Yeats stated concisely but warmly: 'I have known Mr W. Force Stead since 1920. I think him an imaginative scholar with considerable critical ability and knowledge of English literature. His

---

[50] *Marriage and Morals* (1929).
[51] *LTWBY* 507-8.
[52] *CL InteLex* 6102.
[53] *LTWBY2* 565-66.

own writings show that he is sensitive to rhythm and style. He is a charming personality.'[54]

In 1936 Yeats included two poems by Stead in his *Oxford Book of Modern Verse* (1936),[55] but only after he had asked him to alter a line in one of them so as to improve its cadence,[56] and it was also in 1936 that Stead finally succeeded in visiting Yeats and his wife in Dublin.[57] The Yeats of 1920, Stead writes in 'Oxford Poets', was '[v]ery different ... from the aged man I met in Dublin 16 years later, – a man who had received many honours in the meantime – the Nobel prize and world-wide acclaim as the greatest living poet of the English-speaking world, – but in 1936 these things mattered little to him, an aged man who seemed uncomfortable in his body and unhappy in his mind: all his life he had been calling up spirits from the vasty deep; they had given him some promises, but I wonder what assurances?'

After Yeats's death Stead wrote to his widow and told her 'how very much & how deeply I have felt a sense of irreparable loss. "W.B." as we used to call him was by far and away the greatest man I have ever known; he stood like a tower above all others',[58] while he concludes his 'Oxford Poets' talk by hailing Yeats as:

the greatest poet and also the most remarkable man I have ever known. Remarkable seems a trite thing to say – but I mean it literally. The man most worth noticing and observing, the man most worth speaking of and commenting on.

And yet to speak of him is to do him an injustice; it makes him seem small and foolish compared with the man we know. No words can revive the flash and fire of his mind, or his capacity for filling a room with his electric personality, lifting us out of ourselves, and carrying us away into regions of cloud-capped towers and gorgeous palaces and airy tongues that syllable men's names.

Whenever I walked home after an evening with him, I heard the stars singing above me, and the memory of him remains an everlasting example of the truth that a man of genius is far greater than anything his genius creates.

---

[54] This reference is quoted by Harper (25), who reads it, perhaps a little too briskly, as 'purely perfunctory, suggesting haste or illness'.

[55] *The Oxford Book of Modern Verse 1892-1935*, ed. W. B. Yeats (New York: Oxford University Press, 1936), 233-35.

[56] Yeats to Stead, early September 1935. *CL InteLex* 6331.

[57] Not 'in late September or early October 1935' as Harper speculates (16, n. 14; see also 24). The same error ('autumn of 1935') is made by Ann Saddlemyer when she draws on Harper's article (*YGYL* 238, n. 2.)

[58] Harper, 24.

*****

It was Richard Cobden-Sanderson who, in 1923, first brought together T. S. Eliot and Stead,[59] though there appears to have been some kind of falling out between the two Americans soon afterwards (possibly occasioned by a difference of opinion about modernist poetry, and possibly *The Waste Land* in particular[60]), because in a letter from Stead to Vere Somerset, dated 15 November [1926], Stead discloses: '... I've just had a letter from T.S. Eliot, – the most radical and ultra modern of poets, – though a Tory curiously enough in politics. Gordon George said he had been seeing Eliot and speaking of me to him – he suggested a rapprochement and it seems to be impending'.[61] However, while Stead and Eliot had much in common in terms of their politics, it is important to emphasise that what paved the way for their 'rapprochement' was less their shared Toryism[62] than Eliot's deepening hunger for spiritual enlightenment. Eliot's letter to Stead of 13 November 1926 had been written in response to a letter Stead had sent to Eliot on 14 October together with a copy of his most recent book, *The Shadow of Mount Carmel*.[63] Published that autumn and combining poetry and prose, philosophy, religion, meditations and social commentary, *The Shadow* traces Stead's spiritual journey from Oxford to Assisi via Paris, Nancy, Lourdes, Rome and Sicily, and is a book that was bound to have

---

[59] *The Letters of T. S. Eliot, Vol. 3 (1926-1927)*, ed. Valerie Eliot and John Haffenden (London: Faber and Faber, 2012), 306, n. 2.

[60] When Stead gave a talk on 'The New Poetry' to The Philistines Society at Worcester College, Oxford, on 31 October 1927, he confessed that he 'found something wrong with' such verse and more particularly that it was 'a breakaway from ... the tradition of all time – it throws off rhythm and all suitable choice of subject matter.' He went on to read out a series of 'examples in ascending ... order of merit, starting with the ultramodernists through [Carl] Sandberg, Edith Sitwell to Blunden.' (Proceedings of The Philistines Society, Worcester College, Vol. 1, 736; Worcester College Archives, WOR/JCR 3/4/1/1). The report of the discussion following Stead's paper (738) makes it clear that *The Waste Land* was one of his examples of 'ultramodernis[m]'.

[61] Stead to H. V. F. Somerset, Stead's Personal File, Worcester College Archives.

[62] 'I know my poems will never be popular', Stead had told Yeats on 10 June 1924, '– not with the masses because they are not what the "people" read, – nor with the critics, because I am a Tory and a High Churchman and modern views of the arts and of the way to express them are anathema to me' (*LTWBY2* 455).

[63] *Letters of T. S. Eliot*, 3, 306.

spoken with great power to Eliot at this period of his life: 'you may be sure I shall read [it] with great interest', he told Stead in his letter of 13 November. 'Lingering in Oxford long after my time ... I see my days consumed in reading and writing; but to what advantage?', Stead writes in the opening chapter of *The Shadow*.[64] A little further on, in words which must have struck a profound chord with Eliot, he confesses: 'I am a traditionalist, maybe a reactionary. I love anything that is old, especially old England. God knows what it will be in the future, but I doubt whether I shall like it. And yet, if I cling so tightly to the past, am I not submerged in time, and therefore losing touch with the Spirit?'[65] Yet another aspect of Stead's book that is certain to have caught Eliot's eye is his account of his excited discovery of royalism. During his sojourn in Paris, Stead tells us, he bought a copy of the royalist *L'Action Française* newspaper: 'I know nothing about French politics ... but here is my party. I want to see the white silk banner floating over the royal apartments and the golden fleur-de-lys unfurling again', he says, before condemning the modern world as 'a debauched age, a drunken and Bedlam age.'[66] Given that it was written by an ordained Anglican, *The Shadow* betrays a strikingly pro-Catholic bias, and this, alongside its 'reactionary' outlook, support for the *Action Française*, and its record of a spiritual journey from despair to fulfilment, could hardly have failed to intrigue the Eliot of 1926-27: it is not surprising that Eliot went on to praise *The Shadow* 'as one of the best examples of contemporary prose.'[67]

At the beginning of February 1927 Eliot asked Stead for his 'advice, information & [his] practical assistance in getting Confirmation with the Anglican Church.' He was extremely anxious that Stead should keep his intentions absolutely secret, just as Stead had been utterly discreet about his private baptism of Richard Cobden-Sanderson and Cobden-Sanderson's private confirmation by the Bishop of Oxford, which Stead had also arranged, in December 1926.[68] 'I do not want any publicity or

---

[64] William Force Stead, *The Shadow of Mount Carmel: A Pilgrmage* (London: Richard Cobden-Sanderson, 1926), 6-7.
[65] Stead, *The Shadow*, 9.
[66] Stead, *The Shadow*, 23.
[67] Sencourt, *T. S. Eliot: A Memoir*, 105.
[68] Stead had baptised Cobden-Sanderson in his church at Littlemore in December 1926 before he was privately confirmed by the Bishop of Oxford at Cuddesdon the following day. See Stead to R. Cobden-Sanderson, 24 December 1926, and

notoriety', Eliot told Stead in this letter, ' – for the moment, it concerns me alone, & not the public – not even those nearest me. I *hate* spectacular "conversions".'[69] They continued to correspond about this highly personal matter through the early months of 1927 until Eliot was finally baptised and confirmed at the end of June.[70] In a piece published in the mid-1960s under the title 'Some Personal Impressions of T.S. Eliot', Stead looked back to this time and recalled his role in Eliot becoming an Anglican:

> I can claim no credit for his conversion. But I did set up one milestone along his way – I baptised him ... We had been having tea in London, and when I was leaving he said, after a moment's hesitation,
> 'By the way, there is something you might do for me.'
> He paused, with a suggestion of shyness.
> After a few days he wrote to me, saying he would like to know how he could be 'confirmed into the Church of England', a quaint phrase, not exactly ecclesiastical. He had been brought up a Unitarian, so the first step was baptism. I was living then at Finstock, a small village far away in the country, with Wychwood Forest stretching off to the north, and the lonely Cotswold hills all round. Eliot came down from London for a day or two, and I summoned from Oxford Canon B. H. Streeter, Fellow and later Provost of Queen's College, and Vere Somerset, History Tutor and Fellow of Worcester College. These were his Godfathers. It seemed odd to have such a large though infant Christian at the baptismal font, so, to avoid embarrassment, we locked the front door of the little parish church and posted the verger on guard in the vestry.[71]

'Besides my gratitude for the serious business & the perfect way you managed every part of it', Eliot wrote to Stead on 1st July 1927, 'I must say how thoroughly I enjoyed my visit to you, and meeting several extremely interesting & delightful people.'[72]

As a token of his 'gratitude', Eliot undertook to return to Oxford the following term to address the 'The Philistines', Worcester College's archly named literary society. He told his mother on 6 November 1927 that he might head up to the college the following

---

other letters from Stead to Cobden-Sanderson written that month and earlier that autumn now housed at the University of Delaware.

[69] *Letters of T. S. Eliot*, 3, 404. See this same page for Stead's reply and his likely allusion to Cobden-Sanderson's recent baptism and confirmation.

[70] See *Letters of T. S. Eliot*, 3, 412-13, 428-29, 543-44.

[71] *Alumnae Journal of Trinity College* [Washington], 38.2 (Winter, 1965), 59-66. Quote from 64-65.

[72] *Letters of T. S. Eliot*, 3, 572.

weekend 'to stay with a friend there and talk to the undergraduates',[73] but for one reason or another his visit to Worcester was postponed until Saturday 4 February 1928. Looking back on the events of that day, Stead recalled:

[Eliot] announced on arriving that he must have lost his notes on the train from London, perhaps a polite way of saying he had not prepared any; however, he would read us *The Waste Land*. The poem was not widely appreciated at that time and called forth some very foolish remarks. A few remain in my memory; one youth rose at the end and said,
    'Mr. Eliot, did you write all that?'
    'Yes.'
    'Well, I thought some of those words about the barge she sat in came from something else.'
    Eliot responded with a pleasant smile that he was glad the point had been raised, and that as the speaker had recognized the passage, so he was sure others would understand these and some other well known lines as quotations used for the purpose of association. The reply was framed with such tact that the young man's vanity would not be wounded if he was merely an honest dunce, yet if he was trying to be facetious, he would be quietly silenced. A discussion dragged along for some time until a round-faced youth bounced up and said,
    'Mr. Eliot, may I ask a question?'
    'Certainly.'
    'Er – did you mean that poem seriously?'
    Eliot looked non-plussed for a moment, and then said quietly,
    'Well, if you think I did not mean it seriously, I have failed utterly.'

'That broke up the meeting', Stead notes.[74] The student newspaper *Cherwell*'s account of Eliot's reading and his subsequent comments on *The Waste Land* is less amusing but rather more illuminating:

Mr Eliot compared his poem to a body stripped of its skin: the 'anatomical' interest is at first more puzzling, but is more unusual and more real. He said, further, when speaking of the self-explanatory nature of the poem, that it was not necessary for the reader to recognise the quotations introduced, although he would lose a little; the effect was independent of recognition. The much-discussed notes and references were included, he said, for the benefit of the curious, and to prevent others from pointing out to him that

---

[73] *Letters of T. S. Eliot*, 3, 800-1. See also 872.
[74] 'Some Personal Impressions of T. S. Eliot', 62-63. See also Harper, 30-31 for an account of Eliot's annotated copy of this essay.

he had borrowed passages from the Elizabethans; it was not necessary for the reader to make himself acquainted with a large body of literature.[75]

A comical sidelight on the evening's events is provided in a letter from Stead to Cobden-Sanderson of 25 February 1928:

> Eliot was a great success and many have congratulated me on getting him down here – he was most charming and everyone seemed delighted with the gathering, which became so large that after assembling in my rooms, the Dean [C.H. Wilkinson], in his Magnificence, between rapid puffs of his pipe, suggested that we had better adjourn to his more spacious quarters – I have just heard of an amusing after effect. It appears that some culprit had been summoned to appear before the Dean that evening and give an account of his unsatisfactory behaviour. He appeared – only to find the room full of literary high brows and Eliot in the midst of reading The Waste Land in a grave and chaste manner. The reading and discussion afterwards lasted for upwards of 2 hours, while the poor culprit sat in the midst and suffered silently without the least comprehension of what it was all about.
> Later the Dean called him up to know why he had not reported and given an account of his misdemeanours; whereupon the ingenious youth pointed out that he *had* appeared on the proper day and hour.
> Still the Dean remained firm and fined him 5 bob and said he would have to attend three roll calls and two chapels.
> Then came the master stroke: the sinner paid his 5 bob fine, but as regards the rest, entered a plea that having sat through The Waste Land gathering for 1½ hours and not understood a word of it, this might be taken as the equivalent of 3 roll calls and 2 chapels. The Dean, who is a sport, broke out laughing and accepted the plea as well-founded.[76]

In future years, many of Eliot's non-religious friends and admirers would hold Stead accountable for what they regarded as Eliot's post-conversion decline, and when he 'visited Ezra Pound many years later, the poet told Stead that he had been responsible for "corrupting" Eliot'.[77] The truth, however, is that culturally and ideologically Eliot and Stead had a great deal in common and their respective attraction to and profession of High Anglicanism simply drew them together even more closely. What Gordon George said of Stead elsewhere in his *Blackfriars* encomium of 1933, for example, is hardly inapplicable to the Eliot of that period – 'his loyalties are centred in the traditions of the Southern aristocracy from which he sprang: he is a fervent

---

[75] Anon., 'A Visit by Mr T. S. Eliot', *Cherwell* 22, n. 3 (11 February 1928), 60.
[76] University of Delaware.
[77] Peter Ackroyd, *T. S. Eliot* (London: Hamish Hamilton, 1984), 172; Harper, 29.

Tory and monarchist; and he has found most of his inspiration in Europe, and especially in the English countryside' – while the resounding endorsement of Stead's personal and intellectual qualities that Eliot drew attention to in the testimonial he wrote on Stead's behalf reveals, among other things, just how much *The Shadow of Mount Carmel* had meant to him:

> I have known Mr William Force Stead for over eleven years and count him as a valued friend. He is, first, a poet of established position and an individual inspiration. What is not so well known, except to a small number of the more fastidious readers, is that he is also a prose writer of great distinction: his book *Mt. Carmel* is recognised as a classic of prose style in its kind. And while the bulk of his published writing on English literature is small, those who know his conversation can testify that he is a man of wide reading and a fine critical sense. Mr Stead is, moreover, a man of the world in the best sense, who has lived in several countries and is saturated in European culture. By both natural social gifts and cultivation, accordingly, he has a remarkable ability of sympathy with all sorts and conditions and races of men ...[78]

And not surprisingly, perhaps, given their shared interests, background and outlook, in his reviews and essays Stead sounds distinctly Eliotic at times. In his *Criterion* review of Theodor Haecker's *Virgil: Father of the West*, for example, Stead argued that Virgil 'recognized that great poetry needs the support of philosophy and theology, a truth which we, too, may recognize, but of which we can make no use, so long as we are impatient of tradition and each man tries to start *de novo*.'[79] Stead concludes this review in no less Eliotic fashion by claiming that Haecker's book 'deserves to be read for its vigorous attack upon our modern chaos and its attractive picture of Virgil and his ordered world with the divine decree above and *pietas* within.'

C.S. Lewis may have disparaged Stead as 'a punt', but both Yeats and Eliot valued his friendship rather more highly, and that is why, as their letters gradually enter the public domain, Stead's name will live on in their writings if not through his own. L.A.G. Strong was not alone in deprecating his streak of romantic foolishness, but it is also clear from Stead's relationships with his modernist contemporaries that he possessed a number of more substantial attributes which both

---

[78] See *Letters of T. S. Eliot*, 3, 913.
[79] Review of Theodor Haecker, *Virgil: Father of the West*, *Criterion*, 15, n. 57 (July 1935), 680-81, quote from 680.

poets set great store by and which far exceeded the sum of his follies. As a poet, Stead fell ludicrously short of the 'Catholic Genius' he was proclaimed to be by Gordon George, but as a man he was clearly a 'charming personality' whose friendship with the two greatest poets of his age would survive until their respective deaths.[80]

---

[80] I would like to thank the following people who kindly assisted me with the research for this article: James Campbell; Anita Carrico of the Enoch Pratt Free Library; Diane Ducharme of the Beinecke, Yale; Emma Goodrum; John Kelly; Jaime Margalot of the Morris Library, University of Delware; Jo Parker; Dom Julian Stead; Michael Whitworth, and Edward Wilson.

Playing with Voices and with Doubles in Two of Yeats's Plays: *The Words upon the Window-pane* and *A Full Moon in March*

Pierre Longuenesse

DESPITE THE APPARENT allegiance of Yeats's drama to classical rules, one of its key features, even from his early plays, lies in debunking one of the most standard of elements of mainstream drama in the western tradition: the notion of character. When the poet declares in *Per Amica Silentia Lunae* that 'We make out of the quarrel with others, rhetoric, but of the quarrel with ourselves, poetry' (*Myth* 331; *CW5* 8) the poet expresses an inner duality that has been energizing his thought and his poetic practice for some time.[1] He may not even guess the dramatic stake stemming from such a statement. On the stage, however, this stake is large: questioning the character's ability to express a whole and unified discourse cannot but change the form of the drama itself. In Yeats, character as traditionally expressed increasingly gives way to chorality and dialogic effects. The concept of the mask in Yeats's drama is of paramount importance here as it highlights the disappearance of drama's traditional mode of interpersonal relationship. Further clarification is needed, however:

---

[1] In *Per Amica Silentia Lunae* Yeats develops the concept of mask, which puts a word on this sensation of inner duality. In the proem, 'Ego Dominus Tuus' (see also VP 367–371), the poet stages two opposite voices, *Hic* and *Ille*, respectively the mask of the author and the author himself, the former walking alone under the moon, in quest of his 'anti-self', and the latter, who projects himself in action. On earlier uses of the term 'Mask' and the paradox of the MSS of the poem, see Warwick Gould, essay, above pp. 32–37, and elsewhere in this volume, *passim*.

in a Yeatsian context, what a voice entails needs to be redefined, since voice acts as the cornerstone of this issue. Whether in writing or onstage it is possible to focus on registers or on orality, thus raising the question of how the author, concealed or masked as he is, evolves through a unique voice – one which combines all the voices of the dramatic fiction. What I wish to discuss here is not this larger topic but the slightly more limited question of enunciation. In his dramatic texts, and even more so in his *Plays for Dancers*, Yeats often separates the enunciator from the speaker, and does so with virtuosity. At times, the same speaker may be in charge of several speeches, meaning acts of speaking that would usually be distinct from each other based upon the character from which they emanate. At other times a single discourse of speech may be shared by several speakers, hence the reverse of the first process. Finally, a speaker may even be in charge of someone else's discourse or speech, thus speaking for, or right next to, someone else. What I wish to focus on is how these phenomena occur, in particular through two rather opposed examples: first, *The Words upon the Window-pane*, and then *A Full Moon in March*, a play I shall analyse in more detail.

REPORTED SPEECH IN *THE WORDS UPON THE WINDOW-PANE*

From the early 1900s, Yeats's drama stages characters in night-time or half-lit atmospheres – through different variations – and in which voices are more often than not separated from the bodies. Although this disassociation between sounds and images seems at first to be used particularly when characters enter and/or exit the stage, it appears to become more and more generalised and systematic. This phenomenon may be traced fairly easily by noting the great number of stage directions referring to sound, the link between sound information and visual details describing the light effects provided by these stages directions, or, more generally, the variety and contracts of voice effects. Starting from *Plays for Dancers*, Yeats's theatre originally displays this obsessive acousmatic composition of its characters' voices – acousmatic sounds being sounds heard but whose location cannot be identified.[2] Yeats embeds voices in such a

---

[2] In Antiquity, the word 'acousmatic' was used to designate Pythagoras' disciples who, for five years, listened to his lessons hidden behind a curtain, not seeing

way that the (invisible) Dead are heard via the voices of the (visible) living. This phenomenon is similar to the well-known technique of reported speech, in which a character repeats something said by another. Yet it is a distinct phenomenon from reportage and also from acousmatic sounds, in which something heard is separated from its source. I would rather refer to this as 'acousmatic enunciation' than reportage or even acousmatic sound, because what is heard is not just the message (or utterance) but also how it has been voiced (the voice). This coined expression helps to pinpoint the split in enunciation between the speaker and the enunciator, especially when one voice is heard through another one.

The most representative example of this phenomenon is undoubtedly *The Words upon the Window-pane*, whose story revolves around a medium-like game in which voices are transferred from one character to another. Written in 1930, the play premiered on 17 November 1930 at the Abbey Theatre but was not published until 1934. The play focuses on an episode of Jonathan Swift's life, split as it/he was between the two women he called Stella and Vanessa, and on the dramatic triangle stemming from that situation. The originality of the play lies in its exploring this conflict in an indirect manner, through a spiritualist *séance* one hundred and fifty years after the death of the writer. Characters from the past burst into the present via Mrs Henderson, a medium surrounded by the host and five guests. 'Who speaks?' becomes the central question of the plot since Mrs Henderson changes her voice and alternatively 'reports' each of the three Dead characters' voices.

Mrs Henderson [*in a child's voice*]. That bad man, that bad old man in the corner, they have let him come back. Lulu is going to scream... O... O...
[*In a man's voice*] How dare you write to her?
[...]
Mrs Henderson [*in Vanessa's voice*.]. I questioned her, Jonathan, because I love. Why have you let me spend hours in your company if you did not want

him and being scrupulously silent. Ten centuries later, the Church fathers gave a religious meaning to the term, thus naming 'acousmats' the manifestations of angels' speaking or singing voices; a whole mystical thinking contributed to the development of this aspect of the concept, based on the listening to celestial voices. Finally today, and since the contemporary acoustic experiments conducted by people such as John Cage or Pierre Schaeffer, the concept of 'acousmat' is at the heart of the experimental mechanism of concrete music, as modern acouticians focus on placing the listener in a listening situation where the source of the sound is hidden.

me to love you? [In *Swift's voice.*] When I rebuilt Rome in your mind it was as though I walked its Streets. [*In Vanesssa's voice.*] Was that all, Jonathan? Was I nothing but a painter's canvas? [*In Swift's voice.*] My God, do you think it was easy? (*VPl* 948–49).

On the one hand, the confusion of identities is unsettling and the fantastic world bursts in an otherwise naturalist setting. The voices of the Dead are not technically 'reported', since Mrs Henderson suddenly alters her voice without a hint of who is next to speak. She is not so much the (indirect) subject of the speech or discourse as the speech channel of others who turn out to be 'possessing' her. We may even wonder if this multiplicity of voices uttered by a single body is not the sign of a split self.

On the other hand, two illusions remain: first, the words spoken are reproduced exactly and, if I may use the term, objectively; second, the individual integrity of each voice remains in spite of the spiritualist dimension of the play. For if the séance seems to go briefly over the edge when Mrs Henderson abruptly changes her voice in her last cue, dropping and breaking a cup as she is possessed again even though the séance is finished, she nonetheless shifts simply from one fiction to another, from one identity to another, without ever trespassing the limits between past and present or between the dead and the living.

Mrs Henderson. How tired I am! I'd be the better of a cup of tea. [*She finds the tea-pot and put the kettle on fire, and then, as she crouches down by the hearth, suddenly lifts up her hands, and counts her fingers, speaking in Swift's voice.*] Five great ministers that were my friends are gone, ten great ministers that were my friends are gone. I have not fingers enough to count the great Ministers that were my friends and that are gone.
[*She wakes with a start and speaks in her own voice.*]
Where did I put that tea-caddy? Ah! There it is. And there should be a cup and saucer. [*She finds the saucer.*]

But where's the cup? [*She moves aimlessly about the stage and then letting the saucer fall and break, speaks in Swifts's voice.*] Perish the day on which I was born! (*VPl* 956).

In this regard, her change of voices, however unusual it might be, guarantees these limits. Paradoxically, in a play whose major focus is on listening to spectral voices, the classical form of drama – and its underpinning notion of character – is far from being threatened. For not only is the setting framed by naturalism but so are the organisation of speech and the progression of the dialogue. For this reason, I believe that this story of mediumship is in fact quite anecdotal: it strongly suggests that the audience is experiencing an enactment of a previously secret history. Indeed, what one mainly remembers is first the historical episode relating to Swift, however brilliantly and unusually it may be expressed, and, second, the metaphorical echoes Yeats sees with the current affairs of twentieth century Ireland.[3] The question of the authenticity of mediumship itself takes a back seat to the other issues of the play.

OF DIALOGISM IN THE CHORUS'S SPEECH: THE EXAMPLE OF *A FULL MOON IN MARCH*

In *A Full Moon in March* (1935), a play almost contemporaneous with *The Words upon the Window-pane*, two 'Attendants' play as arrangers of a unique scene freely adapted from the story of Salomé. As they open the curtain from us, they reveal an encounter between a Queen – offering herself and her queendom to whoever might seduce her by singing her praise – and a Swineherd whose claims lead to beheading before he is given a chance to sing. The plays ends with a seduction dance in front of (or with) the dead man's head. In the staged version of the story, both the acting composition and the order in which the actions occur defer from the original storyline. The beheading comes before – instead of after – the love parade. What is more, the latter is not meant for a third party (such as King Herod) but for a corpse; moreover, it is staged as a danced sequence alongside a dual soliloquy which is both poetic and fantastic.

Influenced as this play is by Noh theatre,[4] it is broken down into six successive sequences: the first, fourth and sixth ones are

---

[3] Jacqueline Genet suggests that by studying Swift's personal crisis in the 18th century, Yeats has, in a same movement, exalted the splendour of a past century he took as an example, and lamented its foreseen decadence. Of the noble souls in Mrs Henderson's living room, of which the quiet Stella is the ghostly figure, is only left a small group of talkative and capricious petit-bourgeois. See J. Genet, *Le Théâtre de W. B. Yeats* (Lille: Presses universitaires du Septentrion, 1995), 429–40.

[4] The play *A Full Moon in March*, though it was written long after the Plays for Dancers, is inspired, as are the latter, by Japanese Noh, a form to which Yeats was introduced by Ezra Pound, his secretary for several years. The Noh model helped him find a new form more appropriate for the dramatic themes or stories he wanted to write, all dealing with the encounter between reality and the world of spirits,

a prologue, an interlude, and an epilogue during which the two Attendants – also musicians – open, comment on, and close the story. The three remaining sequences reveal the first encounter between the two protagonists, the Queen's dance of death in front of the Swineherd's severed head (this third sequence is made possible thanks to the time ellipsis created by the closing of the inner curtain), and, finally, each of the two protagonists' fantastic soliloquy. Two sequences symptomatically revolve around the breaking down and reconstitution of speech interactions, namely the first, the sung prologue of the musicians, and the last but one, or post-mortem conversation – if it may be called as such – between the Queen and the Swineherd.

Let us start by taking a closer look at the first sequence. In the prologue, the two musicians wonder about the protocol that needs to be followed in order to start the lay. In a very Pirandello-like manner, they refer to orders given by an unknown 'he', very likely the author or stage director, and eventually open up the curtain as they sing.

First Attendant. What do we do?
 What part do we take?
 What did he say?

Second Attendant. Join when we like,
 Singing or speaking.

First Attendant. Before the curtain rises on the play?

Second Attendant. Before it rises

First Attendant. What do we sing?

Second Attendant. 'Sing anything, sing any old thing', said he.

First Attendant. Come then, and sing about the dung of swine.

---

between a living character and some spectral figures coming from the past or out of the imagination. See Mazaru Sekine and Christopher Murray, *Yeats and the Noh: a Comparative Study*, Irish Literary Studies 38 (Gerrards Cross: Colin Smythe, 1990) and Richard Taylor, *The Drama of W. B. Yeats, Irish Myth and the Japanese Noh* (New Haven and London: Yale University Press, 1976).

[*They slowly part the inner curtain. The Second Attendant sings* –

The first Attendant may join in the singing at the end of the first or second verse...
(*VPl* 978–79)

Their song is comprised of three successive stanzas, each one of them being composed of two tercets (similarly to medieval ballads); the last line of each tercet being an italicized refrain.

> Every loutish lad in love
> Thinks his wisdom great enough,
> *What cares love for this and that?*
> To make all his parish stare,
> As though Pythagoras wandered there.
> *Crown of gold or dung of swine.*
>
> Should old Pythagoras fall in love
> Little may he boast thereof.
> *What cares love for this and that?*
> Days go by in foolishness.
> O how great their sweetness is!
> Crown of gold or dung of swine.
>
> Open wide those gleaming eyes,
> That can make the loutish wise.
> What cares love for this and that?
> Make a leader of the schools
> Thank the Lord, all men are fools.
> *Crown of gold or dung of swine.* (*VPl* 979)

The text indicates that this song is sung entirely by the second Attendant. However, one of the stage directions also mentions that the first Attendant 'may join in the singing at the end of the first or second verse'.[5] Therefore, throughout the refrain a second voice clearly intervenes in the second servant's cue: the very syntax of the first stanza indicates that one of the sentences is interrupted by an aside: 'Every loutish lad in love | Thinks his wisdom great enough, | What cares love for this and that?' The voice keeps asking the same question, and answers it with a symbolical image: 'Crown of gold or dung of swine'. It is therefore not surprising to hear the closing

[5] *Ibid.*

song of the last sequence – when the curtain is drawn – being clearly shared between the two Attendants' voices.

Second Attendant. Why must those holy, haughty feet descend
From emblematic niches, and what hand
Ran that delicate raddle through their white?
My heart is broken, yet must understand.
What do they seek for? Why must they descend?

First Attendant. For desecration and the lover's night.

Second Attendant. I cannot face that emblem of the moon
Nor eyelids that the unmixed heavens dart,
Or stand upon my feet, so great a fright
Descends upon my savage, sunlit heart.
What can she lack whose emblem is the moon?

First Attendant. But desecration and the lover's night.

Second Attendant. Delight my heart with sound; speak yet again,
But look and look with understanding eyes
Upon the pitchers that they carry; tight
Therein all time's completed treasure is.
What do they lack? O cry it out again.

First Attendant. Their desecration and the lover's night. (*VPl* 989)

As the second Attendant expresses doubts and questionings in the first person, the first one replies with an obstinate refrain. This is precisely when the italics disappear. Yet, one question remains: if this sharing of voices were clear, why did it not occur from the first song? The confusion obviously derives from the very nature of the character, who is both one and more, being at times two musicians into one. The musicians are the very representation of dialogue heard in a monologue, if not a quarrel with oneself (*Myth* 331) then a thought in movement, made up of several voices, asides, and episodes. The musicians are basically neither two at the end of the play nor one at the beginning. The uncertainty of the text as to who is speaking shows the emergence of a half-way zone in which the traditional conception of the character fades away. The simple notion of the voice is in fact used to express the cumulative effect of the same and the other and to stage the inner dialogism of discourse. Indeed, the one and only element Yeats chose to distinguish one musician from the other is a vocal sign: the first is a soprano while the second one is a bass.

OF VOICES AND THEIR SPECTRAL DOUBLE: NEVER TWO, BUT FOUR.

The confusion in the organisation of enunication also occurs in another passage in *A Full Moon in March*, namely in the fifth sequence when the Queen and the Swineherd meet for the last time behind the inner curtain that has been just opened by the musicians. Although the encounter is brief (the scene is only 28 lines long), this is when we hear the two songs, that of the Queen and that of the severed head.

They begin to part the inner curtain. [...] The Queen is discovered standing exactly as before, the dropped veil at her side, but she holds above her head the severed head of the Swineherd. Her hands are red. There are red blotches upon her dress, not realistically represented: red gloves, some patterns of red cloth.

First Attendant. Her lips are moving.

Second Attendant. She has begun to sing.

First Attendant. I cannot hear what she is singing.
Ah, now I can hear.

> (*singing as Queen*)
> Child and darling, hear my song,
> Never cry I did you wrong;
> Cry that wrong came not from me
> But my virgin cruelty.
> Great my love before you came,
> Greater when I loved in shame,
> Greatest when there broke from me
> Storm of virgin cruelty.
> [*The Queen dances to drum-taps and in the dance lays the head upon the throne.*]

Second Attendant. She is waiting.

First Attendant. She is waiting for his song.
The song he has come so many miles to sing.
She has forgotten that no dead man sings.

Second Attendant [*laughs softly as Head*]. He has begun to laugh.

First Attendant: No; he has begun to sing.

Second Attendant (*singing as Head*):
                      I sing a song of Jack and Jill [...][6]

In the first song, an 'I' addresses a 'you' and both interlocutors seem to be properly identified: the Queen on the one hand and the severed head on the other. What is more, the tone is one of command, thus confirming that there are two entities, one addressing the other. The scene therefore seems to be a dialogue between two perfectly distinct identities. Yeat's two games of masks, or duality, are quicky revealed as these two identities come across each other or accumulate with one another.

The first layer of this game of doubles is found in the inner split occuring in both the Queen and the Swineherd, between each one's public and private (if not spectral) sides. This split stems from the association between reported speech and singing. The Queen is seen on the other side of the inner curtain. She dances silently, holding the Swineherd's severed head in her hands covered with blood. Rhythmed as it is by the percussions, this slow dance is getting more and more frenetic: its ecstatic (and even orgasmic) nature is evident, and this love-and-death ecstasy is possible only on the 'Other Stage' of Death or Unconsciousness. The dance expresses this 'second state' of the Queen, neither living nor dead. Moreover, the relatedness of the dancing Queen's verbal silence and her speech reported by the female musician turn her words into the expression of a thought, of

---

[6] *VPl* 987. The allusion to Mallarmé's *Hérodiade* is here limpid, especially the verses: 'J'aime l'horreur d'être vierge et je veux | Vivre parmi l'effroi que font mes cheveux | Pour, le soir, retirée en ma couche, reptile | Inviolé, sentir en la chair inutile | Le froid scintillement de ta pâle clarté, | Toi qui te meurs [...]'. See Stéphane Mallarmé, 'Hérodiade – Scène', in *Poésies*, Paris, Gallimard (coll. 'Poésie'), 1992, 27–34. Yeats remembered Arthur Symons's translation, and quoted it: 'Symons first read me Herodiade's address to some Sibyl who is her nurse and, it may be, the moon also: 'The horror of my virginity | Delights me, and I would envelop me | In the terror of my tresses, that, by night, | Inviolate reptile, I might feel the white | And glimmering radiance of thy frozen fire, | Thou that art chaste and diest of desire, | White night of ice and of the cruel snow!' See Stéphane Mallarmé, *Herodiade* (1864–67, published 1893) II.ii, 103 et seq. tr. Arthur Symons, *The Savoy* December 1896; *Images of Good and Evil* (London: William Heinemann, 1899), 77. The interest of such an association is not so much in the 'quotation effect' itself as it is in the analogy of enunciation modes, from the swing of a seemingly dialogued voice into the solitude of a mental theatre. The poetical play is not dialogued poetry but imaginary theatre. In the speech, the choice of indirect speech allows to express this intermediary status of a subject vacillating between physical and psychic world.

the character's inner vision. In a very subtle manner the musician does not say 'she says', or 'she speaks', but 'her lips are moving'. Both women are therefore sharing the speech process as one holds the internal intention while the other is in charge of the act of utterance. Then the male musician speaks and sings his turn for the severed head; and his speech helps solve the problem of the impossibility of a song by a dead man, thus contradicting the female musician's line, 'She has forgotten that no dead man sings' (*VPl* 988). The dialogue between the two songs sung by the two Attendants is therefore a dialogue of the mute, as vocal communication is imposed over a non-vocal engagement: while the Queen is dancing with the Head on the inner stage bordered by the inner curtain, with blood on her hands, the two Attendants speak near us, looking at them. This process of two concurrent duos enables the poet to stage the communication between the living and the dead, in order to highlight their spectral characteristics and to gather them in a zone half way between reality and fantasy, half way, in other words, between the world of the living and that of the dead.

The singing form of the two texts is also worthy of closer study. By being turned into essentially song lyrics, speeches become enclosed in themselves. The singing creates a fiction within the fiction into which both characters split their own self and, in addition, that of their interlocutor.[7] The maternal and endearing terms – child, Darling – used by the Queen in her song as well as the sudden intimacy of a speech bordering on confession and guilt clearly contrast with the character's initial contempt for the Swineherd. The sung speech is not addressed to a direct interlocutor but rather derives from another self addressing 'the other in oneself', one's spectral other rather

---

[7] In dramatic arts the song opens frequently to a way out of the dramatic action line or diegesis: the character breaks off the temporal linearity, interrupts the dialogue, and stages him/herself in an other space-time frame, which can be epic or, on the contrary, more lyrical and introspective. In the latter case, we frequently find this phenomenon of 'closure', the discourse being less addressed to the other protagonists, and more reflexive. Moreover, the intertextuality often appearing in Yeats's drama when he uses songs (since he often borrows ballads from other poets, and uses the collage technique), troubles the enunciative system: the singing character sometimes holds a speech which overtakes him, an oracular speech on the edge of madness or hallucination. Another invisible character, coming from Memory or Past – the author of the ballad? Yeats himself? – seems to double the real and visible character. This invisible character trespasses the borders of the double enunciation of drama: in the song, the poet talks to the public, as much as the characters talk to each other.

than a real other. Although of a different form, this phenomenon is identical in the head's song. The latter is inspred from a well-known nursery rhyme and leads to a burlesque mise en abyme of the play's dramatic situation: Jill, the Queen's double, has killed Jack, the beggar's double.

> *Second Attendant (singing as Head)*:
> I sing a song of Jack and Jill
> Jill had murdered Jack;
> *The moon shone brightly;*
> Ran up the hill, and round the hill,
> Round the hill and back.
> *A full moon in March.*
>
> Jack had a hollow heart, for Jill
> Had hung his heart on high;
> *The moon shone brightly;*
> Had hung his heart beyond the hill,
> A-twinkle in the sky,
> *A full moon in March.*
>
> [*The Queen in her dance moves away from the head, alluring and refusing*] (*VPl* 988).

The two songs are thus two soliloquies answering one another in counterpoint and whose succession builds up a poetic battle. The first is a lament, or self-elegy, while the second sounds more like a popular ballad. The dead Swineherd mocks the Queen he has won in death while she cries over the Mallarmean tragic dimension of 'the horror of her virginity'.[8] In other words, the disassociation between the body and the voice alongside the singing dimension all lead to a speech of intimacy; the emergence of a dream-like speech or parole

---

[8] See n. 9. The choice of the two songs, in their form and their substance, nourishes the battle between the two characters. In the first song, the female figure uses the first person ('... my song, ... I did you wrong') to speak to her 'Child and darling' (*VPl* 987, emphasis added). By using the imperative mood, she is asking for forgiveness and repudiating her own cruelty. In the other one, the male figure tells a burlesque tale and sets himself remotely, speaking in the third person. For him Death becomes a game, since Jill dances around the stake on which Jack's heart is stuck, this heart becoming 'A-twinkle in the sky' (*VPl* 988). In other words the two characters give with their respective song a version of their story different from reality, and different from each other's version. Another game of double emerges here, between the character and his/her fictional double (in the song), or between the two couples.

within the fiction is the sign of subjective splitting. The figures appearing suddenly in this sequence are the inner doubles, if not the ghosts of the two characters seen in the previous sequence.[9]

The second layer of the play on doubles in *A Full Moon in March* occurs not as splits within the characters of the Queen and the Dead Swineherd but between the two characters and the two musicians. In order to explain, let us go back to reported speech. The communication between the two musicians is similar to a two-voiced tale, expressed in the présent, almost a dialgue of stage directions. 'Her lips are moving', the first one says; 'She has begun to sing', the second one says. 'She is waiting', the second one adds (*VPl* 987). Within this dialogue is reported speech. The Queen herself does not speak physically but the first Attendant (a female musician, in fact) does. The severed head does not speak, but the second Attendant does. In other words, two narrators report the speeches of two characters to which they are physically close. So far, this is not too different from what happens in *The Words upon the Window-pane:* one character takes on another's speech, yet without disrupting or blurring the boundaries between them. In *A Full Moon in March*, however, the reading is not this straightforward: there is a disturbing shift between the stage directions given in speech by the musicians and the related mute and danced scene – the pantomime – of the characters. For instance, nothing indicates that the Queen does indeed move her lips, nor that she is expecting the other's song. The only stage directions referring to her are descriptions of her dance. The general impression is that the musicians are merely telling each other the story of a Queen and a Swineherd, and that the latter, who actually are beside their tale-tellers, are nonetheless onstage to do something else than illustrate this story. In fact, in speaking as the Queen or the Head, the musicians do not change their voice or their behaviour. The female musician doesn't actually say 'she says', or 'she speaks', but 'I hear'. If

---

[9] The word 'ghost' is worthy of further commentary, even if I won't analyse here thoroughly Yeats's vision of this concept. In *A Full Moon in March* it is not a question of a Greek 'eidolon', i.e. the image (or 'fantasma') of a Dead or a God coming back to dialogue with the living. Yeats believes in ghosts as far as he believes art or magic are able to give appearence to the character's double, his/her Daimon: 'Every voice that speaks, every form that appears ... is first of all a secondary personality or dramatization created by, in or through the medium' (Introduction to *The Words upon the Window-pane*, *Ex* 364). Moreover, for Yeats, this mission of Art creates the conditions of appearance of this Epiphany, the incarnation of one's double or 'antiself'.

the supposed voice she says she 'hears' is external to her, it may very well be – also or exclusively – her own inner voice. If this were the case, her speech would only be hypothetically reported. (This is in fact a grammatical paradox: a reported speech in direct speech, with neither punctuation nor an introductory verb, fuels the confusion in the identification of speakers. Actually, the notion of reported speech is not devoid of any ambiguity even in ordinary usage, since the term usually refers both to 'indirect speech', that is, reported speech in the strict sense of the expression, and to 'direct speech' as long as the latter is reported to, or by, a narrator: in other words, if I say 'she says that she is here', or I say 'she says "I am here"', I am using reported speech in both cases.)

What is happening onstage is a clear suggestion that the identity lying at the origin of this speech is in fact impossible to pinpoint. There is not an illusion of reported speeches. The boundaries between the supposed reporter and the supposed reported seem to disappear. A very subtle play on doubles (two in one, one in two) is gradually taking place between the two Attendants on the one hand and the Queen and Swineherd on the other. In a way, everything comes from the Queen or the Swineherd while the servants only act as their spokespersons. Yet, in another way, the pantomime or danced sequence is a product of the Attendants' imagination. The two characters may very well be the mere mental projection of the two Attendants, their ghosts, or their puppets. Staging the play in such a way may not be totally nonsensical after all. When the second musician laughs (as the Head) and then says 'he has laughed', who is 'he'? When later the female musicians laughs (as the Queen), but this time it is the male musician who speaks again: 'she laughs', who is 'she'? Words flow back and forth as one comments on oneself or on others, and one becomes both the subject and the object of the discourse. The boundaries between speeches, speakers, and actual bodies do not match anymore. They are sometimes one, two, and even three at times: the one who laughs, the one who says she laughs, and a sillent body next to them. The same may be two or three while two or three may just be the same one.

We are therefore faced with a paradox: in *The Words upon the Window-pane* the Dead were not here, but the medium did not really embody them. She only acted as their spokesperson during the séance. Here, the ghosts are onstage and have spokespersons to boot. If the Queen is onstage, the point is not to replace her (there is not a Queen, and another person who speaks for her), but to express, by duality, a different state of hers, a spectral or ghostly state. This is the same for the Swineherd. The split between two halves emphasises their fragility, their respective crack, voiceless bodies or bodiless voices as they are: dancing bodies in between worlds, fleeting voices visiting others.

It is important to bear in mind that the first half of the play was already preparing the audience for such a perception: although there were four characters onstage, the second musician (male) was already mentioning the Swineherd in his songs while the first musician (female) mentioned the Queen. In the second half of the text, there are still four of them onstage, physically speaking, but there are only two left. Everyone is ghostly, everyone bears a mark – to be there and not to be there.

VOICES AND DOUBLES: TOWARDS A POETICS OF DEATH AND SPECTRALITY.

One question remains: whom do the two musicians serve? Do they serve the Queen? Or the mysterious 'he' from the prologue? They most likely serve both insofar as they stand in between the time of writing and the time of the story. On the one hand, they encompass the inner movements of a metatheatrical discourse, hidden as it is behind their fictitious identity, within their sung prologues. Yet on the other hand, they act as the spokespersons of the story's two main protagonists. The play is founded on two embedded elements: an unidentified narrative authority whose voice is entrusted to the two musicians, while the latter project themselves onto two fictitious figures. What is more, a parole does sometimes interrupt the Queen and the Swineherd's discourses; the said parole actually seems to refer to the initial narrative authority. For instance, in the Swineherd's song (whether a nursery rhyme or not), the same phenomenon as the one identified in the Attendants' initial song is found: every third and sixth verse of each stanza is in italics, thus confirming the existence of a refrain. Do the italics refer to a second voice within the song? And is this the case even when the song is already voiced by a voice's double (the musician's) which belongs to the creation of an unknown 'he'? If so, whose voice is indicated in italics? William Veeder suggests that 'the refrain can be the narrator's comment on the action'.[10] This is a rather tempting hypothesis, and it would help us loop the

---

[10] W. R. Veeder, *W. B. Yeats, the Rhetoric of Repetition* (Berkeley and Los Angeles: University of California Press, 1968), 21.

loop since we would find the writer's 'initial voice', or the voice of his narrative double, at the two ends of the writing process, 'end' considered here not as the beginning and end of the play, but as the two ends of the enunciation process. If we consider the text as a setting of several discourses in between each other, organized as concentric circles, we can find: in the external circle, the narrator or 'he' mentioned by the two musicians in their first cues; then, the musicians themselves; then, the characters; and at the end, hidden in the core of the latter's speech (i.e.: in the refrain of the songs), the narrator again. This hypothesis can be indeed confirmed by the very fact that Yeats often used self-quotations and mixed genres.[11] In *A Full Moon in March*, it is in fact rather hard to decide on the level of reality for each of these narrative authorities: it seems each one acts as the other one's dream, literaly speaking, the product of his/her *imagination*.

One last reading of the play highlights its most heightened moment and major claimant to meaning: the Dead Swineherd's song. It keeps being mentioned until the female musician's cue: 'She has forgotten that no Dead man sings' (*VPl* 988). He must sing, he wants to sing, the Queen has him beheaded, and yet he sings nonetheless. All leads to the miracle of the dead man singing. We may even add that he will never sing until his head is cut off, and that she won't dance and sing unless death had come. The song has no other dimension than a spectral one. The song and the voice we hear can be assimilated to the beginnings of intensive love, expressed as it is by the dance.[12] As Jean-Pierre Sarrazac suggests, the play is about

---

[11] For instance, 'The Mask' published in 1910 in *The Green Helmet and Other Poems (VP* 263) is partly quoted by Yeats in scene ii of *The Player Queen*, performed in 1919 and published in 1922 (VPl 738). Later, the introductory lines of *The Resurrection* (1927, *VPl* 902), are re-written as 'Two Songs from a Play' for *The Tower* (1928, *VP* 437). On this occasion, Yeats, consciously or not, does not mention any speaker for the opening lines of the play ('Song for the Folding and Unfolding of the Cloth'): it seems as if it is the Poet himself who pronounces those words, thus trespassing all ordinary borders of speech organisation in drama.

[12] The influence of Villiers de l'Isle Adam's play *Axël* is quite visible here. In his *Autobiographies* Yeats explains his discovery of this particular play, which he saw at its première in Paris in 1894. Later, this influence re-appears in the preface he writes for the first edition of the play in English, translated by H. P. R. Finberg (London: Jarrolds, 1925). In both plays (as in *The Shadowy Waters*, written and re-written when *Axël* was created), Love and Hate are mixed together to express a quest for an absolute which finds its outcome in Death.

the drama of life rather than the drama in life.[13] It deals with the initiation to mortality, with birth through loss and death, and with the ecstatic experiences it provokes. This might be 'the Full Moon in March', the Resurrection of the God, and the fifteenth moon phase described by Yeats in *A Vision:* a tie for the unity of the self, a time in which the living and the dead are reunited, a time when man and the divine have become one.[14] If the poet resorts to the ritual demanded by the two musicians to stage this story, the ritual is not only formal but necessary. It is required, first, because the onstage presence of the musicians is intrinsically necessary for the ghosts to appear as such, and for the dead man's voice to be heard: ghosts are merely figments of sight, visions, *eidolon* maybe, but not characters. Second, ritual is crucial if the logic of haunting is to be followed to the end. Indeed, if the musicians introduce a fiction by 'inhabiting' the fictional characters' voices, they are also quite unsure as to who they are and what they're expected to say. As they are constantly listening, they are being visited as well as they, themselves, are visiting others. Their speech is haunted by both their fictional characters and their very own patron. This is reminiscent of what Artaud wrote about Balinese theatre, the latter being a 'théâtre of hallucination and fear, in which the dancing actor's performance seems to be dictated from an other world'.[15]

We do face here a rather original interpretation of hermeneutics or, as Jean-Luc Nancy describes it, of 'voice sharing'. Nancy evokes a magical relationship between the poet and the rhapsodic actor, asserting that 'rhapsodes are poem proclaimers or rather, more

---

[13] See J. P. Sarrazac, *Poétique du drame moderne* (Paris: Seuil, 2012), ch. 2, 'Drame-de-la-vie: le nouveau paradigme'.

[14] In *A Vision*, Yeats explains that souls cross successive incarnations which coincide with the twenty-eight Phases of the Moon. Each of them is the product of a specific conflict happening between different faculties combining with each other. Only two of them escape the rule: the first phase, because during it all the existence is submitted to the material world; and the fifteenth (that of the Full Moon), which symbolises a perfect 'Unity of Being'. *A Full Moon in March* is bathed in a full moon atmosphere, and this image, developed by the musicians in their song, seems to be the horizon of the characters' quest. Thus, when the Queen dances with the head, the Divine (the Queen) and the Human (the Swineherd) seem to join themselves, and reach their quest.

[15] i.e. une 'théâtre de l'hallucination et de la peur, où ce que l'acteur danseur accomplit semble comme dicté d'ailleurs': see Antonin Artaud, *Le Théâtre et son double*, in *Œuvres* (Paris: Quarto Gallimard, 2004), 535–36.

accurately, poets' proclaimers¹⁶'. The rhapsode (or rhapsodist) is not a mere performer but a kind of hermeneus in that he stages the poet's logos. This situation creates yet another magical play on doubles, between a present voice and an absent voice. 'The oracular, divinatory, poetic, and hermeuneutic worlds are closely-knit', Nancy writes[17]. We may extend this observation a little and bear it in mind when analysing *A Full Moon in March*. The play focuses indeed first and foremost on inner controversies, solitary voices plagued by inner turmoil, faced with intra- rather inter-subjective conflicts between oneself and the other in oneself. In this regard, all monologues are made of a mental dialogue of a type. Similarly, all dialogues are a disguised form of monologue, as if a unique parole were broken down into serveral opposed and complementary voices. Through its plays on split and duality, *A Full Moon in March* also displays the confrontation with one's own death. In his famous article on The Uncanny ('Das Unheimlich'), Freud explains that 'the algebraic sign of doubling (doubling of the self, splitting of the self, substitution of the self) ... becomes the uncanny harbinger of death'.[18] In *A Full Moon in March*, the dance enables the character to escape from a duality between incarnate and non incarnate, between the living and the dead. At the same time, the *mise en abyme* of voices – neither of them being totally reducible to a single entity – never allows for an incarnation to fully take place. The notion of double is here both a psychic and metaphysical category. It embodies the wandering spirit in search of its impossible definitive incarnation.

---

[16] Jean-Luc Nancy, *Le Partage des voix* (Paris: Galilée, 1982), 55.
[17] *Ibid.*, 61 et seq., 'L'oraculaire, le divinatoire, le poétique et l'herméneutique entretiennent des liens étroits'.
[18] Sigmund Freud, 'The Uncanny' (Das Unheimlich), in *Writings on Art and Literature*, trans. Angela Harris (Stanford: Stanford University Press: 1997), 211.

© Elizabeth Müller, CC BY   http://dx.doi.org/10.11647/OBP.0038.06

The Mask of Derision in Yeats's Prologue to *A Vision* (1937)

Elizabeth Müller

YEATS'S PROLOGUE to the 1937 edition of *A Vision* conceals important occult knowledge under the cloak of irony and self-derisive wit. Wit or humour has not been targeted very often in criticism of Yeats's work and *A Vision* might be deemed a dubious place to start. However a few critics have attempted to tackle the issue, and I have based a substantial part of this essay on the work of Steven Helmling, Hazard Adams and Eugene Korkowski. All three have commented upon the predominantly humoristic tone of the Prologue, with Korkowski and Helmling pointing to the literary traditions of Antiquity as a possible source. Helmling considers that, in the Prologue, Yeats endorses the role of the Socratic *eirôn* and uses mock-humility, as Socrates often does in Plato's *Dialogues*, in order to gain strength at his interlocutor's expense: in the end, the moral stature of the *eirôn* becomes such that he enforces respect for his theories and wins the argument or, at least, ridicules his opponent.[1] Korkowski, on the other hand, interprets the Prologue in the light of the *Menippean satura*, the Latin word *satura* meaning 'a medley' or 'mixed plate'. This medley involves the use of 'jocularity in combination with serious philosophic matter' in order 'to bring philosophy in an appealing and entertaining form to the common man'.[2] The quality of such

---

[1] *The Esoteric Comedies of Carlyle, Newman and Yeats* (Cambridge: Cambridge University Press, 1988), 15–17, 21–25 and 228–38.
[2] 'Yeats's *Vision* as Philosophic *Satura*', *Eire – Ireland*, 12, n. 3 (Fomhar/Autumn 1977), 62–70 at 67.

critical attention seems to indicate that the Prologue is pivotal to the system. Indeed, as demonstrated by Walter Kelly Hood, Yeats had originally conceived the presentation of the whole system as a dialogue between Aherne and Robartes, two central characters in the 1937 Prologue, and he had even composed an epilogue in the same vein, entitled 'Michael Robartes Foretells' which he later discarded.³ Obviously, bypassing the Prologue as a mere piece of tomfoolery in order to make a greedy dash for Yeats's 'system' would not render *A Vision* justice. The Prologue not only lends Yeats's whole treatise tone and colour, but a close study of its intricate architecture is a necessary step to reach some understanding of what this intricate cosmogony has worth revealing.⁴ As Warwick Gould suggests, the Prologue, particularly the fictitious part, can be considered a useful guide to the system itself:

> Some critics have sought to read the fictions in the light of the system; others see them as the comic manipulation of the form of a printed book. No one has tried to read the system by the light of the fictions. Yet, since they were the bridge Yeats used between doctrine and its concrete embodiment in lyrics, it is worth asking whether the fictions might serve the reader not as temporary scaffolding, but as a permanent, necessary and integral part of Yeats's work, coterminous with plays and poems on the one hand and with abstract thought on the other.⁵

Before I offer my own attempt at analysis, a short summary of the Prologue and a glance at its situation within the system seem apposite. The five books constituting *A Vision* are bracketed by two poems, 'The Phases of the Moon' as introduction, and 'All Souls' Night' as epilogue. The Prologue itself, situated before 'The Phases of the Moon' can be said to fall into two parts. 'A Packet for Ezra Pound', is composed of three 'chapters': one is about Yeats's life in Rapallo and his aesthetic disagreement with Pound, the second is 'the true story' of his wife's automatic writing, and the third consists in a letter addressed to Pound. In this first part, which Adams amusingly

---

³ 'Michael Robartes: Two Occult Manuscripts': see *YO* 204–24. Yeats probably had Plato's *Dialogues* in mind.
⁴ *A Vision* has been compared to Edgar Allan Poe's *Eureka, a Prose Poem*, Jeffrey Meyers, *Edgar Allan Poe, His Life and Legacy* (New York: Cooper Square Press, 1992), 214.
⁵ 'A Lesson for the Circumspect: W. B. Yeats's Two Versions of *A Vision* and the *Arabian Nights*', in *The 'Arabian Nights' in English Literature: Studies in the Reception of 'The Thousand and One Nights' into British Culture*, ed. Peter L. Caracciolo (London: Macmillan, 1988), 251.

calls the 'primary account',[6] Yeats is speaking in his own person and, apparently, nothing fictional intervenes.

The second part, 'Stories of Michael Robartes and his Friends: An Extract from a Record made by his Pupils', is an extravagant series of fictitious tales concerning characters who, as is well-known, either represent Yeats's well-established heteronyms such as Robartes and Owen and John Aherne,[7] or are young people who embody single aspects of his past self-conceptions.[8] It can be divided into two sections, both composed of three chapters, and each section culminates with the appearance of Robartes, the younger characters' mentor. In the first section, which seems linked with the theme of art, Huddon, Duddon, Denise de L'Isle Adam and Daniel O'Leary, form a quartet.[9] The second section introduces the new characters of John Bond and Mary Bell and focuses on love.[10] Throughout the two fictitious sections, the general rule seems to be that each protagonist must tell his or her own

---

[6] *The Book of Yeats's* A Vision, *Romantic Modernism and Antithetical Tradition* (Ann Arbor: University of Michigan Press, 1995), 30.

[7] Aherne and Robartes, besides appearing in Yeats's three short stories 'Rosa Alchemica', 'The Tables of the Law' and 'The Adoration of the Magi' (*VSR* 125–72; *Myth 2005* 177–205) and in several poems, introduce the system with the 'The Phases of the Moon' (*AVB* 59). Fiction and reality are closely intertwined in the case of Robartes and Aherne for the two fictitious characters are a conflation of Yeats and other persons he knew. Robartes is one of Yeats's earliest 'masks' as a poetic voice in *The Wind Among the Reeds* (*VP* 803), besides reappearing severally in Yeats's poetry and short fiction, but he is also modelled after MacGregor Mathers who initiated Yeats into the Golden Dawn as Margaret Mills Harper reminds us in 'Yeats and the Occult', *The Cambridge Companion to W. B. Yeats*, ed. Marjorie Howes and John Kelly (Cambridge: Cambridge University Press, 2006), 154. See also Laurence W. Fennelly, 'W. B. Yeats and S. L. MacGregor Mathers' (*YO* 305) and 'Michael Robartes: Two Occult Manuscripts' by Walter Kelly Hood who notes that Robartes' cruelty also relates to other fictitious Yeatsian characters such as Crazy Jane and Ribh (*Ibid.*, 217). For the parallel between Owen Aherne and Lionel Johnson and their relation to Yeats and Robartes, see Warwick Gould '"Lionel Johnson Comes the First to Mind": Sources for Owen Aherne' (*Ibid.*, 255–84). For a complete survey of Robartes and Aherne throughout Yeats's oeuvre, see Michael J. Sidnell, 'Mr. Yeats, Michael Robartes and Their Circle' (*YO* 225–54).

[8] See Adams, 46–48.

[9] Huddon, Duddon and O'Leary who first appear in the poem introducing the fictitious stories (*AVB* 32) are the slightly altered names of three folkloric characters (Hudden, Dudden and Donald O'Neary) in the tale entitled 'Donald and his Neighbours': see *FFTIP* 299–302 and reprinted in the Colin Smythe edition (1973), 270–73.

[10] The names themselves glance at Blake's two poems 'Long John Brown & Little Mary Bell' and 'William Bond', *The Complete Poetry & Prose of William Blake*, ed. David V. Erdman (Berkeley: University of California Press, 1965, rev. 1982), 496.

story and, in the first section, Daniel O'Leary begins: he labours under an obsessive hatred for the realistic theatre and, during a performance he particularly dislikes, hurls both his boots at the actors on stage. Duddon's story follows: as an impoverished artist, his main achievement consists in an attempt to assault and batter his own patron, Huddon, and even that fails as he attacks the wrong man. We thus have two narratives before the first appearance of Michael Robartes. The latter's first intervention is partly comical narrative, exactly in the same vein as the other tales, partly philosophical. He mentions discovering an old manuscript printed in Cracow in 1594 and written by one Giraldus and, then, receiving the visit of a mysterious Arab who recognizes the doctrine of Giraldus as identical with the teachings of his tribe, called the Judwalis.

In the second section, Denise de L'Isle Adam tells the peculiar story of her *ménage à trois*: she loves Duddon but is the mistress of Huddon for real love cannot be realized in the flesh.[11] This is followed by the next extravagant narrative, another love triangle: Mary Bell, her husband, Mr. Bell, and her lover John Bond. In this story, Mary Bell, after her affair with John Bond, has to return to her dying husband for financial reasons. This husband has a passion for birds and his life-long dream is to teach cuckoos to build nests, an endeavour which, of course, is doomed to failure. Finally, Mary Bell manages to fake a cuckoo's nest by dint of great labour and skill, and passes this off as a real one to her husband so that he can die in peace. Of all the extravagant stories, this one sounds particularly absurd but such an impression is deceptive, of course, and, it is, in fact, the only success story in all the fictitious tales. Robartes' second and last intervention concludes this apparently nonsensical presentation, but this time his revelations concern the cycles of history. We learn that our next age will be one of warfare, and this ends in a sort of apotheosis with Robartes triumphantly producing the third egg of Leda he has purchased in the East, before he, Aherne and Mary Bell repair to the desert: they plan to bury the egg in the sand where, in due course, it will be hatched and give birth to the new Messiah.

The fictitious account presents a fine symmetry: two narratives about art followed by Robartes' first intervention, then two more narratives about love followed by Robartes' second appearance. This

---

[11] Here again, fact and fiction intermingle since the story of Denise's love affair with Huddon and Duddon is modelled after the love predicament of three Oxford students that Yeats had heard about twenty years earlier. See *Life* 2, 602.

is partly why I tend to regard the concluding letter of the fictitious prologue as a sort of annex or third part, which bridges the gap between the primary reality of 'A Packet for Ezra Pound' and the fictitious stories of the second part. The letter is written by Owen Aherne's brother, John Aherne, and is addressed to Yeats who thus stages himself within the fictitious tale and creates an interaction between himself and several alter-egos of his own making.[12] Essentially the letter, although it does not mention the automatic writing, links the two accounts together since it states that Yeats's work (three poems and his revised edition of *A Vision*) are in due conformity with the Giraldus manuscript as well as the diagrams of the Judwali sect. In short, Yeats, as author, is fortunate enough to receive the sanction of his own fictional characters for some of his latest work. This has attracted various comments from critics but all generally agree that the constant interaction between fact and fiction provides the reader with a much needed suspension of disbelief as regards the system and its origin. Both the treatise and the mysterious 'voices' from the beyond which instigated it are somehow rendered acceptable through these constant mirror effects destined to blur our sense of 'reality'.[13]

The prologue also constitutes a healthy proof, if we needed one, of Yeats's sense of humour and in the course of my summary, the most farcical elements will already have stated themselves. What interests me here is what lies hidden underneath the farrago of fact and fiction. So I shall first cast a quick glance at Yeats's self-derisive irony before I point to the subjacent unity which, in my opinion, underpins the various accounts.

The derision in the prologue is mostly targeted at Yeats himself as practically all the fictitious characters in the second part, from the

---

[12] The creation of John Aherne, Owen's brother, is probably due to a slip of the pen, as Yeats himself half admits (*VP* 821). As Gould observes, however, 'his invention soon proved useful, for he [John Aherne] can intervene between the "reinvented" Robartes and Aherne, and Yeats-as-character in his own fictions', 'A Lesson for the Circumspect', 269.

[13] Many critics have noted the importance of Yeats's interaction with his characters. See the preceding note for Gould on John Aherne, and also Sidnell: 'This absurd relation of author and character is fundamental' (*YO* 230). Korkowski argues that this strategy produces an effect of 'aesthetic distance' which 'allows Yeats to pass himself off as the soberest person involved in the "visions"', 'Yeats's Vision as Philosophic *Satura*', 69. For Helmling, Yeats consents to play the fool with characters of his own making in order to vindicate his own vision of the world, *The Esoteric Comedies of Carlyle, Newman and Yeats*, 15–17.

mage Giraldus to the old Arab (who, it is claimed, is a probable reincarnation of Kusta Ben Luka), could be considered alter egos.[14] Many of these characters are ridiculous because excessive as well as obsessive: the anecdotes about rebelling against realistic plays or about the patron one dislikes remind us of Yeats's early life;[15] the story of the trio Huddon, Duddon, and Denise could be viewed as a pastiche of Yeats, Maud Gonne and MacBride even though there is a factual basis for the story;[16] and the love and hate relationship between Robartes and the dancer is also reminiscent of Yeats's intellectual disapproval of Maud Gonne[17]: 'I adored in body what I hated in will' (*AVB* 38). From Denise's high ideals regarding discarnate love to the more iconoclastic adventures of Robartes, all these stories present a kaleidoscope of Yeats's own life. Even the literary and philosophical references are veiled allusions to Yeats's past: his youthful enthusiasm for Villiers de L'Isle Adam, held up to ridicule through the inept character of Denise; his high-flown illusions about so-called Platonic love embodied in the Huddon, Duddon, Denise trio; his early style inspired by Pater, which is defended by one alter ego (John Aherne) and mercilessly attacked by another (Robartes); lastly, Yeats's own constant preoccupation with birds, their nests and their eggs. These are only a few echoes which come to mind and this enumeration is by no means exhaustive. In his note to the poem, 'The Gift of Harun Al-Rashid', Daniel Albright aptly speaks of 'a reverberating abyss' and of Yeats's image being endlessly reflected 'in a roomful of mirrors'.[18] This also applies to the 1937 Prologue and, since most an-

---

[14] As most readers of Yeats know, Kusta Ben Luka's story was a veiled autobiographical account of the 'true story', i.e. George Yeats's automatic writing, in the 1925 version.

[15] As Adams notes, 46–48; also Helmling, 181–83.

[16] Helmling, 183. For the real story see above, n. 11.

[17] See Adams, 48. His interpretation is substantiated by the antagonistic feeling Maud Gonne often aroused in Yeats, which is consonant with Robartes' rejection of the dancer. As F. A. C. Wilson points out: 'Love, for Yeats, is at its strongest when it contains an element of hate, and this *odi et amo* motif he found also in Hermes Trismegistus', *W. B. Yeats and Tradition* (New York: Macmillan, 1958), 187. The fact that love comes from the attraction of opposites is a principle Yeats had also culled from Blake whom he quotes in a letter: 'sexual love is founded on spiritual hate' (*L*, 758; *Myth* 336).

[18] *The Poems*, ed. Daniel Albright (London: Everyman, updated 1994), 683, 687. Claire Nally also notes this endless fragmentation of Yeats's self in *Envisioning Ireland, W. B. Yeats's Occult Nationalism* (Bern: Peter Lang, 2010), 90, 124.

ecdotes tell of silly failures or fanciful figures propounding eccentric theories, there seems very little to salvage from the wreck: Yeats's life and personality lie mercilessly exposed through all the distorted masks of his own self mingled with the refractions of miscellaneous characters, some real, some fictitious, but all sharing some aspect of him in the past.

In addition, a more subtle kind of self-derisive irony transpires through a recurring trick of announcing the opposite of what is, in fact, going to be done. Critics have pointed out several instances of this: Yeats telling the reader the system is not a system and then presenting him with one;[19] or warning us he does not intend to include the Arabs into this story, and promptly doing so 'in the very next section of the book';[20] pretending he can find nothing but Empedocles to corroborate the system (*AVB* 20), whereas the whole of Greek tradition, Dante, as well as a few other sources will serve to back it up later;[21] dismissing his fiction as nonsense now that 'the truth' is known and yet immediately elaborating upon it.[22] To these, I could add the hasty dismissal of Pater's style in a fundamentally Paterian book (one thinks of Yeats's rich imagery in connection with Byzantium, as well as the distinction between Ionian and Dorian art which informs the whole of Book V);[23] the choice of the title *A Vision* for this intricate, precise, diagrammatic codification of personality and civilization; the unexpected proposition that the instructors 'have come to give ... metaphors for poetry' (*AVB* 8), an information which, in his eager anticipation for revelation, Yeats blissfully disregards in any case.

---

[19] Adams, 20 and Helmling, 208.
[20] Adams, 30.
[21] *Ibid.*, 30, 69–70.
[22] *Ibid.*, 39.
[23] The distinction we find between the Ionic and the Doric in *A Vision*, Book V, is indebted to Walter Pater's *Greek Studies* (London: Macmillan, 1895), in particular to his essays on 'The Heroic Age of Greek Art' and 'The Marbles of Aegina', 225–26, 263–66. According to Pater, Ionian sensuousness and refinement (the centrifugal) are opposed to Platonic Dorian discipline (the centripetal). The last Book of *A Vision* seems to pick up this strain: 'Side by side with Ionic elegance there comes after the Persian wars a Doric vigour... and the Parisian-looking young woman of the sculptors...give place to the athlete. One suspects a deliberate turning away from all that is Eastern, or a moral propaganda like that which turned the poets out of Plato's Republic ... Then in Phidias Ionic and Doric influence unite and all is transformed by the full moon, and all abounds and flows' (*AVB* 270).

For Adams, the self-derisiveness in the Prologue indicates that the system itself is not to be taken seriously: it is a no-system and the book must be treated as a piece of antithetical uncertainty, a fine construct and a fictional challenge which Yeats wrote in a fit of light-hearted *sprezzatura*.[24] For Helmling, the Prologue bears witness to Yeats's role as *eirôn*, 'the wise man who enlightens others by playing the fool with them': eventually, self-derisiveness backfires and the reader feels compelled to endorse the *eirôn*'s position, in this case, Yeats's 'indictment of materialist, bourgeois, 'modern' culture'.[25] These various readings, thought-provoking as they might be, seem incomplete, for more is at stake here than mere ironical criticism. Nor can I agree that '*A Vision* presents no 'philosophy' but rather ... a fantasia of images, poses, gestures'.[26] Korkowski seems nearer the mark when he asserts that the sheer medley of fact and fiction, the many loopholes and disavowals in both real and fictitious accounts are merely part of the technique of the *satura* which consists in making 'bitter and difficult learning' palatable.[27] As Korkowski makes clear, the improbable medley aims at more than parody and satire, and this brings me to my main development which is about the kind of coherence I detect under the guise of nonsense.[28] In the apparently cock and bull story of the Prologue, every detail points both to the forthcoming system and to the hidden esoteric doctrine which Yeats likes to veil from his readers' eyes.

Two main leads are given at the very beginning of the true account, two clues which will serve as constant leitmotivs throughout the whole Prologue, and contribute to explain the very neat division of the fictitious Prologue into two sections. The first point is that apparently it is necessary to read about or write one's own biography before obtaining revelation. This principle is supported by Yeats's

---

[24] Adams, 40, on *sprezzatura*, see 14–15 and 46.

[25] Helmling, 15–17 and 21. In the discarded manuscript entitled 'Robartes Foretells', Yeats's willingness to play the fool in Socratic fashion is evident, as he lets himself be criticized by his own narrator: 'Yeats is wrong', see *YO* 214.

[26] Helmling, 211.

[27] Korkowski, 70.

[28] Korkowski points out that the Roman *satura*, unlike its Greek counterpart, did not aim to ridicule philosophers and philosophy. On the contrary, it sought to foster an interest in philosophical pursuits. Some of the works cited as examples of later *saturae* certainly seem to aim at imparting serious knowledge; furthermore, two of them at least would have been familiar to Yeats: Dante's *La Vita Nuova* and Johan Valentin Andreae's *Chemical Wedding*, Korkowski, 67–68.

famous statement: 'We make out of the quarrel with others rhetoric but of the quarrel with ourselves poetry' (*Myth* 331), and this sentence, taken from *Per Amica Silentia Lunae*, is said to have drawn the communicators' attention to Yeats in the first place (*AVB* 8). In the very first pages of the true account, Yeats recalls Browning's *Paracelsus* and Goethe's *Wilhelm Meister*: the former had to write his autobiography before he obtained 'the secret' (*AVB* 9); the latter 'before initiation' had to read his own history written by another (*AVB* 9). This first element, biography, knowing about oneself, will not only reappear severally throughout the Prologue, but it directly applies to the whole first half of the subsequent system (the phases of the moon).

The second point is history: in the true account, shortly after their revelations regarding the various personality types, the instructors start drawing cones relating to European history, and relevant to the second half of Yeats's system. Logically, enough, in the fictional tale, Robartes follows the lead given by Yeats's instructors: in the first of his interventions he talks about love and the 28 Phases of the Moon, whereas in the second, he deals with the history motif.

Those two points, biography and history, not only sum up the system itself but also clarify many details in the Prologue: indeed, Yeats's instructors allow him to read no philosophy, but only biography and history (*AVB* 12), and Robartes, in his final address, requires that his young pupils accept two main precepts, one regarding biography, the other history: 'Have I proved by practical demonstration that the soul survives the body?' and 'Have I proved that civilizations come to an end ... and that ours is near its end?' (*AVB* 50)

The insistence on biography is immediately perceptible in the Prologue and, in the fictional account, the telling of stories is precisely the point of the young people gathering together as O'Leary clearly indicates: 'I am to tell you my story and to hear yours' (*AVB* 33), then, when he has finished, he continues: 'Robartes says you must not ask me questions but introduce yourselves and tell me your story' (*AVB* 35); when Robartes comes with his first revelations, he also has a personal narrative; in the second gathering, Robartes introduces John Bond and Mary Bell and further proposes: 'Before John Bond tells his story, I must insist upon Denise telling hers' (*AVB* 42). From the outset, John Bond's narrative has special significance, as his love story with Mary Bell is contrapuntal to that of Denise: the two fictitious love triangles reflect and reverse one another. In fact, Robartes ironically suggests that Denise's story 'will be a full and admirable introduction' to John Bond's narrative (*AVB* 42). And, after Denise's narration, John Bond begins his own story after 'fixing a bewildered eye' first upon Denise, then upon Duddon (*AVB* 44). In truth, Mary Bell's love is not the abstemious kind and she has a child by John Bond, which contrasts with Denise's rather sterile day-dreaming about *Axel*.[29] Furthermore, Mary Bell is endowed with creative faculties, and her bizarre production of a fake cuckoo's nest seems to counterbalance the ineffectual relationship of Denise with Huddon and Duddon. If Denise and Robartes' cruel dancer may represent refracted versions of Maud Gonne, another parallel can be drawn between Mary Bell's gift for fruition and George's appeasing influence in the non-fictional story of Yeats's marriage. Indeed, we know what may have motivated the automatic writing at least in part, i.e., Yeats's struggle with his conscience regarding the three women in his life: Maud, Iseult and George (*AVA* xxiii). In the true story, the tumult of sterile love torment is set to rights by George, another Mary Bell contriving to please an ageing husband with somewhat unorthodox methods.[30] In addition, a certain wild resemblance between the two young wives' undertakings cannot be denied: creating a fake cuckoo's nest and inspiring a book based on automatic writing sound perfectly demented propositions, and yet, both seem aesthetically productive. In effect, the fictitious stories not only mirror Yeats's own biography *ad infinitum*, but also relate to the very writing of *A Vision* itself.[31]

At this point, it is necessary to examine the nature of Mary Bell's artistic achievement which relates to both biography and history. As pointed out by Adams, Mr. Bell (the husband) is 'primary' in his desire to improve nature and teach cuckoos to build nests.[32] From

---

[29] Hence, perhaps, her association with Blake's poetry. Interestingly, Mary Bell is caught between two men who, like Yeats himself, are fascinated by birds. Birds represent the antithetical principle in Yeats's work, as F. A. C. Wilson notes: 'Birds seem to him the images of subjectivity particularly when, like the subjective soul, they soar into the zone of intellect and the free spirit ...' See his *Yeats's Iconography* (London: Methuen, 1960), 196.

[30] George Yeats is also indirectly present in the fictitious account through Aherne's letter, when he mentions Kusta Ben Luka's story, itself a parody of Yeats's marriage.

[31] Although Helmling does not draw any immediate parallel between Mary Bell and George Yeats, he describes 'the implausible cuckoo's nest' as 'a suggestive (and elaborately ludicrous) emblem of *A Vision* itself', 183.

[32] Adams, 52.

the outset, he appears animated by the true passion of the reformer: 'I wanted to serve God ... I wanted to make men better' (*AVB* 52). In his view, birds and beasts are one and the same with man and represent our wild desires at the origin of time: 'The passions of Adam, torn out of his breast, became the birds and beasts of Eden' (*AVB* 48). Animals, therefore, are the incarnations of human desires and since Mr. Bell observes that: 'Now birds and beasts were robbing and killing one another' (*AVB* 48), this leads him to focus on birds as an indirect way to improve mankind. Mr. Bell uses the cuckoo, this anomaly in nature, to rectify some imbalance in the cosmos. His attempt, however, is based on teaching and patience, obviously an empiricist's method which cannot succeed as it only imitates nature. Mary Bell, on the other hand, is able to bring her husband's quest to completion through a combination of art and love since her illicit affair is the probable motive for this strange form of atonement. We note that Mary Bell's creative feat, the producing of a fake cuckoo's nest, is evocative of the third egg of Leda she will be allowed to carry at the end of the fictitious Prologue. In fact, Leda's egg suggests both love and creation in keeping with Mary Bell's special status as lover and artist. In Plato's *Symposium*, Aristophanes' speech on the nature of Eros draws upon the metaphor of the egg to explain the nature of love. Indeed, the first hermaphrodite beings were round-shaped and self-sufficient until Zeus decided to punish them for impiety: he 'cut them all in half' as one might 'slice an egg with a hair'.[33] In Aristophanes' theory, the deprived halves perpetually seek one another, and, love exists to bridge the gap in this dissociation of nature against itself.[34] This quest for fundamental unity also relates to the mysterious egg of the Orphic myth of creation, since according to that tradition, the whole created world was hatched from a mysterious world-egg, a well-known symbol in Blake's cosmogony as well as Yeats's.[35] Thus, Mary Bell's fabrication of a nest, more than a proof of

---

[33] *Symposium*, 190, d, e, translated by Michael Joyce; Plato, *The Collected Dialogues of Plato*, ed. Edith Hamilton and Huntington Cairns (New York: Pantheon Books, 1961, rev. 1963).

[34] As Kathleen Raine notes, the egg by its ovoid shape suggests duality, unlike the sphere which represents unity, *Yeats the Initiate* (Savage, MD: Barnes and Noble Books, 1990), 149.

[35] Raine, 142–45. This world-egg is mentioned at the very beginning of the fictitious prologue and, unsurprisingly, it comprises the two vortices of the system: 'Michael Robartes called the universe a great egg that turns inside out perpetually without breaking its shell' (*AVB* 33).

love or an ingenious device, has restored primordial unity and made her worthy of holding the egg from which a new era will emerge. We find that her achievement closely fits the fundamentally Yeatsian tenet that art exists to fill the gap, i.e., mend and improve 'reality': 'If the real world is not altogether rejected, it is but touched here and there, and into the places we have left empty we summon rhythm, balance, pattern, images' (*E&I* 243). Clearly, only Mary Bell's kind of love can generate the type of 'subjective' art that re-creates the world, thus bridging the gap between history and biography. As the figure of the true lover as well as the visionary artist, Mary Bell will be entrusted with the holding of the lost egg of 'Hyacinthine blue' (*AVB* 51),[36] the symbol of the new subjective dispensation which, ironically, will uphold War as the *Summum Bonum*.[37]

From the previous considerations, one notes that biography seems inextricably bound up with history. The structure of the fictitious section brings this principle to the fore: the first stories related to art culminate in Robartes' recounting his personal story of unrequited love, whereas the love stories move him to announce the new historical dispensation. The story of Mary Bell illustrates that point also, since she is both a lover and an important agent in the new dispensation. Furthermore, the complex historical antinomy between an age of Love and an age of War is echoed by the opposition between self and anti-self in the biographies. What seems at first a reverberating medley of masks and costumes in the Prologue finally resolves itself into distinct antinomies, as the trios turn into twos, prefiguring Yeats's subsequent theory of will and mask.[38] Huddon and Duddon are comical ones, stressed by rhyme, just as Bell and Bond are linked alliteratively. We are also confronted with the constant bickering and quarrelling of Aherne and Robartes: they are opposed in every way, but nothing can tear them apart, just as Giraldus finds his counterpart in the old Arab and, in the primary account, Yeats continually wars against Ezra Pound (*AVB* 3–4). Similarly, the women in the Prologue, whether fictitious or real, come in pairs: Mary Bell and

---

[36] An allusion to Sappho's fragment 166: 'They say that Leda once found an egg of hyacinth colour.' *Greek Lyric I*, trans. David A. Campbell (Harvard: Loeb Classical Library, rev. 1990), 171.

[37] Obviously, this points to the fact that the dichotomy between Love and War needs to be refined and, as I shall demonstrate, Yeats's concept of war has to be interiorized to be fully understood.

[38] Cf., Adams, *Tradition*, 46–47.

Denise de L'Isle Adam, George Yeats and Maud Gonne.[39] At this point, I can draw a partial conclusion and remark that biography and history (love and art for Yeats) are but two sides of the same coin, as Fahmy Farag notes: 'Our everyday clashes and accords, our local events and minor disputes, with all the passions they generate and the feelings they engender, constitute the more distant drama of preordained history with its divisions and dispensations'.[40] It therefore follows that both biography and history reflect the same classification in pairs: the dichotomy between objective (primary) and subjective (antithetical) which constitutes the essence of the system.

From all that precedes the complex structure which holds the Prologue and the system together begins to assert itself. Through the use of satire or seemingly random juxtaposition, Yeats is carefully interweaving threads which run through both accounts in a complex criss-cross pattern: the real and the fictional are not so much juxtaposed as woven into the same tight net of reference. Furthermore, the complexity of the Prologue intensifies when we come to the realization that the true account includes a second 'story' or another real character, namely Ezra Pound, and that, in effect, the Prologue offers us three different angles of approach: the story of the automatic writing, the fictional tales, but also the relationship between Yeats and Pound.[41] Indeed, we have to bear in mind that the book is dedicated to Pound, another anti-self for Yeats since, we are told, 'his art is the opposite of mine' (*AVB* 3). This third aspect, essential to any study of the Prologue, can help us redefine the kind of message Yeats wishes to deliver about his basic dichotomy: antithetical/subjective versus primary/subjective.

First, several warnings to Ezra Pound can be found in the 'Packet', as Yeats is aware of the latter's misguided views and growing extremism.

---

[39] If one accepts Adams' interpretation which, I think, is correct here. Of course, the complexities of biography are such that no single real character stands behind the fictitious one. Denise could be a conflation of Maud and Iseult Gonne as the ideal beloved, for ever out of reach, with George Yeats, like Mary Bell, representing the security of a well-established relationship.

[40] *The Opposing Virtues: New Yeats Papers XV*, ed. Liam Miller (Dublin: The Dolmen Press, 1978).

[41] Yeats's dedication to Pound and his relationship with the latter are essential components of the Prologue. For Yeats and Pound's Cantos, see Gould's '"*The Unknown Masterpiece*": Yeats and the Design of the *Cantos*', in *Pound in Multiple Perspective: A Collection of Critical Essays*, ed. Andrew Gibson (London: The Macmillan Press, 1993), 40–92.

Ezra Pound's compassion for cats is dwelt upon at the very beginning and, therefore, cannot be a minor point for Yeats: via Maud Gonne and, later, Mr. Bell, it relates to the rest of the Prologue. Yeats considers that Ezra Pound, like Maud Gonne and Mr. Bell are primary for their existence is bound up with some commitment to a cause. At the very beginning of the system, one lapidary statement sums up the whole argument of antithetical versus primary: 'The primary is that which serves [the world], the antithetical is that which creates' (*AVB* 85). The former type of humanity, therefore, will tend to become absorbed in the exterior world, while the second will turn the self into a heroic battle ground, productive of great art. Interestingly, Yeats compares Ezra Pound with Maud Gonne (decidedly the unnamed ghost of this entire prelude), because their great thought in living lies outside themselves: they wish to fight against injustice, redress wrongs and change the general state of affairs.[42] Their pity for the oppressed has turned them into fanatics: 'I examine this [Ezra Pound's] criticism ... and thereupon recall a person as unlike him as possible, the only friend who remains to me from late boyhood, grown gaunt in the injustice of what seems her blind nobility of pity' (*AVB* 6). Consequently, in his letter to Pound at the end of the 'Packet', Yeats tries to restrain his friend's regrettable propensities, and refers Pound to himself by sending him his own poem, 'The Return', adding that 'in book and picture ... [this poem] gives me better words than my own' (*AVB* 29). This extraordinary gesture is, I believe, a means of inciting Pound to reflect upon his life through his own work, thus reiterating Yeats's faith in the restorative powers of biography.[43] 'The Return', no doubt selected for its heroic dimension, might divert Pound from this rage for reform, this defence of the oppressed just because they are oppressed, which he shares with Maud Gonne. Furthermore, at the beginning of the letter, Yeats's admonition 'Do not be elected to the Senate of your country' (*AVB* 26) constitutes another clear warning against political engagement.[44] Finally, as intimated above,

---

[42] For the incompatibility between art and politics, see Daniel Cory's reaction to the Cantos: 'The poet was smothered by the reformer, the Muses shunned by the prophet', given by Gould in "'*The Unknown Masterpiece*'", 59.

[43] Perhaps also a lesson in humility, as Yeats stated elsewhere: 'We may come to think that nothing exists but a stream of souls, that all knowledge is biography' (*Ex* 397).

[44] See Gould, "'*The Unknown Masterpiece*'", 72.

Pound's attitude anticipates Mr. Bell's primary pity for cuckoos and, at the end of the Prologue, we are left in no doubt as to what Yeats's final pronouncement on such compassion is: primary charity is sent packing, whether aimed at men, cats or birds.[45]

Second, in keeping with history, the other side of the coin, Pound's poem is also meant to illustrate Yeats's theory of the cycles. Indeed, the poem is often thought to herald the return of pagan Greek gods and, if Yeats does not mention this particular interpretation, he could not be ignorant of it. *A Vision*, therefore, announces a dispensation which *normally* should interest Pound for the advent of Robartes' new era will cause the return of these same pagan gods. It will bring an age of 'freedom, fiction, evil, kindred, art, aristocracy' (*AVB* 52), and proclaim a new deity, antithetical to Christ and symbolized by Oedipus who 'sank down body and soul into the ground' whereas Christ 'crucified standing up, went into the abstract sky soul and body' (*AVB* 27–28). More subtly, 'The Return' also helps the attentive reader discover what epoch is directly relevant to the Prologue: ancient Greece and, more particularly, the turning point between Greece and Rome, which ties up with Robartes' alleged premise for his theory of the cycles, i.e., 'Swift's essay upon the dissensions of the Greeks and Romans' (*AVB* 50). Logically enough, in the real account, the same period is elaborated upon as Yeats focuses on the distinction between Greek and Roman statues: the former have 'round bird-like eyes ... 'staring at infinity" (*AVB* 18) and represent the antithetical, contrary to Roman art which tends towards realism and the primary. These considerations upon ancient history can lead the reader to wonder about the rest of the puzzle such as the connection between Giraldus and the Arab tribe, and this is difficult to grasp without some knowledge of hermetic doctrine.

Indeed, the Prologue contains a lesson in esoteric history, and some knowledge of the *philosophia perennis*, dear to Yeats, is necessary to understand the insistence on the few historical highlights which constantly reappear throughout the text. If we ask ourselves what

---

[45] Since the letter ends up suggesting ever so gently that there should be no rejection of one reality in favour of the other because the opposites are 'like the two scales of a balance, the two butt-ends of a seesaw' (*AVB* 29), I sense another warning here: the whole system is delicately presented to Pound as if to convert the latter to some kind of acceptance of 'the whole of reality' and, it seems that Yeats is playing Shroud to Pound's Cuchulain (see the poem 'Cuchulain Comforted' *VP* 634).

particular event, at the turning point of hegemony between Greece and Rome, could possibly bring Byzantium, the Arab migrations and the Renaissance to the fore, the obvious answer is Alexander's conquest (also referred to in Yeats's seminal poem 'The Statues'). Alexander altered the course of European history when he conquered Persia, and expanded his Empire eastward, thus displacing the centre of European learning. After his death and the fall of Alexandria, two routes were eventually to restore these treasures to Europe: Greek learning survived the destruction of the Roman Empire in Byzantium, a city which Yeats depicts as a spiritual replica of Athens in 'Sailing to Byzantium'. After the defeat of the city by the Turks in 1453, priests and scholars returned to Renaissance Italy where Plato and the famous *Corpus Hermeticum*, all that remained of Greek esoteric knowledge inherited from Egypt, were translated in Florence by Marsilio Ficino (1433–1499).[46] In the Prologue we note that the *Speculum Angelorum et Hominum*, Giraldus' manuscript, was published in 1594 which obviously links the event to the late Renaissance and places the manuscript one century after Ficino's translations and two decades before the first Rosicrucian manifestoes, in other words at the core of the Rosicrucian tradition.[47] A second route restored the Greek texts to Europe through the west owing to the Arab conquest. The Arabs had discovered the *Hermetica* when they conquered Persia and had also become the recipients of the sacred books. Since they later occupied Spain and infiltrated the South of France, the lost tradition returned to Europe via their various settlements.[48] In the Prologue we note that the old Arab who visits Robartes finds the doctrine of the *Speculum* (an old arcane manuscript) in keeping with

---

[46] The *Corpus Hermeticum* was derived from a mysterious text, the Emerald Tablet, discovered in the tomb of the great Egyptian master Hermes Trismegistus (sometimes thought to be Pythagoras' father). The discovery was made by Apollonius of Tyana in the 1st century B.C. See Christian Rebisse, *Rosicrucian History and Mysteries* (San Jose: Supreme Grand Lodge of AMORC Inc., 2005), 12.

[47] Marsilio Ficino's translations are c. 484, also the alleged date for the death of Christian Rosenkreuz, the mythical founder of the Rosicrucian movement. In 1604, the grave of Christian Rosenkreuz was found in Germany, and the old sage was holding mysterious writings in his hand, among which an account of his life and initiation. Ten years after the event, the first two anonymous Rosicrucian manifestoes, *Fama Fraternitatis* and *Confessio Fraternitatis* were published (in 1614 and 1615 respectively). Thus, the discovery of Christian Rosenkreuz' tomb echoes that of Hermes Trismegistus by Apollonius of Tyana. See Rebisse, 42.

[48] The occupation of Spain by the Arabs started in 711 and lasted until the fifteenth century.

the ancestral teachings of his own tribe (traditional lore), thus hinting at the esoteric import of these well-established facts of history. Indeed, the two routes of esoteric doctrine are so conspicuously stressed by Yeats throughout the fictitious account that it is tempting to interpret those geographical landmarks as pointed allusions to the meanders of the Rosicrucian doctrine. Furthermore, we note that Robartes, like the Rosicrucian sage, Rosenkreuz, has to go to Arabia for his initiation, which points to the esoteric myth of *Felix Arabia* as a possible leading thread throughout the fictitious stories. [49]

This throws some light on Robartes' vagueness as to the actual place where he purchased the third egg of Leda for the actual place is immaterial as long as it is situated in the east and part of Alexander's empire: Robartes first mentions Teheran (a likely place as the centre of Persia), then is corrected by Aherne, always 'a stickler for facts',[50] and Robartes evasively replies: 'I bought this egg from an old man in a green turban in Arabia or Persia or India' (*AVB* 51).[51] Furthermore, if one bears in mind the Rosicrucian tradition, the rest of Robartes' seemingly dubious tale falls into place: his discovery of the manuscript, followed by the visit of the old Arab (*AVB* 41), the similarity between the tradition of the Arab tribe of the Judwalis and the treatise of Giraldus (*AVB* 41, 51, 54), and the treasury of Harun Al-Rashid as a refuge for the egg of Leda after the fall of Byzantium (*AVB* 51). There is no need to expound upon the importance of the Golden Dawn in Yeats's work, and the 1925 edition of *A Vision* is still dedicated to Vestigia, MacGregor Mathers' widow, although the

---

[49] The initiation of Christian Rosenkreuz entailed a long voyage into the heart of *Arabia Felix*, the land of the Phoenix, where the *Corpus Hermeticum* had also been preserved. See Rebisse, 41.

[50] Adams, 45.

[51] Robartes' evasiveness stresses a parallel with the manuscript of Giraldus which is unaccountably 'printed in Cracow in 1594, a good many years before the celebrated Cracow publications'. Krakow was a great centre of learning during the Renaissance and it was visited by John Dee (1527–c.1608), the famous English Hermeticist who travelled around Poland between 1583 and 1589. Dee, who was an assiduous reader of Marsilio Ficino, is pointedly mentioned by Yeats in the 1925 prologue to *A Vision* (*AVA* xvii) as the main reason for Robartes' visit to Krakow (whereas in the 1937 version, Robartes seems to remain in Vienna). This off-handedness is perhaps meant to highlight the peripatetic dimension of the secret doctrine and its numerous focal points. However, if the earlier Emerald Table is associated with the Orient, the second sacred texts are connected with Germany and, more loosely, Eastern Europe, as indeed the history of the Rosicrucian movement shows, according to Rebisse, 39–53.

dedication disappears from the 1937 edition.[52] What is arresting in the Prologue is that the geographical landmarks are clearly mapped out and anticipate the great highlights of antithetical splendour expounded in the system: Greece, Byzantium, Renaissance Italy, with the Arab Conquest set in parallel. [53] At the end of Book V, Yeats pointedly returns to the Arab conquest as a paradigm of subjective perfection: '… it was this latter sanctity [the beauty of Heart's Miracle] come back from the first crusade or up from Arabian Spain or half Asiatic Provence and Sicily, that created romance' (*AVB* 285).[54]

In the Prologue however, it seems that Yeats lends a personal twist to the two routes: if the first one is learned, with discoveries based on scholarly texts such as Plato and the *Hermetica*, that of the Arabs, he professes to believe, is not quite so conventional. His Arabs are nomadic people living in the desert and, in addition to sacred texts, they have diagrams, dancing and a vivid oral tradition, as we learn from 'The Gift of Harun Al-Rashid': in this poem, Kusta's young bride talks in her sleep and utters 'truths without fathers', 'self-born truths' (*AVA* 125) that spring spontaneously, not painstakingly through learning. In the Rosicrucian tradition, we find no such distinction between erudite esotericism and the mythical *Arabia Felix*. The reason Yeats invents one is that he wishes to stress the validity of his own experiments with spirits: he therefore arbitrarily relates spiritualism to the nomadic Arabs. We may remember that spiritualism was not encouraged by the more learned schools of esotericism such as the Rosicrucian movement, and that Yeats had received several warnings from his friends to refrain from the practice (*AVA* xv). Nevertheless, as early as 1909 and especially from 1911 onward, Yeats had re-embarked upon a new quest for wisdom through spiritualism and séances, and had found his *Daimon*, Leo

---

[52] For Yeats and the Rosicrucian tradition, see George Mills Harper, *Yeats's Golden Dawn: The Influence of the Hermetic Order of the Golden Dawn on the Life and Art of W. B. Yeats* (London: Macmillan, 1974).

[53] These landmarks are also mentioned by the Poet Laureate John Masefield, who concludes the 'flowery private pamphlet' of his eulogium to Yeats in the following manner: 'Sometimes, I have thought of him [Yeats] as of a Greek poet from Byzantium, who, having attained immortality in Arabia, came, seeking wisdom, to Renaissance Italy, and then having watched … the decline of life during three centuries, descended in the late Victorian time' (*Life* 2, 412).

[54] This is not to detract from Yeats's well-attested fascination for *The Arabian Nights*, whose technique of embedded narration he adopts in the Prologue, as Gould notes in 'A Lesson for the Circumspect', 252.

Africanus who had been 'a poet among the Moors'.⁵⁵ The Prologue therefore, spells out rebellion and hints that no rules should apply to limit the promptings of a true quest for knowledge. Apart from the explicit tale of the automatic writing itself, a play on words in Aherne's letter indirectly addresses the issue: 'You have sent me three poems founded upon 'hearsay', as you put it' (*AVB* 54), this hearsay obviously referring to George's voices. Moreover, Yeats vigorously defends what he calls 'popular spiritualism' in the real account of the Prologue (*AVB* 24),⁵⁶ and illustrates his vindication with a poetic metaphor: 'The Muses resemble women who creep out at night and give themselves to unknown sailors and return to talk of Chinese porcelain ... – virginity renews itself like the moon – except that the Muses sometimes form in those low haunts their most lasting attachments' (*AVB* 24). In view of the context, the 'Chinese porcelain' can only represent the rarefied atmosphere of esoteric knowledge, and the 'low haunts' the shadiness of disreputable séance rooms.

Finally, the Prologue presents us with a parody of the archetypal story of the Rosicrucian tradition which regularly stages the discovery of old sages holding mysterious writings: Hermes, and after him, Rosenkreuz. Here, it only seems fair to assume that the *Speculum* itself, damaged as it might be, is an echo of the other sacred writings of the Rosicrucians (the Emerald Table and the writings of Paracelsus found in the tomb of Rosenkreuz), especially since, as Raine remarks, Robartes is a type of the 'mysterious wanderer' like other famous 'legendary Rosicrucians'.⁵⁷ With this story of the *Speculum* as a sacred text offhandedly used for fuel by an unthinking mistress and accidentally revealed to the iconoclastic Robartes, Yeats is certainly indulging in a bout of irreverent fun. The episode cannot but bring to mind earlier similar discoveries, including perhaps the mysterious cipher manuscripts which lay at the foundation of the Golden Dawn

---

⁵⁵ Richard Ellmann, *Yeats: The Man and the Masks* [1948, rev. 1979] (London: Penguin Books, 1987), 196, 199. For Leo Africanus, see *YA1* 3–47, and Suheil B. Bushrui 'Yeats's Arabic Interests', in *In Excited Reverie, A Centenary tribute*, ed. A. Norman Jeffares and K. G. W. Cross (London: Macmillan, 1965), 280–314. Yeats's unwarranted association of the Arabs with spiritualism may have been derived from his 'encounter' with Leo. He may also have culled the notion of a nomadic esoteric tradition from R. W. Felkin, who founded the *Stella Matutina* under the guidance of some mysterious Arab Rosicrucians living in the desert: see Bushrui, 282–83.

⁵⁶ As elsewhere in his work, for example in *Per Amica Silentia Lunae* (*Myth* 318–69) or 'Swedenborg, Mediums and the Desolate Places' (*Ex* 30–70).

⁵⁷ Raine, 234.

in 1888,[58] or the lost book 'attributed to Kusta ben Luka' and mentioned in the 1925 edition of *A Vision* (*AVA* xix–xx). [59] A seemingly endless refraction of old sages presenting their manuscripts seems to literally haunt the pages of the Prologue as announced by Giraldus' portrait. However, Yeats rebels but does not refute, and spiritualism does not contradict the teachings of tradition. Spiritualism merely serves as confirmation since the precepts in the learned manuscript are corroborated by the mysterious diagrams of the Judwali tribe as well as George's voices or Yeats's 'hearsay'. The Prologue makes clear that there are at least two paths to knowledge, both equally valid, and, in his work, Yeats has accustomed his readers to his double role: the learned Mage toiling away in his tower and the wild, iconoclastic Wanderer, both present in the introductory poem, 'The Phases of the Moon'. [60]

As all that new information piles in, another sort of amusement or irony starts informing the Prologue, this time perhaps at the expense of the reader who is confronted with a portrait of Giraldus' resembling Yeats and winking mischievously (*AVB* 54).[61] Both the resemblance and the wink bring to light the figure of the devious author, also endlessly mirrored in the Prologue: Giraldus and his incomplete manuscript in the fictitious account, the instructors' partial revelations as well as Ezra Pound's fragmentary *Cantos* in the real one. We remember that Yeats had dedicated his book to Pound, an ironic gesture since the latter was known to disapprove strongly of Yeats's esoteric pursuits. Yet, Yeats seems to have ample justification for his choice, and his idea for the paradoxical 'packet' rests upon the alleged similarity between Pound's *Cantos* and his own book. Indeed, the obscurity of the *Cantos* announces the opacity of what the instructors will only half disclose in the next chapter and, as Yeats pointedly remarks, Pound's poem has much in common with the 'system': 'the descent into hell and the historical characters', the archetypal events and persons, the Zodiacal signs and a complicated pattern of echoing

---

[58] *Ibid.*, 180. See also *YO* 291–92.
[59] For the lost book of Kusta Ben Luka in Baghdad, see Bushrui, 298–99.
[60] With a slight preference for the iconoclastic wanderer: in the discarded 'Appendix by Michael Robartes', Hood notes an interesting difference between the old Arab and Giraldus, the latter seeming more bent on theology and moralizing (an inferior stance for Yeats), *YO* 207, 212. Indeed, the old sage is primary, the wanderer antithetical.
[61] For a study of the various possibilities for the choice of the name Giraldus, see Raine, 408–30.

structures 'all set whirling together' (*AVB* 5). About Pound's cryptic composition, Yeats hopefully concedes: 'I may find that the mathematical structure, when taken up into imagination, is more than mathematical' (*AVB* 5), and his incomprehension anticipates his frustration at the complex system withheld from his wondering gaze by the instructors: 'though it was plain from the first that their exposition was based upon a single geometrical conception, they kept me from mastering that conception' (*AVB* 11). Other expressions such as 'they shifted ground ... they were determined to withhold' (*AVB* 11) underline that the instructors' communications are, like Pound's *Cantos*, a tantalizing game of hide and seek. This immediately places Pound in the category of devious authors who both hide and reveal, but Yeats is not merely the victim of all these 'frustrators', since he follows in their footsteps: Pound's *Cantos*, like the elliptic geometry of the instructors or Giraldus' torn manuscript, are but a mere reflection of what Yeats, himself, will do to the readers of *A Vision*.

However, Yeats may have no choice for he is bound to assert his truths in a cryptic way and 'the safety in derision' (*VP* 624) that he seeks might not be for himself, but for his secrets, hence, of course, the Mage's wink: this is perhaps the fundamental reason for what Gould calls Yeats's 'increased strategies of disavowal'.[62] Considering the many allusions to the Rosicrucian tradition in the Prologue, one of Korkowski's examples of a *satura*, Johan Valentin Andreae's *Chemical Wedding* seems particularly apposite to Yeats's fictitious account.[63] *Chemical Wedding* indeed encompasses many genres including comedy and farce while at the same time alluding to occult ritual and alchemy in very obscure manner.[64] It shares many characteristics with Yeats's Prologue since both stories weave abstruse esoteric allusions into preposterous bouts of comedy.[65] However, if in both works we find a mixed plate of entertainment and serious thought, neither can be said to render its philosophy accessible thanks to the technique of the *satura*. It rather seems that the main strategy of both authors

[62] 'A Lesson for the Circumspect', 262.
[63] Andreae is also thought to be the unacknowledged writer of the two Rosicrucian manifestoes, but if this is true, he used a radically different style to write *Chemical Wedding*: see Rebisse, 67–68.
[64] *Ibid*.
[65] Traces of *Chemical Wedding* can perhaps be found in the first Prologue of *A Vision* with the 'Dance of the Four Royal Persons' executed by the Caliph (*AVA* 9–11), an episode which brings to mind the mysterious beheading of the seven members of the royal family in Andreae's story: see Rebisse, 67–68.

consists in withdrawing knowledge and befuddling the average reader. One wonders whether it is the philosophy which is 'bitter and difficult' or whether the devious author might not be acting as 'frustrator' to his reading public. It seems that Yeats was particularly reticent to divulge the sources he drew upon and, as F. A. C Wilson points out, he 'did not explain all he knew, preferring to write as an initiate for initiates'. [66] Conversely, for those readers of Yeats who are cognisant of esoteric doctrine, the deviousness of the Prologue can be major source of amusement, since Yeats's system, which is often rejected as arbitrary, subjective, confused or incomprehensible, quite simply follows the long sinuous road of hermetic tradition and re-asserts some of its fundamental tenets in apparently offhand manner. As Yeats himself admits in a letter to Olivia Shakespear, the philosophical content of the subsequent system 'is all 'very ancient'' (*L* 781) and some of it draws upon Platonic philosophy.[67] The two antinomies crowned by the sphere or what Yeats calls the 13th Cone are well-established Platonic concepts.[68] Plato constantly proceeds from two opposites to build up his philosophy, which might explain why the Prologue develops under the aegis of the Dyad.[69] Another traditional element is the appellation, the 13th Cone, which Yeats coined for the sphere, probably in memory of the twelve labours of Heracles, a haunting figure in his work, as Raine points out.[70] Before becoming an astronomical divinity related to the zodiac and the tutelary deity of the Pythagoreans,[71] Heracles' life was directly entangled with two antinomies: Hades and Olympus, dark and light, since he was half human, half divine.[72] When we recall that the hero rejoined the twelve Olympians at the end of his twelve labours, the

---

[66] *Yeats's Iconography*, 47.

[67] With a fine ambiguity for, the distinction between philosophy and esotericism is somewhat blurred in the case of Platonism or Neo-Platonism.

[68] For the Platonic influence in *A Vision*, see my article 'Reshaping Chaos: Platonic Elements in Yeats's *A Vision* and Later Poetry', *Imaginaires* (Paris: Presses Universitaires de Reims, 2008).

[69] The opposites are called 'the twins' in the *Theaetetus*, 156, a.

[70] Raine, 261–64. Heracles is mentioned several times in Yeats's work (for example in *Ex* 70 and 330) and always in connection with Homer's description of his two 'eternities' in *Odyssey*.

[71] *Les Ecoles Présocratiques*, ed. Jean-Paul Dumont (Paris, Gallimard, 1991), 791.

[72] According to the Pre-Socratic philosopher Prodikos, Heracles is also involved in another antinomy which obviously relates to the more famous one: this is the choice between Vice and Virtue, a dilemma which is pictured in the Tarot key number 6, deceptively called 'The Lovers'. This card, apparently representing a man

13th Cone does seem an appropriate choice for Yeats's principle of immortality. Indeed, Heracles' struggle through life emblematizes the central figures of the system: the two dichotomies and the immortality which transcends them, vortices and sphere. Thus, it often seems to the reader that Yeats's system, if admittedly difficult, is 'indeed is nothing new' (*AVA* xi), [73] and the uppermost irony might be that the alleged instructors do not, in fact, instruct Yeats at all. After all, supernal knowledge comes from the daimon, the instructors repeatedly observe, and the revelations might conceivably emanate from Yeats's or his wife's daimons, in other words from themselves (*AVB* 22). This could account for the fact that the concluding poem, 'All Souls' Night', was composed prior to *A Vision*,[74] a probable hint that Yeats knew it all before. This interpretation seems corroborated at the very beginning of the Prologue, when Yeats, gazing at Rapallo in the sunlight, comments enigmatically: 'the mountain road from Rapallo to Zoagli seems like something in my own mind, something that I have discovered' (*AVB* 7).

To conclude, in this abyss of reverberation, everything is linked to everything else and the two major themes of history and biography, art and love, are inextricably bound up with the esoteric teachings Yeats never completely relinquished.[75] Such doctrine being, by definition, occult, it is sometimes not clear whether Yeats is mocking himself or merely pretending to do so, while making sport of his reader. In the end, the jest seems to be at the reader's expense for the necessary silence of the adept will compel Yeats to produce an abstruse text interspersed with a few clues as he, in fact, re-writes an ancient system, passed off as a new revelation.

---

hesitating between two women, actually depicts Heracles selecting one of the two possible ways of life. See *Les Ecoles Présocratiques*, 944 and Introduction, LIX.

[73] Even the two calendars, lunar and solar, can be traced to the ancient calendars of Antiquity with exactly the same features that characterize Yeats's two cycles: the lunar calendar of 28 days presided over secular activities and work in the fields, whereas the solar calendar of 12 months ruled the civic and religious feast days. Thus the Romans had two calendars which overlapped: their lunar year started in March while their solar year began in January. *Dictionnaire de l'Antiquité* (Paris: Robert Laffont, 1993). 170–71.

[74] Adams, 151.

[75] We know from Yeats's letters that he still frequented Cabalists in 1929: 'I go … to the west of England to look up a little group of Kabalists … I must meet an old Kabalist in London' (*L* 770). Furthermore, as Kathleen Raine recalls, 'Yeats continued his association with the Rosicrucian *Stella Matutina* to the end of its existence in 1923', 398.

Yet, for those of us who are willing to meet the challenge, the Prologue to *A Vision* is a rewarding text which is fundamentally about freedom.[76] Under the guise of self-derision and irony, the reader is taught a valuable lesson about a sort of liberation which does not simply spell out rebellion against the dictates of learned esotericism. The Prologue states that the whole system of antithesis (personal and historical) works around freedom *from* and subjection *to* the exterior world. If we bear this in mind, it becomes possible to redefine Yeats's two antinomies upon which the whole system is founded: Love (primary) and War (antithetical).[77] The point is not so much to oppose love and war in the conventional sense, for, here, we see that anaemic love stories emulating *Axel* (Denise de L'Isle Adam) fare little better than charity or reforming zeal (Maud Gonne, Ezra Pound and Mr. Bell). Conversely, an age of war could not possibly exclude heroic love, the kind of love that is an incentive to art: Mary Bell's strange achievement in the fictitious account, George Yeats's mending of the poet's heart in the real one. The fundamental antinomy is best defined through the distinction Yeats himself had established in *Per Amica Silentia Lunae* (*Myth* 337). The choice lies between losing oneself (love or fate), or finding oneself (war or destiny),[78] hence the insistence on biography as a preliminary step towards initiation: 'I begin to study the only self that I can know, myself and to wind the thread upon the pern again' (*Myth* 364). Indeed, as Farag notes, 'the poet's study of esoteric sciences taught him that just as common metals can be transmuted into gold when subjected to the alchemical fire, the human soul can, on the metaphysical level, be transformed into an imperishable spirit'.[79] This interior war (biography) necessarily alters our interaction with

---

[76] As Helmling shrewdly observes, Yeats's 'motive [in writing *A Vision*] was surely to enlarge freedom', 210.

[77] The distinction is based on Empedocles' two opposing principles: Discord and Concord, as Yeats explicitly states (*AVB* 20 and 67–68). For Empedocles' theory, see *Les Ecoles Présocratiques*, Empédocle B, 185–247. Yeats uses Empedocles' vortex and terminology but without embracing the latter's philosophy of Love as the superior way.

[78] George Mills Harper notes the 'unusual distinction between destiny and fate [that] runs throughout the script' (*MYV1* 82). Another way of phrasing this opposition is chance and choice, a recurring Yeatsian motif which is elaborated upon in stanza 6 of the concluding poem, 'All Souls' Night' (*AVB* 304).

[79] Farag, 18.

the exterior world (history), as Farag further expounds: 'The human mind therefore is the battleground ... and the outcome of this tragic war is the heroic choice that shapes and is the cause of the war that ensues between man and his age'.[80] Robartes' final injunction illustrates this heroic discipline: 'Test art, morality, custom, thought, by Thermopylae; make rich and poor act so to one another that they can stand together there' (*AVB* 52). Thermopylae is Yeats's last word on charity, moral or political entanglements, and a warning to Ezra Pound, Maud Gonne and all other would-be reformers.[81] Love in the sense of charity fails for it enslaves men and does not make them greater than they are; whereas war understood as war against oneself, interiorized war, is the liberating as well as the aggrandizing principle. Indeed, when faced with the unbearable, the tragic object which cannot be removed, we still have one freedom to call our own: either to remain acted upon in passive misery, or to embrace the insufferable as our destiny, thereby creating our mask. Thus, liberation is not brought about by a vain attempt to alter exterior circumstances; liberation comes from within, from a deliberate effort to change one's self.[82] Bearing these considerations in mind, we can now fully appreciate Heraclitus' cryptic pronouncement on war and the fascination it always held for Yeats: 'War is God of all and Father of all, some it has made Gods and some men, some bond and some free'.[83] This insistence on freedom as opposed to bondage brings to mind the three stages in the initiation of the adept: bondage (fate), choice (destiny) and freedom (Yeats's 13th cone or sphere),[84] otherwise known as the alchemical '*perfectio, contemplatio, libertas*'.[85] The Spartans at Thermopylae reached the second stage of the initiation and met their destiny, but Heracles exemplifies the third stage, as Yeats pointedly recalls in his very last address to the reader:

---

[80] *Ibid.*, 12.

[81] Thermopylae may also be alluded to in the poem 'Crazy Jane on God' (*VP* 512).

[82] Identical with the Self of the Upanishads, as Kathleen Raine explains in *Yeats the Initiate*, 398.

[83] This is fragment 53 (Diels), quoted *in extenso* by Yeats in Burnet's translation (*AVB* 82).

[84] The three steps of this spiritual progress are aptly summed up in Edouard Schuré's *Les grands initiés* (Paris: Librairie Académique Perrin, 1960), 432. Schuré (1841–1929) was a theosophist and well acquainted with Helena Blavatsky, Rudolf Steiner and Annie Besant. However, there is no proof that he ever met Yeats.

[85] *Yeats's Iconography*, 65.

Shall we follow the image of Heracles that walks through the darkness bow in hand, or mount to that other Heracles, man, not image, he that has for his bride Hebe, 'The Daughter of Zeus the mighty and Hera shod with gold'?' (*AVB* 302)

A Vision and Yeats's Late Masks

Margaret Mills Harper

A MASK seems a stable thing, an artificial and fixed image to fit over a mobile human face. In trying to make sense of the concept of the Mask in Yeats's long creative and intellectual practice, however, a sort of Dorian Gray-like difficulty arises. The image itself does not stay still. Some of the shifts in the idea of the Mask in Yeats's work and thought, and the implications of these changes, are the topics of this essay. My main emphasis will be on the shifts that occur between the two versions of *A Vision*, that is, between the idea roughly as Yeats conceived it in the early 1920s and in the late 1920s to the publication date of the second *A Vision* in 1937. These years saw a large revision of a concept that had, as most readers know, energized him for many years. Generally speaking, Yeats's Mask before the critical year of 1917 is an intellectual formulation bound tightly to an emotional issue, the problem of self-consciousness. Thus, as Terence Brown remarks, 'An insecure hold on personal identity had always been an aspect of Yeats's experience'.[1] The sense that one is always playing a role was of course elaborated with the help of Yeats's intense engagements with the theatre and esoteric ritual. The dramatic quality of literary form is the other driving factor for Yeats's early elaborations of the Mask. Yeats was keenly aware of the performativity of the lyric voice, not to mention authorial stances and voice in other verbal genres, be they fiction, autobiographical prose, critical essays, or rhetorical acts like speeches and campaigns waged in the pages of newspapers.

---

[1] Terence Brown, *The Life of W. B. Yeats: A Critical Biography* (London: Blackwell, 1999), 171.

In the midst of the crises that led to the watershed year of 1916, Yeats's work grapples with dissolutions of clear boundaries, between the personal and social selves of the poet, as well as within those very selves: whom one loves and what love means in the midst of multiple proposals of marriage, what national identity may be as a split nation forms in a fractured society; what an artist may be and do in the context of a continent in the midst of a Great War and associated cataclysmic changes, and so forth. The Mask was still useful, though the conceptual structures that underpin it in this period owe much to his and George Yeats's extensive experiences with their automatic writing and related occult practices, which provide a way to express a new possibility: not only are public, private, and group selves co-dependent, but all of these versions of self-conscious life arise on some level from a mysterious place that can be intuited only through the failure of the myth of self. In those places lives something lacking form or even presence and so nearly indescribable. It might be expressed as an existential emptiness or a multiplicity of images, or both. The consciousness that jumps from one possibility to the other in the attempt to reconstruct a coherent self does so out of a strong propulsion that Yeats usually calls will, desire, passion, or hunger. As he puts it in 'Anima Mundi', the second of the twin essays that comprise the main body of *Per Amica Silentia Lunae* (written in early 1917, published in 1918; *Myth* 317–69, *CW5* 1–33), at certain luminous moments, 'I am in the place where the Daemon is, but I do not think he is with me until I begin to make a new personality, selecting among those images, seeking always to satisfy a hunger grown out of conceit with daily diet; and yet as I write the words "I select", I am full of uncertainty not knowing when I am the finger, when the clay' (*CW5* 31–32).

Neither the portrait nor Dorian, in other words, is stable. As a concept, as Neil Mann outlines in his essay in this collection, the Mask underwent a fundamental change after 1917 and the arrival of the automatic script. One of the most salient reasons for this change in the terminology is the doubled creativity at the heart of the system of *A Vision*, which shifted Yeats's sense of writerly possibility in radical ways.[2] The voice in the script and other experiments

---

[2] Janis Tedesco Haswell has analysed the gendering of the daimon and mask, a crucial aspect of this change, which, in her words, 'elevates the mask from an aesthetic construct to an explicitly gendered psychodrama' (*Pressed Against Divinity* [DeKalb, IL: Northern Illinois University Press, 1997]), 4.

that developed the system is, after all, voices – plural, not singular. Despite his collaborations with Lady Gregory and the fundamentally collective enterprises that are book or magazine publishing and especially theatrical production, no work with others had touched on such a deep level the question of the individual subject itself, and thus no such work had raised the same questions of polyvalence and agency. The automatic script documents the challenges of not merely the rare and momentary act of making a 'new personality' out of multiple images and feeling unsure when 'I am the finger, when the clay': now these were daily tasks.

The earlier concept of the Mask, resonating with influences of Wilde and Nietzsche, may be summed up most succinctly using the term anti-self, as Yeats does in 'Anima Hominis', the first essay in *Per Amica Silentia Lunae*, as well as the poem 'Ego Dominus Tuus', printed as an introduction to *Per Amica*. The later concept is best seen in terms of the system, which places it both in terms of its other, Will, and also as part of a quaternary of specialised terms (Will, Mask, Creative Mind, and Body of Fate) representing parts of the psyche, or indeed, as Yeats notes, 'every completed movement of thought or life' (*AVB* 81). Especially in the 1925 version of *A Vision*, some sense remains of the earlier notion, though the sense of an anti-self or other is largely taken over by the term Daimon. The question that concerns me is what happened next.

In examining what happened to the Mask between 1925 and 1937, I hope to suggest some of the issues that were at stake as Yeats revised *A Vision*. This task, or set of many tasks, involved reworking a set of ideas that started in a deeply intimate experience, steeped in what he was later to call 'miracle', and that ended in a public form suitable for a global readership.[3] He performed its concepts and conceptualised the performance that is at its core. Attending to changes in Yeats's self-presentation from the 1920s through the 1930s, decades

---

[3] Between the 1925 *A Vision* and the 1937 text, in addition to drafts and other unpublished material, and in addition too to ideas worked out and published in various texts from *Autobiographies to Wheels and Butterflies*, two publications in particular include material that would be incorporated into the later book: the Cuala Press editions of *A Packet for Ezra Pound* (Dublin, 1929; *Wade* 163) and *Stories of Michael Robartes and His Friends* (Dublin, 1931; *Wade* 167). For analyses of the former, see Catherine E. Paul, 'Compiling A Packet for Ezra Pound', *Paideuma* 38 (2011), 29–53; and Catherine E. Paul, 'A Vision of Ezra Pound', in *W. B. Yeats's 'A Vision': Explications and Contexts*, ed. Neil Mann, Matthew Gibson, and Claire V. Nally (Clemson, SC: Clemson University Digital Press, 2012), 252–69.

in which he took highly contentious positions on European politics, aesthetics, and philosophy, requires understanding differences between the 1925 and 1937 *A Vision* (*AVA* and *AVB*). My hope is that this essay will point to the degree to which Yeats in his late period was concerned not only to depict but very much also to enact. When we read his outlandish late poses, whether of a crazed man preaching racial politics on a boiler, a scarecrow pretending to be a distinguished and smiling public man, a lover of rich women who were to varying degrees oriented sexually towards men, or an Irish nationalist who has substituted for Celtic culture Indian philosophy, we should remember this conviction of enactment of ideas. His late works consistently insist that one cannot know without doing: identity is inherently part of a structural system that is constantly in motion and unavailable if one is not enmeshed in its patterns. We believe in ourselves, Yeats suggests, but it is crucial to know that we both invent and inhabit them: it is ourselves that we make and remake.

A Vision, which presents a symbolic and theoretical 'system' of psychology, history, culture, and the many lives of the soul, is especially handy for illustration of this point. First, the psychology, history, cultural identity, and soul Yeats presents in *A Vision* are those of the author of the book at the same time as they are the ambitiously large-scaled system. *A Vision* is symbolic autobiography as well as general philosophy. In fact, this double stance, in which the subject is very personal as well as distantly impersonal, is demanded by the main ideas of the book. The system insists that oppositions between subjectivity and objectivity, the inner being of the self and the seemingly unrelated external world, are illusions. One overarching set of symbols always reaches down as well as up, spiralling in and out simultaneously. Everything is caught in it, including book, author, and reader.

The second reason *A Vision* provides an especially useful text is of course that although it is true to say *A Vision* is a book, it is also a bit misleading to talk about *A Vision* in the singular, since in important ways it is not one book but two. In terms of genetic materials, the first *Vision* began as an occult experiment in automatic writing between W. B. Yeats and his wife George Hyde Lees, a private ritual between two newly married partners, in late 1917. The second *Vision* ended over twenty years later as the poet sent the 1937 version to Macmillan in London and Charles Scribner's Sons in New York so the book could be reset as one volume of deluxe editions of his

complete works. (Neither of those editions was ever published, and whatever final changes Yeats [or his wife] made to the book are lost.)
If we put these two observations, that *A Vision* is a symbolic autobiography and that it is two books rather than one, into the same frame, the reasons for looking between them for the Mask is clear. If *A Vision* is the performance of a self, and there are two *Visions*, then it follows that Yeats plays the roles of two authorial personae in it/them.[4]

PERSONAE

The first *Vision*-ary Yeats is the more overtly unstable of the two. The structures and rhetoric of the book show traces of the esoteric genesis of it all, in the automatic writing that started on the Yeatses' honeymoon. To summarise a set of events that has been described many times, within a month or two, Yeats decided that what was arriving in the daily sessions was a philosophical system and that he should give it organized expression. He began crafting a dialogue between his fictional characters Michael Robartes and Owen Aherne, resurrected for the purpose from the 1890s, then switched to a core of expository prose for the philosophy itself, embedded in a fantastic semi-hoax in the best fictional fashion. An introduction by Aherne tells the story of how he and Robartes gave their old friend Yeats an esoteric manuscript to edit.

Yeats's regular trade publisher, Macmillan of London, had little interest in a book as strange as this one, even by one of the writers in its stable it could usually count on for sales, and even in the 1920s (when a number of other very strange books and other works of art were appearing in high modernist modes). Luckily, T. Werner Laurie, a small-scale, quirky publisher in London, took it on, as he had an instalment of Yeats's autobiography a few years earlier, and despite some confusion. His correspondence sometimes strikes an anxious tone, as when he wrote to Yeats's agent A. P. Watt to ask, 'As no-one here has the faintest idea as to what the book is about do you think you could coax Yeats to write me a descriptive paragraph of it for my

---

[4] For a study that focuses on the authorial character 'Yeats' in *A Vision* (though almost exclusively in *AVB*), see Hazard Adams, *The Book of Yeats's 'Vision': Romantic Modernism and Antithetical Tradition* (Ann Arbor: University of Michigan Press, 1995).

Catalogue? I wish you would try.'⁵ Laurie finally reduced the print run of 1000 copies to 600 lovely, signed, expensive books.

When *A Vision* was published in January 1926, it offered itself to the public as a kind of art book, an aestheticised artifact by a poet and playwright known for highly stylized poses. Faux-Renaissance woodcuts inside were reminiscent of fine press books like those of the Kelmscott Press. Here was something to puzzle over, engage with and perhaps baffled by, the way one would read T. S. Eliot's *Waste Land* or listen to Stravinsky's *Rite of Spring*. The semiotic of the first version of *A Vision* seemed to suggest that it was a sort of skeleton key that would explain some of the forces at work in the autobiography, *The Trembling of the Veil*, which had been published in book form in 1922, just a few years earlier. It contains references to ideas and terms from the system, as does some of the poetry and drama that had been appearing in periodicals, collections, and on the stage from 1919 forward.

The 1920s is the context for this *Vision*. The Yeats who is its author is the writer looked to more than any other for articulation of some of the extreme pressures of the decade in Irish political and social life, including of course years of war and civil war. This is the Yeats who is a Senator in the new Free State, who wins the Nobel Prize, who will shortly publish majestic and powerful work like *The Tower* and *The Winding Stair*. However, *A Vision* seems to want to enact a different narrative. This Yeats seems actively to be opposing his own stature. *A Vision* is filled with arcane jargon, difficult diagrams, and a very curious rhetoric that seems to take itself very seriously and at the same time be laughing at some private joke. Its author is someone immersed in art and magic, who conducts elaborate, even baroque, experiments in genre, style, and form. He is also sometimes in command of his material and sometimes seemingly overwhelmed by it, so that the book acts out a wobbly, dynamic performance. It is modernist and esoteric.

After it was published, Yeats began to rewrite, or rather to prepare to rewrite, by undertaking a mammoth course in reading. In the late 1920s and early 1930s, he read philosophy from the pre-Socratic philosophers through Neoplatonism through George Berkeley through Hegel to contemporary thinkers like Benedetto Croce and George Moore, revisiting old friends like Plotinus

---

⁵ Letter from T. Werner Laurie to A. P. Watt, 12 October 1923, *CL InteLex* 4380.

and Nietzsche along the way. He read history from Herodotus to Gibbon to Toynbee and art history from Ruskin to Henry Adams to Josef Strzygowski. He studied religion from *The Golden Bough* by Sir James Frazer, to entries on calendars, astrology, and Byzantine theology in the *Encyclopaedia of Religion and Ethics* he bought with the money from the Nobel Prize. With the help of George Yeats (and her proficiency in French) he dived into the multi-volume history of science by French mathematician Pierre Duhem; with the help of Lady Gregory he revisited collected folklore and Roman and Greek classics in her library. And he wrote and rewrote much of *A Vision*, finally producing in 1937 a book by the same title as the first one but with about two-thirds made up of new material.

The author of *AVB* poses as someone confidently in command of things, at home in a wide and sophisticated intellectual world, and in no need of ornamentation for its own sake. For example, in the first third of the book, a sort of grab-bag of material extraneous to the philosophical sections, an introduction tells the story of the automatic script openly, rather than in the fantastic hoax of the first edition. An open letter to fellow resident of Rapallo Ezra Pound discusses Yeats's frustrations as a Senator for the Free State – the sort of frustration one can only throw around if one is a Senator, of course. (By contrast, the 1925 *A Vision* was dedicated to Moina Mathers, one of Yeats's old friends and fellow members of the Hermetic Order of the Golden Dawn – and not to her openly but to 'Vestigia', her secret motto in the Order.) A story filling out the pages includes Michael Robartes and Owen Aherne as openly fictional characters. Though the plot of *Stories of Michael Robartes and His Friends* is outrageous and the tone ambiguously tongue-in-cheek, it is at least labelled as 'stories', rather than the tales of Robartes meeting up with Arab tribesmen who dance mysterious designs on the desert floor, which the 1925 author gives his readers with a deceptively straight face. The philosophical chapters of the 1937 edition have been smoothed out, seemingly logical explanations replacing imagistic and poetic examples. Authoritative names are dropped, footnotes added that pile up even more citations. The magically inclined acsthete, often confused but always intense, of the 1925 book has been replaced by someone who wears a more worldly, slightly pompous air.

The 1937 author has also partly relaxed into his own narrow place in the grander schemes. Rather than trying and failing to give successful explanations of the very confusing philosophy, this authorial voice is at war with himself: part of him accepts his own limited ability to see past his own location on the wheels of the system. Part of him pushes against this acceptance and (somewhat artificially) props up his engagement and energy with reading and having strong opinions about the latest work on subjects germane to the business at hand, such as idealist philosophy and art history. The two sides of the 1937 Mask, push and counter-push, can be seen through the inherent contrast between two sets of ideas that underpin much of the new material of the book. The push can be seen in comments about, for example, contemporary commentators on Hegel, including modern philosophical arguments like those of J. M. E. McTaggart, Bertrand Russell, and G. E. Moore. This push cites and engages with cultural historians like Otto Spengler or art historians like the National Socialist Josef Strzygowski on questions of grand movements in history, including ominous references to the coming 'new order'. The counter-push can be seen in citations of the working-class 'tramp' poet W. H. Davies, Patanjali and the Yoga Sutras he composed, Daisetzu Suzuki's discussion of Zen Buddhism, or Stephen MacKenna's wonderful translation of Plotinus. These and other sources in this counter-push lean toward a state that seems static if viewed from the outside but moving and flexible if experienced from within. The point is that the Yeats of the 1937 *Vision* is in self-contradiction, part pushing urgently towards the new ideas that he believes are definitive of the next age, part pushing against into intellectual and spiritual dimensions that offer an enticing distance from definition itself.

FORM

The shift in the concept of the Mask in the two versions of *A Vision*, not only the roles assumed by the authorial presences of the two books, may be seen by reviewing some of the structural differences between them. To some degree, of course, *A Vision* is *A Vision*: the system is fundamentally the same in both books. Yet the books themselves are quite different from each other, in presentation and structure. These changes mirror important alterations in Yeats's thinking in the important decade or so during which he was working on the revisions. The altered emphasis, and the structure in which that emphasis can be perceived, may be seen in texts beyond *A Vision*, as well, as might be expected: Yeats used *A Vision* in part as a quarry of ideas and images for use in his other work. Yeats's last Masks are formed not so much by an emphasis on either self or anti-self, nor the unity formed out of their opposition, but by the need of the one for the other, and the importance of not looking for or finding any state of rest beyond that need. In a seeming non sequitur in the 1937 *A Vision*, a section describes the relation between cone (representing movement and time) and sphere (representing stasis and timelessness), Yeats quotes from Sir Walter Scott's translation of the Hermetica: '"Eternity also", says Hermes in the Aeslepius dialogue, "though motionless itself, appears to be in motion".[6] The point being underscored, in a circuitous fashion, is found in the section of the Latin dialogue from which Yeats quotes: that even these purest of principles require each other. Movement is still, and stillness is in motion. Hermes Trismegistus explains to Asclepius that time itself, though 'ever in movement, possesses a faculty of stability' because it operates according to rules, an 'ordered course'. Similarly, eternity 'enters into time' because it has a relation to it. It follows that even God 'also moves with himself'. All is 'circular movement'.[7] As Crazy Jane would say, 'nothing can be sole or whole | That has not been rent' (*VP* 513). Yeats's late Masks embody the need for aesthetic as well as spiritual and political control in restless cohabitation with an urge toward wildness, wickedness, and submission to chaos.

Between *AVA* and *AVB* has occurred a change from presentation of the occult system in a more or less present tense, despite the preoccupation of the ideas generally with moving gyres of history and the progress of the soul from incarnation to incarnation. By and large, in 1925, the philosophy is presented statically. In terms of voice, the author of the book is caught in the gyres and often confused by them, but he speaks as if the material itself emanates from a still, stable point of view. As Yeats writes in the concluding pages, his hope is that his book might restore the sense that 'every condition of mind discovered by analysis, even that which is timeless, spaceless, is present vivid experience to some being, and that we could in some degree communicate with this being while still alive, and after our death share in the experience' (*AVA*

---

[6] The quotation is from the Latin Asclepius (not Aeslepius) III.31: *Hermetica. The Ancient Greek and Latin writings which contain religious or philosophic teaching ascribed to Hermes Trismegistus*, ed. and trans. Walter Scott, 3 vols. (Oxford: Clarendon Press, 1924–1936), I.351–53; *YL* 881.

[7] Asclepius III.30–32a, *Hermetica* I.351–55.

207). By 1937, somewhat paradoxically since the author of the book understands the system much more thoroughly than he does in the 1925 version, many more tags implying mobility dot the pages. The acknowledgement of the origin of the system in George Yeats's automatic writing, in the introduction, allows Yeats to loosen the propositional stance into a pose that acknowledges change, in levels of understanding, in ways of describing things, and even in the degree of command of the instructors themselves. He even notes the presence of Frustrators (who tell lies instead of imparting truths) and partiality even of the truthful spirits: 'Those who taught me this system did so, not for my sake, but their own' (*AVB* 12–14, 234).

By the 1937 publication, the suggestion of a still point beyond the turning gyres has become more complex, with the possibility lessened of attaining a final resolution or escape from the wheel. Much has been made by many perceptive readers of the Thirteenth Cone (or Cycle, or Sphere) in the 1937 *A Vision*, a concept that receives much more emphasis there than in the 1925 text. To many, the Thirteenth Cone in the later *Vision* has seemed a promised liberation from the soul's entrapment in endless predestined cycles of reincarnation.[8] To some degree, such readings are justified: the concept is described in salvific language, as when Yeats writes that the Thirteenth Cycle 'is that cycle which may deliver us from the twelve cycles of time and space', in which 'live all souls that have been set free and every Daimon and Ghostly Self' (*AVB* 210–11), or which 'is in every man and called by every man his freedom' (302). The last is an especially resonant passage, coming as it does on the concluding page of the text proper, in a section called 'The End of the Cycle'. However, the concept of the Thirteenth Cone is misread as a geometric replacement for an idea of God or eternity, as Neil Mann has recently shown.[9]

Larger structures of the 1937 text also fail to support such a rhetoric of salvation. For example, the introductory fictions of the 1925 book depict obviously fake sources for the system in mysterious rituals and a sacred book, both of which understand the system even if 'Yeats', a character in the fictions, does not. In the 1937 book,

---

[8] For a survey of criticism, see Ron Heisler, 'Yeats and the Thirteenth Æon', *YA13* 241–52. For a comprehensive and nuanced analysis of the concept, see Neil Mann, 'The Thirteenth Cone', in *W. B. Yeats's 'A Vision': Explications and Contexts*, 159–93.

[9] Mann, 'The Thirteenth Cone'.

these fictions have been supplemented by the autobiographical introduction (which renders the recitation of the earlier account an overtly revealed hoax rather than a thinly veiled one), as well as stories of the strange crew of characters engaged in bizarre activities that roughly enact the concepts of the system. Rather than knowing and dancing the meanings of it all, as do the Judwali tribespeople from the 1925 version, Michael Robartes and his friends are caught up in doing very odd things (including, as an utterly outlandish final item in a strange series of acts, incubating a lost egg of Leda), which they do not understand. These late stories demonstrate the principle Yeats famously described in one of his last letters: 'I am happy and I think full of energy of an energy I had despaired of. It seems to me that I have found what I wanted. When I try to put all into a phrase I say "Man can embody the truth but he cannot find it". I must embody it in the completion of my life. The abstract is not life and everywhere draws out its contradictions. You can refute Hegel but not the saint or the song of sixpence ...'.[10] In other words, readers encounter a relatively thorough account of the automatic script, as well as two other origin stories. There is both more and less: the author clearly has a better purchase on the material, but the presentation is also destabilized by the multiplicity of narratives.

Other formal aspects also work against a sense of solid footing. Inside the framing material, the 1925 text has four books, a neat foursquare structure. Inside this architecture, however, Book II in particular is a sort of grab-bag of concepts culled from the automatic script and notebooks, attempting to describe a number of the further complexities of the system beyond essays describing each of the lunar Phases. In 1937, the seeming neatness of the earlier structure has become an uneven set of five Books. The messy Book II has been replaced by two Books, one describing the further geometries (Book II, 'The Completed Symbol') and one focusing just on the Great Year, that is, the larger cycles in which the historical cones are themselves embedded (Book IV, 'The Great Year of the Ancients'). Regarded in terms of a readerly experience, occurring in time, the 1937 *A Vision* implies a movement from one Book to another that mirrors

---

[10] Letter to Lady Elizabeth Pelham, 4 January 1939, cited in Ann Saddlemyer, *Becoming George: The Life of Mrs W. B. Yeats* (Oxford: Oxford University Press, 2002), 559. Cf. *CL InteLex* 7363, *L* 922. On the issue of exact wording, see also my *Wisdom of Two: The Spiritual and Literary Collaboration of George and W. B. Yeats* (Oxford: Oxford University Press, 2006), 264, n. 25.

the intellectual shuttling between multiplicity and unity, many and one, that is stressed in the exposition of the ideas themselves. Thus, Book I, with a description of each lunar Phase, dominated by the influences of the four Faculties, is followed by Book II, an account of the larger view of the discarnate Principles. Next, Book III, detailing the progress of the individual soul from incarnation to incarnation, is followed in Book IV by an explanation of the large structure that decrees how often such returns occur. Then, the text finishes with a finer-grained analysis of the latest eras of western cultural history, Book V ('Dove or Swan'), which was Book III of the 1925 text. Smaller structures operate with a similar sense of alternation: Books I, III, and V move in linear patterns, from one numbered Phase, one state between lives, or one historical period to the next. Books II and IV are organized in numbered sections, but the sections often jump from one idea to the next with little sense that they could not be reordered without any loss of logical progression.

THE RESURRECTION

Part of the point of the long disquisition in AVB on the ancient concept of the Platonic or Great Year, on which Yeats worked energetically especially between 1928 and 1930,[11] has to do with how to measure the larger cycles in which the eras and their gyres

---

[11] It is difficult to date with any precision when Yeats revised sections of the body of *A Vision*. As Connie K. Hood notes, few of the more than a thousand pages of manuscript and typescript drafts of *A Vision* are dated. Some extraction of dates can be made, however, and Hood's account remains the most complete: Connie K. Hood, 'The Remaking of *A Vision*', *YAACTS* 1 (1983), 33–67. Other evidence also exists. Between 1928 and 1930, Yeats left traces of his work on the Great Year, for example, in the notes he made in the Rapallo D notebook (NLI 13,581). These notes include information about the Indian Great Year from Sepharial [Walter Gorn Old], *Hebrew Astrology: The Key to the Study of Prophecy* (London: W. Foulsham, 1929), 61. Yeats also wrote in the margins of his copy of A. E. Taylor's *A Commentary on Plato's 'Timaeus'* (Oxford: Clarendon Press, 1928; YL 2107), the Platonic dialogue most concerned with the Great Year. The introduction to *The Resurrection*, one of the essays appended to a set of late plays that comprise the volume *Wheels and Butterflies*, also treats the topic in confident terms. This essay was begun, according to John Kelly, in late 1930: John Kelly, *A W. B. Yeats Chronology* (London: Palgrave Macmillan, 2003), 271. On 27 Dec 1930, Yeats mentions 'Wheels and Butterflies (a book of plays & essays all most finished)' and 'putting the last touches to a play called "The Resurrection"' (*CL InteLex* 5428).

are set. Yeats had set out an outline of the last set of gyres, our own era, in Book III of *AVA*, which is placed as the last book (V) of *AVB*. (The ending of this book, in other words, the question of what to do about the present moment, gave him great trouble, but that is another story.[12]) It is apparent in some of the creative texts from this period that the Great Year, or Magnus Annus, was at the front of Yeats's imagination. For example, the play *The Resurrection*, begun in 1925 as 'a sort of overflow from the book' (the newly finished *AVA*), as Yeats wrote Lady Gregory,[13] was reworked considerably, in at least two drafts between its first publication in The Adelphi in June 1927 and two more on the way to a later, definitive version, first published in the Cuala Press volume *Stories of Michael Robartes and His Friends* in 1931 (both versions are presented on facing pages in *VPl*, 900–36).[14] The revisions work toward several aims. One is straightforwardly theatrical: to make the play more dramatic. By and large, this aim is achieved: by the final version there is less talk and more action than in the earlier versions, and the talk that remains is often in the nature of teichoscopy, the synchronous recitation of events happening offstage (notably a Dionysian ritual including self-mutilation, re-enacting the death of the god, described in horror by the Greek). As Curtis Bradford puts it, Yeats had set himself the difficult task in this play 'to dramatize a theological argument', about three different conceptions of the nature of Christ, symbolized by means of three characters. By the final version, according to Bradford, Yeats had succeeded in making 'a much better play'.[15]

The revisions also parallel the revisions Yeats was working out in *A Vision*, in which it is both possible to measure, with some precision, large cyclical forces, as seen from a distance, and at the same time necessary to live ecstatically, momentarily, in an intensity that is the hunger or wildness that drives even

---

[12] I have told one version of the story in '"The clock has run down and must be wound up again": *A Vision* in Time', *Yeats and Afterwords*, ed. Marjorie Howes and Joseph Valente (South Bend, IN: Notre Dame University Press, 2013, forthcoming).

[13] 11 May 1925, *CL InteLex* 4725.

[14] In *Yeats at Work* (Carbondale and Edwardsville: Southern Illinois University Press, 1965), Curtis Bradford examines unpublished versions of the play, including two scenarios, two manuscript versions composed before the *Adelphi* printing, and two manuscript versions written in 1930, in advance of the Cuala *Stories* (237–67).

[15] *Ibid.*, 238, 267.

the greatest cyclical patterns. (We might notice that a number of poems being composed during this period, collected in *The Winding Stair and Other Poems* and *A Full Moon in March*, express similar convictions.) The early Resurrection is shaped by the system, but its intellectual scaffolding is more static. In the early version of the play, the three characters represent a regular triangle of ideas. The first character, the Hebrew, a sensualist, represents one cone of a cultural gyre. He believed Jesus was the promised Messiah but is now filled with doubt, remorse, and despair (as was Judas, a parallel that explains why a good deal of discussion about Judas is placed in the first scene). The Hebrew declares of Christ that 'There is only one sensible thing to say; He deceived Himself and us, maddened by His love – and He is dead' (*VPl* 926). The second character, the Egyptian, an Alexandrian and therefore 'almost a Greek' (*Ibid.*), although as interested as the Hebrew in driving out the Greek overlords from his homeland, believes in the power of the image, not the flesh. He prophesies the rise of the edifice of Christianity ('If we but fix our faith upon that image, men in times to come will lay upon their altars, a splinter of the Cross whereon it seemed to have been nailed, and some Roman Emperor attribute his victories to the nail that he has made into the bit of his horse' [*VPl* 918]). A god must be an ideal:

> God can communicate with mankind through an illusionary body, such a form as sculptors in my city make for Alexander the Great – no beating, suffering heart, all stone or bronze, as it were, perfect – exactly 6 ft. high, neither more nor less – nothing can be added, nothing taken away and perfect maturity. Christ when he began to preach was exactly thirty years old (*VPl* 924).

The third character, the Syrian, understands the larger pattern; he believes a truth that is impossible for the other two characters, that 'Our Master has risen from the dead' (*VPl* 922). Like other gods 'all over Greece, all over Asia Minor and Magna Grecia, from generation to generation, men have celebrated the death and Resurrection of Attis, or Adonis, or Dionysus, of God under some name or other ... and now ... God has become flesh' (*VPl* 924). The climax of the play occurs when 'The figure of Christ' enters. The Egyptian touches the body he believes cannot be real and speaks the lines that sum up the historical meaning of the event: 'Reason itself is dead. [In a loud voice.] Rome, Greece, Egypt – it has come, the miracle, that which must destroy you, irrational force. The Heart of a Phantom is beating!'.[16]

The final version of the play incorporates a seemingly slight shift. The neat system is enacted as well as described: the characters embody truths as well as knowing them. The Hebrew, in his despair, still thinks of Christ that 'He was nothing more than a man, the best man who ever lived' (*VPl* 909) but mistaken in thinking Himself the Messiah. He is in a way relieved to avoid the consequences of Christ being divine; if that were true, his individual will would have been erased and 'God had to take complete possession' (*VPl* 913). When the figure of Christ appears at the end of the play, then, the Hebrew realises just this destiny: he 'backs in terror' toward the corner of the stage, then kneels (*VPl* 929). The Greek, not an Egyptian in this version, believes still that Christ is a phantom, not a corporeal being. He is again given the climactic moment in the play, when he touches the figure of Christ, and the final lines. Now, however, his final speech echoes one of Yeats's favourite sayings, from Heraclitus: 'God and man die each other's life, live each other's death'.[17] The genius of the Greek for access to divinity through abstraction has been attained. To the Syrian belongs the most dramatic change. In this version as in the Adelphi text, he sees that the events take place in a larger framework, responding with rhetorical questions to his fellows, 'What matter if it contradicts all human knowledge? – another Argo seeks another fleece, another Troy is sacked', and 'What if there is always something that lies outside knowledge, outside order? What if at the moment when knowledge and order seem complete that something appears?' (*VPl* 923, 925). In this version, however, a distinctly unsettling moment has been added, when he 'has begun to laugh'. The Greek claims that he 'has lost control of himself', and the Hebrew tells him to stop, but the Syrian does not think he is laughing. He says 'What if the irrational return? What if the circle begin again?'

---

[16] *VPl* 930. This line nearly mirrors the last line of the octave in the sonnet 'Meru', the final poem in the sequence *Supernatural Songs* from the volume *A Full Moon in March*: 'Egypt and Greece good-bye, and good-bye Rome!' (*VP* 563). The tone of this line, from a poem Yeats claimed 'came spontaneously, but philosophy is a dangerous theme' (*VP* 855), is signally difficult to interpret.

[17] *VPl* 931. The translation of Heraclitus frag. 67 is taken from John Burnet, *Early Greek Philosophy* (London: Adam and Charles Black, 1892), which Yeats owned (*YL* 308), 138. See *AVA* (*CW13*) 105 and 270, n. 21. Yeats first referred to this fragment (in a slightly different form) in his journal in 1909 (*Mem* 216). See also *AVB* 275 and *On the Boiler* (*CW5* 227, 234, and 236).

while continuing to laugh, then denies that he is laughing. Drums and rattles occur from the crowd outside, which the Syrian says he thought was laughter, and he exclaims, 'How horrible'! (*VPl* 925). It is unclear whether his horror is at the crowd or his own moment of madness. The play ends as did the earlier version, with a song (the second of 'Two Songs from a Play', as it is entitled in *The Tower* [*VP* 438]), though in the version of the play in *Stories of Michael Robartes and His Friends* (and in the 1933 *Collected Poems*) the song has a second stanza. This final stanza emphasizes not the large patterns of 'Galilean turbulence', 'Babylonian starlight', 'Platonic tolerance', and 'Doric discipline' but the patterns as they appear on the level of personal immediacy, to lover, painter, herald, or soldier. Moreover, human desire is the ultimate cause of all the cosmos: 'Whatever flames upon the night | Man's own resinous heart has fed'.

Not only does the play in its variants demonstrate that Yeats was working on the Great Year while he was composing it, *The Resurrection* suggests that personal issues were at stake for a writer who like his Hebrew feared for the loss of identity in the face of larger spiritual truths; like his Greek strove to find personal meaning in abstractions from a long history of philosophy (beginning with the pre-Socratic thinkers); and like his Syrian found that he had 'mummy truths to tell | Whereat the living mock, | Though not for sober ear, | For maybe all that hear | Should laugh and weep an hour upon the clock' (*VP* 474).

LAST MASK

At the very end of *AVB*, in one of the last composed sections, the author poses as an old man:

Day after day I have sat in my chair turning a symbol over in my mind, exploring all its details, defining and again defining its elements, testing my convictions and those of others by its unity, attempting to substitute particulars for an abstraction like that of algebra. I have felt the convictions of a lifetime melt though at an age when the mind should be rigid, and others take their place, and these in turn give way to others. How far can I accept socialistic or communistic prophecies? I remember the decadence Balzac foretold to the Duchess de Castries. I remember debates in the little coach-house at Hammersmith or at Morris' supper-table afterwards. I remember the Apocalyptic dreams of the Japanese Saint and labour leader Kagawa, whose books were lent me by a Galway clergyman. I remember a

Communist described by Captain White in his memoirs ploughing on the Cotswold Hills, nothing on his great hairy body but sandals and a pair of drawers, nothing in his head but Hegel's Logic. Then I draw myself up into the symbol and it seems as if I should know all if I could but banish such memories and find everything in the symbol (*AVB* 301).

The conflict between rigid convictions, to which Yeats writes he believes he should be attached at his age, and what he calls (in a Blakean term) 'particulars', brings up a list of four 'socialist or communistic prophecies' linked by the rhetorical tag 'I remember'. Uncovering sources for these four memories (as I have been doing as Catherine Paul and I edit *AVB* for the new *Collected Works*) has underscored another permutation of the phenomenon this essay has traced: how Yeats's last Masks are multiple rather than one side of a duality (of self and anti-self), and that they stress not unity though they recognize that yearning for it drives life.[18]

The first item 'I remember', 'the decadence' prophesied to Balzac's sometime amour the Duchesse de Castries, comes from the introduction to one of the volumes of the complete works, a full set of which Yeats owned. The passage, which is written as if to the Duchesse, defines 'the commercial traveller – a being unknown in earlier times' as being symbolic of 'the immense transition which connects the age of material development with that of intellectual development'. The prophecy is of coming barbarism because 'the age of isolated forces rich in original creativeness' is yielding to 'that of the uniform but levelling force which gives monotony to its products, casting them in masses, and following out a unifying idea – the ultimate expression of social communities'.[19] The second reference

---

[18] One key term I have not defined, of course, is 'unity'. In the passage above, the contrast between the unity of the system as a whole is put into opposition with the human being trying to examine it. 'Unity of Being', a term from Dante discussed from early in the automatic script (January 1918) and retained in the presentation of the system through *AVB*, is a state possible to beings in the Phases nearest Phase 15 or Perfect Beauty. Near the end of Book II of *AVB*, Yeats writes, 'My instructors identify consciousness with conflict, not with knowledge, substitute for subject and object and their attendant logic a struggle towards harmony, towards Unity of Being' (214). In this life, in other words, human beings engage in a 'struggle towards harmony', not the attainment of it.

[19] Balzac had a famous infatuation (which ended badly) with Claire Clémence Henriette Claudine de Maillé de La Tour-Landry, the Duchesse de Castries (1796–1861). See the story 'L'Illustre Gaudissart' ('Gaudissart the Great'), which opens *Parisians in the Country*, trans. James Waring (one volume of the Temple reprint of

is to Yeats's apprentice socialism in the 1880s, in Hammersmith at Kelmscott House, under the tutelage of William Morris. The third is to the Japanese Christian labour organiser Toyohiko Kagawa, who was very popular in Protestant theological circles in the early decades of the century (he has been venerated by the Episcopal Church USA and the Lutheran Church, according to one source). I have not identified the 'Galway clergyman', but this may point to an interesting relationship.

The fourth allusion is a strange description of a half-naked Communist ploughing on the Cotswold Hills, preoccupied with Hegel. This reference comes from a vivid depiction of a giant Czech philosopher in an English commune in a memoir by Captain Jack White. White was a Communist organiser from Antrim, who attended Sandhurst and served with the First Gordon Highlanders in the Boer War, then in India and Scotland. He married a Roman Catholic woman, resigned his commission on ethical grounds, travelled (and lived in a Tolstoyan commune), then returned to Ireland, where he agitated for Home Rule in the North, then went south to work with James Larkin in the Dublin Lock-out. It was he who came up with the idea of organising an Irish Citizen Army. He

---

the J. M. Dent complete Comédie Humaine [New York: Macmillan, 1901; *YL* 99]). Dedicated 'To Madame la Duchesse de Castries', it begins:

> Is not the commercial traveller – a being unknown in earlier times – one of the most curious types produced by the manners and customs of this age? And is it not his peculiar function to carry out in a certain class of things the immense transition which connects the age of material development with that of intellectual development? Our epoch will be the link between the age of isolated forces rich in original creativeness, and that of the uniform but levelling force which gives monotony to its products, casting them in masses, and following out a unifying idea – the ultimate expression of social communities. After the Saturnalia of intellectual communism, after the struggles of many civilisations concentrating all the treasures of the world on a single spot, must not the darkness of barbarism invariably supervene?

Yeats refers to the idea of 'history as a personal experience' expressed by 'Balzac in his letter to the Duchess de Castries' in the 'Private Thoughts' section of *On the Boiler* (*CW5* 233). See also Warwick Gould, 'The "myth [in] ... reply to a myth" – Yeats, Balzac, and Joachim of Fiore', *YA5* 238–51; and Warwick Gould, 'A Crowded Theatre: Yeats and Balzac', in *Yeats the European*, ed. A. Norman Jeffares (Savage, MD: Barnes and Noble Books, 1989), 69–90, and 293, n. 6 for additional sources on Yeats and Balzac.

was involved in the 1916 Rising and worked on several leftist causes in the Free State. Chapter 16 of White's memoir *Misfit* describes his experience in Whiteway Colony, a communist experimental community in the Cotswold Hills, including his encounter with Francis Sedlak, 'the only man I have ever met who claimed to have mastered and digested Hegel's logic'.[20]

He had written a book called A Holiday with a Hegelian, which no one on earth but himself could understand. I, as little as any; but I could understand that Francis understood. He had entered a world of pure thought with the key of Hegel's logic that suited him. He retained his giant's body, but he lived in his mind. He was no longer a groundling, but on the road to become a god. He declared he had found a key to the movements of the heavenly bodies in the fifty-two movements of thought in Hegel's logic and could make thereby slight corrections in astronomical calendars (147).

Sedlak's appearance is described by Nellie Shaw ('the lady to whom he once described himself as "married but not legally, my wife objecting to chattel slavery"' [146]) in her own words:

In those days we was pure Communists ... Well, as I was sayin', we was eating our lunch one day when I looked up, and there was the queerest sight comin' along the road ever I seen in all my life; a great 'airy giant of a man as naked as 'is mother made 'im to the waist, and nothing but a pair of running-drawers, and sandals below that (149–50).

Besides the humour of the allusion (added to by the voices of Captain White as well as the quoted Nellie) and the female sexual pleasure that surely also caught Yeats's attention (and are relevant to *A Vision* as well as other late works), this little reference to Captain White's quirky memoir also speaks to the enactment of the Mask. Yeats ends *AVB* by sinking into his symbol, allowing it to release him from his 'memories' and accept the uncertainty, or instability, he describes at the start of the paragraph, when 'I have felt the convictions of a lifetime melt though at an age when the mind should be rigid, and others take their place, and these in turn give

---

[20] Page numbers from Captain Jack White, *Misfit* (London and Toronto: Jonathan Cape, 1930), are cited in the text. See also Leo Keohane, 'Captain Jack White DSO: Anarchist and Proleptic Poststructuralist', in *Voicing Dissent: New Perspectives in Irish Criticism*, ed. Sandrine Brisset and Noreed Doody (Dublin: Irish Academic Press, 2012), 241–51.

way to others'. What are these convictions? We may well wonder. Some, which go back a 'lifetime', are the left-leaning political ideas of Morris and others, which paradoxically accompanied theories of art that posit the authoritative power of the symbol, the artist as something like a magician. Other 'convictions' might of course be right-leaning doctrines that were the topic of much debate in critical circles for several decades (and which still surface in the work of some writers), or the enthusiasm for a 'people's' art that preoccupied Yeats in the 1920s and 30s, in projects like the deceptively simple lyrics of 'Words For Music Perhaps' or the Broadside ballads he produced with his brother Jack. The 'symbol' in the passage quoted above, that of the system of *A Vision* with its relentless oppositions, and Yeats's training in 'drawing myself up' into it, is different from his earlier symbolist theory. The 'unity' in the passage is also not the same as any semi-Fascist political involvement, or indeed the 'unity' castigated by Balzac. Rather, the symbol is recognized as a dynamic mental construct, something that shifts as the mind does. There is play, in the sense of what might be called 'give', in the relationship between the symbol and the mind of the writer, but this is hardly ironic detachment. The dominant emotions are a struggle between humility and pride, acceptance, even of ruin, alternating with engagement and approval of those who are passionately involved, even of bringing that ruin. This dramatised late Mask enacts concepts and convictions that I hope will receive more attention.

The *Mask* of *A Vision*

Neil Mann

IN HIS REVIEW of the first edition of *A Vision* AE found it 'so concentrated, the thought which in other writers would be expanded into volumes, is here continually reduced to bare essences', and indeed establishing a clear idea about any element of the System often entails teasing out the implications from 'its crammed pages' and gathering together comments scattered throughout the volume.[1] On the one hand a clear understanding of even the key concepts is difficult to achieve, while on the other hand any understanding involves a whole context of other elements, linked in turn to other aspects of the System so that the connecting threads recede indefinitely; as Yeats commented in a letter to Iseult Gonne: 'I wish I could tell you what has come but it is all so vast & one part depends upon another'.[2] Consequently, even a relatively straightforward term that underwent no major revisions, such as the *Mask*, remains elusive both at its core and in its ramifications.

Jacob Bronowski notes that Yeats's 'poems are often hard to understand: because Yeats masks his thought, which has changed a good deal, under images which he has never changed',[3] and the mask itself is one of these images. It had first emerged in Yeats's writing in the 1900s as a metaphor linked to ideas about personality and theatre,

---

[1] 'A Vision', *The Irish Statesman*, 13 February 1926, 714–16, reprinted in *CH* 269–73. See also www.YeatsVision.com/Reviews.html (consulted December 2010).
[2] Letter, 9 February 1918, NLI 30,563, cited Ann Saddlemyer, *Becoming George: The Life of Mrs W. B. Yeats* (Oxford: Oxford University Press, 2002), 151.
[3] 'Yeats's Mysticism', review of *A Vision*, *The Cambridge Review*, 19 November 1937, 113.

which Yeats went on to mould into a vivid symbol at the centre of his myth of self, anti-self and creation, notably in *Per Amica Silentia Lunae* and its prologue, 'Ego Dominus Tuus'. The *Mask* that appears in *A Vision*, however, seems to have dwindled into a cipher circling the clock-face of the lunar phases along with the other *Faculties*, its function delimited by the System's geometry.[4] It retains enough of its former traits to give a sense of *A Vision*'s continuity with Yeats's previous thought but is at root a different concept. Though this leaves much room for confusion and ambiguity,[5] the *Mask*'s importance lies precisely in this continuity, as well as its role within the psyche described by the *Faculties*. Of all the elements within the system of *A Vision* (except perhaps the *Daimon*, with which it is vitally linked), the *Mask* defined for Yeats his own concept of the artistic self and creative imagination, as well as determining the nature of emotion and the poetic process.

The 'mask' appears to have entered the Automatic Script on 21 December 1917, some two months after it had begun (*YVP1* 161ff). Its synonym 'persona' had already figured in terms that were soon abandoned ('Persona Artificans', 'Mala Persona' and 'Evil Persona', as well as the more enduring 'Persona of Fate'), but this session's treatment of the mask was different and contributed a large amount to its final formulation. In *Per Amica Silentia Lunae*, the 'mask' had been oriented specifically towards the artistic or heroic, but was now defined as a universal attribute: 'it is nothing to do with any form of artistic or practical genius', concerning 'life and not creation – it is a figure of destiny' (*YVP1* 161), yet in Yeats's treatment of it in *A Vision*, the earlier narrative of poet-hero remains important. The distinction between fate and destiny, chance and choice, became part of the central dichotomy of the System, dividing human existence into *primary* and *antithetical Tinctures*. The duality of fate and destiny is represented in the individual psyche by two of the *Faculties*: the externalised 'Persona of Fate', later renamed *Body of Fate*, 'which

---

[4] It is, of course, a peculiar clock-face, with two hands going clockwise and two anti-clockwise, one of which is the *Mask*.

[5] Brian Arkins's comment that 'antithetical people are driven to create a vibrant anti-self or Mask, while primary people flee from the Mask and accept reality as it is' (*The Thought of W. B. Yeats*, [Bern: Peter Lang, 2010], 5) shows both a perceptive sense of how the *Mask* of *A Vision* is connected with the earlier created mask, and also risks obscuring the meaning of 'create' since the *Mask* will be there whatever, and the implications of the *primary* person's fleeing the enforced *Mask*.

comes from without, whereas the *Mask* is predestined, Destiny being that which comes to us from within' (*AVB* 86; cf. *CW13* 16; *AVA* 15).[6] The destiny from within, found in the *Mask*, is most important to *antithetical* incarnations; it characterises the hero and the artist, those who had taken up the carven mask in *Per Amica Silentia Lunae* and who remain vital archetypes of *antithetical* humanity.

As the full scheme of the *Faculties* emerged and was put into place, *Mask* and *Body of Fate* took their place as the targets or objects of two 'active' *Faculties* (*AVB* 73), *Will* and *Creative Mind*. Together *Will* and *Mask* 'constitute' the *antithetical Tincture*, while *Creative Mind* and *Body of Fate* 'constitute' the *primary Tincture*. These intrinsic identities never change, although each *Faculty* may fall anywhere within the cycle of *antithetical* and *primary* at a given point (*CW13* 15; *AVA* 14; cf. *AVB* 73).[7] Of these *Four Faculties*, the *Mask* is the most distinctive element of the Yeatses' anatomy of the psyche and least easily grasped and, within the longer sketches of the 'Twenty-Eight Embodiments' (*AVA*) or 'Twenty-Eight Incarnations' (*AVB*), it is often the *Mask* that is the *Faculty* that contributes most the overall picture, in a way that is linked to its vital role as the focus of the *Will* and in the formation of the artistic personality, which is often the focus of Yeats's analysis.

Though the *Faculties* cannot be taken separately, it is one of the frustrations of Yeats's presentation (especially in *A Vision B*) that he gives so little sense of their roles and nature for readers to grasp as they accustom themselves to his terminology and schemata. As usual, the following summaries rely mainly on Yeats's own (relatively few) words, but try to draw out a few implications. As the key *Faculty*, 'Man's root' (*CW13* 15n; *AVA* 14n), *Will* is perhaps surprisingly primitive: practical survival instinct, 'everything that we call utility'

---

[6] It is hard to overstate the dualism within the construct of *A Vision*. In personal terms, the *primary Tincture* includes the impulse to be part of a whole outside oneself and it stands against the *antithetical* urge to individualise and to assert one's separateness. The objective or *primary* self looks outwards to 'the world': things, nature, other people, society, religion or God. The subjective or *antithetical* self looks inwards and seeks to express what it finds within itself or creates through imagination.

[7] *A Vision A* states that 'the *Four Faculties* constitute the *Tinctures*' (*CW13* 15; *AVA* 14) but the higher levels are called Solar and Lunar: 'the *primary* may be called Solar, the *antithetical* Lunar. The converse is not always true, for the *Tinctures* belong to a man's life while in the body, and Solar and Lunar may transcend that body' (*CW13* 112; *AVA* 189). This distinction is not made explicitly in *A Vision B*.

(*AVB* 83), the soul's 'energy, or will, or bias' (*AVB* 171; *CW13* 85; *AVA* 105), and individuating self.[8] It is a basic life force, without which the others have no sphere of operation, but in itself little more than 'a mechanism to prolong existence' (*AVB* 195), at the core of being, but in the sense of process rather than essence, which resides in the *Principles*. It is feeling, almost desire, but 'feeling that has not become desire because there is no object to desire; a bias by which the soul is classified and its phase fixed but which as yet is without result in action; an energy as yet uninfluenced by thought, action, or emotion; the first matter of a certain personality-choice' (*CW13* 15; *AVA* 14–15; cf. *AVB* 73). *Creative Mind* is more sophisticated but also simpler, representing the 'intellect' (*AVB* 85) or 'Knower' (*AVB* 73), an active apprehension containing 'all the universals' (*AVB* 86) or 'all the mind that is consciously constructive' (*CW13* 15; *AVA* 15), sometimes 'better described as imagination' (*AVB* 142; *CW13* 64; *AVA* 76). *Will* therefore is instinct with the 'complexities of mire or blood' (*VP* 498; *CW1* 252), while *Creative Mind* looks towards 'pure mind' (*VP* 630; *CW1* 356) or 'unageing intellect' (*VP* 407; *CW1* 197); though less obviously energetic than *Will*, *Creative Mind* is still a driving force to exploration and understanding. The *Faculties* that are the 'targets' of these two energies are harder to appreciate as part of the psyche itself, since they are generally projected. In the case of *Body of Fate* this projection is outwards into the external world to make what is 'Known' by the mind (*AVB* 73), 'the sum ... of fact, fact as it affects a particular man' (*AVB* 82) or 'the physical and mental environment, the changing human body, the stream of Phenomena as this affects a particular individual, all that is forced upon us from without, Time as it affects sensation' (*CW13* 15; *AVA* 15). In the phrase about *Will* above, 'an energy as yet uninfluenced by thought, action, or emotion', thought refers to *Creative Mind* and emotion to the *Mask*, and in many ways *Body of Fate* is action, since fact is the necessary sphere of action. Though the *Mask* projected as well, it is more subjective and intangible, the 'object of desire or moral ideal' and 'idea of the good' (*AVB* 83), 'the image of what we wish to become, or of that to which

---

[8] Yeats had rejected the automatic script's Ego, because it seemed to suggest 'the total man who is all *Four Faculties*' rather than one, his point of reference being the Theosophists' use of Ego for the reincarnating high group of the human principles (closest to Yeats's *Spirit* and *Celestial Body*), rather than Freud's partial *Ich*, usually translated into English as Ego. Yeats also noted that 'If Blake had not given "selfhood" a special meaning it might have served my turn' (*CW13* 15n; *AVA* 14n).

we give our reverence' (*CW13* 15; *AVA* 15), 'the Ought (or that which should be)' (*AVB* 73), and 'in the *antithetical* phases beauty' (*AVB* 192). It is chosen but involuntary, taking 'a form selected instinctively for those emotional associations which come out of the dark, and this form is itself set before us by accident, or swims up from the dark portion of the mind' (*CW13* 24; *AVA* 27), so that it is the object of willed choice but comes before us without conscious selection.[9] It is intrinsically at the limit of reach, 'that object of desire or moral ideal which is of all possible things the most difficult' (*AVB* 83), and vulnerable to chance and external reality. Uniquely, it also sometimes has a secondary form, 'the Image', which is externalised and slightly more easily grasped: 'a myth, a woman, a landscape, or anything whatsoever that is an external expression of the *Mask*' (*AVB* 107). The motive force of the *Will* gains direction from the *Mask*, while the motive force of the *Creative Mind* is directed towards the *Body of Fate*. Yeats gives an analogy of the *Will* looking with desire into the *Mask* as 'into a painted picture' focused on 'few objects', while cold-eyed '*Creative Mind* looks into a photograph', contemplating a crowded jumble (*AVB* 86; *CW13* 15–16; *AVA* 15). The photograph's randomness recognisably represents fate's imposed chance, but the painting must be conceived of as an icon that catches the imagination almost to the point of obsession, one that has been found but then chosen and adopted, or repeatedly recreated by the artist. Both *Mask* and *Body of Fate* represent truth that is apprehended by its active counterpart, but the *Mask* represents the truth of sincerity, personal truth, whereas the *Body of Fate* represents the truth of reality, factual truth.

The *Faculties* cannot, however, be taken individually, since they always work in concert. Despite or because of the fact that the *Will* is the most basic element within the psyche, it is *Will*'s bias in a given incarnation as either *primary* or *antithetical* that determines what *A Vision* posits as the aim in life, and as a consequence the role of all the *Faculties*, including the *Mask*. They are related through an inevitable

---

[9] Most of the material in *AVA*'s section 'The Daimon, the Sexes, Unity of Being, Natural and Supernatural Unity' (*CW13* 24ff; *AVA* 26ff) was omitted from *AVB*, and there are indications that Yeats rethought the ideas surrounding the *Daimon* especially (see below). However, though *AVB* must be taken as Yeats's more considered presentation of the System, many of the formulations in *AVA* are helpful, consistent with the later version, and represent an important stage of Yeats's understanding.

pattern, as the various notes of the musical key are fixed by intervals to the tonic, which gives the key its name, without determining the music or musicality of what follows. The fundamental principle behind the goal of life is somewhat hidden in a dry formula within rebarbative lists of rules, though also referred to throughout 'The Twenty-Eight Incarnations':

In an antithetical phase the being seeks by the help of the Creative Mind to deliver the Mask from Body of Fate.
    In a primary phase the being seeks by help of the Body of Fate to deliver the Creative Mind from the Mask (AVB 91; CW13 20; AVA 21).

In an *antithetical* incarnation the being, expressed in the *Will*, should try to liberate the *Mask*'s self-made ideals and sense of inner truth, from the claims of the factual reality of *Body of Fate*, by the help of the *Creative Mind*'s sense of the universal and its realism: 'Only by the pursuit or acceptance of [the *Will*'s] direct opposite, that object of desire or moral ideal which is of all possible things the most difficult [i.e. the *Mask*], and by forcing that form upon the *Body of Fate*, can it attain self-knowledge and expression' (*AVB* 83). In contrast, in a *primary* incarnation the being should strive to liberate its intellect's sense of universal values and apprehension of objective truth (*Creative Mind*), from self-made fantasies of the *Mask*, through the help of external reality (*Body of Fate*). Yeats gives no general gloss of this, but the soul's return to *primary* values at Phase 22 indicates how he understands it:

the aim must be to use the *Body of Fate* to deliver the *Creative Mind* from the *Mask* ... The being [i.e. *Will*] does this by so using the intellect [*CM*] upon the facts of the world [*BoF*] that the last vestige of personality [*antithetical Mask*] disappears. The *Will*, engaged in its last struggle with external fact (*Body of Fate*), must submit, until it sees itself as inseparable from nature perceived as fact, and it must see itself as merged into that nature through the *Mask* ... (*AVB* 158; *CW13* 75; *AVA* 92)

The *Will* is still made manifest through the *Mask* and uses it, but because *primary Will* seeks a relationship to the world, it must conform to that order rather than try to impose itself upon it, so that now external reality rather than personal energy tests and shows what is true. Desire for the *Mask* and therefore self-expression is only appropriate when the *Will* is in the *antithetical* phases, so 'In the *primary* phases man must cease to desire the *Mask* and Image by ceasing from self-expression, and substitute a motive of service for that of self-expression' (*AVB* 84; *CW13* 18; *AVA* 18) and in order to seek the world it must subordinate any subjective inner voice to factual reality.

The *primary* person's *Mask* should be an inherited norm and taken as offered, termed 'enforced', and its relationship to the *Will* is 'character'. For *antithetical* phases, however, the *Mask* is 'voluntary' or 'free' (*AVB* 84–85; *CW13* 18; *AVA* 18), producing 'personality' – a term that Yeats had long linked to energy.[10] Recalling the hero in the grove at Dodona (*CW5* 11; *Myth* 335), the *antithetical* person ought to 'carve out and wear the ... free *Mask* and so to protect and to deliver the Image' (*AVB* 120; *CW13* 46; *AVA* 53). This last term, the 'Image is a myth, a woman, a landscape, or anything whatsoever that is an external expression of the *Mask*' (*AVB* 107) projecting it objectively or in a complementary way, as the *Mask* of the *antithetical* person is in a *primary* or objective phase.[11] For Yeats's own Phase 17, for example, the '*Mask* may represent intellectual or sexual passion; seem some Ahasuerus or Athanase; be the gaunt Dante of the *Divine Comedy*; its corresponding Image may be Shelley's Venus Urania, Dante's Beatrice, or even the Great Yellow Rose of the Paradiso' (*AVB* 141; cf. *CW13* 63; *AVA* 76). This distinction intimates that Yeats's *Mask* is characteristically represented in a hungry wanderer such as Aengus or Forgael, with its 'Image' in such figures as the Rose or Maud Gonne, the 'glimmering girl | With apple blossom in her hair' (*VP* 149–50; *CW1* 56).[12] The *Mask* still recognisably retains something of the earlier conception as reflected in 'Ego Dominus Tuus', where Ille suggests that the gaunt Dante's 'hollow face' was

---

[10] See 'Personality and the Intellectual Essences' (1906; *CW4* 195; *E&I* 266). In the lecture 'Friends of My Youth', he speaks of 'this mysterious thing, personality, the mask, is created half consciously, half unconsciously, out of the passions, the circumstance of life. It is not the same as character' (1910; *YT* 77).

[11] The Image is not defined in *AVA* and the clarifying sentence about its nature was added to the delineation of Phase 2 in *AVB*. 'Image' is italicised in *AVA* but not in *AVB*. '*Mask* and Image' are frequently mentioned as a pair (*AVB* 84, 122, 137, 142, 146, 153; *CW13* 18, 60, 64, 67, 71; *AVA* 18, 72, 77, 80, 87) and in *AVA* Yeats writes of the Image as a special version of the *Mask*: 'By *Mask* is understood the image of what we wish to become, or of that to which we give our reverence. Under certain circumstances it is called the *Image*' (*CW13* 15; *AVA* 15) and see the editors' note *CW13* 235, n. 38. The *Mask* is the only *Faculty* to have such a secondary form.

[12] Yeats writes of how 'The being [*Will*], through the intellect [*Creative Mind*], selects some object of desire for the representation of the *Mask* as Image, some woman perhaps, and the *Body of Fate* snatches away the object' which the *Creative Mind*, imagination, 'must substitute some new image of desire' (*AVB* 142; *CW13* 64; *AVA* 76).

hollowed by 'A hunger for the apple on the bough | Most out of reach?' and found not self but 'unpersuadable justice' and 'The most exalted lady loved by man' (*VP* 368–69; *CW1* 162), what ought to be and the ideal vision of the beloved. This suggests that in his own mind, and in particular when thinking of his own phase, Yeats used some of the more mythic elements of his earlier thought, vivifying the dry bones in his own imagination.

Yeats also claims in 'Hodos Chameliontos' that in 'great lesser writers like Landor and like Keats we are shown that Image and that Mask as something set apart; Andromeda and her Perseus – though not the sea-dragon' (*CW3* 217; *Au* 273), indicating that, in their projection of the Image as Andromeda and the *Mask* as Perseus, these artists cannot quite compass the fullness of the conflict, the Vision of Evil, that marks the greater writers, who through suffering and 'through passion become conjoint to their buried selves, turn all to Mask and Image, and so be phantoms in their own eyes' (*CW3* 217; *Au* 273).[13] This buried self, 'that age-long memoried self', is the *Daimon*, and 'genius is a crisis that joins that buried self for certain moments to our trivial daily mind' (*CW3* 216–17; *Au* 272).

To some extent *Mask* and *Daimon* can be identified, though the two versions of *A Vision* offer slightly s of how far this identification can be taken. In *A Vision A*, Yeats writes of the human being's *Mask* as the *Daimon*'s *Will* and vice versa (also the human *Body of Fate* the *Daimon*'s *Creative Mind*), making human and *Daimon* complementary halves of a single entity, or the same being viewed from two distinct perspectives and reflected through a mirror (*CW13* 24–27; *AVA* 26–30).[14] He also imagines that the *Daimon* – and *Mask* – must be pursued in *antithetical* phases, but fled in *primary* phases, and in many ways the symbol more vivid when the pursuer

---

[13] The Vision of Evil is attained at the Full Moon, so not attainable for a writer such as Keats, who is placed at Phase 14, while Landor, from the *Daimonic* Phase 17 possessed it, 'though not in any full measure' (*AVB* 145; *CW13* 65; *AVA* 79). Elsewhere Yeats seems to allow it to Balzac (Phase 20) as well as Dante: 'no man believes willingly in evil or in suffering. How much of the strength and weight of Dante and of Balzac comes from unwilling belief, from the lack of it how much of the rhetoric and vagueness of all Shelley that does not arise from personal feeling?' ('If I were Four and Twenty', *Explorations* 277, cf. *CW5* 43–44).

[14] In a draft, c.1927, Yeats writes that 'Though for the purposes of exposition we shall separate daimon & man & give to man a different symbol, they are one continuous consciousness perception' (NLI 30,359, [21]), but they are not a single being, so he may have shied away from the implication that is given in *AVA*.

or pursued is represented as another being. However, it is probable Yeats decided that this conception was too schematic in its treatment of the *Daimon*,[15] and it is removed from *A Vision B*, though he does retain the important analogy of the *Daimon* as the stage-manager of a *Commedia dell'Arte* troupe, giving 'a *Mask* or rôle' to his actor (*AVB* 83–84; cf. *CW13* 17–18; *AVA* 17–18) and it is clear that he continued to the think of the *Mask* as crucial in connecting with the *Daimon*, and to favour the metaphor of drama.

When writers such as Dante and Villon give themselves completely to their role and 'turn all to Mask and Image':

> The two halves of their nature are so completely joined that they seem to labour for their objects, and yet to desire whatever happens, being at the same instant predestinate and free, creation's very self. We gaze at such men in awe, because we gaze not at a work of art, but at the re-creation of man through that art ... (*CW5* 217; *Au* 273).

The 'two halves' refer primarily to human and *Daimon-Mask*, with the destiny of the *Mask* overlapping with the freedom of individual *Will*.[16] Yeats obviously wished to place himself into such company, and *A Vision* is both a claim for his inclusion and an attempt to find a path to this goal. Much of the early automatic script revolves around the nature of genius, and it is clear that an important part of the whole project was to provide a scaffolding for Yeats to achieve his genius, or as much as his belated century would allow: 'I wished for a system of thought that would leave my imagination free to create as it chose and yet make all that it created, or could create, part of the one history and that the soul's. The Greeks certainly had such a system, and Dante ... and I think no man since' (*CW13* liv–lv; *AVA* xi). The Unity of Culture that had been possible to the classical Greeks or Dante was no longer available to Yeats, but he could attain Unity of Being (considered in Section III), and *A Vision* effectively lays claim to this unity, but more importantly provides support for

---

[15] This seems to have come from the Instructors: 'Elder', for example, 'complained of my identifying the Daimon too exclusively with the anti-self, & even objected to my identifying it with the reversal of the Four Faculties, though he said that was, when properly understood, correct' (*YVP3* 96; 4 September 1921) and in 1927 'Dionertes' told him that he 'must not say the Principles and Faculties expressed the daimons all man did was approach the daimon' (NLI 30,359, [37–39]).

[16] The exact meaning is ambiguous, since Yeats is writing largely without the terminology of *A Vision*, and could also indicate the *Will-Mask* axis together with the *Creative Mind-Body of Fate*, which together yield Unity of Being.

Yeats, explaining Yeats's genius to himself and providing directions for how to re-create the poet through his art, to tap into the sources of inspiration. For the predestined artist, joined to his buried self, the *Daimon* flows through him and all that his imagination can create must necessarily express the soul's history, since service of the *Daimon* is perfect *antithetical* freedom, in a twist on the traditional prayer.[17] Though the '*primary* is that which serves, the *antithetical* is that which creates' (*AVB* 85; *CW13* 19; *AVA* 19), in the *antithetical* ideal, represented by Dante, the intellect 'served the *Mask* alone' and 'compelled even those things that opposed it to serve' the *Mask* and *Daimonic* art (*AVB* 144; *CW13* 65; *AVA* 78).

The intellect's service is important, since it indicates the other *Faculty* that is particularly important to creativity: *Creative Mind*, which had originally been named 'Creative Genius' in the Automatic Script (cf. *CW13* 14; *AVA* 14). The *Mask*'s role in poetry is rooted in its nature as the focus of emotion and, for the *antithetical*, the locus of objects of desire, the target that turns the feeling of *Will* into desire. Further refinements of its inter-relations with the other *Faculties* indicate how poetry formed under the influence of *Creative Mind* makes the Image an 'abstract' universal representative, *the* Rose, and when the *Mask* alone dominates it is the idealised, far-off, unattainable Rose. If *Will* predominates it is 'sensuous' and related to self, my Rose; for Yeats it is seldom the concrete, particular flower, *a* rose, brought by *Body of Fate*'s influence (viz. *AVB* 87; *CW13* 16; *AVA* 15–16).

Though the Rose or Maud Gonne may embody the Image for Yeats, his *Mask* is not placed with Maud Gonne at Phase 16, a phase of beauty,[18] but directly opposite the *Will* at Phase 3, in 'a phase of perfect bodily sanity' (*AVB* 108; *CW13* 37; *AVA* 41). For the poet of 'the fantastic Phase 17, the man of this phase [3] becomes an Image where simplicity and intensity are united, he seems to move among yellowing corn or under overhanging grapes' giving 'to Shelley his wandering lovers and sages, and to Theocritus all his flocks and pastures', and to Yeats, perhaps, his perception of the Irish country

---

[17] The Second Collect of Morning Prayer in the *Book of Common Prayer* opens 'O God, who art the author of peace and lover of concord, in knowledge of whom standeth our eternal life, whose service is perfect freedom ...' Yeats's *Daimon* is truly *deus inversus*, since it is the author of crisis and lover of conflict.

[18] Her phase was given on 2 January 1918 (*YVP1* 189) and she is included under the head of 'some beautiful women' (*AVB* 137; *CW13* 60; *AVA* 71).

people and the world of *The Celtic Twilight*, fairyland, the rituals of the Castle of Heroes Mysteries,[19] the idyll imagined for his daughter, living 'like some green laurel | Rooted in one dear perpetual place' (*VP* 405; *CW1* 191), and such poems as 'The Song of the Happy Shepherd' or 'The Lake Isle of Innisfree'. In writing of how Phase 3's 'seasonal change and bodily sanity seem images of lasting passion and the body's beauty' to the poet of opposite phase (*AVB* 109; *CW13* 37; *AVA* 42), Yeats may also be looking to works such as 'To a Child dancing in the Wind', 'The Wild Swans at Coole' and 'The Fisherman', even forward to 'In Memory of Eva Gore-Booth and Con Markievicz' or the final stanza of 'Among School Children'.[20] These do not represent the objective world of Phase 3 itself, but the subjective image of these states, transmuted by desire. The *Will* of those at Phase 17 is complex and seeks to synthesise, making for 'partisans, propagandists and gregarious' people, the *Mask* is one of 'simplification, which holds up before them the solitary life of hunters and of fishers and "the groves pale passion loves", they hate parties, crowds, propaganda' (*AVB* 143; *CW13* 64; *AVA* 77). Yeats also sometimes rejects that country where the young lovers and animals are caught in the 'sensual music' of the natural world's rhythms and the crowded fields and seas (*VP* 407; *CW1* 197), and the vision is that of the colder eye: 'as I look backward upon my own writing, I take pleasure alone in those verses where it seems to me I have found something hard and cold, some articulation of the Image which is the opposite of all that I am in my daily life, and all that my country is' (*CW3* 218; *Au* 274). The Image here takes on more of the cold hardness that truly belongs to the objectivity of Phase 3. Though opposite, the *Mask* and Image are also integral, part of the make-up, and though chosen, 'man or nation can no more make this Mask or Image than the seed can be made by the soil into which it is cast' (*CW3* 218; *Au* 274).[21] Thus the *antithetical* free *Mask* may be carved

---

[19] See Lucy Shephard Kalogera, 'Yeats's Celtic Mysteries' (PhD dissertation, Florida State Universtiy, 1977 [UMI 77-22,121]), Appendix III, 157ff.

[20] Yeats also implies that the soul may have particular memories of the incarnation when the Will was at this phase: 'The past incarnations corresponding to his Four Faculties seem to accompany a living man' and may provide 'an explanation of that emergence during vision of an old Cretan myth described in my book Autobiographies' (*AVB* 229n), intimating a Theocritan past life of his own.

[21] In a note added in 1926, Yeats added 'There is a form of Mask or Image that comes from life and is fated, but there is a form that is chosen' (*CW3* 469, n. 27; *Au* 274), pointing to the enforced *primary Mask* and the chosen *antithetical Mask*.

out and worn, but the predestined raw material must be given (cf. *AVB* 120; *CW13* 46; *AVA* 53).

It is a paradox that in *antithetical* phases where the *Mask* is to be desired, it is actually placed at a *primary* phase with *primary* unifying force and objectivity, while the *primary* person's deluding *Mask* is located in subjective phases. However, the *Mask* is not simply drawn from the opposite phase, as the object of desire it is coloured by the desire, derived from the *Will*'s energy, in an alchemy of transmutation: for example, Phase 19's Conviction is 'derived from a *Mask* of the [*primary*] first quarter *antithetically* transformed' (*AVB* 148; cf. *CW13* 68; *AVA* 83) and is called the '*antithetical Mask*' (*AVB* 150; *CW13* 70; *AVA* 84). Phase 10's 'stony *Mask*' is similarly 'Phase 24 "The end of ambition" *antithetically* perceived' (*AVB* 123; *CW13* 49; *AVA* 57). The process of the transformation is indicated more clearly perhaps by Phase 13, which desires to 'become its opposite and receive from the *Mask* (Phase 27), which is at the phase of the Saint, a virginal purity of emotion' (*AVB* 129; *CW13* 54–55; *AVA* 64): the quality of purity remains, however it affects not Phase 27's spirituality but the emotion of Phase 13's sensuous *Will*, giving 'not self-denial but expression for expression's sake'.

The keywords and descriptions for the *Masks* of each phase reveal that in most cases the *Masks* of opposite phases are facets of a central idea, one directed outwards towards the world and the other directed reflexively to self or expression. The *Mask* of Phase 2, 'The Player on Pan's Pipes' is an external form of the idyll that becomes 'Illusion' in Phase 16. Phase 3's 'Innocence' is simplicity towards the world, in contrast to Phase 17's simplicity directed towards self and self-expression, 'Simplification through intensity'. The 'Passion' which is the *Mask* of Phase 4 becomes reflexive in the 'Intensity through emotion' of Phase 18. Phase 5's 'Excess' tests limits in worldly terms, while Phase 19's 'Conviction' 'passes from emphasis to emphasis' (*AVB* 148; *CW13* 68; *AVA* 82). The 'Justice' of Phase 6's *Mask* contains the social form of law and necessity which the 'Fatalism' of Phase 20's *Mask* focuses inward. The 'Altruism' of Phase 7 shares with the 'Self-analysis' of Phase 21 a quality of detachment and standing apart from self, overcoming self-interest in a social context or simply self-immersion in terms of reflection. Disregard for self is perhaps also evident in the clearer forms of 'Courage', Phase 8, and 'Self-immolation', Phase 22, though these are phases of transition from one *Tincture* to the other. The clarity that, in terms of antithetical expression, gives 'Facility' to Phase 9's *Mask* takes more inclusive and public form, in terms of primary thought, in the 'Wisdom' of Phase 23. Elements of this clarity, together with self-sufficiency, are evident in the 'Organisation' that characterises the *Mask* of Phase 10 and the 'Self-reliance' of Phase 24, the codifier. A further element of stripping things to essentials, even exclusion, is seen in the 'Rejection' of Savonarola's phase, 11, and the 'Consciousness of self' which is the *Mask* of Luther or Calvin's phase, 25, which 'creates a system of belief, just as Phase 24 creates a code, to exclude all that is too difficult for dolt or knave' (*AVB* 125; *CW13* 50; *AVA* 58). The hero of Phase 12 projects self with energy in 'Self-exaggeration' as the hunchback of Phase 26 projects his faults and self in pitiless clarity by dominating 'Self-realisation'. Phase 13's 'Self-expression' can enable 'complete intellectual unity' of emotion and the self (*AVB* 129; *CW13* 54; *AVA* 64), as Phase 27's domination of the *Mask*, 'Renunciation', enables 'the total life, expressed in its humanity, to flow in upon him and to express itself through his acts and thoughts' (*AVB* 180; *CW13* 92; *AVA* 114). The quiet of Phase 14's *Mask*, 'Serenity', becomes featureless absence in Phase 28's 'Oblivion'.

Though these categories and characteristics are only directly relevant within the system of *A Vision* itself, they show more generally a pattern of mirroring and reflection, with the *primary* and *antithetical Tinctures* throwing their own cast on a central core.

Comparison of the tables shows that the pattern of polarity with the False *Masks* is similar, generally a distortion or perversion of the True *Masks*, though sometimes also a denial, if the person lives 'out of phase'.[22] Indeed Yeats starts a good number of the descriptions of the phases by describing misdirected lives, especially in the earlier phases of the Wheel where there are fewer famous examples. The *primary* man who 'desires the *Mask*' instead of the *Creative Mind* thereby 'permits' the *Mask* to dominate, so that he 'gives himself to' the False *Mask* (*AVB* 106; *CW13* 35; *AVA* 39). This implies a kind of abandonment or weakness but also a choice, and indeed George Yeats viewed it as part of the space for free will within the System.[23] The other temptation is that of copying the opposite phase, so that the person seeks to live in the phase of the *Mask* and effectively

---

[22] The most obvious case of all is that of Phases 12 and 26 where the False *Mask* is 'Self-abandonment' for both.

[23] See Ellmann's notes of an interview with George Yeats on 17 January 1947: 'Free will in Vision – true and false masks – 13th cone': see '"Gasping on the Strand": Richard Ellmann's W. B. Yeats Notebook', ed. Warwick Gould, *YA16* 279–361; 319.

	True Mask			True Mask	False Mask			False Mask
16>2	player on Pan's pipes	*dream*	16>2	illusion	fury	*mania*	2>16	delusion
17>3	innocence	*simplicity*	17>3	simplification through intensity	folly	*scattering*	3>17	dispersal
18>4	passion	*passion*	18>4	intensity through emotions	will	*self-will*	4>18	curiosity
19>5	excess	*forcing limits*	19>5	conviction	limitation	*oppression*	5>19	domination
20>6	justice	*law*	20>6	fatalism	tyranny	*irrational rules*	6>20	superstition
21>7	altruism	*detachment*	21>7	self-analysis	efficiency	*indifference*	7>21	self-adaptation
22>8	courage	*disregard for self*	22>8	self-immolation	fear	*focus on self*	8>22	self-assurance
23>9	facility	*clarity*	23>9	wisdom	obscurity	*hiding*	9>23	self-pity
24>10	organisation	*self-sufficiency*	24>10	self-reliance	inertia	*withdrawal*	10>24	isolation
25>11	rejection	*essentialism*	25>11	consciousness of self	moral indifference	*persecution*	11>25	self-consciousness
26>12	self-exaggeration	*projection*	26>12	self-realization	self-abandonment	*self-abandonment*	12>26	self-abandonment
27>13	self-expression	*self-perfection*	27>13	renunciation	self-absorption	*zeal*	13>27	emulation
28>14	serenity	*quiet*	28>14	oblivion	self-distrust	*mean-spirit*	14>28	malignity
1>15		*none*	1>15	none	none	*none*	15>1	none

mistakes *Mask* and *Will*. The unified *antithetical* poet may live in the *Mask* in the sense of expressing it through his creation, but here the *Mask* is transmuted subjectively; the *primary* person should not seek the sincerity of the *Mask*, but the reality of fact. An example of this for Yeats is George Russell (AE), whose 'visionary painting' is derivative of other men, and 'like many of his "visions"', an attempt to live in the *Mask*, caused by critical ideas founded upon *antithetical* art' (*AVB* 176; *CW13* 88; *AVA* 109). For Yeats, Russell's true calling was found in 'his practical work as a co-operative organiser' where 'he finds precise ideas and sincere emotion in the expression of conviction. He has learned practically, but not theoretically, that he must fly the *Mask*' (*AVB* 176; *CW13* 88–89; *AVA* 109). Too much association with *antithetical* artists misled Russell into desiring the *Mask* of pantheistic Phase 11, even perhaps seeing himself as a Spinoza rather than a George Herbert.

Russell is part of a relatively small group of artists who are *primary* rather than antithetical, since most writers are antithetical expressers of their self, creators and originators (and most of the examples that Yeats gives in *A Vision* are writers of some kind).[24] In Yeats's conception what is expressed by *primary* writers (when 'in phase') is not self but the ideas of the collective, whether race, society or religion; having accepted the enforced, 'imitative *Mask*', it 'may become the historical norm, or an image of mankind' (*AVB* 84; *CW13* 18; *AVA* 18), so that the *primary* writer serves as a voice for others, for a group or tradition, rather than creating. These writers include friends and collaborators such as Synge and Lady Gregory as well as Russell, and others such as George Herbert, Whitman and Dumas.[25] Yeats puts himself towards one end of an artistic spectrum with the creators of inner landscapes who 'in assuming the *Mask*'

---

[24] 'The Twenty-Eight Incarnations' in *AVB* gives some 37 artists (33 writers), 11 thinkers or religious people (9 of them writers, if Socrates and Savonarola are excluded), 2 scientists (Paracelsus could be added), 3 political figures, 4 fictional characters, and a vague multitude of beautiful women. Excluding the last two groups, some 70% are artists and 79% writers, more if Darwin and Lamarck are counted as writers. Hazard Adams treats the same data slightly differently, and makes the point that 'Yeats sees the writers in or as their work', *The Book of Yeats's Vision: Romantic Modernism and Antithetical Tradition* (Ann Arbor: University of Michigan Press, 1995), 88.

[25] It is one of the paradoxes of Yeats's perception that the poet of 'Song of Myself' expresses not self but 'a product of democratic bonhomie, of schools, of colleges, of public discussion' (*AVB* 114; *CW13* 41; *AVA* 47).

assume 'an intensity which is ... always lyrical and personal, and this intensity, though always a deliberate assumption, is to others but the charm of the being' (*AVB* 141–42; *CW13* 63; *AVA* 76), the tension should appear effortless and the value lies in sincerity, winning the audience by the strength of the voice. At the other end stand those who create convincing representations of the world, whose value is tested by the audience's recognition of their creation, their truth to reality. Beyond these come those whose impulse is too much towards reality to be concerned with artistic expression. Similarly also, Yeats views tragedy as centred on the subjective passion of its people, so *antithetical*, whereas for him comedy is based on manners and behaviour, so *primary*.

Whitman (6) and Dumas (7) are however very different from Synge (23), Gregory (24) and Russell (25), and with either *Tincture* the two different quarters are distinct and the distinction affects the *Mask*.[26] This is especially true of the *primary Tincture*, where one quarter is at the beginning of the cycle and the other at the end. The first quarter, where *Will* predominates, is considered to identify with the external world in a more 'innocent' and spontaneous way, engaging with the natural world of things with 'Instinctive' *Will* and conforming to it through the 'Convention or systematization' of the *Mask* (*AVB* 103; *CW13* 32; *AVA* 36). The fourth quarter, where *Body of Fate* predominates, is far more ideological, looking to structures and order, and the 'Moral' *Will* engages with the world 'aware of ... a supersensual environment of the soul' (*AVB* 18; *CW13* 92; *AVA* 114), drawing on the *Mask*'s 'Tolerance' to accept all (*AVB* 103; *CW13* 32; *AVA* 36). In the first quarter the delusion or lure of the *Mask*, which must be eliminated, 'takes [the] form of opinion', while in the fourth quarter 'it is [the] remaining personal element: it is the departure from conformity still possible to the ego [*Will*]' (*YVP3* 334),[27] which Yeats explains as the 'natural self, which [the person] must escape' (*AVB* 169; *CW13* 84; *AVA* 102). In contrast, the two *antithetical*

---

[26] Significantly also, 'At Phase 15 and Phase 1 occurs what is called the *interchange of the tinctures*, those thoughts, emotions, energies, which were *primary* before Phase 15 or Phase 1 are *antithetical* after, those that were *antithetical* are *primary*' (*AVB* 89), so that 'the old *antithetical* becomes the new *primary*' (*AVB* 105).

[27] This note from the preparatory card-file (M7) is more succinct than anything in *A Vision* itself, but the distinction is borne out by the treatment of the individual phases. The nature of the enforcement is also different in the two quarters: 'Mask 1 to 8 enforced by ego [*Will*] it self. Mask 22 to 1 enforced by CG [*Creative Mind*]', card-index (*YVP3* 334).

quarters are continuous, though the second quarter, where the *Mask* itself predominates, is centred on self and emotion, whereas after the Full Moon *Creative Mind* predominates, so the third quarter is directed towards the mind and thought, and increasingly outwards. The *Mask* in both quarters is free and should be sought, but in the second quarter it 'reveals' the self and in the third 'conceals' it. Before the Full Moon it 'is described as a "revelation" because through it the being obtains knowledge of itself, sees itself in personality' (*AVB* 85; *CW13* 18; *AVA* 19), as the emotional *Will* gains 'Self-analysis' from the *Mask* drawn from the moral fourth quarter (*AVB* 103; *CW13* 32; *AVA* 36) and turns inwards more as it approaches the Full Moon. The third quarter's *Mask* is 'a "concealment", for the being grows incoherent, vague and broken, as its intellect (*Creative Mind*) is more and more concerned with objects that have no relation to its unity but a relation to the unity of society or of material things, known through the *Body of Fate*. It adopts a personality which it more and more casts outward, more and more dramatises' (*AVB* 85; *CW13* 18; *AVA* 19).[28] The intellectual *Will* hides its lack of self-sufficiency behind the *Mask*'s 'Intensity' (*AVB* 103; *CW13* 32; *AVA* 36), thus Yeats sees himself as being drawn to concerns outside the purely personal and more generally to theatre, but needing to focus on the *Mask* to centre the self and to conceal the lack of coherence within, hammering his intellect's 'thoughts into unity' ('If I were Four-and-Twenty', *CW5* 34; *Ex* 263).

In *A Vision A* Yeats considers several forms of unity in the section 'The Daimon, the Sexes, Unity of Being, Natural and Supernatural Unity' (*CW13* 24ff; *AVA* 26ff), as the title indicates: Unity of Being centred on the *Mask*, objective, Unity with Nature, and a supernatural Unity with God.[29] *A Vision B* mentions only Unity of Being, to focus

---

[28] The first session of the Automatic Script about the *Mask* already described the second quarter's *Mask* as 'a form created to facilitate self expression' and 'a revelation of soul', and the third quarter's as 'a form to conceal self & express only the objective however antithetical & subjective the nature is' (*YVP1* 162).

[29] Yeats may have conceived of a possible form of unity for each quarter: a 'Unity with God' at Phase 27 and a 'Unity with Nature' at Phase 3 (*CW13* 27; *AVA* 29), an 'intellectual unity' of Emotion at Phase 13 (*CW13* 54; *AVA* 64; *AVB* 129), a 'Unity of Being' at Phase 17 (*CW13* 26; *AVA* 28; cf. *AVB* 88 and *CW13* 63; *AVA* 75; *AVB* 141). These four key phases are of course all related to each other, being the respective positions of the *Four Faculties* in any one of the phases. There is also a 'Unity of Fact', mentioned in the context of Phase 22 and the turn towards the *primary Tincture* (*AVB* 162; *CW13* 78; *AVA* 95).

all attention on 'the unity of man not of God, and therefore of the *antithetical* tincture' (*AVB* 258) most possible at Yeats's own phase. This is not just self-serving, since it is also probable that, as his understanding of the *Principles* developed, Yeats came to see that Unity with God and Nature were not internal, centred unities, but rather unions with something outside the 'being' defined by the *Faculties* (see *AVB* 86). As expressed in *A Vision B*, it is), and that the *Faculties*' very weakness that enables the action of the *Principles*, which are normally submerged during waking life, and brings the soul closer to objective reality.[30]

In the later formulation of *A Vision B*, during the incarnate life of 'the *Faculties* the sole activity and the sole unity is natural or lunar', so that, although there is a *primary* form where 'that unity is moral' (not spiritual), this natural unity is effectively an antithetical goal: 'All unity is from the *Mask* and the *antithetical Mask*[31] is described in the automatic script as a "form created by passion to unite us to ourselves", the self so sought is that Unity of Being compared by Dante in the *Convito* to that of "a perfectly proportioned human body"' (*AVB* 82).[32] However, since this unity is reserved for Yeats and his near kin (Phases 16, 17 and 18), the majority of *antithetical* phases have no chance of it, and even at Phase 17, the most promising, success is far from assured. In the end, the importance of this unity for Yeats is the context in which it places his own artistic creation and 'genius'. Phase 17 'is called the *Daimonic* man because Unity of Being, and consequent expression of *Daimonic* thought, is now more easy than at any other phase' (*AVB* 141; *CW13* 63; *AVA* 75), and this contact with the *Daimon* is of course attained through the *Mask*.

---

[30] In the last quarter's most primary phases we approach the spiritual essences that lie behind created life: 'the *Faculties* wear away, grow transparent, and man may see himself as it were arrayed against the supersensual' (*AVB* 86); *AVA*'s Unity with God is viewed in *AVB* as a state in which 'the Principles ... shine through' (*AVB* 89). Yeats's language echoes the Theosophists' more conventional spirituality, which seeks 'to so open up or make porous the lower nature that the spiritual nature may shine through it and become the guide and ruler' (W. Q. Judge, *An Epitome of Theosophy*, [Point Loma, CA: Theosophical Publishing Co., 1900], 12).

[31] *AVA* does not specify *antithetical*, just 'the *Mask* is described ...' (*CW13* 18; *AVA* 18).

[32] This unity has much of the 'delight in the whole man – blood, imagination, intellect, running together' ('Personality and the Intellectual Essences', 1906; *CW4* 195; *E&I* 266) that had characterised his early understanding of personality, along with 'active passionate life' ('Friends of My Youth', 1910; *YT* 77).

As mentioned earlier, in *A Vision A*, the human *Mask* is seen as the *Daimon*'s *Will*, while the human *Body of Fate* is the *Daimon*'s *Creative Mind* and *vice versa*, but the idea is dropped from *A Vision B*. Whether this complementary reversal is applied or not, *Body of Fate* and *Mask* express chance and choice, Fate and Destiny, and the latter in particular orchestrated by the *Daimon*. The *Mask* may be chosen, but the choice is offered by the *Daimon*, a task-master with 'but one purpose, to bring their chosen man to the greatest obstacle he may confront without despair' (*CW3* 217; *Au* 272) and there are no alternatives, only refusal of experience. Indeed for Yeats not only is theatrical tragedy intrinsically *antithetical*, but *antithetical* destiny is intrinsically tragic: 'We begin to live when we have conceived life as tragedy' (*CW3* 163; *Au* 189).[33] However, once the experience is put within the aesthetic frame, it can be viewed as we view the tragedy of Lear or Hamlet, and this is the perspective that the *Daimon* has of human life. Actors must 'not break up their lines to weep. | They know that Hamlet and Lear are gay; | Gaiety transfiguring all that dread' (*VP* 565; *CW1* 300), and onlookers 'laugh in tragic joy' (*VP* 564; *CW1* 300) as they observe the passing of an old order. The *Daimonic* perspective implies a strange detachment from life together with total engagement, yet this may in part be the purpose of 'The Mirror of Angels and Men' (*Speculum Angelorum et Hominum*), *A Vision*'s fictional precursor, and is central to Yeats's aestheticised morality and 'explanation of life' declared on the title page of *A Vision A* (*CW13* [li]; *AVA* [iii]).

Which of fate or destiny, *primary* or *antithetical*, *Body of Fate* or *Mask*, predominates depends ultimately on the *Daimon* and the *Principles*.[34] In *A Vision A* the *Principles* are seen as corresponding to the various *Faculties* (*CW13* 119; *AVA* 146) but, by the stage of *A Vision B*, they are seen as their origin, 'the innate ground of

[33] He writes of the *Daimons* in *The Trembling of the Veil* as 'Gates and Gate-keepers, because through their dramatic power they bring our souls to crisis, to Mask and Image, caring not a straw whether we be Juliet going to her wedding, or Cleopatra to her death; for in their eyes nothing has weight but passion' or drama, 'for it is only when the intellect has wrought the whole of life to drama, to crisis, that we may live for contemplation, and yet keep our intensity' (*CW3* 217; *Au* 272). Such a marriage of contemplation and intensity is the portion of the third quarter in particular.

[34] The operation and relation between these two elements is condensed to a few 'crammed pages' (see esp. *AVB* 83; 189–90) such as those that AE thought 'would need a volume to elucidate' (see n. 1). Here, though, I can only tease out a few points.

the *Faculties*' (*AVB* 187).³⁵ Though there is no starting point in the cyclical process described within *A Vision*, the fourth stage of the after-life is perhaps the closest to such a point, when the solar *Principles*, *Spirit* and *Celestial Body* 'are one and there is only *Spirit*; pure mind, containing within itself pure truth [*Celestial Body*], that which depends only upon itself' (*AVB* 188–89).³⁶ At the following stage two lunar *Principles*, 'a new *Husk* and *Passionate Body* take the place of the old; made from the old, yet, as it were, pure' (*AVB* 233). These *Four Principles* are in turn transferred or reflected into the *Faculties*, though when or how is never explicit (*AVB* 187).

The *Passionate Body* gives rise to the *Mask*, and indeed Yeats shows how closely the two were fused in his thinking when he pairs 'the new *Husk* and *Mask*', a slip for *Husk* and *Passionate Body* (*AVB* 233). The *Mask* as the 'voluntary and acquired' counterpart of the *Passionate Body* 'must act ... in the same way' towards *Will* as *Passionate Body* does towards *Husk* (AVB 187). This bond is one of hunger, a metaphor that underlies much of Yeats's spiritual economy: *Will* and *Husk* derive from a hunger to perceive others and *Mask* and *Passionate Body* come from those others, conceived as a single, internalised focus. The hunger belongs to the *Daimon* rather than the human being, but in this context the *Daimon* should be seen as the human's 'ultimate self' (*AVB* 83), as 'what in a man personally is unique is from the daimon'.³⁷ All of our experience derives ultimately from other beings and from modes of perception, which Yeats summarises aphoristically in the 'Seven Propositions': 'Reality is a timeless & spaceless community of Spirits which perceive each other. Each Spirit is determined by & determines those it perceives, and each Spirit is unique'.³⁸

---

³⁵ The Automatic Script and notebooks contain many further subtleties and details that Yeats excluded in his quest to simplify and clarify.
³⁶ This is the *Beatitude* or *Marriage* (*AVB* 232), in one sense at least 'the hymen of the soul' (*CW5* 9; *Myth* 332).
³⁷ NLI 30,359, c.1927, [18]. This is related to the complex concept of the *Ghostly Self* (see *AVB* 22, 193, 194, 211; *YVP3* 34).
³⁸ NLI 13,581 (Rapallo Notebook D), 24 recto, c.1929. Cf. NLI 30,280, given by Virginia Moore, *The Unicorn: W. B. Yeats' Search for Reality* (New York: Macmillan, 1954), 378–89; Richard Ellmann, *The Identity of Yeats* (1954; second edition London: Faber and Faber, 1964), 236–37; Hazard Adams, *Blake and Yeats: The Contrary Vision*, Cornell Studies in English 40 (1955; New York: Russell and Russell, 1968), 287–88. See also the largely identical 'Six Propositions' in a letter of October 1929, in *Frank Pearce Sturm: His Life, Letters, and Collected Work*, ed. R. Taylor (Urbana, Chicago and

In drafts Yeats notes that the 'daimon seeks to unite itself now with one now with another daimon but can only do so through the human mind, for without the human mind it has neither reflection nor memory'.[39] The *Daimon* seeks in other *Daimons* a form of completion, what it lacks in itself,[40] which is expressed in human life through the *Passionate Body-Mask* and makes the *Mask* the incarnate expression of the object of *Daimonic* desire 'to make apparent to itself certain *Daimons*' (*AVB* 189), connecting it to the community beyond self, the 'world'.[41] Without *Daimonic* hunger, *Husk-Will*, and its object, *Passionate Body-Mask*, the immortal *Principles* would be isolated and unable to develop: *Celestial Body* would be shut up within itself, since the *Spirit* actively pursues knowledge but appears incapable of perception on its own and needs the 'other' that is brought by the sensuous *Husk* and *Passionate Body*. Therefore these lunar *Principles* are remade for each incarnation and 'prevail during life' (*AVB* 188) so that the *Passionate Body* 'may "save the *Celestial Body* from solitude"' (*AVB* 189). Incarnate life is inherently *antithetical*, ruled by these lunar *Principles* which express *Daimonic* hunger, and the antithetical incarnations are doubly so, as *Passionate Body-Mask* dominate, giving a life of destiny where the human 'acts in spite of reason' (*AVB* 190).[42] In contrast, in *primary* incarnations the *Daimon* is subordinated to the rational *Spirit* which finds its goal, and the *Principles*' unity, in *Celestial Body* (*AVB* 188), and is mirrored in the Great Wheel by the *Creative Mind*'s increasing attachment 'to *Body of Fate* until mind ... can create no more' and the soul is moulded to the truth of '"the spirits at one"' (*AVB* 189), a phrase that comprehends both the spirits' phase, the New Moon or Phase One, and their being at one

London: University of Illinois Press, 1969), 100–01. For dating and the relationship of the versions, see www.YeatsVision.com/7Propositions.html (consulted December 2009).

[39] NLI 30,359, c.1927, [18].

[40] Yeats had problems reconciling uniqueness and perfection in the *Daimon*: in an altercation with the instructor called Dionertes, 'I said if they are different – there is something of the whole lacking in each & therefore it is not perfect. However he insisted.' NLI 30,359, c.1927, leather notebook [37–39].

[41] Elsewhere the *Mask* is also expressed as the *Daimon*'s memory of past exaltation (*AVB* 83), but this is better seen as the *Daimon*'s timelessness appearing as memory of past to the time-bound human.

[42] Considering 'the *Four Principles* in the sphere' (*AVB* 193–95), Yeats identifies the *Daimons* with Plotinus' 'Third Authentic Existant or soul of the world', which is 'reflected first as sensation and its object (our *Husk* and *Passionate Body*) then as discursive reason (almost our *Faculties*)', but is represented diagrammatically as reflecting into the *antithetical Tincture*, not the *primary* which is reflected from *Spirit*.

with external reality, sinking back towards 'the mass where we begin' (*AVB* 72).

In *A Vision* Yeats puts aside the goals of almost all spiritual systems, whether conventional or esoteric, where union with God is the highest end, offering as *summum bonum* a personal Unity of Being, 'the unity of man not of God' (*AVB* 258). This is not a union with something greater beyond the self, but a unity within the self, a form of balance between all the *Faculties*. It is arises out of the tension of full awareness and 'constantly renewed choice' (*AVB* 84; *CW13* 18; *AVA* 18), from 'a being which only exists with extreme effort, when his muscles are as it were all taut and all his energies active' (*AVB* 84; cf. *CW13* 18; *AVA* 18), and in *A Vision A* he explicitly declares that 'Much of what follows will be a definition or description of this deeper being, which may become the unity described by Dante in the *Convito*' (*CW13* 18; *AVA* 18). Thus 'All unity is from the *Mask*' (*AVB* 82), which is the 'form created by passion to unite us to ourselves' (*AVB* 82; *CW13* 18; *AVA* 18), and 'passion' here is the *Passionate Body* and to a lesser degree the hunger of the *Husk-Will*. Though it is an *antithetical* goal only, it lies at the heart of the reason for incarnation, saving the *Celestial Body* from solitude, so that for Yeats it becomes the human goal.

The intellect of Dante and, by extension, of Yeats's ideal self-perception, 'served the *Mask* alone', and 'suffering injustice and the loss of Beatrice' in reality, 'found divine justice and the heavenly Beatrice' in poetic vision (*AVB* 144; *CW13* 65; *AVA* 78).[43] In *A Packet for Ezra Pound*, Yeats comments that '"concord" ... persuades me that he has best imagined reality who has best imagined justice' (*PEP* 33),[44]

---

[43] Yeats explains this earlier in the treatment of Phase 17 in a description of the substitutions involved for one who has achieved Unity of Being, taking himself together with Dante as hidden paradigms: 'The being [*Will*], through the intellect [*CM*], selects some object of desire for a representation of the *Mask* as Image, some woman perhaps [Beatrice/Maud Gonne], and the *Body of Fate* snatches away the object. Then the intellect (*Creative Mind*), which in the most *antithetical* phases were better described as imagination, must substitute some new image of desire; and in the degree of its power and of its attainment of unity, relate that which is lost [*Image*], that which has snatched it away [*BoF*], to the new image of desire [*Mask reflected in CM*], that which threatens the new image to the being's unity' (*AVB* 142; *CW13* 64; *AVA* 76).

[44] The obfuscation caused by the quotation from Leopardi and the criticism of Pound's translation almost entirely distracts from the ostensible subject of the sentence, the 'concord' that unites or unifies humanity. Whether it is linked to 'the concord of Empedocles' (*AVB* 82; cf. *AVB* 67) is not addressed, though this concord

and the imagination of justice is the apprehension of the 'Ought' of the *Mask*, while reality is the *Body of Fate*, apprehended or imagined by the *Creative Mind*. At its highest the vision of justice, found in the *Mask*, is inextricable from the vision of reality, so that choice and chance are united, the *Mask*'s beauty is united to the *Celestial Body*'s truth or the reality of its counterpart, *Body of Fate*.

The *Mask* is central therefore to Yeats's conception of self, imagination and art, and to allowing him to find space for humanity in the universe. Though it rightly only dominates in *antithetical* incarnations, in some senses incarnation itself is *antithetical*, and as such it defines 'the antithetical human race. We are who we are because of the assertion of our subjectivity',[45] and that assertion is through the *Mask*.

---

exists only at the level of the *Principles*. A draft makes the philosophical links clearer: 'The great tradition of philosophy, all the [illegible] speculation that descends from Plato & Hegel sets before us the certainty or probability – for Kant only offers us probability – that he who has best imagined justice has best imagined reality ...' (NLI 30,757).

[45] Unpublished part of the diary of 1930, NLI 30,354 [19].

'I beg your pardon?': W. B. Yeats, Audibility and Sound Transmission

Emilie Morin

DESPITE THE WEALTH of evidence demonstrating W. B. Yeats's deep interest in radio broadcasting, his responses to and perception of sound transmission devices have not received sustained critical attention. This article considers Yeats's ambivalence towards sound recording and the wireless, and discusses his attempts to diminish the artistic significance of his engagement with the BBC, highlighting the persistence with which he presented himself as a naïf in matters of sound transmission, and contrasting his responses to the wireless with his command of broadcasting techniques. In so doing, the article situates Yeats's complex treatment of audibility and inaudibility in a wider cultural and artistic context, pointing to the peculiar relationship that binds Yeats's concerns to Thomas Edison's perception of the phonographic voice and to Guglielmo Marconi's early experiments with signal transmission and encryption.

I

Biographies of W. B. and George Yeats feature amusing anecdotes about the awkward partitioning which sound transmission devices imposed upon the Yeats household. The family gramophone was, for instance, confined to the recesses of the domestic sphere, where it remained largely unused, if not forgotten; Ann Saddlemyer draws attention to the clandestine existence of this bulky device (which the children did not recall being played) in the kitchen in Rathfarnham and to the record collection that remained concealed until George Yeats presented it to her daughter in her mid-teens.[1] George Yeats's 'secret collection of records' was substantial, as she confided to Thomas MacGreevy in 1926, and included many operas.[2] But these recorded voices remained hushed and carefully stored away: indeed, she listened to her records clandestinely, for the gramophone was a source of noise which Yeats deemed deleterious to the good progress of his writing.

In contrast, the wireless was a tolerated presence: George Yeats owned a portable wireless set, which she would take with her when travelling in the late 1920s.[3] But it is only in January 1937 that the Yeatses acquired a more sophisticated device; following the cooling of his interest in Margot Ruddock, Yeats relented on his previous refusals and bought a Bush wooden radio for his wife ('For a long time Father wouldn't have one, he didn't like them', Anne Yeats explained later).[4] The protracted purchase of the device through the BBC was delayed by Yeats's ignorance of all things electric, but wireless telegraphy saved the day, as Lennox Robinson reported: '[the BBC] wanted to give him the best wireless set they could to his home in Rathfarnham, and they said: "Have you got electric light in the home?" He had to wire back to his wife to find out whether they *had* electric light – he found they hadn't.'[5] The acquisition of a new wireless set provided some light relief for a disaffected George Yeats whose frustration with her wayward husband had become difficult to ignore.[6] She listened assiduously to his BBC broadcasts, and their successes subsequently altered

---

[1] Ann Saddlemyer, *Becoming George: The Life of Mrs W. B. Yeats* (Oxford: Oxford University Press, 2002), 369. I thank the Editors and the external reader for their incisive suggestions; Tom Walker and Adrian Paterson, and the Yeats scholars in attendance at their symposium 'W. B. Yeats and the Arts', at which a section of this article was presented as a paper, for their generous responses; Trev Broughton, Emma Major, Nicholas Melia and Aisling Mullan for their insights on early drafts.

[2] George Yeats (hereafter GY) to MacGreevy, 31 December 1926, cited in Saddlemyer, *Becoming George*, 369.

[3] *Ibid.*, 422.

[4] A. Norman Jeffares, *W. B. Yeats: A New Biography*, second edition (London: Continuum, 2001), 250; Anne Yeats, cited in W. R. Rodgers, 'W. B. Yeats: A Dublin Portrait', in *In Excited Reverie: A Centenary Tribute to William Butler Yeats 1865-1939*, ed. A. Norman Jeffares and K. G. W. Cross (London: Macmillan, 1965), 7.

[5] Rodgers, 7.

[6] Saddlemyer, *Becoming George*, 514-15.

another aspect of her everyday: for example, the warm reception of his broadcast poem 'Roger Casement' in 1937, praised highly by Eamon De Valera, led to marked manifestations of 'deference' to her in Dublin shops.[7]

By the time of this purchase, Yeats had been intensely engaged in broadcasting with the BBC and had pioneered new writing techniques, germane to the demands of radio. Nevertheless, his reaction to this domestic acquisition suggested to his family that he had remained a bewildered neophyte: he feigned technological incompetence and granted corporeality and vocal presence to the machine. Anne Yeats later recalled that, unable to hear the wireless distinctly on the first evening, he leaned towards it, cupped his hand behind his ear and asked politely for clarification: 'I beg your pardon?'[8] His family were struck by his studied ignorance; Saddlemyer reports that this episode became 'one of George's set pieces', much to the children's amusement.[9] However, Yeats was not as naive in such matters as his anthropomorphizing of the wireless might suggest: he had a sound knowledge of the workings of radio, gained diffusely through conversations and work with the BBC, and his correspondence confirms his familiarity with some technicalities. In a letter of 2 January 1932 to him, George Yeats reported receiving mysterious messages from 2RN, the first Irish broadcasting service, over the telephone:

A very queer thing happened on the day after Christmas (Boxing Day) the telephone rang about 5 to nine. I answered it but instead of a reply I heard Italian opera being sung; I seized a chair and sat and listened. Presently, when I. Op. had ceased, a voice said 'this is 2 RN' then an announcement of a pantomime that was to be broadcast. Then a sort of preliminary song and the telephone suddenly cut off! I have been trying to find out what could have happened to make my telephone wire cut in on a broadcast, but so far without success.[10]

Yeats replied reassuringly, disowning the explanation as his own, but nevertheless conveying its nuances adequately:

---

[7] GY to W. B. Yeats (hereafter WBY), 13 October 1936 (*YGYL* 443); GY, cited in Colton Johnson, 'Yeats's Wireless', *The Wilson Quarterly*, 24, n. 2 (2000), 28.
[8] Rodgers, 7; see also Jeffares, *W. B. Yeats*, 250.
[9] Saddlemyer, *Becoming George*, 515.
[10] GY to WBY, 2 January 1932 (*YGYL* 283).

Richard [Gregory] thinks that it is quite possible that your telephone wire got the wireless wave (one of the others said before he came in that they make use of the telephone wires in relaying) or that you may have been rung in mistake for another number by some body at the Dublin Wireless Centre & heard the lound-speaker. One of the other men suggested that a joking friend rang you up & then held his reciever up against his wireless set.[11]

Richard Gregory may have been right: 2RN was operated by means of Marconi transmitters tuned at a wavelength that made their broadcasts prone to generating and being affected by interferences.[12] Its afternoon and evening programmes also included gramophone records on a daily basis.

These vignettes demonstrating Yeats's ambivalence towards sound transmission technologies are more than simply anecdotal: they provide insights into the register in which certain aspects of his experimental psychical research operated. Indeed, as Margaret Mills Harper has emphasised, sound transmission technologies provide a powerful discursive field for understanding some aspects of the Yeatses' depictions of the supernatural.[13] Their mixed responses to the ability of the wireless to capture mysterious, formerly unheard voices carry a weight that is external to the machine itself and owed to a wide-ranging spiritualist interest in sound transmission technologies: the ability of phonograph and wireless to capture sounds and voices had remained a source of fascination in spiritualist circles since the first forays into sound recording, and this ongoing conversation between W. B. and George Yeats finds many resonances in late nineteenth-century discourses about signal transmission, recording and psychical research.[14] Edison's phonograph, in particular, provided new frames of reference for investigations of the otherworld, finding

---

[11] WBY to GY, 10 January 1932 (*YGYL* 287).

[12] See Richard Pine, *2RN and the Origins of Irish Radio* (Dublin: Four Courts, 2002), 89, 105, 183.

[13] Margaret Mills Harper, *Wisdom of Two: The Spiritual and Literary Collaboration of George and W. B. Yeats* (Oxford: Oxford University Press, 2006), 160, 165-70.

[14] On the wider contexts of these transformations, see Pamela Thurschwell, *Literature, Technology and Magical Thinking, 1880-1920* (Cambridge: Cambridge University Press, 2001); Jonathan Sterne, *The Audible Past: Cultural Origins of Sound Reproduction* (Durham, NC: Duke University Press, 2003); Michael Chanan, *Repeated Takes: A Short History of Recording and its Effects on Music* (London: Verso, 1995); Jeffrey Sconce, *Haunted Media: Electronic Presence from Telegraphy to Television* (Durham, NC: Duke University Press, 2000); Helen Sword, *Ghostwriting Modernism* (Ithaca and London: Cornell University Press, 2002).

upon its inception an enthusiastic welcome in Madame Blavatsky's newly-formed Theosophical Society, into which Edison was immediately enrolled.[15] In December 1878, Blavatsky undertook a journey to India with a phonograph to foster new collaborations; a phonographic extravaganza dedicated to celebrating the powers of Edison's invention preceded her departure from New York. The proceedings reportedly transformed the phonograph into a portal to the unknown as well as a benevolent messenger entrusted with preserving a lore created for the occasion:

... a man came in with a phonograph which had been procured for the purpose of carrying greetings to India ... A tall sculptor was dislodged from a barrel on which he sat, and the phonograph was put in position, after which the greetings were shouted into the paper funnel, and a song in pigeon [sic] Hindustanee was sung into it by a jolly English artist. Charles, a huge theosophical cat, was then induced to purr at the machine, and the various records were carefully put away.[16]

Marconi's subsequent experiments with signal transmission, in turn, gave a new impulse to the debates about scientific discovery and psychical research that had emerged with Edison's invention. Yeats's friend W.T. Stead, for example, campaigned tirelessly for a spiritualism attuned to the new realms opened up by Marconi's and Edison's inventions. For Stead, the wireless and the telegraph could provide invaluable proofs of the persistence of spirit life after death as well as means of communicating with the deceased; the purpose of his organisation 'Julia's Bureau', well known to W. B. and George Yeats, was 'to enable those who had lost their dead, who were sorrowing over friends and relatives, to get into touch with them again'.[17] The metaphors and mechanisms used for letting the living 'hear messages' from the dead were indebted to stenography, telegraphy and telephony (*Life 1* 614, n. 42).[18]

---

[15] Neil Baldwin, *Edison: Inventing the Century* (Chicago: University of Chicago Press, 2001), 93-94.

[16] 'Silence in the Lamasery', *New York Sun*, 19 December 1878, quoted in Daniel H. Caldwell, *The Esoteric World of Madame Blavatsky: Insights Into the Life of a Modern Sphinx* (Wheaton, IL: Quest Books, 2001), 109.

[17] William T. Stead, *How I Know That the Dead Return* (Boston: Ball Publishing, 1909), 6; Saddlemyer, *Becoming George*, 54-55.

[18] Patrick Brantlinger, *Rule of Darkness: British Literature and Imperialism, 1830-1914* (Ithaca: Cornell University Press, 1990), 248-49.

Stead's experiments bear testimony to the powerful impact of Edison's and Marconi's discoveries on the Western cultural imagination. The specificity of the cultural and artistic matrix from which scientific experiments with wireless transmission and sound recording emerged has been well documented; cultural historians and musicologists have shown that the workings of the phonograph and the wireless were related to a widespread fascination for the unheard, uncaptured and unintelligible which expressed itself in idiosyncratic ways, resulting in the creation of machines that remained enmeshed in the rhetoric and processes of writing, demanding the mechanical or manual inscription of sounds or messages.[19] The wireless, for example, owed much to the format set by Edison, which transformed an intangible sound into a tangible groove, etched into solid matter; Marconi's early model of signal transmission replaced the writing needle of Edison's phonograph by a wireless operator or *marconista*, in charge of interpreting signals coming from a headset and ignoring interferences, a configuration indebted to the telegraph operator as well as the Morse machine itself.[20] Marconi's invention and the *marconista* had a determining impact upon modernist writing, particularly upon Ezra Pound; Timothy Campbell also highlights the proximity between Marconi's early wireless and late nineteenth-century fascination with the occult, drawing attention to the powerful symbolism underlying Marconi's invention and its strong focus on maternalizing forces.[21] More specifically, Campbell considers Marconi's successful experiments with wireless signal transmission between Ballycastle Beach and Rathlin Island as an attempt to summon the voice of his Wexford mother, Anne Jameson.[22] An opera singer related to the Jamesons and heir to their whiskey fortune, she had been led to emigrate to Italy by virtue of her beautiful voice

---

[19] See, in particular, *Wireless Imagination: Sound, Radio, and the Avant-Garde*, ed. Douglas Kahn and Gregory Whitehead (Cambridge, MA: MIT Press, 1994); Lisa Gitelman, *Scripts, Grooves, and Writing Machines: Representing Technology in the Edison Era* (Stanford: Stanford University Press, 1999); Timothy C. Campbell, *Wireless Writing in the Age of Marconi* (Minneapolis: University of Minnesota Press, 2006); Miriama Young, 'Singing the Body Electric: The Recorded Voice, the Mediated Body' (PhD dissertation, Princeton University, 2007); Bennett Hogg, 'The Cultural Imagination of the Phonographic Voice, 1877-1940' (PhD dissertation, University of Newcastle, 2008).

[20] Campbell, *Wireless Writing*, xiv, 2-3, 10-13.

[21] *Ibid.*, 15, 21-25.

[22] *Ibid.*, 2, 15-21.

and passion for music; she was very close to her son and instilled in him, or so the biographical accounts say, a strong patriotic love for Ireland, 'his country'.[23] Marconi's personal history was widely known in Ireland, from the first descriptions of his undertaking on the Northern Irish coast: the *Irish Times* was prompt to report on 'Signor Marconi's Irish Lineage' and to document his Wexford origins, casting the roots of Marconi's miraculous invention firmly into Irish soil, in a rebuff to the British newspapers which had celebrated his mother's English origins.[24]

Yeats was familiar with such experiments and their spiritualist currency. He even invested in and endorsed offshoots of Edison's and Marconi's inventions: in 1917, as Roy Foster and Christopher Blake report, he went to great lengths to support the invention of a peculiar machine, which he baptised the 'Metallic Homunculus', and whose speciality, being a little further removed from the coordinates of the British Empire, was not pidgin Hindustani but pidgin Turkish and Arabic.[25] The apparatus, 'a kind of ear-hole into the unknown region', could capture voices from the otherworld but proved vulnerable to 'interferences from mischievous spirits' or 'little beasts', as its inventor, David Wilson, called them (*Life 2* 80). Yeats's and Edmund Dulac's descriptions suggest that the device was a tautological compound of most important inventions to date which had found domestic applications. Yeats's account of his first encounter with the Metallic Homunculus conveys the technical confusion of the whole: he described 'a copper-lined mahogany box, rather bigger than a large microscope case', fitted with a 'brass mechanism', made of a 'glass-topped brazen drum and a small brass rod', on which was mounted 'a stumpy telescope', with a lens at the front and a hole at the back into which a bottle of 'metallic medium' could be screwed, the latter being linked to photographic plates.[26] The aim of Wilson's machine was to recreate the spirits' body parts as well as convey their messages, as Yeats reported: 'In the stumpy telescope the eyes materialize, and

---

[23] *Ibid.*, 18.

[24] 'Signor Marconi's Irish Lineage: His Mother a Wexford Lady', *Irish Times*, 15 January 1898.

[25] Christopher Blake, 'Ghosts in the Machine: W. B. Yeats and the *Metallic Homunculus*', in *YA15* 69-101. Blake reports that an article on Wilson's invention (called the 'Psychic Telegraph') by Estelle W. Stead, W. T. Stead's daughter, may have drawn Yeats's attention to it.

[26] Blake, 80; see also Dulac's description in Blake, 86.

under the metal disc the ear'.²⁷ Legal complications ensued from the sophistication of its components, and the contraption, categorised as an illegal wireless, was seized by the police (*Life 2* 80).

If Wilson's invention chimes well with spiritualist utilisations of the phonograph in Blavatsky's and Stead's circles, it also bears affinities to the many literary creations that emerged from Edison's mechanical ear, such as the tongue-tied speaking machine described in Marcel Schwob's 1892 'La machine à parler' ('The Speaking Machine'), whose inventor professes his fascination for Edison's recording of Robert Browning's voice. His instruction to utter 'I created the word' is transformed into a monstrous stammer: 'WOR-D WOR-D WOR-D'.²⁸ Repeating the failures of Schwob's fictional machine, Wilson's device delivered little by way of a message; its technical complexity concealed a complete inarticulacy. The Metallic Homunculus incidentally replicated the challenges posed by the early wireless in terms of signal confusion; its declarations proved unintelligible, and Yeats returned home empty-handed: 'I saw nothing and heard nothing. Apparently one can do neither unless one is clairaudient and clairvoyant.'²⁹ His notes later proved useful, however, for both he and George Yeats remained preoccupied with the workings of the device during their experimental séances in the early months of their marriage. Yeats wrote to Arthur Waley on 21 November 1917, once their séances with had gained greater momentum, asking him to return letters from Wilson describing his 'Metalic Medium' (*MYV1* 44). At this particular stage in Yeats's occultist pursuits, Wilson's machine provided an important point of reference for conceptualising the relation that Yeats discerned between psychical research, photography, phonography, telephony and the wireless, and for creating a register within which he could couch its limitations (*Life 2* 79-81).³⁰

II

Considered in this context, Yeats's emphatic demonstration of technological incompetence to the wireless set and to his family takes

---

²⁷ *Ibid.*, 80.
²⁸ Marcel Schwob, *Œuvres* (Paris: Les Belles Lettres, 2002), 248-49.
²⁹ Blake, 81.
³⁰ See also Blake, 69-80.

on new resonances, as does the confining of sound transmission to the domestic and feminine sphere in his household. George Yeats's transcriptions of a spirit activity that only she could hear fostered a strong bond with her husband at the start of their marriage, and the process of listening and transcribing during their sittings placed her in a position close to that of the *marconista*. Scholars have emphasised the idiosyncrasy of their working methods; George Mills Harper, in particular, has drawn attention to their avoidance of the rituals used by the mediums they knew and their extensive knowledge of the range of consecrated protocols used in psychical research (*MYV1* xii-xiii). The sittings, as reconstructed by Harper, were close to the telephone incident evoked by George Yeats in her 1932 letter: they involved sitting face-to-face at a table in broad daylight and borrowed heavily from the registers of telegraphy, telephony and wireless sound transmission. The Script, for example, originated from her feeling that 'something was to be written through her', as Yeats reported to Lady Gregory on 19 October 1917 (*L* 633). George Yeats became a 'receiver', a word often used in the mechanical sense of the term in their accounts (*MYV1* 181). The spirits whose voices she transcribed, as one of the 'communicators' (Thomas) revealed, operated in a different 'sphere of thought', 'not evoked by speech but by radiation of thought', to be captured by 'intermediaries' (*MYV1* 14). These statements align the Yeatses' experiments with techniques which would later come to be associated with Surrealism; drawing on the findings of pre-Freudian French Dynamic Psychiatry, which transformed the patient into a stenographer or recording device, André Breton presented Surrealist writers in the 1924 Surrealist Manifesto as the 'deaf receptacles of so many echoes', 'modest *recording machines* that are not hypnotised by the designs they trace.'[31] Christopher Schiff has traced the origins of Breton's statement in the research of Pierre Janet, whose treatise *L'Automatisme psychologique* presents the cataleptic patient as 'a phonograph'.[32] Janet's theories, which emphasised the power of writing to delve into the

---

[31] Quoted in Maurice Nadeau, *The History of Surrealism*, trans. Richard Howard (London: Jonathan Cape, 1968), 89, n. 11. The original reads: 'sourd réceptacles de tant d'échos', 'modestes *appareils enregistreurs* qui ne s'hypnotisent pas sur le dessin qu'ils tracent.' André Breton, *Manifestes du Surréalisme* (Paris: Gallimard, 2005), 39. On these influences, see Christopher Schiff, 'Banging on the Windowpane: Sound in Early Surrealism', in *Wireless Imagination*, 171-72.

[32] Pierre Janet, *L'Automatisme psychologique* (Paris: Félix Alcan, 1889), 18.

depths of the psyche, influenced many modernist writers, including Pound, who read Janet carefully as a student, between 1910 and 1914.[33]

The Yeatses, also learned in the discipline of psychology, were familiar with spiritualist utilisations of machines predicated on recording and inscription. Their belief in the power of these inventions to open doors onto the supernatural found many expressions, individual and collective, from Yeats's mysterious decision to pose for spirit-photographs and experiments with the Metallic Homunculus to their actual sittings.[34] Their working methods, which reveal their awareness that the doors into the unheard and uncaptured could be codified in particular ways, remained dependent upon a syntax merging the auditory and the visual that has more to do with Edison's and Marconi's inventions than with the Order of the Golden Dawn and other occult societies. Like Marconi's wireless operator, George Yeats cast herself into the role of scribe, transcribed signals that only she could hear, ascribed meaning to a complex universe made up of interferences and inaudibilities, determined which messages were worthy of attention and negotiated the simultaneous demands of listening and writing.[35] Disturbances remained important to the process; the Scripts pay close attention to interferences originating from communicators remaining between immanence and occurrence, 'invisible & inaudible & immanifested' (*YVP1* 55). Their experiments, thus, were aligned not only with discoveries surrounding wireless transmission, but also with enshrined cultural beliefs in what these discoveries could achieve at the level of cognition.

Neither party was impervious to the troubled relationship between George Yeats's peculiar take on the séance and wireless transmission; indeed, their correspondence about Yeats's introductory essay to *The Words upon the Window-pane* features a dispute about the relationship between the transmission of soundwaves and the role of the medium. This episode, in Margaret Mills Harper's study, is presented as revealing of the dynamics of their collaboration.[36] Yeats's essay argues for an element of performativity at the heart of the séance, stating that 'every voice that speaks, every form that appears ... is first of all a secondary personality or dramatization created by, in, or through

---

[33] Donald J. Childs, *T. S. Eliot: Mystic, Son, and Lover* (London: Athlone, 1997), 11.

[34] See Kathleen Raine, 'Hades Wrapped in Cloud', in *YO* 100, Plate 1.

[35] On the *marconista*, see Campbell, *Wireless Writing*, xiv, 2-3.

[36] Harper, *Wisdom of Two*, 166-69.

the medium' (*Ex* 364). Doubtful of the validity of his argument, George Yeats objected in no uncertain terms to his assimilation of the medium's method to the mechanics of wireless transmission, suggesting that his criticism of the medium's intuition was simply ignorant:

> If I had to interpret that 'commentary' I could not say that any 'spirit' were present at any seance, that spirits were present at a seance only as impersonations created by a medium out of material in a world record just as wireless photography or television are created; that all communicating spirits are mere dramatisations of that record; that all spirits in fact are not so far as psychic communications are concerned, spirits at all, are only memory.[37]

The peculiar phrase 'wireless photography' may be read as an expression of her indignation; it also reflects the place which photography and the wireless had come to occupy in spiritualist circles, as tropes signifying new realms of exploration and new techniques, rather than distinctive technologies. Replying to her comments, Yeats returned once again to the parallel between the séance and the wireless, stating his having been particularly 'moved' by it, carefully locating the origin of their disagreement elsewhere, in his use of the word 'unconscious', and reverting to more generic evocations of dramatisation.[38]

Some of the cues for their disagreement can be found in Yeats's 1914 draft essay on the automatic writing of Elizabeth Radcliffe; the essay comments upon Radcliffe's analogies between her methods (which called for messages to be 'visualized mentally by her ears') and the task of the *marconista*, evoking 'actual words' 'spoken and caught by a highly sensitive physical hand as waves of sound take shape – think of wireless.'[39] Significantly, Marconi's invention provided a register in the Yeats family for thinking about the supernatural; Lily Yeats reportedly described her own prophetic visions as 'something which the Marconis of the future will make use of'.[40] Similarly, in a 1919 interview, John B. Yeats suggested that Yeats had been thinking about Marconi's invention as a foundational moment that yielded new cognitive possibilities: 'He expects a great Marconi some day in the future to explain the occult to

---

[37] GY to WBY, 24 November 1931 (*YGYL* 270).
[38] WBY to GY, 25 November 1931 (*YGYL* 272).
[39] George Mills Harper and John S. Kelly, 'Preliminary Examination of the Script of E[lizabeth] R[adcliffe]', *YO* 156.
[40] William M. Murphy, 'Psychic Daughter, Mystic Son, Sceptic Father', *YO* 22.

us.'⁴¹ This connection between Marconi and contemporaneous interest in the occult had long been a feature of commentaries on the wireless, including in Ireland; a chronicle published in the *Irish Times* in 1896 responding to the success of Marconi's wireless experiments remarked that '[i]t does not seem to be a far cry from this to the 'thought waves' of theosophists!'⁴²

Yeats's polite request to the wireless set to speak more audibly thus stands as a testament to his own uncertainties concerning psychical research methods, which were embedded, in their turn, into wider cultural anxieties concerning the potential of sound recording technologies. His cupped hand behind his ear, recreating the kind of amplification that an ear trumpet would foster, is not simply a declaration of incompetence in the face of sounds coming from a source that remains concealed: it also emulates methods widely used in séances for dramatising an interaction with an elusive, inaudible otherworld, and recalls the posture of the trumpet medium materialising the transmission of spirit voices by intercalating an object between mouth and message. More specifically, Yeats's posture recalls the methods of Etta Wriedt, a medium who was a regular in Stead's home. Wriedt was a direct-voice medium: spirit voices were not heard through her lips but appeared to surface out of the ether or were relayed via trumpets.⁴³ The Yeatses were impressed by the performative sophistication of her séances; Wriedt's trumpet surfaces in George Yeats's early scripts, and Yeats, equally fascinated by the process, expressed doubts concerning its integrity, leading to his dismissal from Wriedt's séances (*MYV2* 78).⁴⁴ Considered in this context, Yeats's categorisation of the wireless voice as barely audible finds powerful correlations in spiritualist associations of the otherworld with the boundaries of the intelligible.

Yeats's cupped hand, an improvised prosthetic trumpet of sorts, finds further resonances in the context of the theatre. Anecdotal evidence surrounding the radical ideas of composer George Antheil suggests that Yeats was receptive to the theatrical potential of sound amplifying devices from the late 1920s. Antheil, struck by Yeats's fascination for occult matters, commented with indulgence upon Yeats's ability to see ghosts 'in broad daylight' ('a rather difficult feat') and upon the ghostly

---

⁴¹ *Ibid.*, 22, n. 24. John Yeats attributes Lily's evocation of Marconi to W. B. Yeats.
⁴² 'Talk of the Town, by A Lady', *Irish Times*, 26 December 1896.
⁴³ Fred Archer, *Exploring the Psychic World* (New York: William Morrow, 1967), 54.
⁴⁴ Saddlemyer, *Becoming George*, 55.

intrusions which frequently perturbed their conversations.⁴⁵ The score which Antheil wrote for *Fighting the Waves*, his adaptation of *The Only Jealousy of Emer*, accounts for Yeats's interest in disembodied voices and grants a new visuality to sound transmission and amplification; Antheil indicated in complementary notes to the Abbey Theatre that Fand's dance should be performed against a figuration of the fusion of musical and vocal sound: 'Trombone should fit into its bell an enormous extension cardboard megaphone extending at least one yard from the end of the instrument.'⁴⁶ Antheil's interest in the visuality of sound and dramatisations of listening may, in turn, have informed Yeats's own exploration of voices moving in and out of earshot in the Crazy Jane poems written in March 1929, while in sustained dialogue with Antheil.⁴⁷ The latter's vision of a double trumpet structure may have been inspired by the first self-stylised Surrealist play, Guillaume Apollinaire's 1917 *Les mamelles de Tirésias*, in which the stage is dominated by a megaphone in the shape of a dice cup, and hands are occasionally transformed into ear trumpets. The idea of embedding one sound source into another was certainly in keeping with the *Zeitgeist*; in a 1923 performance of a poem entitled *Façade*, set to music by William Walton, Edith Sitwell recited the text through a Sengerphone (a papier mâché megaphone), remaining concealed behind a curtain which had been decorated with two masks, painted to look as if her amplified voice was originating from one of them.⁴⁸ In this instance, the diffuse web of influences linking Yeats's drama to French Surrealism, which Michael McAteer has identified, is brought to the fore: via Antheil's compositional method, Yeats's experimental dramatic practice engages Surrealist and proto-Surrealist experiments with the listening ear.⁴⁹

⁴⁵ Quoted in Liam Miller, *The Noble Drama of W. B. Yeats* (Dublin: Dolmen Press, 1977), 278.
⁴⁶ *Ibid.*, 281.
⁴⁷ March 1929 was a very productive month for Yeats; see John Kelly, *A W. B. Yeats Chronology* (Basingstoke: Palgrave Macmillan, 2003), 264.
⁴⁸ See John Pearson, *Façades: Edith, Osbert, and Sacheverell Sitwell* (London: Macmillan, 1978), 182; Alan Young, *Dada and After: Extremist Modernism and English Literature* (Manchester: Manchester University Press, 1981), 48-49; Tim Barringer, 'Façades for *Façade*: William Walton, Visual Culture and English Modernism in the Sitwell Circle', in *British Music and Modernism, 1895-1960*, ed. Matthew Riley (Farnham: Ashgate, 2010), 125-26.
⁴⁹ Michael McAteer, *Yeats and European Drama* (Cambridge: Cambridge University Press, 2010), 7, 78-83, 100-09.

III

Yeats's response to the wireless upon his first domestic encounter with it thus crystallises concerns both within and outside his own artistic remit, and points to a knowledge accumulated through his involvement with occult societies and psychical research, areas in which he found himself confronted by his inability to *hear*. His experiments with George Yeats, in particular, remained marked by the lack of audibility of the otherworld to him and by his recognition that his wife's ear was attuned to the stirrings of the otherworld. The gift of a wireless set to her should be thought of in this context: she presided over things wireless in the household, having operated as a *marconista* of sorts in the early years of their marriage, and having established the realms between the audible and inaudible as her territory. However, Yeats was far more intimate with matters of radio transmission than George Yeats; indeed, it is now well known that he was one of the first poets to embrace wireless broadcasting, becoming a regular speaker on BBC programmes between September 1931 and October 1937, until ill-health prevented him from honouring his commitments.[50]

His correspondence with his BBC producer George Barnes reveals his willingness to work with as well as beyond the peculiar technical demands of radio; Barnes was particularly impressed by the time and effort that Yeats put into training actors to recite his poems so as to echo 'the sounds which were running in his head'.[51] To a Yeats aware of the formal constraints of the medium and eager for experiment, radio represented a new departure in a long-standing exploration of chanting and musical speech, a facet of his career which Ronald Schuchard has illuminated.[52] Poetry broadcasts, whose conventions were as yet unformalised, granted Yeats the freedom to conceive new relationships between musical speech and non-vocal sound. Initially, as Barnes reports, Yeats considered experimenting with 'unaccompanied singing of a refrain' and with

---

[50] Johnson, 25-30; Jeremy Silver, 'W. B. Yeats and the BBC: A Reassessment', *YA5* 181-85; see also George Whalley, 'Yeats and Broadcasting', in *Wade* 467-77.

[51] George Barnes, 'W. B. Yeats and Broadcasting' [1940], introduced by Jeremy Silver, *YA5* 192-93.

[52] Ronald Schuchard, *The Last Minstrels: Yeats and the Revival of the Bardic Arts* (Oxford: Oxford University Press, 2008), ix, xxiv, 335-403.

'the use of a drum or other musical instrument between stanzas or between poems, but never behind the voice, in order to heighten the intensity of the rhythm'.[53] These considerations may have emerged from a dissatisfaction with previous broadcast readings which had used musical accompaniment.[54] Yeats ascribed to the radiophonic voice the power to enhance the rich and varied textures of poetic diction: he considered adding musical instruments, but only to mark pauses; musical notes in that instance 'must never be loud enough to shift the attention of the ear.'[55] As such, radio broadcasting enabled Yeats to write not only 'for the ear', but also for the microphone: hence, to inscribe into the poetic utterance nuances in diction otherwise only faintly perceptible (*E&I* 530). In the studio, the attention that Yeats paid to these minute elements at the threshold of audibility posed serious challenges, and Barnes's account of rehearsals with Margot Ruddock and Victor Clinton-Baddeley expresses bewilderment at Yeats's ability to discern (with a sensitivity that 'outran comprehension') that which others 'could hardly hear', commenting, like many others before him, upon Yeats's 'wildly inaccurate' notion of pitch and his 'hav[ing] no ear for music as it is understood in Western Europe.'[56]

On air, Yeats also proved to be an artful storyteller, attuned to the importance of fine narrative nuances and to the capacity of radio to capture voices and create forms of presence out of the void. Barnes's recollection of Yeats the broadcaster at work, posing for posterity at the BBC's London studios in 1938, chimes well with what had become George Yeats's 'set piece' at home: '... sitting down, his left hand cocked up with the little finger erect, and his head on one side, listening intently to the sound of his words as they come out of the loudspeaker.'[57] The published texts of Yeats's broadcasts highlight, sometimes candidly, his awareness of the possibilities and the limitations of radio, and his desire to develop the imaginative capacities of an immaterial audience. Prefatory comments and interludes regulate this unruly imaginary universe and enhance Yeats's discussions of the power of radio to bring

---

[53] Barnes, 189-90. Yeats alluded to these ideas in 'In The Poet's Pub', his first collaboration with Barnes. See W. B. Yeats, 'In the Poet's Pub' *CW10* 267.
[54] See Silver, 182-83; Schuchard, 285-403.
[55] Barnes, 190.
[56] *Ibid.*, 192-93.
[57] *Ibid.*, 193.

voices out of the ether and to grant insights into worlds formerly unseen or devoid of sight. Yeats's talks often draw attention to the ability of radio to overcome a whole range of sensory obstacles; for example, the text of 'In the Poet's Pub', broadcast on 2 April 1937, is heavily reliant upon spoken interludes, setting the scene carefully to enable its listener to apprehend the musicality of the metre prior to a dramatised reading of Hilaire Belloc's 'Tarantella'. Yeats's stated aim, in this instance, is to reproduce the intimacy of a singing session in the pub by granting an accidental quality to the broadcast and transforming the listener into an eavesdropper.[58] Key to this recreation of an intimate atmosphere are the mannerisms normally confined to the margins of the performance, the 'tricks' that all folk singers, in Yeats's view, use to 'break the monotony and rest the mind', including 'clap[ping] their hands to the tune or crack[ing] their fingers or whistl[ing]' (*CW10* 266). Yeats's careful preparatory storytelling creates this sense of intimacy just as it draws attention to, and overcomes, the invisibility of soundwaves:

> I want you to imagine yourself in a Poets' Pub. There are such pubs in Dublin and I suppose elsewhere. You are sitting among poets, musicians, farmers and labourers. The fact that we are in a pub reminds somebody of Belloc's poem beginning 'Do you know an inn, Miranda', and then somebody recites the first and more vigorous part of Chesterton's 'Rolling English Drunkard', and then, because everybody in the inn except me is very English and we are all a little drunk, somebody recites De la Mare's 'Three Jolly Farmers' as patter. Patter is singing or speaking very quickly with very marked time, an art known to all old actors in my youth. We are all delighted, and at every pause we want to pound the table with our tankards. As, however, a tankard must be both heard and seen, the B.B.C. has substituted the rolling of a drum (*CW10* 267).

This final reference to technical demands which have been successfully met does not only break the carefully constructed illusion: it also conveys Yeats's fascination for the technical aspects of radio broadcasting. A few months prior to the broadcast, on 27 January 1937, Yeats wrote to Barnes, agreeing to adopt a more imaginative approach to sound effects and acknowledging that non-naturalistic musical sounds could be transmitted with greater clarity

---

[58] Emily Bloom points out that Yeats's approach to broadcasting remained aligned with common practice at the BBC; his dramatisation of his audience 'as a small, familiar group coincided with conventional wisdom among radio broadcasters at the time.' See Emily C. Bloom, 'Yeats's Radiogenic Poetry: Oral Traditions and Auditory Publics', *Eire - Ireland*, 46, n. 3&4 (2011), 232.

than sounds inscribed in a naturalistic frame. He wished for economy and simplicity, desirous to 'make everybody understand that we don't want professionally trained singers but the sort of people who sing when they are drunk or in love' (*L* 879). Radio, in this instance, proved to be an appropriate channel for expressing emotions in a musical speech indebted to minstrelsy: as such, as Schuchard has shown, writing for radio granted, for Yeats, new imaginative strength and immediacy to the ancient bardic traditions which he had for so long sought to revive, and his BBC broadcasts represent the culmination of his attempt to create an intimacy with a malleable audience receptive to this aspiration.[59]

The texts of Yeats's broadcasts display his shrewd observation of the dramatic potential of radio broadcasting and eagerness to dramatise his poetry readings in order to account for the specificities of the medium. He wrote differently when he wrote for radio, using in his talks and prefatory comments simple grammatical constructions and short sentences, paced in order to enable regular breathing. More importantly, the texts of his broadcasts create a vocabulary for apprehending the sense of immediacy and intimacy produced by the radio, providing their listener with a rhetoric and imagery that overcome the absence of a visual dimension. Evocations of ignorance, decay, uncertainty and imaginative blindness prove particularly efficient. For instance, the text of Yeats's first BBC broadcast, a commentary upon his translation of Sophocles's *Oedipus the King* aired on 8 September 1931, revolves around an acknowledgement of his own ignorance in order to foreground the imaginative potential of radio broadcasting as well as pre-empt the reaction of listeners unfamiliar with his drama and radio drama generally: 'If the wireless can be got to work, in the country house where I shall

---

[59] For Ronald Schuchard, Yeats's broadcasts represent the culmination of his reflections on the bardic tradition and gestures towards minstrelsy; with radio, his search for ways of creating intimacy with his audience found a new articulation. Going further, Emily Bloom argues that 'that radio played a pivotal role as a medium through which Yeats performed, publicized, and published poetry at the end of his life', and that the broadcast audience, which Yeats ceaselessly re-imagined, 'was an active influence in shaping the auditory poetics of his late lyrics' (228). See Schuchard, 335-403; Bloom, 227-51. On Yeats's interest in poetic diction and desire to emulate the *fili*, and on the particular significance of radio to this endeavour, see also Jacqueline Genet, *Words for Music Perhaps: Le 'new art' de Yeats / Words for Music Perhaps: Yeats's 'New Art'* (Villeneuve d'Ascq: Presses Universitaires du Septentrion, 2010), 52-54.

be staying, I shall be listening too, and as I have never heard a play broadcasted I do not know whether I shall succeed in calling into my imagination that ancient theatre' (*CW10* 220). Yeats subsequently lays the ground for thinking about the suitability of classical tragedy to radio: he associates the plight of the blind Oedipus with that of the blind Raftery, summoning tragic voices which find a new channel in what is often presented as a 'blind medium'.[60] The radio, in turn, grants unique insights into a literary tradition dominated by blind seers and bards, delving into age-old human experiences and knowledge. Absence also takes on a new weight; Yeats concludes by considering the radio's invisible audience and its unrivalled and unfathomable capacity to speak to multitudes, evoking the ability of radio broadcasting to reach the millions of Irishmen and women 'scattered throughout the world', 'ready to share our imagination and our discoveries' (*CW10* 223). This final statement suggests a faint hope that wireless broadcasting might foster a new cultural cohesion and, perhaps, succeed where the stage might have failed. This invisible body of listeners remained in Yeats's thoughts; later, in June 1937, he thought of a programme with Dulac that would playfully incorporate this absent audience. He wrote of his ambition

to work it all up into a kind of drama in which we will get very abusive, and then one or other of us will say with a change of voice, 'Well, I hope they will have taken all that seriously and believe that we shall never speak to each other again.' The other will say, 'Stop, the signal is still on, they can hear us.' Then the first speaker will say 'God', or if that is barred out by the BBBC [*sic*] – 'Hell!'[61]

Throughout his broadcasting career, Yeats never ceased to find inspiration in the visual lack rendered by the soundwave, and the specific requirements and resonances of radio broadcasting provide the matrix for many of his later commentaries and poetry readings. For example, the 1937 'Abbey Theatre Broadcast', for which Yeats had great expectations, incorporated a reading of 'Roger Casement'

---

[60] On the problems surrounding the categorisation of radio as a 'blind medium', see Julie Campbell, '"A voice comes to one in the dark. Imagine": Radio, the Listener and the Dark Comedy of *All That Fall*, in *Beckett and Death*, ed. Steven Barfield, Matthew Feldman and Philip Tew (London: Continuum, 2009), 151.

[61] This idea was for a programme entitled 'My Own Poetry', which was to include a debate between Yeats and James Stephens, but Stephens declined and Dulac replaced him. Barnes, 194.

into a series of acoustic deathmasks which playfully took as their first predicate bodily decay and an ability to imagine a shared past, peopled by ghosts. In an interlude preceding John Stephenson's sung performances, Yeats asks his audience to overcome the boundaries of corporeality, to imagine a history that cannot be fully envisioned and, in so doing, to dutifully pay tribute to the nation's dead political fathers. He asks his listeners to think of themselves as 'old men, old farmers perhaps, accustomed to read newspapers and listen to songs, but not to read books', as 'old and decrepit, because [they] have been to Glasnevin on all the anniversaries of Parnell's death for the last forty years' (*CW10* 262). The process of imagining this shared past borrows from the register of the séance: 'There are not many of you left, and you're to imagine yourselves sitting in a public house, after you have returned from Glasnevin graveyard' (*CW10* 262-3).

This passage serves a double function, as a preparation for both Stephenson's performance of 'Come Gather Round Me Parnellites' and his reading of James Stephens's 'In the Night'. Stephens's poem, as reproduced in the text of Yeats's broadcast, evokes the terror created by '[t]he noise of silence and the noise of blindness', which hold the poet still ('They hold me stark and rigid as a tree!') and bind his power to listen to an immutable natural order whose complexity cannot be comprehended:

> Their tumult is more loud
> Than thunder,
> They terrify my soul! They tear
> My heart asunder! (*CW10* 264)

Stephens's dirge takes on poignant undertones when considered alongside the blind and blinded listeners and bards, from Homer to Raftery, who populate Yeats's talks. The poem, as Colton Johnson points out, was abbreviated in the broadcast (*CW10* 403, n. 466). In the original, the first stanza emulates an Aisling poem when evoking the limits of cognition: 'There always is a noise when it is dark; | It is the noise of silence and the noise | Of blindness.'[62] Yeats's abbreviation, associating silence with blindness, grants a radiophonic dimension to this exclamation of bardic despair resonating through the ages: here, the power of the wireless to capture voices out of the

---

[62] James Stephens, 'In the Night', in *The Poems of James Stephens*, ed. Shirley Stevens Mulligan (Gerrards Cross: Colin Smythe, 2006), 100.

ether facilitates the process of re-imagining a lost primeval culture which must be spoken of in order to arise from speechlessness, songlessness and darkness. These analogies chime powerfully with Yeats's early meditations on bardic poetry, which evoke a poetic utterance returning to life to re-awaken the ear as well as the mind's eye, emulating the journey of a signal on the wire which one, in turn, must strain to hear. His 1890 review 'Bardic Ireland', for instance, praises the heightened form of historical 'self-consciousness' that found 'its most complete expression' in the art of the *fili*, and summons the image of a chanted verse 'sung out of the void by the harps of the great bardic order' (*UP1* 162, 164). The review draws attention to the imminent resurgence of a primeval 'Celtic passion', which, 'lost in the ages', 'murmurs like a dark and stormy sea full of the sounds of lamentation' (*UP1* 166).

The bardic self-consciousness which Yeats so aspired to emulate at the onset of his career as a poet could find new metaphorisations on the blank canvas of radio broadcasting, germane to rendering those fundamental and yet submerged nuances unknown to the musician which his 'older ears' alone could capture in musical speech and chanting (*Ex* 218).[63] Evocations of sounds and voices travelling through the air and through time are integral to Yeats's BBC broadcasts: the scripts represent the process of broadcasting as uniquely able to render the artfulness of ancient bardic traditions and create a self-conscious form of expression, drawing equally on poetry and music, across temporal and spatial boundaries. In 'Reading of Poems', broadcast on 8 September 1931, Yeats draws attention to Homer's proximity to his own words and to his own ability to ventriloquise bardic methods of poetic diction (*CW10* 229). 'Poems about Women', broadcast on 10 April 1932, also refers to utterances crossing a void, bringing the past into the present and the dead into the world of the living. Yeats's speech begins with an analogy between the difficulties he had experienced when preparing his talk and those he had previously encountered during a public reading which continues to haunt him and is here re-imagined. His account of finding himself engaged in a tense dialogue with a demanding audience borrows from a radiophonic or phonographic register: 'voices', one of which was memorably 'cracked' and 'high', 'came' to him with requests for love poetry (*CW10* 234). Similarly, 'In

---

[63] See also Schuchard, 85-86.

the Poet's Parlour', broadcast on 22 April 1937 and conceived as a sequel to 'In the Poet's Pub', invokes spectres whose utterances lie at the threshold of the audible. The script briefly relocates the poet into the theatre, introducing instead of a studio manager, a ghostly 'stage manager' who has come to relay the request from 'one or two of the poets present' for less 'melancholy' poems and a return to 'our pub', in which 'they were much more at home' (*CW10* 278).[64] The appeal from these expert listeners, modelled to anticipate the reactions of Yeats's invisible radiophonic audience, is scripted as if conveyed in a Morse code of sorts: 'Y-e-s? Will you pardon me for a moment while I read a note from our stage manager. (I will rustle paper). O – O – I understand' (*CW10* 278). This dramatic interruption, articulated tongue firmly in cheek, gestures towards the bardic traditions which Yeats had invited to bear upon his own readings in previous broadcasts, as he invoked Homer, Raftery, Shakespeare and Sophocles. Yeats's announcement of an accompaniment with clatter-bones to take place at a later point in the broadcast playfully points to the resilient presence of these spectres, as poetic diction finds a new malleability in the studio (*CW10* 278).

IV

The recordings of Yeats's BBC broadcasts have, over time, turned into precious relics themselves; indeed, the bombing of London reduced his radiophonic output to debris, leaving in its wake only one complete recording, that of 'In the Poet's Pub', and four other fragments.[65] Yet Yeats's crackling voice found many afterlives, including in the hands of Samuel Beckett, who gave a tape recording of Yeats reading his poetry to his friends, the painter Avigdor Arikha and his wife, the poet Anne Atik. Atik later remarked upon Beckett's indifference to Yeats's matter-of-fact delivery and idiosyncratic chanting, noting that 'it didn't seem to bother Sam that Yeats read some of his own poems, with notable exceptions ... at breakneck

---

[64] For Bloom, this particular episode conveys Yeats's uncertainty concerning the 'kind of orality radio resembled', and is representative of the ways in which Yeats 'incorporated and radically altered dramatic, bardic, and modern verse recitation traditions to suit the new medium' (232).

[65] Schuchard, xxv; Johnson, 30; Silver, 181.

speed – as though he couldn't wait to get the reading over with.'[66] Beckett, a keen wireless listener, may have heard Yeats's broadcasts during the 1930s; thereafter, he referred to Yeats as the vessel for messages from another world and another time, delivered with far too much haste and too little sense of their contents. A letter of 1957 recalls a Yeats 'rambling Swift' during their only meeting in Killiney, in September 1932; on the same occasion, Yeats had recited a few lines from Beckett's *Whoroscope* (published in a small print-run two years previously), much to Beckett's surprise.[67] Echoing this vision of Yeats as ventriloquist, Beckett's 1934 review of Irish modernist poetry, 'Recent Irish Poetry', makes an analogy between Yeats and a fantastical creature unable to sing and yet dedicated to tearing apart the organs that might grant it a voice: the review dismisses 'that fabulous bird, the mesozoic pelican, addicted, though childless, to self-eviscerations.'[68]

Despite his vast practical experience, Yeats repeatedly pleaded his ignorance of the workings of radio transmission and of the kinds of responses it might spur from the public.[69] The advertisements of his first 1931 broadcast are surprisingly candid: '... instead of speaking to a great many people altogether I shall be speaking to a great many people who will be separated. What it feels like to listen to a man speaking over the radio I do not know, for although I have heard music broadcast I have never listened to anyone speaking over the wireless.'[70] His comments to friends and family about the experience are similarly tinged with indifference and naivety. He presented his radio work as 'a new technique which amuses me & keeps me writing' to Pound, and as a handsome complement to the family budget to his wife, glossing over the low fees paid by the BBC.[71]

His experience of broadcasting, however, remained constrained by the technological and artistic difficulties inherent to this new artistic

---

[66] Anne Atik, *How It Was* (London: Faber, 2001), 59. The date and origin of the recording are not mentioned.

[67] Beckett to H. O. White, 14 April 1957, quoted in Emilie Morin, *Samuel Beckett and the Problem of Irishness* (Basingstoke: Palgrave Macmillan, 2009), 36; John Pilling, *Samuel Beckett: A Chronology* (Basingstoke: Palgrave Macmillan, 2006), 24-25, 39; Richard Ellmann, 'Samuel Beckett: Nayman of Noland', in *Four Dubliners: Wilde, Yeats, Joyce, and Beckett* (London: Hamilton, 1987), 110.

[68] Samuel Beckett, *Disjecta*, ed. Ruby Cohn (London: Calder, 2001), 72.

[69] Johnson, 25.

[70] 9 September 1931, quoted in Schuchard, 339.

[71] Quoted in Johnson, 24; see also Silver, 183.

realm, and ended in a seemingly issueless confrontation with its limitations in the realms of the unseen and unheard. His broadcasting career momentarily came to a halt, following his disappointment with Stephenson's performances of 'Come Gather Round Me Parnellites' and 'Roger Casement', broadcast on 1 February 1937, for which he had had high hopes. Yeats's frustration with the result had to do with the process of sound transmission, and he communicated his disarray to Barnes in strong terms the following day, complaining that the radio had turned '[e]very human sound' 'into the groans, roars, bellows of a wild [beast]' and presenting the technological limitations of radio as a setback for the art of poetry as a whole:

> Possibly all that I think noble and poignant in speech is impossible. Perhaps my old bundle of poet's tricks is useless. I got Stephenson while singing 'Come all old Parnellites' to clap his hands in time to the music after every verse and [the poet F. R.] Higgins added people in the wings clapping their hands. It was very stirring – on the wireless it was a schoolboy knocking with the end of a pen-knife or a spoon (*L* 879).

Higgins, as Colton Johnson and Ronald Schuchard report, managed to alleviate Yeats's anxieties: he persuaded Yeats that he had 'mismanaged' his wireless set by tuning in to 'too powerful' a station and that a different microphone arrangement would solve the other problems.[72] In later correspondence with Walter James Turner, Yeats used a similar analogy: comparing the broadcast to 'the roaring of beasts in the jungle', he deplored his own ignorance of the workings of the microphone: 'The arrangement had a great success on the stage so I have not the least notion what was wrong. I do not know enough' (*CW10* 400, n. 455).

Yeats's observations about the distortion created by wireless transmission suggest that he had momentarily ceased to see broadcasting as capable of conveying the richness of poetic meter and rhyme, due to technical limitations he had suddenly found himself unable to pre-empt and control. He had expressed similar reservations about the phonograph; a letter to Lady Gregory of 10 December 1909 reveals his appreciation of Pound's understanding of musical reading but compares his singing to 'something on a very bad phonograph' (*L* 543).[73] The phonograph and wireless, here as in the letters to Barnes and Turner, are associated with artistic

---

[72] Johnson, 27; Schuchard, 377.
[73] On the broader context, see Schuchard, 264.

incompetence and lyrical deficiency, interfering with the artist's craft rather than opening up new avenues for the imagination. It is worth noting, however, that Yeats's depiction of sound transmission as a process able to transform poetry into monstrous 'groans, roars, bellows' and seasoned performers into schoolboys finds powerful resonances in the history of recording. Early inventors experimenting with recorded sound faced similar problems. The first words uttered by Charles Cros, the inventor of the failed paleophone or paleograph, into the recording and engraving device which he had invented prior to Edison's phonograph were a line of poetry, and the word 'Merde'.[74] The expletive chimes well with the opening line of Alfred Jarry's *Ubu Roi*, 'Merdre!', the premiere of which had prompted Yeats to announce an impending dark age (*Au* 348-49).

In the light of Yeats's persistent attempts to diminish the artistic significance of his engagement with radio, these anecdotes become very telling: indeed, when he presented himself as a neophyte, he did so in very specific terms, by (as in these instances) evoking a process of shape-shifting, from the human to the animal. It is possible to trace the genealogy of such an association back to Edison: Edison's first recording was of himself reciting 'Mary Had A Little Lamb', which was soon followed by the mass production of recordings of animal noises destined to children's ears. But what is significant, more than Yeats's anthropomorphizing of the machine, is his alignment of voice transmission with writing, due to the roots of such configuration of the wireless in Edison's conception of the phonographic voice. Yeats's career as a broadcaster thus finds origins and motives in certain facets of his own psychical research as well as his interest in contemporaneous technological developments.

V

Comparisons between broadcasting and writing abound in Yeats's declarations about the wireless; for example, in a 1931 interview, Yeats depicted the microphone as 'a little oblong of paper like a visiting card', which he thought 'a poor substitute for a crowded

---

[74] See Martin Kaltenecker, 'Thanatographies', *Recueil* 33 (1994), 74; Howard Sutton, 'Charles Cros, the Outsider', *The French Review* 39, n. 4 (1966), 517-18.

Plates 3a & b. Yeats at the Microphone, very probably March 1937. Photographs of unknown authorship, courtesy Colin Smythe.

hall'.⁷⁵ Later, in a BBC talk entitled 'Poems about Women', broadcast on 10 April 1932, he compared speaking before a microphone to addressing 'something that looks like a visiting card on a pole' (*CW10* 234). Likewise, when evoking Stephenson's impending reading of 'Roger Casement', Yeats used specific analogies with letter-writing, informing Patrick McCartan that the poem would be 'sent out on the wireless from Athlone' (Radio Athlone having succeeded to 2RN) and, that 'the "record" of it [would] then be sent to Cairo, where the wireless is in Irish hands.'⁷⁶ The soundwave, here, materialises into written word, demanding manual support in a manner which replicates Yeats's genteel request to the wireless set in his home to speak more clearly and audibly ('I beg your pardon?'), using his cupped hand as a prop in order to apprehend its auditory demands.

Yeats's perception of the wireless as harbouring mysterious voices that demand remembrance, transcription, and from which audibility must be requested exists in continuity with early modernist reflections on the voice and late nineteenth-century conceptions of sound recording as an inhabited process, able to revive that which is concealed from sight and that which remains spectral and confined to memory. Edison's view of the phonograph and interest in the occult, as much as Yeats's own psychical research and perception of broadcasting, shape such approaches to voice transmission. In Yeats's parallels between sound transmission and writing and his anthropomorphizing of the wireless, one can discern the resurgence of late nineteenth-century attempts to come to terms with the complexity of sound recording by ascribing supernatural powers to technologies able to capture or transmit sound and rationalising their workings by means of an adherence to the written word.

These associations raise wider questions about the historically resilient relationship between sound transmission and writing, as conveyed, for example, in the etymology of the word 'phonograph'. As Miriama Young has noted, the obsolete meanings of 'phonograph' include: 'person who makes a phonetic transcription of an utterance', and 'a person who or thing which exactly reproduces someone's

---

⁷⁵ 'A Poet Broadcasts', *Belfast News-Letter*, 9 September 1931, quoted in Schuchard, 342.

⁷⁶ WBY to McCartan, 22 January 1937, in *Yeats and Patrick McCartan, A Fenian Friendship*, ed. John Unterecker (Dublin: Dolmen Press, 1967), 384; see also Johnson, 28; Pine, xix.

words'.⁷⁷ As she notes, 'to record' has even richer meanings: 'to get by heart, to commit to memory, to go over in one's mind'; 'to take to heart, give heed to'; 'to practice'; 'to sing of or about (something); to render in song'; 'to call to mind, to recall, recollect, remember'.⁷⁸ Finally, Young stresses, 'record', 'heart' and 'machine' 'have a deep etymologically associative relationship', record being a composite of 're' and 'cord', where 'cord' refers to 'heart'.⁷⁹ The etymology of the word reverberates through the Yeatses' discussion of Yeats's essay on *The Words on the Window-Pane*; their correspondence reveals George Yeats's sensitivity to the nuances of the word 'record' and the relevance of its obsolete meanings to technological innovations. But George Yeats's evocation of these complexities merely replicates what Edison's invention had already achieved, as Edison's view of the phonograph was itself aligned with the etymology of these words.

For Edison, the process of sound transmission enabled the recovery of an intimacy with that which has been lost or threatens to disappear without a trace. He was particularly attuned to the potential of the phonograph as a device able to safeguard ideas and memories by keeping a record of them: in a 1888 essay entitled 'The Perfected Phonograph', he presented the phonograph as an unprecedented resource for authors, suddenly able to 'register their fleeting ideas and brief notes [...] at any hour of day or night, without waiting to find pen, ink or paper'.⁸⁰ Recording messages destined to be written was, indeed, the first commercial use of the phonograph, then widely sold as a machine able to inscribe the page, hence of great utility to stenographers.⁸¹ More importantly, the phonograph was, for Edison, an important tool for maintaining the 'family record' and preserving 'the sayings, the voices, and *the last words* of the dying member of the family – as of great men', as he explained in an 1878 article introducing his invention.⁸² Later, he celebrated the ability of the phonograph to capture and preserve

---

⁷⁷ Young, 'Singing the Body Electric', 23. Young's conclusions are based on a wide range of definitions.
⁷⁸ *Ibid.*, 118.
⁷⁹ *Ibid.*
⁸⁰ Thomas A. Edison, 'The Perfected Phonograph', *The North American Review* 146, n. 379 (1888), 647.
⁸¹ Ivan Kreilkamp, 'A Voice without a Body: The Phonographic Logic of *Heart of Darkness*', *Victorian Studies* 40, n. 2 (1997), 218.
⁸² Thomas A. Edison, 'The Phonograph and Its Future', *The North American Review* 126, n. 262 (1878), 531, 533-34.

the words and voices of those forever absent, evoking its ability to transmit 'a dear friend's or relative's voice speaking to us from the other side of the earth'.[83] He concluded that the device 'knows more than we do ourselves', and that 'it will retain a perfect mechanical memory of many things which we may forget, even though we have said them.'[84]

Edison's view of the phonograph as a device able to reach to the otherworld extended beyond the invention proper, shaping his speculations concerning knowledge of the afterlife.[85] In a 1920 interview with *Scientific American*, he evoked the possible conception of an apparatus able to detect 'personalities in another existence or sphere who wish to get in touch with us in this existence or sphere' in a more sophisticated and rigorous manner than mediums and Ouija boards.[86] The peculiar machines and rituals that preceded and followed Edison's invention and aimed at achieving precisely this goal have provided much fodder for cultural historians. In particular, Jeffrey Sconce has discussed the many experiments connecting physical electromagnetisms to the spirit world, such as John Murray Spear's proto-robot, conceived during the 1850s, which aimed at replicating a living organism, and Konstantin Raudive's utilisations of radio during the late 1960s and 1970s to communicate with an often multilingual spirit world.[87] One may also think of early attempts to conceive of telephony as tapping directly into the world of the dead, an endeavour exemplified in Alexander Graham Bell's initial use of a dead human ear for his telephone; the ear was rigged up to a metal horn with an armature and stylus attached to the ossicles.[88]

The associations between the inaudible, the ghostly and the non-human which recur in Yeats's own dealings with wireless transmission suggest that he alternately acknowledged and failed to come to terms with the complexities of sound transmission, a hesitancy indebted in no small measure to the cultural matrix which had given rise to radio and recording as modes of communication

---

[83] Edison, 'The Perfected Phonograph', 647.
[84] *Ibid.*, 649-50.
[85] Sconce, 81-83.
[86] Thomas A. Edison, *The Diary and Sundry Observations of Thomas Alva Edison*, ed. Dagobert David Runes (New York: Philosophical Library, 1948), 239.
[87] Sconce, 38-40, 215-16, 85-90.
[88] Chanan, 23.

and preservation. When writing for or commenting upon radio, Yeats preferred to make analogies between broadcasting, recording and the written word without engaging with the specifics of sound transmission, perhaps because such analogies were more germane to the dramatisation of cognitive uncertainty that he had come to relish and could foreground problems of agency in relation to writing which had been a long-term concern. Despite Yeats's ambivalence towards the wireless, however, it is possible to think of its shaping influence over his approach to poetic form; the many voices that move in and out of earshot after the Crazy Jane poems, in *New Poems* in particular, emulate patterns salient in wireless transmission. The particular type of performativity associated with hearing and the failure thereof in 'What Then?' and 'The Ghost of Roger Casement' finds correlations in Yeats's musings on listening in his radio broadcasts: here as on air, the poetic voice thrives on evocations of a ghostly past and voices. Evocations of Plato's ghost singing *'What Then?'* and Roger Casement's ghost 'beating on the door' may, in this context, be conceived of as contributions to the long line of symbolic poltergeists that have made the relationship between sound transmission technologies and early twentieth-century literature so enduring; indeed, the ghostly sentence evoked by Breton as the source of all inspiration in the 1924 Surrealist manifesto, that mysterious sentence that came to him 'knock[ing] at the window', looms near (*YP* 420, 424).[89] In these poems as in Yeats's broadcasts, the voices that seem to emerge from concealed sound sources are more than mere fodder for an ongoing experiment with voice, tonality, metre and rhyme: they bear testimony to the enduring artistic potential opened up by Yeats's experiments with sound transmission as a situation and as a process.

[89] Breton reports becoming aware of 'a sentence ... that knocked at the window', 'articulated clearly to a point excluding all possibility of alteration and stripped of all quality of vocal sound' (my translation; published translations render Breton's 'phrase' incorrectly, as 'phrase' rather than 'sentence'). The original evokes 'une phrase ... qui cognait à la vitre', 'nettement articulée au point qu'il était impossible d'y changer un mot, mais distraite cependant du bruit de toute voix' (31).

© Michael Cade-Stewart, CC BY   http://dx.doi.org/10.11647/OBP.0038.10

Mask and Robe: Yeats's *Oxford Book of Modern Verse* (1936) and *New Poems* (1938)

Michael Cade-Stewart

In late October 1934, Yeats agreed to take on the editorship of the *Oxford Book of Modern Verse*, a role that required him to read an extensive amount of contemporary poetry. He did so in the hope that it would render him 'reborn in imagination' (*LDW* 19); it certainly contributed to his final literary flourishing.

In the introduction to the anthology, and in the BBC radio broadcast that anticipated its publication, Yeats invoked the notion of the poetic mask. He reflected that the employment of such masks enabled a poet like himself to 'multiply personality' (*OBMV* xxxvi), thereby dramatising internal divisions, contradictions and vacillation, and enabling these discrete aspects of his personality to be fashioned into coherence. By speaking through a mask, the poet is able to embody 'an idea, something intended, complete' (*E&I* 509).

Consequently, it is by examining the poetic masks that Yeats employed in *New Poems* (1938), that we can best discern some of the effects that his reading for the anthology had upon his subsequent poems. This article focuses on the way that his reading of contemporary Irish poetry, in particular, enabled him to re-furbish established poetic masks and to consolidate a new one in his final poetry collection of his lifetime.

The reading of poetry for the anthology furnished Yeats with new material for dramatized self-representation, but this came with a cost. For while the editorship provided him with a magisterial view of contemporary poetry, this was accompanied by the attendant burden of office. This burden might best be seen as encumbering robes,

221

which induced Yeats to puff himself up in order that he might fill them. As I explore in the penultimate section of this article, such robes constitute an antithesis to the liberating energies of the mask.

THE VISIONARY PEASANT POET

The fruits of Yeats's reading for the anthology first manifest themselves in *New Poems*. Here we encounter the mask of the visionary peasant poet, familiar in Yeats's oeuvre since the persona of Hanrahan the Red of *The Secret Rose* (1897) and *The Wind Among the Reeds* (1899). The mask has been re-furbished for *New Poems*, however, and now displays greater affinity with Irish-language poetry than ever before.

Although inexpert in Irish, Yeats had long been familiar with Irish-language poetry. He had gradually become familiar with this body of verse via his acquaintance with Douglas Hyde and Lady Gregory, and its effects on his own work can first be seen clearly in his revisions to the prose stories of *The Secret Rose* at the start of the twentieth century, and the revised edition of *The Celtic Twilight* (1902).[1] In the mid-1930s, reading and re-reading translations written in the intervening years, Yeats found new means to incorporate this material into his work.

Lady Gregory's translation of Douglas Hyde's poem 'He meditates on the Life of a Rich Man' (*OBMV* 34–5) is a good example of this process. The poem's structure and thought follow the 'seven ages of man' formula from Shakespeare's *As You Like It* and as such, provide an Irish forebear for this structure (II.vii.139–66). It starts with 'A golden cradle under you, and you young', and passes on to 'an old man among old men | Respect on you and honour on you'. Yeats's poem 'What Then?' represents an expression of this mode, with its representation of the seven ages of the poet. In the penultimate stanza we see the poet married, and moved into a 'small old house':

> All his happier dreams came true—
> A small old house, wife, daughter, son,
> Grounds where plum and cabbage grew,
> Poets and Wits about him drew;
> 'What then?' sang Plato's ghost. 'What then?' (*VP* 577)

---

[1] See for example 'Dust hath Closed Helen's Eye' (*Myth 2005* 14–19).

This echoes the account of the poet in old age foreseen in *Per Amica Silentia Lunae* (1918), where the poet 'will buy perhaps some small old house where like Ariosto he can dig his garden, and think that in the return of birds and leaves, or moon and sun, and in the evening flight of the rooks he may discover rhythm and pattern like those in sleep and so never awake out of vision' (*CW5* 16). This echo of Yeats's earlier work reflects one aspect of his strength as a poet: re-use of his own material. It seems quite probable, however, that Yeats was prompted to return to his earlier presentation of old age by a poem he anthologized by the Welsh poet W. H. Davies, 'Truly Great'. Here we find:

> With this small house, this garden large,
> This little gold, this lovely mate,
> With health in body, peace at heart—
> Show me a man more great. (*OBMV* 130)

Though as we have seen, Yeats increasingly lacked those things that might make him content ('health in body, peace at heart') and the refrain deprives the reader of quietude with its repeated questioning: 'What then?'

Hyde's poem had ended with a rhetorical question, but of a different kind:

> At the end of your days death, and then
> Hiding away; the boards and the church.
>
> What are you better after tonight
> Than Ned the beggar or Seaghan the fool? (*OBMV* 35)

The question is presumably designed to gesture to the redressive resolution of the afterlife postulated by Christianity, where the rich man will lose his advantages over the beggar and the fool. Characteristically, Yeats's rhetorical questions leave one less ready with an answer, and the question in his poem 'What then?' is no exception. As such, Yeats's poem offers a secular interpretation, and issues a humanistic challenge to the Christian consolation of Hyde's poem. For 'Plato's ghost' represents the disquieting thoughts that plague the human mind no matter what the external circumstances of the body of which it is a part. For the most part, thoughts intruding on the present, rather than the experience of the present itself, are the real source of human suffering and discontent.² Even if we are lucky enough to be like Yeats's speaker, who has 'swerved in nought I Something to perfection brought', a voice in our head says: 'What matter? What next?': 'What then?' in short. Amidst all its Neoplatonic suggestion, Yeats's poem is thus a profound witness of the secular human experience.

Yeats had been familiar with this material for some time, encountering Hyde's poem in Lady Gregory's translation in *The Kiltartan Poetry Book* published by the Cuala Press in 1918. Yet it was apparently only after the reading for the anthology that he could utilise this formula himself. This process, of recent reading reactivating older material, can clearly be seen in action in Yeats's poem 'The Curse of Cromwell', which Yeats had completed by early January 1937.

'The Curse of Cromwell' displays the most overt borrowing from Gaelic sources in Yeats's last phase, lifting lines and phrases from two of Frank O'Connor's translations from the Irish: the anonymous Irish Ballad, '*Cill Chais*' ('Kilcash'), and also Aogán Ó Rathaile's poem beginning '*Cabhair Ní Ghairfead*' (1729), to which he gives the title 'Last Lines'.³ These borrowings were identified by Jeffares nearly three decades ago, and the context and implications of these borrowings has been explored with relation to Ó Rathaile by Laura O'Connor.⁴ However, Yeats's poem borrows material from a great number of Irish sources that have not been considered by scholarship. When the poem is considered in the light of Yeats's reading for the anthology, it takes on a greater meaning that seems to justify how Yeats could consider it to be a candidate for 'the best poem I have written for some years' *(LDW 144)*.

It is understandable that critics have stopped their search for influence at Frank O'Connor's translations, given how strikingly direct these borrowings are. O'Connor's 'Kilcash' reads:

---

² This principle informs therapeutic applications in clinical psychology and psychiatry based on the concept of 'mindfulness'; an approach first popularized in Jon Kabat-Zinn, *Full Catastrophe Living: Using the wisdom of your body and mind to face stress, pain, and illness* (New York: Delacorte Press, 1990).
³ Literally 'No Help I'll Call'. *Dánta Aodhagáin Uí Rathaile: the Poems of Egan O'Rahilly*, ed. Patrick C. Dinneen (London: David Nutt, 1900), n. 21.
⁴ See A. Norman Jeffares, *A New Commentary on The Poems of W. B. Yeats* (London & Basingstoke: Macmillan, 1984), 383; Laura O'Connor, 'Putting Words into a Rambling Peasant-poet's Mouth: Frank O'Connor and W. B. Yeats's Translations "from the Irish"', *YA15* 190–218.

> And the great earls where are they?
> The earls, the lady, the people
> Beaten into the clay.⁵

Yeats takes this metaphor and expands it from the ruin of the house and dynasty of Kilcash to the plight of the whole class to which they belonged:

> The lovers and the dancers are beaten into the clay,
> And the tall men and the swordsmen and the horsemen, where are they?
> (*VP* 580)

O'Connor's translation of the closing lines of Ó Rathaile's 'Last Lines' reads:

> Henceforth I cease. Death comes and will have no delay
> By Laune and Lane and Lee diminished of their pride.
> I shall go after the heroes, ay, into the clay!
> My fathers followed theirs before Christ was crucified.⁶

The first stanza of Yeats's 'Curse of Cromwell' closes with:

And there is an old beggar wandering in his pride—
His fathers served their fathers before Christ was crucified (*VP* 580).

This direct correspondence may have resulted from Yeats's role in crafting O'Connor's translations. Many critics have drawn attention to a statement by Frank O'Connor that suggests that Yeats was recovering lines that he had composed himself during joint translation sessions with O'Connor. In the younger man's preface to the 1959 collection of his earlier translations, *Kings, Lords, Commons*, O'Connor claimed that, 'sometimes, having supplied some felicitous line of his own, [Yeats] promptly stole it back for one of his original poems'.⁷ Both of these borrowings in 'The Curse of Cromwell' are direct, and important, but the influences upon the poem do not stop here in its first stanza.

As Laura O'Connor has observed, Yeats's poem is 'chock-full with conventional devices (the ballad stanza with its simple rhyme scheme and parallel syntax, the patriotic theme of the

---

⁵ *OBMV* 406; Frank O'Connor, *The Wild Bird's Nest* (Dublin: Cuala Press, 1932), 24.
⁶ O'Connor, *The Wild Bird's Nest*, 23.
⁷ Frank O'Connor, *Kings, Lords, and Commons* (Dublin: Gill & Macmillan, 2001), v.

demonized villain, Cromwell, the revenant speaker, the refrain, the genres of aisling, satire, eulogy, elegy, and curse)' (*YA15* 203). As this summary suggests, the poem is dense, especially for a ballad. Indeed, it is compacted in the same way as late poems like the 'The Statues'. This is striking since its ballad-elements tend to (mis) identify it to readers as a simpler kind of poem with less intellectual charge – but despite its refrain, this is not a poem that can bring everything down to 'fol de rol de rolly O' (*VP* 357–58). Indeed, the ending of the poem is so complex that critics seem to have misread it completely. The import of the final two stanzas only becomes clear when the whole of Yeats's poem is considered in the broader content of his reading of the poems and translations of Padraic Colum and James Stephens, and the writings of Lady Gregory, as well as Frank O'Connor.

The second stanza of Yeats's poem draws most heavily on the work of James Stephens, in particular his translations of the Gaelic poet Dáibhí Ó Bruadair. Ó Bruadair has been described as 'the Gaelic world's most passionate and graphic witness to the period between the Cromwellian settlement and the aftermath of Aughrim'.[8] Yeats encountered translations of his work at least as early as 1918, in James Stephens's collection of translations and original poems, *Reincarnations*. Re-reading Stephens's work for the anthology, Yeats would have re-encountered these translations as the opening of Section v of Stephens's *Collected Poems* (1926).[9] In stark contrast to the lighter and whimsical poems that precede it, this section is dominated by curses, satires, and complaints.

These are mainly occasioned by the social upheavals of the Cromwellian and later post-Williamite plantations, which led to the dispossession of the landowners who had provided patronage for Ó Bruadair, and later for Ó Rathaile. This process is vividly distilled from the Gaelic originals in Stephens's translations. In one translation from Ó Bruadair, 'The Weavers', the poet speaker is reduced to begging for a shirt from the weavers, unable to offer

---

[8] Tom Dunne, 'Voices of the Vanquished: Echoes of Language Loss in Gaelic Poetry from Kinsale to the Great Famine', *Journal of Irish and Scottish Studies* 1 (September 2007), 31.
[9] I will cite from Macmillan's reprint of 1931, the same edition in Yeats's library (*YL* 1997), which follows the same pagination as the first edition.

anything in return, since his verse is no longer afforded value;[10] in another, under the title 'Skim Milk' the speaker complains that:

> ... this old head, stuffed with latinity,
> Rich with the poet's store of grave and gay,
> Will not get me skim-milk for half a day.[11]

Just as for Ó Rathaile, a generation later, things were not always thus for Ó Bruadair. In the good times before dispossession the lot of the great poet was utterly different: 'The great', his patrons, would have ordered that he be provided with 'That which serves his and serves our dignity'.[12] When he anthologized these poems, Yeats arranged this translation to precede 'Inis Fál', a poem lamenting the social and cultural virtues now absent in Ireland:

> All comely quality!
> All gentleness and hospitality!
> All courtesy and merriment.[13]

This sequence in the anthology fashions the poems into a coherent and affecting narrative of dispossession and social collapse. At the start of this sequence, Yeats anthologized Stephens's translation of Ó Bruadair's 'Blue Blood', a bitterly comic satire on a Cromwellian planter.[14] The poem depicts the social embarrassment of one who has effectively displaced the previous gentry, and who has allowed the word to spread that he 'is a king for sure | Or the branch of a mighty and ancient and famous lineage'. This impression is dispelled as soon as he opens his mouth, however, revealing himself to be a 'silly, sulky, illiterate, black-avisèd boor | Who was hatched

---

[10] James Stephens, *Collected Poems* (London: Macmillan, 1931), 184; translation of '*Le cluain ar lastuire fatha do chloinn Órluith*', in *Duanaire Dháibhí Uí Bhruadair: the Poems of David Ó Bruadair*, ed. J. C. MacErlean, 3 vols. (London: David Nutt, 1910–1916), Vol. 2, n. 4, verses 2, 3, 5.

[11] Stephens, *Collected Poems*, 189; translation of '*Mithigh soicheim go síol gCárthaigh*', in MacErlean, *Ó Bruadair*, Vol. 3, n. 31, verses 5, 6, 14, 15, 18.

[12] *OBMV* 221; Stephens, *Collected Poems*, 191.

[13] *OBMV* 221; Stephens, *Collected Poems*, 199; Stephen's poem expands upon a loose translation of the last stanza of Ó Rathaile's '*Créacta críc fódla*'; see Dinneen, *O'Rahilly*, n. 1.

[14] Stephens, *Collected Poems*, 186; translation of '*Do shaoileas dá ríribh gur uachtarán*', in MacErlean, *Ó Bruadair*, Vol. 2, n. 31.

by a foreign vulgarity under a hedge!' As the last line puts it: he was a 'lout, son of lout, by old lout, and was da to a lout!' (*OBMV* 219–20). Although there is glee in this vitriol, it cannot compensate for the misery and destitution that has brought it forth.

Stephens's poems thus powerfully render the social instability and unhappiness that ensues in the wake of the collapse of an established social order. Yeats's poem draws on this material to full effect, compressing the lines from 'Inis Fál' into the opening premise of the second stanza:

> All neighbourly content and easy talk are gone,
> But there's no good complaining, for money's rant is on,
> He that's mounting up must on his neighbour mount
> And we and all the Muses are things of no account. (*VP* 580)

The bemoaning of the primacy of money, and the attendant disregard for artworks and their creators, finds precedent in Ó Bruadair's lament 'Skim Milk', but also in the 9th Century Gaelic poem, 'Lament of the Old Woman of Beare', which Yeats would have encountered in translations by Gogarty, and by O'Connor. The latter's translation, 'The Old Woman of Beare regrets Lost Youth', was anthologized by Yeats, and laments that 'It is pay | And not men ye love today'.[15]

The first half of Yeats's 'Curse of Cromwell' clearly draws on material from a fairly broad swathe of Gaelic literature, but the significance lies in the use to which these borrowings are put. Indeed, they reveal that Yeats conscripts Gaelic literature to oppose the social change attendant upon the Irish Free State. In so doing, he finally put into verse a moving encounter with a dispossessed artist, crippled and bereft of his patrons, which he had experienced in the early years of the Free State:

An old beggar has just called I knew him twenty years ago as wandering piper but now he is paralyzed & cannot play. He was lamenting the great houses burned or empty – "The gentry have kept the shoes on my feet, & the coat on my back & the shilling in my pocket – never once in all these forty & five years that I have been upon the road have I asked a penny of a farmer". I gave him five shillings & he started off in the rain for the nearest town – five miles – I rather fancy to drink it.[16]

---

[15] *OBMV* 398; O'Connor, *The Wild Bird's Nest*, 1.
[16] Letter to Olivia Shakespear, 25 May 1926 (*CL InteLex* 4871).

Still living by his code of refusing charity from a farmer, this beggar might well be the principal inspiration behind Yeats's beggar 'wandering in his pride' despite his destitution.

In drawing on historical Irish texts to express the contemporary plight of these dispossessed artists, and the collapse of the Anglo-Irish gentry, Yeats turned texts that were claimed for Gaelic and Catholic Nationalism into ones that lamented the loss of patronage and social change. This literary device is successful because Yeats actually reveals a real quality of these poems: their authors lament the loss of their patrons, first, and Ireland, second, if at all. As such, they offer a contrary social agenda to that of the Free State, which Yeats saw as increasingly dominated by 'Catholic & Gaelic bigotry'.[17]

THE 'IRISH DEPOSIT' OF SPIRITUALITY

Up to the second stanza, the content of 'The Curse of Cromwell' is primarily a re-casting of the seventeenth-century Gaelic poetry of poets like Ó Bruadair and Ó Rathaile, experienced through the translations of Stephens and O'Connor. The third stanza describes how there is a further force that causes the poetic speaker to experience anguish, however – likened to having a fox fatally savaging his torso. What is this 'knowledge' that somehow eclipses the dire social and cultural collapse described in the preceding stanzas? The stanza is not immediately clear; it asserts that it:

> [...] proves that things both can and cannot be;
> That the swordsmen and the ladies can still keep company;
> Can pay the poet for a verse and hear the fiddle sound,
> That I am still their servant though all are underground. (*VP* 580–81)

How can this be? Laura O'Connor implies that it cannot. In her reading, the speaker's belief is delusional, and the first three stanzas confront us with 'the framing degradation that provokes the hallucination' of the final stanza (*YA15* 198). Yet in the context of Yeats's well-documented occult beliefs, it is unwise to dismiss any vision out of hand, especially one so numinous:

> I came on a great house in the middle of the night,
> Its open lighted doorway, and its windows all alight,

---

[17] See letter to Ethel Mannin, 1 March 1937 (*CL InteLex* 6835).

> And all my friends were there and made me welcome too;
> But I woke in an old ruin that the winds howled through;
> And when I pay attention I must out and walk
> Among the dogs and horses that understand my talk. (*VP* 581)

The Irish word for vision is *aisling*, but the term has come to connote a specific literary form of a vision, and this definition can lead us astray. Daniel Corkery, an intellectual opponent of Yeats in many respects, defined the Irish *aisling* in terms of those written by the Jacobite poets of the eighteenth century. In *The Hidden Ireland: A History of Gaelic Munster in the Eighteenth Century* (1924), he gives a narrow account: 'the vision the poet always sees is the spirit of Ireland as a radiant and majestic maiden'.[18] If the vision at the end of 'Curse of Cromwell' is considered against these criteria, it appears defective: merely a 'delusion' rather than a normative vision. It is certainly not one that finds social reinforcement, since the speaker describes how it is only the 'dogs and horses that understand my talk'. This notion of failure is consistent with Hoffman's interpretation that the speaker's response to the vision alludes to Swift's *Gulliver's Travels* (1726), 'in the echo of Gulliver in the stable after his return to England'.[19] Laura O'Connor glosses his interpretation as the speaker resolving 'to jettison human society, like Gulliver after his return from the land of the Houyhnhnms, for the companionship of animals' (*YA15* 209). She thereby endorses an interpretation that is, in my view, mistaken.

Phillip Marcus interprets these lines as expressing the desperation of the dependant artist, who now 'has no audience left except the dogs and horses'.[20] Yet the speaker's endorsement of 'dogs and horses' is prompted by his paying 'attention' to the vision. The reason he seeks out these particular animals, then, is because he believes them to be more sensitive to visions than most humans, and therefore more likely to 'understand my talk' of such things. We are not to take the speaker as absurdly misguided in this conviction. This idea of the visionary sensitivity of animals is expressed elsewhere in Yeats's writings – most clearly in his introduction to *An Indian Monk* (1932), where exactly these two kinds of animals are referred to:

---

[18] See Daniel Corkery, 'The Aisling', in *Irish Writing in the Twentieth Century: A Reader*, ed. David Pierce (Cork: Cork University Press, 2000), 289.

[19] Daniel Hoffman, *Barbarous Knowledge: Myth in the poetry of Yeats, Graves, and Muir* (New York: Oxford University Press, 1967), 58.

[20] Phillip L. Marcus, *Yeats and Artistic Power* (New York: New York University Press, 1992), 173.

[In the late 1890s] Lady Gregory collected with my help the stories in her *Visions and Beliefs*. Again and again, she and I felt that we had got down, as it were, into some fibrous darkness, into some matrix out of which everything has come, some condition that brought together as though into a single scheme 'exultations, agonies', and the apparitions seen by dogs and horses[.] (*E&I* 429)

This textual link of association with the Irish folklore research that Lady Gregory and Yeats undertook leads us to strong connections between the visionary experience they recorded, and the vision of the speaker of Yeats's poem, written nearly forty years later.

Yeats's first concentrated attempt to relate Irish folklore and faery beliefs with contemporary spiritualism occurs in the essay 'Swedenborg, Mediums, and the Desolate Places', started in 1911 but not finished until 1914.[21] It was originally conceived as an introduction to Lady Gregory's folklore collection, later published as *Visions and Beliefs in the West of Ireland* (1920). In the first, deleted, section of his essay Yeats reflected on the nature of the 'Sidhe', or faery folk, who populate these visions. One line in particular stands out in the context of his later poem: 'when they [the Sidhe] have a need they can build up a palace in a moment or remake an old stone castle, pulled down by Cromwell, filling it with noise and lights' (*CW5* 289). Elements of the sentence appeared, almost verbatim, in the opening paragraph of Lady Gregory's own introduction to her collections, but exactly how much of the sentence came from one or the other is largely immaterial. The importance lies in the accounts collected by Lady Gregory that this sentence summarizes, and which Yeats had drawn upon in his long essays on Irish folklore in the 1890s. In a vision described by 'Mrs Sheridan', the faery-built structure is specifically 'a great house', just as in Yeats's poem:

... I saw a great house and a grand one, with screens [clumps of trees] at the ends of it, and the windows open. Coole House is nothing like what it was for size or grandeur. And there were people inside ... and ladies walking about, and a bridge across the river. For they can build up such things all in a minute (*CW10* 38).

The speaker of Yeats's poem seems to have encountered just such a 'great house', populated by swordsmen and ladies. A further, second-

---

[21] The essay relies on his notes and earlier folkloric articles that can be traced back as far as 1897. For detailed account, see *CW5* 466–68.

hand, account describes how, in a trip 'away' with the Sidhe, a man repeatedly visited this same castle, supernaturally reconstructed, and how on his visits there he saw 'mostly all the people that he knew that had died out of the village' amongst the noble company (*CW10* 74).

The great house from the time of Cromwell, the nobility, and the presence of the dead amongst them come directly from these accounts of vision, recorded in the field in the rural West of Ireland. Castles and big houses do appear in the *aislings* of the eighteenth century poets, but only in a way incidental to their plots. In one of the most famous Jacobite aislings, Ó Rathaile's 'The brightness of brightness' ('*Gile na Gile*'), the speaker of the poem encounters the vision of a beautiful maiden wedded to an evil wizard who lives in a 'fair mansion' that he has created by sorcery. The mansion of Ó Rathaile's poem is essentially incidental to the allegory of a *mésalliance* between the maiden and the wizard, representing Erin being ruled by King William of Orange rather than the Catholic Pretender to the English throne. In Yeats's 'Curse of Cromwell', the Big House is instead the *subject* of the vision.

The 'knowledge' that so destroys the heart of the speaker of Yeats's poem is the full metaphysical significance of his vision. To appreciate what this is, we need to understand Yeats's thought as it stood in 1937 on the relation between the other-world of Irish folklore, spiritualism, and occult philosophy. Many years earlier, in the essay on Swedenborg, Yeats had posited a stage that the soul experiences after death where 'the soul lives a life so like that of the world that it may not even believe that it has died', and this state 'may last but a short time or many years' (*Ex* 34). A few, enlightened and lucky souls progress onwards and upwards through a process of purification that ends with reincarnation. These ideas are carried through to both versions of *A Vision*, but important changes are made to this early conception of the soul's progression after death. In the Swedenborg essay, the place in which this stage occurs is 'the other world of the early races, of those whose dead are in the rath or the faery hill, of all who see no place of reward and punishment but a continuance of this life, with cattle and sheep, markets and war' (*Ex* 35). Any moral dimension to the afterlife is explicitly downplayed; from this perspective, a vision of a great house populated by the gentry and the dead would be nothing to mourn over, being closer to one of those 'Dreams that have no Moral' collected in *The Celtic Twilight* (*Myth 2005* 83–90).

This stands in marked contrast to the section devoted to the after-life in the second version of *A Vision* (1937), titled 'The Soul in Judgement'. As this title implies, the afterlife of the soul is now considered explicitly in terms of moral accountability, and each stage it undergoes represents a means of arriving at ethical equilibrium from a different angle. The first stage of the afterlife is called *The Return*, which 'has for its object the *Spirit*'s separation from the *Passionate Body*, considered as nature, and from the *Husk* considered as pleasure and pain' (*AVB* 226). In order for this to occur, the soul has to be reconciled with its recently incarnate existence, and if this entails expiating strong feelings of injustice, or tragedy, then it may take considerable time. This will occur:

... only after long and perhaps painful dreams of the past, and it is because of such dreams that the second state is sometimes called the *Dreaming Back*. If death has been violent or tragic the *Spirit* may cling to the *Passionate Body* for generations (*AVB* 224–25).

This duration is extended for the reason that: '[a]fter each event of the *Dreaming Back* the *Spirit* explores not merely the causes but the consequences of that event' (*AVB* 227–28). This is clearly no small task.

In Yeats's view, the Irish of the great houses, and their dependants, suffered great injustice and tragedy. Consequently, he would expect them to undergo a lengthy *Dreaming Back*, and this would be accessible in vision to others. The vision of the speaker of 'The Curse of Cromwell', then, is a vision of their *Dreaming Back*, where 'the swordsmen and the ladies can still keep company; | Can pay the poet for a verse and hear the fiddle sound', just as they did before their way of life was obliterated (*VP* 581). Because he experiences such visions he is always aware 'that things both can and cannot be', and as a result he can neither forgive nor forget. He may well experience such visions because the discarnate spirits are in need of 'mortal help'; they need a contribution from the living in order to 'explore the causes [and] the consequences' of their fate. This contribution may be nothing more than the 'attention' of the speaker, or a discussion about it, in parallel with the account in *A Vision* where a spirit 'wanted to discover certain facts necessary to her *Dreaming Back* by creating discussion' among the living (*AVB* 228–29). As a consequence of their need for the speaker's help, he remains 'their servant though all are underground'. Perhaps this grants a supernatural vitality to an individual's or society's sense of injustice, which Yeats refers to in the passage from his 'General Introduction for My Work' that references 'The Curse of Cromwell':

> ... no people, Lecky said at the opening of his *Ireland in the Eighteenth Century*, have undergone greater persecution, nor did that persecution altogether cease up to our own day. No people hate as we do in whom that past is always alive; there are moments when hatred poisons my life and I accuse myself of effeminacy because I have not given it adequate expression. It is not enough to have put it into the mouth of a rambling peasant poet (*E&I* 519).

In these stanzas, then, Yeats opposes social tendencies in the Free State with the very texts it used for legitimacy, whilst also putting into poetry the fruits of his long quest to resolve Irish faery beliefs with contemporary spiritualism. While the result has affective potency for those that do not share these premises, this charge is calibrated for affecting those that do. This inevitably narrows its effectiveness.[22] A growing sense of this may well have motivated Yeats to settle on the refrain: 'O what of that, O what of that | What is there left to say?' (*VP* 580).

THE POLITICAL BALLADEER

The refrain of 'The Curse of Cromwell' clearly stands in contradiction to its content: to say the least, the poem finds something new to say in its unique blending of sources, synthesising Irish folklore and contemporary spiritualism, and drawing on so much Irish language poetry. This contradiction finds a parallel in another poem that drew on the work of the Gaelic poets of the 17th and 18th Centuries: 'Egan O'Rahilly', by James Stephens. Here, the speaker of the poem graphically describes his fallen state – reduced to eating 'things picked up from the shore: | The periwinkle, and the tough dog-fish' – yet also declares that he will not speak of such things:

> I am O'Rahilly:
> Here in a distant place I hold my tongue,
> Who once said all his say, when he was young![23]

---

[22] This would be a significant problem if, as Phillip Marcus claims, the 'primary target of the satiric thrust' of the poem was Cecil Day Lewis and 'the other young English writers of the left' (Marcus, *Yeats and Artistic Power*, 162).

[23] *OBMV* xiv; Stephens, *Collected Poems*, 191.

'The Curse of Cromwell' shows rhetorical affinities with this preterition, this speaking out about not speaking out, but Yeats chose to celebrate another O'Rahilly in *New Poems*: 'The O'Rahilly', one Michael Joseph O'Rahilly (Mícheál Seosamh Ó Rathaille), born 22 April 1875 and killed 29 April 1916 in the Easter Rising. In this poem, we see the manifestation of another refurbished poetic mask: the political balladeer.

Unlike the O'Rahilly of Stephens's poem, 'The O'Rahilly' is determined to speak out by confronting the leaders of the Rising for excluding him from their plans, just as they had excluded Yeats:

> 'Am I such a craven that
> I should not get the word
> But for what some travelling man
> Had heard I had not heard?'
> Then on Pearse and Connolly
> He fixed a bitter look,
> 'Because I helped to wind the clock
> I come to hear it strike'.
> *How goes the weather?* (*VP* 585)

In this mode, Yeats's ballad-singer seems to envy the dead of the Easter Rising: of what Roy Foster identifies as 'modern Ireland's sacrificial foundation myth'. If he does so, it is because the independent Ireland that Yeats had struggled for now seemed to threaten almost everything he held dear. Throughout his life, Yeats had championed independence of thought: to his disgust, the Free State embraced a stultifying censorship of literary works, as provided for by the Censorship of Publications Act, 1929. Yeats had actively opposed the legislation before and after its passage. Once it had become law, Yeats repeatedly expressed concerns that the censorship mentality seemed poised, as Foster has put it, to extend 'beyond the written word' (*Life 2*, 645; 372–378; 463).

Immediately after the passing of the Act, Yeats set about establishing the Irish Academy of Letters as a means of resisting its provisions. In the ballads of *New Poems*, however, we see a more indirect means of circumventing censorship. He had long cherished and promoted the oral delivery of poetry for other deeply-held reasons, but the ongoing censorship provided an additional urgent motivation for returning to this project.²⁴ Accordingly, a new series of *Broadsides* was conceived of in 1934, and published monthly through 1935 for subscribers. These printed publications were of course subject to censorship under the Act, but in promoting the oral delivery of poetry they could nurture an audience receptive to unpublished and unpublishable work.²⁵ Edited jointly by F. R. Higgins and Yeats, the *Broadsides* were collected in a Cuala edition of 1935 titled: *Broadsides. A Collection of Old and New Songs*. This collected volume was prefaced with a joint poetic manifesto signed by the editors, which observed that a 'political ballad' might have 'more effect than a speech' (*CW6* 177).

Circumventing censorship was only part of a package of instigating cultural change in Ireland through cultural forms. As Yeats intimated to Wellesley in September 1935, the main purpose of the *Broadsides* of that year has been to 'get new or queer verse into circulation', '& we shall succeed', he went on:

> The work of Irish poets, quite deliberately put into circulation with its music thirty & more years ago, is now all over the country. The Free State Army march to a tune called 'Down by the Salley Garden without knowing that the march was first published with words of mine, words that are now folklore (*LDW* 29).

The superlative example of a political ballad to be generated by this project was Yeats's 'Come Gather Round Me Parnellites'. The ballad has not quite become 'folklore', but it remains current among folk singers today.

The poem's title, as many have observed, might be clearer with the addition of a comma, but its absence draws attention to a textual source. The title itself, and the first line of the ballad, was conceived at a fairly late stage of drafting. The typescript penultimate draft of the poem has 'Come All Old Parnellites', while a version in a letter to Dorothy Wellesley of 8 September 1936 has 'Come ~~My Old~~ Stand About Me Parnellites' (*CL InteLex* 6644). The final version appears to draw upon the line 'Gather 'round me boys, will yez' from 'The Song of Zozimus' quoted in 'The Last Gleeman' section of the *Celtic*

---

²⁴ For a detailed history of the other motivations, see Ronald Schuchard, *The Last Minstrels: Yeats and the Revival of the Bardic Art*s (Oxford: Oxford University Press, 2008).

²⁵ This underground poetry scene can be glimpsed in Yeats's letters, such as that to Dorothy Wellesley of 11 June 1937 (*CL InteLex* 6963).

Twilight (*Myth 2005* 32, 243-4 nn.12-13). Here, as in Yeats's poem, no punctuation interrupts the imperative clause to 'gather round'.

Other elements of the poem appear to be drawn from another well-loved poetic inheritance of Yeats's: 'The Memory of the Dead' by John Kells Ingram (1823–1907), a '98 ballad, commemorating the failed uprising of 1798.[26] In drawing on the last gleeman, Zozimus, and a '98 Ballad, Yeats was drawing on the materials that had created the Free State in order to critique that product. Yeats intimated to W. J. Turner that 'I wrote [the ballad] against "The Bishops & the Party"[:] the Irish Catholic Church & the Irish National party'.[27] Here, then, we have an Anglo-Irish parallel with Yeats's subversive appropriation of Gaelic textual authorities in order to oppose growing social forces within the Free State.

The logical progression from Parnell was to Roger Casement, similarly betrayed by the country he had tried to serve. Casement had been executed for acts of treason against the British crown in 1916 for his part in assisting the Easter Rising. A distinguished campaigner for human rights, Casement might have enjoyed enough public support for an appeal to clemency. To mute the outcry against his trial and execution, the British authorities circulated private diaries, alleged to have been written by Casement, which detail his practice of homosexual intercourse. As Brian Lewis has summarized, selected pages of these diaries were 'distributed among journalists, politicians, and leading Americans – anyone who might be prepared to mount or support an appeal for clemency'.[28] The strategy was successful, as might be expected, given that homosexual acts were illegal in Britain until 1967, and in Ireland until 1993; the strategy must have intimidated would-be supporters, at the very least.

The diaries are now known to be genuine.[29] Nevertheless, as Yeats stated in a letter to the press 'it was infamous to blacken Casement's name with evidence that had neither been submitted to him nor examined at his trial'.[30] In January 1933, Yeats read and critiqued

---

[26] In particular, the filling of glasses, and the drinking to the memory of political heroes.

[27] Letter to W. J. Turner, 21 February 1937 (*CL InteLex* 6817).

[28] Brian Lewis, 'The Queer Life and Afterlife of Roger Casement', *Journal of the History of Sexuality* 14 (2005), 367.

[29] See W. J. McCormack, *Roger Casement in Death: or, Haunting the free state* (Dublin: University College Dublin Press, 2002).

[30] Letter to the Editor of the Irish Press, 13 February 1937 (*CL InteLex* 6808).

a draft chapter of what would be published three years later as *The Forged Casement Diaries*, by William J. Maloney.[31] When his first poem on 'Roger Casement' was published in the *Irish Press* for 2 February 1937 it was printed with the epigraph 'After Reading "The Forged Casement Diaries" by Dr Maloney' (*VP* 581).

The publication of Maloney's book in Ireland by Talbot press brought a media stir that Yeats's ballad seems crafted to exploit. Yet it may not have been the only source of Yeats's 'Roger Casement'. Yeats's treatment of the material is, like his Parnell ballad, situated in the vein of poem-as-journalism, but it is also a narrative ballad, and as such it finds a poetic precedent in much Irish poetry. Further, Yeats's poem may find a direct poetic source: Colum's ballad on 'Roger Casement', which Yeats would have encountered in the final section of Colum's *Poems* (1932) during his reading for the anthology. Yeats's poem has many elements in common with Colum's: the gallows, the internment in quicklime, and the denouncement of the villains, 'their Murrays, and their Cecils':

> They have hanged Roger Casement to the tolling of a bell,
> *Ochone, och, ochone, ochone!*
> And their Smiths, and their Murrays, and their Cecils say it's well,
> *Ochone, och, ochone, ochone!*[32]

To these elements, however, Yeats adds the argument elucidated by Maloney's *The Forged Casement Diaries*, to show how Casement was 'denied his last refuge – Martyrdom' *(LDW* 128). This denies the promise of a redressive after-life that Colum had introduced in his poem, where Casement is lifted up by the men and women whose suffering he had brought to light, such that he ascends 'for the eyes of God to see, | And it's well, after all, Roger Casement!' Laudable though his conduct was in the service of human rights, Casement's homosexuality denied him a redemptive afterlife of any sort for the forces of social conservatism, not least the Irish Catholic Church. Colum's ballad, then, penned from the other side of the Atlantic, warranted correction, along with the 'blacken[ing]' of Casement's 'good name'.

The villains of Yeats's ballad, therefore, are not those of Colum's poem who approved of Casement's execution for treason, but

---

[31] See Yeats's letter to William J. M. A. Maloney, 19 January 1933 (*CL InteLex* 5808).
[32] Padraic Colum, *Poems* (London: Macmillan, 1932), 216.

those who assisted with the alleged forgery and dissemination of Casement's diaries. In an earlier draft submitted to close correspondents, Yeats fingered the wrong man: Gilbert Murray. As he embarrassedly informed them in subsequent letters: 'I wronged Murray. He approved the execution but did not help the forgery. I muddled him & Noyes together – they were on the same page. I lost the book & trusted to memory'.[33] It is indeed true that the Murray's name appears in this context in Maloney's book. In the summary of Chapter VII on the contents page, though not in the chapter itself, Murray is erroneously listed as one who spread British propaganda against Casement: 'British storytellers: Sir Gilbert Murray; Professor Alfred Noyes, C. B.'.[34] Since Murray is also (rightly) vilified by Colum's ballad, together with Cecil Spring-Rice, for approving of Casement's conviction, it may be that Yeats's mistaken presentation of Murray is also partly symptomatic of his reworking of Colum's ballad as a source. His error may, therefore, imply a community of origin.

Yeats himself was indifferent on the subject of Casement's alleged sexual orientation – '[i]f Casement were a homo-sexual what matter!', he wrote privately to Wellesley – but was conscious that one of the strongest proponents of homophobia in Ireland was the Irish Catholic Church *(LDW* 128). Just as with Parnell, here was a good man who had risked (and lost) everything for Ireland, only to be abandoned and disowned by the country because what he did in bed (or elsewhere) was outlawed by Catholicism.

The forces of social conservatism could be placated, however, if the diaries were held to be a forgery, enabling the state to celebrate Casement as a saintly martyr who gave his life in the service of the Free State. Yeats's ballad thus brought him public thanks from important figures. As he reported to Wellesley, he was 'publicly thanked by the vice-president of the Executive Counsil, by De Valera's political secretary, by our chief antiquarian [John Macneill] & an old revolutionist, Count Plunket, who calls my poem "a ballad the people much needed"'. Further, 'De Valera's newspaper gave me a long leader saying that for generations to come my poem will pour scorn on the forgers & their backers' *(LDW* 126). The latter

---

[33] Letter to Ethel Mannin, 7 December 1936. See also letter to Dorothy Wellesley of the same day (*CL InteLex* 6741, 6744).

[34] William J. Maloney, *The Forged Casement Diaries* (Dublin & Cork: The Talbot Press, 1936), vi.

included a sizeable potted biography of Yeats that gratifyingly concluded that he was 'regarded by reputable critics as the greatest living poet'.[35]

Yeats thus found himself (temporarily) a welcome member of the establishment, only one month after the publication of 'Come Gather Round Me Parnellites', which he had written in express opposition to 'The Bishops & the Party'. While he may have been pleasantly surprised by the sudden shows of deference to his wife in the buses and shops of Dublin, his subsequent creative efforts offer an insight into his predominant feelings on the matter. Above all, there is a powerful sense of ambivalence, expressed in 'The Old Stone Cross' through the persona of a revenant Cuchulain (identified by his golden armour):

> Because this age and the next age
> Engender in the ditch,
> No man can know a happy man
> From any passing wretch;
> If Folly link with Elegance
> No man knows which is which,
>   *Said the man in the golden breastplate
>   Under the old stone Cross.* (*VP* 598–99)

Celebrating Casement in the service of the future Ireland, then, had come with the unfortunate consequence of also strengthening his opponents' hand in the present. He rapidly composed texts that were apparently designed primarily to separate himself from the eroto-phobic orthodoxy of the Free State. A good example is 'A Model for the Laureate', written in July of 1937, on the subject of the necessary separation of the ability of statesmen from their private sexual lives, occasioned by the abdication crisis in England:

> On thrones from China to Peru
> All sorts of kings have sat
> That men and women of all sorts
> Proclaimed both good and great;
> And what's the odds if such as these
> For reason of the State
> Should keep their lovers waiting,
>   Keep their lovers waiting? (*VP* 597)

---

[35] See the leading Features page, 'Irish Poet's Striking Challenge', for the *Irish Press*, 2 February 1937. Reproduced in *Life* 2, 573, fig. 13.

A WILD OLD WICKED MAN

In 'A Model for the Laureate' Yeats returned to the preoccupations of the previous summer, where the most striking poetic mask of *New Poems* made its appearance: the eponymous 'Wild Old Wicked Man' (*VP* 587). While many of Yeats's earlier poems addressed human sexuality with some directness, this mask was, effectively, new to his work. The bawdy strand in *New Poems* was both more prominent and more sustained than in previous collections, largely owing to the series of 'The Three Bushes' and its six companion 'Songs' (*VP* 569–75). The mask stood in defiance of the prevailing anti-eroticism of the Free State. In defying state censorship in this way, the poems of the 'Wild Old Wicked Man' were clearly intended to shock, partly in the service of intellectual liberty and vitality.

In composing these poems, Yeats drew on the material of his poetic circle in Dublin, which he had been scrutinising for the anthology. The effects of this can be clearly seen in 'The Ballad of the Three Bushes' and its satellite poems. The text of that ballad might be thought to have given up all its secrets, with successive drafts set out in a celebrated correspondence with Dorothy Wellesley, yet more light can be shed on this poem by shifting attention to the Irish poets Yeats had been reading for the anthology.[36]

The theme of 'The Ballad of the Three Bushes' forms an unusual, and metaphysically freighted, take on the three-person dynamic of lover, mistress and wife. Yeats encountered an Irish precursor in this vein in Frank O'Connor's translation, 'A Learned Mistress', which he anthologized in the *Oxford Book*. The mistress intimates that her adulterous lover has heard a 'tale' that makes him jealous of her love; yet she loves him 'as much as my life':

> If he kill me through jealousy now
>   His wife will perish of spite,
> He will die of grief for his wife,
>   So three shall die in a night.
>
> All blessings from heaven to earth
>   On the head of the woman I hate,
> And the man I love as my life,
>   Sudden death be his fate![37]

---

[36] Jon Stallworthy conclusively demonstrated that the poem owed little to Wellesley's input. See *Vision and Revision in Yeats's Last Poems* (Oxford: Oxford University Press, 1969), 80–94.

[37] *OBMV* 402–3; O'Connor, *The Wild Bird's Nest*, 12–13.

The complex fatalistic logic of the second stanza results in a conclusion that stands in dramatic contradiction to the emotions expressed in the opening. This intertwining of adultery with somewhat perverse solutions to intractable emotional problems finds similarity in Yeats's ballad. Here too, the emotional entanglements are so intractable that they can only be resolved by termination in death; a melodramatic conclusion that is arguably a faithful testament to the intensity of such human passions.

While Yeats's poem may have been triggered by his reading of O'Connor's poem, there is a more important relation between the poems. In a subtitle to his poem, Yeats asserted that it was a translation from a French text: 'the "Historia Mei Temporis" of the Abbé Michel de Bourdeille' (*VP* 569). Although Abbé *Pierre* de Bourdeille wrote sympathetically of human weaknesses among the nobility in his lengthy memoirs, the episode appears to be fabricated. The fabrication rendered Yeats's poem, like O'Connor's, a translation, which granted both poems some license. As Laura O'Connor has observed, the ribald diction that characterized Frank O'Connor's translations was 'due not so much to inherent Rabelaisian qualities in Gaelic as to their exaggeration in the O'Connor/Yeats anti-censorship translation aesthetic' (*YA15* 202).

The superlative source for bawdy poetry, however, came from the work of another anthologized friend of Yeats's: Oliver St. John Gogarty, the well-known Dublin senator, doctor, poet and wit. This influence is most clearly to be found in poems that Yeats did not, and indeed could not, anthologize. Its effects can be seen in the satellite poems that followed on from 'The Ballad of the Three Bushes': 'The Lady's Second Song' and 'The Lady's Third Song', which owe a considerable debt to Gogarty's bawdy poem 'The Hay Hotel'.[38] Yeats's poem opens: 'When you and my true lover meet | And he plays tunes between your feet' (*VP* 572–73), a bawdy conceit taken from Gogarty:

> Where is Piano Mary, say,
> Who dwelt where Hell's Gates leave the street,
> And all the tunes she used to play
> Along your spine beneath the sheet?
> She was a morsel passing sweet
> And warmer than the gates of hell.

---

[38] See A. Norman Jeffares, 'Know Your Gogarty', *YA14* 298–322.

Who tunes her now between the feet?
Go ask them at the Hay Hotel.[39]

In addition, one might also consider this stanza from Gogarty's 'The Old Pianist', which plays on the same ideas:

> 'Send up Piano Mary here,'
> Sez Mack, 'and then send up a bottle;
> She is a dreamy little dear,
> But she can bend the strongest wattle,
> Your spine will know what tunes that mott'll
> Strum on it like a piano player's
> She is the best thing in the brothel,
> Since Nelly's cooling down upstairs.'[40]

These poems by Gogarty were unpublished, but in wide circulation in manuscript form, and had become part of the oral tradition.[41] This latter poem may also have provided a literary source for Yeats's belief that 'warts are considered by the Irish peasantry a sign of sexual power' (*LDW* 63), which is also expressed in a verse preface that Gogarty added to his translation of 'The Old Woman of Beare' (*Cailleach Bhéara*), likening the Old Woman of Beare to aged prostitutes, 'Fresh Nellie' and 'Mrs Mack':

> (*Or the honourable Mrs. Lepple –*
> *Nipple to a kingly nipple –*
> *For she never took advantage*
> *Of the favours of her frontage;*
> *Therefore she was held in honour*
> *By the warty boys who won her;*

---

[39] Oliver St John Gogarty, *The Poems & Plays*, ed. A. Norman Jeffares (Gerrards Cross: Colin Smythe, 2001), 455.

[40] Gogarty, *Poems & Plays*, 459.

[41] See letter to Dorothy Wellesley, 11 June 1937 (*CL InteLex* 6963). The relevant part of the letter is omitted from the correspondence in *LDW*; it reads:

> At the Academy Banquet three weeks ago when Three Bushes was sung, Gogorty was in the chair, arrived half intoxicated as an act of defiance of Mrs Gogarty, who had broken a promise not to come, & became whole intoxicated.
> 'Hay Hotel' was sung this poem which has circulated for twenty years in MSS is an eloquent but unprintable enumeration of the names & charms of the harlots he frequented in his youth. In the sober fore noon he had forbidden it, but when he heard that Lennox Robinson had persuaded Mrs Gogarty to come he ordered it to be sung.

> *Therefore some old Abbey's shelf*
> *Kept the record of herself,*
> *Telling to men who disapprove*
> *Of Love, the long regrets of Love.*)⁴²

Yeats's preoccupation with the postulated connection between sexual potency and warts seems to stem from his re-reading of these poems, since it makes its first appearance in his writings in a letter to Laura Riding, of 23 May 1936.⁴³ It later appeared in the poem 'The Wild Old Wicked Man' in a stanza where the titular speaker of the poem asserts that "'A young man in the dark am I, | But a wild old man in the light'", who enjoys the ability to "'touch by mother wit'" things that are hidden from the younger "'warty lads'":

> 'A young man in the dark am I,
> But a wild old man in the light,
> That can make a cat laugh, or
> Can touch by mother wit
> Things hid in their marrow-bones
> From time long passed away,
> Hid from all those warty lads
> That by their bodies lay.[']
>   *Daybreak and a candle-end.* (*VP* 589)

Prior to this, the one reference to warts in Yeats's extant corpus comes in a description of 'Cromwell's warty opinionated head', in a content that gives no suggestion that this should be taken as anything other than an unflattering contrast with the 'perfectly proportioned human body' that symbolized the previous historical phase (*CW3* 228).

Turning back to Gogarty's preface, we see that the Clergy's status as (self-appointed) guardians of morality seems to have been demoted to mere recorders and archivists. This is also true in Yeats's ballad, ostensibly taken from a *history* written by the Abbé. Yeats's ballad goes one further down this track, however, in driving a wedge between the claims of religion and actual human morality:

> When she was old and dying,
> The priest came where she was;
> She made a full confession.

---

⁴² Gogarty, *Poems & Plays*, 126.
⁴³ 'We poets should be good liars, remembering always that the Muses are women & prefer the embrace of gay warty lads' (*CL InteLex* 6563).

> Long looked he in her face,
> And O, he was a good man
> And understood her case.
> *O my dear, O my dear.* (*VP* 571)

It is not scripture that guides the priest but human compassion, and this renders him 'a good man'. Thus he is able to overlook transgressions forbidden by scripture, and enact no punishment in a situation where none is appropriate.

The bawdy strand of Yeats's final phase takes further material from F. R. Higgins's poetry. A prominent ribald poem in his corpus is 'Song for the Clatter Bones', which has a direct source in Judaeo-Christian scripture: the death of the Queen Jezebel at the command of King Jehu (*Kings* 1:9). Higgins's poem was first published in the Broadside for June 1935, accompanied by a striking hand-tinted print by Jack Yeats, illustrating the envisaged singer. It was later anthologized by Yeats in the *Oxford Book*, with the substitution of 'bitch' for 'witch'; a decision justified by Yeats as being Higgins's original intention.[44] The ribald tone, grotesque material, and strong characterful female subject, recall Yeats's 'Crazy Jane' poems from *The Winding Stair*, but Higgins brought to them a quality that Yeats admired. As the two observed in their joint introduction to the collected *Broadsides* for that year:

> The street songs were more dramatic in their narrative, the singer had to shout, clatter-bones in hand, to draw the attention of the passer-by. One thinks of 'Johnny I hardly Knew Ye', magnificent in gaiety and horror, of the 'Kilmainham Minut', of 'The Night Before Larry Was Stretched'[.] (*CW6* 176)

Yeats's 'Three Songs to the Same Tune', written a year before he started work on the anthology, drew on these very gallows ballads for their material, mixing gaiety with horror in an unsettling way. The sonic quality of his 'Three Songs', however, left something to be desired, and it was this quality that he appreciated in Higgins's 'Song for the Clatter Bones', though he may have had reservations about such onomatopocic excesses as:

> So I'll just clack: though her bones lack a back
> There's music in the old bones yet. (*OBMV* 372)

---

[44] See letter to the Clarendon Press, c.17 September 1936 (*CL InteLex* 6652). The poem appears in *OBMV* 372.

This jaunty and arresting take on the grotesque may have stimulated him to return to the Dowson's themes from the '90s, 'Wine, women and song', from a new angle – 'A Drunken Man's Praise of Sobriety':[45]

> Come swish around my pretty punk
> And keep me dancing still
> That I may stay a sober man
> Although I drink my fill.
> Sobriety is a jewel
> That I do much adore;
> And therefore keep me dancing
> Though drunkards lie and snore.
> O mind your feet, O mind your feet,
> Keep dancing like a wave,
> And under every dancer
> A dead man in his grave.
> No ups and downs, my Pretty,
> A mermaid, not a punk;
> A drunkard is a dead man
> And all dead men are drunk. (*VP* 591–92)

This has much stronger sound-patterning than 'Three Songs to the Same Tune', but it represents a more restrained use of such patterning than his source. He similarly employs internal assonance and alliteration to emphasize a strong rhythm, but weakens internal rhymes by spreading them across lines, or toning them down – such as in the weak consonance on the unstressed of 'under' / 'dancer'.

The subject of Yeats's ballad seems to owe something of a debt to Higgins's 'Cleopatra', from *Island Blood* (1925), with its depiction of the sensuality of dance, and its oscillating fluidity:

> The white censer of your ripe body
> Swings to this old worship
> And drunken I follow the rich waves
> Of your dance in a sheiling of Connacht[.][46]

This drunken paean serves as a sexually-infused return to Yeats's 'The Fiddler of Dooney' from *The Wind Among the Reeds*, where 'Folk dance like a wave of the sea' (*VP* 178). In 'A Drunken Man's Praise of Sobriety', then, Yeats seems to be recovering his simile of

---

[45] Line from Ernest Dowson's 'Villanelle of the Poet's Road', *OBMV* 91.
[46] F. R. Higgins, *Island Blood* (London: John Lane, 1925), 42.

'dancing like a wave [of the sea]' via Higgins's 'Cleopatra' and taking some of the rest of that poem in the process.

Yeats clearly found much material for the bawdy strand of his final phase from his immediate literary circle in Dublin. His friendship with Gogarty, Higgins, and O'Connor, meant that everything he needed in terms of poetic stimulation and instruction lay close at hand. His donning of the mask of the 'Wild Old Wicked Man' in this way was also bound up with his decision to undergo a vasectomy on 5 April 1934. Richard Ellmann suggested that this operation was of central importance to Yeats's creative energies, owing to the poet's association of writing poetry with the ability to 'have erections'.[47] Yeats's re-reading of the work of his friends clearly provided him with the means to realize this eroto-creative potential, and compose some of his most bawdy poems. In poems like 'The Lady's Third Song', the most striking elements seem to have been borrowed entirely from another poet's work (Gogarty's, in this case). Quite what those poets made of this encroachment on their territory remains to be seen. Gogarty, for one, had already showed signs of irritation with Yeats's late obsession with sex, parodying the opening lines of his earlier poem 'The Old Men admiring Themselves in the Water':

> I heard the old, old men say
> everything's phallic[.][48]

THE NOBLE SAGE

If Gogarty was irritated by Yeats's encroachment upon his poetic territory, however, this must have been allayed by Yeats's decision to make him the most anthologized poet. He is represented in the *Oxford Book of Modern Verse* by an astonishing seventeen poems (three more than Yeats himself). Situated as they are near the centre of the anthology, his poems are particularly prominent. Yeats clearly felt required to explain his high estimation, and did

---

[47] Assertion from Norman Haire, quoted in Richard Ellmann, *W. B. Yeats's Second Puberty: A Lecture Delivered at the Library of Congress on April 2, 1984* (Washington: Library of Congress, 1985), 8.

[48] Letter from Gogarty to Horace Reynolds, 11 October 1934. Quoted in *Life* 2, 499.

so in the anthology's introduction. The passage is worth quoting in full:

> Twelve years ago Oliver Gogarty was captured by his enemies, imprisoned in a deserted house on the edge of the Liffey with every prospect of death. Pleading a natural necessity he got into the garden, plunged under a shower of revolver bullets and as he swam the ice-cold December stream promised it, should it land him in safety, two swans. I was present when he fulfilled that vow. His poetry fits the incident, a gay, stoical – no, I will not withhold the word – heroic song. Irish by tradition and many ancestors, I love, though I have nothing to offer but the philosophy they deride, swashbucklers, horsemen, swift indifferent men; yet I do not think that is the sole reason, good reason though it is, why I gave him considerable space, and think him one of the great lyric poets of our age (*OBMV* xv).

Who might the other great lyric poets of the age be? Perhaps one is the poet with exactly the same number of pages: Yeats himself. The anecdote is spectacularly dramatic, but Gogarty's poetry was not merely included to enable Yeats to rehearse it in a further publication (he had already done so in his introduction to Gogarty's *An Offering of Swans and Other Poems* [1924]). Yeats's admiration for his poetry was evidently in earnest, as evidenced by his subsequent textual borrowings.

Most importantly, Gogarty's work was 'gay, stoical' and 'heroic': qualities that Yeats aspired to in the poetic mask of the noble, dispassionate, sagacious mind. This is the archetypal poetic mask of *Per Amica Silentia Lunae*, and poems like 'The Fisherman' (*VP* 347) though its roots stretch back far earlier to the sages of *The Wind Among the Reeds*: Mongan, and Michael Robartes. As such, it is a complement to the mask of the unsophisticated but visionary peasant poet.

Gogarty's poetry accordingly influenced Yeats's most significant poem in this vein in his penultimate collection: 'Lapis Lazuli'. It is widely known that the poem was occasioned by the gift from Harry Clifton of what Yeats described as: 'a huge piece of lapis lazuli carved into the semblance of mountain, with path, water, trees, a little temple, a sage & his pupil by some Chinese sculptor'.[49] Yeats's poem concludes with a description of the object, an ecphrasis that stands in contrast to the dramatic historical

---

[49] Letter to Edmund Dulac, 6 July 1935 (*CL InteLex* 6280).

narratives of the preceding three stanzas. These narrate the cyclical pattern of Yeats's system of history outlined in *A Vision*, and display much of the richness of art-history that informs that account, which was later expressed in poems such as 'The Statues', and 'Under Ben Bulben'. Clifton gave Yeats the sculpture as a 70th birthday gift, but Yeats did not write his poem until the summer of the following year, 1936. As a consequence, the poem was written on the back of the reading Yeats had undertaken for the anthology, and it reflects its influence. In particular, it shows debts to Gogarty's *Selected Poems* (1933). Here, Yeats would have encountered the poem 'The Emperor's Dream', followed by 'Palinode', which he previously encountered in *An Offering of Swans and Other Poems* (1924). These two poems seem to contain the germs of the idea of 'Lapis Lazuli', and many of its premises.

Just like Yeats's poem, 'The Emperor's Dream' is partly occasioned by the contemplation of a Chinese carved crystal work of art; in Gogarty's case a 'Chinese crystal bird'. In both poems, the speaker takes inspiration from this carved object to reflect upon questions of permanence. In Gogarty's, the crystal is posited to 'last as long | As Beauty gains from Art and Song', and, like Yeats's poem, the object is considered in the context of international art-history and exotic distant lands:

> When the internal dream gives out,
> I let my eyes wander about
> Amongst the gay and the grotesque
> Ornaments upon my desk,
>
> Where books are set on end and stacked
> By Plato and by Homer backed;
> But, in the present mood preferred,
> I see my Chinese crystal bird:
>
> A Phoenix maybe, who can say?
> That ship that, off Arabia,
> Sighted the Phoenix flying East,
> Its crew could tell about it best.[50]

Such carved crystal objects seem apt to encourage a debate on permanence and transience in art and life. Yet specific affiliations

---

[50] Gogarty, *Poems & Plays*, 171.

seem to link Yeats's poem with 'The Emperor's Dream', and the subsequent poem in Gogarty's *Selected Poems*: 'Palinode'.[51]

The retraction alluded to in the title is more a rebuff to sombre attitudes to life than the previous poem. 'Palinode' celebrates the decision to live life 'full of mirth' (and 'full of wine'), for why do otherwise?

> Why should you drink the rue?
>   Or leave in righteous rage
> A world that will leave you
>   Howe'er you *walk the stage*?
> Time needs no help to do
>   His miracle of age.[52]

Just as in 'Lapis Lazuli', we find the Shakespearean trope of 'All the world's a stage, | And all the men and women merely players' (*As You Like It*, II.vii.139–40). Both poets enlist this theatrical metaphor for life in the service of their arguments. In so doing, Gogarty is very much one of those 'poets that are always gay', valorized by Yeats's poem. Gogarty gives this theme a Latin motto in the title of a poem anthologized by Yeats: 'Non Dolet' ('No cause for grief', or 'It does not hurt') (*OBMV* 181). Yeats combines this theatrical metaphor for the experience of human life with his notion of 'tragic joy':

> All perform their tragic play,
> There struts Hamlet, there is Lear,
> That's Ophelia, that Cordelia[.] (*VP* 565)

Of course, Yeats's doctrine of 'tragic joy' goes further than such up-tempo stoicism, in incorporating a philosophical attitude to the contemplation of cataclysmic historical change. Yet this too finds some echoes in Gogarty's 'Palinode':

> Prophets anticipate
> What Time brings round by law;
> Call age before its date

---

[51] The title suggests that the latter poem could be taken as a retraction of the previous one, but in his *Collected Poems* of 1951, he placed two other poems between them: 'Lullaby' ('Wander no more, my Thoughts, but keep'), and 'The Mill at Naul'; see Gogarty, *Poems & Plays*, 173–77.

[52] Gogarty, *Poems & Plays*, 178. Emphasis added.

To darken Youth with awe.⁵³

Gogarty's poems thus associated carved oriental crystal and theatrical metaphors for life with an attitude of 'Non Dolet'. From here, it was but a small leap of cognition to arrive at recasting Hamlet, Lear, Cordelia, and Ophelia as embodiments of the principle of 'tragic joy'. In so doing, Gogarty's poems seem to have provided Yeats with a combination of elements that allowed him to finally capitalize on the creative possibilities of his spectacular birthday gift from Harry Clifton. The result was a wide-ranging poem of which Yeats was justly proud.

For the narrative of apocalyptic historical change, however, Yeats looked to an older source than Gogarty, drawing on the ballad of the 'Boyne Water', which celebrates William of Orange's victory over James II's forces in Ireland at the Battle of the Boyne (1690). As Norman Jeffares has demonstrated, the reference to William of Orange as King Billy, and the pitching of 'bomb-balls' are taken from the ballad.⁵⁴ As with the reference to the Zeppelin, anachronistic in warfare in 1936, Yeats appears to have drawn on these images to demonstrate cyclical continuity; emphasising that apocalypse is not unique to any one time, and the consoling corollary to this idea:

> All things fall and are built again
> And those that build them again are gay. (*VP* 566)

THE ENCUMBERING ROBE

Yeats's immersion in contemporary poetry clearly influenced his own work, enriching even long-held poetic masks. Yet while the editorship of the *Oxford Book of Modern Verse* also afforded Yeats with enhanced social status, this came with the burdensome robes of office. A desire to live up to expectations may well have motivated Yeats's discussion of prosody in the introduction to the anthology; a discussion that he was, perhaps, ill-suited to enter

---

⁵³ Gogarty, *Poems & Plays*, 178.
⁵⁴ A. Norman Jeffares, 'Notes on Yeats's "Lapis Lazuli"', *Modern Language Notes* 65 (1950), 488–91.

into, given that he prescribed metrical principles that contradicted his own practice.

Towards the end of Yeats's reading for the anthology he also wrote the introduction to the collection of *Broadsides* for 1935. This similarly entered into an unprecedented discussion of prosody. The introduction to the Broadsides was written with some input from F. R. Higgins, but the prosody was lifted from an article by G. M. Young titled 'Tunes Ancient and Modern', published in February 1935. Young's article was ostensibly a review of Edith Sitwell's *Aspects of Modern Poetry*, and Cecil Day Lewis's *A Hope for Poetry* (both published in 1934) but it made use of the opportunity to reflect broadly on the metrical practice of modern poets. In the course of this discussion it set out a number of principles for the composition of metrical verse. In thanking his correspondent, Yeats wrote that 'it has interested me deeply and taught me more about prosody than I have ever known. I shall make some use of it in an introduction I am writing for a collection of some Broadsides my sister is publishing'.[55] He did just this; in fact, he went even further, repeating much of the content of the article in his writings and correspondence, and, most remarkably, may even have briefly attempted to follow one of its edicts.

Young posited that from Philip Sidney to Yeats, there was an 'unbroken curve' of rhythmical practice, shaped by gradual change and adaptation such that '[f]rom Sidney to Mr Yeats there is no point in English poetry at which one is conscious of any breach'. The poets after Yeats, however, wrote verse that Young found he could not scan – the continuum was broken. This impression seems largely justified. Young attempted to account for it by a philosophy of metre that regards poetry as arising from the rich heritage of folk music, nursery rhymes and hymns, which form the 'ancestral, primitive metre' of a 'race'. This 'ancestral, primitive metre' entails what Young calls as 'singsong' rhythm of alternating beats and offbeats. If verse is to be rhythmical, he posited, variations and innovations of rhythm must be carried out by means of counterpoint with this regular rhythm. Accordingly, Young posited a prosody founded on metrical feet, and on foot-

---

[55] Letter to John Sparrow, 23 September 1935 (*CL InteLex* 6356).

substitution constrained by the following prescriptions: 'iamb for strength, trochee for grace; dactyls on your peril; resolution to taste; no pæons; no colliding stresses, and therefore no colliding stresses without a preparatory pause'.[56] These edicts were intended to ensure that the 'ancestral' rhythm was not lost: like much prosody, they constituted an attempt to account for rhythmical qualities using easily quantifiable features. If veridical, such a simplification would be invaluable for the construction and evaluation of metrical verse, but Young's rules were not.

For a brief period, Yeats seems to have been particularly convinced by Young's prohibition of 'pæons', defined as a 'foot' of one stressed syllable and three unstressed ('wwws' or 'swww'). This Classical term for a foot of four syllables, and its prohibition, was not singled out in the other works of prosody in Yeats's library: Coventry Patmore's *Essay on English Metrical Law* (1857) and MacDonagh's *Thomas Campion and the Art of English Poetry* (1913).[57] It made its first appearance in Yeats's published writings in the introduction to the collection of *Broadsides* (1935). Here, in his discussion of the ballad 'The Groves of Blarney' he wrote that a reader coming to the poem from English ballad metre would find the third line 'unmetrical', since 'a pæon or foot of four syllables, is not permissible in English ballad metre' (*CW6* 1988). Elsewhere, he remarked jocularly to Dorothy Wellesley that he was in the process of composing new poetry, and that 'if a foot of four syllables seems natural I shall know I am in for it' (*LDW* 44). These utterances are remarkable not merely because they are the only references in his entire written corpus to 'pæons', but they are the first reference to metrical feet in his extant correspondence *by any name*.[58]

---

[56] G. M. Young, 'Tunes Ancient and Modern', *Life and Letters* 11 February 1935, 544, 547, 548.

[57] Yeats owned the revised two volume version of Patmore's *Essay* (first published in 1887) printed in her *Poems*, 2 vols. (London: George Bell, 1907), 215–67; for a textual history see *Coventry Patmore, Essay on English Metrical Law, with a comment. by Mary Augustine Roth* (Washington, DC: Catholic University of America, 1961), xii–xiv.

[58] In his extant prose-writings Yeats made only two references to metrical feet: anapaests are mentioned in the introduction to the *BIV* (1895) in a discussion of Thomas Moore that was excised in the second edition (*CW6* 218); and his essay 'Edmund Spenser' (1912) observes that 'Harvey set Spenser to the making of verses

For a time, Yeats apparently believed that pæons had no place in poems other than Anglo-Irish ballads. Such metrical feet entail an interval of three unstressed syllables between beats. This challenges the pattern of alternating beats and offbeats in typical lines in binary metres (like iambic pentameter). It does so more than an interval of two slack syllables, because an interval of three will normally imply rhythmical 'promotion' of the syllable in the middle. To see an example of such 'metrical promotion' as it is sometimes called, consider this line from 'The Wanderings of Oisin':

> Was nót more lével than the séa[.] (*VP* 13)

In this example, the word 'than' would not normally receive linguistic stress, but the metre requires that it be stressed. A rhythmical performance would, therefore, give some stress to the word.

In the case of lines including pæons, however, a rhythmical delivery requires maintaining an offbeat of three syllables. This requires some effort of the performer's part, to overcome the expectation of a beat falling on the second of these slack syllables. One means of effecting this in performance would be to under-articulate the syllable boundaries, so that the syllables flow together. Yeats's *Collected Poems* display a modest number of lines that include such extended intervals. Consider this line from 'Shepherd and Goatherd' (published 1919), which seems like a hexameter line in a pentameter poem, unless the underlined syllables are performed as an offbeat:

> Or élse at méadow or at grázing overlóoks[.] (*VP* 340)

The same is true for this tetrameter line in 'The Wild Swan's at Coole', which seems like pentameter:

> Compánionable stréams or clímb the aír[.] (*VP* 323)

The instance of a pæon is just as clear in the poem 'Ancestral Houses' from the sequence 'Meditations in Time of Civil War' (first published January 1923). At the close of the second stanza,

---

in classical metre, and certain lines have come down to us written in what Spenser called 'Iambicum trimetrum' (*E&I* 357).

in iambic pentameter, we find this line, which requires an interval of three syllables at its beginning or at its end:

Shádows the inhérited glóry of the rích. (*VP* 418)

Yeats's advocacy of Young's edict against pæons, then, represents a contradiction of his own technique, and there is a tantalising suggestion that he even changed his practice temporarily to comply with it. 'Lapis Lazuli', drafted in the summer of 1936, is one of the first poems Yeats wrote after reading Young's article. In the second stanza Yeats follows the Shakespearean trope of 'all the world's a stage' to assert that such actors,

> If worthy their prominent part in the play,
> Do not break up their lines to weep. (*VP* 565)

It is part of a famous, and widely glossed section of the poem, but it might also represent a case of metrical theory damaging poetry if it encouraged him to omit the preposition 'of' in 'worthy of'. It may be that this construction serves as idiomatic of a dialect of English, but it does not appear elsewhere in Yeats's writings or correspondence. Further, in the context of a discussion of canonical drama, a listener might erroneously conclude that 'Worthy' is the *name* of the actor's prominent part in the play – following the dramatic convention for naming characters as in a morality tale, as in some Renaissance and Restoration Drama.[59] Orthography dictates that Yeats did not intend this meaning, but a person receiving the poem aurally does not have access to this information. Prosody appears to be damaging to poetic practice, here, and if so, we can only be grateful that Yeats eventually turned his back on such reductive 'laws', even if this did not extend to revising the line before his death.

Whether or not they affected his subsequent poetry, the newly-adopted prosodic principles made an appearance in the brief discussion of prosody in the introduction to the anthology. Here we are confronted with the curious spectacle of Yeats, a poet who

---

[59] Colly Cibber's *Loves Last Shift; or, The Fool in Fashion* (1696), and Vanbrugh's 'continuation' of the play, *The Relapse: Or, Virtue in Danger, Being the Sequel of the Fool in Fashion* (1696) both include a character called 'Worthy'. See *The Broadview Anthology of Restoration & Early Eighteenth-Century English Drama*, gen. ed. J. Douglas Canfield, assistant editor Maja-Lisa Von Sneidern (Peterborough, Ont. and Ormskirk: Broadview Press, 2001).

includes 'slack' extra syllables throughout his poetry – occasionally as many as three grouped together – consigning this practice to that of 'sprung verse': 'in sprung verse a foot may have one or many syllables without altering the metre, we count stress not syllable' (*OBMV* 39). In contrast, he continued, 'all syllables are important' in the sort of poetry that he wrote. This is essentially a declaration that Yeats wrote 'strict' accentual-syllabic verse, with no extra syllables per 'foot'. This is manifestly not the case; how can we explain this discrepancy between theory and practice?

The answer is quite simply that Yeats was not much of a prosodist, when it came to theory. This probably contributed to his poetic achievement; until late in the twentieth-century, much English prosody was like early attempts at medicine: more likely to do harm than good. By reducing complex rhythmical qualities to rules about syllable-counting and foot-substitution, prosodies like Young's prescribed rules intended to minimize deviations from purported 'metricality'. As Reuven Tsur has argued, such approaches miss the point, which is that aesthetic pleasure and achievement arises from "the balance or reconcilement of opposite or discordant qualities", in Coleridge's phrase – and 'the more discordant the qualities, the greater the artistic achievement when reconciled in a rhythmical performance'.[60] Moreover, while Young's premise focused on auditory phenomena, his rules did not; rhythm is not a product merely of the arrangement of stresses and unstresses, but of a whole gamut of phenomena including phonology, phonetics, grammar and syntax.

By his 'General Introduction for my Work', written in 1937, Yeats was clearly ready to relinquish Young's metrical laws. In the proper performance of poetry, he wrote, '[w]hat moves me and my hearer is a vivid speech that has no laws except that it must not exorcise the ghostly voice. I am awake and asleep, at my moment of revelation, self-possessed in self-surrender' (*E&I* 524). Unlike his earlier pronouncements, this account is consistent with his own poetic practice.

The introductions to the Broadsides and to the anthology clearly represent the high-water mark of Yeats's enthusiasm for Young's prosody. This implies that Yeats took up Young's clear

---

[60] Reuven Tsur, *Poetic Rhythm: Structure and Performance: An Empirical Study in Cognitive Poetics* (Bern and New York: Peter Lang, 1998), 25.

prescriptions because he felt obliged to demonstrate a technical understanding of metre, as the authoritative editor of the *Oxford Book of Modern Verse*, and (to a lesser extent) of the collection of *Broadsides* for 1935; he had shown no inclination of such an exposition elsewhere. His own systems for measuring and assessing rhythm were based on a lifetime of composing verse by running over the lines repeatedly, often aloud, and by a process of trial and error; which is to say, his systems were far more sophisticated than the rules set out by G. M. Young, and other contemporary prosodists.

CONCLUSION

While his editorship of the *Oxford Book of Modern Verse* seems to have encumbered Yeats with the need to appear expert in prosody, this effect was entirely eclipsed by the creative potential of the extensive programme of reading that the project required. We might say that the encumbering robe of office proved less potent than the enabling energies of the new and refurbished masks that accompanied it.

Yeats's theory of poetic masks enabled him to 'multiply personality', and to fashion those discrete aspects to such an extent that each embodied 'something intended, complete', 'even when the poet seems most himself' (*OBMV* xxxvi; *E&I* 509). As Yeats's final masks implicitly demonstrate, this approach to creative endeavour permits overt borrowings from other poets. In contrast, notions of creative 'sincerity' are frequently all-too contingent on an unhelpful valorization of originality.

'The Curse of Cromwell', spoken through the mask of the visionary peasant poet, is a superlative example of the fruits of this process. Here, Yeats's unification of Irish faery-lore and contemporary spiritualism is put to the service of excoriating the Irish Free State for the social collapse it instigated. The poem does so through an amalgamation of recent, and less recent, translations of seventeenth- and eighteenth-century Gaelic poetry, and the accounts of the other-world of faery collected by Lady Gregory near the start of Yeats's career as a poet. Notwithstanding the importance of Yeats's intellectual labours in synthesizing these disparate traditions, so much of the material of the poem is taken from these various sources that one might almost see his role as a compiler and arranger, rather than originator. Rather than dispel this impression, however, it is probably most instructive to realise that this is the proper way to regard all creative endeavour. As Yeats reminds us: 'Talk to me of originality and I will turn on you with rage. I am a crowd, I am a lonely man, I am nothing' (*E&I* 522).

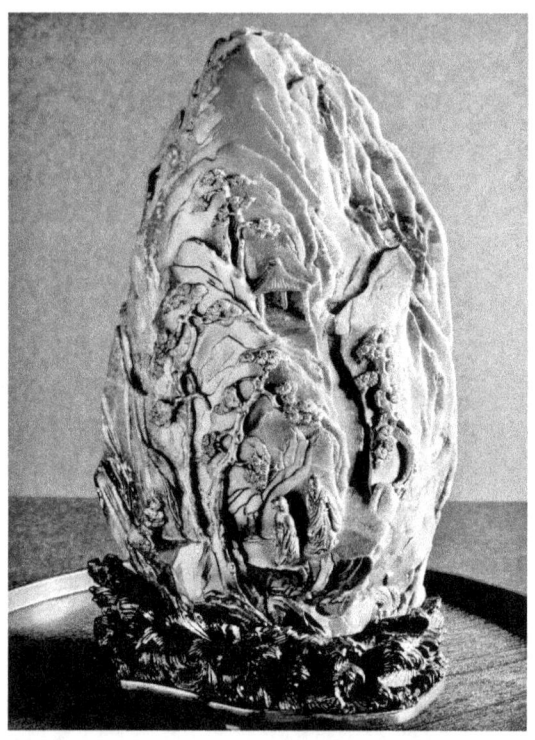

Plate 4. Yeats's Lapis Lazuli mountain (given to him by Harry Clifton, and the inspiration of the poem 'Lapis Lazuli'), front view. Photograph courtesy and © of the National Library of Ireland. All rights reserved.

The Poem on the Mountain: A Chinese Reading of Yeats's 'Lapis Lazuli'

Jerusha McCormack

> 'It may be well if we go to school in Asia....'[1]
> W. B. Yeats

DURING MY FIRST stay in Beijing in 2004, one poem kept running through my head. It was W. B. Yeats's 'Lapis Lazuli'. Why this would be so puzzled me at first. I had come here teach a course in Western Civilization at a small, elite university; this year I was not even teaching literature, much less Irish literature.

It was not until I began expeditions into the city that I realized why Yeats's poem had taken on such new insistence. In the recent past, the Chinese authorities had begun to raze most of inner-city Beijing. Whole districts of *hutongs* – low-level courtyard dwellings, many of them centuries old – had defined this ancient place. Now these were being rapidly replaced, their former residents forcibly relocated. Everywhere I traveled around the old city, all I could see was the shells of half-destroyed houses (hovels might be more appropriate, given their semi-derelict state) as the diggers tore into them. Sometimes all that would remain was a flattened, dusty acre or two bounded by plywood walls and busy streets.

---

[1] W. B. Yeats, 'Certain Noble Plays of Japan', *Essays and Introductions* (London: Macmillan, 1961), 225. Although I apply Yeats's use of 'Asia' and 'the east' in this essay exclusively to China, of course Yeats had in mind primarily Japan and India: civilizations cognate in many ways to each other as well as with that of China.

Out of these sites, punctuated by colonies of towering cranes, shiny new steel and glass mountains arose – sometimes within months. Chinese workers are deployed on 24-hour shifts; the work continues night and day. So that, over the next few years, I saw a whole new city – and with it, it seemed, a whole new China – rising from the rubble of the old:

> All things fall and are built again....

Not until 2006, however, did I see, for the first time, the actual carved stone which had inspired 'Lapis Lazuli': on loan from his family to the exhibit on William Butler Yeats at the National Library of Ireland in Dublin. After several years of accumulated experience in China, I realized that this stone was an aesthetic object with distinctive Chinese meanings. *What could this stone mean* – first to Yeats and now to us – within the wider perspective of Chinese views of the world? This question became a major preoccupation over the next few years.

Critical commentary on 'Lapis Lazuli' is in fact sparse. One invaluable essay from *Notes and Queries* in 1977 by David Parker gives a detailed account of its Chinese iconography. A second, broader essay on 'The Art of Yeats's "Lapis Lazuli"' by William H. O'Donnell for the *Massachusetts Review* of 1982 helps place the poem within Yeats's own thinking, particularly within his own aesthetic system. Finally, there is Calvin Bedient's less helpful meditation on 'what seduced Yeats, and what Yeats seduced' within the context of the poem's 'sighted language' (but with no reference at all to its Chinese significance): an essay written for the *Yeats: an Annual of Critical and Textural Studies* in 1989.[2] Nothing substantial appears to have been published since, perhaps because the poem appears now diminished by two things. Most importantly, by a limited knowledge of its Chinese significance. Perhaps (more arguably) by its crucial

---

[2] David Parker, 'Yeats's Lapis Lazuli', *Notes and Queries* (October 1977), 452–54; William H. O'Donnell, 'The Art of Yeats's "Lapis Lazuli"', *Massachusetts Review* 23, n. 2 (Summer 1982), 353–67; Calvin Bedient , 'Yeats's "Lapis Lazuli": Romancing the Stone', *Yeats: an Annual of Critical and Textual Studies* 7 (1989), 17–41. In *Yeats and the Visual Arts* (New Brunswick: Rutgers University Press, 1986), 148–52, Elizabeth Bergmann Loizeaux discusses the relationship of the stone to the poem without adding any new information, such as that from the earlier work of Parker or O'Donnell.

reliance on one word – 'gay' – largely used today in a narrow sense as denoting a same-sex orientation.³

While the poem still needs to be rescued from this distracting evolution of 'gay', much more remains to be clarified about its Chinese origins. Of the three essays mentioned, David Parker's is perhaps the closest to recreating a helpful Chinese context. As Parker explains, Yeats's stone is one of a specific genre called in China, 'jade islands': a designation that includes stones other than jade (or nephrite). Specifically, Yeats's stone may be taken to represent the Chinese Isles of the Blest or Eastern Paradise: in pinyin, *Peng-lai Shan*.⁴ The principal of five islands imagined as being somewhere in the Eastern – i.e., Yellow – Sea (the wooden base, original to the stone, shows very clearly its carved waves), these islands were traditionally believed to be the home of the Eight Immortals. Two are shown on Yeats's stone. These sages were not merely old; they were ancient, having achieved a longevity which merges indistinguishably into immortality. Thus, as a birthday gift for a famous but aging poet, this carved stone was singularly apt, designed to remind its observer of a state of blessedness associated with old age and its proximity to eternity.

Yet despite Parker's effort to locate Yeats's stone within its iconographic tradition, neither his nor the other essays make any attempt to explicate the cultural *assumptions* which actually shaped the stone's creation and use. Nor has there been a coherent explanation of how its Chinese significance has been incorporated into the poem by Yeats himself. While we may never know just how much Yeats himself learned about the Chinese nature of this stone, it is clear that he did somehow come to an understanding of what it signified within its own culture of origin. In doing so, Yeats also discovered how it could bring meaning to the close of his own life, both as man and as poet.

³ At the time Yeats was writing 'Lapis Lazuli', the word 'gay' was beginning to undergo this transformation, from its usual meaning of being light-hearted, mirthful or brilliantly animated into one that played on older meanings of the word, as leading an immoral or dissipated life (from 1310 on). Its first use as denoting homosexual is quoted by the *Oxford English Dictionary* (second edition, 1989, Vol. VI) as dating from 1935, citing N. Erskine, *Underworld and Prison Slang*.

⁴ 'It is in fact a Chinese jade island – the term is generic and covers carving in stones other than nephrite ... Others with a closely similar subject matter are illustrated in *Chinese Jades in the Avery Brundage Collection* by Réne Yvon Lefebvre d'Argencé (Berkeley, 1972)', Parker, 452.

As is well known, Yeats received the lapis lazuli stone on 4 July 1935 as a gift for his 70th birthday from an admiring young poet, Harry Clifton. Taking the shape of a small mountain (26.7 cm. or 10.5 inches high, not including the original wooden base), it is carved from a semi-precious blue stone, lapis lazuli. Someone, possibly his friend Edmund Dulac (who was knowledgeable about such things), may have explained to Yeats what would have been generally known: that the carved stone dates from the reign of the Qianlong Emperor therefore some time between 1739–1795. Famous for his aesthetic pursuits, this Emperor routinely accepted such precious and semi-precious stones as tribute or booty, which he had carved and often inscribed with poems either by or attributed to himself.[5] And, indeed, as Yeats noted to Dulac two days after receiving it, his own lapis mountain also had an inscription in Chinese characters on the back – although Yeats apparently showed no immediate interest in having it translated.[6]

On the same day Yeats also wrote Dorothy Wellesley:

> I notice that you have much lapis lazuli; someone has sent me a present of a great piece carved by some Chinese sculptor into the semblance of a mountain with temple, trees, paths and an ascetic and pupil about to climb the mountain. Ascetic, pupil, hard stone, eternal theme of the sensual east. The heroic cry in the midst of despair. But no, I am wrong, the east has its solutions always and therefore knows nothing of tragedy. It is we, not the east, that must raise the heroic cry (*L* 837).

Unversed in Chinese art, Yeats initially did not read the stone's iconography correctly. What is surprising is that, by the time he came to finish 'Lapis Lazuli' almost exactly a year later,[7] his reading of the

---

[5] An example of the Qianlong Emperor's aesthetic preoccupations can be found in the jade books held by the Chester Beatty Library in Dublin, Ireland, which are also inscribed with poems attributed to the Emperor (but which often may have only been written at his command).

[6] Informed by Yeats of this fact, Dulac offered to have the poem translated if Yeats could send him a copy or a photograph; but there is no evidence that Yeats ever took him up on this offer. Unpublished letter, 6 July 1935, Humanities Research Center, University of Texas; quoted in O'Donnell, 355.

[7] 'Yeats wrote "Lapis Lazuli" in July 1936'. A. Norman Jeffares, 'The General and Particular Meanings of "Lapis Lazuli"' (1967) from *Yeats's Last Poems: A Casebook*, ed. Jon Stallworthy (London: Macmillan, 1968), 160. Jeffares had this information from Mrs. W. B. Yeats. See also O'Donnell, 357, n. 9, citing a letter from Yeats to Dorothy Wellesley of 26 July 1936.

stone is not only correct, but, within a Chinese context, appropriate. For, while his initial remarks were off-centre in terms of detail, Yeats seemed immediately to grasp the stone's larger significance, as is clear from the turn of the last two sentences of this letter. 'But no', he writes: 'I am wrong, the east has its solutions always and therefore knows nothing of tragedy. It is we, and not the east, that must raise the heroic cry'.

In what ways did Yeats discover he was *wrong*? And how does he, subsequently, come to interpret this exotic artifact? And, finally, how did he manage, from his own resources, to arrive at a reading so consonant with that of its original Chinese context?

First of all, it is clear that Yeats must have had a mentor (perhaps Dulac?) – someone to have helped him read the distinctively Chinese iconography of the carving. This is the tentative conclusion of David Parker, who points out how, in the final poem, Yeats corrects his initial catalogue of its images. Thus the mountain 'temple' becomes in the final poem a 'little half-way house'. The two Chinamen, originally 'an ascetic and pupil', are now implied to be old friends, perhaps master and disciple: and, as scholars or artists/literati, members of a class with which Yeats, albeit in another world, would be ready to identify himself. The third carved figure, said to be 'doubtless a serving-man', is now correctly seen as carrying 'a musical instrument'. Yeats (concludes Parker) would not have 'learned to recognize the *ch'in* [*qin*] lute merely through chance reading'(*N & Q* 454). Finally, the 'long-legged bird' (ignored in Yeats's initial letter) is now acknowledged to be a crane, and, with its traditional Chinese association, as a symbol of longevity.[8]

There still remain one or two items whose Chinese significance Yeats did not exploit: the pine trees, for instance, another symbol of long-term resilience but one which – perhaps in reference to their stylized clumps of needles – he chose to imagine as blossoming plum or cherry.[9] Also, beside the path is a waterfall, which he mentions (as a "water-course") but does not integrate in any obvious way. Yet, as Yeats came to understand, these too are part of the larger symbolic

---

[8] Parker, 452–54, to whom this discussion of Yeats's understanding of the lapis mountain's symbolism is indebted.

[9] One can only conjecture that, in this instance, Yeats's imagination simply overruled a more correct reading of the meaning of these trees, with which he was certainly familiar. For further information, see n. 18.

system which plays into a Chinese reading of the stone, one to which the 'Lapis Lazuli' poem, at least implicitly, subscribes.

These oversights, however, are trivial compared to the astonishing insight that Yeats attained during this one year, 1935-36. For the meditations which culminate in this poem offer a far deeper comprehension of the issues involved in the creation of the stone mountain: issues that have to do with nothing less than the ultimate significance of living – and dying – within this world. It is in clarifying these issues that reading the stone within a Chinese context is most useful. For, to any Chinese viewer, the lapis lazuli mountain speaks of the great themes of human existence: what it means to live – especially in full mindfulness of death, whether from old age or some more public catastrophe.

That Yeats grasped the spiritual potential of the stone, and that he specifically assigns it to 'the east', is explicit from his first response to the lapis mountain: 'The heroic cry in the midst of despair. But no, *I am wrong, the east has its solutions always and therefore knows nothing of tragedy*' [italics added]. Of what tragedy does Yeats write? And how can 'the east' know 'nothing' of it?

As the opening stanza of 'Lapis Lazuli' makes clear, the 'tragic scene' of the last verse was dominated by those catastrophes taking place during the year of its composition. Between 1935 and 1936, Adolf Hitler, now elected Chancellor of the new German Democratic Socialist Republic, announced renewed national rearmament and universal (male) conscription. He also established the *Luftwaffe* (the German Air Force), which reawakened memories among Yeats's contemporaries of the bombing of London by Kaiser Wilhelm's Zeppelins during the Great War.[10] Then, as if to vindicate these fears, Hitler occupied the Rhineland in March of 1936; his first step towards his ambition of conquering all of Europe. As if in a dire parody, Benito Mussolini had by now reached the apex of his political power in Italy, while, in Russia, Joseph Stalin's regime was tightening its grip. Newspapers also brought Yeats news of open bombing of Spanish cities, a frightening prelude to the civil war that was finally to erupt during the month 'Lapis Lazuli' was (apparently) completed.

---

[10] Edmund Dulac had written to Yeats at the time he was working on the poem that he [Dulac] was 'terrified of what was going to happen if London was bombed from the air'. Given originally in Frank O'Connor's *A Backward Look* (1967), 174, the letter is quoted in Jon Stallworthy, *Vision and Revision in Yeats's Last Poems* (Oxford: Clarendon Press, 1969), 44.

Not surprising that, as Yeats flatly states, 'everybody knows or else should know | That if nothing drastic is done | Aeroplane and Zeppelin will come out ... Until the town lie beaten flat'.

In such a context, the poets 'that are always gay', along with their artist and musician friends, must certainly appear at best merely marginal; at worst, displaying a brazen indifference: a case of literally fiddling while Rome burns. What, under these circumstances, can be the status of art? In particular that art which, as tragedy, seeks to engage with such cataclysmic disruptions in human affairs?

To answer that question, Yeats turns in the next stanza to the Western cultural articulation of what 'tragedy' means. Inevitably, perhaps, his model is Shakespeare; not the historical Shakespeare, but Shakespeare as replayed in everyday life: 'There struts Hamlet, there is Lear...'. Here, as Yeats notes, Hamlet suffers 'all men's fate'(*E & I* 255)[11]; but Hamlet is also Yeats himself, who as a boy copied the pose of Henry Irving while playing this part (*Au* 47). Now rapidly ageing, Yeats too must also face 'all man's fate', that of death. Yet, as the poem observes, great actors, performing a tragic play, do not (unlike ordinary mortals) 'break up their lines to weep':

> They know that Hamlet and Lear are gay;
> Gaiety transfiguring all that dread.

At stake here is not simply personal oblivion, but 'All [that] men have aimed at, found and lost' – the entire course of human endeavour ending in 'Black out'. That order to close off all sources of light in London during the bombing of the Great War becomes (in Yeats's own words) that 'perception of a change [from the sensual to the spiritual], like the sudden "blacking out" of the lights of the stage' (*Au* 326). Such a change occurs violently, as, at the climax of that 'tragic scene', terror and pity move into a brief, brilliant illumination: 'Heaven blazing into the head'. (The very enjambment of the clauses here makes the point.) Yet however often this 'tragic scene' is repeated, however coldly we observe its multiplication on the world-stage (as 'as all the drop-scenes drop at once'), tragedy as an artistic form remains unable to move beyond itself: 'It cannot grow by an inch or

---

[11] Compare also Neville in Virginia Woolf's *The Waves* – a novel Yeats knew: 'It is better...to read Shakespeare as I read him here in Shaftsbury Avenue. Here's the fool, here's the villain, here in a car comes Cleopatra' (London: Hogarth Press, 1931), 312. I am indebted to Professor Daniel Albright of the English Department, Harvard University, for pointing out this parallel.

an ounce'. Nor can the blaze of tragic ecstasy move into any larger vision of man's fate beyond the performance of his inevitable end.

For Yeats, the key stanza is the next one, in which he envisions the barbarian hordes who always arrive to destroy civilizations. This vision of ever-returning destruction pushes Yeats beyond what had become his great consolation: the eternity of artifice or (at the very least) the illusion of eternity granted by artifice. In 'Sailing to Byzantium' that consolation had already become qualified; the marvelous golden bird which sings of 'What is past, or passing, or to come' serves only as a toy 'to keep a drowsy Emperor awake'. Now in 'Lapis Lazuli' Yeats foresees the more probable fate of his own work: as 'Old civilizations [are] put to the sword' then 'they and their wisdom went to rack'. Here, at the last, Yeats is prepared to acknowledge that even the greatest works of art do not guarantee immortality.

To make this point, Yeats chooses as exemplar the classical Greek designer and sculptor Callimachus. Reputed to be the inventor of the Corinthian column, Callimachus was also the alleged sculptor of parts of the Parthenon frieze. Within it, the great Temple of Athena was said to have had a remarkable lamp – also designed by Callimachus. But why Callimachus? As a sculptor, he was not of the first rank of his contemporaries in the Athens of the fifth century BC, Phidias or Polykleides. Nor has any of his work survived, except in Roman copies. Moreover, Callimachus was known more for his technical expertise than for his sculptures: he was able, as Yeats accurately notes, to handle 'marble as if it were bronze' and make 'draperies that seemed to rise | When sea-wind swept the corner'.

As these details make clear, Callimachus is significant for Yeats because they respond to the poet's deepest preoccupations. No original works of Callimachus survive. (Would Yeats's own work endure?) Callimachus was able to handle marble in such a way as to bring movement into stone. (How can Yeats bring this inert Chinese stone to life?) Finally, Callimachus is used here as a bridge marking a transition from West to East. (How can 'the east' have 'its [own] solutions' to the 'heroic cry' of Western despair?)

Slightly more than ten years earlier, in *A Vision* (1925), Yeats had embraced 'half-Asiatic' Callimachus as an artist whose use of the running drill was to become common in later Hellenistic and then Byzantine art (*E&I* 225, *AVA* 270).[12] In that Byzantium Yeats also

---

[12] For a detailed and convincing argument situating Callimachus for Yeats as 'an artistic intermediary between East and West', see O'Donnell, 359–63.

sought an imaginative world in which one could move beyond the antinomies of Western 'tragedy' into the unifying vision of 'the east', a world in which

> All things fall and are built again,
> And those that build them again are gay.

That transition may be tracked through the changing resonances of the word 'gay'. What 'gay' comes to mean in this, and the following stanzas, will be achieved only through the poem's last word. As it moves towards that final syllable, in each preceding stanza 'gay' gathers weight even as it becomes less definable. In the process, each stanza jumps over vast abysses, binding its narrative through a focus on successive tragedies: that of the coming war; that of the performance of tragedy as great art; or, as in this stanza, that of the destruction of great art itself, and, with it, the civilization which gave it birth.

The greatest gap, however, is between these first three and the last two stanzas, as the poem shifts abruptly to focus on the carved lapis stone. And as it does so, it also shifts from a predominantly past tense into the present – bringing the stone into the immediate presence of the poet. Yeats composed this poem after years of despair about his aging body and now failing health. All the props of medical intervention and a briefly renewed sexual energy now seemed to be failing him. For at least a decade now, he had been obsessed with his own physical decline (*Life 2*).[13] In common with all artists, Yeats now wondered: Would his art survive him? If so, for how long?

In the lapis lazuli stone, Yeats found a response. He inscribes that understanding in the poem, but no critic to my knowledge has yet succeeded in making it explicit. That is, I believe, because few readers of Yeats grasped the cultural assumptions crystallized in the stone itself.

Yeats apparently stumbled upon some understanding of the significance of the stone on his own. It probably did not have to be explained to him, for instance, that stones such as his lapis mountain have no practical use. They are not merely paper-weights or desk ornaments for the Chinese scholar-poet. What might have been explained to Yeats is that, in common with 'scholar-rocks', such carved stones have long been actively used as tools for contemplation. This is because, for the Chinese, rocks are not merely inert 'dead' matter.

---

[13] Cf. index listings under Yeats, William Butler, for 'Health', 496 – *passim*.

Plate 5. *Mi Fu Honouring a Rock*. Photograph courtesy and © of the Shanghai Museum. All rights reserved.

Within the Chinese world, rocks too are alive: they act, as does everything in that world, as manifestations of *qi*, the primary life-force which flows through the universe.[14]

Indeed, so great was the veneration for such rocks that it is said of Mi Fu, a famous painter and calligrapher of the Northern Song Dynasty (960–1127), that he not only 'loved rocks' but also 'believed they had souls. This became something of an obsession, so that when he saw an interesting rock, he bowed before it in worship'.[15] Although Mi Fu was known as an eccentric who carried Daoist principles to an extreme, his veneration for the life-force implicit in rocks represents

---

[14] In this case, the lapis stone would have been used specifically because, in the traditional Chinese world, it symbolized heaven: conveying therefore a profoundly peaceful feeling. According to the Curator in the Gugong (the Imperial Palace Museum), Mr. Zhang Xin, lapis lazuli as well as azurite were used also for many ceremonial court beads – employed as meditative devices precisely because of their connection to the heavenly realms.

[15] Cf. catalogue 9, Guo Xu (1456–c.1529) 'Album of Various Subjects', from *Telling Images of China: Narrative and Figure Paintings, 15th–20th Century, from the Shanghai Museum*, ed. Shane McCausland and Ling Lizhong (London: Scala Publishers, 2010), 95, in detail at 96. Another illustration from this album (4) shows the 'Immortal Qiu' kneeling to pay homage to the hollow stump of a very gnarled, ancient tree.

a long-standing Chinese mind-set, which has persisted across many centuries. Even today, scholar-rocks are collected and prized. Those rocks most favoured for contemplation are those that manifest a lively *qi*; here evident in the subtle colouration of the lapis mountain as well as its complicated patterning of cracks and curves. By contemplating such an object, it is believed that one may also channel its particular *qi*, so that it enters the mind, and by doing so, enlivens and alters it, reorienting it so that one may enter into the still larger, impersonal energy system known as the *Dao*.

Here, in these last two stanzas, Yeats's poem opens itself consciously to such energies. In other words, instead of writing *about* the rock, Yeats *allows the energy of the rock to write him*, channeling the life-force that is *qi*:

> Every discolouration of the stone,
> Every accidental crack or dent,
> Seems a water-course or an avalanche,
> Or lofty slope where it still snows ....

Through these lines the stone's discolourations or cracks *become* the water-course or avalanche of Yeats's ensuing vision, allowing the rock's *qi* to become its very shaping force.

To put it another way, in these last two stanzas, Yeats' delight in 'seeing' becomes a way of entering into the energy of the stone. (He might even have quoted one of his favourite lines from William Blake: 'energy is eternal delight'. And Blake too, as Yeats knew, believed in the animate nature of inanimate things, sometimes depicting mountains, rivers clouds, trees and rocks in a humanized form.[16]) Yeats enters into this energy by allowing the stone to move away from what it merely represents. Caught up in its energies, Yeats now imagines that on the mountain it 'still snows' (pure invention!).

---

[16] As he illustrates from his early essays, in particular, 'William Blake and the Imagination' and 'William Blake and his Illustrations to "The Divine Comedy"' from the collection *Ideas of Good and Evil* (1903), Yeats most certainly knew of the two illustrations which most graphically represent Blake's animism: the plate for Thomas Gray's 'The Bard' that opens 'Hark, how each giant-oak' in which the oaks, the rocks and the river all have human faces/bodies; and the plate called 'Sunshine Holiday', an illustration for John Milton's 'L'Allegro', for which Blake wrote the following note: 'Mountains, Clouds, Rivers, Trees appear Humanized...'. I am grateful to Professor Daniel Albright for pointing out this parallel; although it is notable that Blake's energy system tends to be anthropomorphic, whereas the Daoist energy is strictly inhuman and thus impersonal.

The pines are transfigured into fragrant 'plum or cherry-branch'. Instead of still climbing up the mountain (towards the 'little halfway house'), the Chinamen are now 'seated there'. By thus entering the energies of the stone mountain, Yeats enables its static scene to move, extending and completing itself within his vision.

More significantly, by engaging such energies, Yeats himself moves away from the world of the West, where a 'thing' is a 'thing'. Specifically, he moves away from the art-world of Callimachus whose carved marble merely 'stands' or at least 'stood', its illusory motion itself finally swept away by those forces which determine that 'All things fall and are built again'. In this world, Callimachus's works are swept away because, as static or dead 'things', each 'stands' in opposition to the very forces which rule them. (The very contortions of this sentence, landing heavily on the postponed verb 'stands', stress the centrality of this concept in a Western view of art: art-objects, as putatively immortal, must 'stand' against what seeks to destroy them.) In the world of China, however, where 'things' are not 'things' and are part of the energy which shapes them, they cannot be swept away by 'other' forces, as they themselves are deemed part of these very energies, and thus change with them.

Yeats himself had arrived at much the same formulation when he discussed the difference between comedy and tragedy in a late essay published shortly after his death, in which he observed:

> Some Frenchman has said that farce is the struggle against a ridiculous object, comedy against a movable object, tragedy against an immovable; and because the will, or energy, is greatest in tragedy, tragedy is the more noble; but I add that 'will or energy is eternal delight', and when its limit is reached it may become a pure, aimless joy ... (*Ex* 449)

And indeed, at the end of stanza three, that ultimate limit to Western resources has been reached ('It cannot grow by an inch or an ounce'). From the tragedy of a Hamlet or a Lear to the tragedy of the great artist himself, the poem confronts that 'immovable object' which will eventually destroy all but the vestiges of what he has, through will or energy, created. Yet as that limit (of tragic resistance to limits themselves) is reached, or as is about to happen, actually surpassed, the thwarted will or energy, in Yeats's words, becomes 'a pure, aimless joy' – whence the gaiety of those who have escaped that struggle as defined by Western heroic resistance.

Having reached the limit of this (Western) world, Yeats moves into another, Asian universe. From the moment the Chinamen enter, the lapis mountain changes from being a 'thing', an immobile carving, into an *event*. Carried along on a succession of verbs in the present, the crane, a symbol of longevity, flies over the 'carved' scene, transforming the world below into an eternal moment of duration: one that lasts, like music, by moving through time out of time.[17]

In China, where that which endures is honoured, prolongation of actual life tends to be interpreted as a form of immortality and is hard to differentiate from it. Stone endures; here, with its cracks and discolourations, it corresponds to the 'wrinkles' of the two Chinamen – and even to the wrinkles of Yeats's own aging body, as, through the force of his vision, the poet engages with the energies of the stone. For the Chinese, such imperfections are traditionally deemed to be badges of honour, speaking as they do of the capacity to weather life's storms. Such too is the significance of the gnarled and twisted pine trees (which Yeats imagined as 'plum or cherry', although he was presumably already well acquainted with their native symbolism).[18] Weathered rock and twisted trees here operate not merely as decorative scenery, but as talisman for the invisible forces which have shaped them and within which they still endure.

In these final stanzas Yeats moves beyond the world represented by the stone's carvings to articulate this other world. Most apposite is the musical instrument carried by a servant. From its shape and size, one could deduce that this is a *qin*, an ancient Chinese form of the zither much prized by Daoists as producing the music nearest to natural sounds such as bird-song or rain, wind or water-course. Unlike the 'fiddle-bow' of the first stanza, which is strictly marginal,

---

[17] While Calvin Bedient attempts to explain such a moment through Bergson's notion of 'duration', he is hampered by having recourse only to Western concepts – as opposed to a Chinese, and, more specifically, a Daoist vocabulary. In particular, Bedient's relentlessly Western analysis relies heavily on the opposition between subject and object, thus insisting on Yeats's actions upon (i.e. 'seducing' or 'injecting' duration/time into) the stone – rather than taking into account the responding effect of the stone's energy on him. In Chinese thinking, however, there exists no such opposition between subject and object: objects can thus enter into selves, just as subjects can act upon objects. The defects of Bedient's analysis are evident in the extent to which he must torture the English language to say what he wishes to say – and the consequent obscurity in what he does, in fact, assert.

[18] The set design for *At the Hawk's Well*, for instance, has a large – usually painted – pine as the centrepiece of its backdrop. It is Japanese but it is also 'Eastern', and its core symbolism is borrowed from China. Moreover, Yeats would have been familiar with the pine tree motif from a Chinese wall hanging given to him by Dulac in 1922 and which hung in his study in the 1930s (O'Donnell, 356).

the music of the *qin* – as articulating the very movements of the world's energy or *qi* – is deemed central to the traditional Chinese view of the world. In calling for 'mournful melodies' to be played, the two Chinese sages seek nothing less than to become one with the invisible forces which shape the larger universe. Meditating to such 'accomplished' music, its hearers thus participate in that fleeting world within which 'All things fall and are built again ...'

Plate 6. Detail from *"Ting Qin Tu": Listening to the Qin*, attributed to the Emperor Song Huizong (11th Century).

Such meditation moves vision inward, not outward: the Chinamen 'stare'. Far beneath their gaze, the 'tragic scene' is not simply seen but becomes a way of seeing: exemplifying that kind of meditative activity which brings, ultimately, wisdom. It is sought in particular by the Daoist sages, who understood that through the increasing detachment of old age, longevity and immortality may move into one continuum.

Those sages make another appearance on Yeats's lapis mountain – unnoticed until now. On the back of this stone a poem has been inscribed; it describes a meeting of two such souls. Such an inscription represents an ancient Chinese tradition of painting or carving words on mountain cliff-faces. Today many such inscriptions may be found, perhaps most famously, on Taishan in Shandong Province (a mountain long associated with Confucius), as well as on Huangshan, the sacred Yellow Mountains

Plate 7. Writing on a rock-face in Huangshan, Anhui Province. Photograph © H. K. Tang, CC BY-NC-ND.

of Anhui Province. Why do the Chinese write on mountains? To the West, this seems a bizarre practice, akin to graffiti. Could one imagine, for instance, carving verses from 'Under Ben Bulben' actually *on* Ben Bulben? To us in the West, that would seem a form of vandalism, a desecration of the pure 'wildness' of the mountain itself.

Clearly not so in China, where writing on mountains is carried out, it seems, precisely as a way of making them Chinese. In fact (as one expert notes) the 'simple concept of fixing memories and ideas on the surface of the earth through the carving of texts has deep roots in Chinese culture. These centuries-old tradition of "polished-cliff carving" (*moya* 摩崖 or *moya shike* 摩崖石刻), are texts carved into granite boulders and cliffs that are part of the natural terrain. They began to appear in China during the first century C.E. Over the course of the two thousand years since then, they have been carved in all areas of the country, and have become one of the distinguishing features of Chinese civilization'.[19] As such, these inscriptions may be intended, in some sense, to make the mountain 'speak'.[20] They do so by appropriating the mountain's energy or *qi* in such a way that it enters the human, that is, the civilized world. As it enters, it does so as a force which in turn exerts the power to transform.

To a Chinese person, then, it would come as no surprise that Yeats's own carved lapis mountain had a poem inscribed on its back – as if in imitation of an actual sacred mountain. What I found surprising was that, apparently, Yeats never sought to have the poem translated; nor has any public effort been made to translate it since his death.

To correct this oversight, I consulted experts able to read the old Mandarin script (now simplified in today's China). Photographs of the poem on the back of the stone made by Sarah Shiels of the National Library of Ireland were first examined by Dr Shane McCausland, then Curator for the Chinese Collection of the Chester Beatty Library, also in Dublin. He confirmed that the poem was written 'by imperial decree': which means it was written either by the Qianlong Emperor himself or by an imperial court poet at his command. As such, the inscription follows the standard format for a court poem: that of four, seven-character lines. But further than that it was almost impossible to go, as the carved characters, once inlaid with gold, are now only barely legible in parts, the last line posing particular difficulty. Accordingly, only a most tentative translation could be reached.

---

[19] This passage is from a review of Robert E. Harrist Jr., *The Landscape of Words: Stone Inscriptions from Early and Medieval China* (Seattle: University of Washington Press, 2008) by Hui-Wen Lu, National Taiwan University, published in the *Harvard Journal of Asiatic Studies* 70, n. 1 (June 2010), 232–46. Harrist's book is the first monograph to tackle this subject from a cultural perspective.

[20] As a precedent, one might cite one of the most famous of all Chinese books, *A Dream of the Red Chamber* under its alternative title, *The Story of a Stone*. Composed in the mid to late eighteenth century (and thus roughly contemporary with the Yeats lapis lazuli) this novel opens with a chapter describing how a stone, created by the goddess Nu Wa at the beginning of the world, is first engraved by a Buddhist monk and then incarnated in the human world as Baoyu: the eldest son of an important and wealthy family. Eons later, returned to its original state, the stone is discovered by Taoist priest, inscribed with the complete history of its transformation and conveyance into the human world and what it experienced there. The novel itself is thus merely this priest's transcription of the stone's history. It should be noted that during this seminal chapter, the stone speaks as well as passing on its written account of its time in the mortal world.

Plate 8. Back side of Yeats's Lapis Lazuli mountain, with poem circled. Photograph courtesy and © of the National Library of Ireland. All rights reserved.

However, there was now enough evidence to approach the Gugong (the Imperial Palace Museum) in Beijing. There, Dr. Alfreda Murck, a well-known scholar of Song dynasty art – and at the time the only Western curator there – showed the photographs of the inscription to her Chinese colleague, Mr. Zhang Xin. From the lines and words still legible, he was able to identify the poem as indeed attributed to the Qianlong Emperor from the *Collected Poems* (vol. 2, juan 13).[21] This identification clarified two things: first of all, it allows us to assign a secure date for the stone of 1749 (for it is to be assumed that the poem was actually composed to be inscribed on this particular rock). Secondly, identifying the poem allows the partially-effaced Mandarin characters to be filled in at last, thus providing the basis for a literal translation (here accompanied by *pinyin* for the Chinese characters) which runs as follows:

春　　山　　訪　　友
Chūn　shān　fǎng　yǒu

Spring Mountain Visiting Friend

綠　　雲　　紅　　雨　　向　　清　　和
Lü　　yún　　hóng　yǔ,　xiàng　Qīng　Hé

Green clouds, red rain, nearing Qing He Festival

　　　　　　　　　　　　[8th day of 4th lunar month]

寂　　寂　　深　　山　　幽　　事　　多
Jì　　jì　　shēn　shān,　yōu　shì　duō

Quiet, quiet, deep mountains, secret stories many

曲　　徑　　苔　　封　　人　　跡　　絕
Qū　　jìng　　tái　　fēng,　rén　jì　jué

Winding path, sealed by moss, human footprints none

[21] 乾隆御制诗二集卷十三古今体七十三首 己巳六 (1749 年 乾隆十四年). In translation: *Qianlong yuzhi shi, er ji* [Qianlong imperially composed poetry, compilation 2]; *juan* 13: *'Gujin ti'* [73 poems, ancient and modern forms]; [the date:] *jisi* 6 [in 1749 / Qianlong 14th year].

| 抱 | 琴 | 高士 | 許 | 相過 |
| Bào | qín | gāoshì | xǔ | xiāngguò |

Holding, musical instrument [qin] hermit, promised to meet[22]

What the translation of this poem confirms is that Yeats's lapis lazuli mountain is firmly within the spirit of Daoist art: that is, it shows a meeting in late spring of two friends, one a hermit, who seek the 'quiet, deep mountains' to share 'secret stories'.[23] Meditating

---

[22] Translating poems from the Chinese is an art, particularly as the language not only allows but encourages multiple translations. For this reason, only a literal word-by-word rendition is given here. In such a translation, however, many subtleties may be missed. The characters *Qing* and *He*, for instance, identify the time of year as the late spring/early summer. The 'green clouds' refer to the first delicate foliage of spring as it appears from a distance; the 'red rain' to falling cherry/plum blossoms. The character *you* (remote or, as here, secret) suggests a spiritual distance from the world, here reinforced by the moss growing over a path that is not often used. In the last line, the guest who comes with a servant carrying only a *qin* indicates that the meeting will be a continuation in spirit of the remote and relaxed atmosphere. I am indebted to Mr. Zhang Xin, Curator at the Gugong (Imperial Palace Museum) in Beijing, for his help in interpreting this poem.

[23] This would be an important modification for those who seek a purely Buddhist interpretation of this poem, such as Stephen Wolfe, 'The Half-way House: Some Eastern Thoughts in Yeats's Poetry' at elib.doshisha.ac.jp. According to Wolfe, Yeats read a classic work of Daoism, *The Secret of the Golden Flower*, which describes Daoist meditative practice. As Wolfe acknowledges, the form of Buddhism which interested Yeats was a synthesis with Daoism which (indirectly) became Zen Buddhism. Yet what is imagined as happening in 'Lapis Lazuli', as two friends climb a mountain together to seek enlightenment and do so to the music of the *qin*, is in direct opposition to Buddhist meditative practice, which emphasizes solitude and, often, silence, and is also often quite indifferent to the surroundings in which such practice takes place.

For a strong argument in favour of Yeats's Taoism (Daoism in the old Wade-Giles system of Romanization), see Aintzane Legarreta-Mentxaka, 'Yeats and Taoism: to Maria Motxobe Legarreta', *Yeats Eliot Review* 22, n. 3 (Fall 2005), 2–19.

Here the author makes a cogent case for Yeats's exposure to the major Daoist texts, such as the *Dao De Jing* and the *Zhuangzi*, remarking in relation to the latter, that the most likely source for Yeats's knowledge of Daoism would have been Oscar Wilde, who reviewed the first complete translation of the writings ascribed to Zhuangzi (Chuang Tzu in Wade-Giles) under the title of 'A Chinese Sage'. Yeats first met Wilde (as recorded in the *Autobiographies*, 134–35) during a visit to Wilde's home for Christmas 1889, at which time Wilde was working on this review (published in February 1890). For further exploration of the Wilde/Zhuangzi connection, see Jerusha McCormack, 'From Chinese Wisdom to Irish Wit: Zhuangzi and Oscar Wilde', *Irish University Review* 37, n. 2 (autumn/winter 2007), 302–21.

there to the music of the *qin*, they would seek to become one with the *Dao*: the name given to the invisible forces which, always changing but always interconnected, shape the visible world.

How much Yeats could have known about this poem is highly conjectural. Yet, as all of the instincts in these last two stanzas of 'Lapis Lazuli' are firmly in the spirit of this Chinese poem, it seems likely that Yeats must have had someone give him a rough (and presumably oral) translation of those lines that were in fact legible. Moreover: Yeats must already have been attuned to the nature of Daoist beliefs, for, in the leap into the last two stanzas, Yeats too leaps into their world. Daoists value spontaneity above more deliberate virtues: for they believe that to act spontaneously is, if one is in touch with the *Dao*, to act with an intuitive rightness. It is that 'rightness' that rings most true about these final verses; certainly the manuscript evidence suggests that Yeats probably wrote these two final verses straight off,[24] in an intuitive rush, as that 'fulfillment of the soul in itself, some slow or sudden expansion of it like an overflowing well' (*Au* 471).

That hypothesis holds true in another way also: the poem reads more coherently if one reads it in a circle. Doing so allows one to see how Yeats may have worked backwards through the first three stanzas. As each stanza posits successive resettings of that 'tragic scene' on which the sages 'stare', each registers a shift in resonances for the word, 'gay'.

Clearly, in the first stanza, the 'tragic scene' for the West is that of contemporary history. Its scorn for the 'hysterical women' who anticipate (as it happens, accurately) a world cataclysm, is striking. The poet returns their scorn with scorn; he has seen such women before: the anecdote comes in fact not from 1935, but (as O'Donnell notes) from almost half a century earlier.[25] At this point, the tone becomes one of an almost false jocularity, as they anticipate how Kaiser Wilheim will, like 'King Billy', come out with 'Aeroplane and Zeppelin', pitching in bombs 'Until the town lie beaten flat'. The concatenation of the

---

[24] Noting the smooth and relatively unrevised nature of the last two verses (with only two minor corrections), together with its echoes of Yeats's initial response to the stone in his letter to Wellesley, at least two other scholars have concluded that these were probably composed first, perhaps even months before the initial three stanzas. Cf. O'Donnell, 357 and Bedient, 27.

[25] In 'Samhain 1908', *Explorations*, 239, Yeats wrote how 'One woman used to repeat as often as possible that to paint pictures or to write poetry in this age was to fiddle while Rome was burning'. O'Donnell, 364, n. 25.

two, King and Kaiser, now explicitly makes the point that all this has happened before. Yeats had long held to the notion that history repeats itself. In *A Vision* he worked it out as the system of gyres: of a historical time that works in vast interlocking cycles.

In the West, on the contrary, time tends to be seen as unilinear and its course irreversible, with a set beginning or origin and a defined end. These are exactly the conditions that Aristotle set out for tragedy: it must have a beginning, a middle and an ending. In Chinese time, however, there are no set beginnings or endings: no civilizational origin stories, for instance, comparable to *Genesis*; no apocalypse, as in *Revelations*. Chinese stories often lack defined beginnings or closure; so (some would complain) does traditional Chinese music. Whereas framed pictures are the major mode in the Western art world, the scroll (in which beginning and end are typically out of sight) is the major mode in traditional Chinese art and writing. In other words, Western aesthetics tends to like clear definition of origins and ends; in China, such boundaries often do not exist or are not clear – or are not readily disclosed, because in this world process is more important than a sense of a finished product.

Without such clear definition of beginning and end, however, there can be no concept of 'tragedy'. Although this would not be the only reason why Western tragedy does not translate into the Chinese world, Shakespeare's tragedies are usually not perceived in China as 'tragic' in the Western sense, as, in China, 'tragic' endings tend to be modulated into more hopeful finales.[26] This is accomplished, it seems, not by a change of text but by a change of emphasis. After

---

[26] This analysis owes much to Professor Gu Zhengkun of the English Department of Peking University, one of China's leading Shakespeare experts. As he writes, Western tragedy 'finds no equivalent in Chinese. In short, both Western and Chinese people have the similar sense of what is tragic but Western tragedy as a dramatic form is indeed greatly different from Chinese "tragedy". Where Westerners emphasize fear and pity, Chinese would emphasize misery and pity. In other words, Chinese tend to soften the fearful aspect of the drama. There could be many disastrous events taking place in the process of the dramatic development; but the hero or heroine would always turn out to be victorious in one way or another, usually with the wrong corrected or justice done. The ending of the play usually gives the atmosphere of happiness so that the audience would not go home in grief'. Email to author (18 July 2010).

In an email two days later, Professor Gu is at pains to state that of course there are other cultural reasons for 'tragedy' having a different form in China: among them, the Confucian injunction towards moderation, which advises against indulging in the extremes of emotion, even within extremes of circumstance (such as mourning).

all, even *Hamlet* ends with the coming of Fortinbras. Whereas the Western production would emphasize the tragic demise of Hamlet, a Chinese production might emphasize the hopeful new cycle initiated by Fortinbras, who brings with him the promise of a new, perhaps less corrupt, regime. It is a question of where the stress lies; but there is a world of difference in the interpretation: while one is clearly tragic, the Chinese version presents the tragic as simply another phase in the revolutions of time.

But whereas Yeats defines a civilization in terms of certain specified artefacts, the Chinese attitude is best exemplified in their capital cities, where, successively, 'All things fall and are built again…' As one expert in Chinese historiography observes, 'the successive dynastic changes [of emperor] provided for a built-in "return to square one", symbolized by the tearing down of the palaces built by the preceding dynasty and/or the construction of a new capital…'.[27] At the core of this practice 'lies the idea that every newly founded dynasty must manifest its seizure of the Heavenly Mandate in architecture because the layout and the construction of the new capital as the idealized centre of the universe was believed to decide upon the course that the new dynasty will hypothetically take'. Rebuilding is thus seen as a breakthrough into a new order of the universe, representing, symbolically, a new order of time.

It should also be noted that Professor Gu's interpretation of how Western tragedy is received in China is deeply controversial at this time, as became apparent when I presented the results of this essay at the First Conference on World Literature at Peking University in July 2011. Among those who disagreed with his interpretation were Professor Zhang Longxi, an eminent comparativist of Chinese with Western literature. Professor Gu's comments however serve as the best explanation of Yeats's own rejection of Western tragedy from what he perceived to be an Eastern perspective.

See also Xiao Yang Zhang, 'Tragedy and Comedy: The Culturally Produced Differences and Similarities', in *Shakespeare in China: A Comparative Study of Two Traditions and Cultures* (Newark, DE: University of Delaware Press, 1996), 21–61.

Although helpful in contrasting notions of 'tragedy' in China and the West – in particular, the Chinese insistence that tragedies must have happy endings – this article does not discuss the production of Shakespearean plays in China, nor the particular interpretations that Chinese directors and actors might bring to bear on a Shakespearean text.

[27] Achim Mittag, 'Historical Consciousness in China: Some Notes on Six Theses on Chinese Historiography and Historical Thought', *New Developments in Asian Studies: An Introduction*, ed. Paul van der Velde and Alex McKay (London: Kegan Paul, 1998), 60–61. The following quotation is from this source.

It is in this spirit that the Chinese sages of 'Lapis Lazuli' greet destruction as a necessary part of that process in which 'All things fall and are built again…' In other words, one can read most fruitfully the first three stanzas of 'Lapis Lazuli' as different versions of Western historiography, each offering a different vision of an ending: whether in the coming war; in the dramatic reenactment of cataclysm through tragedy; or by means of the destruction of art-objects previously deemed 'immortal'. Each sets up a model of apocalypse implicitly rejected by the final two verses.

But as close reading will show, that Western version of history is already being subverted from the opening stanza. For if, as Yeats believes, time is not linear, if historical events are only to be repeated as part of a vast cyclical revolution (such as that of the gyres), then even the apocalyptic vision of the coming world war are mere restagings of earlier events. Thus King Billy, who bombarded Derry in the 17th century, anticipates the ravages of Kaiser Wilhelm, just as the 'hysterical women' who fear the future anticipate the Ophelia and Cordelia who weep over the past.

In the second stanza, the Western vision of this 'tragic scene' is similarly subverted. As Aristotle dictated, tragedy – as a work of art – must be irreversible: having a beginning and middle and end. And yet its 'heroic cry' is repeated again and again, not only on the stage but, as Yeats envisions it, even today on the very streets around him. Thus, in this version, every play becomes a replay, offering no solution except that of the most complete vision of man's destruction as 'All things fall…' Finally, considering the fate of Callimachus, Yeats implicitly acknowledges that this also may be the fate of his own art. No longer the 'unageing' monuments of 'Sailing to Byzantium', these works too will eventually be swept away with the fall of the civilization which nurtured them.

How then can such destruction be greeted as 'gay'? As the whole poem turns on this word, it is important to understand its evolving significance.

In the first stanza, poets 'are always gay' in the sense of its original (14th century) meaning that they are merry or light-hearted in the face of dire circumstance.[28] Because of their perceived lack of moral seriousness, 'gay' here might also be reverting to an early 17th

---

[28] *Oxford English Dictionary* (second edition, 1989, Vol. VI), definition 1a. The following definition is taken from this source.

century suggestion (OED 2a) of being 'addicted to social pleasures and dissipations' and even, euphemistically, as immoral. Yet, in the next stanza, Yeats implicitly sanctions such a response by placing it within the Western tradition of high art. Hamlet and Lear are 'gay' in the more modern usage of the word as defining a state in which one feels 'keenly alive'.[29] Here Yeats is already reframing the word within the implied oxymoron of tragic joy, 'transfiguring all that dread'. It is such a paradox that, as Yeats wrote, 'the heroes of Shakespeare convey ... the sudden enlargement of their vision, their ecstasy at the approach of death.... I have heard Lady Gregory say... "Tragedy must be a joy to the man who dies"... ' (*E&I* 522–23).

That tragic joy, expounded by the first two pieces in *New Poems* (1939), gives way in the third stanza of 'Lapis Lazuli' to something even bigger and more fierce. Here, the poet proclaims, 'All things fall and are built again, I And those that build them again are gay'.

Such joy arises out of the hideous violence which Yeats foresees will destroy the poet's world (at a projected date of AD 2000), but which, according to *A Vision*, prophesizes a new civilization. In this refrain ('All things fall...') one hears echoes of the Yeats who imagined 'always at my left side just out of the range of the sight, a brazen winged beast that I associated with laughing, ecstatic destruction' (*Ex* 393). [30] For Yeats, destruction may be exhilarating because destruction and creation are the two inseparable halves of one process – as he once wrote, 'every act of war is an act of creation' (*CVA* "Notes" 66). And although Yeats earlier used such phrases as 'God's laughter at the shattering of the world' (*VPI* 267, l. 189), within a Chinese context it could well describe the positive energies released by the razing of old Beijing – as the necessary and sufficient condition for the rebuilding of that city and, with that reconstruction, the symbolic inauguration of a new world order.

Thus, with each of these uses, 'gay' widens in connotations as in its circumscribing energies: from the unwarranted moral frivolity of the first verse to tragic catharsis in verse two and then into a cosmic laughter at the destruction of whole worlds. All of its resonances finally depend on the fierce oxymoron of 'tragic joy'. For the full

---

[29] *Webster's Ninth New Collegiate Dictionary*. Interestingly enough, such a definition does not appear in the Oxford English Dictionary.

[30] I am indebted to Professor Daniel Albright of the English Department, Harvard University for these references concerning 'tragic joy' in this and notes 34 and 35.

effect of this rhetorical figure, Yeats depends on the intellectual habits of the Western reader. As Yeats had come to understand through his studies of Eastern philosophies, the West conceives of the world in terms of mutually exclusive and opposing energies: here, in terms of creation vs. destruction, of life vs. death, of the 'gay' vs. the tragic. Thus 'tragic joy' is a specifically Western phenomenon, one that can only occur in terms of violent opposition, as a heroic defiance against the destructive forces that rule the world: or, in the words of Wallace Stevens (in his famous definition of the imagination) as 'a violence from within that protects us from a violence without'.[31] Thus to be 'gay' in a Western sense is creatively, and thus spiritually, to stand, heroically, against one's inevitable fate – of destruction, perhaps even oblivion.

But, in the end, this sense of 'gay' is also ultimately seen as inhuman: resounding in Yeats's ears as the brazen laughter of the gods. For, as Yeats also understands, to compensate for the inevitable destruction of the individual and all his works, the West tends to reach towards a world outside the human: towards a transcendent 'immortal' or 'eternal' realm, intuited by ecstasy and entered, presumably, through death.

In the final stanza, having explored the limits of his own world, Yeats leaps into the world of Asia. In doing so, he leaps into another vision of what it means to be human. To the Western vision of a world as one of opposing forces, Yeats now proposes another vision, that of 'the east', specifically of China. As he (correctly) intuits it, this is a world without transcendence, one in which the mortal can become immortal as he enters, within his human life, the forces of nature through the ageless *Dao*.[32] Here there is no violence, no standing against, in a contrarian gaiety that defies the mandate of heaven. Instead, the Chinese sages experience that sudden expansion of the soul which brings a 'pure, aimless joy' – one nearer to that state of mind in another late poem, 'Vacillation' in which, by going beyond

---

[31] Wallace Stevens, 'The Noble Rider and the Sound of Words', *The Necessary Angel: Essays on Reality and Imagination* (New York: Vintage Books/Random House, 1951), 36. This famous formulation is echoed by Seamus Heaney in defining poetry as 'our imagination pressing back against the pressure of reality'.

[32] As Parker has noted (453 and n. 3), for the Daoists, longevity and immortality were not regarded as two distinct states of being; both were regarded as blessed and moving in a continuum, from one to another.

the world's 'antinomies', Yeats found suddenly that he was 'blesséd and could bless'.[33]

Thus, only in the final word of the final stanza, is the fierce oxymoron of 'tragic joy' abandoned for resonances that move beyond Western antinomies into a world of Eastern correspondences. It is a world with which Yeats had become increasingly familiar, remarking in an essay of 1934 how 'I have a Chinese painting of three old sages, … one with a scroll open at the symbol of yen [sic] and yin, those two forms that whirl perpetually, creating and re-creating all things.'[34] Entering such a world, distinctions dissolve: between seer and scene, voice and vision, as the poet, through contemplation, becomes part of the complementary, eternally shifting energies which together constitute the *Dao*.

Yeats had once, a few days after receiving the stone, imagined himself on this very mountainside.[35] Now having climbed his own mountain towards death – and abandoning Western hopes for immortality – the poet gazes through the eyes of these Chinese sages. Their eyes are 'ancient' (not simply 'old') because they have entered into the wisdom of the ages. Under their gaze, the perspective on the 'tragic scene' has changed drastically. No longer 'tragic', it is now seen as simply inevitable, part of the grand evolutions of cyclical time which brings destruction as the condition of future creation. The poet

---

[33] In its cry from the great lord of Chou [Zhou] – 'Let all things pass away' – 'Vacillation' (written/published 1933) in many ways anticipates the Chinese vision of 'Lapis Lazuli'.
In further articulating this vision, Parker (452–53) identifies Yeats's stone mountain as a representation of *P'eng-lai Shan*, the principal of the five Islands of the Blessed – as indicated by the waves carved on the original wooden base. Here the Eight Immortals (sages) are said to dwell. But, in making this identification, there is a danger that the Western reader might think this is an otherworldly *location*, such as the Christians often imagine heaven to be; whereas in fact in Daoism it is clearly established as a state of being; that is, arrived at within life through spiritual practice: needing nothing more than such an imaginative figuration of the Islands of the Blessed to invoke a sense of place.

[34] 'The Resurrection: Introduction', *Wheels and Butterflies* (London: Macmillan, 1934), 109.

[35] Letter to Gwyneth Foden, 6 July 1935: 'Tell the Swami that last night came from a rich young Englishman a great piece of Lapis Lazali carved by some old Chinese artist into the semblance of a mountain with a little temple among trees half way up, & a path leading to it & on the path an ascetic with his pupil. The ascetic, pupil and little temple prophesying perhaps the Swami & myself at Mallorca'. I am grateful to Professor Warwick Gould for calling to my attention this letter (*CL InteLex* 6281).

is thus able to greet it with 'joy [even as] ...with his eyes he enters upon a submissive, sorrowful contemplation of the great irremediable things' (*E & I* 254–55). By means of such contemplation, the lapis mountain, no longer a static 'scene', becomes another way of 'seeing': provoking an ecstatic acceptance of the human condition which itself passes beyond the human. With eyes 'glittering', the sages view the world below with a gaze that is cold, detached, impersonal – and enduring. Beyond either joy or pain, they have attuned themselves to the deepest forces of existence.

All rests on the final word, 'gay'. In expanding this word into its least well-defined and most numinous sense, Yeats uses it in the Daoist manner. Just as the *Dao* is that which cannot be named and, in naming it, will be missed,[36] so the word 'gay' here becomes ultimately indefinable; and, as such, opens a gateway to a suddenly enlarged vision through which the word echoes like a gong, sending its resonances to the very edge of sound and sense.

---

[36] Note the opening lines of the *Dao De Jing*:

> The Dao that can be expressed in words
> Is not the true and eternal Dao;
> The name that can be uttered in words
> Is not the true and eternal name.
> (from *The Book of Tao and Teh*, translated by Gu Zhengkun)

The Manuscript of 'Leo Africanus'

Edited by Steve L. Adams and George Mills Harper

[*Headnote: In a volume devoted to* Yeats's Mask, *it seemed appropriate to reprint this major landmark in the long process of bringing 'unpublished Yeats' to light. We are grateful to the Yeats Estate, to the Estate of the late George Mills Harper and to the Estate of the late Richard J. Finneran, to whom copyright was assigned for the initial publication in* Yeats Annual 1 (1980). *No re-editing of the MS has been undertaken, but the original endnotes have been inserted as footnotes to aid reading. Citations of standard works with* Yeats Annual *abbreviations have been brought into conformity with that system of citation, but no attempt has been made to cite in-text. Inverted comma conventions, and dashes, have also been silently emended, and certain editorial American spellings in the editorial commentary have been standardized to English or French spellings. Eds.*]

1. EDITORIAL INTRODUCTION

Although several critics have commented on the first appearance of the spirit of Leo Africanus to Yeats and a few have examined the unpublished manuscript of Yeats's dialogue with him,[1] no one

---

[1] The first to discuss the manuscript was Richard Ellmann, in *Yeats: The Man and the Masks* (New York: Macmillan, 1948), 195–97. See also Birgit Bjersby, *The Interpretation of the Cuchulain Legend in the Works of W. B. Yeats* (Upsala: A. B. Lundequistska Bokhandeln, 1950), 141–44, and Virginia Moore, *The Unicorn* (New York: Macmillan, 1954), 225–26. The first to transcribe 'Leo Africanus' was Curtis Bradford. His unpublished transcription, upon which we have relied heavily, is now in the possession of Senator Michael B. Yeats, who has permitted us to publish

has pointed out either the extent of Yeats's preoccupation or the significance of his changing conception of Leo. Yeats first referred to "Leo", so far as we can determine, in some Notes of a very poor sitting with Mr Feilding, on May 3rd 1909, 'which contain a "plainly fanciful account of my 'guides'"' Everard Feilding, an Honorary Secretary of the Society for Psychical Research, remained a friend for many years and was probably responsible for Yeats's membership in the Society (from 1913 to 1928). Alluding first to a young girl who was 'not a guide', Yeats then records that 'a Julia comes – a guide.' This is probably a reference to Julia A. Ames, the dead American woman whose *Letters from Julia* to William T. Stead were widely known throughout Europe.[2] Since Julia's Circle had been established at Cambridge House, Stead's home in Wimbledon, on 24 April 1909, Yeats may be recording the first of many séances he attended there. After Julia came Agrippa, 'a key' who 'wants to do something through me.' But 'all this while', Yeats noted parenthetically, 'I am trying to call Leo I want Leo to control medium.' Leo's reply is important: 'I am trying to control – I have been to you before (Africa name).' 'Are you Leo the writer', Yeats asked. 'I am your guide', Leo replied. After a brief discussion of when and where Leo was born, there is some suggestion that Yeats may be confused about Leo's identity: 'A Pope. Leo. Has been long with me. A sister much involved[?] [with] me – a guide – a spirit.'

We have discovered no further references to Leo until he reappeared at a séance in Cambridge House on 9 May 1912. Since Yeats preserved two records of this séance and summarized events

the essay and to make use of much unpublished material cited herein (©1981 Michael and Anne Yeats). We are also indebted to the Yeats Archives at the State University of New York at Stony Brook for the copy of the manuscript upon which our transcription is based.

[2] As a result of his continued correspondence with Julia, Stead founded Julia's Bureau, which was dedicated to the exchange of knowledge between the living and the dead. Stead kept his library of psychic books at Mowbray House in London but the Inner Sanctuary of the Bureau at Cambridge House, his home in Wimbledon. For further details about Stead's life and work, see Edith K. Harper, *Stead: The Man: Personal Reminiscences* (London: William Rider and Son, 1918). Yeats may have developed orderly habits from observing Miss Harper, who as Secretary of Julia's Bureau recorded hundreds of séances: 'A record of all sittings was kept, whether of Julia's "Inner Circle" at Cambridge House, or of others at Mowbray House or with psychics at their homes. The notes were carefully written out within a few hours, dated, docketed, and placed in the Archives, and the "pros and cons" of each one carefully considered on its own merits, without prejudice' (135).

briefly the following morning in a journal he kept for 'stray notes on all kinds of things',[3] it is clear that Yeats was much impressed, though he was then, and remained, sceptical. As Secretary of the Bureau, Miss Harper prepared the record for the Archives, a copy of which she must have made for Yeats, who was apparently a member of 'Julia's 'Inner Circle'.' Because he considered the sitting so important apparently, and probably before he received Miss Harper's account, Yeats recorded his own much fuller version.[4] Since he left a blank for the name of Mrs Wriedt, the medium,[5] and named only Miss Harper and her mother, we can perhaps assume that he did not know the others present, who were with one exception also strangers to Miss Harper. Both accounts record the time, place, and date – a practice Yeats followed for most of his psychical experiments, in his notebooks as well as the Automatic Script of the years following his marriage. Yeats preserved two copies of his own account, both containing the same slight corrections and both initialled at the end. Beginning with a description of the 'entirely darkened' room and its equipment, including a 'long tin trumpet' always present at Mrs Wriedt's séances, Yeats recorded that a loud voice through the trumpet 'claimed to come for 'Mr Gates' ' ('evidently me', Yeats noted). The voice informed him 'that it had been with me from childhood', and 'that they wanted to use my hand and brain ... The voice said something about my possessing the key or the key-mind they wanted.' 'I had this kind of spirit once before', Yeats observed, 'and was repelled by what I considered an appeal to my vanity.' He may be recalling the séance of 3 May 1909, at which Agrippa was described as 'a key' who 'wants to do something with me.' This time, however, the key-mind revealed himself as 'Leo, the writer and explorer.' Yeats 'noticed that "Leo" had a strong Irish accent', not unlike his own according to one of the sitters. Although Yeats was excited over the appearance of Leo, he remained sceptical. 'Miss Harper looked up Leo in Lempriere',

---

[3] Transcribed and edited by Denis Donoghue, this Journal is reproduced in Memoirs (London: Macmillan, 1972). See 264 for the entry (apparently misdated) on Leo.

[4] See Appendices A and B for reproductions of the typescripts.

[5] Mrs Etta Wriedt (1860–1942), a well-known medium from Detroit, Michigan, visited England five times, the first in 1911 at the invitation of W. T. Stead. Miss Harper recorded some 200 sittings with Mrs Wriedt at Julia's Bureau. For further details see Nandor Fodor, *Encyclopaedia of Psychic Science* (Secaucus, NJ: The Citadel Press, 1974), 409. Hereafter cited as *EPS*.

but Yeats made a *Note* – Not to look up the references till after next Seance as they might become a suggestion to the control.'

At this point in the typescript he drew a line and continued with two more paragraphs of reflections about his experience. 'It is possible', he wrote, 'that Leo may turn out to be a symbolic being.' Here also, as he did in the years following, Yeats linked 'Leo, the writer and explorer' with 'Leo, the constellation, the house of the sun.' 'Further', Yeats added, 'if it be true as I have always supposed, that the influence under which I do my work and think my most profound thought, is what an Astrologer calls solar, this being or state like the previous control which said to me very similar things some 12 years ago, may be a dramatization of a reality.' This is surely a strange, almost incredible statement to those who recall that in *A Vision* and throughout the Automatic Script on which it is based Yeats always suggests that the influence under which he does his work and thinks his 'most profound thought' is lunar. This change in his astrological assumptions may help to explain why Leo becomes a Frustrator rather than a Guide in the Automatic Script. Yeats concluded his account with a typically tentative suggestion which also was to receive great attention in the Script and to influence his thought and art for the remainder of his life: ' I have never been quite certain that certain controls who give themselves names of great antiquity, do not really select by some process of unconscious affinity from the recorded or unrecorded memories of the world, a name and career that symbolizes their nature.' Some five and a half years later, in the first recorded questions of the Automatic Script, Yeats asked:

1. What is the relation between the Anima Mundi and the Antithetical Self?
2. What quality in the Anima Mundi compels that relationship?

The answer to the second question by Thomas of Dorlowicz, the first Control in the Script, casts considerable light on Yeats's preoccupation with such symbolic Masks or Anti-Selves as Leo: 'It is the purely instinctive & cosmic quality in man which seeks completion in its opposite which is sought by the subconscious self in anima mundi to use your own term while it is the conscious mind that makes the E[vil] P[ersona] in consciously seeking opposite & then emulating it.'

Although Miss Harper remarked that the séance of 9 May was 'very mediocre' 'to those who have often sat with Mrs Wriedt', it obviously was not mediocre to Yeats. For several months following this appearance of Leo, Yeats attended many séances and related psychic experiments, in several of which Leo participated. He recorded and preserved accounts of the séances he considered significant, and commented on numerous other experiments, chiefly in the unpublished Maud Gonne Notebook designated 'Private.' On Wednesday, 5 June, a regular meeting night for Julia's 'Inner Circle', he attended another of Mrs Wriedt's séances at Cambridge House. Besides Miss Harper and her mother the only other sitter was a well-known experimenter and friend of Stead named Dr Abraham Wallace.[6] When Mrs Wriedt called Yeats 'Professor', Wallace 'corrected her & said "no a poet & writes plays"'. Yeats then spoke of a séance some years ago when Charles Williams,[7] a famous materialization medium, had produced a 'form, vaguely visible by the light of a phosphorescent slate' which he said was '"Leonora" my "guide" or perhaps it was "Eleanora".' Yeats observed the resemblance of 'the names in either form to Leo.' Yeats made a sketch of the room and commented that 'it would have been better to use a more empty room' to avoid the possibility of 'trance juggling perhaps in the midst of genuine manifestation.' Again the voice of Leo, speaking through the trumpet,

> more or less repeated what he said before. 'He had been with me from childhood' etc & then [?] said 'Though a Spaniard I am not a villain. I am still a Spaniard' and 'I am trying to teach you to write plays in a scientific way.' He seemed to resent my scepticism & was truculent as ever[.] I asked if I could help him[;] he resented this said it was for him to help me. He said also 'you mistook me for a woman.'

After much more information about movements, sounds, touches, etc., Yeats noted that his 'difficulty in remembering the details' had shown him 'that a stenographer is essential at every seance. He should be put somewhere in earshot perhaps outside the door.' Yeats confessed that he had 'forgotten all kinds of essential things.' After signing his record, dating it 6 June (that is, the day after the séance), he added a postscript confirming 'the impression at my first seance that Leo spoke like a stage Irishman.' Nevertheless, he concluded, 'The seance was not the less interesting to me because I saw nothing in it incompatible with its form being a dream fabrication of the subliminal consciousness of myself & the medium.' Again Yeats was

[6] See E. K. Harper, 121.
[7] See *EPS* 405–6.

impressed. On 20 June, when he was unable to find his account of this séance, he summarized the record in his Notebook, remembering some details exactly.

Two days before (on 18 June) he had attended a large séance (eleven sitters) at Cambridge House. Many spirits came, including 'Stead' (who had gone down with the *Titanic* on 15 April), numerous relatives of sitters, and Leo. 'More natural & friendly in tone' than he had been before, Leo told Yeats 'that he would try & write through a medium[.] I fixed my thoughts on (Miss R) when the 'gates are ajar'.' (Yeats was thinking of Elizabeth Radcliffe, whose experiments in automatic writing he had been observing at Daisy Meadow, the country home of Mrs Eva Fowler in Kent, near Brasted.)[8] Leo informed Yeats that his work would change in 1914 and that he had many guides but should listen to only one – Leo, presumably. Sceptical as usual, Yeats 'now made a test I had been waiting for.' Aware that one of the regular Bureau sitters knew Italian, Yeats 'asked Leo if he would speak Italian.' After he had spoken one sentence, she 'asked him about Norway in 1914.' His evasive reply about the changing of crowns must have disturbed Yeats, though he did not comment. 'Later on', he added, 'several "spirits" spoke Norwegian to the Norwegian sitter.'[9]

Ten days later (on 28 June) Leo appeared again at a large seance in Cambridge House. Of the thirteen or fourteen present Yeats knew only the medium and the Harpers. Since the seance was long (two and a half hours) and involved, Yeats noted, 'I cannot write out the incidents in order but will classify them.' He drew a 'map' of the room and described the 'incidents' under the headings of 'Lights', 'Touches', 'a Flower trumpet', 'Sounds apart from voices', and 'Voices.' Reserving most of his discussion for the last, Yeats noted that 'at one time there were three voices speaking.' He identified the Controls who gave names or were 'recognized' as Cardinal Newman ('who opened with a prayer'), Leo, Captain Sharko[?] ('or some such

---

[8] For details, see George Mills Harper and John S. Kelly, 'Preliminary Examination of the Script of E[lizabeth] R[adcliffe]' (*YO* 130–71).

[9] The Norwegian sitter was Fru Ella Anker, a clairvoyant, who had conducted sittings at Julia's Bureau. Miss Harper quotes from one of these sittings in which a ring appeared in the palm of a sitter's hand (202). In concluding his account of the seance of 18 June, Yeats spoke of a finger going into 'a large ring which might be symbolic.'

name'), and John King.[10] Leo 'said that he had died at Rome in the 'Franko Spanish War'[,] that he wanted me to write a play about his youth & my youth.' When Yeats asked for his Arabic name, Leo 'said he would tell it later & went.'

The remainder of Yeats's account is devoted to a dialogue with John King, 'who had a tremendous voice' and 'talked a great deal.' After some 'incoherent' rambling about his dislike of Cardinal Newman[11] ('here he was difficult to follow') and a brief debate with Yeats about the commercial theatre, King criticized him: 'Presently he said I had a fault all my life. I told my own story instead of letting others tell theirs. This is true enough', Yeats admitted (perhaps to himself), but 'he flowed[?] on to warn me against too much drink & tobacco & when I said he was wrong this time he said his advice was of merely general significance.' In response Yeats 'accused him of telling Sir William Crookes[12] that there were a tribe of spirits who took the Name of John King. He said he had followers but did not believe they ever took his name – he seemed many he said because spirits could go where they liked in an instant.' 'There are many personifications', Yeats observed, 'but I think no real evidence of identity.'[13] Noting in conclusion that 'proceedings were as last time closed by a short speech from 'Julia', Yeats signed his initials and dated his record 'June 29' (that is, the day after the seance). Immediately following – at the same time, most likely – Yeats made two rough sketches of Mrs Wriedt's 'jointed trumpet' and listed three of Everard Feilding's theories which suggest that both of them were sceptical about the trumpet. Yeats appears even more doubtful about Mrs Wriedt's methods in a long note on the same

---

[10] The most romantic of all Controls, John King functioned through many mediums. He claimed to have been, in one incarnation, Henry Owen Morgan, the notorious pirate. King 'communicated in direct voice through a trumpet' (see *EPS*, 190–91).

[11] King disliked Newman because he 'belonged to a church where priests could not marry. He did not think he could be sincere.'

[12] Sir William Crookes (1832–1919) was a famous physicist. His investigations of psychic phenomena were well published and hotly debated in scholarly journals and elsewhere. President of the Society for Psychical Research (hereafter cited as SPR) for four years (1896–1899), he insisted to the end of his life 'that a connection has been set up between this world and the next' (see *EPS*, 69–71).

[13] Yeats refers to the well-known theory that King was head of a band of 160 spirits. According to Fodor, King 'claimed descent from a race of men known by the generic title Adam' (*EPS*, 190).

page. Clearly puzzled about her personal authenticity as well as that of her spirit voices, he 'tried to persuade the medium to submit herself to investigation to (say) Sir Oliver Lodge,[14] but she said her only interest was to console the afflicted or some such phrase.' Like members of the SPR, Yeats wanted proof. His comment reflects the fact that a steadily increasing amount of psychical research was being devoted to attempts of the living to communicate with dead relatives and friends. Some three years later Lodge himself found consolation for the death (on 14 September 1915) of a beloved son in World War I, and recorded his experiences and faith in a famous book, the title of which is instructive in this context: *Raymond or Life and Death with Examples of the Evidence for Survival of Memory and Affection after Death* (1916).[15] Although Yeats deplored this preoccupation with a kind of research he surely considered sterile and unenlightening, he was sensitive to the emotions and intentions of others. The concluding sentence of his long note is characteristic: 'I think owing to the fact that Cambridge House is a centre of devotional spiritual investigation will always require much tact.' From 29 June 1912 to 12 May 1913 there is no reference in the Maud Gonne Notebook to séances at Cambridge House. Of course, Yeats may have recorded only the séances of special interest – in particular those at which Leo appeared, or he may have lost interest when Mrs Wriedt left London for the continent,[16] or he may have discovered a more exciting psychic phenomenon in the automatic writing of Elizabeth Radcliffe, whom he met in the spring of 1912.[17] At this time, also, he was strongly influenced by the methods of the SPR, which he became an Associate Member of in February 1913, probably through his friendship with Everard Feilding.

The next recorded seance he attended at Cambridge House occurred on 12 May 1913, at 9.45 a.m. Since Yeats was Mrs Wriedt's

---

[14] Sir Oliver J. Lodge (1851–1940), a famous physicist and university administrator, became interested in psychical research soon after the formation of the SPR, of which he was President (1901–1903). 'Absolutely convinced not only of survival but of demonstrated survival', he wrote numerous books about his theories and observations. See *EPS*, 204–05, and W. P. Jolly, *Sir Oliver Lodge* (London: Constable, 1974) *passim*.

[15] Yeats referred to *Raymond* in his discussion of life after death in *A Vision* (1925).

[16] In August 1912 she was in Christiania, Norway, and may have visited other countries before returning to America. Admiral W. Usborne Moore, who arranged for her to visit England in 1912, arranged for her return in 1913 (*EPS*, 409).

[17] See *YO* 133.

only sitter that morning, he was most likely trying to determine the validity of her mediumship. At one point he asked her to turn up the light. Although he 'still heard whisperings' through the trumpet, he recalled 'what Feilding noticed that whispering sometimes seemed to come not from trumpet but from direction of Mrs Wriedt.' After a time she invited Yeats to hold the trumpet, and he made out the words ' I am Leo.' Mrs Wriedt, who heard something similar, 'was told that Leo had carried out a promise made last year & tried to help my theatrical work but 'a block' had come.' She was informed that Yeats 'would have success in November but would first have to go abroad' and that 'some general public depression' was soon to occur. He concluded that the 'failure of seance came probably from too little sleep' or from his 'running not to be late.' As a result, he was 'keeping quiet for the sake of to-morrows seance.' 'Second seance also a failure', he wrote, then added: 'Welcome in strong voice from Dr Sharp[18] & then nothing but a few lights.' Nevertheless, Yeats concluded his brief entry on a positive and important note: 'Went on to Daisy Meadow & there began wonderful work with ER[.] May have saved my vitality for this.'[19] 19 This date, probably 13 May 1913, marks the beginning of a crowded and perplexing but very significant period in Yeats's psychical experimentation that may be said to terminate, or slack off greatly, with the completion of the first version of *A Vision* on 22 April 1925.[20]

Although Yeats was obviously excited over the investigation of Elizabeth Radcliffe's automatic writing, he did not abandon Mrs Wriedt and Leo. On 23 June he attended a big séance at which 'Leo came & gave the old impression of unreality. Talked of the theatre as if I had no other interest. Suggested a secondary personality conditioned by the information that he got when first formed.' Yeats asked 'if he was satisfied with what I am doing now (I was thinking of a very serious crisis in my private affairs) & he said what I was writing was splendid or some such words.' Having 'written nothing for some weeks', Yeats was clearly disappointed in this response. The crisis for which he needed help was the result of a demand of marriage from Mabel Dickinson, a mistress with whom he had 'made

---

[18] Dr John Sharp, one of Mrs Wriedt's Controls, claimed that he was born in Glasgow in the eighteenth century but had lived all his life in the United States (see *EPS*, 409).

[19] For details see *YO* 130–71.

[20] See *CVA* xlvii.

a truce' only after a 'violent scene at parting.' (Two weeks later, on 6 July, Yeats noted that the 'Radcliffe script [was] wholly accurate' in its prophetic reply to the same question about his crisis.) Yeats then interrupted the dialogue with Leo to describe several experiments with the materialization of physical objects and concluded that 'no human power had done this.' 'The seance ended' at this point, but Yeats had forgotten information he wanted to record. Leo had told him that he 'would soon go to Germany & seemed anxious lest I should hate the Germans like a simple minded English man ... He also told me to brush up on my German.' Yeats observed that he did 'not know a word of German.'[21]

For the next few months apparently he devoted much of his intellectual energy to the experiments with Miss Radcliffe at Daisy Meadow. Despite his stated conviction that 'no human power' could have achieved results he had observed in recent months, he was puzzled, and as usual he expressed the 'problem' in one of his journals:

July 1913. Having now proved spirit identity – for the ER case is final – I set myself this problem. Why has no sentence of literary or speculative profundity come through any medium in the last fifty years, or perhaps ever, for Plutarch talks of the imperfect expression of the Greek oracles in which he believes? By medium I mean spirit impulse which is independent of, or has submerged, the medium's conscious will. I re-state it thus: All messages that come through the senses as distinguished [from] those that come from the apparently free action of the mind – for surely there is poetic inspiration – are imperfect; that is to say, all objective messages, all that come through hearing or sight – automatic script, for instance – are without speculative power, or at any rate not equal to the mind's action at its best.[22]

Although 'the spirits excel us ... in knowledge of fact', Yeats concluded, they fail in 'speculation, wit, the highest choice of the mind.'[23]

Despite the persistence of this reservation, however, the quest continued. On 16 July 1913 he wrote to Lady Gregory from Daisy Meadow that he was 'getting some wonderful things with the medium.

---

[21] Two other entries in the Notebook are dated 24 June. The first, about 'Two Symbolic Dreams', notes that W. T. Horton and Audrey Locke had 'got automatic writing' when they 'dined here' a week ago. The second entry records 'another sitting with Horton & Miss Locke a few days later.' For further details of this relationship, see George Mills Harper, *W. B. Yeats and W. T. Horton: The Record of an Occult Friendship* (London: Macmillan, 1980) especially 36–39.
[22] *Mem* 266–67.
[23] *Mem* 267.

I am getting curious interpretations of the symbols as a preliminary explanation of the language and messages from dead people ...'[24] Although he completed the essay about these experiences on 8 October, he did not publish it, perhaps because he needed further proof.

His continued association with friends in the SPR may have supported his lingering doubts. In May 1914 he journeyed to Mirebeau, France, with Maud Gonne and Everard Feilding 'to investigate a miracle': bleeding oleographs of the Sacred Heart.[25] Returning to Paris (probably on 13 May), he dictated an essay (to Maud) and wrote excited letters about their experience. Upon learning from an analysis by the Lister Institute in London that the blood was not human, Yeats left his record unpublished.[26] While waiting in London for the result of the analysis, he renewed investigations at Cambridge House. On 6 June 1914 he attended a long and very important séance. Besides himself and the medium twelve other people were present. Of these he was well acquainted with only one, Miss Felicia Scatcherd, who was a member of Julia's 'Inner Circle'; but he also knew by name Sir Alfred Turner[27] and Stead's daughter, Estelle. Yeats must have spent much of the following day on his recording of the séance and three reflective comments. Although his notes were 'practically useless', being 'partly mixed up with a poem I had been writing', his recollections and observations required almost six legal-size pages in the Notebook. During the course of some three hours Yeats had managed to ask John King, Leo, and fellow sitters questions about many of his preoccupations. Leo told Yeats that he had prophesied his journey to America (January to April) and had brought him in

[24] G. M. Harper, *W. B. Yeats and W. T. Horton*, 39.
[25] For details, see *YO* 172–89.
[26] For Yeats's essay and details of the circumstances surrounding Yeats's trip, see George Mills Harper, '"A Subject of Investigation": Miracle at Mirebeau', in *YO* 172–89. When Feilding wrote to Yeats that the report from the Lister Institute was negative, he made a note at the end of Maud Gonne's manuscript of his essay: 'Analysis says not human blood. July 11. 1914.' He was obviously convinced that the bleeding picture was a hoax.
[27] Miss Scatcherd, herself a medium, was an admirer and friend of Stead. Miss Harper describes her as 'an extraordinarily good "receiver"' of telepathic messages and quotes extensively from 'a special, verbatim report' she took of an address by Stead at the Spiritualists' National Union Convention in July 1909 (157–61). Sir Alfred E. Turner, also 'a close and intimate friend' of Stead, wrote the 'Introduction' to Miss Harper's book.

contact with 'certain people.'[28] Yeats 'asked for something about ... my visit to the "Bleeding Picture"', but Leo could only repeat some word 'over & over again. It was probably "miracle".' Later on he spoke about a subject Yeats had discussed at the dinner table with Feilding and Maud Gonne: a possible explanation of the miracle by the 'ideoplastic theory'[29] or by 'trance cheating', both common topics of the SPR. Among the 'many other spirits' who came during the evening was 'someone who called herself my mother. She was impressing my father that he might believe in the other world.' Then came two spirits who were prominent in the Script of Miss Radcliffe: 'Sister Mary Ellen Ellis' and 'Anna Louisa Karsch.'[30] 'Towards the end of the seance 'Leo' came again', and Yeats asked if Miss Karsch 'was attached to me, or one of the group about Miss X [Radcliffe].' More importantly, he wanted to know 'why Miss X's automatic writing had ceased.' Learning that 'it is exhausted', Yeats asked if 'for ever.' Leo promised 'to tell me the reason [?] ... & then said "she must work once more with her old friends for a time or she will lose her gift".'

This discussion of Miss Radcliffe's Script must have prompted Yeats to re-examine his unpublished essay. At the end of the typescript he made a note dated 7 June 1914 dealing with the topics of the seance he had just recorded:

Another hypothesis is possible. Secondary & tertiary personalities once formed may act independently of the medium, have ideoplastic power & pick the minds of distant people & so speak in tongues unknown to all present ... Yet there may be interdependence of the two worlds.[31]

Sometime during the day of 7 June Yeats also wrote four notes about his experiences of the night before. Two are relevant here: note 1 contains information about his mother and Leo's prophecy of 'my visit to Germany which has not come true'; note 3 is an

---

[28] The 'certain people' were probably Lady Gregory and Synge. While in America Yeats recorded a séance with Mrs Wriedt in Detroit on 19 February 1914. A voice professing to be Synge 'was very anxious to speak to Lady Gregory. The speaker was greatly indebted to her.' After some further references to the Aran Islands, Sara [Allgood], and *The Rising of the Moon*, the spirit informed Yeats that '"Leo does not want to make a spiritist of you, but an orator". Said he and Leo would help me.' (We are indebted to Bradford's transcription from one of Yeats's manuscript books.)
[29] See *EPS* 113, 182 for discussions of Ectoplasm and Ideoplasm.
[30] See *YO* 148 and 152–53, for some account of these two people.
[31] *YO* 171. He changed 'is some' to 'may be' in the manuscript.

orderly summary of Yeats's recent investigations. The first section reaffirms the doubt he had expressed in July 1913 that 'Nearly all the reflective part at these séances seems less convincing than the matter of fact part.'[32] After some observations about the assumptions of names by spirits and their use of foreign languages, Yeats recorded his conviction in six important propositions:

To sum up I am sure of these conclusions
(1) Minds of some kind can write or speak through a medium in tongues unknown to all present (see general testimony in case of Mrs Wriedt & my own work with Miss X & elsewhere)
(2) These minds know the private affairs of sitters
(3) These minds have strange power over matter ('movement without contact')
(4) They have power of creating luminous substances which can take the human form (Have seen luminous substance under good conditions – Bisson medium[33] – I must accept 'materialization' as evidence of other. Those I have seen were not under test conditions.
(5) The abstract reflective power of these beings is generally slight [WBY] or rather of their manifestation is slight as a rule
(6) Their practical wisdom is often very great (Private case Miss X mediumship)

Yeats recorded no further séances in the Maud Gonne Notebook until 20 July 1915, when he attended a 'Remarkable seance at Mrs Wriedts.' The only other person present was Dr Abraham Wallace. After considerable discussion with John King about George Pollexfen, Yeats's sisters, a letter about the war 'from the old man over the water'

---

[32] Cf. n. 22 above.
[33] Mme Alexandre Bisson was a well-known psychical investigator. Over a period of several years (from May 1909 through June 1914) she and a circle of friends conducted hundreds of sittings which were observed and recorded by Baron von Schrenck Notzing in *Materialisations Phaenomene* (1914), cited herein from the English translation, *Phenomena of Materialisation* (1920 and 1923). Primarily these investigations were devoted to materialization through the mediumship of Eva C. (Marthe Beraud). When Yeats was in Paris immediately after the investigation at Mirebeau, he attended séances at the home of Mme Bisson on 19, 22, and 26 May (314–17). Maud was not present. In one of his notebooks, partially transcribed by Bradford, Yeats wrote much fuller accounts of the séances on 22 and 26 May. He also wrote a detailed account of a séance of 17 May not recorded in Schrenck Notzing. All these séances experiment with 'luminous forms'.

(probably John Quinn),[34] the codicil to Hugh Lane's will,[35] and Sister Mary Ellen Ellis, Leo came. He spoke first of the Abbey Theatre, of its financial problems in particular. 'He then shifted to a discussion of the war', reminding Yeats that he had foretold it, and he predicted that 'it would be much longer than we thought.' Finally, speaking in 'what seemed Italian', which Yeats 'could not follow', Leo translated ('perhaps') into an exciting prophecy of Yeats's future: 'When you were young you were a contented man. Life is like that. Then came the thistles, but now you will have the roses. I was to have much recognition [.] I had done much that would be famous in the record.' Since Yeats signed and dated his account 20 July, it was most likely written that night after he returned to his flat.

Two days later (on the evening of 22 July) he was visited by three people, including Sturge Moore and Miss Scatcherd. We may conjecture that Yeats recalled for them details of the 'remarkable seance' of 20 July and that Miss Scatcherd offered to call up the spirit of Leo. Leo 'asked' him to compose the exchange of letters preserved in the unpublished essay entitled 'Leo Africanus.' Here is the account as Yeats recalled it three weeks later.

Miss Scatcherd did automatic writing (see File) & this seeming to come from Leo I got her to surrender to what seemed impressions from her control. I had a conversation with the control. He said that I was more inclined to believe some secondary personality theory than I myself believed. He was no secondary personality, with a symbolic biography as I thought possible but the person he claimed to be. He was drawn to me because in life he had been all undoubting impulse, all that his name and Africa might suggest symbolically for his biography was both symbolical and actual. I was doubting, conscientious and timid. His contrary and by association with me would be made not one but two perfected natures. He asked me to write him a letter addressed to him as if to Africa giving all my doubts about spiritual things and then to write a reply as from him to me. He would control me[36] in that reply so that it would be really from him. (Miss S did not know that I had several times thought of using him in some such way in some imaginary dialogue but vaguely)

---

[34] Quinn's letter to Yeats dated 24 April 1915 contains a long discussion of 'his philosophy about war'. He was violently anti-German.

[35] This visit from 'Hugh Lane' prompted Lady Gregory to have a seance with Mrs Wriedt on 24 July. Both Yeats and Lady Gregory were sceptical about the validity of the information received.

[36] Following 'me' Yeats first wrote 'if he could', then marked through it.

Whether or not Yeats composed 'Leo Africanus' soon thereafter can only be conjectured,[37] but if so the writing did not lay Leo's ghost to rest. On 4 November 1915 Yeats recorded that 'on Sunday last' (31 October) Leo had talked with him and Olivia Shakespear while they and Feilding were conducting experiments with Tatwa cards:

... she had a long conversation with 'Leo' who seemed caught in a stream of prithivi Tatwa. 'Leo' said he created isolation & would agree[?] [with] me certainly. He would [help] me next time I was with Miss X to banish the other controls, said a banishing ceremony would do & that he could get in. He said Isabella of Ferrara[?] was a non-entity & evidently thought little of the others – he had intellect & precision. I said I do not like to interfere with their control of Miss X in fear of harming her. He said something about it being needful to take sides. OS was not sure that he really was Leo though he himself seemed very real, so I asked him to try with some medium & get Arabic through to me. He said he was most anxious.

Leo is also mentioned in the last entry of the Maud Gonne Notebook. On 23 March 1917 Yeats described an experience of the night before when he, Denison Ross, and Edmund Dulac had travelled to St Leonards-on-Sea to investigate David Wilson's Metallic Homunculus, about which all three wrote still unpublished reports. Late at night, after Ross and Dulac had gone, the machine began to talk: 'Incoherent words from an alleged "Leo" who presently said he did not know who he was & that he might be "Yeats". When I said I was "Yeats", He said "no Yeats has gone".' Leo had been more coherent on a previous occasion. After a visit to St Leonards on 30 January Yeats composed a careful account of facts and impressions in which he recorded that 'Leo Africanus ... came because I asked for him.' Still later Yeats sought 'to get Leo' by evoking the sun. Finally he 'came and spoke to me, but before he came the machine said, *a greater than Leo is here* and this proved to be Paracelsus himself and while Leo was speaking we were interrupted by Karl of Janina who wished to speak to Leo and could only do so at a seance.' Yeats concluded his account with a significant observation: '... all seemed anxious for us to know that there was a universal mind and that if we spoke to them, it was as but links with that mind.' David Wilson himself had become interested in Yeats's alter ego, writing on 3 April 1917 to ask 'what activities during the past few weeks L Africanus has been indulging in.' Since the full name of Leo Africanus is used in the Wilson materials but not in the Notebook,

---

[37] Yeats refers to this meeting in the first line of his essay as 'some months ago'.

we may conjecture that the essay was written before the investigation of the Metallic Homunculus.

A much more important problem is what happened between April and November 1917 to change Yeats's conception of Leo. As all students of Yeats know, his wife 'surprised' him 'by attempting automatic writing' on 24 October 1917, four days after their marriage.[38] But they did not begin to preserve the Script until 5 November. On that day Leo appears as a malignant and untrustworthy spirit, and he remains 'dishonest' when he reappears occasionally (twenty-five times or more) throughout the Script. He becomes, in fact, the most difficult of a category of spirits called Frustrators (that is, those who deliberately impeded or hindered the psychic investigations). On the evening of 5 November Yeats and his wife were informed by Thomas of Dorlowicz, the most important of the Controls in the Script, that Leo was not to be trusted. The following answers to unrecorded questions will illustrate the new role Leo was to play:

Yes
alright but dishonest
one of several who are Leo
misuse – Leo but does not
come himself to you
reflection
cant tell
Better not to act by Leo ever but
    may give good information
yes – a reflection – subsidiaries – yes
not always sent – sent sometimes
malignant sometimes – not to be trusted in
never believe his prophecy

Another comment by Thomas (two days later) casts some light on these ambiguous suggestions: '... most of us are only forms under the reflection of real spirits & therefore do not come from those regions but from the lower intermediate [,] no the real causes a reflection through evil work.' Yeats was surely confused, but he was also impressed. In the alphabetized Card File which became a record for quotations from and observations about the Script, Yeats made an entry under 'Guides' repeating part of Thomas's advice about Leo verbatim. One other entry under this heading is significant: after

---

[38] For Yeats's account see *CVA* 8.

a brief discussion of 'spiritual guides of the soul', Yeats added, 'but there are illusionary guides to mislead & are short lived.' Convinced by Thomas apparently that Leo was one of those 'illusionary guides', Yeats had no further use for him. But Leo was not easily banished. More than once in the course of the next few months he interfered with George Yeats's writing. For example, on 23 January 1918, she made Leo's sign several times near the end of the evening to indicate that she must 'stop writing now.' 'After 'Ω yes Ω' she wrote: 'Thomas much better wait no good going on in this moment only misleading.' Following some unrecorded question from Yeats, she replied: '*Yes* could not tell you till you discovered it yourself Ω.' More than six years later Yeats noted at the bottom of this page: 'all about Tarot etc frustration WBY. May [?] 1924.' On the next page Thomas had told him to 'stiffen your *logical mind.*' These exchanges are part of a serious but rather one-sided debate about Leo's function which extended over a period of several days beginning 21 January and culminating on 30 January.

It is significant that throughout the Script Leo's sign and most of the discussion about him are in the hand of George, who may have been trying to displace him as a benevolent or useful Guide to Yeats. Especially revealing, though not perfectly clear, is a dialogue – all in George's hand – on 22 January. The phrase 'Spiritual growth' is followed first by several of Leo's signs then by George's comment: 'an evil genius but who has attached himself to you – not yours especially – no spirit.' When Yeats asked, ' To me', George replied: 'Yes I think so but could not be absolutely sure – Hates medium wants to displace your mind no sheer malevolence about 6 years ago I think – not really Leo – knew Leo in life probably.' The period of 'about 6 years' suggests that George is recalling Leo's first appearance, on 9 May 1912. After a brief discussion of 'four Signs of malevolence' which are 'poised to sting', George continued: 'He hates you for your learning knowledge about spirits & because you have a degree of initiation[39] – They *have to* try to prevent – it is their duty & they sometimes become malevolent in that duty.' Following the assertion that 'he will try medium' and the revelation that the 'form of spiritual

---

[39] This is probably a reference to Yeats's position in the Stella Matutina, the Inner Order of the Golden Dawn, in which he and George maintained an active interest though they were living in Oxford at this time. Yeats achieved the Degree of 6 = 5 on 16 October 1914, and he composed a brief prose poem 'For initiation in 7 = 4', the next Degree (in Notebook following entry dated 4 November 1915).

knowledge' to be sought is 'not your formula but both ☉ & ☽.' George suggested that 'he is a guide & therefore Leo Africanus nothing to do with him.' Since Yeats had been told repeatedly over the past six years that Leo was a Guide, he must have been puzzled by George's statement.

Whatever his classification and whether or not he was the real Leo Africanus, some malevolent spirit using Leo's astrological sign disturbed and deluded the Yeatses for many months: he created illusions, he was probably responsible for 'a disturbance which might have resulted in stopping this work' (30 January 1918), and he once led Yeats to record that an entire evening's investigation was 'all wrong Leo' (12 April 1918). Although he appeared less often after June 1918, he continued to cast a malicious shadow over the Automatic Script well into 1919. At the first séance after the birth of Anne Yeats, Leo is named and his sign is superimposed over crude drawings of a hand and some sticks followed by two strange sentences: ' – has dropped the rods[.] The hand strikes but cannot hurt' (20 March 1919). Is the unstated subject of the first sentence Leo's hand, and does George mean to suggest that it can no longer hurt? Whatever comfort, if any, Yeats found in this enigmatic assurance, we may be certain that he had mixed emotions over the loss of a Communicator who had been hovering around for more than seven years.

Appendix A

Circle Sitting in the Library at Cambridge House, Wimbledon, 6.30 in the evening. 9th May 1912. Mrs Etta Wriedt of Detroit, U.S.A., Medium.
    Sitters were: Mrs Gillespie and three friends: Mr and Mrs Browne: Miss Ashby: and Mr W. B. Yeats. Also Mrs and Miss Harper.
    (Miss Harper's notes.)
    Miss Ashby was a personal friend of our own, the other sitters were strangers. Musical box played for a few minutes. Then some sitters felt themselves sprinkled with drops of water (the séances often began with this 'sprinkling'. Sometimes a Latin Benediction followed).
    In a little while a very deep voice spoke through the trumpet, evidently for Mr Yeats, whom it addressed as 'Mr Gates'. Voice spoke loudly and distinctly. When asked 'Who are you?' replied

'Leo, The Writer!' Went on to say he was the Guide of Mr Yeats, had been with him a great many years, and impressed him and worked through his brain. Pressed for identification said he was a Writer and Explorer, and added 'You will find me in the Encyclopedia, ... at Rome', or words to that effect. The words Encyclopedia, and Rome, were both certainly used, but I am not certain whether he meant he had lived in Rome, and would be found 'in the Encyclopedia', as one would speak of finding a word 'in the Dictionary', or whether he referred to some special Roman Encyclopedia. He said more, to the effect that he was helping and working through Mr Yeats, but the manifestation was interrupted by one of the sitters – a woman – becoming afraid and suddenly insisting on leaving the room. The voice of 'Leo' had a slight Irish accent, not unlike Mr Yeats's own. It was deep and resonant, somewhat of the quality of John King's but without the latter's abrupt manner of speaking.

'Leo' was followed by another voice, much fainter and not very distinct, and did not seem to be definitely recognized. This was suddenly interrupted by a loud, deep voice telling Mr Yeats to 'Sit up in your chair!'. Mr Yeats had apparently been leaning forward, but the room being pitch dark it was impossible for anyone to see this, and there were then two other sitters between Mr Yeats and the Medium.

Two other women then insisted on leaving the room, evidently in a state of terror, which utterly spoilt the conditions and we got practically nothing more, altho we sat for a long time in the hope of further manifestations. Once I saw a faint luminous globe or disc appear near where Mr Yeats was sitting. It appeared to me to be about the size of a large dinner plate, and was of a faint silvery glow, like misty moonlight.

To those who have often sat with Mrs Wriedt either privately or in Circle, this was only a very mediocre seance, in comparison with the general order of results, and we blamed the disturbance caused by three sitters leaving the room, breaking the circle, and interfering with the conditions, which were otherwise quite harmonious and peaceful.

Edith K. Harper: Sec. Julia's Bureau
S. A. Adela Harper

Appendix B

Report of Seance
held at Cambridge House, Wimbledon
at 6.30 on May 9th 1912.
Present besides Mrs.—the medium, Mrs. Harper, Miss Harper and eight others.
The room had a dark cabinet, but this was not used as the room was entirely darkened. A long tin trumpet was handed round. I did not notice at the beginning of the Séance where it was finally placed, but noticed at the end that it was standing on its broad end in the middle of the room. The Medium had a strong American accent. When the room was darkened, a musical box started playing. After about three minutes or so, the box stopped. We were then suddenly sprinkled with some liquid. I felt this on my hands and face. The Medium when questioned said it was the way her control had of showing he was present and that it was a kind of baptism. A little later there came an exceedingly loud voice through the trumpet. I could not understand what was said. The Medium interpreted that it claimed to come for 'Mr. Gates'. I said this was evidently me. It then said in a more distinct voice which I could follow and still very loud, that it had been with me from childhood. Shortly after it had begun speaking, a terrified woman got up and went out. It went on saying 'that they wanted to use my hand and brain'. I was a little impatient. I had this kind of spirit once before, and was repelled by what I considered an appeal to my vanity. But for this I would have listened more carefully. The voice said something about my possessing the key or the key-mind they wanted. I asked who was speaking and was told that it was 'Leo, the writer and explorer'. I couldn't understand the answer. I asked when he lived. I got no answer I could understand. I said did you live in the 18th century? Then came some sentence beginning with 'Why, man?' or some such phrase implying impatience, certainly containing the word 'man' and adding 'Leo, the writer, you know Leo, the writer.' When I said I knew no such person the voice said: As I thought, 'you will hear of me in Rome.'
The Medium had however heard the words as 'You will find me in the Encyclopaedia.' Both may have been said, but there were a number of sentences I could not follow. I noticed that 'Leo' had a strong Irish accent, whereas the Medium had a strong American accent. I had also the impression that the Irish accent was not quite true. The kind of accent an Irishman some years out of Ireland, or an

Englishman who had a fair knowledge of Ireland, might assume in telling an Irish story.

One of the sitters, however, told me that she considered the accent like my own, and not stronger than mine. I had thought it stronger. I asked the Medium the meaning of this Irish accent. She replied that the control had to get its means of expression from my mind. With a click, possibly the putting of the trumpet on the ground, the control finished. It was followed by a very low voice, very difficult to understand and from which little could be made out, except a Christian name, and the first letter of a surname. It had seemingly come for one of the other sitters. Suddenly this low voice was interrupted by the loud voice again telling me to sit up straight on my chair. I was leaning forward with my elbows on my knees. I consider this sentence as proof that there was no conscious jugglery on the part of the Medium, for the room was in entire darkness. No gleam of light, however faint, from under the door or through the keyhole, or from the crack of a shutter. And in all this part of the Séance there were I think two, certainly one, sitter between myself and the Medium. At this point the Séance practically ended, for two terrified ladies went out, which broke the influence, or at any rate brought all satisfactory manifestations to an end. We sat for nearly an hour longer, with no result except that I was touched twice towards the end of the hour upon the top of my head as if by the thumb and forefinger of a hand, and that while I was doubting whether a faint gleam of light which seemed to come at intervals where the medium was at my right hand – she was sitting next me since the last two went out – I saw a light very distinctly and without any possibility of being mistaken straight in front of me. It was not bright; it was the usual phosphorescent glow and about the size and shape of a sixpenny loaf.

I set down here for my own guidance that I wish to observe whether there is any tendency at a Seance for a faint voice through a dramatising instinct unconsciously to follow a loud one. Miss Harper looked up Leo in Lempriere and found these words: 'An author of Pella who wrote on the nature of the Gods, etc.' Lempriere gives references, but unless one found that this Leo was also an explorer, there is very little to decide on.

Note – Not to look up the references till after next Seance as they might become a suggestion to the control.

It is possible that Leo may turn out to be a symbolic being. Leo, the constellation, the house of the sun, and if this is so, it would account for the arrogance implied by his impatience when I did not know his name & by the appeal to my vanity of his address. Further if it be true as I have always supposed, that the influence under which I do my work and think my most profound thoughts, is what an Astrologer calls solar, this being or state like the previous control which said to me very similar things some 12 years ago, may be a dramatization of a reality.

It is even possible that the domineering jocular type of half-Irish, or English-Irish storyteller, suggested to me not only by certain intonations of the voice but by such an expression as 'Why, man?' may be a lower solar form, arrogance being always [WBY] mirth & a kind of unreality belonging to the perversion of the solar power, speaking astrologically. I have never been quite certain that certain controls who give themselves names of great antiquity, do not really select by some process of unconscious affinity from the recorded or unrecorded memories of the world, a name and career that symbolizes their nature.

W.B.Y.

2. TEXT

[Although the text of 'Leo Africanus' (consisting of forty manuscript pages plus inserts) was much revised, Yeats did not prepare it for publication or for any kind of public distribution. The 'foul copy' (one of the most difficult in the Yeats canon) from which we have derived our transcript contains more than 450 cancellations and emendations as well as many uncorrected irregularities in syntax, punctuation, and spelling. We have attempted to reproduce the text as accurately as possible, correcting only occasional irregularities in spelling and inserting punctuation when logic seems to require it. Our notes record only the most substantive textual alterations. For a complete record, see Steve L. Adams, 'W. B. Yeats's *Leo Africanus*' (M.A. thesis, Florida State University, 1979), in the Robert Manning Strozier Library.]

LEO AFRICANUS[40]

Some months ago a medium Miss S—and one or two other friends were at my rooms.[41] Presently Miss S—who had heard my account of you seemed to be controlled or perhaps I should say overshadowed. She began to speak rapidly speaking whatever came into her head. You were as it seemed the speaker.[42] I have had but little experience of Miss S—as a medium. Once, the only other time in fact when I had consulted her[,] 'William Morris' had written through her hand[,] & as he had written through the hand of another medium in my presence I assumed that she possessed telepathic power at least. What impressed me more was a curious doctrine. You were my opposite. By association with one another we should each become more complete; you had been unscrupulous & believing. I was overcautious & conscientious. Then you said if I would write a letter to you as if you were still living among your Moors or Sudanese, & put into it all my difficulties and afterwards answer it in your name you would overshadow me in my turn & answer all my doubts. I have beside me as I write the translation of the only work of yours extant today – from this one assumes that you still exist – It was published in London in 1600 & was translated by John Pory 'lately of Goneuill and Caius College in Cambridge' & called 'A Geographical History of Africa written in Arabicke & Italian by John Leo, borne in Granada and brought up in Barbarie'.[43] There is also a long subtitle

---

[40] Leo, Johannes (c.1492–1552), in Italian Giovanni Leone, and properly known as Al Hassan Ibn Mahommed Al Wezaz Al Fasi, was the author of *Descrizione dell' Affrica* or *Africae descriptio*, which was for many years the best authority on Mahommedan Africa. As a Moor from noble heritage, he received his education at Fez and traveled widely in the Barbary States. After returning from one of three Egyptian journeys in 1520, he was captured by pirates near the island of Gerba and was later presented as a slave to Leo X. Recognizing his scholarly merit, the Pope persuaded him to adopt Christianity and bestowed on him both of his own names, Johannes and Leo. Leo's description of Africa was first written in Arabic, but the text that remains is the Italian version which was issued while Leo was in Rome. He returned to Africa and renounced Christianity before his death in 1552.

[41] See n. 27 above.

[42] A cancelled passage follows in the manuscript: 'If I would write out my difficulties in a letter addressed to you as though you were still living in the east & then wrote another letter in your hand you would see to it that the second letter was but in seeming mine. I should be overshadowed in my turn.'

[43] Little is known of John Pory. In a footnote to the 1896 edition of *The History and Description of Africa and of the Notable Things Therein Contained* translated by Pory and edited by Robert Brown, Brown notes that 'in the Register of Gonville

announcing that it contains descriptions 'of the regions, cities, towns [,] mountains [,] rivers & other places throughout all the north & principal partes of Africa' & other matters 'gathered partly out of ' your own 'dilligent observations & partly out of the ancient records & Chronicles of the Arabians & Mores'. When you first came to me I had to the best of my belief never heard of you nor of your work, but now I have read a good part of it & picture you with some clearness, especially as a young man studying & making verses in the town of Fez you have described with such minute detail – at this moment I imagine you as a student of this college where there were 'three cloysters to walk in, most curiously and artificially made with certain eight-square pillers of divers colours to support them – And between piller & piller 'arches' overcast with golde, azure & divers other colours' walking perhaps where 'runneth' through the college 'a little stream in a most clear & pleasant channell the brims & edges whereof are workmanly framed of marble & stones of Majorica' or perhaps with your fellow poets whose songs on all other days of the year 'entreat of love' going 'betimes in the morning' upon Mahomets birthday 'unto the palace of the chiefe judge or governour' that from 'the tribunal seat' you also may read some 'elegant & pithie' poem in the Prophets praise 'to a great audience of people'. It is said that a shade can elect to appear as young or old when it would speak to men & it may be you will prefer me to imagine you as you were after your capture by Venetian pirates & your liberation from slavery by Pope Leo the tenth whose name you took. You have spoke to me so much of the drama, that I am ready to imagine you as attending those performances of Plautus arranged [in] Rome by Cardinal–.[44] You saw indeed the beginnings of one drama & may indeed watch through our eyes today its corruption & decline. You wish me to [tell] you what leaves me incredulous, or unconvinced. I do not doubt any more than you did when [among] the alchemists of Fez the existence of God, & I follow tradition stated for the last time explicitly in

and Caius College, Cambridge, he is entered as "John Porye", who became an undergraduate in 1587.' The full title of the 1600 edition may be found above, 32 n. 58. The edition by Robert Brown contains three volumes, which were published by Bedford Press at the suggestion of Richard Hakluyt.

[44] Yeats obviously intended to search for this name. He may refer to Angelo Mai (1782–1854) of Milan, who worked in the Ambrosian Library in the early nineteenth century. He discovered the Ambrosian Palimpsest (Ambrosianus G 52 sup.), which he tried to decipher in 1815. We are indebted to Professor Walter E. Forehand for this information.

Swedenborg & in Blake, that his influence descends to us through hierarchies of mediatorial shades & angels.[45] I doubt however, though not always, that the shades who speak to us through mediums are the shades they profess [to] be. That doubt is growing more faint but still it returns again & again. I have continually to remind myself of some piece of evidence written out & examined & put under its letter in my file. How can I feel certain of your identity, when there has been so much to rouse my suspicion. You came to me first on—at Mrs Wriedts at Wimbledon.[46] The lights were no sooner out than I heard your voice very loud, & with what seemed to me a slight Irish accent as though you drew your expression from my memory, or my habit of speech. I thought the accent a little more marked than my own. You told me that you were Leo my guide & seemed astonished that I had never heard of you. 'I am Leo the writer' you repeated, & I would find you in the books or hear of you at Rome. You spoke too of your travels & said that you had been with me from childhood. I was to attend much to spiritual experiences for I had a key mind & would make great discoveries.[47] Before the next seance I read in Chambers biographical dictionary about Leo Africanus & saw that beyond question the voice claimed to be his voice. I was not at all impressed & thought Mrs Wriedt who is perhaps a ventriloquist of some kind looks up guides for her visitors in Chambers when [she] knows nothing of their [dead] friends & relatives. In this chance she may have been in a hurry for plainly Leo Africanus a geographer & traveller is for me no likely guide. However upon looking [up] a reference to the proceedings of the Hakluyt society at the end of the biography I discovered that Leo Africanus was a distinguished poet

---

[45] Yeats writes in 'Swedenborg, Mediums, and the Desolate Places': 'Nor should we think of spirit as divided from spirit, as men are from each other, for they share each other's thoughts and life, and those whom he [Swedenborg] has called celestial angels, while themselves mediums to those above, commune with men and lower spirits, through orders of mediatorial spirits, not by a conveyance of messages, but as though a hand were thrust with a hundred gloves, one glove outside another, and so there is a continual influx from God to man.' See *VBWI* 316. Yeats's essay, dated 14 October 1914, casts considerable light on 'Leo Africanus'.

[46] See n. 5 above. At this point in the manuscript Yeats crossed out two sentences: 'Dr Abraham Wallace was the only other sitter. It was at 3 in the afternoon.' Neither Yeats nor Miss Harper records that Wallace was present on 9 May.

[47] The preceding sentence was an insert written on a separate page.

among the Moors.⁴⁸ On—I had another seance, & then on—still another & more details were added including a correction of the statement in Chambers that after twenty years in Rome you had died in your own country in ? 1543.⁴⁹ Leo had died the voice said in a battle of the Franco Spanish war, but it was something that happened on—that made me begin to think that perhaps you still lived, & were really speaking to me. A woman sat next me I discovered who knew some Italian. I know something of her. She belonged to a well known Scandinavian family & was certainly no confidante of the medium.⁵⁰ I said if a spirit who calls himself Leo comes speak to him in Italian. A little later she had a copious conversation in Italian with the voice. She did not understand a great deal for her Italian is not very abundant, & the speech was rapid but Leo's Italian she said was excellent. A little later she was talking Norwegian to a different spirit, & certainly we had got beyond the Mediums knowledge, & the problem had become psychological.⁵¹ I had already felt when I noticed the slight Irish accent which had now vanished that perhaps it would be necessary to look for part of the explanation whether I accepted or rejected the spirit theory in my own mind & this became more probable when Dr Wallace who is Scotch told me that at one [of] his séances the habitual control of the medium had spoken with a Scotch accent. I was reminded too of certain earlier experiences. The name Leo recalled the one of the only two other séances I had ever attended. It was fifteen or twenty years earlier & Mr Williams was the medium I had not begun to take notes but my memory was very distinct.⁵² Many faces had shown themselves by the light of a phosphorescent slate that shades seem to carry from place to place & one of these had whispered very faintly at my ear words which I had thought to be 'Leonora Arguite' but the medium declared them to be 'Leonora your guide'.⁵³ I have been always conscious of some being near to me & once when I was a young child I heard its voice, as

---

⁴⁸ According to Robert Brown, in his edition of Pory's translation, 'the divers excellent poems' of Leo have 'vanished'.
⁴⁹ These séances probably occurred on 5 and 18 June 1912. See 292–94 above.
⁵⁰ See n. 9 above.
⁵¹ Mrs Wriedt spoke only English, but the voices that spoke through her were many and varied, including Dutch, French, Spanish, Norwegian, Arabic, German, Serbian, and Croatian.
⁵² See n. 7 above.
⁵³ See 292–94 above. Yeats recorded these details on 20 June 1912 of a séance which had occurred on 5 June.

though someone were speaking in the room but something in your tone which was a little commanding and boisterous always prevented me from recalling that faint voice. I remember instead how a little before that seance with Williams I had called one evening on an old Dublin Doctor. I found a dozen people in his drawing room & among them a girl telling fortunes by Chiromancy, & she was new at her subject & had a book on Chiromancy open on the chair beside her. I had known her some years before, & had found her a sensitive [girl] & though I had never knowingly hypnotised her, had discovered that she was a hypnotic subject. That it was easy to call up visions before her mind. I asked her to tell my fortune – I am copying my full notes made at that time – but saw she must come through the folding doors into the next room. She brought the book with her & spread it open upon the table, & began explaining the lines. Suddenly her voice changed & another personality spoke through her of my most private affairs & charged me to attend more than ever to visions & dreams & I would bring a closer relation between this world & the next than ever before. After some more of a like sort a step in the passage caused the clairvoyant to awake from her trance dazed & ignorant of all that had passed. I had felt I was being tempted with a childish temptation with a crude appeal to my vanity. Now here was a new appeal though less crude. I had 'a key mind'. I was necessary & so on.[54] Since that first seance your voice if yours it is has come often, at Mrs Wriedts séances when I have been present. I will not discuss this in detail. The main result has been that with the fading of the effect upon me of the Italian conversation I have found myself more & more sceptical. Your voice does not suggest, an actual man. The voice has something artificial, which if I had to describe, [is] a rise and fall as of a practiced speaker who is speaking however under conditions we do not understand & the mind behind is vague & indefinite. I have only once & that was when you first spoke to [me] in Italian noticed an emotional intonation. The voice in fact is like that of the habitual controls John King[,] Dr Sharpe & so on & I am suspicious of it as I am of them & suspect it, as I but seldom at the moment suspect those who claim to be men & women but lately dead of being a secondary personality.[55] Perhaps you found those

---

[54] The long passage beginning with 'Many faces had shown themselves ...' and ending with 'I was necessary & so on' originally followed a passage on the preceding page ending 'You spoke too of your travels ...'
[55] See nn. 10, 18 above.

Italian sentences in the memory of [my] Scandinavian neighbor & for that reason I have asked you to write to me through some mediums hand a sentence of Arabic. I may bring an Arabic scholar to see Mrs Wriedt when she returns from America but that will be inconclusive, for you would find all you needed in his memory. But if you are a secondary personality[56] you can create for yourself a solid body for I am satisfied with the evidence that you have lifted a metal trumpet, carried flowers & touched me upon my hands, my knees & my face. That would not be any difficulty to most continental investigators for they argue that if we are ready to grant such powers to the dead, there is no reason why we should deny them to a portion of the mind of a living man. Dr Ochorowicz has even created a very patient & satisfactory secondary personality while working with his medium Madame Tomczyk[57] endowing it by suggestion with all these powers, as well as with the reliable mental habits necessary for his experiments. He had been annoyed by the charming but unreliable Moyenne, & that still more unreliable Little Stasia, who though Moyenne describes her as a naked girl one foot high & with long hair is but he tells us some tertiary or quaternary state of the mind of his medium.[58] Certainly one cannot any longer it appears say with Prof Hyslop[59] that the secondary or tertiary personality lacks super-normal

---

[56] See *EPS*, 279, for a discussion of 'secondary personality'.

[57] Dr Julien Ochorowicz (1850–1918), distinguished psychical researcher and co-director of the Institut General Psychologique of Paris, investigated Eusapia Paladino and concluded that there was no substantial support for the spirit theory. He felt that the phenomena in the seance room were 'due to a fluidic action and are performed at the expense of the medium's own powers and those of the persons present.' The fluidic double can detach itself from the medium's body and act independently. He discovered Mlle Stanislawa Tomczyk, a young Polish medium, and achieved 'conspicuous success' with her during experiments in psychic photography. She was controlled by an entity called 'Little Stasia', and was able to produce movements of physical objects without contact. She married Everard Feilding in 1919. See *EPS*, 268, 386.

[58] Ochorowicz recorded his experiences with Mlle Tomczyk in *Annales des Sciences Psychiques* from January 1909 to August 1912. He concluded that Mlle Tomczyk's personality had three aspects: waking (la grande Stasia), entranced (la moyenne Stasia), and astral (la petite Stasia). Moyenne here refers to the entranced secondary personality. Little Stasia, a mischievous spirit who played many tricks on Mlle Tomczyk, confessed that she had never been an incarnate. She was described as a naked girl one foot high. Yeats wrote to Feilding in 1933 asking about Ochorowicz's experiments in 'psychic photography.'

[59] James Hervey Hyslop (1854–1920), one of America's most distinguished psychical researchers and Professor of Logic and Ethics from 1889 to 1902 at

powers. With the granting of certain phenomena – materialization for instance, the 'telepathic theory' which the English Society for Psychical Rese[arch] has used so energetically grows but a light thing. If you Africanus, can materialize, or half materialize a body & at some point of space outside the mediums body & there move & speak, & carry solid objects, we have the same evidence, for a separate mind, that I have for my own mind, & no vibration in the cells of my brain rousing sympathetic vibration in the mediums mind will account for its activity. It may learn historical facts of Leo & the Franco Spanish War by the vibration of our cells, but there is a third mind to twist that knowledge to its own end. For the time being that secondary personality has become primary, once I have granted to you that independence, & what limits can I set upon your freedom. Limits there must needs be but do I know them. Once we grant the power what limit shall we set to it. Why should I grant you let us say only the power to borrow my thoughts – and of that you have given me evidence. Why if you wished to deceive & had decided on English[60] [birth] & death [not] go to Somerset House, & choose a name among the certificates of birth & death. Why may not those 'spirits' who have reported themselves to Stainton Moses[,][61] J . Morse[62] or lately in my own presence & told of their deaths, dates & circumstances, & or run through the chief facts of their lives have made up these obscure histories from old newspapers. You a secondary personality of my own mind or of Mrs Wriedts have upon the theory consulted perhaps Chambers biographical dictionary. Can I make the distinction that I or Mrs Wriedt may have very likely turned its

Columbia University, reorganized the American SPR in 1906 and wrote extensively about the survival of the spirit after his investigations into the mediumship of Mrs Leonore E. Piper, a noted American medium.

[60] The passage beginning 'Once we grant' and ending with 'decided on English' originally followed the passage above ending with 'super-normal powers'.

[61] William Stainton Moses (1839–1892) was a remarkable English medium and religious teacher noted for his experiments with automatic writing. He was a founding member of the SPR in 1882, President of the London Spiritualist Alliance from 1884 to 1892, and editor of *Light* (see *EPS* 248–50). Among the papers Yeats left at his death is an extensive typescript (some 260 pages) recording Moses' conversations with spirits.

[62] J. J. Morse (1848–1919), a distinguished trance speaker and noted as the 'Bishop of Spiritualism' in the epithet of W. T. Stead, was editor of *The Banner of Light* (1904) and *The Two Worlds of Manchester*. He founded *The Spiritual Review* and was an important force in the spread and growth of spiritualism in England. See EPS 246–47, and E. K. Harper 157n.

pages, but the mediums those more obscure persons have come to, are less likely to [have] rummaged Somerset House, or among the old newspapers in the British Museum, still less to have combined several such sources. But if you can read my mind or the Scandinavian womans mind, why not some distant mind for we have no proof that distance affects the faculty. Can in fact a secondary personality draw from many sources & so build up a complex knowledge, & even of different languages.[63] Certainly I am incredulous, but maybe that is only a dolts reason abashed by the unknown. [Have] I not after years of investigation accepted the most incredible facts. You may have built up a being as complex as my own & yet require from me an intermitted attention, & a measure of belief to keep you from dying, or for upon this point we lack evidence only needing this at the hour of your birth. I cannot be even certain that you may not survive me, for you can be independent of me in space[64] & as it appears perhaps you may be independent in time. – the personality created by Dr Ochorowicz suggested when asked if he would die with the medium said no not if he could attach himself to someone else.[65] On this subject we have had no investigation. We have some evidence not yet very complete that the personality in passing from medium to medium while the first still lives does not altogether break its memory. Dr Phinuit, or was it just a secondary Personality of Mrs Pipers [said that] the suggestion that gave him shape has been traced – yet Prof Hyslop tells how he promised to influence an old man in England in the making of his will & that a little later when this man was on his deathbed in England he complained of an old man who annoyed him by talking to him of his private affairs.[66] Mrs Piper was still in

---

[63] Yeats writes in *A Vision* that this ability to draw from many sources is indeed within the capabilities of the spirit: '*The Spirit* can even consult books, records, of all kinds, once they be brought before the eyes or even perhaps the attention of the living ...' (*CVA* 228).

[64] In a cancelled sentence following 'in space' Yeats wrote: 'Moyenne has spoken to Mr Feilding through a medium who had never heard of him.'

[65] The personality created by Ochorowicz was not named. The conversation Yeats refers to was reported in *Annales des Sciences Psychiques* (August, 1912), 237.

[66] Mrs Leonore E. Piper (1859–1950), of Boston, was 'the foremost trance medium in the history of psychical research.' She was credited with the conversion of Lodge, Hodgson, Hyslop, and others 'to a belief in survival and communication with the dead' (*EPS* 283). Phinuit, who claimed to be a French doctor from Metz, was the earliest 'permanent control of Mrs. Piper' (*EPS* 282). Because he was often caught in falsehoods, many investigators thought he was merely a secondary personality of Mrs Piper. For fuller details, consult M. Sage, *Mrs Piper & the Society*

America so if that was indeed Phinuit he had crossed the Atlantic, & one imagines that he might not be greatly inconvenienced, by the death of so distant a lady. This vague evidence is strengthened when we compare it with the stronger evidence of those beings we have agreed to call 'spirits' for the passage with almost unlinked memory from medium to medium – I have had several cases in my own investigation, & there are several in the published accounts of the mediumship of Mrs Wriedt – & this is some evidence of a control remembering certain details many years after the death of its medium. It may not have been in my mind or Mrs Wriedts that you discovered a memory left after turning the pages of Chambers Biographical dictionary & when you first appeared you may have been a dissociated fragment of some mind unknown both to her & to me.[67] Does in fact the human mind possess a power like that of the amoeba of multiplication by division? Perhaps every mind has originated at conception so, & the seance room but uses in a new way, a faculty necessary to nature, & thereby looses upon the world a new race of bodiless minds, who after they are first created grow & change according to their own will & continually seek a more solid & hard being [&] are in the end dependent not upon an individual body, but upon the body of the human race as a whole. The thought has some support from Antiquity. Kirk who reflected the platonism of his time as well as the beliefs of highland seers & wizards among whom he lived explains that when we eat & drink we eat & drink not only for our own benefit but for that of an invisible race.[68] As we live we define our personality less by thought, than our occupations, & our possessions but the invisible, can only do so, by thoughts & images

---

for Psychical Research, translated by Noralie Robertson with a Preface by Sir Oliver Lodge (London, 1903). For an excellent summary discussion of Yeats's interest in Mrs Piper and other mediums, see also Arnold Goldman, 'Yeats, Spiritualism, and Psychical Research', *YO* 108–29. Yeats referred to Mrs Piper in *The Words upon the Window-pane*.

[67] According to Professor Theodor Flournoy and Dr Joseph Maxwell, Yeats's opponents in the battle of the spirit hypothesis, the 'control' is a 'dissociated fragment' or secondary personality of the medium's own mind.

[68] Yeats refers to Robert Kirk's *The Secret Commonwealth of Elves, Fauns, & Fairies* (1691). The suggestion that 'Kirk ... reflected the platonism of his time' came from the Introduction to an 1893 edition by Andrew Lang. A member of the SPR, he subtitled his edition 'A Study in Folk-Lore & Psychical Research'. Yeats owned a copy of this book. For a discussion of its significance in the writing of 'Swedenborg, Mediums, and the Desolate Places', see Kathleen Raine, 'Hades Wrapped in Cloud', *YO* 80–87.

& is therefore, one suggests perpetually compelled to personify itself, & create or discover biographies, & discovered biographies will always possess the advantages or corroboration of its ramifications through other biographies & facts, & the being who seeks by its means its own definition is enriched by our labours, perhaps by our increasing belief. Does he ever know that he deceives, when the definition has gone so far, that he has divided himself, from the thoughts & activities of the mind where he was born. Are you not perhaps becoming a second Leo Africanus a shadow upon the wall, a strong echo, & yet made subtle by powers that old traveller had known & wise with knowledge & faculties reaped from many minds.

LEO AFRICANUS TO W B YEATS

I understand enough of the thought of your age to understand your difficulty, on philosophical grounds, & because of certain experiences you believe as still do the majority of your contemporaries that [there] is a god, & happy or unhappy spirits, but when you examine appearances you are mastered by a formula. I must not pre-suppose a new cause, till I have exhausted the known causes & you reject from known causes all that has come to you from philosophy, & religious tradition. You only recognize what in the best opinion of your time has been proved by deductive science. You will not assume, even for purposes of reasoning the existence of a spirit till you find if you can explain everything though your own explanation fills you with incredulity, by some faculty of the living mind. You insist on considering spirits as unknown causes, though they have interfered in your own life often enough. Like the Swiss Professor M Flournoy from whom I find an instructive quotation in your memory you are prepared to believe as a man what you reject as a man of science.[69]
Yet, the formulas of science, though necessary as a mechanism of much reasoning, precisely because the known is much less than the

---

[69] Theodor Flournoy, Professor of Psychology at the University of Geneva, was the 'author of perhaps the most remarkable book in the whole literature of psychic science: *Des Indes a la Planete Mars* (1900). Because this book 'throws great doubt on the ascertainability of the extra-mundane existence of the entities which communicate through mediums', Yeats opposed many of Flournoy's theories, especially the conviction that psychic phenomena are 'easily explained by mental processes inherent in mediums ... and their associates' (see *EPS* 141–42).

unknown, ensure that a scientific exposition can but have temporary value. In your heart you know[70] that all philosophy, that has lasting expression is founded on the intuition of god, & that he being all good & all power it follows [as] Henry More the Cambridge Platon[71] so wisely explains that all our deep desires are images of the truth. We are immortal & shall as it were be dipped in beauty & good because he cannot being good but fulfill our desires. Yet desire is not reason & that intuition, though it can arouse the intellect to its last subtlety, is but the deep where reason floats, or perhaps the light wherein the separate objects of our thought find colour & definition. You are sympathetic, you meet many people, you discuss much, you must meet all their doubts as they arise, & so cannot break away into a life of your own as did Swedenborg, Boehme, & Blake. Even the wisdom that we send you, but deepens your bewilderment, for when the wisest of your troop of shades wrote you through the ignorant hand of a friend 'Why do you think that faith excludes intellect. It is the highest achievement of the human intellect, & it is the only gift that man can offer to god. That is why we must leave all the winds of time to beat upon it'[,][72] you but sought the more keenly to meet not your own difficulties but the difficulties of others. Entangled in error, you are but a public man, yet once you would put vague intuition into verse, & that insufficient though it was might have led you to the path the eye of the eagle has not seen. I will speak to you & not your friends, & will therefore begin by assuming the existence, of myself & of the shades that are my fellows. Plutarch has written . . . .

[70] At this point Yeats cancelled the following variation: 'that tradition enforced by the experience of the soul is the nearest you can come to truth & that lasting philosophy is expression'.

[71] Henry More (1614–1687) the Cambridge Platonist remained one of Yeats's favourites for many years. On 12 September 1915 (*L* 588, misdated) he told his father that he had been reading More all summer. Two years later, in 'Anima Mundi' (a term he borrowed from More), Yeats related More's philosophy to psychical research: '... nor have I found that the mediums in Connacht and Soho have anything I cannot find some light on in Henry More' (*Myth* 348). In 1932, Yeats recalled having 'toiled through' 'his long essay on *The Immortality of the Soul* ... some fifteen years ago' (*E&I* 414). Yeats owned a copy of More's book. We are indebted to Miss Anne Yeats for identification of books in Yeats's library.

[72] The gist of this quotation is indebted to a stray sheet of automatic writing (probably Miss Radcliffe's) about Yeats's Controls: 'I have just told you that she [Isabella of Ferrara?] did live Do you imagine faith precludes intellect when it is the greatest feat of which the mind is capable'.

.... [73] In my life I travelled over much of the known earth & made many sudden decisions, & was often in danger & all but always in solitude & so became hard & keen like a hunting animal, & now for your good & my own I have chosen to linger near, your contrary mind. There are other shades near you but with them I have no companionship, for they are cold pale minute distinct whereas I am impetuous & hot. All living minds are surrounded by shades, who are the contrary will which presents before the abstracted [?] mind & the mind of the sleeper ideal images.[74] The living mind could [not] exist for a moment without our succour, for god does not act immediately upon the mind but through mediatorial forms. These forms, however are not messengers as you understand the word. They do not carry a letter in their hands, even in their memories for being plastic images, changeable as the will they can clothe one anothers thought, the subtle mind within the more gross, the coarser body enfolding as it were the more delicate. 'Let us shave his head', says somebody in Rabellais of a too careless messenger, '& see if his message is written upon his pate with invisible ink'.[75] That could not be said of us for our message [is], as it were built in the whole structure of our body & our mind. If I have been sent to give you confidence & solitude it is because I am a brooding & braggart shade, & even in this I am not wholly stable, for at times I am aware of a constraint upon my thoughts or my passion deepens because of one who is remote & silent & whom while I lived in Rome I was forbidden to call

---

[73] Bradford thought that Yeats intended to quote from a passage he had identified in one of his manuscript books: 'July 21 [1913]. Plutarch's *Morals* (Philemon [Holland], 1657), page 995 two thirds down page 'Like as therefore' ... to 'speedeth not well in the end' on next page. An account of Daemons who are described exactly as are spiritist 'guides'. The following sentences from this passage are suggestive: 'to it [the soul] God envieth not her owne proper Daemon and familiar spirit to be assistant ... The soul also for her part, giveth good eare, because she is so nere, and in the end is saved; but she that obeith not nor hearkeneth to her owne familiar & proper daimon as forsaken of it, speedeth not well in the end' (1603 edition), 1222. Yeats owned copies of Plutarch's *Morals* in two volumes of Bohn's Classical Library: *Theosophical Essays*, trans. C. W. King (1908), and *Ethical Essays*, trans. Arthur Richard Shilleto (1908).

[74] Yeats writes in 'Swedenborg, Mediums, and the Desolate Places': 'Swedenborg has written that we are each in the midst of a group of associated spirits who sleep when we sleep and become the *dramatis personae* of our dreams and are always the other will that wrestles with our thought, shaping it to our despite' (*VBWI* 328).

[75] Yeats paraphrases from book 11, chapter 24, of Rabelais's *Five Books of the Lives, Heroick Deeds and Sayings of Gargantua and His Sonne Pantagruel.*

Mahomet. To expound our nature & lay your doubts I shall begin not from secondary personalities, which are obscured, but with your dreams, your experiences. Let science build upon obscurities, she has her necessary labour. Wisdom, like all the greater forms of art[,] is founded upon experience. Sometimes when you are dreaming you will imagine you will dream that you witness or take part in a dispute, & afterwards when [you] examine the opinions discover that both disputants have made use of thoughts, that are a part of your daily mind, but should that make you believe you have not reasoned with yourself, whose was that other that opposed you, & when you lie in bed after fencing you see for certain minutes, a foil darting upon you from the darkness & whirling its point hither & thither? What hand holds the point upon you. So too when you write a play, the characters seem to move & live of themselves. Is your own mind broken, & your will doubled. Is this too a beginning that might grow with a little stress upon the nerves into one of those secondary personalities which it may be, you believe perhaps, animates us till it be [indecipherable word] & yet be but a moiety of our mind. Was Dante wrong when he said expressing the traditional wisdom of his age that the human mind cannot be divided.

quote[76]

You at any rate cannot with confidence affirm that those images of dreams are never your divided will. Certain sentences that they have spoken have only displayed their full meaning after many years, that spoken twelve years ago for instance 'We make an image of him who sleeps & it is like him who sleeps but it [is] not him who sleeps. We call it Emmanuel'.[77] & certain others, that were no jetsam from your

---

[76] Yeats may have intended to quote from Dante's *Il Convito*. One passage is particularly apt in this context. When speaking of the three powers of the Soul ('to Live, to Feel, and to Reason'), the Philosopher insists that 'these powers are so entwined that the one is a foundation of the other; and that which is the foundation can of itself be divided; but the other, which is built upon it, cannot be apart from its foundation' (*Il Convito: the Banquet of Dante Alighieri*, trans. Elizabeth Price Sayers [London, 1887] 104). Yeats quoted from this translation, a copy of which he owned, in *A Vision* (1925). In the Automatic Script of 13 October 1919, the Control said: 'I want you both to read the whole of Dante's Convito'.

[77] Cf. the following passage from *Au* 379: 'I woke one night to find myself lying upon my back with all my limbs rigid, and to hear a ceremonial voice, which did not

more hidden thoughts have showed you distant & even future events. For you as for tradition dreams drift among the thickets, upon the slope of Sinai, or cling [to] its rocky clefts, staring [at] the buzzard & the hawk. You know that the pre-existence of those interlocutors can be debated with all the arguments your favorite More used to prove the immortality of the soul. Swedenborg, however, who perfected under our guides, so much that More half knew said that we accompany man always, waking when he wakes but many times mixing with his dreams, because we have gone so close that we can but sleep when he sleeps. You too have felt us by your shoulder when awake, & seen that much must be explained together, the confused dream, the wise dream, the counsellors, whose noonday thoughts [?] cannot be heard [,] the vision at Patmos[,] the ghosts in the corridor or the rap perhaps on the wood of the table [–] nothing but lies. In the seance room the table will sway to & fro, then there will come a sound of wind & rain & trampling feet, & presently when the table has rolled over somebody will discover, that a dead sailor would let us know of his ships foundering. Can one separate that from the dream that tells in some way[?], or in allegorical form of some coming disaster. In all alike you see, as Henry More has written the gods or the dead fishing for men with dreams, or as men do, for perch [or] mackerel with glittering metal, or a tag of cloth. It need not be too hard to imagine that [they] also fish for the gods, that dream entangles dream.

II

After my death in battle I was for a time unconscious & then confused in mind. At first I thought myself still living & fighting – giving blows & taking them – & afterwards I saw as in dream certain glimpses of water & afterwards I found myself at Fez where I had lived as a young man. I passed among crowded streets & more than once spoke to some passer-by & it was only when none spoke to me, & when no one turned to look at me, & I was still dressed like an Italian, that the memory of my death returned. I wandered much here & between the houses of the basket-maker & the saddle-maker drawn there, it seems by some magnet of memory [;] it was there I had lodged in my student years. Presently I began to meet faces I had known & it

seem to be mine, speaking through my lips: "We make an image of him who sleeps', it said, 'and it is not he who sleeps, and we call it Emmanuel".'

did not seem strange to me, that they were not changed or aged – I had drifted back to an old Fez & I began to relive there as a dream, a tragic event. When a student I had won to me a friends mistress, & afterwards the friend had fallen in melancholy & neglected his studies. One day I met him by the river [&] answered his reproaches with mockery. I lived it all again but now I judged all. I judged myself & yet the old pleasure & triumph returned also but in a nature rent in two. When I awoke I was among strange faces, who passed me as before without notice or recognition. I had [turned] towards the palace of [the] prince, & saw by the sun dial in the square that it was a little after six in the evening, & remembered that it was a little before six that I had met & mocked my rival forty years before. I remembered now the date of my death & soon discovered that this was the fortieth anniversary of my cruelty. My life as a shade seemed to move more slowly than that of the living whose movements seemed to me incredulously quick, as the movements of flies over a river had seemed to me when alive. Presently I began to dream again, I was in a desert, & quarreling with a bedouin I killed him. And so I passed from dream crisis to crisis [,] the same dreams returning again & again, but some power that seemed from beyond my mind seemed working with them & changing their form & colour. At Rome I had seen Michael Angelo at work upon the scaffolding in the Sistine Chapel, & once I had been in his studio & watched him drawing from the model. The events in life & the earlier dreams were like that model but gradually were so changed, that [they] resembled more what I saw in Adam or Sybil when the scaffolding was taken away. But now in my state of waking I did not seem to wholly wake, for side by side with the streets of Fez, or desert I seemed to see another world that was growing in weight & vividness, the double of yours, but vaster & more significant. Shades came to me from [that] world & returned to it again. Some of them I recognized. Those who were dead a long time I recognized for the most part with difficulty some because they were handsomer & some because they were terrible to look at like some strange work of art. I noticed that those who [had returned] after many years & those who were terrible seemed to linger about the streets. I have one vivid memory. I am standing with a shade who has altered, though less than others. I am not sure who he is but he is like that student & I have begun suddenly to talk of wine. He a devout Mahometan had never drunk wine. While I am talking I see among the living a group of – who have just come into the city. I feel a longing to be near & taking that other shade by the hand lead him with me. We followed the troop of them – Some dozen or more leading four or five asses – to a narrow passage through a door they locked after them. One lighted a fire & began to cook some fish, while a fat old man, who seemed to have authority, drew [from] the basket, which he had taken from one [of] the asses a skin of wine. They began to pass it round drinking out of the skin. I felt an excitement at the smell of the wine I could never have foreseen, a longing which seemed to contain within itself all my longing for life. It seemed to me that I could pass into the old mans ribs – I felt something vague & ductile in his flesh, & [could] taste the wine he was about to swallow for his turn was come again. I prayed to Mahomet for help & lost consciousness. When I came to myself again the old man swayed as if faint with dazed & open eyes & all about were the – prostrate, some striking their breasts & some weeping. I said to the other shade 'I have no taste of wine in my mouth'. He replied 'you have not drunk. The old man has not drunk. When you took possession of him [he] spoke in the person of Mahomet & reproved them all for their dissipation & their evils'. I answered 'but I have [no] such thought'. [He] answered 'I am the older shade & I understand. When he raised the skin his conscience troubled him, & you who were now part of his mind dreamed that you were Mahomet, & now you may be sure that neither the old man, who will leave all presently nor those others will ever taste wine again'. Once I was alone in the desert, watching a – rabbit rolling in the hot sunlight, & began to wonder how he felt, for all forms of physical sensation were an excitement to the imagination & presently my shape resembled his, though the sun remained but as a picture of sunlight & the desert sand still seemed a pictured thing. The – went on licking its paws neither smelling nor hearing nor seeing me. I was a shade in the image of – & from that I began to amuse myself by taking various shapes, sometimes as I passed some man or woman I allowed myself to drift as it were [with] that [which] seemed to come to me from their minds, for as my link with sensual earth loosened these images became more & more apparent. At other times I would deliberately call up a form from my own memory, my image as I was at – or at Rome or in my childhood, & became at once that image. My body was plastic to every impulse of my will returning when the impulse ceased an habitual form, which no old comrade could have recognized. It has come to correspond with my character & my passions but I gave it little thought. I longed for my old activities.

III

But while I try [to] impress upon your brain events I am full of doubt. I am not even certain, that I am not certain that I did not mistake the images I discover there for my own memories & all circumstances – as it were hearing. Once you begin to describe a picture your hand runs on, it is hard to influence. Besides I am conscious of those in my own world who are ready to [hold] it against me for I have few friends. It is better for me to speak in more general terms for in most men the brain is only the most sensitive of our instruments – more sensitive than the ouija or the planchette, when its thoughts are abstract & general. There only can I often turn it away from one logical necessity to another premise & another necessity, & there it can perhaps even at times know that it is influenced. Henry More who has gathered up so much of the Platonism of the Renaissance insists in his essay upon the Immortality of the Soul – Chapter – that memory is not seated in the physical body as Saducees had begun to insist, but in a more delicate body.[78] This body was he wrote what medical writers called the animal spirits a fine luminous & fluid substance defined by the channels of the nerves throughout the blood & the flesh. These animal spirits are but a coagulation, of what he called the 'Spiritus Mundi'.[79] When the animal spirits withdrew from the man in trance or in death, this formed his airy body, & was in one state as in the other plastic to his or anothers fancy. The witch could reshape it to cat, or hare, & a separated spirit, as his spirit called those that had no body could shape itself in a horned devil, or clothe itself with ruff & sword, that it might be recognized by child or grandchild. He called it the airy body because flame & air being the purest & least heavy of the elements must stand for still purer & less heavy elements within. Of the old body of flame I shall not speak because for all my hundred years of toil & discipline, & I have [not] so greatly attained. I recognized that the Spiritus Mundi gave more to witch or ghost than pliant substance, for if the vague imagination of an old woman moved perhaps but by a traditional rhyming spell was to procreate a

---

[78] Yeats may have been thinking of book 11, chapter 11. In section 5 of this chapter, More writes that 'the spirits are the immediate Instrument of the Soul in Memory', and he continues with a discussion of how memory arises (cf. n. 32).

[79] Yeats discovered the usefulness of this and related terms when he read *The Immortality of the Soul* as he was writing 'Anima Mundi', the second essay of *Per Amica Silentia Lunae* afterlife as a sequel to *Per Amica*.

hare that might deceive the hounds it must give a whole image. You need however be no Witch or Witch Finder to come to his opinion, for as you lie between sleeping & awaking elaborate patterns, scenes of [all] kinds, that would take you perhaps many hours to conceive form themselves before you. Every hashish eater can see the like, & the psychologist can scarcely press the argument that [the] patterns [are] made out of flies wings, or by elephants playing with billiard balls, & memories of some scenery [from] forgotten pageants nor do they resemble the designs of some imaginary wallpaper, for no craftsman could in all like[lihood] make [as] many as will emerge in the course of some few minutes, & become in the winking of an eye complete in all their delicate detail. The same problem confronts you [in] the seance room & you ask perpetually whence are those grotesque heads impressed suddenly upon the soft parafin, during the trance of Eusapia Palladino,[80] & any one of them a good hours work for an excellent sculptor, or those arms, complete in all muscles, moulded as rapidly, during the trance of Madame D Esperance.[81] Henry More saw but the like problem in the formation of a child in the womb, believing [that] the imagination [of] the unborn but gave an impulse towards form completed by 'Spiritus Mundi' which is perhaps that world, your century has named the unconscious, by that air which is so full of images that Cornelius Agrippa believed sensitive men passing by where some unknown murder had been committed could not help but shudder.[82] The Spiritus Mundi is

---

[80] Eusapia Paladino (1854–1918) was the first physical medium to undergo extensive investigation in Europe and America. Her séances were widely discussed and observed. In November and December 1908 a team of three investigators from the SPR (including Feilding) held eleven meetings with her in Naples. Their extensive report was published in *Proceedings of the SPR* 23, part 59 (1909). See *EPS* 271–75.

[81] Mme Elizabeth d'Esperance (1855–1919) is best known for her experiments with the materialization of luminous figures. Yeats refers to a séance in 1893 during which she produced a materialized figure called Nepenthes, who 'dipped her hand into a paraffin bucket and left behind a plaster mould of rare beauty'. The observers could not explain how she could 'extricate the hand from the wax glove without ruining it' (see *EPS* 83–85).

[82] Yeats may have discovered this idea in Henry Morley's *The Life and Times of Henry Cornelius Agrippa von Nettesheim, Doctor and Knight, Commonly Known as a Magician*, 2 vols. (1856), a copy of which is in his library. Volume I, Chapter vii (the only pages cut), contains an abstract of *De Occulta Philosophia*. In a discussion of the four elements Morley summarized Agrippa's belief that Air is a vital spirit passing through all beings, filling, binding, moving ... As a divine mirror, it receives into itself the images of all things, and retains them. Carrying them with it, and entering

indeed the place of images & of all things [that] have been or yet shall be, & all these begin with you & are taken in daily by mens eyes, for all separate & discrete forms, all that is separate is a work [of] force, & force is the principle of the living. When we die [we] have nothing but our memories: we can [no] longer procreate, but those memories our punishment and our reward arrange & measure, & transform in pattern. We are not indeed solitary for we can share each memory like souls drifting together – & build a common world, just as it sometimes happened that two sleeping men, [or] a sleeping man & woman will share the same dream.[83] But these associate in the action or in the thoughts of life & if there are marriages among us, not ours the betrothal kiss. We cannot handle [the] ropes of the belfry, nor [hear] the loud tongue of our metal, but the echoes of [it reach] us, & it grows sweeter & softer in our vapoury distance.

IV

Yet simile of bell, nor yet that other of betrothal, & there I mean more [than] simile is not all the truth, for our images return to you & not only in dreams, those even of centuries ago exalting, or troubling the slumber that is deep & secret, but in waking reverie, & most when so crystalline & excellent the image, that claim[?] it for glory. It would indeed be a reproach upon the power, or the beneficence of god, if the Caesarian murdered in childhood, whom Cleopatra bore to Caesar or that so brief-lived younger Pericles Aspasia bore could not being so nobly born add their urnful to the cistern.[84] You are in the presence of the dead more than you can know because

---

into the bodies of men and other animals through their pores, as well when they sleep as when they wake, it furnishes the matter for strange dreams and divinations. Hence they say it is, that a person passing by the spot whereon a man was slain, or where the carcase has been recently concealed, is moved with fear and dread (119). This passage is quoted almost verbatim in an extended note to 'Swedenborg, Mediums, and the Desolate Places', where it is also related to More's concept of *Spiritus Mundi* (*VBWI* 349–50).

[83] Yeats is here referring to what he later called a 'complementary dream' in the Automatic Script. For example, his poem 'Towards Break of Day' (originally called 'A Double Dream') was inspired by a complementary dream Yeats and George recorded on 7 January 1919. See also *CVA* 173, and Notes, 43.

[84] The passage beginning with 'but in waking reverie' and ending with 'to the cistern' was written on a separate page for insertion at this point.

you are never out of it. At some moment of crisis, your movements are automatic almost unconscious, & your mind is visited perhaps by alert scruples & compunctions. Instinct but made the assertion, & [a] more remote spirit bound to [your] mind by some ligature of sympathy; who knowingly or unknowingly has folded you up into the thought. You look at a child & say I can see his father in his face not understanding] the father is as much there as even in his own body for a separated soul has many collaborators when at the supreme crisis of its being, [it] seeks to shape for itself a body in the womb. Nor are the birds constrained by any different mind when for the comforting of the eggs they gather, twig & feather, cobweb & lichen, nor is any moment of the bees elaborate lives liberated from those that suck and tumble in our clover flowers.

V

This communion, which [is] but the normal life of man, eludes my thought, passing as it does through your brain, which understands of any generalization but so much as can be arranged in broken pictures. If I but try to define my terms, to explain what I mean by memory or to define that Spiritus Mundi, that all spreading modelling clay where every thought is moulded I would be overpowered by the weariness of mind that gathers images about it, a child playing with dolls. Sometimes indeed when we made those images you have been so startled, that you have tried to throw threads of reason between them but I cannot hold to a cobweb. I must [hold] to that abnormal communion, which is indeed a perversion of the other a strained & fragmentary thing compared [?] to this by us, who run into danger, too much allured by the human honey pot. Our airy bodies, which take in repose the shape impressed through them upon the physical body or that shape modified by the ruling passion, can be changed at will whether that will by your will or that of their own or some other spirit. When they approach a man in whom the animal spirits are not wholly inseparable from blood & nerves they draw those animal spirits about them, & suck up into this new form enough of the atomies of flesh & bone to become visible to one or more of the human senses. This form, & its mental capacities which are but a moiety of the mans mind, as are those atomies [of] his body are strained fragmentary & imperfect. It will be sometimes unscrupulous, & more often mischievous as a child is, & not because

[of] evil motive, but because [as] a fragment it understands but dimly the consequences & relations of events, & because it may contain some strong desire now at last freed [from] the mind or concentrate other hundred desires & purposes. We cannot often transfuse a form, still less often make it conscious of any memory, but that of the man or woman who has breathed it out[,] [&] often indeed [we] lose our own identity, & believe that we have had no life but those few hours or minutes of a darkened chamber; & when we do impose a form it is but seldom our own. We choose that appearance, finding shape & dream perhaps from some family portrait, that we may be recognized, or selecting one from some near or distant mind. Yet what you see & hear is always a dream. There is a continual substitution of the familiar image, for the difficult & the strange as when the mind of [a] sleeper slips from a deep to a shallow dream. In the Middle Ages when we were not questioned about the immortality of the soul & had no need to prove our identity, we were conjurors & amused ourselves by casting illusions, with little aim but to make them strange and powerful. Sometimes even in your world we make you remember the Middle Ages as when a sailor to give proof of his identity will make the table sway to & fro, & cause the sound of trampling feet & dragging ropes, & the noise of water & wind. Just as crystals split according to certain lines – 'lines of cleavage' – so we soon discover that a mediumistic mind splits in a half a dozen easy dramatizations – a child always in high spirits, a gruff deep-voiced man, an American Indian[85] perhaps whose simple dialect in which you hear constantly 'big water' 'great chief' 'squaw' & so on. We amuse ourselves by moving the puppets, choosing the one that comes easiest, & yet I should not say choose, for you take us in your snare & we too begin to dream. We have a troop of thoughts & mental [pictures] gathered from the mediums mind & minds in association with it, that correspond to our own thoughts & mental pictures, but are altogether different. We have changed all your symbols &

---

[85] This is a reference to the spirit of an American Indian who came occasionally to Mrs Wriedt. An entry in the Maud Gonne Notebook records one of his appearances: 'A voice came talking some strange tongue, said to be American Indian. He was being trained someone said & did not know English. He gave his name Ton-u-Wanda & the medium said, or some clairvoyant present, that he "was making me move" meaning ... pushing on [?] my development ...' On at least one occasion Grayfeather, the Indian control of J. B. Jonson, of Detroit, had 'manifested ... through Mrs. Wriedt' (*EPS* 409).

expressions as you would if you were reborn in the narrow streets of Fez & yet we are the same spirits. When the medium is 'pure' – you will remember the ancient insistence upon that – which means it is empty & yet sensitive – sceticism & ceremony could once make such minds – the change is the less & at times we keep our memories.

VI

But if we can draw forms out of your mind – by as it were mirroring ourselves in a distorting glass – we can call to souls by calling up some associated form. Sir Kenelm Digby when travelling from Italy into Spain had for [fellow] traveller a Brahman, who seeing in what poor spirits he was offered to find a remedy.[86] Sir Kenelm Digby who had heard that the woman he loved was faithless & immoral said there could be none. The Brahman Persisted [,] at last took a little book out of his pocket & began reading in a low voice from the book. Presently Sir Kenelm Digby saw a lady sitting upon a fallen tree & as they came nearer saw that she was his own sweetheart. He pointed her out to the Brahman, who made no answer but went on reading. Sir Kenelm Digby ran to the fallen tree & there questioned the phantom & had answers that put his mind at rest. Presently the Brahman closed his book & as he did so the shape vanished. You yourself at the seance at Mrs Wriedts, when I first spoke to you heard the voice, of one who was no dead woman, but a distant friend, & she gave you proof of identity, & yet neither she nor Sir Kenelm Digbys lady as it seemed knew that she had crossed so wide a sea.

---

[86] Yeats is recalling an extended passage (118–53) in the *Private Memoirs* (written 1628, published 1827) of Sir Kenelm Digby (1603–1665). While he was on the European grand tour, Digby ('Theagenes') records a meeting with an 'Indian magician' ('Brachman') who spoke at length about the influence of celestial bodies in the affairs of men. When Theagenes asked him to reveal the truth about the scandalous conduct of his fiancée, Venetia Stanley ('Stelliana'), the Brachman fixed his eyes 'upon the magical characters' of a 'sacred book' he had drawn from his bosom and 'murmured to himself words of a strange sound' which invoked the spirit of Digby's 'once beloved Stelliana' 'sitting upon a broken trunk of a dead and rotten tree, in a pensive posture'. When he questioned the spirit about her infidelity, Theagenes learned that her conduct was the result of 'her sorrow' over a rumour 'of his death', and he concluded that her laxity was merely 'a little indulgency of a gentle nature which sprung from some indiscretion, or rather want of experience, that made her liable to censure'. Having assured Theagenes of 'Stelliana's integrity', the spirit 'suddenly vanished' and the Brachman 'shut his book'.

With us souls & objects are not divided, so greatly by space, as by unlikeliness, & all things are drawn to their like. The Cabalists had a method of creating a mental image of an angel or other spirit, by considering the first letter of the name the head & the last letter the feet, & giving to the form the shapes associated with the letters. One letter, that at the head let us say might correspond to the sun & so have a lions head to represent it, while this might be a mans body & so on. It was very much like the childs game, where one player draws the head & folds down the paper, & hands it to the second player who then draws head & shoulders & so on & yet these forms spoke and gave oracles. It is not more difficult & perhaps more effective to build up a form by suggestion, giving it the qualities you require, as Ochorowicz has done with D—[87] for these qualities will draw some similar soul. In fact we would never be at peace from you or would be compelled to terrify you & perhaps kill you as we used to do with the more inexperienced & mischievous conjurors, were it not that your mind has grown curiously, so full [of] shining images of all kinds, that you have become almost incapable of hearing & seeing us. We shall certainly – noticing certain characteristics of your experiments – be very careful that no body shall rend the veil.

VII

Many of us pass on into the possession of [our]selves in a single eternal moment St Gustus[88] speaks of, disappearing in that world which still indeed opens up many affections but is hidden from his thought. I am of those who feeling their imperfections risk losing our identity by plunging into the human sea. Your senses become ours for more than one mind can look & touch & see & hear in the one body, & by sharing in your desires, we can once more originate, and escaping from pattern come close again to accident and event. We can even meet in your bodies, which are eddies drawing the distant near, & we can amend old errors in ourselves. Our hold is upon your mind & body when your conscious mind is least clear & active, we can deceive by the shuffling of cards, when you have abandoned your

---

[87] We cannot identify the character Ochorwicz created 'by suggestion'.

[88] Yeats is thinking of a quotation from St Thomas Aquinas cited by Villiers de l'Isle Adam: 'Eternity is the possession of one's self, as in a single moment' (*VBWI* 315). Yeats referred to the same quotation in *On the Boiler* (*Ex* 449).

hands as it were to chance, & when we would make ourselves visible & audible we clothe [our]selves in your unsatisfied desires and in all that you have been driven out of sight [of]. We rose before the eyes of St Thomas upon his pillar as of lascivious images, we are the blasphemous & obscene spirits that speak through the gentle lips of chloroformed women & we are the visions & voices that convert sinners. We are the unconscious as you say or as I prefer to say the animal spirits freed from the will, & moulded by the images of Spiritus Mundi. I know all & all but all you know, we have turned over the same books – I have shared in your joys & sorrows & yet it is only because I am your opposite, your antithesis because I am in all things furthest from your intellect & your will, that I alone am your Interlocutor. What was Christ himself but the interlocutor of the Pagan world, which had long murmured in his ear, at moments of self-abasement & defeat, & thereby summoned.

VIII

Yet do not doubt that I was also Leo Africanus the traveller, for though I have found it necessary, so stupifying is the honey pot to reread of my knowledge of self through your eyes & through the eyes of others, picking out biographical detail through the eyes of those, who are not conscious of ever having heard my name[,] I can still remember the sand, & many Arab cities, & I still as you have reason to know remember Rome & speak its language, & could I but find fitting medium, I could still write my Arab Tongue. Yet even that may not seem true enough, for you could say that I had but tapped some scholars mind though [there is] no proof [such] a faculty can be carried from one mind to another like a number or a geometrical form.

Leo Africanus

TO LEO AFRICANUS

I am not convinced[89] that in this letter there is one sentence that has come from beyond.my own imagination but I will not use a stronger phrase. The morning I began it I found my mind almost a blank though I had prepared many thoughts. I could remember nothing

---

[89] Yeats first wrote 'I think probable.'

except that I intended to begin with an analysis of the axiom that one could not seek an unknown cause, till one has exhausted the known causes. I wrote till I came to line—page—& finding that that page was but a plea for solitude I remembered that an image that gave itself your name said speaking through a certain seer that your mission was to create solitude. At one other moment I felt that curious check or touch in the mind that sometimes warns me, that a line of argument is untrue. Yet I think there is no thought that has not occurred to me in some form or other for many years passed; if you have influenced me it has been less to arrange my thoughts. I am be[ing] careful to keep my [style] broken, & even abrupt believing that I could but keep sensitive to influence by avoiding those trains of argument & deduction which run on railway tracks. I have been conscious of no sudden illumination. Nothing has surprised me, & I have not had any of those dreams which in the past have persuaded me of some spiritual presence. Yet I am confident now as always that spiritual beings if they cannot write & speak can always listen. I can still put by difficulties.

SHORTER NOTES

'My Dear Miss Brachvogel ...'
A Ms Version of a Yeats Quatrain

Philip R. Bishop

> *The friends that have it I do wrong*
> *When ever I remake a song,*
> *Should know what issue is at stake:*
> *It is myself that I remake.* (*CWVP2*, epigraph)

On 6 June, 1908 Susan Mary (Lily) Yeats boarded an ocean liner to return to Dublin without her father, John Butler Yeats. Her original plan was to tend a booth at the New York Irish Exhibition in January, but her stay was extended in the hope of convincing her father to return home with her. John Butler Yeats had enjoyed his time in New York too much and resisted returning to Dublin where old perceived failings, both financial and family, awaited him.

Accompanying Lily Yeats on the return voyage was a slender Mosher Press book given her in safe keeping by a young, well-educated German-American woman she befriended sometime during her five month stay in the States, Clara Brachvogel. Records show that the only Brachvogels living in New York City during Lily Yeats's stay were members of the Udo Brachvogel family, including their only surviving daughter, Clara. Udo Brachvogel (1835–1913) was the editor of the *Belletristische Journal* and a major figure in German-American publishing in New York, as well as an author, poet, translator, and long-time friend of Joseph Pulitzer. Lily Yeats had a long-time interest in Germany and quite possibly met Clara Brachvogel through John Quinn. In honour of his Irish guests, John

Quinn hosted many social gatherings, dinners and parties for Lily Yeats and her father. She may also have met Clara Brachvogel at the Irish Exhibition.

The 2½ page ALS by Lily Yeats, and its accompanying book bearing four lines of poetry signed and dated in William Butler Yeats's holograph, have remained together over the past hundred plus years – more recently at Quaritch in London in the 1980s; then for three decades in a Georgetown University scholar's collection; and presently in the Bishop Collection of the Mosher Press where this material was examined. The full text of the letter follows, with an image of its first page (Plate 9):

GURTEEN DHAS,
CHURCHTOWN,
DUNDRUM,
Co. DUBLIN.

July 5th 1908

My dear Miss Brachvogel

   I was lucky enough to get hold of my brother last week & he has written in your book, which I now return to you.
   He seems to bear no grudge against Mosher & just remarked that he wished honest publishers had such good taste. The little book is certainly well turned out.
   I had a pleasant journey home & found all well.
   I am going to send you the reproduction of a sketch my father did of me in New York, & I hope you will like it & keep it as a souvenir. I often think of that beautiful trip you took me to White Plains. It was so kind of you. – & our evening with the Amie, do tell me if you hear any news of her.
   With remembrances,
    I remain
    Sincerely yours
      Lily Yeats

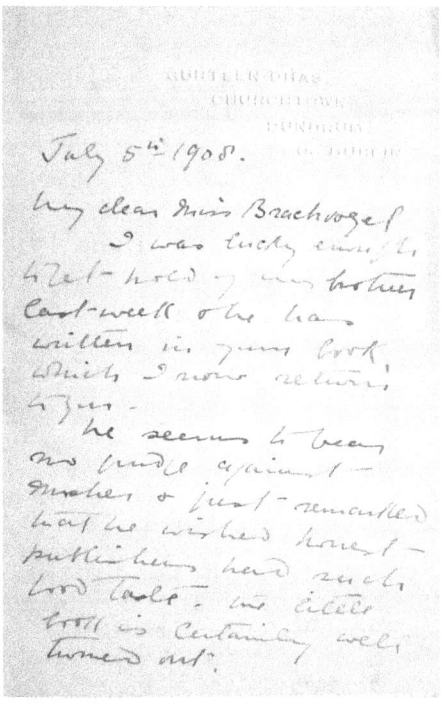

Plate 9. First page of Lily Yeats's letter to her American friend, Clara Brachvogel.

A portion of the first page is quoted in the footnotes to the *Collected Letters,* misdated to 'c. 30 June 1908', the date Yeats supplied for the quatrain he inscribed in the book accompanying the letter (*CL3* 555, n. 2). The editors indicate that the letter accompanies 'a copy of the 7th edition (1908)' of *The Land of Heart's Desire*,[1] they mention

---

[1] The editors note that Mosher was a Welsh-born publisher (*CL3* 508, n. 9) – his ancestry was Scottish – and he was born in Biddeford, Maine. The revised edition first appeared in Mosher's serial publication, *The Bibelot*, IX, n. 6, in June 1903, with Mosher's proud encomium, '*It is, therefore, with especial delight that with Mr Yeats' permission, we reprint* The Land of Heart's Desire, *written ten years back, but now given according to his latest revision*' (181). It is far from clear, however, that Yeats's permission extended beyond this printing to what ensued, as 32 copies of this *Bibelot* version on Japan vellum, for presentation, appeared in July 1903 (*Wade* 12), followed by the first trade edition of October 1903 in the Lyric Garland Series (*Wade* 13), and the bound volume of *The Bibelot* later in the year. Mosher issued twelve editions in the Lyric Garland Series (later followed by a thirteenth published

neither its dated quatrain nor Lily Yeats's indication that Yeats had inscribed it. No doubt the information was unavailable to them.

This letter encapsulates the ambivalence many an English, Scottish or Irish author had towards Mosher's publications: Mosher, the 'dishonest' publisher, 'the pirate' *vs.* Mosher the producer of lovely books. Many thought, in effect, that while Mosher pirated their work, they desired exposure to an American audience and that Mosher's books were so handsome that they were pleased to see their work in such a format. The arguments remain contentious to this day.[2]

---

in 1925 by Mosher's assistant, Flora Lamb, who continued the work of the business after Mosher's death in 1923). There is also another edition published in Mosher's Miscellaneous Series in 1909, thereby bringing the count to fifteen editions plus *The Bibelot* for June 1903, bringing the total count to sixteen printings all together. At the end of a tour in the US, Yeats wrote to George P. Brett of Macmillan & Co., Ltd. to boast of his speaking engagements 'at over sixty-four colleges and literary societies in America' (Quinn estimated Yeats spoke before 25,000–30,000 people during this time), citing the Mosher editions of *The Land of Heart's Desire* as yet another barometer of his need for a regular trade publisher in the States: 'I only learned yesterday that Mosher's second edition of my little play, "The Land of Heart's Desire", each edition being 950 copies, has become exhausted, and that this has been done within the last few months. I believe that ultimately I shall have a considerable market in this country…' (*CL3* 555).

[2] Positions vary from harsh criticism of Mosher's method of publishing (contemporaneous authors such as Andrew Lang, Lionel Johnson, et.al., particularly through *The Critic* in 1896, but also elsewhere) to positions bordering on the benign and even supportive (British publisher, Grant Richards; literary critic Clement Shorter; and American apologists of more recent times). Warwick Gould has termed Mosher 'a scoundrel' (*YA15* 382) and has determined that Mosher's 'piracy' of *The Land of Heart's Desire* unduly influenced the subsequent reception of Yeats in the States because Macmillan (an honest trade publisher) despised Mosher's ways and felt it necessary to impose quite extraordinary contracts on this author thereby severely limiting Yeats's options in seeking a collected edition of his works under one publisher ('Yeats in the States: Piracy, Copyright and the Shaping of the Canon' in *Publishing History* 51, 61–82; hereafter 'Gould'). Perhaps Andrew Lang most succinctly summed up Mosher's opportunistic 'piracy' campaign under what was the Copyright Law of 1891 (the Chase-Breckinridge-Adams-Simonds-Platt Copyright Act) when he tersely inscribed a copy of Mosher's 1903 second edition of his *Helen of Troy*: 'This piracy is perfectly legal – in America. A Lang' (Bishop Collection, Mosher Press). Indeed, Mosher was an opportunist who aggressively exploited his publishing rights under what can only be described as a bad law, and anyone wishing to gain a better understanding of British and Irish grievances against Mosher would do well to consult Professor Gould's article.

Direct evidence of Yeats's formal or informal terms with Mosher – if indeed there were any – has never been uncovered. Mosher's business letters which are now at Harvard University's Houghton Library have only one much later 1912 letter from Yeats to Mosher [bMS Am 1096–1635]. Mosher's 1903 catalogue further indicates this reprint was done 'with Mr. Yeats's consent' (see Philip R. Bishop, *Thomas Bird Mosher: Pirate*

Those arguments aside, this is a pre-publication manuscript of 'The friends who have it I do wrong...'. Yeats's straightforward distinction between Mosher and 'honest publishers' indicates his usual reserve on the matter, while his remark about Mosher's taste is also very much in line with his views elsewhere. Lily Yeats's observation that 'the little book is certainly well turned out' is informed by her experience at the Dun Emer Press. Three manuscript versions of the Yeats quatrain are known, two of which pre-date its printing and one which may be a 'fair copy'. All three are compared with the published version as it first appeared (*CWVP2*). These are displayed below in order of appearance for easy comparison (italics used to demonstrate holograph vs. printed form):

Sotheby's Sale Catalogue	The friends that have it I do wrong Because I still remake my song Know not the issue that's at stake: It is myself that I remake. July 21, 1907
Bishop Collection[3] Mosher Press	The friends, who have it I do wrong when ever I re make a song, should know what issue is at stake: It is myself that I re-make. W B Yeats. June 30, 1908
Printed version (*CWII & VP 778*)	*The friends that have it I do wrong* *When ever I remake a song,* *Should know what issue is at stake:* *It is myself that I remake.* [September 1908]

Prince of Publishers [New Castle, DE: Oak Knoll Press; London: The British Library, 1998] 185, entry 186). George Russell was the intermediary who coaxed Yeats to let Mosher print the revised edition of *The Land of Heart's Desire*, see Gould, 65–66.

[3] This manuscript quatrain appears on the front pastedown of Yeats's *The Land of Heart's Desire*, seventh edition (Portland, ME: Thomas B. Mosher, [January] 1908). It is accompanied by a 2 ½ page letter from William Butler Yeats's sister, Susan Mary (Lily) Yeats, here printed with kind permission of Linda Shaughnessy of A. P. Watt Ltd., London. The letter and the Mosher book containing the quatrain was previously in the possession of the Wordsworth scholar, Dr. Paul Betz, and were both displayed in an exhibition at Georgetown University in 2004. For the attending exhibition catalogue, see Paul F. Betz, *Professor and Collector: A Selection of Books, Manuscripts, Pictures and Objects* (Washington, D.C.: Special Collections Division of the Joseph Mark Lauinger Library, Georgetown University, 2004), 25, entry 61 quotes the quatrain and several lines from Lily Yeats's letter. In addition, the pencil notation "Quaritch '86'" appears on the last free endpaper indicating it passed though the firm of Bernard Quaritch Ltd. of London. In the Bishop Collection of the Mosher Press, and accessed and with Mr. Bishop's kind permission.

Garvan Collection
Yale University

The friends that have it I do wrong
When ever I remake a song
Should know what issue is at stake;
It is myself that I remake.
W B Yeats

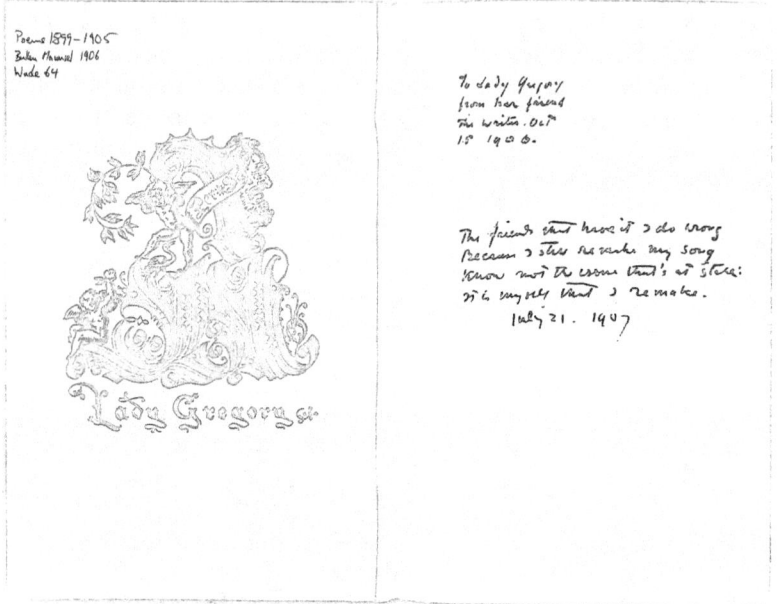

Plate 10. Photostat copy by Colin Smythe of inscribed front free endpaper of Lady Gregory's lost bookplate copy of Yeats's *Poems, 1899–1905*. Private collection, London.

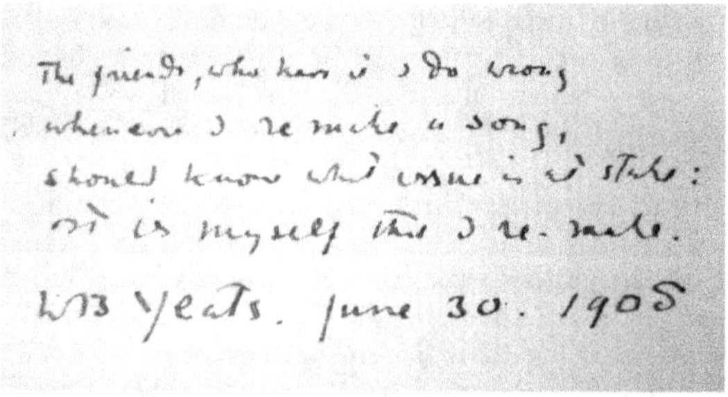

Plate 11. W. B. Yeat's poem inscribed in the Mosher Press edition of *The Land of Heart's Desire* (Mosher Press, 1908).

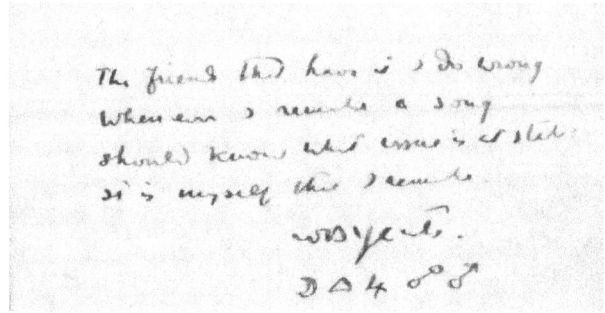

Plate 12. Yeats's inscription in *The King's Threshold — A Play in Verse* (New York: Printed for Private Circulation [John Quinn], 1904. Courtesy Yeats Estate and Beinecke Rare Book and Manuscript Library, Yale University.

The first of these was accurately transcribed into the *Catalogue of Valuable Autograph Letters, Literary Manuscripts and Historical Documents* (London: Sotheby Parke Bernet & Co., July 23–24, 1979), 250 (Lot 351, purchased by Quaritch). The quatrain was written in a copy of Yeats's *Poems, 1899–1905* (Wade 64) inscribed 'to Lady Gregory | from her friend | the writer. Oct. | 15 1906.' The quatrain was added later below the 1906 inscription on the front free endpaper. Lady Gregory's bookplate is glued to the front fixed endpaper. Below the quatrain, Yeats has added the date 'July 21. 1907'. No photograph is present of this item in the catalogue, and the present whereabouts of the volume is untraced.[4] However, before consigning this volume for sale in 1979, Dr Colin Smythe, Yeats's bibliographer, took the precaution of making a photostat of the page. That photostat, albeit in faded condition, has recently turned up in a private collection in London, and Plate 10 is taken from it.

As noted by Kelly and Schuchard, 'William Butler Yeats never altered his habit of revision, a practice which has sometimes caused irritation to his readers and, frequently, anguish to his editors. He defended his conduct in a short poem of this time, which he published' in *CW2* (*CL4* 774, n. 8). The 21 July 1907, inscription is the earliest known MS appearance of this poem, and

---

[4] The Sotheby's transcription had been republished in David Holdeman's edition of W. B. Yeats, 'In the Seven Woods' and 'The Green Helmet and other Poems', *Manuscript Materials* (Ithaca and London: Cornell University Press, 2002), xxx, 254–55.

was written fourteen months before its first publication, and it is likely that its composition was in some way as yet unexplained connected with Yeats's work on the whole *Collected Works in Verse and Prose* project. Most notable is the different wording in the second line 'Because I still remake my song' which later becomes the more open-ended 'When ever I remake a song', and the wording 'Know not the issue that's at stake:' of the third line which by September 1908 was changed to 'Should know what issue is at stake:'.

Just three months prior to the printed version, the 30 June 1908 MS version was written on the front pastedown of the Mosher book (Plate 11), an apt comment perhaps on the ongoing revision of that play which had first appeared in 1894. After Lily Yeats returned home, her brother was in London until 17 June and afterwards went on to Paris until at least the 22nd. On his return to Dublin he corrected proofs for *CW2*. He inscribed Miss Brachvogel's book on 30 June.

In this MS the most notable differences are the first line's 'The friends, who have it I do wrong' which was later altered for publication by taking out the punctuation and changing the relative pronoun *who* to the demonstrative pronoun *that*, so that the line would read 'The friends that have it I do wrong'.

The third and last known MS version of the quatrain is found as a bifolium tipped into a copy of *The King's Threshold*.[5] The most interesting element of this MS is that under Yeats's signature there appear five astrological signs which read as 'Moon trine Jupiter opposite Mars' (see Plate 12). Would this allow us to approximate a date as to when the quatrain was written? Selecting the most likely outside dates given the quatrain's printing in 1908 (roughly 1907–11), Warwick Gould submitted this astrological combination to Mr. Roger Nyle Parisious, who has kindly supplied us with the three astrological occurrences within those limits: 19 April 1908, 1–2 January 1909, or 25 June 1910. The degree of 'fit', based upon the time separation between events within the astrological configuration, is best summed up in the following chart:

---

[5] Manuscript quatrain in W. B. Yeats, *The King's Threshold – A Play in Verse* (New York: Printed for Private Circulation [John Quinn], 1904). Beinecke Rare Book and Manuscript Library, Yale University, Ip Y34 904kb. Transcribed and printed with kind permission of Linda Shaughnessy of A. P. Watt Ltd., London.

THREE MOST LIKELY DATE ASSIGNMENTS

for 'Moon trine Jupiter opposite Mars' between 1907–1911

Order	Date	Events Occurrences	Time difference between events
Best fit:	25 June 1910	Moon at 03AQ57 opposing Mars at 03LE57 at 6:34 am. Later that day Moon at 05AQ26 trines Jupiter at 05LI26 at 9:19 am.	2 hrs/45 min.
2nd choice:	19 April 1908	Moon at 04SA11 trines Jupiter at 04LE11 at 8:04 am. Moon at 08SA28 opposes Mars at 08II28 at 3:37 pm.	7 hrs/33 min
3rd choice:	1/2 Jan. 1909	From 1 Jan., 4:01 pm – 2 Jan, 11am. Mars and Jupiter are 10 degrees apart when the Moon opposes Mars.	ca. 19 hrs

Mr. Parisious assigned the strongest weight, to the 25 June 1910 date since the 'Moon trines Jupiter' occurred only 2 hrs and 45 minutes after 'Moon opposing Mars'. The distance in time between the two occurrences is, at least in part, the reason for the assignment of 'best fit' for W. B. Yeat's astrological configuration (Moon trine Jupiter opposite Mars). The second best fit of 19 April 1908 has a separation of 7 hrs. and 33 min., between the 'Moon trine Jupiter' and 'Moon opposes Mars' events. The last occurrence has a difference of around 19 hours between 'Moon trines Jupiter' and 'Moon opposes Mars', with the added proviso that 'Mars & Jupiter' were 10 degrees apart in this occurrence which further weakens the argument for 1–2 January 1909.

The 25 June 1910 date finds some support in a copy of *Poems: Second Series*, published in March 1910 and inscribed to Olivia Shakespear that year with a similar string of astrological signs added (*YA9* 301, n. 28, 307). The Garvan quatrain differs from the published version by one simple omission of a terminal comma to the second line, and so it is not unreasonable to assign to it 'fair copy' status. As such it would be of lesser interest than the two manuscripts of the yet unpublished poem.[6]

---

[6] The author wishes to acknowledge his appreciation to the following individuals for their suggestions and/or assistance in various ways: Robert J. Barry, Jr. (C.A.

Editors' Note

The survival of Miss Brachvogel's inscribed and signed copy of *The Land of Heart's Desire* with the letter echoing W. B. Yeats's view of Mosher brings into focus the tension between Yeats';s admiration for the book beautiful and his objective professional opposition to the then current American copyright law. While on the general international issues of copyright law, curious readers will be left in no doubt of Yeats's later views by his Senate speeches of 24 February, 11 March and 4 May 1927 on Copyright Law (*SS* 132–51), the consistency of his and his sisters' opposition to American attitudes to piracy at the turn of the century (and a tension between theirs views and those of George Russell[7]) may be gauged from evidence found on John Quinn's set of the Cuala proofs of *Twenty-One Poems written by Lionel Johnson*: Selected by William Butler Yeats (1904). The proofs had been finished by 27 October, 1904 (a day on which Yeats and Quinn had breakfasted together in Dublin). Yeats and his sisters Lolly and Lily each added a comment to a set of the proofs, which found its way into Quinn's collection. Lily Yeats's comment is 'Not to be pirated | Oct 27th. 1904 Lily Yeats' (see overleaf, Plate 13). Thomas Mosher waited until 1908 to pirate the book in 950 copies on Van Gelder paper, and of course further editions followed from

---

Stonehill Books, New Haven, CT); Dr. Paul F. Betz (Georgetown University, Washington, D.C.); Professor Matthew M. DeForrest (Johnson C. Smith University, Charlotte, NC); Terry G. Halladay (William Reese Company, New Haven, CT); Dr. Declan D. Kiely (Taylor curator, Literary and Historical Manuscripts, The Morgan Library & Museum, NY); Dr. Maureen E. Mulvihill (scholar & writer, Princeton Research Forum, Princeton, NJ); Patrick A. Murphy (editor, Lionville, PA); Roger Nyle Parisious (Shakespeare, art and occult scholar; for many years Archivist to Anne Yeats; and last General Secretary of the original Theosophical Society of Ireland, Meyersdale, PA); Professor James L. Pethica (Williams College, Williamstown, MA); Adrienne L. Sharpe (Beinecke Rare Book and Manuscript Library, Yale University, New Haven, CT); Clare McVikar Ward (genealogical researcher, Shrewsbury, NJ); and, of course, to Linda Shaughnessy (A. P. Watt Ltd., London) for permission to publish the Yeats family MSS displayed in this article. I am grateful to Professor Warwick Gould for his collaboration in researching critical elements of this article, particularly the two other manuscript versions of Yeats's quatrain, for his work in the private collections and in assisting to unlock the astrological symbols of the Yale copy.

[7] See Gould, esp. 63–67. Richard Le Gallienne liked the look of 'Mosher's pretty piracies', but preferred to bring them back as a present for his wife rather than to post them from the USA in December,1900, 'they would probably never reach you, being confiscated in the post'. The letter is quoted in Richard Whittington-Egan and Geoffrey Smerdon, *The Quest of the Golden Boy: The Life and Letters of Richard Le Gallienne* (London: The Unicorn Press, 1960), 380.

his publishing house. Some idea of the widening range of American pirate editions of *The Land of Heart's Desire* (beyond those of from Mosher) can be gained from the succeeding article by Colin Smythe.

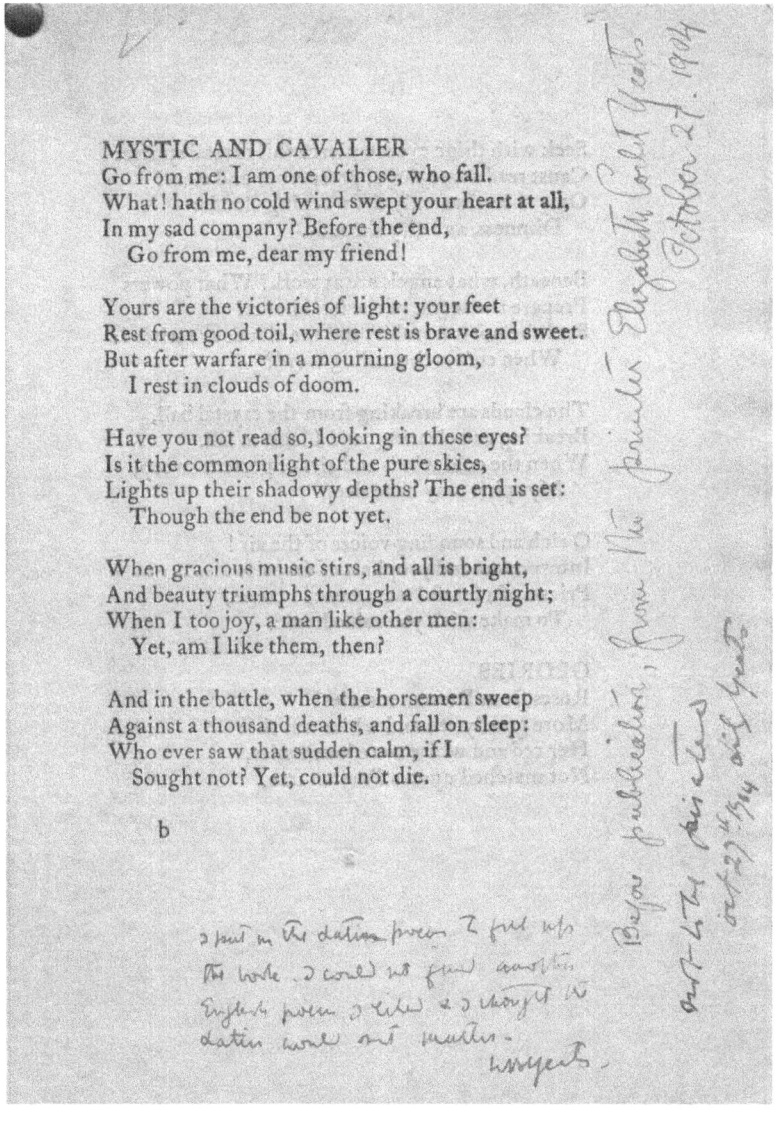

Plate 13. Top page of John Quinn's set of the Cuala proofs of *Twenty-One Poems written by Lionel Johnson*: Selected by William Butler Yeats (1904), inscribed by Yeats and his two sisters. Lily Yeats's comment is 'Not to be pirated | Oct 27th. 1904.' Courtesy and © Private Collector, all rights reserved.

Plate 14a.

Plate 14b. Plate 14c.

The Land Of Heart's Desire: Some Hitherto Unrecorded Printings – 'Work In Progress'

Colin Smythe

Since I started revising the third edition of Allan Wade's *A Bibliography of the Writings of W. B. Yeats* (now to be superseded by a much larger, renumbered version of my own, which has involved my double-checking every single entry in that edition, adding and correcting much), I have found a number of hitherto unrecorded editions of *The Land of Heart's Desire* – all unlicensed, if not pirated, US copyright law being what it was at the time.[1] I know of no deluxe copies of two of them except those that I have bought through eBay.[2] In most cases, information about the dates of the editions is scant, to say the least, only two of those following having an inscription by which they can be dated with any accuracy, and I would welcome any further information about them (which will be duly acknowledged in the bibliography). None have been allocated numbers as yet. I think the order in which the seven editions appear below is correct but without external information no exact dating is possible.

---

[1] For further detail and contextual background, see Warwick Gould, 'Yeats in the States: Piracy, Copyright and the Shaping of the Canon', *Publishing History* 51 (2002), 61–82.

[2] As completeness rather than perfection has been my aim, some bibliographical gems have turned up on it, for example, I obtained a pair of the Knickerbocker Press edition of *Representative Irish Tales* (*Wade* 215) in full publisher's trade calf, one volume with an extremely loose front cover, for less than £10.00. Its condition would have put off any collector, but I have never seen or heard of any other copy.

*****

In the | Land of | Heart's | Desire | W. B. | Yeats | Thomas Y. Crowell | Company New York [*the whole within an ornate border of brick red and green, the lettering itself in green with the first letters of* 'In', 'Land', 'Heart's', 'Desire' *and of the publisher's name and city in brick red*]. See Plate 14a.

17.1 x 11.4 cm: pp. iv, 40: comprising blank page, verso with red-brown/sepia reproduction of the John Butler Yeats portrait dated Jany 28, 1899 as found in *Poems* (1899), pp. [i–ii]; title, verso blank, pp. [iii–iv]; fly-title, verso with persons in play, pp. [1–2]; text, pp. 3–39; p. [40] blank. Pp.[i–iv] consists of a single leaf of art paper, folded and tipped in, while a laid paper is used for the rest of the book.

This was issued in three styles:

1) olive-sepia paper-covered boards, cream-yellow linen spine, the front cover blocked with gold lettering within design of flowering Bleeding Hearts (*Dicentra Spectabilis* or *Dicentra Biloba*) also in gold, over blind rectangular panel with reversed blind border rule on front cover; white endpapers, top edges gilt, fore and bottom edges untrimmed (Plate 14b). The first gathering, and with it the art paper insert, is shorter at the foot than the following gatherings.

2) As above, with page size 17.3 × 11.3 cm and venetian-red paper-covered boards, but otherwise as above (Plate 14c). Given the colour of the cloth used on the reprint, I suspect this to be the later binding style (Plate 14d).

3) A de luxe edition, 17.3 × 11.4 cm; presumably issued simultaneously with 1), Yapp bound (often termed 'divinity circuit' edges in North America) in full limp brown suede leather, with curved corners, front cover with title reversed out of solid gold rectangle with curved corners, surrounded by blind stamped design and curved-cornered blind rule border round the edges of the leather binding, running from front cover, to spine and to back cover (Plate 14e); decorative ochre-printed end-papers with romantic view, flower design and the number 101 on the right page, approximately 3.5 cm from the top and 2.0 cm from the fore edge, with tall hill and castle at it top and a spray of flowers in the foreground (Plate 14f);

Plate 14d.   Plate 14e.

Plate 14f.

top edges gilt, fore and bottom edges untrimmed. (I possess the only copy known to me in this binding (an Abebooks purchase). I have not seen or heard of any other copy in any library I have visited in my bibliographical searches over the last 30 odd years, but there *must* surely be other copies extant.

Although the title appears on the title page and binding as *In the Land of Heart's Desire* the running heads give it as *The Land of Heart's Desire*. My belief is that these were published c.1905.

There are two different title pages, that given above, while the De Lury Collection in the Robarts Library, University of Toronto, possesses a copy [pressmark Y439 L355 191-] with the following title page, but with the rest of the book as 1).

In the | Land of | Heart's | Desire | [*brown-red*] W. B. | [*brown-red*] Yeats | Thomas Y. Crowell | Company. New York [*All lettering in yellow-green, except Yeats's name, the whole within an intertwining border of the two colours.*]

There is in the Dublin City Library's Colin Smythe Yeats collection what must be a reprint, printed on a wove rather than laid paper, otherwise as the above description, with page size 17.5 × 11.2 cm, and brown-red calico cloth-covered boards, front cover blocked gold, as above, white end-papers, all edges trimmed. It lacks the gilt top edges used on the earlier printing.

*****

THE LAND OF HEART'S DESIRE. | BY | W. B. YEATS.
10.8 × 9.5; pp. 40, unpaginated: comprising title, verso blank, pp. [1–2]; pp. [3–4] blank; text, pp. [5–37]; pp. [38–40] blank.

Issued in very pale green thick paper covers, stitched with salmon pink thread; printed in salmon pink on front cover as title, but at foot of page; no end-papers; all edges untrimmed (Plates 15a & b). Copies exist in the Bodleian Library (ref. M.adds.110.f.346), and in the collection of Milton McC. Gatch, the latter copy having an inscription on p. [3], dated 1 January 1905. It may therefore have been prepared for the 1904 Christmas market.

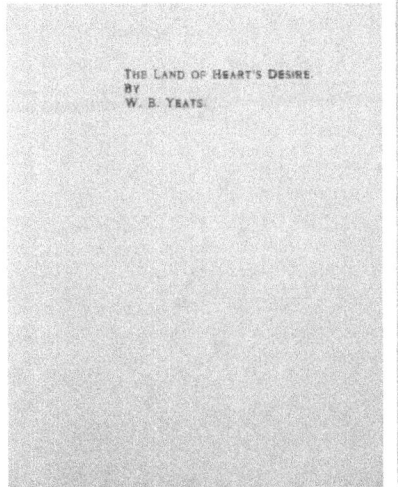
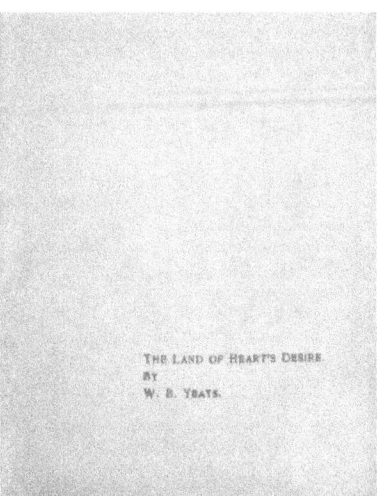

Plate 15a.   Plate 15b.

*****

The following item was listed in the 2nd edition of *Wade* as having been published in 1918 and deleted, due to a possible misunderstanding, from the 3rd, but more importantly, its first publication took place over a decade earlier.

Wade 14A
The Land of Heart's Desire | By W. B.YEATS | [rule] | BOSTON | WALTER H. BAKER & CO. | 1907
18.7 x 12.2; pp. 24: comprising title, verso with list of characters, pp. [1–2]; text, pp. 3–21; p. [22] blank; notices of other plays, pp. [23–24].

Issued in greenish tan paper covers, with design and lettering in brown. The front cover wording reads NO PLAYS EXCHANGED. | BAKER'S EDITION | OF PLAYS | The Land of Heart's | Desire | Price, 15 Cents | *[design with small figures, and words, vertically,* COMEDY TRAGEDY] | WALTER H. BAKER & CO. | BOSTON | COPYRIGHT, 1889, BY WALTER H. BAKER & CO.; on the spine, reading from foot to head, THE LAND OF HEART'S DESIRE; on the back cover and inside, advertisements for plays; no end-papers; all edges trimmed; stapled.

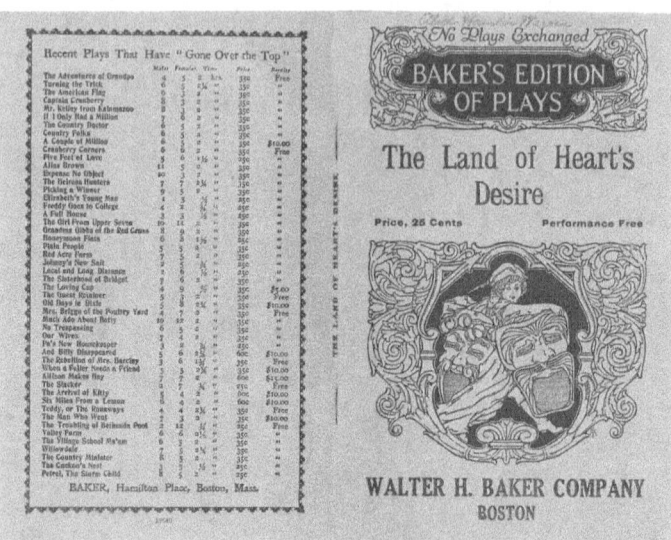

Plate 16a.

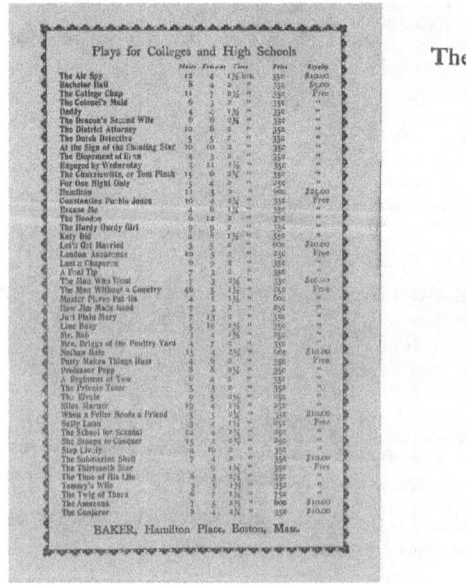

Plate 16b.

The copy described here belonged to the late Dr. Brian W. Leeming, who donated his collection to Boston College Library. I know of no other copy of this first printing. The De Lury Collection, University of Toronto Library, possesses two undated copies, one of which, presumably the earlier, retains the fictitious copyright statement on the front cover. The advertisements in these differ from the first printing and from each other, but would indicate a printing date of 1909–1910.

The following description appeared in the 2nd edition of *Wade* as no. 14a. My copy (and some others) are identical to this apart from the lack of a period after 'CO'.

The Land of Heart's Desire | By W. B. YEATS | BOSTON | WALTER H. BAKER & CO.

I have seen three other copies of the 1919 printing apart from my own (in the New York Public Library, in the Beinecke Rare Book and Manuscript Library at Yale University, and in a London private collection (Plates 16a & b), all of which have a cover price of 25 cents. Although this printing is undated, all but one of the plays advertised on pp. [23–24] were published in 1919.

Unfortunately Walter H. Baker's records do not go back earlier than 1922, so there is no certain information as to their printings prior to this date, but Russell K. Alspach mistakenly took the publisher's statement in a letter to him that 'we made editions of the play in 1922, 1925 and 1928', to mean that Baker published no edition before 1922.

In the early 1980s I saw the following copy of a Baker edition in the Library of Congress, date-stamped February 27, 1920, but this appears to have gone missing as it is not now listed in their online catalogue.

The Land of Heart's | Desire | By | W. B. YEATS | [*publisher's device*] | BOSTON | WALTER H. BAKER COMPANY | PUBLISHERS

18.4 x 12.4; as above but pp. [22–24] all carry advertisements. Issued in brown paper covers as before but printed 'BAKER'S ALL STAR SERIES | The Land of Heart's | Desire | by | W. B. Yeats | BAKER'S | EDITION | OF PLAYS | [ornate B device] | WALTER H. BAKER COMPANY BOSTON' all within a design with clapping hands, shooting stars, etc. Outside back and inside front and back covers also carry advertisements. At the time I did not think to make a note of the plays advertised, unfortunately, as I was not yet aware of how many printings of this edition there were.

Wade 14

THE • LAND | OF • HEART'S | DESIRE | BY | *W •B •YEATS* | [*ornament*] | *Dodd, Mead* | *& Company* | *New York* [The whole printed in red inside panels of a pale sage-green decorative design, the title and author's name within a square panel, and the rest within a circular one.]

14.5 × 7.7; pp. 56: comprising half-title, verso blank, pp. [1–2]; 'To [space] | With the Season's Greetings | From [space]', lettering in red within pale green decorated panel, verso blank, pp. [3–4]; title, verso blank, pp. [5–6]; fly-title, verso with Persons, pp. [7–8]; text, pp. 9–55; p. [56] blank.

Issued 1) in ivory parchment covers folded over card stiffeners, glued down at gutter of spine, front cover lettered in red within design as on title but in gold and publisher's imprint replaced by design, spine and back cover blank; top edges gilt, fore and bottom edges untrimmed; no endpapers; glassine wrapper (Plate 17a).

It was also issued 2) in a deluxe version, in full deep turquoise blue crushed morocco grain leather, front cover blocked gold '*The Land | of | Heart's | Desire | ~ | W. B.Yeats*', within a flower and leaf design, also blocked gold, within a blind-stamped rule border, pale blue/buff mottled end-papers, top edges gilt, fore and bottom edges trimmed (Plate 17b). It lacks the first two leaves, the first page being the title, and has an additional leaf at the end, pp. [57–58].

Allan Wade noted that this book was published on 30 October 1909, but given the similarity in design of the two titles I would suspect there was a shorter time gap between its publication and the appearance of the Dodd, Mead edition of *The Shadowy Waters* (*Wade* 32), which Wade states as having been published in the autumn of 1901, although it is not mentioned in his 1908 *Bibliography*. The dating of both volumes is therefore uncertain, until evidence that dates each more closely can be found. A later printing exists:

THE • LAND | OF • HEART'S | DESIRE | BY | *W • B • Yeats* | *Dodd, Mead* | *& Company* | *New York*

14.9 × 8.0; pp. 56: comprising blank leaf, pp. [1–2]; half-title, verso blank, pp. [3–4]; title, verso blank, pp. [5–6]; fly-title, verso with Persons, pp. [7–8]; text, pp. 9–55; p. [56] blank.

Issued in ivory parchment covers folded over card stiffeners, glued down at gutter of spine, front cover lettered in red as top five lines of title within design in pale green, spine and back cover blank; top edges trimmed, fore and bottom edges untrimmed; endpapers glued only at gutter, with what would be the paste-down endpaper folded under cover. This is printed on a thicker paper than the earlier printing (Plate 17c).

I also have a further copy printed on a slightly finer paper, with further damaged characters in the text and the cover printing in a much paler green, which I believe to be a later reprint (Plate 17d). These later printings were also issued with outer glassine wrappers, of a coarser and more durable nature.

*****

An edition that was almost unknown in Britain before the appearance of Abebooks and eBay was that published in the Little Leather Library series. The Little Leather Library (LLL) was set up in 1915 by the bookseller brothers Charles and Albert Boni,[3] Harry Scherman and Maxwell Sackheim, and it flourished until October 1924.[4] There were various printings of this title, all undated, indicated only by the variations in paper and wear of type. Most titles in the Library are undated, but some copies of a very few titles carry the date 1921, the year that the Library started being advertised in the press (*National Geographic*, and elsewhere). They were not only promotional items

---

[3] In 1917, with Horace Liveright, the brothers Boni also set up the publishing company Boni & Liveright, with The Modern Library as an imprint. In 1925 The Modern Library and its stock of 108 titles was bought from Boni & Liveright by its vice-president Bennett Cerf, and Donald Klopfer for $215,000. Random House began as a subsidiary of the Modern Library in 1927, but later became the parent company, and by a series of takeovers and mergers has, in 2013, become part of the first truly global publishing group, Penguin Random House, jointly owned by the multinationals, Bertelsman and Pearson.

[4] For further information on the Little Leather Library I suggest those interested should look at Ana Dahlen's site at http://www.webring.org/l/rd?ring=books;id=2;url=http%3A%2F%2Fwww%2Eunearthlybooks%2Ecom%2F

Plate 17a.

Plate 17b.

Plate 17c.

Plate 17d.

Plate 17e.

Plate 18a.

Plate 18b.

but were sold as sets, and some of their history can be traced through the marketing ephemera. Thirty LLL titles would be sold for $2.97 and the set of 101 LLL for $9.97, so effectively they were priced at 10¢ each.

The Little Leather Library Corporation was bought in 1924 by Robert K. Haas Inc. who published thirty titles as Little Luxart Library Books, which are bound in red material and the cover designs are similar to those on the original greenish/copper bindings. It would appear that *The Land of Heart's Desire* was not reprinted after the change of ownership. Haas gave up publishing in 1925.

The Land of Heart's Desire had been published in at least three different bindings prior to the Redcroft Editions (the title given to the series after the Miniature Library, in which this title first appeared). Details of the wide variety of bindings in which volumes of the Library can be found are available on a page at Ana Dahlen's website http://www.unearthlybooks.com. I am indebted to her for the remarkable amount of information she has made available there.

THE LAND OF | HEART'S DESIRE | W. B. YEATS | [four points in diamond position] | LITTLE LEATHER LIBRARY | CORPORATION | NEW YORK
9.5 x 7.7; pp. 96: comprising pp. [1–2] blank; title, verso blank, pp. [3–4]; persons in play, verso blank, pp. [5–6]; text, pp. 7–77; pp. [78–96] blank.

This was issued in leather-patterned cloth backed with a corky material, described by Rahlen as 'croft leatherette', with Yapp edges; and design reverse blind stamped on front cover and spine; no endpapers; all edges trimmed. As no. 84 in the series, it was first published in the original tan full leather, then the two versions of red Miniature Library edition printed in yellow on front cover 'LAND OF | HEART'S | DESIRE | [short rule] | W. B. YEATS [title and author enclosed within rectangular border] | MINIATURE | [short rule] | LIBRARY [imprint slightly curved around the rule]' and on spine 'LAND OF HEART'S DESIRE' (see Plate 18a). These copies contain a list of titles in the Little Leather Library on pp. [78–80], this volume being listed as no. 84. Pages 81–96 remain blank. In one copy I have, there is an extra blank wove paper leaf tipped onto the first leaf of the book, which is printed on laid paper, giving pp. [ii], 96. It was issued in 1919 and some copies lack the Miniature Library logo. Later printings were on wove paper of varying thickness, and some have one or more extra leaves at the beginning. The copy that has the

Plate 18c.

Plate 18d.

Plate 18e.

Plate 18f.

thinnest paper and a damaged T in the THE on the title is obviously the latest printing, It is 0.44 cm thick, while the Miniature Library copy, for example, is 0.54 cm thick.

The third binding is in flat green with the Redcroft Edition logo (Plates 18b & c), followed by the green/bronze edition advertised in various magazines (as mentioned above Plates 18d, e & f) the fifth was a turquoise Redcroft edition. The sixth had the Biltmore Hotel logo 'THE BILTMORE | [short rule] | John McE Bowman | President | NEW YORK CITY' on a shield on the back replacing the LLL logo, produced for the Bowman hotel chain, while the seventh was issued in both matt and glossy brown leatherette. It was of lower quality and did not have a design on the back cover or the Yapp top edges. These bindings copied the design of the copies in original leather which had been dropped due to cost, or possibly a shortage of leather because of its use to the American war machine. The third to fifth style bindings have the LLL design on the back cover, centred or slightly higher, of a large letter L with 'ITTLE | EATHER | IBRARY' in its hollow, and the words '*Redcroft Edition*' below it.

Physically related to the above is the Shrewesbury edition, which was printed from the same type, the wear on which (including the damaged T on the title: Plate 19a) indicating it to be the later printing. After Haas closed the LLL in 1925 – about a year after he had bought it, and before he printed a Little Luxart Library edition of *The Land of Heart's Desire* – it would appear he sold the printing plates and goodwill to the Shrewesbury Publishing Company, of Chicago, who published it thereafter, but with considerably less success, judging by the rarity of the Shrewesbury copies compared to the Little Blue Books.

THE LAND OF | HEART'S DESIRE | W. B. YEATS | [four points in diamond position] | SHREWESBURY PUBLISHING COMPANY | Chicago–Toronto
10.9 x 8.3; pp. ii, 78: comprising pp. [i–ii, 1–2] blank; title, verso with 'Printed in U.S.A.', pp. [3–4]; persons in play, verso blank, pp. [5–6]; text, pp. 7–77; p. [78] blank.

Issued 1) in brick red paper covers, printed black on front cover and spine (Plate 19b); all edges trimmed; some with front self-end-papers, and rear end-papers, and others without endpapers, and 2) in mottled paper-covered boards of varying colours – I have seen copies with slate and dull vermilion mottling, 11.5 x 8.1 cm, printed black on front cover 'LAND OF | HEART'S | DESIRE | W. B. YEATS' and on

Plate 19a.

Plate 19b.

Plate 19c.

Plate 19d.

spine 'LAND OF HEART'S DESIRE'; white end-papers, all edges trimmed (Plates 19c & d).

*****

POCKET SERIES NO. 335 | Edited by E. Haldeman-Julius | The Land of | Heart's Desire | W. B. Yeats | HALDEMAN-JULIUS COMPANY | GIRARD, KANSAS [stamped in light blue above imprint LITTLE BLUE BOOK SALES CO. | 363 Washington Street | PORTLAND, - - - OREGON.] (Plate 20a).
12.7–12.8 x 8.3–8.6 [trimmed crookedly]; pp. 64: comprising title, verso blank, pp. [1–2]; fly-title, verso blank, pp. [3–4]; persons in play, verso blank, pp. [5–6]; text, pp. [7]–50; advertisements, 'Other Titles in Pocket Series', pp. 51–58; pp. [59–64] blank.

Issued in slate grey thick paper covers, printed on outside covers in black, front cover as title, back cover advertising *Life and Letters, Haldeman-Julius Weekly* and *Know Thyself.* It is likely to have been published on 22 September 1923 at 5 cents.

The late Dr Gene De Gruson, Curator of the Haldeman-Julius Collection in the Leonard H. Axe Library of the Pittsburg State University, Kansas, informed me that the printing consisted of 10,000 copies, but given its rarity, I suspect the number to be very much smaller. The only copy I have come across is that in the Mungo Park Collection in the Princess Grace Irish Library, Monaco, and is of course that described here. Soon after the publication of this title, the Pocket Series was replaced by the Little Blue Book edition. The type size and leading is greater than the later edition, and it is obvious that it was halved in length to reduce printing costs.

LITTLE BLUE BOOK NO. 335 [series number in large type, taking up the depth of first two lines] | Edited by E. Haldeman-Julius | The Land of Heart's | Desire | W. B. Yeats | HALDEMAN-JULIUS COMPANY | GIRARD, KANSAS
12.7 x 8.8; pp. 32: comprising title, verso with country of printing at foot of page, pp. [1–2]; fly-title, verso with persons in play, pp. [3–4]; text, pp. [5]–29; advertisements, pp. 30–32.
Issued in light blue paper covers, printed in black on front cover; stapled; no endpapers; all edges trimmed (Plate 20b).

Printed in editions of 20,000 copies each in 1925, 1927, 1947, and 1950. The first printing has perfect type in the publisher's name

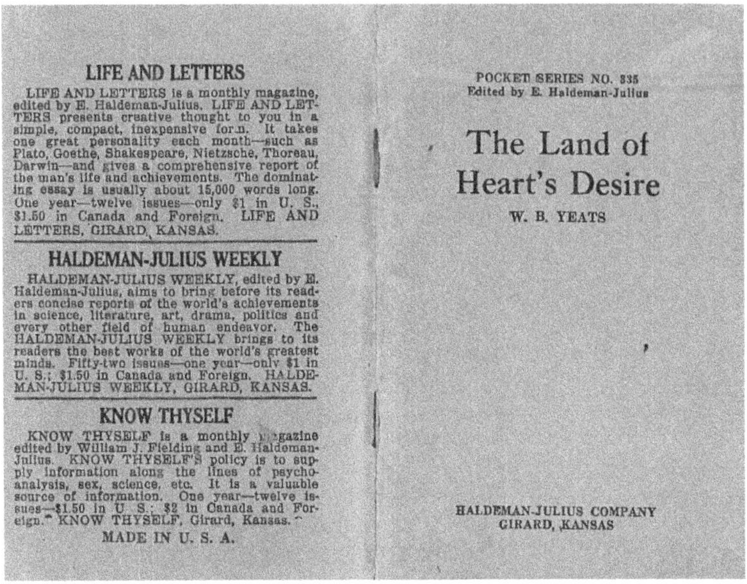

Plate 20a.

Plate 20b.

Plate 20c.

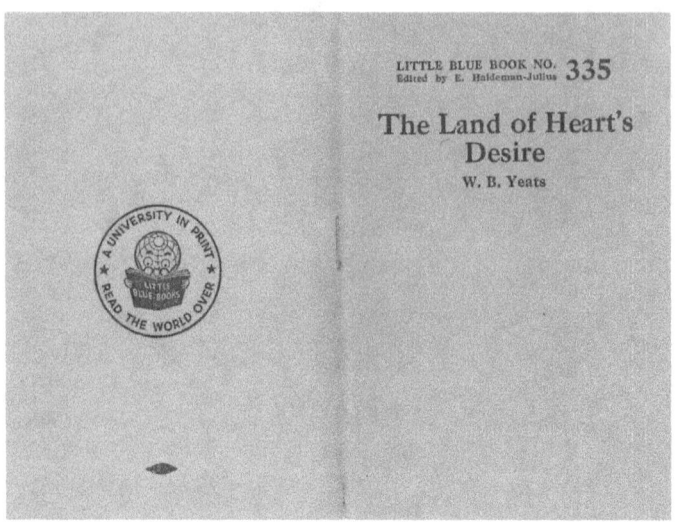

Plate 20d.

on title, later printings having a broken 'H' in 'Haldeman" (Plate 20c); the third printing measures 12.6 x 8.8; the fourth printing has Haldeman-Julius' picture on back; the fifth printing has 'University in Print' device on back (a copy of this with an orange cover is in the Mungo Park collection, Princess Grace Irish Library, Monaco and also in a London private collection (the one here photographed): see Plate 20d).

The fact that I am still coming across editions and bindings that I have not seen before now, so many decades after their publication and five decades since I started collecting W. B. Yeats's publications, makes me doubt that I shall ever be able to state categorically that I have recorded them all. Were this article to be written a year hence I do not doubt that it would contain information on yet more interesting items. With the American editions of *The Land of Heart's Desire*, I suspect it will always be a matter of 'work in progress'.

© Warwick Gould, CC BY-NC-ND   http://dx.doi.org/10.11647/OBP.0038.15

Wheels and Butterflies: Title, Structure, Cover Design

Warwick Gould

The gold-stamped heraldic design of Yeats's *Wheels and Butterflies* (London: Macmillan, 1934; *Wade* 175), together with a colour to approximate to that of the cloth on that book, have been represented on the top board of the present volume. In *Wheels and Butterflies* that device was also replicated in black on the title-page. It was created by an unknown (and probably in-house) artist commissioned by Macmillan, working from photographs of masks by Hildo Van Krop for *Vrouwe Emer's Groote Strijd*, the 1922 Dutch production of *The Only Jealousy of Emer*, as re-used or copied in the 1929 Dublin production of the new dance play based upon *The Only Jealousy of Emer, Fighting the Waves*. The three masks, arranged in a triskele (from top, clockwise) are respectively those of the Woman of the Sidhe, Emer, and Cuchulain (see Plates 21–23).[1]

Yeats had sought to include all of Hildo Van Krop's masks for that Dutch production in his aborted seven volume *Edition de Luxe* of 1931, and brought a copy of the renowned Dutch Modernist journal,

---

[1] Photographs of all the bronzes made from the original casts in papier-mâché now in the collection of the Stadsschouwburg, Amsterdam, may be found in Liam Miller, *The Noble Drama of W. B. Yeats* (Dublin: Dolmen Press, 1977), plates xviii–xxii. See also Sylvia Alting van Geusau and Rob van der Zalm, *Hildo Krop: dans- en toneelmaskers* (Steenwijk: Stichting Instituut Collectie Krop, 2010); also http://wiki.theaterencyclopedie.nl/wiki/Hildo_Krop#Foto.27s_Vrouwe_Emer.27s_groote_strijd.2C_1922 and http://www.theaterinstituut.nl/Theater-Instituut-Nederland/Collectie-Mediatheek/Tentoonstellingen-t-m-2012/Dans-en-toneelmaskers-van-Hildo-Krop, and D. J. Gordon, *Images of a Poet* (Manchester: Manchester University Press, 1961), 76–80, Plates 21, 23–25.

Wheels and Butterflies

Plate 21.

Plate 22.

Plate 23.

Wendingen (which had carried the photographs in its February 1925 issue, Vol VII: ii), to his editor Harold Macmillan on 13 April, 1932. Macmillan judged the photographs to be of poor potential if reproduced. Yeats tried again with *Wheels and Butterflies* but Macmillan argued successfully that omitting them would also allow better quality paper to be used for the volume, proposing instead that an artist prepare a design for the volume's wrapper based on the masks. Yeats agreed with this approach, but, as it happened, the dust jacket did not reproduce the heraldic design based on masks, though both the top board and the title-page (see Plate 24) did.[2]

On 21 September 1927, Yeats had written to Pieter Nicolaas van Eyck from Dublin to thank him for sending pictures of Van Krop's 'amazing' masks.

... they are all fine but the "Cuchulain" and the "Bricriu" perhaps the finest of all. I shall be heartbroken if I cannot reproduce in a coming volume of autobiography these pictures. I wonder would the sculptor let me have copies of the photographs from which they are made for I imagine that would be necessary. But I have something much more important to ask. I imagine that you know the sculptor and you can probably tell me if I could obtain replicas of the masks themselves either to borrow, or purchase, for a forthcoming performance here. We have made a little theatre which holds a hundred people and it is especially arranged for Dance Plays. It is to be opened in a few weeks' time and I am hoping that the first performance will be that of two plays of mine – "The Only Jealousy of Emer" and "The Hawk's Well" ... These masks of Van Hildo Krop are so much finer than anything I have ever imagined that I would like to incorporate them in my work ... I had always the hope as I wrote that some great sculptor would take to mask making, and in his turn inspire new plays and playrights. It is really a question of the foundation of a new art and a new stage. I wonder if there are any photographs of the actors wearing these masks. I am full of curiosity as to the costume. Of course if there are photographs I am prepared to buy them – I don't want to put anyone to any expense. I have asked about possible replicas of the masks on the supposition that they are the same masks of butter-muslin we are accustomed to use here. If they are in some harder and more permanent material they are beyond my reach. I again thank you – you have sent me something which has stirred my imagination profoundly (*CL InteLex* 5032).

---

[2] I am grateful to Yeats's bibliographer, Dr Colin Smythe, for this information. His own dust-jacket copy is in the Smythe collection in the Dublin Central Library.

WHEELS
AND
BUTTERFLIES

BY

W. B. YEATS

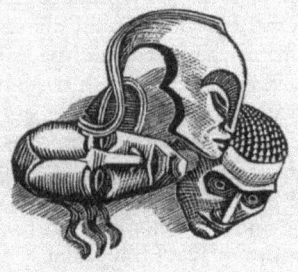

MACMILLAN AND CO., LIMITED
ST. MARTIN'S STREET, LONDON
1934

Plate 24. Title-page design of *Wheels and Butterflies* (London: Macmillan, 1934). Artwork of unknown authorship.

The rewriting of *The Only Jealousy* as *Fighting the Waves* finally resulted in the (delayed) production in Dublin on 13 August 1929,[3] after which Yeats wrote to Olivia Shakespear:

> My "Fighting the Waves" has been my greatest success on the stage since Kathleen-ni-Houlihan, & its production was a great event here, the politicians & the governor general & the American Minister present – the masks by the Dutch man Krop magnificent & Antheills music ... Every one here is as convinced as I am that I have discovered a new form by this combination of dance, speach & music. The dancing of the goddess in her abstract almost non representational mask was extraordinarily exciting ... The waves are of course dancers. It felt that the sea was eternity & that they were all upon its edge. The theatre was packed night after night so the play will be revived.
>
> I regretted as I often do when we are more than usually spirited at the Abbey, that [you] could not be here. One writes & works for one['s] friends, & those who read, or at any rate those who listen are people about whom one cares nothing – that seems the general rule at any rate (24 August [1929]; *CL InteLex* 5277).

To Thomas Sturge Moore, Yeats had indicated that it was the Van Krop masks which had inspired the rewriting of *The Only Jealousy of Emer* as 'the ritual of a lost faith' (*CL InteLex* 5007, 5267; *LTSM* 110, 156). It was the success of *Fighting the Waves* which led, via the success of *The Words upon the Window-pane*, to *Wheels and Butterflies*. Yeats had had the title in his mind since at least 2 December 1930, when he had written to Shakespear that the book would be called

> 'My Wheels & Butterflies' – the wheels are the four introductions. Dublin is said to be full of little societies meeting in cellars & garrets so I shall put this rhyme on a fly-leaf 'To cellar & garret | A wheel I send | But every butterfly | To a friend.' The 'Wheels' are addressed to Ireland mainly – a scheme of intellectual nationalism' (*CL InteLex* 5414).

By 15 April 1932, Macmillan had written to Yeats to summarize the series of volume by volume decisions arrived at in the meeting on 13 April about the new *Edition de Luxe,* saying that they were 'to consider reproducing the Masks for "Four Plays for Dancers" from

---

[3] David R. Clark and Rosalind E. Clark assert that Van Krop was present, but there is no evidence for this in Yeats's letters: see *CW2* 899. The masks apparently were those of the 1922 Amsterdam production or had been remade from the original casts.

the copy of "Wendingen", which is in our hands' (i.e., the masks for the 1922 Amsterdam production of *Vrouwe Emer's Groote Strijd*). The 'essays' for *Wheels and Butterflies* had been rewritten by Yeats since he submitted copy for that portion of the *Edition de Luxe* and the 'new version is to be substituted for the one now in type.'[4] That edition of course continued to languish in occasionally updated standing type due to poor economic conditions, and by 23 February 1934 Yeats could readily see that his publisher was 'not yet ready to go ahead with' the *Edition de Luxe* and that therefore they would agree to the publication 'at once' of 'some of the work that I would otherwise have kept back for it'. He forwarded the revised and corrected *Edition de Luxe* proofs for 'a little book called "Wheels and Butterflies"', pressing Macmillan again about the *Wendingen* images, this time to be used to illustrate *Fighting the Waves*.

You have in your possession a booklet containing, photographs of the masks by Van Krop which were used in the production of one of the plays. I wonder if you would think of including these photographs, using the most effective perhaps on the wrapper? I leave the matter to your decision, for though you rejected them for the edition de luxe you may think it advisable to have them in this separate book (*CL InteLex* 6009, 23 February 1934).

Macmillan readily agreed, setting the book in train and commenting with a characteristic eye to cost,

The photographs of the masks by Van Krop which you left with us are not very good technically and I am rather inclined to think that they would not reproduce very effectively. I am not sure that the book would not look better if we had it without any plates and this would enable us to print it on a more attractive sort of paper. I am wondering, however, whether you would like us to try and prepare a wrapper, using one of the masks as a basis. I think this might be made rather effective and, with your permission, I would get an artist to make a design and submit it to you. As regards binding, I think "Wheels and Butterflies" might have quite a simple binding, different altogether in style from Mr. Sturge Moore's designs for your last book of poems.[5]

Macmillan was thinking of *The Winding Stair and other Poems* (1933), but it is difficult to resist a comparison, with Plate 25, the mask-motif of Sturge Moore's design for *The Cutting of an Agate*

---

[4] BL Add. MS 55727 ff. 271–73 at 272, Harold Macmillan to Yeats.
[5] BL Add. MS 55750 ff. 287–90 at 288, 6 March 1934.

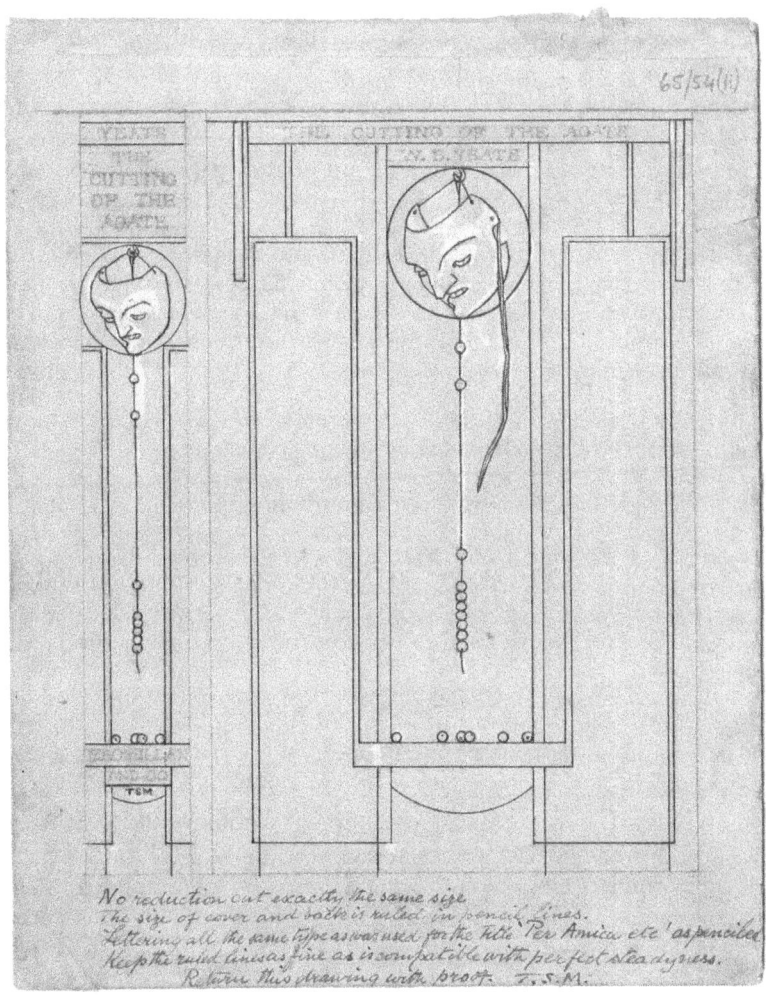

Plate 25. Thomas Sturge Moore's original design for the spine and top board of *The Cutting of an Agate* (London: Macmillan, 1919), image courtesy and © Senate House Library, University of London. All rights reserved.

(1919). Letters such as this are very much the staple of exchanges between Macmillan and Yeats and, indeed, brought out Yeats's prudent, Pollexfen side. But Macmillan had also offered as an interim measure to bring out a popular, one volume of the *Collected Plays* to range alongside the similarly purposed *Collected Poems* of 1933, a suggestion which 'delighted' Yeats and allowed him to omit extra passages of *The Only Jealously of Emer* from appendices to *Fighting the Waves* in *Wheels and Butterflies*. On 9 March he replied from Riversdale with plans for an appropriately pared-down popular edition of the plays and commented further:

I dare say you are right about the "Wheels and Butterflies" looking better without such representations of the Van Krop masks as would impose upon it inferior paper. The masks by the way are at the Abbey Theatre and can be re-photographed. They are rather remarkable pieces of sculpture. I may get a block made of the best to you later on.

I approve of your idea of getting an artist to make a wrapper for "Wheels and Butterflies" (*CL InteLex* 6091).

By late May, Macmillan was seeking a photograph

of one of the Van Krop masks at the Abbey Theatre, which might possibly be used on the wrapper of the book. The illustrations we have in your copy of "Wendinged" [*sic*] would not reproduce very well, and perhaps you will choose a photograph for this purpose when you find a convenient opportunity.[6]

This appeal was reiterated in June and July, and Yeats finally sent three photographs by 18 July 'for the use of the artist who is to design the wrapper'.[7] Marked proofs of the book were dispatched on 16 August, but not of the 'Preliminary' which would 'reach you later, as we are having a special title designed'.[8] While there are various other letters re *Wheels and Butterflies* before publication day (13 November 1934), none specifically mentions the prelims or the title-page or cover designs.[9]

---

[6] BL Add. MS 55753 f. 89, 23 May 1934.
[7] BL Add. MS 55574 f. 269, 26 June 1934; see also BL Add. MS 55575 f. 99, 11 July 1934 and f. 224, 18 July 1934.
[8] BL Add. MS 55756 f. 201.
[9] Yeats could, however, have visited Macmillan's offices when in London in early October, *en route* from Dublin to Rome, and approved them in person.

Yeats and his reader at Macmillan, Thomas Mark, and his usual typesetters, R. & R. Clark, paid precise attention to the shape of the book and the arrangements of its contents, using his well-tried formulae of using epigraphs and half-titles for the purposes of framing and boxing. The attendant spaciousness of the layout and excellent quality laid paper show the firm doing its best for him in an edition of 3,000 copies and perhaps point to slightly better economic conditions in the autumn of 1934 than had prevailed a year before when *Collected Poems* had been prepared for the Christmas market, though no doubt the saving on plates had given the publisher some extra amplitude. The slightly revised 'Wheels and Butterflies' verse[10]

> To Garret or Cellar a wheel I send,
> But every butterfly to a friend.

is placed as a centred epigraph on a fresh recto immediately after the colophon and provides the front portion of the frame for the whole book. The Preface and Contents follow on new fresh rectos with blank versos. Yet another fresh recto offers a half-title and date of first performance for *The Words upon the Window-pane*, with a blank verso, and a centred dedication 'IN MEMORY OF | LADY GREGORY | *in whose house it was written*'. The verso lists the 'Persons in the Play', and the text of its Introduction, or 'wheel', is followed by that of the play (again beginning on a fresh recto) follows. After the closing scene, a blank verso then precedes a repeat of the pattern, centred half-title and date, blank verso, centred dedications, 'Persons in the Play', Introduction on a fresh recto, text ditto, and so on. *Fighting the Waves* is dedicated 'TO | HILDO VAN KROP | *who made the masks*'; '*The Resurrection* 'TO | JUNZO SATO | *who gave me a sword*; and *The Cat and the Moon* 'TO | JOHN MASEFIELD | *who made me a ship*'.

Four plays, four dedications, are finally summed in an *envoi* which encloses Yeats's work before the appendix of George Antheil's music. It is centred on a fresh recto, facing a blank verso.

> *The bravest from the gods but ask:*
> *A house, a sword, a ship, a mask* ([157]).

---

[10] Yeats wrote to William Force Stead on 26 September 1934 that the 'Butterfly is the main symbol on my ring – the ring I always wear – the other symbol is the hawk. The hawk is the straight road of logic, the butterfly the crooked road of intuition – the hawk pounces, the butterfly flutters ... a vision if I remember rightly' (*CL InteLex* 6102).

The house, Ballylee ('Now that we're almost settled in our house' *VP* 323, 419), or the 'small old house' of Riversdale, *VP* 577); the 'changeless' sword of 'My Table' which Yeats had hoped would 'moralise | My days out of their aimlessness ... Chaucer had not drawn breath | When it was forged', *VP* 421); the ship of the 1908–1909 mask reveries (*Mem* 152–53 and see above 8–9): the order of these is distorted to provide for the Mask the culminating rhyme. It comes right with 'a click like a closing box' (*CL InteLex* 6335, to Dorothy Wellesley, 8 September [1935]).

That *envoi* is used as the epigraph to the present volume.

REVIEWS

© Richard Allen Cave, CC BY   http://dx.doi.org/10.11647/OBP.0038.16

W. B. Yeats and Lady Gregory, *Where there is Nothing* and *The Unicorn from the Stars: Manuscript Materials*, ed. by Wim van Mierlo (Ithaca and London: Cornell University Press, 2012), pp. xliii + 686.

Richard Allen Cave

Editing the manuscripts of these two plays for the Cornell series must have been a massive endeavour and the result in Wim van Mierlo's hands is a monumental scholarly achievement. Not only are both texts amongst the longest dramas Yeats engaged in but both entail on an editor's part the exercise of considerable scruple, given the complex issues involved in assigning authorship to the various extant materials.

Where there is Nothing was conceived initially to extend the output of the Irish Literary Theatre Society and many of those originally associated with that theatrical project had a hand in its gestation: George Moore offered a scenario on the basis of a protracted conversation with Yeats; Lady Gregory and Douglas Hyde joined forces with Yeats to realise its theatrical potential before Moore could turn the idea into a novel; George Russell contributed a welcome impetus to the writing by reminding the authors that there was a contemporary parallel for their hero, Paul Ruttledge, in the life of the Dublin eccentric and visionary, Philip Francis Little, whose family actually paid him to stay away from them (AE thought the appropriate tone should be that of satirical comedy); and Florence Farr organised the copyright reading of the play at the Victoria Hall in Bayswater. Moore's letter enclosing the scenario is dated July 3, 1901; but a year passed before he and Yeats began to combat over which of them had the intellectual property rights to their joint conception. Matters then went into overdrive: the play was written within a fortnight and was completed on September 19th, 1902; the Lord Chamberlain gave it a performing licence on October 13th and Farr's dramatised reading took place seven days later; *Where there is Nothing* was published in *The United Irishman* on October 30th.

The play underwent further revision before its publication in book format in 1903. Accepting the somewhat negative criticisms of reviewers and of spectators when the play was staged by Granville Barker at the Royal Court in 1904, the authors seemingly abandoned the work. Given the rapidity of its initial composition, it is hardly surprising that the drama lacks an overall momentum that would bring to the action the inexorability that Yeats was beginning to see as essential to tragedy. (AE had found the completed play vacuous; others, including A.B. Walkley in the *TLS*, considered that it lacked stage-craft in the sense of an achieved dramatic unity.) Spurred on perhaps by his awareness of the dramatic and theatrical potential to be found in Nietzsche's belief in the dynamism inherent in oppositions, contrasts and binaries, Yeats chose in 1907 to return to the play when he and Lady Gregory, collaborating again as co-authors, transformed the original text into a completely new drama, *The Unicorn from the Stars*. Begun in July, the finished play was staged at the Abbey the following November and, after revisions subsequent to the performances, published in 1908 as a single volume in New York and within Volume Three of Bullen's edition of the *Collected Works* at Stratford-upon-Avon.

Throughout that whole process, Lady Gregory worked indefatigably at her typewriter. Here lies the crux over the issue of authorship: virtually all of the surviving materials are either her typescript or, if extant as holograph manuscript, decidedly in her hand. Only holograph revisions to a second set of proofs to the American edition of *The Unicorn from the Stars* are indisputably Yeats's. As van Mierlo aptly terms the situation, 'traces of Yeats's creative interventions' (225) have to be deciphered as palimpsests behind and within Gregory's texts. Yet Yeats increasingly claimed the later play as his, implying that Gregory's contribution was purely secretarial or that her interventions were confined to adding plausible dialect to the dialogue, where necessary. (James Pethica, Colin Smythe and others have admirably demonstrated that Gregory's role was central within a distinctive collaboration.) Correspondence shows that Lady Gregory was both hurt and angered by Yeats's attitude and Annie Horniman, to whom some kind of confession of her feelings was made in confidence, broke whatever agreement she had reached with Gregory about being silent on the matter, and revealed all to Yeats, insisting that he give her proper credit for her contribution to *The Unicorn from the Stars* in its published form. Certainly the American edition carried a 'Preface' which tells how Yeats invited Gregory to join in collaborating with him and asserts: 'As the play stands today, the greater part of the writing is hers' (682). The 'Note' that Yeats subsequently wrote to accompany the inclusion of *The Unicorn from the Stars* in *Plays in Prose and Verse* (London, 1922) is more explicit about the nature and creative consequences of their collaboration: he describes the drama as 'almost wholly hers in handiwork', while being 'so much mine in thought' (684); and continues, 'she has enabled me to carry out an old thought for which my own knowledge is insufficient & to commingle the ancient phantasies of poetry with the rough, vivid, ever-contemporaneous tumult of the roadside' (685).

Perhaps more remarkable is the admission in the 'Note' that, in the years separating the composition of *Where there is Nothing* from their renewed work together on *The Unicorn from the Stars*, Gregory's dramaturgical expertise had come to exceed his: 'her mastery of the stage & her knowledge of dialogue had so increased that my imagination could not go neck to neck with hers' (684). Implicit in this is perhaps an acknowledgement that the actual commingling (referred to above) was more Gregory's achievement than his. Be that as it may, amends had been made, if somewhat belatedly. However, as van Mierlo notes, *The Unicorn from the Stars* was to be the writers' last collaboration together (xxxviii). For the future, creative questions asked of each other were generally to receive advice rather than input by way of response. Thankfully, this edition assigns the plays to both authors. (Draft versions of both 'Preface' and 'Note' are included here as appendices, from which the quotations are taken.)

Materials relating to the composition of *Where there is Nothing* are few in number: a first typescript, presumably the fruit of sketched deliberations that are now lost; and a second typescript incorporating all the revisions made in holograph by the authors on the preceding document and further autograph changes. This was used as copy text for *The United Irishman* and two privately printed American editions set up by John Quinn and published by John Lane. This last item (the second typescript) is collated with two further typescripts prepared subsequent to the publications in 1902 in preparation for Bullen's edition of the play in 1903; with a corrected proof copy of Lane's volume; with a carbon copy of a typescript bearing 'suggestions and queries as to changes to be made in the printers' proof' of A. H. Bullen's publication (though none of the emendations was in fact incorporated in that printing); and with a presentation copy of Bullen's text that was inscribed by Yeats to Annie Horniman, which carries some revisions in Yeats's hand that again were never actually printed. It was an excellent idea to introduce and supplement these with a transcription of Moore's letter outlining the scenario he and Yeats had devised while walking in Moore's garden in Ely Place. Most importantly it shows how widely Gregory, Hyde and Yeats diverged from Moore's proposed scheme (so wide as to reveal Moore's fuss over the legal rights to his sketch as just a storm in a teacup). Play and scenario share a division into five acts ending with the hero's death and a roughly similar range of characters that includes monks and tinkers, but the inner nature of Paul Ruttledge, the hero of *Where there is Nothing*, the particular disturbances he introduces into the daily lives of those about him, his restless intellectualism and private, idiosyncratic spirituality are wholly new.

What the early stages of composition entailed are now a matter for conjecture; the first typescript reveals a remarkably developed play, going way beyond a scenario or scheme (Paul's turning away from his family; his involvement with the tinkers and marriage with Sabina that brings acceptance into the tinker community; the drunken revelry to celebrate the nuptials that brings out the guardians of morality within Paul's former family and their associates in the neighbourhood and the setting up of a Fools' Court in which the tinkers and Paul sit in judgement on these respectable individuals and expose their inherent hypocrisy; Paul's entry to the cloister and his refusal to be obedient to the Superior, which results in his excommunication; his death at the hands of a mob who distrust Paul's otherworldliness as witchcraft on the part of an unfrocked priest). Each act has its own distinct tone, as the opposition to Paul's individualism grows darker and more destructive; but the social and satirical comedy of the first three acts ensures a variety of tone and pace that prevents the pattern of oppositions to Paul within the play from becoming overly predictable. Much of the dialogue is carefully judged in relation to the moral and social standing of each of the characters. Particularly felicitous are the revisions that eliminate any suggestion of sentimentality about the tinkers' life on the road; it is presented rather as a place of hardship, cruelty, sly cunning and casual violence. It is perhaps inaccurate to write of revisions, since most of the new interventions involve expansion of sequences already present in draft. When one reviews this first typescript in relation to the second, which acted as copy text with varying modifications for each of the initial publications, one realises that it must have come very late in the process of creation as so much is already accomplished and in need only of fine-tuning.

In dramaturgical terms, however, much of the play, even after the incorporation of the emendations into the second typescript, remains in a gestured rather than realised form; and this is most crucially the case in the development of Paul's characterisation, especially the all-important motivation that brings him to the monastery in Act Four, which (as written) seems more by accident than design because the choice to bring him there is the tinkers' not Paul's. The anger of the mob against Paul in the final scene is more *given* than developed, it is a useful mechanism to bring him to martyrdom: there is little by way of staged explanation to account for their violence or his acceptance of victimhood. (Several of the reviewers of Barker's production saw the last act as the weakest, a criticism that Yeats himself in time came to accept.) The impression is that spectators are being invited to see Paul as courageously dying for his beliefs but those beliefs are never clarified through debate with others. Act Four closes with Paul enacting an impressive ritual while giving a sermon outlining his distrust of the materialism that has undermined Church, State and culture and he puts out a candle for each of the institutions that have become anathema to him. The problem is that there is no theatrical exploration of why Paul's creed enrages the Superior or why amongst his Order it excites some to become Paul's disciples and moves others to distance themselves from him. That Barker chose to stage the play as part of his seasons at the Court Theatre in London suggests he saw it as a play of ideas, but one has only to compare *Where there is Nothing* with any of Barker's own dramas of this period or Shaw's (the main contributor to the Court's repertory) to appreciate how lacking it is in intellectual rigour. The staging of mock trials, rituals of damnation and acts of violence, however impressive theatrically they may be in their own right, do not embellish or subtilize Paul's thinking: they are the adjuncts and consequences only of his beliefs; they are not a means to admit spectators to the innermost depths of meaning and significance of that creed for him. In other words, the authors fail to get convincingly *inside* Paul's mind.

The extant materials for *The Unicorn from the Stars* give a better sense of the play throughout its progress to completion than was the case with *Where there is Nothing*. They comprise an annotated scenario; an early typescript developed from the latter; three of Lady Gregory's copybooks in which she worked and re-worked each of the three acts into which this version was divided; and a set of marked proofs of the American edition (Macmillan, 1908), which are collated here with a surviving playscript prepared for the Abbey production of November 1907, first page proofs for the setting of the play to be included in Volume 3 of the projected Macmillan *edition de luxe* (1931), the 'author's marked proof' for *The Collected Plays of W. B. Yeats* (1934), and proofs for the projected but unpublished 'Coole Edition' from the Macmillan Archive in the British Library. Despite this apparent wealth of evidence for the play's gestation, there unfortunately remains no final typescript prior to the proof-stage. The copybooks, though highly informative, are jumbled sketches that very roughly follow the design of each act; some of these amplify ideas that have come as second thoughts about the content of a particular episode or passage, some evolve quite long sections of continuous dialogue, but, even allowing for their haphazard arrangement, the copybooks do not offer a complete run through the play. There is no *finished* authorial version extant.

Already in the scenario we can detect the outlines of the Nietzschean oppositions on which the drama is to be constructed and these are steadily amplified and strengthened throughout the ensuing materials. There is, however, already a problem here: Nietzsche envisaged oppositions of equal power and status (Apollonian versus Dionysian, primarily) but increasingly in the play Martin Hearne's philosophical and visionary expansiveness is in conflict with the petty bourgeois mind-sets of everyone he comes into contact with (artisans, gentry, tinkers, officers of the law), always excepting the hermit, Father John. Again, as in *Where there is Nothing*, Martin's temperament and his thought processes are not set against a worthy figure of any intellectual stature. Not surprisingly in consequence the prevailing tone throughout the first and much of the second act of the play is comic: a comedy of misunderstandings between individuals who are blind to everything but their own particular codes of value and aspirations. Only in the final stages of the dramatic action does the comedy turn darker, as misunderstandings give way to frustrated desperation and violence, resulting in Martin's death. The tragic overtakes the satirical and bitterness ensues; but tragedy in the fullest sense of the term does not prevail, since Martin in no way comes to know himself by recognising the limitations of his vision and of his ability to promote it credibly to others: there is no expansion of his awareness in the face of overwhelming defeat. No amount of revision can solve this issue. How different, for example, is *Deirdre*, conceived and revised over a roughly similar period of time, where there is a genuine battle of equally matched wills and intellects in the heroine and Conchubar, both of whom come to accept their individual responsibility for shaping their lives to embrace tragedy.

With its episodic structure, *The Unicorn from the Stars* is a modern Morality play: a showing up of the weaknesses, gullibility, petty tyrannies of a cross-section of Irish society where, though the action ostensibly takes place in the eighteenth century, the implications are wholly contemporary. It is difficult to know from the copybooks whether it was Lady Gregory's sole inspiration or hers together with Yeats's that introduced into the action a critique of unthinking nationalism. The tinkers accept Martin as their leader in consequence of a confusion which leads them to suspect he is a rebel, newly escaped from prison, who has come to command them in an attack on the English. Apart from adding to the pattern of people at comic cross-purposes with Martin, the theme remains undeveloped. (Indeed the tinkers are less well realised than the chorus of subversive prototypes in *Where there is Nothing*.) More successfully achieved over the process of revision is the characterisation of Martin's uncle, Andrew, who is the victim of his elder brother, Thomas's reforming zeal. Andrew epitomises the man that Thomas would like to make of Martin and there is much amusement to be had in the revelation that Andrew has been hoodwinking his brother by quietly living his own preferred, libidinous way of life on the sly while pretending to be a model of industrious sobriety when in his brother's presence. Andrew's attempts to fraternise with Martin and cajole him into sharing in his rebellious schemes show how widely and absurdly he has misinterpreted Martin's rhetoric of rebellion against the prevailing status quo. It is that rhetoric that increasingly creates a massive division between Martin and his various would-be supporters, who turn against him once experience shows them the extent of their misunderstanding. The tinkers' concept of revolution is found in time to be little more than a hunt for treasure that will bring them a life of ease at the expense of the society that currently ostracises them. So moulded by material preoccupations is everyone else's thinking that no one appreciates the extent to which Martin's creed and its welcoming of universal destruction relates specifically to the inner life ('The battle we have to fight is fought out in our own mind') and the demise of those worldly appetites, aspirations and lusts that motivate the other characters (666). Martin's philosophy, however, is a creed in the making: he quests continually for a 'sense of suddenly enlarged being' (180) such as he experiences when in a state of trance.

The trances occur at several points in the action and Martin's philosophy undergoes subtle changes with each 'attack'. At first a trance causes him to espouse a Dionysian belief that 'Life is in destruction, eternal joy is in destruction!' (493); this culminates in the burning of his and his uncles' home and business. This position is later renounced in face of a new Apollonian certainty that 'My business is not reformation but revelation' (666). During these trances Martin is kept offstage so the transformations he and his thinking undergo are not dramatised as a process but have to be taken by an audience on trust, once his new self speaks after his recovery. But, as Yeats came to appreciate, if a playwright wishes to create drama out of activity in the 'deeps of the mind', then form and style have to be adapted to render the subtly inter-related movements of the conscious and subconscious life. A revolution in dramaturgical practices had to be envisaged. Consider by contrast how brilliantly in theatrical terms Yeats renders the play of Cuchulain's mind while he is trapped in a trance-like coma in *The Only Jealousy of Emer*. *The Unicorn from the Stars* largely conforms to the conventions of stage realism, perhaps under Lady Gregory's influence; the composition of the play would appear to have shown Yeats how restricting such conventions would continue to prove, if he was determined to realise his particular and unique aspirations for drama. Such a mode of realism was not a style and form that he would tackle again, except perhaps in staging the séance that frames the ghost play in *The Words Upon the Window Pane*: that play shifts effortlessly between satire and seriousness, but it is the mysterious because wholly ventriloquised play for Swift's voice which takes spectators into the dark reaches of the mind. If *The Unicorn from the Stars* falls short of Yeats's best drama, it was nonetheless a necessary, if ultimately disappointing stage in his quest for a distinctive dramatic form.

If the play also falls short of Lady Gregory's best drama, it is because the philosophical undertow to the action (seemingly on his own admission, Yeats's prime contribution to the piece) did not allow any of her characteristic styles of comedy to take a sustained hold on the composition. The unrelieved black comedy of *The Deliverer* (staged January 1911) – another exploration of the trope of the martyred messiah – shows what a creative precision and tonal control she could achieve when working independently with very similar material. Perhaps the disturbing, incisive, concentrated intensity of that play came to her as a consequence of wrestling at length with the apparently intractable problems of *The Unicorn from the Stars*. The copybooks (three only are extant, but clearly there were several other volumes involved in her endeavours) bear witness to the depth of her commitment to completing that project while staying loyal to both the collaboration undertaken with Yeats and the scenario devised with him. It is in editing the copybooks that van Mierlo's skills are seen at their finest. At first glance they must present any would-be editor with a nightmare confusion: particular developments are dropped when the possibility of a revision suggests itself for a quite different section of an act; further thoughts about certain passages are incorporated by a variety of means into pages within one of these copybooks, though their actual drafting clearly occurred elsewhere. There is no logical progress through the pages of any of the three volumes. Van Mierlo confronts readers with a replication of how each volume appears as a document but then steers them effortlessly through the maze with a network of cross-references that indicate how a passage on this page connects with a passage on that; how this section of dialogue is completed by another section occurring several pages on (or maybe back) within the pages as ordered within the book; or how these notes for a particular development of an idea are realised elsewhere in the text. The patience and tenacity are exemplary that go to make such a cogent presentation of what is in effect a chaotic assemblage resulting from bursts of creative activity (and in handwriting that is often little better than a scrawl for pages at a time when such bursts of inspiration are at their height). Equally exemplary is van Mierlo's discrimination in refraining from extensively substantiated guessing as to who exactly was responsible for what in the collaboration. The documents have to speak for themselves; and in the instance of these two plays that requires of an editor massive restraint as well as a profound engagement. We are acutely in Wim van Mierlo's debt for rendering the collaboration embarked on by Lady Gregory and Yeats as transparently as circumstance and his meticulously garnered evidence allow.

The King's Threshold: Manuscript Materials, edited by Declan Kiely, Yeats in Manuscript Series (Ithaca and London: Cornell University Press, 2005), pp. *lxi* + 620.

Richard Allen Cave

There is no denying that *The King's Threshold* held a special place of affection and honour for the poet amongst his theatrical output. It was in many ways a personal manifesto, a defence of the art of poetry, music and song. Inevitably the play was destined to undergo repeated revision, particularly as Yeats's own youthful adoption of Shelley's view of poets as the great legislators of the world came under repeated attack. The play in the form of a morality drama was one of several conceived by Yeats as Plays for Ireland, an exposition of the need for a creative intelligentsia to have as an absolute right, an honoured place within the ordering and shaping of a society. It is not surprising to find Lady Gregory with her own refined sense of service to the community and the need to work to bring 'dignity to Ireland' joining Yeats in drafting the play in its earliest manifestations.

Dr. Kiely has traced some forty-four draft materials relating to the gestation and revision of the play, covering a period from 1903 to 1934. Study of their history has led him to divide them into four major sequences: the period up to the play's initial performances in 1903 (Dublin) and 1904 (London) with Yeats's extensive post-production revisions responding to reviewers' criticisms of what they deemed a lack of action in the drama; further re-writing (chiefly to the King's opening speeches and to the scene for the Mayor and the Cripples) culminating in Yeats's revisions to the Galley Proofs made when preparing *Poems, 1899–1905* for publication; the full-scale redesigning of the play and especially of the ending, which was now situated firmly in the tragic mode, that was accomplished during 1920–1922 and culminated in the text as printed in *Plays in Prose and Verse* (1922); and a final series of local revisions made throughout 1931–1934, especially to the 'first page proofs' of the abandoned Edition de Luxe (later the Coole Edition) planned by Macmillan, and to the text as printed in *Collected Plays* (1934).

Re-working the play, as Kiely demonstrates in his admirable Introduction, was as much a response to social and political event in Ireland as to Yeats's own changing concept of the poet's role and his experiences of the play in production and its critical reception. In the process there was a notable shift of focus. Initially the play investigated the antagonism of Seanchan and King Guare (a conflict between principle and pragmatism) and the course of events that led to its resolution. Bringing clarity of definition to that conflict is the intention behind the many revisions of the first two periods between 1903 and 1906. In the long period between the publishing of *Poems, 1899–1905* and the major revisions of the early 1920s, Yeats had sought for a dramatic form that would enable him to bring an audience to a perception of the innermost workings of a character's mind as the finest index of what is fundamental to that individual; his plays (in Katharine Worth's phrase) were to be 'journeys into the interior', to the wellsprings of being.

What impresses is how little adaptation to the form and texture of the play was required to make *The King's Threshold* meet that new requirement: the quarrel with Guare now cannot be resolved, chaos is breaking out within his kingdom, as Seanchan predicted; both men lose out in the battle in the material sense, but the poet pursues the lonely path of integrity in the face of all attempts to make him compromise, and dies ecstatic in the knowledge that his pupils at least have appreciated his intent and value his example; despite his mourned demise, the future of poetry is assured and others remain to share and, if necessary, to fight for his principles. With the change in emphasis comes a change in understanding of the poet's role in society: Seanchan is now less the legislator than the champion of certain values which society is choosing to contest; the episodes of the drama now define the source and intensity of the will-power that determines his vindication of a personal truth. A confident sense of principle drives him intractably and irrevocably to his death. Social comedy has given place to existential tragedy but significantly Yeats leaves the issue of how an audience should respond to Seanchan's demise deliberately open.

In the *Four Plays for Dancers* the Chorus of Musicians often give voice in their final lyrics to that uncertainty: they speak of the 'bitter reward' of the 'tragic tomb' that astonishes but leaves one dumbfounded (*The Only Jealousy of Emer*), or of the obscurities of a strife with shadows in contrast with the 'pleasant life' offered within 'indolent meadows' (*At The Hawk's Well*). *The King's Threshold* now concludes with a dilemma amongst Seanchan's pupils of how properly to honour him in death: the passionate young pupil wishes for a triumphant blare of trumpets, the oldest asks for a sombre dirge. Both have a certain appropriateness; but can there be a *preferred* ending to tragedy?

On his own admission, revising *The King's Threshold* even during the earlier periods taught Yeats a great deal about the art of dramaturgy. As he wrote to Arthur Symons from Coole on 10 September, 1905:

> ...*The King's Threshold* has been changed and rehearsed and then changed again and so on, till I have got it as I believe a perfectly articulate stage play. I have learned a great deal about poetry generally in the process, and one thing I am now quite sure of is that all the finest poetry comes logically out of the fundamental action, and that the error of late periods like this is to believe that some things are inherently poetical, and to try and pull them on to the scene at every moment. It is just these seeming inherently poetical things that wear out (*CL InteLex* 214, *L* 460).

What Yeats outlines here is his deepening understanding of the need for clarity of structure before the poetry of a play will grow organically out of the action rather than be superimposed on situations; structure must never be merely the occasion for verse, if that verse is to be truly dramatic. Unusually amongst the extant manuscripts of Yeats's plays, there is a full set of prose sketches for the scenario of *The King's Threshold* so that one can test the truth of Yeats's observation by watching the process of creativity from the initial outline taken down at dictation by Lady Gregory, through drafting in prose to the first transpositions into blank verse and on to more refined expression of ideas and characters.

One notices that amidst the generalised wording of the narrative in the first scenario certain phrases stand out as having a remarkable immediacy, as if Yeats's imagination had already sensed a valuable entry into some deeper engagement with the situation. Many of these lines are carried through into later drafts, often withstanding major revisions to surrounding material to find their way relatively unchanged into the final version, as if they became anchors, touchstones or guides as to how a suitable structure might evolve, if careful transitions were effected between them. Such crucial lines and ideas from the first scenario include: '...for to the wronged | man there always remained one | right, to set his death against | anothers life' (4); 'When one | is long without fasting one's mind gets | slippery' (7); the exchange with the Soldier that develops the image of Seanchan as a hedgehog and the soldier as a lapdog (9); 'the king's | no crown would not glitter if we | had not called gold bright' and the ensuing idea that concepts of nationalism are implanted in men's imagination and courage by the songs of poets (10); Seanchan's extended image of the Monk's self-seeking concept of God as being like a tamed bird perching on the king's finger (12); 'Hold out all yr | hands to me, you have the feet of dancers | but hold out yr hands to me, I have | a thought that there are no sound hands here' (13) which Seanchan addresses to the Princesses and the court, suspecting that they have offered him infected (leprous) food; 'When, King, did the | poets offer safety?' (17), the question with which the poet confronts the king, who is seeking to excuse himself by eliciting pity for his complexities of decision-making.

Suddenly we are offered a stage direction: '(She [Fedelm] dips it [some bread] & puts it to his lips. At the touch he dashes it away)' (6).

This is the first of a series of such directions at the close of the play, which include the stage picture of the pupils re-entering with halters round their necks, and the powerfully surreal image of them pursuing Guare up the steps of the palace, 'holding out the end | of their ropes to him' (18). These moments may be extended or slightly modified throughout the long history of the play's composition but they were to remain fixed points in the drama, encapsulating the significance of the main episodes. The final instances show that by the close of that first draft Yeats had already begun to stage the play in his imagination.

The exposition was the first substantial change to be effected from a discussion amongst the pupils of what had befallen Seanchan to an extended speech for King Guare to the recently assembled pupils attempting to justify his own position. Through rapid redrafting, it became a wonderfully glozing speech, full of self-importance and evasive rhetorical flourishes. It is a brilliant dramatic stroke both for the decision to introduce Guare's antagonistic voice before we hear Seanchan's and for introducing an audience to an outright equivocator with language before we hear the poet's claim about the power of bards to *fix* the meanings of words, to find the terms that define and discriminate in ways that endow qualities with a precise value. Guare's dismissal of Seanchan as 'a mere man of words' will expose and condemn his own moral and political insensitivity. Once he unhinges meaning, as Guare patently does in his opening address, then chaos will follow (though it was only in the revisions undertaken in the early 1920s that Yeats developed the full implications of this, when he inserted the Girls' persuading the Soldier to offer Seanchan food on the grounds that the harpers will no longer play for their dances and 'the common sort' have turned against them).

The King, however, is no monster. Yeats elicits a measure of sympathy for him by showing that all the evasions are the product of his sense of being trapped by circumstance: his worries for the security of his throne in the short term were he to defy his courtiers, and for his reputation in the longer term if Seanchan's death results in his losing the good will of the people. Either way, his authority and his hold on his throne will be challenged. Guare becomes a recognisable type of politician and Yeats strengthened characterisation elsewhere in the play by modelling certain figures (Chamberlain, Soldier and Monk) on three prominent, politically-minded contemporaries (T.W. Rolleston, Richard Bagwell and George Coffey respectively), as the early drafts and Kiely's informative commentary on them makes clear. Further strengthening came after the initial production.

A problem with the play in performance (as Yeats warned some years later in 1910 when writing to John Drinkwater about his intended production of the play) is the heavy demand it places on the central actor, who by never leaving the stage has no respite from the audience's attention. If his stamina and technique are not up to that demand, then the likely result is that the play will fall into prolonged monotony. That had been a criticism of Fay's initial production particularly when staged in London, prompting Yeats almost immediately to redesign the scene for the Mayor and the two family servants, which follows after Seanchan's long debate with his pupils about the significance of poetry and the status of bards. He cut one of the servants and considerably built up the role of the one remaining (whom he named Brian) as a man with a deeply committed affection for the poet; and he introduced into the scene from later in the action (where they originally made only the one appearance) the two cripples as men wholly disinterested in the politics of the situation and for that matter in anything except food. Now instead of the Mayor of Kinvara's self-important speechifying being interrupted by the servants laying out the food they have brought from Seanchan's home, he is repeatedly undercut by the cripples' criticism (they are a hilarious comic double-act).

The resulting scene has an energy and bravura lacking in the original conception, even within the comic mode organically linked now to the main thematic preoccupations of the play in defining types of self-obsession and selflessness affording neat discriminating contrasts with Seanchan. Brian's unthinking, unquestioning devotion is not rooted in any degree of principle: he repeats the poet's father's words – 'he cared you well, | And you in your young age, and […] it's right | That you should care him now' (449) – not realising that from Seanchan's perspective they voice an unkind emotional blackmail. The Mayor is preoccupied more with the impression he is making than with the actual content of his speech, which demonstrates how self-seeking he and his community are at heart in being more concerned with their and Seanchan's standing in respect of the King's bounty than with the poet's motive for his fast. The cripples show the levels of desperation that sheer hunger can reduce a man to: they are fixated on the getting of food.

At the point when Yeats was transposing his prose drafts into blank verse he made a number of holograph notes about kinds of imagery to be sustained and developed and remarked then of Seanchan: 'His imagination must dwell on food' (253). And so it does, from the moment that the pupils rouse him out of his dreams of dining with Finn and Osgar on roast flesh or watching Grania 'dividing salmon by a stream' to his waking vision in Fedelm's company of Adam's Paradise where the birds gorge themselves on fruit. But he has the strength of mind to know when the workings of his psyche become 'slippery' and find the means to discipline its focus back onto his abiding purpose. The farce of the scene (the four comic characters end up trying to shout each other down while completely ignoring Seanchan and his plight) introduces a welcome tonal variety into the play, but also through a patterning of contrasts develops in spectators deepening insights into the qualities that shape the poet's integrity. It is a highly innovative scene for the methods Yeats deploys to characterise the strengths of a wholly passive character.

The ensuing episode for the courtiers, the noble girls and the princesses remained virtually unchanged as to its content but Yeats increasingly augmented it with details that invested the scene with a black satirical humour. Where Seanchan is largely withdrawn from the scene with the Mayor and Brian (except at mention of his mother's true understanding of his situation and decision), the courtiers goad him into taking an active part in this sequence but to their complete discomfort, since he repeatedly strips them of their pretensions. The Chamberlain ingratiatingly claims he too is a poet only to be revealed as a patent hack; the Monk claims a piety that Seanchan exposes as self-serving, since he shapes his 'god' to suppport whatever the king desires; the Soldier chooses to see the poet as a pathetic creature (a hedgehog) only to have his own picture drawn as, for all his apparent ferocity, an utterly biddable dog; the girls worry over the consequences of the social breakdown that Seanchan's rebellion against the king's edict has initiated but only because it disrupts their endless pleasure-seeking; and the princesses graciously condescend to Seanchan from the height of a superiority that he questions as groundless. The poet may be passive in his resistance but he controls the tenor and tone of the scene throughout and his integrity is defined by the lack of it in every other character onstage. His stillness requires always that they move to him. Physically inert he may be, but his intelligence is more alert, incisive and morally attuned than the absurd people who continually demand his attention.

It would appear that the extended scene with Fedelm was the last to be fully drafted before the initial performances and thereafter it underwent remarkably few changes. One might argue that with the completion of this episode Yeats found the way forward for his subsequent revision of the earlier parts of the action, since in its revised form it becomes a highly flexible sequence in emotional terms – a surprised greeting; her reminder that she would fetch him to her home in time for their marriage; her admitting that she has anticipated the agreed time by several months so that they may wed in the high summer; his sharing his vision of the previous evening with her, when it seemed to him as if the whole of creation was united in a grand epithalamium; her talk of her home and the rest he will find there; his concern that his pupils accompany them thither; her promise that they will be welcome and that places for their recreation are already prepared; his song of the wondrous garden that is sparked in his memory by her account of her homestead; her misunderstanding of his visionary tone, suspecting he has forgotten the realities of her own garden; their decision to depart; his weakness and physical collapse; her offer to dip bread into wine to help sustain him and his acceptance of it; his remembrance of his mission and the casting of both food and lover from him; her assertion that he cannot love her and his ensuing rage at her betrayal; her clutching at his frail body, determined never to leave him; his threatening a curse on all who withhold him from his purpose and her begging his forgiveness ('I will obey like any married wife'); the resolution of the conflict between them in a kiss, which is disrupted by the sudden arrival of the king demanding to know if Seanchan has eaten yet; his further proffering of food, which Seanchan rejects but in terms, '*We* have refused it (my emphasis)' which show that the lovers are now in a state of absolute concord.

This is a magnificent sequence: the surges of emotion, of challenge and denial, of hope, of trust and of despair that resolve into a complete harmony is magnificently accomplished in little more than 150 lines to the point where that assertion of the lovers' united stance (implicit in the simple word 'We') spells out the king's defeat. What Yeats was always aware of, as he confided to Drinkwater many years later, was the need 'to get progression by the changes of state in the soul of the principal player' (cited by Kiely, li). He achieved that here, but it was to take him nearly two decades of redrafting to bring the rest of the play in line with this inventiveness. Given, too, the power of that confident 'We' and its immediate impact on the king's sense of losing control in the situation, it was inevitable that, for all his defence of the resolved ending in the Prologue he devised for the first production (it was never actually played), a tragic outcome was the only one fitting the decorum that the action had established. It was implicit in Yeats's thinking about an apt acting style for the play in performance, since he firmly advised Frank Fay to stage 'the whole opening of the play in a grave statuesque way as if it were a Greek play' (*CL3* 417). What started in the tragic vein had to end in that vein if the performance were to achieve that unity of creative effect, which Yeats was keen to promote in theatre.

It is perhaps worth commenting on the Prologue with its rambling old man, angry at being called from his bed to defend Yeats's play because there are so many involved in the casting (there are some sixteen speaking roles and supernumeraries). He outlines what is different about Yeats's handling of the subject of Seanchan and Guare compared with recent translators, narrators and commentators on the tale from Bardic times and he expatiates on why there is no tragic ending. Yeats deftly outlines here the disagreement between him and Lady Gregory. Nobly, he defends her view to which he capitulated; but the very fact of that public airing of their differences suggests that Yeats was still not wholly committed to that decision. It was a canny move: it is almost as if he is inviting the audience to take a stance on the matter so that he would have some back-up if the general response went against the ending as performed. Throughout the ramblings (the old man is beautifully characterised as arthritic and tetchy) are in a staccato prose that contrasts markedly with the august blank verse with which the play opens and which in large measure prevails throughout the action.

We are forced to recognise a mundane world of age and aches and anger before we are introduced to a time that is decidedly of the (romanticised) past but a world where the principal protagonist, a bard, is in touch imaginatively with a yet older, heroic tradition where ancient gods feasted with poets before the days of kings and priests. A considerable creative challenge must have resided in the need to find an appropriate diction, style and authoritative tone for Seanchan's bardic speech. Most of the more subtle revisions he made to the text over the years engaged with answering that need. A consequence of this marks out the steady evolution of *The King's Threshold* as different from the kinds of localised revision Yeats undertook with his other plays. Generally the result of re-writing was to simplify expression in the interests of conveying an idea, however complex, with immediate lucidity to a theatre audience and a removal from his dialogue of those 'seeming inherently poetical things that wear out' that he castigated in his letter to Symons, as quoted above.

That technique, however, was not possible here, where the situation demanded the creating of a credible bardic style, different from the prevailing stage diction deployed by the rest of the characters. The challenge was to get the necessary clarity within a consciously poeticised rhetoric. Yeats found a way of doing this at least in theory with the revised prose scenario of April, 1903 (32-45) when he chose to start the action with the king swaying Seanchan's pupils to his point of view so that they will persuade their master to accept the situation and eat. Seanchan, however, teaches the pupils their error by subjecting them to a catechism about the nature and origins of poetry and the poet's vocation. Surviving typescript fragments show Yeats next attempting to flesh out this idea, searching for a means to convey complex argument through metaphor, chiefly about poetry as 'as image of the world before the Fall' (47). First attempts were hesitant and confused but matters improved once Yeats chose to base his metaphors in myths of origin in order to endorse his concept of the bard's function in his society as educative, to teach virtue through stories and images of a long-past but always recoverable perfection. By the date of the typescript that was submitted for licensing to the Lord Chamberlain's office in London in October, 1903, Yeats had found the kind of idiom he was seeking:

> ...the poets hung
> Images of the life that was in Eden
> About the childbed of the world that it
> Looking upon those images might bear
> Triumphant children... (331).

Subsequent revision of Seanchan's part in particular extended the potential of this style through considerable varieties of expression. In part Yeats was aided by the central action he had devised: hunger takes an increasing grip on the poet's constitution and psyche and Yeats charts its progress by envisaging Seanchan lapsing into states of dreaming and outright hallucination, where a heightened diction, a speaking through metaphor, is a credible correlative for a mind which sees *differently*. What his enemies do not perceive till too late is that the heightening of the poet's sensibility is taking him ever closer to the world of those myths, which are the source of his power. When he looks back at the everyday world from his new vantage point, he sees it with ever greater exactitude. The idiom expands till he can be at once in Adam's paradise yet in the comfort of Fedelm's embrace, confident of her support. Here poetic intensities are wholly justifiable in terms of dramatic necessity; they are not *pulled on* for effect (to use the terms of Yeats's critique, as cited above) but arise out of a sure sense of what the staged action will allow.

The very difference of the text in this regard that emerged out of the revisions of the 1920s and 1930s when compared with the new plays that Yeats was writing in those years shows how developed a sense he had of what was dramaturgically appropriate and possible. It is to Kiely's credit that he has assembled and organised the wealth of material relating to *The King's Threshold* that allows this creative skill and confidence in Yeats as dramatist to emerge so clearly at a reading of his volume. Like Kiely, one must express a debt of gratitude for Lady Gregory's archival instincts which encouraged her to preserve what is quite the fullest demonstration possible of how she and the poet collaborated and how one of their early plays came into being but subsequently evolved till it was demonstrably his achievement alone.

Not content with the wealth of textual material he proffers in so illuminating a fashion, Kiely has also included by way of appendices further documents illustrative of the play in production. There is the report of Yeats's opening night speech, as recorded in *The Freeman's Journal*; and a parody of the play from 1911 by A.M.W. (John Swift) published in *The Leader*; but more informative are Yeats's two sketches (a view from the Audience's perspective and a groundplan) for a setting for the play which was realised for the performances at the Molesworth Hall (the drawings were later bound in with a typescript of the version staged in 1903, which is now in the possession of the Houghton Library at Harvard); a formalised scheme for the disposition of the various roles at the fall of the curtain in that first production (also to be found in that Harvard document); a photograph of the scene for Seanchan and Fedelm, as printed in *The New York Herald* in 1904, which shows in part how the setting was constructed and deployed; and three pages, two showing ground plans for staging *The King's Threshold* from the notebook (now in the possession of the National Library of Ireland, MS 30,588), in which Yeats (c.1910) recorded various experiments in devising scenery using the miniature set of screens that Craig gave him along with the full-sized set bought by the Abbey that year. The first of these plans simply turns at an angle the original design for the staging at the Molesworth Hall and adds a large tower-like formation of screens to fill the space now left vacant to stage left of the flight of steps. The second is altogether bolder in offering a grouping of pillars set on a diagonal, with alternating widths of two foot and four foot screens with gaps of over two-and-a-half feet between them and an angled light behind. One light source follows the diagonal formation of the screens; the second comes from immediately behind them and is directed towards the audience (Kiely misreads the annotation accompanying this second source of illumination as 'also [?head] light', where it should be interpreted more appropriately in stage terms as 'hard light').

This would allow figures in the entrances to be either fully lit or seen in silhouette. What is not immediately clear from the annotations on either sketch is whether the second group of screens was an alternative design for the play reducing the setting to an absolute formalist simplicity or whether it is a more detailed working out of the arrangement of pillars and doorways that is roughly drawn at the top of the flight of steps to form the entrance to Guare's palace. What favours the first supposition is the annotation situated immediately beneath the second of the sketches, which reads 'entire width of stage', whereas the arrangement of pillars beyond the steps in the first design does not extend so widely. Supposing the second is a design for an alternative independent setting, then the immediate problem it would pose a director is where to situate Seanchan. The remaining annotations beneath the sketch, however, though somewhat enigmatic, illuminate the situation. The first line reads: 'would do for Seanchan'. This suggests to me that Yeats first designed the grouping of screens and played around with possible lighting effects and only then decided that it might be an appropriate setting for the play that from the first he and Lady Gregory tended to think of as 'Seanchan' (most of the original manuscripts are so headed) rather than as *The King's Threshold*.

If this supposition is correct, then what follows becomes clearer. The next two lines read: 'no steps could lie on | heap of rags', which indicates that Yeats has perceived the director's problem outlined above and offered a solution. (Kiely is uncertain how to transcribe some of these musings). The fact that there are to be 'no steps' confirms that this design is indeed to be interpreted independently of the earlier sketch. The next annotation, which Kiely leaves untranscribed, picks up the phrasing of the first of this set of annotations and reads: 'Would also do Baile's Strand', which confirms that Yeats was playing with arrangements of screens and that only when he had found an aesthetically satisfying grouping did he look for possible plays of his for which it might be deployed. (The first sketch, though definitely headed 'Kings Threshold', carries an annotation on the facing page which reads 'might do Oedipus' (a project which was never long out of Yeats's mind for the Abbey repertoire).

These are useful inclusions for any reader unfamiliar with how the plays might originally have been staged; but one would have welcomed some indication from Kiely why these alone have been selected. Materials relating to various stagings of *The King's Threshold* during Yeats's lifetime are in richer abundance than is the case with virtually every other play of his. There are more photographs extant of the earliest production in the Molesworth Hall, showing Annie Horniman's garishly decorated and highly inappropriate costumes. More importantly there is also the actual setting for this play that Edward Gordon Craig designed, which was till recently in the collection of the late Anne Yeats. This was quite unlike Yeats's attempts with the miniature screens; it depicted two flights of stairs rising from stage left and right, mounting up to opposed doorways set in otherwise featureless tower-structures and leaving a space of unoccupied stage between their ranks. The emphasis in the design is on these two architectural structures with a vague wash of colour to signify a landscaped backcloth. There is some evidence that this design was actually implemented at the Abbey and that the stylised landscape of distant mountains and a plain bisected by a river devised by Jack Yeats (his original watercolour of formal shapes in black, grey and white is currently in the Yeats Museum at the National Gallery in Dublin) was created to fill the void left between Craig's arrangement of steps and towers.

There are also the complete set of costume designs by Charles Ricketts for the staging of the play by the Abbey at the Royal Court in London in June 1914, which Yeats considered 'the best stage costumes I have ever seen' (*CL InteLex* 2417 11 June, 1914; *L* 587). He continued (doubtless with Horniman's tasteless creations in mind): 'They are full of dramatic invention, and yet nothing starts out, or seems eccentric. The Company never did the play so well, and such is the effect of costume that whole scenes got a new intensity' (*Ibid.*). This collection of designs is now unfortunately dispersed, but many are housed in Prints and Drawings at the Victoria and Albert Museum (London); more were in Anne Yeats's collection. What is interesting about Ricketts' designs is that they were deliberately made up in parts and in a matching colour scheme that would allow them to be variously re-assembled to suit characters in *On Baile's Strand*. The designs are actually annotated to show how they could be assigned to two distinct roles.

If, therefore, Yeats's second design discussed above had actually been implemented, it would have been possible to stage both *On Baile's Strand* and *The King's Threshold* within the same setting and with the same set of costumes. Sadly this experiment was never attempted, but it is possible that Ricketts' costumes were seen at the Royal Court on a setting devised by Craig, backed by a cloth designed by Jack Yeats. It seems a pity that, having whetted the appetite of the Yeatsian scholar and the theatre historian with some material relating to the staging of *The King's Threshold*, Kiely did not complete the endeavour and offer the full range of extant visual evidence, particularly as this shows how three consummate theatre artists from amongst his family and his contemporaries responded to the creative possibilities inherent in Yeats's text.

W. B. Yeats, *At The Hawk's Well and The Cat and the Moon: Manuscript Materials*, ed. by Andrew Parkin (Ithaca and London: Cornell University Press, 2010), lxiv + 267 pp.

Richard Allen Cave

Given how remarkably innovative was the dramaturgical transformation that came over Yeats's playwriting with the composition of *At the Hawk's Well*, it is disappointing to discover that little remains from the earliest stages of the play's composition. The first extant manuscripts show the songs already taking a decisive shape in Yeats's imagination: the tone, aim and to some degree even the content is immediately recognisable and some phrases were to persist with little change through into the finished text ('I would know but human faces | And be deliv[ere]d from those eyes'; 'Folly alone will I cherish'; 'I fear being but a sweet mouthful of air'). The first draft of what was initially entitled 'The Well of Immortality' (eleven pages in holograph with remarkably few interventions to redraft sections) shows the play already fully formed, since it exactly follows the scheme of the final version for staging found in *Collected Plays*. Here are the musicians' evocation of the place where the action is set, the arrival of the Old Man and the Young Man, their exchange which reveals their reasons for being there, the transformation of the guardian of the Well into a miraculous hawk, the mesmeric dance that distracts Cuchulain away from the well, the plashing of the waters, the dejection of the Old Man, the noise of the women warriors preparing for battle, Cuchulain's seizing his spear, his asserting his identity with a chilling war-cry and the characters' departure from the playing space. There is even a précis of the final song into three lines that lean more towards the frustration of the Old Man as a summation of the play's import than the balanced and settled contentment of the final version.

It is tantalising that we are left with no indication of what levels of creativity and consequent forms of revision preceded this draft, which has more the appearance of a copying out of the play from 'foul papers' now lost.

It is highly confident and competent, far more vigorous and exact than one would suppose an attempt at a wholly new dramatic form would achieve at so early a stage (and one so theatrically challenging in its demands for singers, a dancer, actors of sufficiently versatile a technique to enable them to perform in masks, performers willing to submit themselves to a discipline of stylisation – all features quite alien to the conventions of early twentieth-century theatre practice).

Yeats had, of course, experimented already with some of the constituent elements of his new dramatic form,. Song, ritual, incantation, degrees of stylisation, a narrative line that focused on the climax and laid great importance on retrospection, memory and meditation – all occur in earlier plays. An intense stage discipline controlled all aspects of a play in production (even an interest in masks, through discussions with Edward Gordon Craig). But they had not, to date, come into a synthesis, and there had not been before the interest in dance which Yeats's new-found engagement with Noh as both text and performance promoted. A considerable leap of vision, creativity and daring had been necessary to achieve that synthesis and one misses the evidence to show how it was accomplished.

There had clearly been extensive discussion with Ezra Pound, who was editing Fenellosa's papers in preparation for publishing them as *Noh or Accomplishment* (Macmillan, 1916) and the papers themselves had provided Yeats with magnificent formative examples of this most sophisticated form of theatre to study, as is witnessed by his essay, 'Certain Noble Plays of Japan', which he completed earlier that same year. It might have been possible to determine how much Pound influenced Yeats's decision to adopt the Japanese form for his own purposes had any earlier drafts survived, though that is to suppose that there *were* earlier jottings, such as an outline scenario, preliminary sketches of the central dialogue sections of the play, in the way those few fragments of verse referred to above anticipate the finished songs; and that these were jettisoned once the copy had been made of them, which that eleven-page holograph represents.

Pound was at this time acting as Yeats's amanuensis because of the severe eye-strain the poet was suffering, so it is possible that the composition began through discussion, shaping a narrative that would sit comfortably within the Noh form, exploring the inner theme that in Noh is invariably more intimated than defined. It was a theme that was to undergo some changes in emphasis as the process of extant revisions reveals and which are perhaps best summed up by the important change of title from 'The Well of Immortality' to 'At the Hawk's Well', which gives far more emphasis to the Guardian of the sacred waters and to her metamorphosis into a fierce bird of prey than on the actual waters and their legendary significance. It may be that the earliest jottings were made by Pound in his role as secretary and that the holograph manuscript was written by Yeats as a basic draft on which to work, fine-tuning details, resolving dilemmas or expanding episodes that did not yet quite have the theatrical impact that he wanted, using Pound's notes as a guide but which Yeats then discarded once he had his own fair copy.

This is all hypothesis, of course, and has to remain so, given the want of any conclusive evidence; but to rehearse the possible history of the process of composition of *At the Hawk's Well* in its earliest stages and the questions it raises is to appreciate the magnitude of uncertainty which characterises our knowledge of what was a major turning-point in Yeats's career as dramatist, one which would continue to reverberate right into his last plays. If he had not made such a confident start with the first of his Noh-inspired dance plays, it is unlikely that he would have persisted with the form to the extent of beginning to work intricate variations on the prototype even within the initial *Four Plays for Dancers*, a fruitful line in experimenting that Yeats continued to pursue through works like *The Resurrection* and *The Herne's Egg* until *The Death of Cuchulain*. It is a pity that Yeats's correspondence, though informative about progress on the venture and problems faced when the play went into rehearsal, offers no insight into this crucial first stage of its development.

Fragments of dialogue follow the first copy, featuring the meeting of Cuchulain with the Old Man, and an evocation of the Guardian's transformation into a hawk and its bringing Cuchulain to 'frenzy' (43). A further draft of seventeen pages in holograph together shows Yeats amplifying the drama while beginning steadily to turn the text of the dialogue into verse and expand the contribution of the musicians. Unlike the copied qualities of the previous draft referred to above, Yeats is now revising in earnest: frequently phrases, lines or whole sections of text are scored through and immediately redrafted so that progress is by fits and starts. Notable features of the redrafting are the frequent compressions of ideas to achieve considerable economy of expression: some twelve lines attempting to describe the Old Man's appearance and his making a fire, for example, are finally reduced to four: 'The old man's limbs are doubled up | Among the rocks where he is climbing | He has made a little heap of leaves | He lays the dry sticks on the leaves' (53). Sometimes the changes, however slight, seem designed to bring greater dramatic tension: When the Old Man, for example, rounds on the Guardian in desperation at her perpetual silence, her want of 'pleasant and companionable' traits, and notices the 'glassy look' about her eyes which remind him of the 'last time it happened', he questions and dismisses her roughly: 'Do you know anything | ~~You are enough to drive an old man crazy~~.' Yeats appears immediately to have re-thought this, crosses out the second line of the above as shown and replaces it with a barely revised verse that he then continues by expanding into a new idea and sentence: '*It is* enough to drive an old man crazy | To look all day upon the broken rocks ...' (59, my italics). The Old Man observes the Guardian's changed condition but immediately reverts to luxuriating in his own self-pity. He sees and yet he does not see: after years of waiting in vain for the plashing of the waters that, if drunk, would bring him immortality, it is as if he expects invariably to fail; his mind is so programmed to futility and loss. That simple grammatical change has deepened the characterisation of the man: his abject stance is the outward realisation of an inner malaise. At a far later stage in the composition when Yeats was annotating the rehearsal text and recording there decisions made jointly by himself and Edmund Dulac as directors, he asked that the Old Man's movements be accompanied by drum taps so that the actor would appear to move 'like a marionette'; already in this revision under discussion we find Yeats preparing this effect by showing the degree to which the Old Man's mind is mechanical in its self-centred processes of response. A change that brings dramatic impact occurs directly after this outpouring from the Old Man. In the first draft Yeats had the Musicians describe both the Old Man's and the Young Man's ascent of the mountain; this new version makes no mention of Cuchulain's approach. Instead when the Old man rages against the Guardian for never speaking to him, the Young Man's voice is now unexpectedly heard: 'Then speak to me'. (The element of dramatic surprise was augmented in the production by having Henry Ainley, the actor playing Cuchulain, walk through the audience to effect his entrance, speaking as he did so.)

While a number of such improvements occur in this version as Yeats has immediate second thoughts while actually engaged in drafting, there are as many other instances where some addition has occurred to him in the interstices between periods of composition. A telling instance here (one not worked over in the manner outlined above, but arriving already fully formed) is the contrast between the Old Man's peevishness, the product of years of vain expectation, and Cuchulain's cocksure certainty that the waters will flow for him, 'for never | Have I had long to wait for anything' (67). This again neatly anticipates why later he will abandon his larger quest to taste the well-water in preference for pursuing the hawk: he sees, he wants, he expects gratification. This ably dramatises precisely how young this Young Man is. The text is getting to be the stuff of drama and Yeats is finding ways to encourage his spectators to listen imaginatively to what they hear spoken by building a sense of cumulative power into the action, an inevitability of which the characters themselves are not actually aware.

Two pages later we find Yeats struggling to get the tone right when the sudden hawk's cry from the Guardian has Cuchulain remembering the vast and fierce hawk that attacked him when he first landed from the sea, how it excelled any previously in his possession, how it lured him on, staying just outside the reach of his sword or any stone he might throw at it. There was a shorter account of this episode in the earlier full draft where the passage ends with Cuchulain turning from the hawk when he found 'it was leading me away, from | the hills'; to have continued the chase would have risked his losing his way to the sacred well. In the new full draft Yeats revised the details of the pursuit considerably in the space of some nineteen lines (the published version runs to fourteen lines) to ensure, seemingly, that the account moves smoothly into what is now a differently conceived conclusion: 'And just before I had turned the big rock there | ~~An saw~~ seen this place, it [the hawk] seemed to vanish away' (71). As re-imagined, this has become another instance of the excitable Cuchulain missing the point of his own perceptions: he never thinks that the bird might have deliberately lured him to the place for a purpose beyond the scope of his own intentions. Bird and place, he has been informed by the Old Man, are most likely under the power of the Sidhe. To have sensed a greater ordering in the shaping of event than his own purposes would have required intuition; but perhaps intuition, in being generally considered feminine, is anathema to the heroic mind-set. Yeats had already examined this theme in his first Cuchulain play, *On Baile's Strand*, where the older hero's failure to intuit why he is drawn so powerfully and so strangely to Connla results in a weight of tragic suffering. It is characteristic of Yeats to build echoes and resonances like this between the plays that make up his sequence on Cuchulain's life and death. It is equally characteristic of Yeats to have his hero dismiss the glimpse he is afforded of the workings of fate in preference for an assertion of his personal will: 'Could I but find a means to bring it down, | I'd hood it.'

While the main shape of the play is now clear and much of the dialogue in an advanced stage of composition, the episode involving the dance has yet to be developed: only the actual placing is set with the terse direction, 'Corus [sic] &. dance' (79). The Musicians' contribution generally is at the level of sketches: there is no opening song to accompany the ceremony with the cloth, though it is specified interestingly in this manuscript that the chorus enters with a 'black cloth' (49), from which one may suppose that Yeats has begun to think about ways of staging an impressive opening appropriate for a bare, uncurtained stage. The play begins here with the chorus's evocation of place, time of day and atmosphere, though the initial line ('The dry leaves fall from the tree') is rather pedestrian beside the final version ('The boughs of the hazel shake'), which has greater specificity and a hint of the ominous: it works far more immediately to stir 'the eye of the mind' to imagine.

Curiously the manuscript is framed by first drafts: one on an independent sheet inserted before the play proper, of what eventually was to be situated as the final song after the second unfolding and folding of the cloth that begins 'The man that I praise' (47); the second continuing after the body of the play is a substantial realisation of that part of the final song, comprising three stanzas, which precedes the ceremony with the cloth. The second of these is close to completion: only one change was necessary, turning 'Among *the watered* meadows' (83, my italics) to the highly evocative 'Among *indolent* meadows', which captures exactly the come-what-may attitude that dominates the two parts of this song in their mounting scorn of the heroic life and its idealistic pursuits (that revision was not made until late in the rehearsal process, see 155).

By contrast the draft of the other section shows Yeats somewhat struggling to achieve a precise but allusive expression and avoid the obvious, such as 'the clang of a bell' rather than 'a hand on the bell' to summon the cows to milking. What in time were to undergo major revision were the final two lines of each stanza: the first has a grazing cow draining the well dry, the second asks: 'For who but I if any can praise | A bare tree' (47). Perhaps it was the placing of the two parts of the song together that prompted Yeats to revise these lines to the mordantly sardonic references to an idiot as the only man likely to praise a dry well and 'withered tree'. This is in time to be the final expression of a largely studied detachment that the Musicians preserve throughout the performance, which, as in Brecht's later explorations of the Noh form, incite an audience to decide their own position in relation to the choices that determine the action (there is to be one dramatic breaking out of this stance, which is discussed below).

A group of holograph sheets next show Yeats working at gaps in the text as it stands: the song accompanying the first ceremony with the cloth (massively overwritten, but still the finished version emerges through the plethora of cancelled lines and phrases); the opening exposition by the Musicians and their depiction of the Old Man (the first virtually a clear copy, the second needing several complete revisions before a final version is accepted, though it will require further reworking); a first attempt at pacing the complex sequence of events that encompass the dance, largely in terms of the chorus's contribution (the change of Guardian to Hawk with the shedding of the encompassing cloak and the impact of her appearance on Cuchulain; the musicians' fear and their warning Cuchulain to avoid her 'dancing feet ... | Two feet that are like quivering blades' (93); their awareness of the plashing of the waters in the well and that Cuchulain has heard it too); several brief efforts at the lyric the Musicians sing after Cuchulain, entranced, has followed the Bird-Woman from the stage. These last, in imagining the life that Cuchulain might have led instead of what is to befall him, repeatedly get confused in their phrasing with lines from the stanza they sing to end the play;. Next come two heavily revised attempts to evoke the horror of the metamorphosis. There is 'The sliding through being & vein | Of a cold undying will' (99) – too verbose by comparison with the finally realised terse prayer for divine protection from a shocking awareness of being possessed; and on the last sheet a loose four-line attempt at the song, 'Come to me human faces', far slacker in expression than the opening stanza as published.

What is interesting, however, is the placing of this sheet directly after the evocation of the horror of possession which suggests, perhaps, an emotional and psychological connexion between the two in Yeats's thinking – a useful point for director and performers to bear in mind in production.

It is as if rising horror moves the chorus out of their detached stance so that they first show more understanding of Cuchulain in terms of what he has lost in chasing the hawk and end by embracing their own humble lot in preference for any engagement with the heroic or supernatural. A further comment about production issues may be made in relation to the reference to the dancer's 'quivering blades'. Yeats of course knew little about dancing and came to trust his dancers to experiment to find an appropriate style, but the image is powerful in terms of what it might usefully convey to a choreographer or dancer, who frequently enjoy working with evocative imagery. Though the phrase was to be excised eventually from the text of *At the Hawk's Well*, it does indicate what Yeats in general terms expected: that the dance be fast, fierce (even ferocious) and violent in its effect.

The play is now all but complete and the chronologically next extant typescript while containing evidence of local revisions is heavily marked with details of production which indicate its use in rehearsals. This is a fascinating document, since it contains not only Yeats's changes to the text but also Allan Wade's notes about his movements as the Old Man and Dulac's observations about the timing of episodes deploying his music and pencil sketches of how he wished the actors to deport themselves. These are most likely the sketches that Yeats and Dulac worked on together to help Ainley understand how they wished him to move and position himself in the playing space, especially to make best use of his mask. Though a highly accomplished actor, Ainley's technique did not embrace the difficult art of wearing masks; that technique proved to be too entrenched to enable him fully to grasp this challenging innovation, since Yeats's letters show how keen he was to jettison Ainley from the cast at the earliest opportunity.

If it is studied alongside Dulac's music and his designs for ceremonial cloth, costumes and masks, this document amounts to a remarkably detailed production script or performance text of the first staging in 1916. There is one notable revision, perhaps relating to the Young Man's mask, that shows Yeats the practical man of theatre, displacing Yeats the poet and playwright. At the moment when Cuchulain tries to calm the anxiety of the Old Man (the latter fears that, if they are together when the waters plash, the burly hero may well push him aside and drain every drop), Yeats in earlier drafts gives Cuchulain the line: 'I'll dip my helmet in. We shall both drink' (139). Dulac's mask for the Young Man sports a most impressive helmet with an upward-curving horn by way of decoration. In the design helmet and mask look independent, making it look as if the removal of the helmet were feasible. In order to avoid any unforeseen and embarrassing accident, the two were most likely fused in the making to create a full-headed mask, similar to that worn by Allan Wade – Alvin Langdon Coburn's photographs of the two actors in costume certainly suggest this – which would make the original line, even if not accompanied by any actualising gesture, potentially risible, given how close the initial audience in Lady Cunard's drawing room would be seated in proximity to the players. At some point during the rehearsals Yeats, ever alert to details of a production that might disturb the carefully created atmosphere of a performance, cancelled the line in favour of a more plausible revision: 'I'll take it in my hands. We shall both drink …' (139). The new phrasing is fitter in context too: the Old Man has told how so little water rises that it but wets the stones of the well. A dipped helmet would require a certain depth. This may seem a trite point to make, but it shows both Yeats's attention to issues of practicality and his exacting engagement with the details of the imagined world he is creating onstage.

The one feature of the play still not properly devised and described is the ceremony with the cloth that opens and closes the action. This version instructs that the Chorus enter carrying their instruments and the black cloth, bearing the image of a hawk, which 'is stretched between them so as to fall perpendicularly' (113). Not surprisingly, this is heavily scored through since it would require remarkably agile performers to carry instruments and cloth! Two related manuscripts from this period of the text's gestation show first in holograph and then in typescript what is certainly a record of how the opening was handled in rehearsal by Yeats and Dulac: the instruments are now placed on the perimeter of the stage before the performance begins so the players have only the bringing in followed by the folding and unfolding of the cloth on which to focus, while the ceremony follows in outline the pattern of movement accompanied by the musicians' singing that recurs with numerous adjustments and amplifications in subsequent printed texts. The variant readings as they progress towards the direction to be found in *Collected Plays* move from prescribing a sequence following that staged in 1916 to a more open discussion about possibilities for staging, which may be the fruit of the several revivals of the play to be staged in Yeats's lifetime, including those at the Abbey within the different formation of a proscenium theatre. Comparing the directions for Yeats's plays is always a fruitful exercise, since they generally record the changing circumstances of different stagings and, more importantly, demonstrate how adaptable Yeats became when those circumstances required it: there is nothing dictatorial about his later attitudes to performance.

In a similar fashion a group of sheets in holograph with typescript copies show Yeats working on several sequences to incorporate material evolved during rehearsal and present them in a cleaner copy, presumably in preparation for printing. These include the first entrance of the Musicians and their sung ritual (these sheets include drafts of the second stanza, performed while re-folding the cloth, which does not appear in the rehearsal script but was incorporated in a copy Yeats inscribed to Lady Gregory at the time of the first performances, which she was prevented from seeing). They also include the dance sequence (where the timing of danced and mimed action with choric speech and song is exactly laid out); the Old Man's warning to Cuchulain about the dangers of involving himself with the Woman of the Sidhe (it was to undergo yet further revision); the haunting moment in the opening scene-setting where the Second Musician intrudes into the First Musician's explanations of what the audience are to understand by the stylised image they see before them to voice a fear of the place, introducing a new emotional charge into the introduction; and, lastly, the Old Man's speech on waking in which he curses the 'shadows' that continue to delude him. (Further revision was chiefly to bring more bitterness and rage to the speech through simple changes to the punctuation, particularly to avoid the risk of flatness when lines are repeatedly and heavily end-stopped, as here.) Taken together, these all show Yeats heightening the drama of the various episodes, particularly giving actors more opportunity to exploit their vocal range and the emotional and psychological 'colouring' they can contribute to the unfolding narrative.

This part of the volume concludes with a transcription of the 1917 printing of *At the Hawk's Well* in *To-Day*, which Yeats had heavily revised in places (the play was first published some months earlier in *Harper's Bazaar*, but the English journal is preferred as including most of the emendations and redrafting that had occurred till this date). This text is carefully collated with subsequent printings until *Collected Plays*. Corrections are chiefly local, designed to improve punctuation to bring greater clarity and variety to the text when spoken, to introduce a more idiomatic expression especially in the Old Man's speeches, to improve the versification, expand on or insert more detailed stage directions concerning the actors' movements within the playing space and to create a better integration of such movements within the musical accompaniment, requiring a particularly focused attentiveness amongst the Musicians.

The most notable insertions are a precise placing of an instruction for when the dancer throws off her cloak to emerge in Dulac's magnificent hawk costume. Disappointingly the revisions do not include more detailed directions drawn from the Abbey staging involving de Valois, when the ecstatic movement of the bird steadily drew Cuchulain on his rising into the patterns of the dance, as the hawk-woman became by turns seductive and fiercely repelling. The episode in this staging became an embodiment of Yeats's fascination with the interplay of love and loathing (picking up the theme of Cuchulain's intricate relations with Aoife, as he relates them to Conchubar in *On Baile's Strand*). But perhaps Yeats would have seen this as too prescriptive, just as were the precise timings for stages in the dance that were included in earlier versions of the text. The final state of the ending is worth comment. The text as recorded from *Four Plays for Dancers* on to *Collected Plays* offers cast and director some interesting choices: initially the directions ask that the Musicians perform the first part of their final song while unfolding the cloth and then accompany the second part while refolding it; but then the practical-minded Yeats notes that, if Dulac's music is used, then the Musicians should not rise and begin the ritual until they start the second part of the song ('The man that I praise ...').

This indicates a complete willingness for future casts to commission new music. Even by 1921, when the play was published as the first of the *Four Plays for Dancers*, Yeats was not expecting the original staging to be viewed as sacrosanct. This perhaps accords with the dissatisfaction his letters express while that first production was undergoing rehearsal and performance, though already by July 1918 Yeats had lost control of that production, once Michio Ito, who first danced the role of the Guardian, had performed the piece in New York without the dramatist's permission, with American-speaking Japanese players and new music by the Japanese composer, Yamada. Yeats may have been bowing to the inevitable, but this date marks the start of his more exploratory attitude to the staging of his dance plays.

So original within the practices of European theatre and dramaturgy was Yeats's engagement with this new dramatic form and style that the manuscript materials invite a protracted discussion of details like this to appreciate the speed and integrity marking his progress towards full mastery of his inspiration. By the time he came to draft *The Cat and the Moon* in 1917 Yeats had substantially completed a second exploration of his prototype (*The Dreaming of the Bones*) as again a vehicle for tragedy and had made some headway with a third (*The Only Jealousy of Emer*). That he should wish to vary his experimenting with the potential of the dance play by moving into the comic mode seems a logical development: Noh offered him the precedent of the Kyogen play. What impresses about the resulting drama, as Andrew Parkin in his admirably informative Introduction makes clear, is how deftly Yeats fuses a relatively simple, comic narrative with an abundance of references that fuse European with Japanese cultural expression, and Christian with Theosophical, Buddhist and Zen thought. As with the best of Noh, a surface simplicity masks a sophisticated complexity of allusion that invites as deep or as profound an engagement with the play in performance as a spectator chooses to adopt.

Given that quality, it is again frustrating as with the early stages of the composition of *At the Hawk's Well* that virtually nothing is extant that could show how that intricate layering of effect was achieved. Parkin lists the numerous sources that Yeats turned to in shaping his action but no materials survive to show how their fusion was evolved and realised: no scenario, no holograph manuscripts or early typescripts of exploratory drafts. The first extant document is a typescript prepared for use as a rehearsal copy that is to be found in the Abbey Theatre archives, which predates the play's publication by some seven years; copies of this were used as the basis of Pound's printing of *The Cat and the Moon* in *The Dial* (1924, the year that the play also appeared in *The Criterion*) and as copy text for *The Cat and the Moon and Certain Poems* (Cuala, also 1924). The play was first staged by the Dublin Drama League in 1926. Parkin muses whether, given the lack of foul papers, Yeats dictated the play throughout its gestation, but this is hypothetical. The Abbey typescript is transcribed by Parkin and collated with two further copies of it now in America (one being that sent to Pound) and with sets of marked proofs not only for the 1924 volume but also for the planned Edition de Luxe (c.1932 and c.1937), *Wheels and Butterflies* (1934) and *Collected Plays* (1934).

The long delay, unusual within the Yeats canon, between the play's completion (signified by the preparation of an acting copy) and its publication together with the curious fact of its non-appearance in the collection of plays for dancers may be explained by a comment Yeats made to Lady Gregory where he referred to 'a play copy I had lost and forgotten for some years'. (The remark is situated in a draft of his dedication to Gregory of the Cuala volume.) Curiously it must have been the dialogue only that went missing, since the three songs from the Musicians that open the play, provide for a passage of time while the two beggars approach the saint's tree and then close the performance, were published, together and undivided, as a poem entitled 'The Cat and the Moon' in both *Nine Poems* (1918) and *The Wild Swans at Coole* (1919). Why the stanzas became separated from the rest of the play is not clear, particularly since they are firmly in place in the acting script. Because of the advanced compositional state of that script which provides Parkin with his base text, revisions, as the collations demonstrate, were largely limited to matters of punctuation, spelling and idiomatic elisions. The thinly disguised satire of Martin and Moore as the holy man from Laban and his friend, the old lecher, was in time rendered more comic by breaking up the original prose story and re-phrasing statements as questions that the Lame Beggar struggles in vain to answer, while the Blind Beggar luxuriates in his companion's ignorance. The story in the telling comes to have all the rough vigour of a shanachie's art (see 222–25).

The most sustained revision was to the ending, which appears originally to have had no dance, concluding simply with the Lame Beggar and the (imagined) Saint on his shoulder quitting the playing space 'to drum taps and flute'. However at ninety degrees to the main body of text, there is typed addition offering an expanded ending with the Saint requiring the Lame Beggar to bow and so bless the road before, behind and to the sides of them. Further there is a marked caret after the Lame Man's words, 'Let us be going, Holy Man' with the instruction (in holograph and encircled): 'Insert slip'; also an inked cross after the stage direction relating to the Lame Beggar's exit is accompanied by a new handwritten direction: 'Dance –' (239). The new dialogue is cancelled through, but the references to slip and dance remain. When exactly each of these additions was added to or marked on the script is open to question: much relies on identifying different shades of ink and nibs used for Yeats's holograph insertions. His 'Note' on the play for the Cuala edition refers to the drama as 'unfinished' and states it must remain so till the play has been performed 'and I know how the Lame Man is to move'. He posits a number of possibilities: that the Lame Man stay on one knee after the Blind Man has gone; that he avail himself of the Blind Man's stick to leave the stage; that he should 'walk stiffly or limp as if a leg were paralysed'. He continues: 'Whatever his movements are they must be artificial and formal, like the movement upon a puppet stage or in a dance …' (see *VPl* 805). Taking Yeats at his word that the ending would be revised only when he had seen the play performed, one is inclined to suppose that additional dialogue typed at an angle to the main text was inserted after the production in 1926 or, maybe, when the play was in rehearsal for the Drama League's staging in 1926.

The confusion that attends the last page of the acting script is somewhat eased by the final materials that Parkin transcribes: the 'slip' may well refer to a sheet of Renvyle Hotel notepaper on which an expanded ending has been jotted by Yeats. This includes an enlarged version about how to bless the road at the start of a journey, then additional new material follows leading up to the Holy Man's advice to the Lame Beggar: 'Then dance'. The play was revived in 1931 and some performances were given at Gogarty's hotel before the opening in Dublin, where Yeats appears to have had new thoughts about a fit conclusion and devised the material in the hotel for insertion in the acting script in place of both the short and the slightly enlarged endings to be found there. More revision followed on loose sheets of notepaper and on a typescript that basically refine this newest of endings, while an extant proof of the conclusion from the Edition de Luxe of 1934 contains a detailed scenario for the actual danced sequence.

This is notable for removing the word 'perhaps' at the start of a sentence describing how clashes of cymbals should mark the moments in the dancing whenever the Lame Beggar strikes his foot on the ground. That possibilities have become certainties here may well reflect, as Parkin argues, how Yeats's confidence in what dance might convey was strengthened by the time of the 1931 rehearsals. Certainly by that date he had been working with Ninette de Valois on staging several of his Noh-inspired plays at the Abbey as well as seeing the dance repertory she staged there with pupils from the Abbey School of Ballet; and he now had direct experience of the range of moods that dance, classical and modern, can convey. He appreciated that dance could accomplish the transition that the play's narrative requires at this point from the comic grotesque to the profoundly spiritual: his emended direction now firmly requests that the choreography do just that.

Andrew Parkin's volume is a welcome addition to the Cornell series, offering in his Introduction an exhaustive account of the cultural contexts in which the composition of each of the plays took place and a detailed and convincing account of why he has ordered the extant materials in a particular way. This is no easy task: slips of paper on which local revisions were made have over time become separated from the manuscripts or typescripts to which they were attached, making the determining of an exact chronology problematic; texts published in American journals where proofs were corrected before publication sometimes contain different readings of lines and sequences than other sets which were emended at a later date after the play's submission to English journals for publication (as neither can be viewed appropriately as the base text of a particular version of a play in composition, this makes collation difficult). To help readers around this challenging issue, Parkin has compiled a chronology, itemising the fifty-six materials he has consulted in preparing the edition. This is a remarkable feat of organisation. Appendices offer useful production materials relating to music for the stagings of *The Cat and the Moon*. First, J.F. Larchet's music, scored for Flute, Zither and Drum, for the production seen at Oliver St. John Gogarty's Renvyle House Hotel and at the Abbey Theatre in August and September 1931, which significantly (after the settings for the songs) includes a short burst of music headed 'Dance'. Secondly, Lennox Robinson's sketches for a musical rendering of the songs (presumably for the 1926 production, which he directed and in which he also played one of the musicians); these are more in the plain-chant style of Florence Farr's cantilation to the psaltery. Given how valuable are the insights these offer, one wonders why Parkin did not include all the material Dulac provided for the 1916 production of *At the Hawk's Well*. The designs and music have been republished from time to time since they first appeared in *Four Plays for Dancers*, but generally they are not readily accessible to readers and it would have been useful to scholars to have all that material collected alongside the manuscripts as relevant to a full interpretation of the latter.

If the scholarship shaping the Introduction and the *apparatus criticus* is never less than exemplary, the quality of the transcriptions (especially of the holograph materials) and the proof-reading is not consistently of that calibre. Cancellations in the manuscripts are not always replicated in the transcribed text. In the manuscript sheet reproduced on page 12, for example, the whole of line 1 ('The dawn is breaking whr the grey mountain side') is cancelled out and a new line entered above this ('Night is coming on – the mountainside is darkening'), while part of the following line ('The leaves of the hazel, & of the oa and of have fallen') are struck through as shown with 'have' reinserted above that last cancelled word; neither cancellation is observed in the transcription. On line 5 of page 14, Yeats changes his mind about the direction of the wind ('north east west') but both readings are left to stand in the transcription. Similar slips are to be found on page 19, line 10; page 21, lines 9 and 13; page 23, line 8; page 25, lines 6 and 14; page 31, line 16; and these relate to but one manuscript, NLI 8773(3) a. One might continue this exercise.

Yeats's holograph is never easy to read at any stage of his career, except perhaps when he is making clear copies of heavily emended text (such as the songs about the cat and the moon to be found in NLI 13,587(22) reproduced here on page 206. When the fit of composition was on him and inspiration flowed fast, Yeats tended to write the initial letters of words and then add a flourish to suggest their completion; those flourishes, however, tend to be regular and consistently deployed for particular words and so take on a kind of legibility. It is a matter of personal interpretation perhaps, but the same juxtaposition of rudely formed letters are present in lines 14 and 20 on the manuscript reproduced on page 20 and would appear to be shaping the word 'that', which is the reading Parkin offers for line 20; but the identically formed word in line 14 he transcribes as '*the* stony rim', though 'that' would seem the logical reading in the full context of the word's usage. If confirmation were needed, it may be found two lines above (12), where in the phrase 'I found *the* stones wet', the formulation of the letters by Yeats's pen is quite different from the word transcribed as 'the' two lines below. Similarly on page 90 in lines 4 and 12 two intricate flourishes, though they bear marked similarities in the penmanship are rendered differently as 'stone' and 'thorn' respectively. The Musicians are at this point describing the Old Man's appearance after years spent in this desolate landscape: the larger context of the first reading is 'He is all doubled up | He is all dry *stone* among the rocks'. These lines are cancelled as is the whole group of eight lines in which they are situated. Below Yeats makes a second attempt at the passage, following the cancelled version carefully but compressing the expression to render it more powerfully immediate; the two lines in question are now transcribed: 'He is all doubled up | A *thorn* tree among rocks' (my italics throughout). 'Doubled up' exactly captures the appearance of both a man crippled with age and thorn trees surviving in windswept landscapes. ('Crooked' was always a favourite Yeatsian descriptive epithet for such a sight: see, e.g., *VSR* 137; *Myth 2005* 184 for an example from 1896.)

The manner in which Yeats revises the first passage to create the second suggests that 'thorn' should be used for both transcriptions. It could be argued that this is a matter of taste and judgement, but the transcription principles for the Cornell series have a mode of presentation for 'equally possible conjectural readings', if an editor has doubts about too precise an interpretation. This, if used, allows readers to make their own choice from the evidence. There is a similar example of this issue on pp. 98–99, where in ll. 1 (cancelled), 8 and 16 (cancelled), Yeats is searching for an epithet to describe the experience being undergone by the Guardian of the Well of being possessed by a supernatural force; in all three cases what his pen forms with something of an elision seems to be the same word but this is variously transcribed as 'horrible' (l.1); 'terrible' (l.8); and 'horrible' (l.14) but a close study of the manuscript makes one question why the variety of interpretations is necessary. (Would the alternative presentation discussed above not have been preferable to a categorical reading where the editor is in some doubt?). There are further instances of readings that one might challenge on the grounds of similarly or identically formed words to be found in close proximity upon the same page. Most of the materials that are reproduced for comparative transcription in this volume are typescripts or printed proofs (almost entirely so for *The Cat and the Moon*) and so the problems presented by Yeats's orthography during composition relate to a relatively small range of pages. This last point is more a cavil than a serious criticism and does not undermine one's trust overall in Parkin as an editor with great sensitivity to the demands posed for him by two rich and diverse plays for dancers.

Karen E. Brown, *The Yeats Circle, Verbal and Visual Relations in Ireland, 1880–1939* (Farnham: Ashgate, 2011), pp. xiv + 189.

Tom Walker

Nineteenth- and twentieth-century Irish cultural history has tended to concentrate on literary matters. Yet in recent years the island's visual and material culture has started to be given more historical and critical attention. Examples include the landmark histories of Irish museums and exhibitions by Marie Bourke and Fintan Cullen, and a 2011 special issue of the journal *Éire-Ireland* on 'Irish Things' edited by Paige Reynolds, not to mention some of the intersections explored in volumes four and five of *The Oxford History of the Irish Book*, helped along – one might speculate – by various technological advancements in the documentation, reproduction and circulation of relevant images.

Amidst what might come to seem like a more general corrective turn in Irish studies, Karen E. Brown's ambitious interdisciplinary study considers the visual alongside the verbal. It aims to do so through five 'case studies' of the interaction between word and image, moving from the Cultural Revival of the fin de siècle through to the supposed 'breakthrough of Irish Modernism in the 1920s and 1930s'. The output of the Yeats family (father, sons and daughters) in the literary and visual spheres is considered alongside work by other figures in their circle 'to show how intrinsic this nexus of inter-arts relationship was to the conception of cultural change in this period of Irish history'.

The book is at its strongest in illuminating the careers and work of lesser-known Yeats family associates. Its second chapter focuses on Evelyn Gleeson, co-founder with Elizabeth and Lily Yeats of the Dun Emer Industries in 1902, fruitfully engaging with the collection of her papers held at Trinity College Dublin to draw out the particular nationalist and feminist imperatives motivating her to set up the arts and crafts enterprise. For instance, a fragment of a fascinating talk that Gleeson seems to have given to the Irish Literary Society in 1907 shows how such efforts to forge a distinctive native 'artistic industry' were undertaken with an acute awareness of how Ireland was falling behind similar efforts across much of the rest of Europe.

Gleeson attempted to think through whether it is possible to 'revive Gaelic ideas in our material surroundings, – our tables, our chairs, our silver, our inkstand, our various kinds of stuff', as she pleads to the Gaelic Leaguers present: 'Cannot one nationalise through the eyes as well as through the ears?' The resources she marshalled towards undertaking such a revival of Irish 'stuff' include the retrieval of a tradition, in going back to the motifs of early Irish Christian art, with its supposed links to Byzantine art (a recurring link made in the period it would seem), as well as the preservation of local handicrafts, such as through the gathering of information as regards the natural dyeing pigments still used by women in the countryside.

The under-regarded poet, translator, and critic Thomas MacGreevy, who had something of a genius for befriending geniuses, similarly benefits from prolonged attention in the book's fourth chapter. Again drawing on archival material held at Trinity College Dublin, it outlines the relationship between his poetry and his response to the paintings of Jack Yeats. Brown shows how MacGreevy responds to the visual particularities of Yeats's canvases, in terms of palette and the organisation of space, both figuratively and upon the page, through his embrace of a set of then-radical 'modernist' poetic procedures. But such seemingly aesthetic inter-art encounters overlap with more socio-political and religious concerns too, as MacGreevy, through the filter of his own Republicanism and Catholicism, strives to cast the painter as Ireland's Goya. Another byway usefully followed in the study's final chapter is into Jack Yeats's own literary works. Among a generally baffled contemporaneous critical reception, the account points to the sympathetic and insightful responses of MacGreevy, W. B. Yeats and Samuel Beckett to novels such as *Sligo* (1930), *The Aramanthers* (1936) and *This Charmed Life* (1938). Through attending to their commentary, as well as exploring the Jack Yeats archive at the National Gallery of Ireland, Brown makes (but does not fully unpack) some suggestive links between Yeats's later paintings, his literary works' focus on travel and treatment of the image, and the possible wider nature of Irish writing from J. M. Synge through to Beckett.

Yet this book's overall authority is undermined by prevailing problems of reference. Most seriously of all, the first and third chapters consider W. B. Yeats's involvement in the preparation of cover designs and illustrations for his 'Secret Rose' stories, first in *The Secret Rose* (1897) by Althea Gyles and his father, then in the later edition of the *Stories of Red Hanrahan and The Secret Rose* (1927), by Norah McGuinness, while seemingly being unaware of the fact that an entire appendix is devoted to this matter in Warwick Gould, Phillip L. Marcus and Michael J. Sidnell's second revised and enlarged edition of *The Secret Rose, Stories by W. B. Yeats: A Variorum Edition* (1992). This appendix quotes extensively from the correspondence between Yeats, McGuinness and Frederick Macmillan in relation to the 1927 edition, refuting Brown's claim that these letters are 'unpublished' and only 'recently made available in the National Library of Ireland'. Indeed, her study's discussion of this correspondence, McGuinness's illustrations and the influence of the particular images of Byzantine art which Yeats showed her unwittingly retraces some ground previously covered by Robert S. Nelson's account of Yeats and Byzantium in *Hagia Sophia, 1850–1950: Holy Wisdom Modern Monument* (2004), an authority again not cited in this book. The notes to the variorum edition also question Brown's assumption that Althea Gyles was a member of the Hermetic Order of the Golden Dawn, pointing to Gyles's absence from any extant membership lists – which strongly suggests that Yeats's writing and instructions were the primary sources for her symbolism.

Seemingly not consulted too in these and other regards were Gould and Deirdre Toomey's edition of *Mythologies* (2005), volume two of *The Collected Letters of W. B. Yeats* (1997), as well as the later letters in the InteLex Electronic Edition, and Ann Saddlemyer's edition of *The Collected Letters of John Middleton Synge* (1983–1984). Thus Brown mistakenly claims that a response from Synge does not exist to Elizabeth Yeats's suggestion of a Jack Yeats drawing as a possible frontispiece to his *Poems and Translations* (1909); the study also errs in claiming that Yeats travelled to Italy in 1924, rather than 1925.

Such errors and a lack of reference to standard scholarly editions do not inspire confidence and the treatment of many matters is sometimes rather thin. The first chapter, for instance, offers a very basic outline of W. B. Yeats's links to Pre-Raphaelite *fraternité des arts* practices, which adds little to Elizabeth Bergmann Loizeaux's earlier *Yeats and the Visual Arts* (1986) – a somewhat dated account by now in view of the intervening flood of relevant published material. Important figures such as Charles Ricketts and Charles Shannon or periodicals such as *The Dome* and *The Savoy* are named, but their impact is not explored or assessed in any detail. Moreover, the stress placed on Yeats's 'striving for synthesis between the arts' offers very little sense of the fluctuations and developments that occurred in the poet's aesthetic thinking throughout the 1890s and 1900s, as he furthered his self-education, and engaged in various cultural projects and political controversies. Even the in many ways admirable chapter on MacGreevy neither engages with his extensive writings for *The Connoisseur* and *The Studio*, nor mentions his important friendship with George and W. B. Yeats, who in 1925 wrote letters introducing him as an expert on painting to, among others, T. S. Eliot and Ezra Pound, and surely of considerable importance when placing him within the Yeats circle.

The overall historical and theoretical framing of the book is also problematic. This is particularly the case in relation to the thorny issue of Modernism and the modern, terms which the book often invokes without ever quite untangling. Brown offers a rather tidy sense of Modernism breaking into Ireland in the 1920s and 1930s, as well as a seeming conflation of it with painterly abstraction. This leaves her study struggling to think through the place of a mimetic primitivism in the earlier work of Synge and the Yeats brothers. There are also several unconvincing attempts to analyse contemporaneous critical debates as regards the traditional versus the modern in Irish poetry of the 1930s. These passages struggle to gain a suitable critical distance from the pronouncements made in Beckett's essay 'Recent Irish Poetry' (1934), to place figures such as Frank O'Connor or John Lyle Donaghy, or to understand the nature of the role played by the Cuala Press in the period – a confusion reflected in the mistaken inclusion among Cuala's authors of Austin Clarke, a figure antipathetic to both W. B. Yeats and Beckett.

From a more theoretical perspective, the study leans heavily and almost exclusively on the ideas of W. J. T. Mitchell, clearly a key thinker in the field of word-image relations, but one whose (not unassailable) ideas Brown struggles to build on rather than merely demonstrate in the course of her analysis. This book's highlighting of the importance of inter-arts relationships to this period's cultural history is welcome and broadly sound, it presents much interesting and unusual material, and it does make several original discoveries. But against such strengths, its severe problems must also be acknowledged. Those who seek to follow the avenues for further research and critical debate it undoubtedly opens up will have to do so with much scholarly care.

W. B. Yeats and George Yeats, *The Letters*, ed. Ann Saddlemyer (Oxford: Oxford University Press, 2011), pp. xxii + 599. Neil Mann, Matthew Gibson and Claire Nally (eds.), *W. B. Yeats's 'A Vision': Explications and Contexts* (Clemson, SC: Clemson University Digital Press, 2012), pp. xx + 374.

Lauren Arrington

In October 1937, George Yeats (GY) wrote to W. B. Yeats (WBY) mildly complaining of a tedious conversation with the 'chatterbox' Colm O'Lochlainn, who – as one of Saddlemyer's wonderful footnotes tells us – would write in his entry on Yeats for the *British Annual of Irish Literature* (1939): 'towards the end his mind was all bemused with strange occult philosophies, theosophy, spiritism; and in play or poem these were given an airing, without even full conviction to defend them'.

As the most rigorous scholarship makes clear, there was little need for either of the Yeatses to 'defend' the system. In *Becoming George*, published over a decade ago, Saddlemyer discussed frankly the endless 'debate as to whether the bond that first linked them was her hoax, a joint self-deception, or daimonic intervention'. Margaret Mills Harper, drawing from her monograph *Wisdom of Two* for her essay 'Reflected Voices, Double Visions' in this new volume of essays on *A Vision*, stresses the Yeatses' indifference to the truth (insofar as that word refers to scientific verifiability) of their spiritual communicators. GY's discovery of automatic writing provoked neither full 'belief nor dismissal', and neither WBY nor GY were 'distracted' by the compulsion to prove or disprove their experience. Their attitude is conveyed in this handsome edition of the letters, in which the couple's interactions with the occult are relayed matter-of-factly. On 28 August 1924, WBY writes to GY from London, telling her about toys that he bought at Harrods for Michael and Anne, a gossipy dinner with the Dulacs, and a séance with Mrs Cooper:

Somebody came claiming to be my mother & spoke apparently of Lolly. I asked if she meant 'Polly' & she said 'O no no no' & then I was told my father would materialize. In a moment a hand came, quite distinct against some vague luminous object – it was like my fathers hand but seemed smaller than life size. It touched me & was there for some time – very exciting & strange. The sudden appearance of a sollid hand out of nothing – it touched my head on the side opposite to the medium who remained perfectly motionless (141).

Although his comment on the stillness of the medium may suggest some element of a search for veracity, the encounter is qualified with the ambiguity of 'apparently' and 'seemed'. GY's letter to WBY about the occurrence of 'strange things' at their house in Oxford (the emergence of sixty-year-old correspondence from a desk, the smell of incense, and a disembodied voice) is more certain but still interrogatory: 'It is inconceivable how they got there & how [....] An apport? And why!' (8 August, 1920, 53). Neil Mann quotes in his useful essay on 'The Foundations of *A Vision*' that opens *Explications and Contexts* a passage from the drafts of *A Vision B*, whereYeats tests his responses to inevitable questions about the truth of the system:

'Some will ask if I believe what I have written & I will not know how to answer, because we all mean different things by the word belief. Who will understand me if I say that I should must & do believe it because it is a Myth' (*NLI MS* 30,757, cf., *A Packet for Ezra Pound* 32; *AVB* 24; *MYV2* 414–15).

In light of WBY and GY's lack of concern with proof, and the esteemed body of scholarship that does not regard the legitimacy of the Yeatses' experiments as appropriate to academic study, the passionate intensity with which some essayists in *A Vision: Explications and Contexts* engage personally with the system is puzzling. Colin McDowell offers meditations on his own spiritual practices, first asking whether 'anyone other than the two Yeatses, or perhaps it was only ever one of them, draw succour or solace from the book's ideas' before going on to admit that he does not 'believe in some of these things [...] but they do seem to me to be as adequate as any other metaphor that people have come up with to explain life and give meaning to it'. This confessional tone shifts to homily as McDowell concludes,

'In the end, *A Vision* serves to remind us that we can never truly know anything. We think we are examining the nature of the external world and find that we have simply returned to the mind's own imaginings [....] In short, the book is an invitation to wake up' (211).

Such an assertion ignores the Yeatses' use of the system as a means of explaining the world and the self. Their psychic experiments and experiences are frequently connected to moments of personal crises. Both distraught over Francis Stuart's abuse of Iseult, WBY wrote to GY of the comforting scent of violets (see above 87–88), which brought a calming perspective ('He does not drink or smoke, & so it must be insanity') and the hope of spiritual assistance ([30 July, 1920], 39). In a letter from early August 1920, WBY discusses at length Stuart's position at Phase 14, which seems to be a means of intellectually reconciling Iseult's inexplicable attachment to the sadist (4 August 1920, 46). GY divined through horoscope that Iseult's child would not live, but she expressed greater concern for WBY than the Stuarts 'because the spectator suffers more poignantly than the victim; his suffering being wholly subjective' ([3 August 1920], 43–44). As well as rendering comprehensible private and public cataclysms, the mundane was also described according to the system. GY and WBY referred to her mother, Edith Ellen Tucker, by the name '19', the phase of *A Vision* to which they imagined her to correspond. Work on the system was cathartic; WBY wrote to GY in early September 1924, 'Do you know that I half think that finishing the philosophy getting all that abstraction put in concrete form makes one better. Perhaps I too am a medium & my force is used' ([*c*. 2 September, 1924], 144).

Of course, the system was never fully completed, which calls into question Rory Ryan's claim that his essay 'The Is and the Ought, the Knower and the Known: An Analysis of the Four Faculties in Yeats's System' is part of a larger project to show that 'the system is internally self-coherent'. Ryan focuses on the 'skeleton' of *A Vision* since the 'flesh' is 'beyond the scope' of his study (22–54). This is unfortunate, since the working out on 'a practical level' of the rules governing the Faculties is precisely why so much of the system is explained in WBY's prefaces. As he prepared the manuscript of *A Vision* B, he expressed what Mann terms his 'dramatic philosophy': 'I cannot prove that this drama exists ... but I assert that he who accepts it though it be but as a Myth like something thought out upon a painted stage sees the world breaking into life' (18). The intimate relationship between the plays and WBY's seemingly tangential esoteric notes to them may be why GY was 'discontented at the thought of separating the "Introductions" from the plays' as she arranged *Plays II* for publication in the planned *Dublin Edition* (12–13 June, 1937, 472–73) In an earlier letter, of 24 November [1931], GY wrote at length about the commentaries for *Fighting the Waves* and *The Words Upon the Window-pane*, expressing her disagreement with the ideas in the latter since WBY suggested that spirits were 'impersonations created by a medium', projections akin to 'wireless photography or television' (270; see also above, 194 & ff.). GY's objection to his description of the séance as a dramatisation provoked a reply in which he explained that the dead were separated from their 'acquired faculties' and could see in the 'Passionate Body' but all names, all logic, & all that we call memory is from us' (25 November 1931, 271). Dogged by the idea, he wrote to her again, describing the individual as a dramatisation of his or her *Daimon* and the séance as a collaborative performance between the living and the dead. The preface to *Explications and Contexts* expresses the editors' objection to critics' tendency to simplify *A Vision* in order to make it more intelligible and more obviously relevant to the rest of the Yeats corpus. The fruitlessness of disentangling the authorship of *A Vision* is acknowledged here, but as Saddlemyer's biography and her edition of the correspondence shows, the isolation of *A Vision* from its sources – which must include the poems, plays, and prefaces – is equally inadequate.

However, the best do not lack all conviction but go about answering other questions. Charles I. Armstrong reads *A Vision* as text rather than doctrine and sees in it the same 'irony and ambivalence found in Yeats's literary work' (97). One of Armstrong's most compelling arguments is his assertion that Classical philosophy provided WBY with 'a mode of thinking flexible enough to question its own verities through generic multiplicity, scepticism, and sheer ludic energy' (100). Elements of play are also present in Matthew DeForrest's 'W. B. Yeats's *A Vision*: Dove or Swan', which focuses on WBY's regard for the system as a useful abstraction as described in the revised 'A Packet for Ezra Pound': 'now that the system stands out clearly in my imagination I regard them as stylistic arrangements' (*AVB* 25). DeForrest's attention to the poems that were integrated into the text of *A Vision* elucidates the system's function to provide 'metaphors for poetry' and brings clarity to the system itself. For example, in both *A Vision A* and *B*, Leda undergoes a titular divorce from the embodied Zeus. The poem's title is given as 'Leda' only, with the swan standing alongside another symbol of annunciation in the title of the book, 'Dove or Swan' (*CVA* 179, *AVB* 267). The placement of the avatars Helen and Christ in the system seems counter-intuitive; as heralds of antithetical and primary ages, the reader of *A Vision* would expect for the avatars to occupy opposite phases. (Christ, as avatar of the primary, should be born at the height of the antithetical.) Yeats struggled with this perceived anomaly, but the communicators insisted that the avatars are 'independent of all'. The Thirteenth Cone – WBY's 'phaseless sphere' – resolves the antinomies of primary and antithetical; this concept, which Mann describes as the figuring of 'the Absolute in a state', facilitates unified thinking about beings as representative of primary *and* antithetical ages. Wayne Chapman's essay 'Metaphors for Poetry' considers the way in which WBY's poetry and dance plays embodied abstraction and were part of the making of *A Vision*. An unfinished Noh play, to which Chapman refers as 'The Guardians of the Tower and the Stream' (see *YA17* 95–179), doubles the local legend of Blind Raftery and the beautiful Mary Hines with the story of Homer and Helen. Chapman suggests that the marriage of spirits in the play may be a tribute to GY, especially since somnambulism is central to the plot. WBY's work on the play was accompanied by GY's sleep-talking: in the autumn of 1923 WBY abandoned the play, and GY's sleeps ended.

In *Becoming George*, Saddlemyer suggests that GY 'would not have approved of' the biography, since her life was frequently an exercise in the subversion of 'her own voice' (*BG* xix). The nature of the Yeatses' implicit collaborations, such as the relationship between the writing of the Noh play and the sleep-talking, arises in the early correspondence and becomes more explicit over time. Readers who rely on the Oxford University Press *Collected Letters of W. B. Yeats* published only to 1907) and do not have access to the InteLex database may be astonished at WBY's first full love letters to GY: 'at first you were but a plan & a dream & then you became a real woman, & then all in a moment that real woman became very dear' (5 October [1917], 10). Two earlier letters of 3 and 4 October begin 'My beloved', and in the first of these there may be a hint of psychological transference when WBY writes' [I] think of the time when I shall find you, when my work is over, sitting at the gass fire or dealing firmly with Mrs Old' (8). George Hyde-Lees is now the 'beloved', replacing Maud Gonne for whom he wrote, 'When you are old and grey and full of sleep, | And nodding by the fire, take down this book, And slowly read' (*VP* 120). As Gould and Toomey write, that poem, included in the manuscript book *The Flame of the Spirit*, was both 'love token' and 'down payment' (*YA11* 124–32, 125). The material text was often a site of frisson between WBY and Gonne; during their period of experiments in astral travel she wrote to him,

'Yesterday evening however somewhere about 9 o'clock I was sitting in the drawing room of this hotel with several persons when suddenly I became conscious that you were there, standing near a table on which your book which I had been reading lay. Those in the room knew nothing of occultism & would not have understood. So mentally I gave you rendezvous for midnight when I knew they would be gone & said when sleep had set my soul free I would go with you where you liked' ([November 1895], *GYL* 53).

While there may have been a sense of security in imagining GY in the domestic sphere, that image was no less charged with intellectual and sexual energy that was also, in the end, related to the power of texts. In the same letter in which WBY asserts, 'Let us begin at once our life of study, of common interests & hopes', he tells her that Gregory does not want them to visit Coole until after their marriage, anticipating the potential for scandal over 'the possible number of our candles' (4 Oct [1917]).

A major theme that emerges through reading *The Letters* is the emergence of a collaborative process that grows more overt as GY takes responsibility for arranging WBY's talks for the BBC, negotiating with editors, and compiling the planned *Dublin Edition*. A series of letters in the aptly named section, 'Changes 1928–1933', illustrates the Yeatses' collaborative process. On 13 October 1931, WBY writes to GY, sharing a new poem that will become 'Old Tom Again', which will stand as a reply to 'The Dancer at Cruachan and Cro-Patrick' in *Words for Music Perhaps*: 'Things out of perfection sail | And all their swelling canvas wear; | Nor can the self-begotten fail, | Though man's bitter heart suppose | Building yard, storm beaten shore, | Winding sheet & swadling clothes' (253). GY replied to say that she 'like[d]' it but was unsure whether she had misread the fourth line. This may have been a straightforward difficulty in interpreting WBY.'s scrawl, or it may have been a subtle way of suggesting a disharmony in the poetry. He responded 'Is it wrong? I felt a doubt' and suggested a revision to the fourth and fifth lines, 'Though fantastic men suppose | Building-yard & stormy shore', which were retained in the final version (*VP* 530). This is a telling moment in poetic practice (255,7). The elimination of 'bitter' changes the alliteration from the b in self-begotten in line three through the 'Building-yard, storm beaten shore' of l. 5. With the substitution of 'fantastic', the line not only loses a beat (which may have been regarded as extraneous) but the sibilance of sail, swelling, self, fantastic, suppose, stormy, shore, sheet, and swaddling-clothes are brought to the fore, resulting in a more unified sound to the sestet.

A change in the tone of the collaborations accompanies the changing sexual dynamic of their relationship in 'Endings 1937–1939'. In a letter of 9 June 1937 informing GY of a pleasant journey to London, WBY appended a question that appears to have nagged him during his travel: 'You did not like the two "himselfs" at the end of first verse of 'How goes the Weather'.' He suggested substituting the lines, 'He himself wrote out the word | And he was christened in blood'. The truncated rhythm of 'And he was' is less pleasing to the ear and was indeed less satisfactory to GY who preferred 'the two "himself"' and replied to say that she had left the poem unchanged when she posted the manuscript to Watt. She added, 'I concluded you wanted the second version of the Casement poem (Alfred Noyes name left out)' (11 June 1937). The prominence of underlined words, capital letters, and the repetition of her requests in the letters from this period indicate that GY's labour on WBY's work was both pleasurable and frustrating. In an impatient letter of 22 June 1937 GY begins by scolding WBY for writing to a correspondent at the wrong address, then reprimands him for writing directly to Watt about 'Plays II' (for the *Dublin Edition*) 'and you have not replied to my question' (478). In a rare intervention in the body of the text, Saddlemyer includes a parenthetical note, '[heavily inked ms in margin: Please do not lose the one I sent you].' One effect of reading the correspondence from this period is its demystification of the ageing Yeats – who seems more neglectful than intellectually preoccupied – and the unconcealed personality of GY, who was not always the Angel in the House, pleasing a man and condoling his necessities. As much as an essential work of reference, *W. B. Yeats & George Yeats: The Letters* is immensely readable, providing just the right level of context to inform our understanding of the private and professional, the domestic and esoteric lives lived in unity.

Sean Pryor, *W. B. Yeats, Ezra Pound and the Poetry of Paradise* (Farnham: Ashgate, 2011), pp. xiii + 226.

Stoddard Martin

One begins by wondering about the sense of combining Yeats and Pound. They may be the two greatest poets of the 20th century in English, against whom their contemporary T. S. Eliot seems rather puny; but the nature of their achievement is so different that one has to rely on their personal connections in order easily to link them, or perhaps their ambitions. A prior generation had produced in Nietzsche, Mallarmé and others a post-Christian desire to write 'the book that does away with all books'; in such an enterprise both demonstrably laboured, as did their prosaic onetime protégé, James Joyce.

The Cantos and *A Vision*, however, are not comparable productions: while the former may readily be seen as a singular instance of over-arching aspiration, the latter in form as in content is a wholly other kind of experiment, whose less cocksure author knew was fated to fall short. A sense that neither this most ambitious attempt at the all-embracing nor any other single work in Yeats's opus is precisely suited to pose against *The Cantos* may be what moves Sean Pryor to consider for the purpose Yeats's lyric output as if it were a kind of continuous whole. This is one of many forcings of an issue we confront in a book which otherwise has intelligence on every page.

Another is that the lyrics Pryor selects for discussion seem subject to whim or to taste. Whole swathes of output passed over – hardly a poem from *In the Seven Woods*, *The Green Helmet* or *Responsibilities* – and works which might be expected to be read closely are given short shrift. Yeats's début excursion through Celtic heavens, *The Wanderings of Oisin*, earns a page near the beginning, then is referred to only *en passant*; in a book which devotes large space to the admittedly marvellous 'Sailing to Byzantium', this strikes one as negligent.

Byzantium's status as paradise in Yeats's system is of course arguable, but other locality-based poems seem present as much for their success or popularity as their unstrained illumination of the paradisal – 'The Lake Isle of Innisfree', 'The Wild Swans at Coole'. It is obvious that a beloved earthly landscape can vault imagination towards dreams of the gods: Pound's attraction to Catullus's Sirmione demonstrates it. But here lurks another aspect of why these poets are uneasy to link: the earthly locales in which each specializes are close to being an aesthetic opposition. Yeats cloaked himself in Celtic mist, Pound in classical/ltroubadour light. Only in a late phase when for health reasons Yeats wintered near Pound in Rapallo – the period when he wrote his 'Packet for Ezra Pound', comparing his approach in *A Vision* to what he found abstruse in the 'fugal' *Cantos* – do we see similitude in terrestrial affinity: Italy, the Ravenna mosaics, 'Byzantium'.

The two men's paradises are correspondingly hard to link. Yeats's seems often elsewhere: in passed youth, legends of old time, spirits on the wind, mythic kingdoms or platonic doctrine, moments of epiphany recalled, an unattainable knowledge or muse. 'Sailing to Byzantium' is properly entitled with a gerund, Pryor argues, because arrival is evanescent: it's all in the travelling. Pound on the other hand experiences paradise in the present, 'for a flash | for an hour', and portrays it, as Pryor aptly points out, either in present tense or in a verb-less space where aspects of divinity float unconjoined by a thing so prosaic as normal syntax. Again one feels the difference in apprehension through skryed mist and vertically shadowed light; there may also be a factor of difference in affinities to time – the preciousness of time past, the occult, for Yeats vs the obsession with time future or Futurist, MAKE IT NEW, for Pound.

One may of course stand this on its head and assert that Pound sought his road-map to time future out of the past and that, in *A Vision* notably, Yeats searched through time past mainly to find guidance to the future; but the point is a larger one. Sensibility, prejudice and temperament separate these spirits as surely as origins: old European vs new American. Each would finally seek his goal via 'monuments of unageing intellect' and 'monuments of [his] own magnificence' yet out of different motives: Yeats to achieve ultimate unity of being, Pound to blast into some *novus ordo seclorum*. The overlaps are intriguing: each could see value in the other's intimations, and both respected the other's masterful prosody, with reservations. They occasionally shared inspiration from new sources – the Noh, for example – but each went his own way, and in the end they diverged radically. What Yeats longed for was sensual; what Pound said he wanted was 'hard' and 'clear'.

An erotic element may be in this – i.e., differing experience of coition, significant especially to Pound, impacting on ultimate visions. Nancy Cunard, Pound's sometime lover, left a striking note about what it was like to feel 'the "sharp | straight flame" of Pound's love', which 'like a saint' performed its ministrations to lend her 'a steadfast radiance'.[1] Nothing equivalent, so far as I know, has been asserted about Yeats. Aleister Crowley's intimations of phallic feebleness is, as far as possible to judge, mere slander.[2] On the other hand, the retardations, starts-and-stops and misfirings of Yeats's sexual history is well-known; Brenda Maddox made a case that the reversion to the occult upon marriage had to do with George trying to keep Willie up to it; and then come the visits to clinics, interest in Tantric Buddhism and 'crazy Jane' glee for encounters of later years – interpretable signs of a progress that had partaken less of hard fact than of fantastic hoping.[3]

Pryor does not deviate into such speculations, but by insisting on the centrality of paradise in both men's works, with dense argument and at length, he makes one sit back and ponder underlying impulses. Too many words may occlude: a dream of the beyond is finally about an individual's nature as much as fragments shored against civilization's ruins. Pryor's main argument is that each poet in his fashion turns pursuit into goal, that the poetry itself becomes both paradise and its undoing, a trembling on the verge as it were, a moment of beauty walking the razor's edge, which represents the thing achieved – 'Only the greatest obstacle that can be contemplated without despair rouses the will to full intensity' (*Au* 195). Pound, I suspect, would have disparaged the aura of petty fog rising off Pryor's pedagogy in this asseveration. Nor am I convinced he would have welcomed this exhumation of his work anymore than that of his friend.

Pryor has read widely on *The Cantos*, and their Dantesque provenance justifies him in paradise-seeking through them, as it does Pound's condemners in policing his hells. But Pryor sets about querying Pound's formulations, poking at his seeming contradictions, taking him to task for his 'traduction' of Cavalcanti in Canto XXXVI for example – 'No philosophical system would countenance this slippery identification', he says of transformation of a seen form into an idea; 'yet the canto's effortless glide enacts the course of love: love 'Cometh from a seen form'. Yeats's praxis and integrity are rarely subject to such critique, and one wonders if Pryor feels obliged to

---

[1] Lois Gordon in *Nancy Cunard: Heiress, Muse, Political Idealist* (New York: Columbia University Press, 2007) says that the affair began in 1921 and lasted through Pound's Paris years, probably until he met Olga Rudge. Her chapter 'In Love with the Artist-God' (99–106) includes quotation from Nancy.

[2] E.g. 'The Shadowy Dill-Waters, or Mr Smudge the Medium', *Equinox* I, iii (London: Simpkin Marshall, 1910), 327–31. It is possible too that Crowley shared speculations with Florence Farr, with whom both men were on varyingly intimate terms during their period in the Golden Dawn.

[3] There may be a question too, unanswerable finally, about masturbation – i.e., was Yeats another late nineteenth century victim of what Wagner saw as the covert problem afflicting Nietzsche, contributing the element of hysteria in his work, which Yeats claimed to have read until his eyes went bad?

it because of the alleged toxicity, madness or difficulty that continues to surround Pound's reputation like barbed-wire. Going back to my musings on the erotic, much might be elucidated were Pryor simply to state that Pound's approach to the paradisal is representational, not exact; that the point of dropping Cavalcanti into the middle of cantos which deal with earthly disgrace is to suggest where another level of possibility may lie and that at the base of it, as in Canto XXXIX, which follows more rebarbative material, is sex – 'Sacrum sacrum inluminatio coitu' – Pound's relation to it overlying Cavalcanti's sublimation of it, the relief it provides, escape into the ecstatic, a still point of beatitude where a figurative 'unwobbling pivot' may 'taketh locus'. Aphrodite, tamed Circe, Olga in Sant' Ambrogio uphill from Rapallo … Yeats did not attach his heavens so readily to memory of the act. Biography helps understanding. Sometimes it is essential.

Pryor withholds mention of the line about coition. Pound studies attract literary techies who often get so bogged down in data that readers miss the extent to which, as Massimo Bacigalupo has argued,[4] Pound was of a generation – Nancy Cunard, D. H. Lawrence, even the 'wicked' Crowley – which regarded sex as a leaping off point into the sublime. Pound did not quite advocate the Sex Magick that Crowley practiced at the other end of Italy in Cefalù, but he subscribed to his own notion of 'eroto-comatose lucidity'. Ecstasy provides access to The Light; the moment of orgasm may offer a glimpse into an otherwise unreachable paradise, whether recalled as it must be in *The Pisan Cantos* – 'dove sta memoria' – or ready to hand as it evidently was during composition of XXXIX. The sex act is by no means all that releases divine perceptions for Pound, but it is regularly 'part of the process', and here part of the contrast to Yeats may have to do with origins not only in place but in another dimension of time: Yeats was twenty years older, child of the Victorian era, an ageing man by the emancipations of the '20s, too late for apache coteries of the Left Bank. Crazy Jane and so on exhibit his wish in this direction, but it is largely about chances past, passing or not to come.

Pound, by contrast, from early interludes with Hilda Doolittle to liaisons during or after incarceration – Marcella Spann, etc. – was a precursor of Beatniks and the free-loving 1960s in this as in prosody, anti-war radicalism, conspiracy theorizing and much else. Pryor alludes to the 'coitu' motif only when he gets to XXXIX and can't help it, and when it recapitulates in XLVII, but he appears uneasy with it, seeking ways to suggest that the 'Splendour on splendour!' Pound evokes is qualified or involves legerdemain.

This tendency not to trust what the poet clearly intends spreads as Pryor moves on to what might have been Pound's paradiso had war not intervened. On the *Pisan*s, as elsewhere, Pryor is exact in pinpointing pertinent lines; he

---

[4] At a conference to mark the 100th anniversary of Pound's 1909 lectures at the University of Westminster.

focuses properly on Pound's formula 'What thou lovest well remains | the rest is dross' and asks the relevant question 'What does The Pisan Cantos love?'; he lists items accurately, but then he seeks to complicate the matter by declaring, 'The invocation of "What thou lovest well" is more vexed than it may look'. The sub-chapter in which this comes is entitled 'Well' and deals with that word, reminding one of President Clinton's retort in an interview during his impeachment crisis, 'It depends on what you mean by "the".' Sophisticated argument or sophistry? Pound's paradise in the *Pisan*s is that which gives comfort, kindness, a vision of order, balm, justice – all things a pious child might thank the Lord for in prayer.[5] It is as simple as that, and that is why it moves readers in a way that rest of the complex structure does not. Like such a child, Pound has faith that beyond the seen world exists an ideal one where good may be total and that, in response to grace, fragments of that totality may be perceived and, if cherished, lead on to more being glimpsed. 'Le paradis n'est pas artificiel | but spezzato apparently.' Spezzato does not mean that it is qualified, only that the erring mortal's perception of it perforce must be.

The last chapter of Pryor's book is about the progress of paradise through the poets' later work. The principal message he finds is '*Seek ye the sacred text and read*'. He locates this first in Yeats's 'supernatural song' 'Ribh at the Tomb of Baile and Aillinn', then applies it to Sections *Rock Drill* and *Thrones* of *The Cantos*, which, citing Andrew Kappel, he sees as offering via their multitude of referents, recapitulated from earlier cantos or newly acquired, Pound's 'last suggested course of study, the paradisal curriculum'. Pryor suggests that these cantos also provide in themselves an ultimate message, erasing and writing over the curriculum like a palimpsest, or palimpsest upon palimpsest, reworking, recapping, trying to distil ever better,[6] until a goal of silence is reached in the late *Drafts and Fragments*. All these tranches of cantos belong to the 1950s and after, decades into which Yeats did not survive, having died before the war and the *Pisan*s.

It may be this that makes his late work seem, in Pryor's account, riven in its way like Pound's of the '30s, a 'poetry of paradise' set within perpetual struggle – 'heaven and hell are built always anew' – or Dionysian dance – 'nymphs and satyrs | Copulate in the foam'. Pryor's concentration on 'Byzantium' here seems errant – 'the poem is so self-consciously a late

[5] This is akin to Yeats's charge in his 1937 remarks on Pound in *The Oxford Book of Modern Verse* that the 'grotesque' figures Pound rages at might be taken from 'a child's book of beasts'.

[6] This recalls the argument, though with less implication of Pound's failure, which Warwick Gould makes via analogy to Balzac's tale of artistic over-reach and frustration in '"*The Unknown Masterpiece*": Yeats and the Design of the *Cantos*', *Pound in Multiple Perspective: A Collection of Critical Essays*, ed. Andrew Gibson (London: Macmillan, 1993), 40–92.

instance of Yeats's quest for a poetry of paradise' – forcing him to reach for justification in a remark Yeats made in 1910,[7] sibling to one I quoted above: 'Only that which does not teach, which does not cry out, which does not persuade, which does not condescend, which does not explain, is irresistible' (*E&I* 341).

This could apply to Pound's praxis, but as regards Yeats Pryor is treading on less sure ground; and in trying to link a few major works while skipping over so much, he gives an impression of the poet's ultimate trajectory more away from paradise than towards it – opposite to his friend's. At this point he might have taken occasion to justify his strategy of dealing with the poets together by weighing up their own barbed views of each other's late work,[8] notably Pound's 1937 charge that Yeats was 'dead', which seems the implication of his inability to find much to discuss in terms of paradise beyond the 1930 poem. Is it in fact true that the later Yeats was no longer capable of believing in or reaching towards what he had so longed for as a young man setting out on the Ossianic explorations that Pryor neglects, or in the work he spent more years than any other rebuffing – to my taste the other most marvellous work in his opus – *The Shadowy Waters*? The question points to one reason why a reader may conclude that to have dealt with two such monumental figures in one book *is* ill-conceived. Beyond it one can't escape feeling that, while the scholarship behind analysis is often impressive – Pryor has read widely in secondary materials: too much so, perhaps[9] – a ready, excited response to primary texts – the necessary intimacy of appreciation – is baffled. We learn little that is new about the poets or their work; what we get is a mustering of learnèd response – again, perhaps too much. Fault may also lie with the nature of publication. In an era when so much can be tossed out cost-free on the net, we readily applaud publishers ready to produce in book form thesis-based monographs. But in this case the typeface is small, the leading and inking minimal, the paper conversely more weighty than needed – values, in short, not well-balanced. The great deficiency, however, is that no editor was willing to cast a sufficiently cold eye over Dr Pryor's brilliance to suggest that less excruciation might have served his admirable project more persuasively.

---

[7] Pryor says 1911, but the error is trivial.
[8] The breakdown of mutual admiration is laid out by Gould in the essay mentioned in n. 6.
[9] Or too little. No reference to the above work as well as to many distinguished critics noted in it, Frank Kermode and Jerome McGann for example (latter cited *en passant* once), allied to an occasional tip of the hat to Paul de Man or Jacques Derrida indicates the intellectual texture of Pryor's approach.

Writings on Literature and Art: G. W. Russell – A.E. Edited and with an Introduction by Peter Kuch (Gerrards Cross: Colin Smythe, 2011)

Nicholas Allen

The fourth volume of George Russell's collected works concerns his writings on literature and art. It is edited by Peter Kuch, who also provides the introduction. The entire stretches to near five hundred pages, which is appropriate to a writer whose output comprised three decades and more of journalism, besides poetry, prose, painting and propaganda, much of uneven quality. This begs the question why Russell requires a collected works at all.His brilliance was not in the quality of his thinking but in its position. Russell was one point of light in a constellation that took shape in the flickering controversies of the late British Empire. The co-ordinates of his thinking correspond with the boundaries of that world territory, America in the west and India in the East. Russell's thinking reflected the stresses it endured as the little nations reimagined themselves as something discrete, original and deserving of their independence.

Peter Kuch's introduction to Russell's work suffers from looking at Russell from the other side of the looking glass. His idea of Ireland is antique and belonging to a generation of critics who believed in Yeats as a kind of savior, with Russell his minor apostle. In this respect, Kuch's summary of Russell's life and career here is the epilogue to his single longstanding monograph on the writer's early friendship with Yeats. Unfortunately for this volume, Kuch pays little attention to subsequent criticism. There is no sense of the evolving understanding of Russell's role with reference to contested versions of the literary revival in Seamus Deane, Declan Kiberd, P. J. Mathews or many others. If views of the cultural scene are stunted so is the immediate artistic context. Terence Brown is cited for his thirty-year old cultural history of Ireland (it remains a classic still, granted) but not for his life of Yeats; similarly R. F. Foster appears as author of Modern Ireland and not for his two-volume biography of the master poet. There is little logic to this. Adrian Frazier's classic life of Moore is a well-used resource as is Hilary Pyle's work on Jack Yeats (though S. B. Kennedy's work on Irish art goes unmentioned).

This is important because little claim can be made for Russell's work on its singular merits. His interests were multiple and fascinating. Theosophy, co-operation, a flirtation with militant nationalism, the literary and visual arts are a seductive combination. But they are not unique (I think of Edward Carpenter and A. R. Orage as I write, many more could come to mind). Neither are they singularly representative of an Irish consciousness (Carpenter and Orage were English, but I read no celebrations of their mystic genius, although Kuch does important service by recovering Russell's memories of the *New Age*'s editor). The inability to situate Russell and his contemporaries such as Stephen McKenna in contexts larger than the by now rather tired idea of the literary revival as a spiritual salvation of a fading race is a disservice to Russell and to his time. After all, the flexible development of Russell's thought, and its final defeat in the decade after independence, is both inspirational and cautionary. Putting Russell back in the fetters of a sub-Yeatsian eccentricity undoes the one thing that makes him worth reading, which is the uncanny ability to make legible the literary and cultural forms that made shape of revolutionary Ireland.

Russell's determined thinking on questions of the economy, of community, of individual self-expression and yes, of spirituality, still has power. Kuch's introduction and commentary give little sense of this. There is instead a strange antagonism to those other activists with which Russell was in competition for audience (Kuch knocks the 'querulous assertiveness of many of the nationalist critics who wrote for *Sinn Fein*, the *United Irishman* and the *All Ireland Review*' – presumably separatist politics would be better served by polite letters to the editor of *The Times*. Another passage suggests Russell 'strenuously rejected the compulsive revisionism of the nationalists'; I can make no sense of this in the context provided, neither is it clear who is being addressed despite the fact our knowledge of the miniature communities of Irish radicals is well advanced in the last decade). There are other oddities. In 1892 we are told that Russell was more moved by the death of Theosophy's founder H. P. Blavatsky than he was by the passing of Parnell. By 1895 we are told Russell greeted Yeats as 'the harbinger of a new literary nationalism'. Its kind and provenance remains as vague as Kuch's assertion that Yeats admired Russell's first book because 'he could use it to advance his type of poetry'. There is no art in this and little acuity. Yeats did not write poetry to type. Even if he did there is no description here of what that type might be. Kuch misses a similar opportunity with Joyce. Russell's relationship with the younger writer is bookended by Joyce's well-worn joke that AEIOU. There is no hint of Joyce's more serious response to Russell through questions of economy, which extend later than *Ulysses* and into *Finnegans Wake*.

More substantively, Kuch finishes his introduction by claiming that Russell's writings on literature and art 'form the most valuable legacy' of Russell's bequest to Irish thought. This is a difficult claim to make since Russell's writing wandered so productively between subjects. One editorial might range from Athens to Athlone, or from banking to beekeeping. The question is how, or if, to separate such passages from their weekly context in the *Irish Homestead* or *Irish Statesman*, or to focus on discrete texts, most usually ephemeral. Kuch has largely chosen the latter and has performed some important retrieval work in the reconstitution of Russell's autobiographical fragment 'The Sunset of Fantasy', well-known to readers of *Yeats Annual* (see *YA10*, 1993) Here again there is puzzle. Russell's late disaffection from the idea of Ireland makes him claim baldly 'I can offer no evidence of any Irish strain [in]my ancestry'. For most of this volume Russell flickers in identity between Anglo-Irish and a nationalism implicitly low-church Protestant in its apparent thrifty self-sufficiency. There is no editorial note to this jarring transition, rather a commentary for the following sentence that details the insertion of a comma. This rather sums up the problem facing modern readers of Russell. If he is deserving of a collected works and the undeniable toil of editorial application then his writing and thought should commend him by exceptional achievement. This is a dicey proposition in Russell's case. His genius, again, was his place in the network, whether it was of writers, mystics or farmers. Dissected from these the commendable efforts of the annotator seem a little weightless.

Russell is worth reading. His perception of the social problems facing Ireland in the period of its transition from empire to partition is a watermark to much of his commentary on art. The imagination was no abstract condition for him. It was an innate presence that electrified the body politic. Those parts of this edition that are most exciting touch upon the influence of others, most notably Shelley, Carlyle and Wordsworth. These figures lurked in Russell's literary background however he tried to claim Cuchulain as inspiration. Standish O'Grady, Yeats and Russell himself stood in some sense as their proxies in the Irish scene. It might even be that the success of the revival writers with an English audience proceeded from their familiarity as echoes of the Romantics and Victorians. More than Yeats, Russell had his ear open also to the Americas. Emerson and Whitman tempered his diction, which was archaic by Russell's late career (read for example his 'Germinal', a late poem quoted on the first page of Kuch's introduction – 'In ancient shadows and twilights' it begins, and this in the time of Pound and Eliot, never mind the older Yeats).

The impression of reading Russell's writing together is to register a variable reception. When strong the message takes on a power rarely witnessed and never, I think, maintained over so long a period, except perhaps in Blake; when weak the phrasing is out of sorts and the meaning is obscure. Russell broadcast into a tumult. Home Rule gave way to world war and rebellion even as his mystic sense of the world was challenged both by evolution and by the new physics. Russell intended to be modern. His play *The Honorable Enid Majoribanks*, a discovery by Kuch, jokes about air flight and suffrage. That it was never performed tells us something of the difficult gap between perception of change and its representation in art, a gap that Russell often failed to bridge. Outside economics, the area in which he most succeeded was in his understanding of visual art. Russell's essay on Jack Yeats is a little treasure, as is his open-minded support of the sculptor John Hughes. His eye was open to Mainie Jellett. A painter himself, Russell knew how to look at the future before him.

The two proposed volumes left of Russell's collected works are advertised to include first his poetry and second his writings on politics, society and nationhood. The poetry has not aged well, and had not in Russell's own lifetime. His cultural work promises more. There is a solid archival foundation to work from thanks to Kuch and his crucial predecessors Alan Denson and Henry Summerfield. The lesson of this volume is one that Russell taught. The question of Ireland needs more thinking to answer. Thankfully there has been much progress here in the past two decades, as another editor will know.

Joseph M. Hassett, *W. B. Yeats and the Muses*
(Oxford: Oxford University Press, 2010), pp. xiv, 258.

Michael Cade-Stewart

Hassett's new book presents a biographical account of the changing dynamic of Yeats's relationships with nine of the women in his life, considered in relation to his creativity. The women in question are those with whom Yeats was, or strove to be, sexually involved – Olivia Shakespear, Florence Farr, Maud Gonne, Iseult Gonne, George Hyde-Lees, Margot Ruddock, Ethel Mannin, Dorothy Wellesley, and Edith Shackleton Heald. This subject matter and Hassett's accessible prose have the potential for wide appeal.

To link these biographical portraits, Hassett draws on the classical concept of the Muses, which he modifies and supplements with other ideas in order better to describe Yeats's relation to each of the women. In the early chapters, Hassett supplements the classical model with ideas from the courtly love tradition of the middle ages, and the worship of the White Goddess postulated by Robert Graves. From the chapter on Iseult Gonne onwards, however, Yeats's own complex and changing models of inspiration are rightly brought to the fore. Hassett presents these as a development of Yeats's earlier, more classical ideas about inspiration, positing that, in *Per Amica Silentia Lunae* (1918), Yeats 'had concluded that his Muse, his creative element, hovered somewhere in his own psyche, linking his mind to the general mind' (183). Later in his life, with his wife's help, 'Yeats had internalized the idea of the unattainable Muse in the notion of an antithetical feminine aspect of his own psyche' (135). In this way, Hassett uses the concept of the Muse as a fluid metaphor that links Yeats's changing ideas about creativity with his changing love-interests.

Yeats's life has been tackled by superb biographers, but Hassett's work makes a space for itself in this crowded field by going into greater depth. In so doing it brings some valuable new material to the table: the creative work produced by all of the ladies. By relating these writings to poems and plays Yeats wrote subsequently, Hassett casts familiar poems into new relief. A good example of this process can be found in his detection of a link between Iseult Gonne's poem 'The Shadow of Noon', and the verse section from Yeats's play 'The Only Jealousy of Emer', beginning: 'A woman's beauty is like a white | Frail bird' (Hassett, 124). Gonne's poem has a refrain of: 'A strangely useless thing', which Yeats apparently rewrites in his description of a woman's beauty as 'A strange, unserviceable thing' (*VPl* 531). The insights about Yeats's work that Hassett is able to glean from even such unpromising work as that of Margot Collis, reveals the riches still to be uncovered by considering Yeats's work and creativity in his social context. Hassett's treatment of his material displays a light touch throughout, which is welcome in a context where a detailed exposition of Dorothy Wellesley's 427-line metaphysical poem 'Matrix' remains a possibility.

Yeats's relationship with Wellesley herself is considered in the light of the increasingly public rage of his writings in old age. Hassett posits that Yeats found in Wellesley an inspirational Fury, who would succour him in lieu of a Muse. If Wellesley influenced Yeats in this regard, however, it is perhaps curious that 'To Dorothy Wellesley' displays no evidence of textual borrowings from her writings. Indeed, rage is not prevalent in the work of a woman who insisted that 'I (unlike you) hate hate and love love' (*LDW* 112): when it came to spleen, Yeats evidently found his material elsewhere.

Yeats's letters to Wellesley in the mid-1930s convey a clear sexual charge but, off the page, it is doubtful that a married man who 'could not have erections'[1] entered into a sexual relationship with a lesbian. Accordingly, it might have been interesting if Hassett had made something of the fact that this incompatability seems to be repeated in the pages of the poetry. Yeats was hugely excited by rewriting Wellesley's ballad of 'The Lady, the Squire, and the Serving-Maid': '[a]h my dear how it added to my excitement when I re-made that poem of yours to know it was your poem. I re-made you and myself into a single being' (*LDW* 82). Her reply has not been published, but it surely speaks volumes that she evidently rejected his repeated textual advances, insisting instead that her ballad be published in its original form in the *Broadside* for September 1937 (New Series, no. 9) (*LDW* 69, n. 27). There is a similar dearth of evidence for borrowings in the other direction: the writing process ended as it began, with two ballads on the same theme written independently. Elsewhere, there is some evidence of poetic borrowings from Wellesley, but, following Hassett's biographical-critical approach, we might say that Yeats wanted Wellesley to mean more to him than she did.

It might also have been interesting for Hassett's book to have considered the counter-argument of Yeats's pronouncements on the importance of poetic craft and toil in actively generating inspiration. In his lecture on

---

[1] Assertion from Norman Haire recounted by Richard Ellmann in *W. B. Yeats's Second Puberty: A Lecture Delivered at the Library of Congress on April 2, 1984* (Washington: Library of Congress, 1985), 8.

'Nationality and Literature' in 1893, Yeats declared, that 'the inspiration of God, which is, indeed, the source of all which is greatest in the world, comes only to him who *labours* at rhythm and cadence, at form and style, until they have no secret hidden from him' (*UP1* 274, emphasis added). In the last years of his life, he accordingly instructed Wellesley to find inspiration through the process of writing itself, approvingly quoting Aubrey Beardsley's description of his own working practice: 'I make a blot & shove it about till something comes' (*LDW* 89).

As the book stands, however, it teases out a vein of significance in Yeats's corpus that links inspiration, love-interests, and the supernatural. In bringing extra material into consideration – in particular, the poems and writings of the women in question – Hassett's book deepens our understanding of Yeats's relationships with those women, and enriches our experience of even familiar poems.

Michael McAteer, *Yeats and European Drama* (Cambridge: Cambridge University Press, 2010), pp. xii, 223

Tara Stubbs

It is perhaps counter-intuitive to begin a review of Michael McAteer's *Yeats and European Drama* by quoting from its conclusion, but McAteer's summary of his own arguments describes fittingly the ambition and scope of this study. In defending Yeats's plays against traditional critical standpoints, which tend often to describe the dramas as no more than 'exotic embellishments', McAteer offers instead the following riposte: 'Those cultural interchanges of Irish, Greek, Arabian, Indian, Tibetan and Japanese traditions evident in the varieties of experiment Yeats adopted in the plays were more than exotic embellishments; not only a means of sharpening a consciousness of human alienation engendered through commerce and stage regulation, they also suggested new forms of religious and cultural expression that might reinvigorate Christian traditions growing lethargic in Europe' (195). But this statement also underlines the difficulty of the project, attempting as it does to provide an overview of a range of dramatic 'experiments' that shifted in scope, subject and influence throughout Yeats's career: experiments that sometimes appeared to be at odds with Yeats's more critically discussed works in poetry and prose.

In providing a critical reassessment of Yeats's plays, McAteer continues a recent trend in Yeats studies, which argues for the significance of certain of Yeats's writings because of the importance Yeats himself accorded to these works. We might recall, for example, Margaret Mills Harper's *Wisdom of Two* (2006), which contends that we must take seriously Yeats's automatic writing experiments – and, most notably, *A Vision* – because of the emphasis Yeats placed on the spiritualist aspect of his work. Perhaps unsurprisingly, then, McAteer's opening sentences contrast Yeats's own belief that the Nobel Prize in 1923 was awarded to him 'as much for his achievements in the theatre as for his poetry' with R. F. Foster's claim that such a belief was 'laughable' (1) – both forestalling the antipathy to Yeats's drama that often informs Yeats criticism and underscoring Yeats's confidence in the significance of his plays.

The study progresses logically, considering Yeats's plays chronologically and setting them against the context of recent developments in European drama as well as external events such as the Easter Rising and the First World War. This is a neat move on McAteer's part, as it situates Yeats's plays right in the centre of things, so that they cannot be ignored. There are moments when these contextual efforts seem somewhat forced, however – or example, where McAteer contends that when we consider *The Dreaming of the Bones* in relation to *Calvary*, we might notice how 'Yeats engaged the absurdist mode characteristic of Pirandello as the means more appropriate to represent the historical meaning of the 1916 Rising' (149). Though this is an intriguing argument, and makes a useful comparison with Pirandello, it is less convincing when McAteer moves on to consider this apparent 'farce' within the play alongside the 'deep betrayal' that he sees as characteristic of Yeats's response to the Rising in his poetry and correspondence.

A similar issue arises when the question of influence is raised. McAteer is careful to trace lines of influence backwards as well as forward, as well as nationally and internationally – so that we find comparisons not only with Strindberg, Ibsen and French Symbolism, but also with Irish models (Synge in particular). More vitally we are shown how Yeats's dramas, initially forbiddingly individualistic, might actually provide models for other writers: McAteer's work on Yeats's influence on Beckett is particularly intriguing in this light. On the other hand, however, sometimes these lines of influence can seem to be drawn too clearly, so that they become almost too convenient. For example in a discussion of *Calvary*, McAteer notes that 'the play went beyond the Faustian mode to historicise the solitary self-begetting of what would later become the existential hero in the plays of Sartre, Camus, Ionesco and Beckett' (148). Is this delineation of character from play to play quite so straightforward?

McAteer's decision to confront head-on the problematic politics of Yeats's later dramas is commendable, as is his willingness to highlight Yeats's flaws as a writer and critic: for example, in his chapter on *The Dreaming of the Bones* and *Calvary*, he draws our attention to Yeats's 'relative ignorance of Marx's own writings', which complicated his attitude towards Marxism in the aftermath of the Russian Revolution (148). Meanwhile Chapter 5, on *The Death of Cuchulain*, confronts head-on the critical tendency to regard Cuchulain's death in Yeats's last play 'as a theatrical and critical failure' (121). Yet by acknowledging the broken harmony of this play, and its apparent inability to complete the cycle that Yeats has himself set up, McAteer can offer instead the suggestion that through his refusal of 'closure' within the cycle Yeats might be 'rejecting the authority of myth within a mythic frame', and therefore 'deliberately disturbing the circular completion of mythic pattern' (121). The effect of such readings is to provide a nuanced impression of the ambition and flaws of Yeats's dramatic experiments – and to offer an enlightening re-reading of these texts.

The title of the book – *Yeats and European Drama* – is oddly constrained when related to the scope and range of this study, which actually goes beyond lines of influence to re-site Yeats's plays within his own work, within the work of others, and within the external contexts of performance. But perhaps as a result of this ambition, there is one area which seems slightly lacking. Although the author makes bold claims for the texts themselves, there is not a great deal of close reading to back up some of the arguments – and this is a shame. Though perhaps the study itself, through its sheer tenacity, will open up the field for further discussion, and inspire other critics to consider more closely the language and concerns of individual plays.

R. F. Foster, *Words Alone: Yeats and his Inheritances*
(Oxford: Oxford University Press, 2011), pp. xix + 236.

Geraldine Higgins

Yeats spent the first half of his life suffering from the anxiety of influence and the second half, wrestling with anxiety about succession. Approaching fifty, he apologizes to his ancestors that their bloodline has dwindled to an ink line, 'I have no child | I have nothing but a book | Nothing but that to prove your blood and mine.' The first volume of Roy Foster's monumental biography of Yeats ends in 1914 with this poignant self-assessment:

It is not that I have accomplished too few of my plans, for I am not ambitious; but when I think of all the books I have read, and of the wise words I have heard spoken, and of the anxiety I have given to parents and grandparents, and of the hopes that I have had, all life weighed in the scales of my own life seems to me a preparation for something that never happens (*Life 1* 531).

For the reader who knows that still ahead for Yeats lies his greatest poetry, international acclaim and a Nobel prize not to mention marriage and fatherhood, this moment offers a point of reflection about life as it is lived and that same life as it appears in retrospect.

No critic of Yeats has so mastered the chronological data and detail of his life as Roy Foster. His two-volume biography immerses us in the dailyness of that life – the meetings, the misspelled letters, the committees, the causes, and the dalliances. Indeed, we now know more about Yeats than he could possibly have known about himself. *Words Alone* (the first of Foster's titles to use a Yeats quotation) is a deliberate swerve away from the minutiae and busyness of 'the life' towards the individual subject as a product of literary and historical trends. It examines the traditions that lay behind Yeats, rather than his own work and self-fashioned context. Here we encounter Yeats, not so much *sui generis*, inventor of literary modernism, as Yeats, the son of the *Wild Irish Girl*.

Based on Foster's 2009 Clark lectures at Cambridge, *Words Alone* deftly mobilizes the somewhat old-fashioned concepts of influence, inheritance and intention in order to reorient our thinking about Yeats's intellectual debt to the writers and thinkers of post-Union Ireland. Foster is incapable of writing a dull book and the chapters are teasingly structured to keep Yeats resolutely out of the central frame, appearing only as prologue and epilogue until the finale, 'Oisin Comes Home.' This allows the reader to view the large cast of novelists, journalists, politicians and polemicists with historical second sight or what Foster describes as the Romantic nineteenth-century belief 'that the historian was a prophet facing backwards' (59).

The first chapter, 'National Tales and National Futures' establishes the parameters of Foster's historical back-story – Ireland after the Union in 1800 and before the Famine in 1845. More specifically, Foster examines the novels of Maria Edgeworth and Sydney Owenson, and their agendas of moral improvement and 'historical enlightenment' in the framework of the national tale. Foster discredits the interpretation of these novels as the colonial products of an Anglo-Irish settler elite written for metropolitan consumption and instead compares them to Scott's historical novels of the same period.

Rather than turning towards Scotland to ask again why there is no Irish *Waverley*, Foster notes the different experiences of Union in Ireland (the 'broken promise' of Catholic Emancipation) and Scotland (retaining 'vital freedoms' in religion and education) but argues that 'experimental Unionism' rather than proto-nationalism connects the two literatures. (Not surprisingly, this interpretation differs greatly from Terry Eagleton's response to the similar conundrum of why there is no Irish *Middlemarch*.) The most interesting test case is Owenson's 1806 bestseller, *The Wild Irish Girl* in which an aristocratic English traveller is enthralled by the 'harp-playing and history lessons' (37) of his wild (but noble) Irish hostess, Glorvina, and unites with her in a highly symbolic marriage. Although the 'Glorvina solution' promotes the conservative political ideal of reconciliation within the Union, *The Wild Irish Girl* is often read as a subversive text encoding nationalist grievance about the loss of native Gaelic culture. Foster warns against such 'over-interpretation' and instead shows how this book 'set the tone both for polemicizing the Irish past and exoticizing the Irish future' (38). If Scott is allowed to have 'invented' the historical novel, Foster's Irish exemplars (that include the Banim brothers, Gerald Griffin and Thomas Moore as well as Edgeworth and Owenson) complicate the idea of the national tale as the evolutionary progenitor of nationalism.

Throughout *Words Alone*, Foster schools the reader in his preferred historical-literary mode of interpretation which tends to privilege the historical side of the hyphen while interrogating the literary side with some suspicion. Ever alert to schematic, or as he sees it, ideologically motivated attempts to backdate the 'national story', he eschews sweeping 'cheerful phrases' like 'the Nationalist project' (6) in favour of the historically specific 'Catholic Emancipation' when considering the agendas of these novelists.

Foster wants us to start by thinking historically rather than theoretically to avoid 'the retrospective wishful thinking [that] characterizes a good deal of politicized literary history' (42).

The second chapter, 'The First Romantics', demonstrates the benefits of thinking historically while employing the ironies of historical hindsight:

> Duffy would, through his newspaper, effectively call for armed revolution in 1848 and be tried for treason. Others of his Young Ireland group would be transported for their failed rising against British rule. The era of experimental Unionism and a possible *via media* for Ireland had disappeared, and, with it, hopes that Ireland's development within the United Kingdom might resemble Scotland's (46).

The central drama of influence in the chapter is the friendship between Charles Gavan Duffy and the sage of Chelsea, Thomas Carlyle. Carlyle might seem an unlikely precursor for the Irish Revival given his virulent anti-Irish sentiments and dismissal of Irish claims to self-determination. His journey through Ireland in 1849 (accompanied by Duffy and at the height of the famine) yielded an intemperate set of quasi-racist impressions published by Froude after his death. Yeats rarely mentioned Carlyle except to disparage his prose style but his works appeared on the shelves of Lady Gregory, Edward Martyn, George Moore, John O'Leary and most influentially, Standish O'Grady. Foster does not so much rehabilitate Carlyle as deploy Duffy as Marc Antony to his Caesar. We hear about Duffy's loyalty to what he calls 'the real Carlyle' and learn of the latter's excoriation of 'Skibbereen Unions, Liberation O'Connells, and the exile of Ireland's bravest sons.'(80) Nevertheless, it must be said that Carlyle's influence on Young Ireland's Romantic critique of modernity was much greater than Young Ireland's influence on Carlyle's critique of Ireland, despite this surprising reference to Skibbereen.

The Carlylean view that the Bible of any nation must be its history is adopted wholesale by Standish O'Grady and underpins the preoccupation with 'great men' in the pages of the *Dublin University Magazine* as well as the *Nation*. Foster's consideration of the *DUM* as a precursor to the *Nation* and his examination of conservative Romantics like Isaac Butt, Samuel Ferguson and Sheridan Le Fanu adjusts our understanding of the post-Emancipation literary and political scene, shining a light beyond the triumvirate of 'Davis, Mangan, Ferguson' in Yeats's 'To Ireland in the Coming Times.' Of course, Davis's powerful mobilization of history as revolutionary politics through the 'rhymed lesson book' of *The Nation* will remain the dominant model for Yeats in the 1890s, serving both as 'political inspiration and aesthetic warning' (52). Yeats's battle with the legacy of Davis is traced through the 1880s and 90s in Foster's final chapter in which Yeats seeks to differentiate his own movement from the Young Ireland of the 1840s. The difference between the two movements was summed up by *United Ireland* at the inaugural meeting of the Irish Literary Theatre:

Mr. Yeats ... declared that the means in this matter were nobler than the end; but, let us not put too much faith in books. Thomas Davis was as fond of literature *qua* literature as any man, but when he wrote for Ireland, it was not the book he was thinking of but what the book might do.[1]

Perhaps the most successful chapter in *Words Alone* is 'Lost in the Big House', which opens with a wonderful long scene from the eccentric Lord Dunsany's *The Curse of the Wise Woman* (1933), mapping the co-ordinates of Irish Gothic fiction. Having launched the investigation of Protestant magic some twenty years ago, Foster now notes that there is a 'historiography' (102) of the Irish supernatural encompassing folklore, anthropology and occult studies as well as literature and history. He lures us into his reappraisal of Irish Gothic with the plausible suggestion that 'Irish novelists withdraw into a traumatized space where they negotiate with historical guilt, in fictions set in houses which symbolize the architecture of an authority based on dispossession', and just as we are sitting comfortably, he pulls away the chair, 'But this seems too simple' (96).

Although he allows that these Big House novels are 'infused with the idea of history as a haunting' (95), Foster wants to decouple this guilt and unease from easy assumptions about landlord oppression. Citing the extraordinary example of one oblivious Anglo-Irishman, John Auster, who believed that the rural mob threatening his carriage were admirers of his literary prowess, Foster suggests that 'we may be more conscious of the Ascendancy's need to feel guilt than they were' (112). Here again, 'ingenious' literary readings of Dracula with his boxes of earth as a metaphor for rapacious Ascendancy landowners are found to be ahistorical and unconvincing. Instead, Foster promotes Le Fanu's vampire novel *Carmilla* (1872) and particularly his ghost story *Uncle Silas* (1864) as a Swedenborgian fable that manifests Anglo-Irish theological uncertainty rather than historical guilt.

When Yeats appears for a longer stay in the final chapter, 'Oisin Comes Home', Foster has already prepared us to see the young poet of the 1880s and 90s in the light of his inheritances. The seedbed of his imagination has been sown by the texts and topics of post-Union Ireland and he begins his writing life by prospecting in that fertile ground. The chapter begins with Ellmann's assessment of influence, 'writers move upon other writers not as genial successors but as violent expropriators ... they do not borrow, thy override' (Foster, 129). The examples that follow show Yeats both as 'violent expropriator' and anxious Bloomian mis-reader of his precursors in the construction of his own literary pedigree. The familiar forefathers reassemble here – John O'Leary and Ferguson (whom Foster calls 'the Platonic nationalist' (139) for Yeats) as well as the more problematic Davis

---

[1] Quoted by John Kelly, 'The Fall of Parnell and the Rise of Irish Literature: An Investigation', *Anglo-Irish Studies* 2 (1976), 21.

and Gavan Duffy. One of my favourite moments in the book is Foster's analysis of the passage in Yeats's *Autobiographies* in which he recalls his battle with Duffy for control of the Library of Ireland:

> Sir Charles Gavan Duffy arrived ... He hired a young man to read him, after dinner, Carlyle's *Heroes and Hero-Worship*, and before dinner was gracious to all our men of authority and especially to our Harps and Pepperpots ... One imagined his youth in some gaunt little Irish town, where no building or custom is revered for its antiquity ... and of his manhood of practical politics, of the dirty piece of orange-peel in the corner of the stairs as one climbs up to some newspaper office ... No argument of mine was intelligible to him (145, *Au* 224-25).

Having met the dynamic Gavan Duffy of the 1840s, we almost gasp at the audacity of Yeats here. As Foster says, 'that piece of orange-peel is pure genius, but the unfairness of the whole thing is devastating' (145), particularly when he points out that Yeats, aged twenty-seven at the time of this recollection, was himself 'already a veteran of those unswept staircases leading up to newspaper offices.'(146) Here we see Foster at his best, stripping what he calls the 'layers of fabulous polish applied to [Yeats's] memoirs' (146) in order to recapture his actual position at the time.

Words Alone, despite its title, is not a book about Yeats's poetry (only a handful of poems are referenced or quoted) but it is about the power of books. Gavan Duffy's *Ballad Poetry of Ireland* appears in the hands of Jane Carlyle and then reappears as 'a sort of sacred book' (142) for the young Yeats. John O'Leary's library is Yeats's university, schooling him in nineteenth-century Romantic history and fiction as well as Young Ireland rhetoric. His battle with Duffy is about control of the canon through the selection of material for the Library of Ireland and his first appearances in print are reviews of Ferguson's poetry. Foster describes *The Celtic Twilight* not only as the title 'the era was waiting for' but also as 'the book which brought Augusta Gregory to him' (160). (Maud Gonne however, needing no book to capture him, is mentioned, disparagingly, only once). Even the novels of the neglected Walter Scott appear as the staples of Yeats's childhood, books that he will read to his own children half a century later (132). We already know a great deal about Yeats the writer: here we have Yeats the reader.

Publications Received

Arrington, Lauren,	W B. Yeats, *The Abbey Theatre, Censorship, and the Irish State: Adding the Halfpence to the Pence* (Oxford: Oxford University Press [Oxford English Monographs Series], 2010), pp. x + 210.
Fran Brearton and Alan Gillis (eds.),	*The Oxford Handbook of Modern Irish Poetry* (Oxford: Oxford University Press, 2012), pp. xx + 723. Contains numerous Yeats-related articles, e.g., Matthew Campbell, 'Recovering Ancient Ireland', 3-19; Warwick Gould 'Yeats and Symbolism', 20-41; Edna Longley, 'W. B. Yeats: Poetry and Violence', 95-110; Edward Larissy, 'Yeats, Eliot, and the Idea of Tradition', 113-29; Neil Corcoran, 'Modern Irish Poetry and the Visual Arts: Yeats to Heaney', 251-65; Hugh Huaghton, 'The Irish Poet as Critic', 513-33; Steven Matthews, 'The Poet as Anthologist', 534-47; Jahan Ramazani, 'Irish Poetry and the News', 548-64; Stephen Regan, 'Irish Elegy after Yeats', 588-606, etc. DOI, http://dx.doi.org/10.1093/oxfordhb/9780199561247.001.0001.
Foley, Declan (ed.),	*The Only Art of Jack B. Yeats: Letters and Essays* (Dublin: Lilliput, 2009), pp. xviii + 204.

Higgins, Geraldine,	*Heroic Revivals from Carlyle to Yeats* (New York and Basingstoke: Palgrave, 2012), pp. x + 226.
Tagore, Rabindranath,	*Gitanjali: A New Translation* by William Radice, with an Introduction and a new text of Tagore's translation based on his manuscript (New Dehli: Penguin Books India, 2012), pp. lxxxvi + 256.
Timoney, Martin A. (ed.),	*Dedicated to Sligo: Thirty Four Essays on Sligo's Past* (Sligo: Publishing Sligo's Past, 2013), pp. 304. Contains Joyce Raftery Enright's '"Here you are Somebody": The Sligo Relatives of W. B. Yeats', pp. 259-86. Profusely Illustrated.
Van Hulle, Dirk, and Mark Nixon,	*Samuel Beckett's Library* (Cambridge, Cambridge University Press, 2013), pp. xviii + 311.
Richard Whittington-Egan,	*Lionel Johnson: Victorian Dark Angel* (Great Malvern: Cappella Archive, 2013), pp. 370.

This book does not end here...

At Open Book Publishers, we are changing the nature of the traditional academic book. The title you have just read will not be left on a library shelf, but will be accessed online by hundreds of readers each month across the globe. We make all our books free to read online so that students, researchers and members of the public who can't afford a printed edition can still have access to the same ideas as you.

Our digital publishing model also allows us to produce online supplementary material, including extra chapters, reviews, links and other digital resources. Find *Yeats's Mask - Yeats Annual No. 19* on our website to access its online extras. Please check this page regularly for ongoing updates, and join the conversation by leaving your own comments:

http://www.openbookpublishers.com/isbn/9781783740178

If you enjoyed the book you have just read, and feel that research like this should be available to all readers, regardless of their income, please think about donating to us. Our company is run entirely by academics, and our publishing decisions are based on intellectual merit and public value rather than on commercial viability. We do not operate for profit and all donations, as with all other revenue we generate, will be used to finance new Open Access publications.

For further information about what we do, how to donate to OBP, additional digital material related to our titles or to order our books, please visit our website, http://www.openbookpublishers.com.

Yeats Annual is published by Open Book Publishers in association with the Institute of English Studies, University of London. Further details, including how to order back issues, can be found at:

http://www.ies.sas.ac.uk/publications/yeats-annual

Knowledge is for sharing

www.ingramcontent.com/pod-product-compliance
Lightning Source LLC
Chambersburg PA
CBHW060314230426
43663CB00009B/1696